Textbook of
PISTOLS *and* REVOLVERS

Long range target practice with the Smith & Wesson .357 Magnum Revolver. The shooting is being done at a range of 200 yards, over the water, so that the splash will indicate the position of any low shots. Note the excellent shooting position, with the hand as high as possible on the grip, and the thumb extended upwards along the left side of the frame, so as to bring the hand as nearly as possible into the line of recoil. Note also the easy and natural position of the body, with the feet spread slightly to brace the body against the wind, yet not too far apart. The marksman is the author's son, Robert.

Textbook of
PISTOLS and REVOLVERS
Their Ammunition, Ballistics and Use

By Major JULIAN S. HATCHER
Ordnance Department, U. S. Army

"Distinguished Pistol Shot", U. S. Army. Member United States Revolver Association. Life Member and Director, National Rifle Association of America. Officer in Charge Experimental Department, Springfield Armory, 1917. Officer in Charge of Manufacture, Springfield Armory, 1919-1921. Officer in Charge Small Arms Ammunition Department, Frankford Arsenal, 1923-1928. Chief of Small Arms Division, Technical Staff, Ordnance Department, 1929. Chief of Small Arms Division, Ordnance Department, Washington, 1929-1933. Chief Ordnance Officer, National Matches, Caldwell, N. J., 1919. Ordnance Officer, National Matches, Camp Perry, 1920-1921. Ordnance Representative, National Matches, Camp Perry, Ohio, 1931

Team Manager and Adjutant
U. S. International Rifle Teams, Switzerland, 1925; Rome, 1927; and Antwerp, 1930

Captain
U. S. Rifle Team, Bisley, England, 1931

Member
U. S. Olympic Games Committee

Author
"Pistols and Revolvers and Their Use"—1927

SHOOTER'S EDITION

Skyhorse Publishing

First published in 1935.
First Skyhorse edition 2015.

Skyhorse Publishing books may be purchased in bulk at special discounts for sales promotion, corporate gifts, fund-raising, or educational purposes. Special editions can also be created to specifications. For details, contact the Special Sales Department, Skyhorse Publishing, 307 West 36th Street, 11th Floor, New York, NY 10018 or info@skyhorsepublishing.com.

Skyhorse® and Skyhorse Publishing® are registered trademarks of Skyhorse Publishing, Inc.®, a Delaware corporation.

Visit our website at www.skyhorsepublishing.com.

10 9 8 7 6 5 4 3 2 1

Library of Congress Cataloging-in-Publication Data is available on file.

Cover design by Richard Rossiter
Cover photo credit Thinkstock

Print ISBN: 978-1-62914-519-8
Ebook ISBN: 978-1-63220-149-2

Printed in the United States of America

TABLE OF CONTENTS

PART 1. ARMS

PART 2. AMMUNITION

PART 3. SHOOTING

INTRODUCTION

While this is a book on firearms, it does not by any means cover the whole subject, for the broad general term "Firearms" is an extremely comprehensive one, which includes every weapon that uses gunpowder, from the heaviest piece of Railway Artillery down to the smallest Vest Pocket Pistol. To treat this whole field, even in an elementary and most perfunctory manner would require many volumes.

Firearms may be divided into the two main classes of Artillery and Small Arms. Small Arms, in turn, comprise several subclasses, such as, *Machine Guns;* rifles and shotguns, or *Shoulder Arms;* and pistols and revolvers, or *Hand Firearms.*

It is this last mentioned class of weapons, pistols and revolvers, or Hand Firearms, that forms the subject of this book. An attempt has been made to tell the reader as much as is possible in one volume about the guns themselves; the different methods of shooting and using them; their mechanism, care and repair; their Interior and Exterior Ballistics; the peculiar suitability of the different kinds for various purposes; the relative effectiveness or stopping power of the various calibers and types of gun and ammunition; and many other related subjects.

In writing on this subject, the author has assumed that the reader may be either a novice who knows nothing whatever about firearms and their use, or an advanced expert who wants a technical reference book where the results of many experiments with pistols and revolvers and their ammunition are tabulated in convenient form. Under these conditions it is inevitable that some of the things included will seem to the advanced reader to be too simple and elementary; while at the same time much that is treated here will seem to the beginner to be too technical.

An earnest effort has been made to combine these various classes of material in such a manner that the advanced reader may omit everything that seems to cover ground that is already familiar, while the beginner should read in each chapter only far enough for his present needs, reserving the more technical parts until familiarity with and interest in the subject of hand firearms and their use will lead him more deeply into the study of everything connected with them and their ammunition.

No effort has been made here to cover the Handloading of Ammunition, for this is a very large subject, and a Textbook of Handloading would be a complete volume in itself. Moreover, such a work is already available, under the title *Handloading Ammunition,* by Mattern, to which the reader who is interested in this subject is referred.

In *Pistols and Revolvers and Their Use,* written by the present author in 1927, a considerable amount of space was given to the history and development of hand firearms and their ammunition. No such material is included in the present *Textbook;* for the amount of live and up-to-date material available was such that the author found himself mainly concerned with the problem of getting all this material into one single volume of reasonable size.

Thus this book is essentially a treatise on *modern* Pistols and Revolvers and their Ammunition, with only such references to and descriptions of the older weapons and cartridges as are considered necessary to illustrate certain technical points under discussion, or to serve as a reference regarding some of the older guns more commonly still in current use.

Annapolis, Maryland
    December, 1934

PART 1

ARMS

CHAPTER 1

MODERN HAND-GUNS—GENERAL INFORMATION

H AND firearms may be divided into various classes according to the mechanical construction, the use for which intended, or the caliber.

When considered from a constructional point of view, they would be classified as single shot pistols or repeating pistols (which includes automatic pistols and revolvers). When considered as to use, they would be classified as:

Military Arms.

Target and Outdoorsman's Arms.

Pocket and Home Defense Arms.

When considered as to caliber, they are named for the diameter of the bullet in hundredths of an inch. Thus the smallest common type is the .22 caliber, in which the bullet is .22 of an inch in diameter and has a 30-grain lead bullet. The largest common type is the .45 caliber, with a 255-grain bullet.

SINGLE SHOT PISTOLS

The old military horse pistols were ordinarily single shot weapons, and in later years single shot cartridge pistols were much used in the army and navy. A sample is the .50 caliber Remington Pistol which is now much prized among target shots for conversion to .22 caliber and use as a target weapon.

While the revolver and automatic pistol have long ago ousted the single shot for military use, it is still a favorite for certain types of target practice. A single shot pistol gives greater accuracy than any other known type because it is not necessary to have a separate cylinder to hold the cartridge as is the case with a revolver, in which the bullet must jump a gap between the cylinder and barrel, nor is it necessary to have the barrel movable as is the case with many automatic pistols. Moreover, the sights

1

on the single shot pistol can be fixed firmly to the barrel instead of being a separate part, such as the slide, as they are on some automatic pistols.

In this country the rules limit the length of barrel of an automatic pistol to ten inches and also limit the distance between sights to the same figure, so that most single shot guns intended for target use have a ten inch barrel and ten inch sight radius. However, there are a number of single shot pistols with six to eight inch barrels, which are used principally as auxiliary arms in hunting, trapping, camping, etc. Moreover a number of target shots are now using barrels of 7 or 8 inches in length in preference to the 10 inch.

Most single shot pistols are shaped like a revolver, with curved handles, but there are some which have been built on the lines of the automatic pistol.

In a gun built for target use, such as the modern single shot pistol, there is no reason for having double action lock-work, hence most of the later ones are of the single action type which conduces to simple lock-work and a quick, clean action that is well suited to getting the best accuracy with a target arm.

Formerly single shot pistols were made in various calibers but now they are made only in .22 caliber.

REPEATING HAND-GUNS

Repeating hand-guns as distinguished from single shot pistols, embrace both revolvers and automatic pistols, and some repeating pistols that are neither revolvers nor automatics. One example is the Fiala repeating pistol which is made like an automatic pistol with a magazine in the handle, though it does not operate automatically. Instead, the breech must be opened and closed by hand each time the gun is fired and the opening and closing of the breech extracts the old cartridge from the barrel and inserts a fresh cartridge from the magazine in the handle.

The revolver in practical form dates from 1836, and is either of the earlier single action type in which the hammer must be cocked by hand for each shot, or of the later double action type in which the hammer may either be cocked by hand for each shot or may be cocked by simply pulling on the trigger.

When a gun, either single or double action, is cocked by hand, the only work that the trigger has to do is to hold the hammer in its cocked position until pressure is applied; then it must release its engagement with the hammer and let the hammer drop. This can be accomplished with very little pressure or work. On the other hand, with a double action gun if the hammer is to be cocked by pulling on the trigger, it is obvious that in the first place a considerable motion of the trigger is necessary in order to lift the hammer and that a considerable amount of work must be done by the trigger finger. Thus shooting a gun "double action" is usually far harder to accomplish with accuracy than shooting "single action." All modern double action guns are made so that they can be operated in the single action style by first cocking the hammer by hand.

The first Colt revolver, patented in 1836, had a single action, and this type of mechanism was so satisfactory that single action revolvers of almost identical lockwork are manufactured and sold in quantities today by the Colt's Patent Fire Arms Mfg. Company. It is interesting to note that only very recently another manufacturer, Harrington & Richardson, has placed on the market a single action .22 caliber target revolver.

AUTOMATIC PISTOLS

All automatic pistols are what is more properly known as "semi-automatic" or "self-loading." An "automatic" gun, strictly speaking, is one that keeps firing as long as the trigger is held, such as the machine gun. But one pistol is made in this way at the present time. The automatic pistol is made so that each time the trigger is pulled, a cartridge is fired, the empty shell thrown out, the hammer cocked and a new cartridge fed into the barrel ready to be fired again by a second pull of the trigger. Merely holding the trigger down will not make the second shot go off. The trigger must be released and then pulled again.

There is a little device in the automatic pistol called the disconnector, which is designed to prevent more than one shot from being fired by a single pull of the trigger. As soon as the slide of the pistol moves to the rear, the disconnector disengages the sear from the trigger so that the trigger must be released and obtain a fresh hold on the sear to make the second shot.

If pistols were made so that they are fully automatic, the whole magazine full of shots would go out in a small fraction of a second as soon as the trigger was pulled. There was a very small Italian-made sub-machine gun tested by the Government during the early part of the war, known as the Villar Perosa. This gun has a magazine containing fifty Luger pistol cartridges and is fully automatic. When the trigger was pulled all fifty shots were fired in a little over a second, so that it just sounds like tearing a piece of canvas instead of like a number of separate shots.

During the early part of the World War an automatic pistol was changed over at Springfield Armory so as to work automatically, with the idea of possibly using such a weapon in aircraft combat. The mechanism functioned so rapidly that when the trigger was pulled all the shots went out at one time and it was hardly possible to distinguish the report of seven shots from one prolonged report. Moreover, the rapidly repeated recoils of these different shots coming one after the other, threw the gun upward

On the firing line at Camp Perry. The National Individual Pistol Match of 1931.

and backward so that it was impossible to hold it down even when using both hands. The writer fired this gun a number of times and it was a very curious sensation to fill the magazine, load the gun, take careful aim at the target, and suddenly find the gun empty and pointing at the sky, regardless of the amount of effort made to hold it down.

In the discussion of pistols, individuals will often be encountered who insist that automatic pistols will fire one shot after another as long as the trigger is held down and the cartridges last. They are entirely mistaken and it will be seen from the above mentioned example that to make a gun this way would be very foolish, for in the first place, it would be, in effect, like having only one shot. The first shot might hit the point of aim but the others would all go wild and they would be fired so quickly that there would be no chance to let go in time to fire a second time.

Automatic pistols date from about 1893 when the Mauser pistol first became prominent. In most small automatic pistols, such as the .25, the .32 and the .380, the breech block is merely held against the head of the cartridge by a strong spring. When the gun is fired, the pressure of the powder gas forces the bullet forward out of the barrel and forces the cartridge backward. But before the cartridge can move backward, it must push the breech block out of the way and this requires comparatively speaking a considerable amount of time. Hence the bullet is gone before the breech actually opens.

The speed at which the breech opens depends largely on the weight of the breech block and the weight of the bullet. The heavier the bullet, the more quickly the breech will open, other things being equal. Hence with very heavy bullets or strong powder charges, it will be necessary to have a large and heavy breech block to make an automatic pistol work satisfactorily on the "blow-back principle" which has just been described.

For this reason most high powered pistols such as the military pistol, have a locked breech; in other words, one that has some sort of device to positively lock the breech block to the barrel until the bullet is gone, the same as the bolt of the Springfield rifle is locked to the barrel by turning the bolt handle down and causing the locking lugs to engage in the recess cut for them.

Of course, in the Springfield rifle it is quite easy to design such a mechanism because the owner of the rifle shuts the bolt and locks it by hand before firing and will have to unlock the bolt by hand after firing. In automatic pistols these operations must be accomplished by the force of the explosion itself. The most common way of doing this is by using the recoiling barrel. The barrel of the gun is mounted so that it can slide backward and forward against the action of a spring. Normally the spring holds the barrel forward and the breech block is locked to the back end of the barrel. However, when the gun is fired the barrel moves back under the force of recoil and this backward motion of the barrel withdraws the bolt or other device which locks the breech block to the barrel.

REVOLVER vs. AUTOMATIC PISTOL

In late years there has been a great deal of discussion as to the relative merits of the revolver and the automatic pistol. A great host of automatic pistols have been invented and manufactured with varying degrees of success. In military sizes the automatics have reached the greatest perfection, and have been adopted by the United States Army, and by many other important armies. In pocket sizes automatic pistols are sold throughout the world in very large numbers. Nevertheless, the revolver has been holding its own during all this period, and is now manufactured in quantities apparently as large as ever. It is difficult to say which is actually better, the revolver or the automatic pistol. Each has its own distinct advantages and disadvantages, which the reader must decide for himself. I will enumerate some of the advantages and disadvantages of each type of weapon.

The revolver has the following advantages:

1. It is an old standard weapon, everyone is used to it, and most everyone knows something about how to handle it.
2. The revolver is safer for inexperienced people to handle and to carry than the automatic pistol.
3. The mechanism of a revolver allows the trigger pull to be better than that of the average automatic.
4. A misfire does not put a revolver out of action.
5. A revolver will handle satisfactorily old or partly deteriorated ammunition which gives reduced velocities that would jam an automatic.

Among the principal disadvantages of a revolver as compared to an automatic are the following:

1. It is more bulky to carry.
2. The grip is generally not as good.
3. It is slower to load.
4. It is hard to clean after firing.
5. It is harder to replace worn or broken parts on a revolver than on an automatic.
6. Replacement of a worn or corroded barrel is a factory job.
7. Worn or poorly made weapons are subject to variable accuracy, due to improperly lining up cylinder or due to not locking cylinder properly in line with barrel.

The advantages of the automatic pistol are:

1. It has a better grip—fits the hand and points naturally.
2. It is more compact for the same power.
3. It is easier to load than a revolver.
4. It is easier to clean.
5. In case of a worn or corroded barrel a new one can be put in at small expense without sending the gun to the factory.
6. It gives a greater number of shots for one loading than a revolver.

7. It gives greater rapidity of fire and greater ease of rapid fire.
8. There is no gas leakage or shaving of bullets.

The automatic pistol, on the other hand, has some serious disadvantages, among which are the following:

1. The ammunition must be perfect. Old and deteriorated ammunition will cause a jam.
2. A misfire stops the functioning of the gun.
3. When the gun is kept loaded for long periods of time the magazine spring is under a tension and may deteriorate, causing trouble.
4. The automatic can not use blanks or reduced loads.
5. It has a poorer trigger pull than the revolver.
6. The magazine action requires a jacketed bullet which is not as good for practical use as a lead bullet.
7. The automatic pistol is more dangerous to handle, especially for inexperienced people, owing to the fact that after one shot it is always cocked and loaded.
8. It is not well adapted to reloading. It throws away the empty shells at each shot.
9. Many automatics eject empty cartridges toward the face, causing flinching.
10. It can not be fired from the hip as it throws cartridges into the shooter's face.
11. It throws out empty cases on the ground to remain as evidence.
12. It can not be fired from the pocket without jamming.
13. In some makes the hammer bites the hand or the slide strikes the hand and causes injury.

By far the most serious of all these disadvantages of the automatic pistol is its inability to use ammunition that is not up to the mark. For a weapon to use under any and all conditions where failure to function may be fatal, and where any and all kinds of ammunition may have to be used, the revolver is still far and away ahead of the automatic pistol, and is likely to remain so indefinitely. It is, therefore, still the choice of explorers and others to whom the possession of a hand arm in functioning condition is of paramount importance.

On the other hand, the automatic pistol is generally considered superior to the revolver for military use, where the ammunition supply is of known quality and spare parts are available.

The .45 Army automatic became extremely popular during the World War, and the experience with this arm at that time thoroughly justified the judgment of the Army authorities in adopting this as the service side arm for all branches of the Army. For home defense use the small pocket automatic, which is usually hammerless, has the disadvantage of frequently lying for long periods of time with the magazine full of cartridges and the safety on. The magazine spring and mainspring may thus be kept under compression for perhaps years at a time. If at the same time the ammunition deteriorates from age, the result may be that the arm will not function when needed. Moreover, these small automatics always have safeties, which are an excellent thing for one who uses these guns enough to know all about how they function; but if one of these weapons becomes needed in an emergency by some member of the household who does not know much about using hand arms, it may very well occur, and has occurred, that the user was not familiar with the method of manipulating the safety and therefore could not fire the gun. These disadvantages are not shared by the revolver.

We will now consider the different classes of hand firearms according to the uses for which they are intended.

MILITARY ARMS

Most armies and navies use a heavy caliber automatic pistol or revolver as the service sidearm. These guns are usually of .38, .45 or .455 caliber. Opinion as to relative desirability seems to be about equally divided between revolvers and automatic pistols. The United States Government's standard sidearm is the caliber .45 Colt Automatic. The Germans use the 9 m/m Luger which is a .38 caliber. The British have for many years used .455 automatic pistols in the navy and the .455 service revolver in the army; but it is understood that they are now considering the adoption of a .38 caliber revolver as their service sidearm.

Most military revolvers and automatic pistols have fixed sights and are strong and rugged in construction. Naturally they are much used in target shooting as there are many competitions which require the use of the standard government arm, but in general, military arms are not especially designed for target practice and, therefore, lack the adjustable sights and the fine lock-work that characterizes those especially built for target use.

TARGET AND OUTDOORSMAN'S GUNS

Target handarms run all the way from .22 caliber up to .45 and are of all weights and sizes. They include single shot pistols, revolvers, and automatics.

In recent years, however, there has been a strong tendency for target practice with revolvers or automatic pistols to follow three distinct lines. First, the .22 caliber, which is just target shooting reduced to the ultimate in convenience, safety and simplicity, using the lightest possible cartridge that is capable of extreme accuracy, that is, the .22 Long Rifle. In the .22 caliber target practice, slow fire with single shot pistols preponderates.

Then there is a type of target shooting which originated from the needs and requirements of the police and peace officers. This usually involves both slow and rapid fire with revolvers and automatic pistols of .38 or larger caliber, having adjustable sights.

Then there is the military pistol shooting which also involves slow and rapid fire with strictly military guns having sights which are not adjustable.

In considering the arms used for target practice we find, therefore, that they include guns of almost every size and shape.

The weapon which is most purely a target gun is the single shot pistol now made only in .22 caliber. Single shot pistols are usually made with 10-inch barrels so as to get the advantage of all that the rules allow in barrel length and sight radius; though recently shorter barrels are coming into favor and now many target pistols have seven inch barrels. All target revolvers and pistols have adjustable sights and usually they have many other aids to accurate shooting, such as specially fine trigger pull, curved or checked triggers, etc.

The principal automatic pistol in the special target class is the Colt Woodsman .22 which is made with either a 6½ or a 4½ inch barrel. Target revolvers usually have 6, 6½ or 7½ inch barrels.

Recently Smith & Wesson in placing on the market their .38/44 Outdoorsman revolver, made the following statement: "An Outdoorsman's revolver is one that uses a cartridge having high velocity, flat trajectory for unknown ranges that can only be estimated, wind-bucking qualities above the average, and shock-power far above the expectancy of the caliber; that has a clean crisp trigger pull so that it can be shot accurately; that has a barrel not only long enough to insure ample distance between the sights, but also so weighed and balanced as to avoid any effect of either undue weight or muzzle lightness. It must have sights with perpendicular and parallel sharp edges so no reflected light will affect the shooter's aim; they must be of such design that they most easily adapt themselves to various visions and must be adjustable to the individual, and, when adjusted, remain unchanged; and, above all, this revolver must be the utmost in reliability and accuracy."

Smith & Wesson also called their K-.22 heavy frame revolver an "outdoorsman's revolver." It will be seen, therefore, that an outdoorsman's revolver, as described by Smith & Wesson, is the same as a target revolver except for the use of "a high velocity, flat trajectory cartridge with shock power far above the expectancy of the caliber." In other words, according to this definition, an outdoorsman's revolver is nothing more or less than a target revolver which is designed to use not only the regular target cartridge, but an ultra-high velocity cartridge such as the .38/44 or the high-speed .22. Accordingly, outdoorsman's revolvers will in this book be considered with target revolvers.

POCKET AND HOME DEFENSE ARMS

These are automatic pistols or revolvers, usually of .38, .32 or .25 caliber which are adapted to the use of detectives, policemen, peace officers, and others who may want to carry a revolver in the pocket; or for the citizen or householder who may need a gun for personal or home defense. Guns of this class usually have fixed sights and barrels ranging from two to four inches in length. Many of the revolvers are hammerless; in other words, double-action revolvers with hammer concealed so that they may be fired merely by a long pull on the trigger. While as mentioned above, guns of this type usually have fixed sights, there are matches in the U.S.R.A. for pocket revolvers and generally the guns used in these matches have sights that are adjustable.

MISCELLANEOUS GUNS

Among the miscellaneous weapons that might be mentioned here is the Thompson Sub-Machine gun which, while it is not a pistol in any sense of the word, nevertheless uses the caliber .45 pistol cartridge.

Then there are special pistols made for shooting blank cartridges for starting races, athletic events, etc. Most of these use .22 caliber blank cartridges. Some of them, such as the Walther, sold by A. F. Stoeger, Inc., of New York, use a special .22 caliber blank cartridge, made very very short, and crimped, so that it is shaped very differently from any ball cartridge. Thus the gun can be made so that ball cartridges cannot be used in it. For this reason it can be sold without a permit in many states which do not allow the sale of pistols and revolvers.

These blank cartridge pistols are often made so that there is no opening at all in the muzzle of the gun, and the noise and smoke escapes through a hole in the top of the frame. Thus if the gun is pointed at some person and discharged, no damage can be done by sparks and particles of powder being blown in the victim's face, as might very well happen when a blank cartridge is discharged directly at a person in an ordinary gun. Recently the authorities of one of our large cities raided an establishment suspected of unlawful activities, and among other suspicious articles, found one of these small blank cartridge pistols, with the hole in the top of the frame, and no hole in the muzzle. They had never seen one of them before, and were so much mystified by their find, that they wrote to the War Department for information, which was furnished by the author, to whom the communication was referred to answer.

AIR PISTOLS

There are on the market several different makes of air pistols, suitable for target practice, and very convenient because of the lack of noise, smoke, and smell, and the fact that they do not have to be cleaned. These guns all operate by the sudden compression of air in a cylinder by a spring-driven piston released by the trigger. The air escapes through the barrel, driving the bullet before it.

As the power available is limited by the necessity of making the mechanism sufficiently light and compact to be contained in a pistol, only very small and light bullets can be used, and they cannot be given a very high velocity. Nevertheless, the results obtained make the better air pistols very respectable weapons to use against small animals, such as rats, mice, etc., and they are excellent for target practice indoors. The power of the small bullet is such that it will penetrate a half inch or more into flesh, and these guns must therefore be used with all the safety precautions customary with firearms.

Air pistols are in general made in two calibers, .177 and .22. They are rifled, and shoot the same pellet that is used in the famous B.S.A. (Birmingham Small Arms) Air Rifle, and in the Webley and Crossman air rifles. The pellets are shaped like an hour glass, with a front section which rides on the rifling, a middle section, or "waist" of smaller diameter, and a flared rear section, or "skirt" which engages the rifling. This shape reduces the resistance of forcing the ball into engagement with the rifling, and permits the attainment of higher velocities.

These pellets have a hollow base, and the opening extends almost to the front end. Thus their weight is very small in comparison with their air resistance, and this gives them a very low "ballistic coefficient," which means that they lose speed very rapidly during their flight through the air. Actually they slow down enough to become harmless at a distance of 100 yards, and this fact makes them very useful for target practice and shooting around the yard and garden, as safety is assured if the user will only assure himself that all is clear for a distance of 100 yards in front of the gun.

The .177 pellet weighs 8.2 grains, and the .22 pellet weighs 15

Not a "firearm," but excellent for pistol practice. The Webley Air Pistol.

grains. In the Webley pistol, interchangeable barrels may be had to shoot either size of pellet in the same pistol. As the energy delivered by the charge of compressed air is the same, regardless of which barrel is used, it follows that the .177 pellet will have higher velocity and penetration than the .22, but the latter will have more shock power when used against small animals, such as mice, etc.

A .22 caliber B.S.A. rifle gives a muzzle velocity of 435 foot seconds, corresponding to a muzzle energy of 6.3 foot pounds. The Crossman air rifle, pumped up to six strokes of the lever, gives a velocity of 492 foot seconds or a muzzle energy of 8 foot pounds. With the Webley air pistol the .22 pellet gives a muzzle velocity of 273 foot seconds with a muzzle energy of 3 foot pounds, and the .177 air pistol tested by me gave 367 foot seconds velocity and a muzzle energy of 3 foot pounds. For the purpose of comparison, it may be stated that the muzzle energy of the .22 short is 54 foot pounds.

Of the several air pistols on the market, the Webley is perhaps the most popular. The handle and trigger are attached to the air cylinder, which lies just above the hand of the firer, and forms the main bulk of the gun. The barrel lies just above the air cylinder, and is hinged at the front end. By releasing the catch at the rear end of the gun, and lifting the barrel, the arm is cocked, through the action of a linkage connected to the barrel and connected with the piston through a slot in the top of the cylinder. Cocking involves drawing the air piston forward against the compression of a strong coiled spring contained in the front of the air cylinder. At the forward limit of its motion the piston is caught and retained by the sear. While the barrel is thus in the raised position, the pellet is inserted in the breech, and when the barrel is closed, the gun is ready to shoot. The Webley air pistol weights 2 lbs., has a seven inch barrel, and an adjustable rear sight. The barrel is rifled with seven grooves, right hand twist, one turn in 15 inches. The grooves are very wide with narrow lands between them. This adds to the velocity by reducing the force required to start the lands to cutting in the skirt of the bullet.

These Webley air pistols are very accurate, but they have a peculiar springy recoil due to the inertia reaction of the heavy piston which is driven backward in the air chamber of the gun when the trigger is released. The recoil is, therefore, negative; that is, the pistol tends to jump forward and downward slightly instead of backward and upward as in ordinary firearms. The recoil, while disturbing, is very much less in intensity than that in a regular firearm. With practice excellent shooting can be done with these guns in spite of the jump above mentioned, and I have seen a group shot at 25 feet distance that could be covered with a dime.

Another well known air pistol is the Haenel, made in two types, single shot and repeating. The single shot type sells for slightly less than the Webley, the repeating type for slightly more. These guns are shaped almost exactly like the Luger and are a very pleasant type of gun to aim but rather difficult to cock on account of the fact that the cocking is done by swinging the grip backward which affords a rather poor leverage for the work of compressing the spring.

In these guns, the barrel is hinged to the frame, and may be tipped downward against the action of a spring detent to expose the breech for cleaning or loading. This action is entirely independent of the action of cocking the mainspring and air piston by using the handle as a lever. The Haenel Air pistol has a 4¼ inch barrel, with 12 lands and grooves of equal width, right hand twist, one turn in 18 inches. Weight, 2 lbs., 6 ounces.

A much cheaper air pistol, which does not shoot as hard as the Webley, but nevertheless is very satisfactory for target practice,

The "Haenel" Air Pistol. This gun, modeled on the shape of the Luger Pistol, is cocked by grasping the barrel with one hand and the stock with the other, and swinging the stock to the rear, first pressing the catch in front of the trigger guard. The barrel is then tipped down for the insertion of the pellet.

is the Hubertus. In this gun, as in the Webley and the Haenel, the air cylinder lies over the handle, and contains the piston and the action spring. However, in this gun, the barrel lies in front of the air cylinder, and the cocking of the mechanism is accomplished by pushing in on the muzzle of the barrel. The breech end of the barrel is attached to a disc of steel against which the piston comes to rest when the gun is discharged. Pushing in on the barrel forces this disc against the piston, driving it back to the rear of the cylinder, against the main spring, which is compressed by this action. When the piston is cocked and caught by the sear, a lock can be released to allow the barrel and the forward part of the air cylinder to be tipped. This exposes the breech of the barrel, into which a pellet can then be inserted, after which the barrel is grasped by a corrugated portion near the muzzle, and drawn forward to its original position, the cylinder is tipped down and latched, and the gun is ready tc shoot. As a safety feature, the latch which unlocks the barrel so that it can be tipped down for loading also locks the trigger so that there is no danger of releasing the piston while the arm is open. Weight of the gun,

The "Hubertus Air Pistol." This inexpensive air pistol has a rifled barrel, and shoots the .177 air rifle bullets with very satisfactory accuracy. With the barrel extended as shown, the gun is in the firing position.

22 ounces. Barrel length 5 inches. Accuracy at 25 feet, a group of ten shots ¾ inch in diameter.

There are several other air pistols on the market, and all of them are useful for target shooting at short distances.

PISTOLS FOR SHOT SHELLS

Several different makers supply a single shot pistol chambered for the .410 gauge shot shell or the .23 gauge shot shell. Among these may be mentioned the Harrington & Richardson Handy Gun and the No. 35 Stevens Autoshot. Both of these guns are furnished in either 8-inch or 12¼-inch barrels and have a tip-up breech loading action.

The Harrington & Richardson catalog states in reference to the Handy Gun: "The sawed off shotgun has long been recognized as an extremely effective weapon at short range. The new Handy Gun is offered as a weapon of defense for the home, office and bank and as a small game gun for the hunter. Also for the automobilist for protection against holdups. When shooting in the dark or from a moving vehicle, making aim difficult or impossible, the spreading charge of shot has several chances of scoring as against one chance for a single bullet. A second shot can be fired very quickly, the automatic ejector throwing the fired shell clear of the gun."

Another weapon of the same category, but more powerful, is the Ithaca Autoburglar gun. This is nothing more or less than a 20-gauge double barrel shotgun, sawed off to 12¼ inches in barrel length and with the shoulder stock replaced by a pistol grip. The reason for the 12¼ inch length is that in some states the laws define a pistol as a gun with a barrel not over 12 inches in length. However, these laws are subject to constant change and it is not safe to rely on any such ruling.

A good example of the manner in which the firearms maker or user may be affected by the frequently changing legal requirements is afforded by the Federal Firearms Act of June 26, 1934. This law, which is intended to discourage the manufacture or sale of certain articles frequently used by gangsters, places a heavy tax on the manufacture or sale of the articles in question, and requires all owners of such articles to register them with the Collector of Internal Revenue. The articles affected are machine guns, mufflers or silencers for firearms, and any gun, except a pistol or revolver, which has a barrel length of less than 18 inches. The Harrington & Richardson Handy Gun has been decided to be a weapon within the meaning of this act, and in consequence, a tax of $200.00 must be paid whenever one of these guns is sold or transferred.

THE DIFFERENT MAKES

There are two firms in this country and one in England who are prominent among all makers of hand firearms in the world for the excellent design and high grade of their product. These firms are Smith & Wesson, of Springfield, Massachusetts, the Colt's Patent Fire Arms Manufacturing Company, of Hartford, Connecticut, and Webley & Scott, of Birmingham, England. All these firms manufacture both revolvers and automatic pistols.

Pocket automatic pistols of high grade were also manufactured by the Remington Arms Company and by the Savage Arms Company but have been discontinued by both of these firms, though Remington still makes a double barreled .41 caliber Deringer.

High grade super-accurate single shot target pistols and target revolvers of .22 caliber are made by the Harrington & Richardson Arms Company, of Worcester, Massachusetts. Pocket revolvers of .22, .32, and .38 caliber are also made by Harrington & Richardson as well as by the Iver Johnson Arms & Cycle Co. of Fitchburg, Mass.

CHAPTER 2

TARGET AND OUTDOORSMAN'S GUNS

TARGET shooting with the pistol or revolver is a sport which enjoys a large and rapidly growing popularity. Competition is vigorous and the great National Championships which are awarded every year are keenly contested. It is only natural, therefore, that the weapons intended specifically for use in this sport should be of the best possible design for the one purpose of getting the highest target accuracy. Sights, trigger pull, barrel length, etc., are determined solely from the viewpoint of the target range. For this reason the target weapon has a longer barrel, lighter trigger pull, smoother action and more delicate sights than have the military and pocket arms.

In the race for accuracy we might expect to see freak arms of all kinds used in target shooting, but this is prevented by certain definite rules by which our two great shooting organizations control the type of arm that may be used in their matches. For example, no barrel may be more than ten inches long; the sights must be not over ten inches apart; the trigger pull must be not less than two pounds for single shot pistols and two and one-half pounds for revolvers. These and other restrictions define pretty closely the general characteristics of the arm to be used, but within these rules the individual variations may be enormous as will be seen by referring to some of the illustrations accompanying this chapter.

Among the different types of gun that are used for strictly target work may be mentioned single shot pistols, automatic pistols and revolvers. The single shot pistol is capable of somewhat greater accuracy than is either the revolver or the automatic, and for this reason it is the finest of all target arms, and it is easier to make high scores with it than with the others. However, the revolver and the automatic are more practical arms than the single shot pistol, and, moreover, they are capable of very great accuracy; so great that some of the highest scores on record are held by the revolver. Therefore, to make the sport more interesting and varied, and to give the user of each type a chance for the title with his own particular arm, there are matches in which the revolver or automatic may be used and from which the single shot pistol is excluded. The different varieties of target arm will now be described.

SINGLE SHOT TARGET PISTOLS

The single shot target pistol is a very fine type of gun for the man who is just starting to learn shooting. One reason for this is that it is much safer than either an automatic or a revolver. A single-shot pistol which must be reloaded after every shot and which remains empty most of the time, is the arm to start off with. In using the revolver, and even more in using an automatic pistol, there is a natural tendency to shoot too fast and to fire too many shots, because it is so easy to go ahead and shoot.

The single-shot pistol must be reloaded after each shot, which rests the user between shots and allows him to gain familiarity with the action by the repeated handling thus made necessary.

This arm is also free from the danger sometimes present when a beginner starts with an automatic pistol. This is the danger that he may become rattled and pull the trigger again unconsciously, thus firing another shot. This can not happen with a single-shot pistol and even if the weapon should be dropped upon firing, no harm is done. Moreover, the single-shot action is easier to clean and keep in proper condition than the six shooter or the automatic.

Another reason why this is a good gun for the beginner, is the fact that it shoots the .22-caliber cartridge which is economical and does not have a serious recoil and report to confuse the issue of learning to shoot.

Stevens Target Pistols

Many years ago the J. Stevens Arms & Tool Company of Chicopee Falls, Massachusetts, began to make target pistols, and in the days of Paine and Bennett these arms became celebrated. Their popularity continued until about 1904 or 1905. They were made in several weights; the heaviest being known as the Lord model, with a very massive barrel; the Conlin model, with a finger spur, and the Gould model, were somewhat lighter; and the Diamond model was the lightest of all. These guns were all of the "tip-up" variety, opened by pressing in a button on the left side. The front sight was a bead, or "Paine" type; the rear sight was a round notch on a flat spring adjustable for elevation by means of a serrated wedge. There was no adjustment for windage except by driving the rear sight to one side or the other in its slot with a hammer. These sight adjustments were very crude indeed as compared with the modern screw controlled sights which are fitted on all first class target pistols today. In these old Stevens pistols the hammer had to be put at half cock before the action could be opened or shut; otherwise the firing pin interfered with the end of the barrel. These guns were years ahead of their time in the matter of size. Though they were made in .22 caliber, they had a full man sized grip, which no other American .22 caliber arm did until very recently.

The first target pistol ever owned by the writer was a Stevens Diamond model and much ammunition was burned in it. None of these old guns are now made, but the company still produces a gun very much like the old Gould model, and with the same action. This is called the "Off-hand Model" or the "No. 35." This gun is furnished in 6″ and 8″ barrel only and is also made for shot shells in .410 caliber.

The Stevens No. 10 Target Pistol

After the World War, Stevens produced a new model, looking like an automatic, and having an improved rear sight, adjustable for windage and elevation. The barrel tips up to load, and is held shut by a lock on the left side. This lock is cam shaped so that it automatically takes up any play and prevents looseness from developing. This gun is what might be called semi-hammerless. The hammer is enclosed inside the frame, but has a rod with a knob on the end of it by which it may be cocked.

This is an extremely well balanced gun which feels quite comfortable in the hand. The trigger pull is excellent. In this modern gun the Stevens Company has lived up to its old time reputation for accuracy, as these No. 10 pistols are capable of making 1¼ inch groups at 50 yards from machine rest. Barrel length, 8 inches. Weight, 36 ounces.

The Smith & Wesson Perfected Target Pistol

For many years the Smith & Wesson Perfected Target Pistol was the outstanding arm in its class and enjoyed almost a complete monopoly of the favor of the great target shots. Its popularity was deserved, for it had unexcelled accuracy and superb lockwork, and year after year the winners in the big matches would be found using this gun. It originated as an extra barrel for the Smith & Wesson .32 caliber single action revolver. This revolver had a hinged frame with a tip-up action, and at one time the company marketed a combination set consisting of the .32 caliber revolver and an extra single shot barrel which could be put on the revolver frame by taking out the joint screw and removing the barrel and cylinder and inserting in its place the single barrel. With the target barrel in place the appearance of the gun plainly indicated that it was intended primarily as a revolver, for the revolver has a lip on each side of the frame to back up the cartridges in the cylinder, and when the single shot barrel was in place these lips of course remained on the frame, giving rather an odd look to the gun.

As the single shot feature became more popular the company marketed the single shot pistol alone and the lips on the frame were omitted. The lock-work was of the single action type, which, of course, is all that is needed on a single shot target pistol. This gun was known as the Model of 1891. Finally, some years later, Smith & Wesson designed a new lock-work for their double action arms and as this was thought to give a more perfect trigger pull, it was incorporated in the target pistol, although of course there was no need for the double action feature of the lock-work. This gun was designed to take full advantage of the rule regarding barrel length and distance between sights, so the barrel is exactly ten inches long and the distance between sights is ten inches. The gun weighs twenty-five ounces and the barrel tips up to load.

Frequently someone familiar with pistol shooting may be heard to speak of the "Olympic Model" Smith & Wesson .22 and it may be well to explain the meaning of that term. At the time of the Olympic Games in 1920, Mr. A. L. Woodworth of the Springfield Revolver Club, who is also an experimental engineer at Springfield Armory, made a number of experiments with .22 caliber rifling and determined that the bore of the Smith & Wesson single shot pistol, which was .226 in diameter, was slightly too large for the very highest possible accuracy. After a number of experiments it was found that a .223 bore and a very tight chamber with the rifling extended back so that it would cut into the bullet when the cartridge was inserted in the chamber would give considerably improved accuracy. Ever since 1921 this construction has been standard with Smith & Wesson. T. K. Lee called the gun with the new bore and chamber the "Olympic" .22 because they were used to equip the Olympic Team of 1920. As often happens in such cases, the name stuck to the gun and the Smith & Wesson pistols made with this smaller bore are called the "Olympic" Smith & Wesson to distinguish them from the older ones. In using this Olympic Smith & Wesson it will be noted that the cartridge cannot be pushed all the way in the chamber but stops when it is about a sixteenth of an inch from being all the way in. This is where the rifling comes against the lead bullet and at this point an additional extra pressure must be put on the cartridge to force it home.

While this arm perhaps holds more target records than any other pistol that has ever been designed, it is of course by no means perfect. In the first place the gun was built with the receiver of a small .32 caliber revolver as a foundation. The .32 caliber frame has a handle that is not large enough for the hand of the average target shot and to overcome this difficulty large wooden grips were fitted over this small handle. However, the relation of these target grips to the trigger is influenced by the small size of the frame to which they must be fitted and for this reason the grip on this pistol has never been entirely satisfactory; one of the worst disadvantages being that there is not enough space between the frame and the back of the trigger guard to accommodate the middle finger. The difficulty encountered with the grip of this gun is reflected by the fact that many users either make special grips or build up and pad out the regular ones in some way.

In spite of the disadvantages above mentioned this Smith & Wesson perfected target pistol was for many years the stand-by of the match shots in the "Any Pistol Class" and for years was the standard target arm. The barrel is superbly accurate. Groups of less than an inch in diameter at fifty yards have repeatedly been made from machine rests with this gun. In using this pistol keep the joint screw well tightened up, otherwise looseness may develop between the frame and the barrel which will have a bad effect on accuracy. Also when closing the gun be sure that the latch is pressed down firmly as the rear sight is carried on the latch and unless this precaution is observed variations in elevation may occur. The manufacture of this gun was discontinued in 1923 on the advent of the Straight Line Target Pistol.

Smith & Wesson Straight Line Target Pistol

Smith & Wesson had long recognized the disadvantages mentioned above as applying to the Perfected model, and in 1923 they brought out a new model which was called the Straight Line Target Pistol, the result of an earnest and very commendable attempt to produce an up-to-date and highly improved target gun which would eliminate the disadvantages of their former model. In producing this arm the great Smith & Wesson organization started in from the ground up to design a gun which would be solely and entirely a single shot target pistol with every feature determined only by the requirements of target shooting. To begin with, none of the older models were considered in making this new gun and it was not built on the receiver of any other arm as a foundation as was the previous model. Instead the handle was first designed to as nearly as possible fit the hand of the average shooter. This handle was made of a typical automatic pistol shape and was given the proper slant so that when the arm of the shooter is extended the barrel of the pistol will point horizontally.

Then after the handle was decided on the design was further completed so as to place the barrel of the pistol as close down to the line of the shooter's arm as possible. This barrel was of course

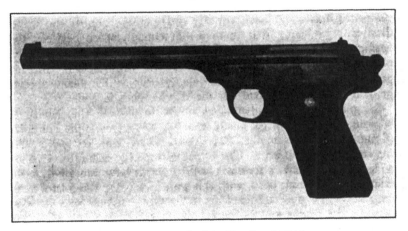

The Smith and Wesson Straight Line Target Pistol.

made ten inches in length and was bored and rifled exactly as was the old Olympic model which has never been improved upon for inherent accuracy. The barrel was fitted to swing sideways for loading and both front and rear sights are mounted on the barrel itself so that there is no chance of relative motion between the sights as is the case when the front sight is mounted on the barrel and the rear sight on the receiver of a jointed frame pistol. The firing mechanism is an innovation in that the usual swinging hammer is discarded and for it is substituted a striker moving in a straight line parallel with the barrel.

The distance between sights is 9¼ inches, and the rear sight is adjustable for both elevation and windage. The elevation screw has a "click" for every half turn, which prevents the adjustment from accidentally becoming changed. The number of threads, 40 per inch, on the elevation and windage screws, and the distance between sights, has been so chosen that one turn of the adjusting screw will move the shot group one inch on the target for each ten yards of range. For example, at twenty yards, a turn of the screw will move the group 2 inches, and a half turn will move it one inch. The pistol weighs 34 ounces, and is put up in a pressed steel case with a ramrod and a screw-driver.

It is a peculiar and unfortunate thing that this Straight Line Pistol has never attained anything like the same popularity that was enjoyed by its predecessor, the old Perfected Model. This is to be regretted because shooters are often to be heard blaming the companies for ultra-conservatism and for being afraid to put money into production of a new model. Certainly it is to the shooter's advantage when a company does bring out something new and improved but it costs the company a great deal of money to do so and when after such an effort the company finds itself losing money and realizes that the new model is not as popular as the old one then it does not help to get any more improvements adopted.

It has always been somewhat of a mystery why the Straight Line did not take with the shooting public as well as did its predecessor; but the fact remains that it is easier to make good scores with the old Perfected Model with all its disadvantages than it is with the Straight Line with all of its supposed improvements. There is not the slightest doubt in the world that the Straight Line Pistol has a superbly accurate barrel, but something about the design makes it somewhat hard to get out of this gun all the accuracy that it possesses. My own opinion is that it is probably due to the fact that the reach to the trigger is too short. When I shoot this gun the trigger comes on the second joint of the index finger and it is difficult to let-off a trigger with this part of the finger without losing some of the necessary sensitiveness and control. Moreover, the angle of the grip is such that the barrel has a distinct tendency to point downward when the arm is extended naturally toward the target. This means that there is always a constant, though perhaps imperceptible, effort expended in keeping the barrel brought up into the proper line, and there is always a tendency for any relaxation or twitching to cause a low shot.

The Colt Camp Perry Model

For many years nearly all the leading slow fire shots in the "Any Pistol" class used the Smith & Wesson Perfected Target Pistol, and there was no other target pistol to be had which was at all comparable with it; while in the revolver class there were highly satisfactory target arms made by both Smith & Wesson and The Colt's Patent Firearms Manufacturing Company. With many revolver shots the Colt guns, such as the Officer's Model .38 and the New Service Target .44 were favorites. Many of these shooters repeatedly urged the Colt Company to produce a single shot

Upper: The Improved Colt's Camp Perry Model Single Shot Target Pistol. This gun has the same grip and is built on the same frame as the Officer's Model Revolver in the .22 and .38 Calibers.

Lower: The Colt Camp Perry Model .22 Caliber Target Pistol with the grip and side plate removed to show the simplified single action mechanism. The lever on the left operates the Positive Lock, a safety Device to prevent accidental discharge in case the gun is dropped or the hammer receives a blow from any cause.

target pistol also. Finally, at the National Matches of 1921 a few members of the Marine Corps team were observed to be shooting a new .22 caliber single shot target pistol made on the same frame as the Officer's Model .38. The cylinder of the revolver is replaced by a flat block containing the breech end of the barrel. This block, carrying the barrel is hinged to swing to the left for loading just the same as the cylinder in the revolver does.

This new gun had something that the shooters of the country had long been demanding, which was a .22 caliber target arm with a full sized frame. It seems self-evident that the size and shape of the grip on any pistol or revolver should be determined by the average size of the hands of the users; but strangely enough pistol and revolver manufacturers had for years seemingly determined the size of the handle on any gun by the size of the cartridge the gun was intended to shoot. For all .22 caliber guns were made on a tiny frame with a tiny handle, suitable for a race of men about three feet tall; the .32 calibers were made on a small frame with a handle about right for a race of men about four and one-half feet tall. Only the larger guns such as the .38 specials and the .45's had grips about right for the present race of humans.

The new Colt pistol was called the Camp Perry Model. It had a ten inch barrel, ten inch sight radius, and a fine large grip with a very favorable balance and a weight of 34 ounces, which is about right for a target gun of this kind. Though the gun exactly resembles the revolver in outside appearance, the lockwork is entirely different, being simplified as much as possible and especially constructed for a clean, crisp trigger pull and fast hammer action. In the Spring of 1934 the gun described above was superseded by a new and improved model, with an eight inch barrel instead of the ten inch barrel formerly used, and with a shorter hammer fall and consequently faster lock time. The new model also has the barrel increased slightly in diameter so as to retain the weight and balance. Moreover the trigger has been redesigned so as to be more slender and not so curved.

This is an excellent single shot pistol and will appeal especially to the revolver shot, for this gun has the same weight, appearance, grip and balance as the target revolver, so that matches shot with this gun serve as practice for the revolver, and vice versa. The reader will note, perhaps with surprise, that this gun now has a barrel shorter than the full ten inches allowed by the rules. In past years target pistol shots assumed as a matter of course that the best accuracy would be obtained by using the longest possible barrel allowable; but recently a conviction, shared by the author, that a shorter barrel frequently gives better results, has been gaining headway.

The Harrington & Richardson U.S.R.A. Model

This is the most popular target pistol on the market today. In fact, it now holds the pre-eminent position in the "Any Pistol" class that was formerly held by the Smith & Wesson Perfected .22; and the rather strange thing about this fact is that the company that produces this gun has until recent years specialized in very inexpensive revolvers and shotguns and has never, until lately, entered the target shooting field.

Though, as mentioned above, the company made only very inexpensive guns, they had a large trade and a capable management, and all that they needed to be a factor among the makers of target arms was a clever designer with an intimate knowledge of the target shooting game and a management with sufficient breadth of view to take advantage of his knowledge. The designer they found in the person of Mr. Walter Roper, and they already had a manager with broad vision in the form of Mr. John M. Harrington. This combination has enabled the firm to take a position second to none in the excellence of their .22 caliber target weapons.

When this company first decided to go into the single-shot pistol game they were somewhat fortunate in being able to approach the problem from an unprejudiced viewpoint, because it was a new line to them and they did not have any model which was suitable for working over into a single-shot pistol. Thus, they had to start from the ground up, and therefore they were enabled to make their model to fit target pistol requirements as they saw them, without any factors of expediency to influence their decision.

With any single-shot pistol there are two factors that enter into the size of groups to be obtained. One is the mechanical accuracy of the gun itself, and the other, and by far the more important one, is the personal accuracy of the user. This factor that I have called "personal accuracy" depends upon several things, but assuming that a man is what is generally known as an excellent shot, and that he knows all about aiming and sighting, holding and trigger pull, still there is another factor that enters very strongly into his ability to perform with a pistol, and that is having a gun which will actually fit his hand and enable him to take a comfortable shooting stance; in other words, having a gun whose shape, balance and grip will do their maximum in helping the shooter to do his best.

Usually the errors of the shooter are so much greater than those of the gun, that I sometimes think this factor of fit and balance is the most important of all for a single-shot pistol.

In the past the unsuitable grip or handle on most of the single-shot pistols available has been a source of a great deal of dissatisfaction. One of the very finest target pistols hitherto available originated as a combination set consisting of a small revolver and an additional single-shot pistol barrel to be put on after removal of the revolver barrel and cylinder. In this gun the grip was entirely too small. As an expedient to overcome this trouble a special target grip was furnished to slip over the revolver frame, and this helped considerably, but still left a great deal to be desired, as the space between the trigger guard and frame was too small and narrow to accommodate the middle finger of the right hand, which would naturally go into this space on gripping the pistol. Many shooters found it necessary to fill this space up with a wooden block or with a piece of soft rubber, or some other filling material.

Now Walter Roper knew all these things very well and he decided first, to find a way to produce a pistol barrel with the finest possible mechanical accuracy; and second, to build this super-accurate barrel into a target pistol with a grip that would fit John Shooter as he is without the addition of gadgets, padding fastened on with tire tape, special stocks, or anything of the kind. The remarkable thing about this whole business is how well he succeeded.

From his experience in the arms business, Mr. Roper believed that the best way to develop really fine accuracy in the first place and to keep it that way in the later manufacture is to use a machine rest that will eliminate the human factor in testing for that accuracy. For years it had been considered almost impossible to make a really reliable machine rest for pistols and revolvers, and it still is something that has never been satisfactorily done for the larger calibers; but it can be done for the .22, and Mr. Roper proceeded to do it.

With the aid of the machine rest the accuracy of the barrel was developed to the point where all shots touch at 20 yards, and one inch groups at 50 yards are the rule. Moreover, this machine rest is used in a routine way in the factory for the regular production of guns, and each gun made is tested on the machine rest and must perform satisfactorily or it will not be accepted.

Having thus conquered the question of accuracy, the matter of grip and fit remained. It was observed that most shooters fill up the space behind the trigger guard, so a projection was provided on the trigger guard to fill this space and provide a surface to rest on the middle finger. Then the metal frame of the handle was so designed that the machining necessary to make a piece of wood fit on this frame was reduced to a minimum and could be done very cheaply. Thus the company was enabled to furnish several different shapes of wooden grips all adapted to be used

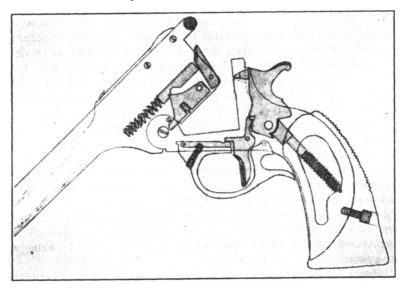

X-ray sketch by the author to show the mechanism in the latest U.S.R.A. Model Harrington & Richardson Single Shot Pistol. Note the double point on the trigger. One point is used for the full cock position, which does the fine work of shooting, while another point is used for the half-cock notch, which has to do the heavy work of keeping the arm safe. The screw in front of the trigger guard will change the weight of the trigger pull.

on the same gun, so that the user would be sure to find a grip to his liking, without having a special one made up. Five main shapes of grips are furnished. No. 1 is the regular grip like the one shown in the sketch. No. 2 is somewhat thicker and fatter. No. 3 is similar to No. 2, and in addition has a lip projecting upward at the top of the grip behind the hammer to keep the hand from slipping up on the grip. No. 4 is shaped somewhat like the handle of the old single action Colt revolvers. No. 5 is the so-called Free Pistol type with the bottom of the grip extended well to the rear. There is also one called No. 3-No. 5 which is a No. 5 grip having at the top a lip like that on the No. 3 style.

One of the most important innovations in this gun is the lock-work. Previous single-shot pistols, especially those based on revolver design, usually have quite a long siow hammer fall, as compared with this one. A long hammer fall has a very bad effect on scores because it gives time for the gun to move after the trigger has been pulled and before the cartridge explodes. A heavy hammer is bad because it jars the gun and sets up vibrations which affect the bullet delivery from the barrel.

In designing the lock-work for this gun, the makers did not take a revolver lock and readapt it, but started out all new and designed a non-jarring speed lock with extremely short hammer throw, which makes it lightning-fast. The lack of jar in this lock-work is really remarkable. The makers recommend placing a dime on the front sight and then trying to snap the gun without displacing the dime. This is an extremely difficult test, but it can be done.

The accompanying X-ray drawing shows the lock-work used in this gun, and it will be observed that it differs remarkably from the common revolver type of lock. It will be observed that the lock-work is extremely simple, which conduces to an excellent trigger pull. Moreover, the trigger pull is easily reduced by stoning in case it is desired to use the gun for free-pistol shooting.

Among the other mechanical improvements on this gun, not the least important is the fact that the frame closes up absolutely tight so that the head of the cartridge is fully enclosed, and thus there is no danger of having the heads blow out and cut the firer's fingers, as has happened in the past, and which is still more likely to happen with the new high-speed ammunition. Incidentally, it may be mentioned that this H. & R. gun is safe for use with this new ammunition.

In some guns the mistake has been made of having the striker or hammer nose hit that part of the cartridge which rests on the extractor. This is a bad mistake, as caliber .22 ammunition is notoriously sensitive to changes in ignition, and anything that tends to cushion the hammer blow will adversely affect the accuracy. In this U. S. R. A. Model, this mistake was carefully avoided, and the part of the primer that is hit is held solidly against the frame.

The sights are of the Patridge type, and both are mounted on the barrel so there is no chance of misalignment, as there is when one sight is mounted on the barrel and the other on the frame. All adjustments are made on the rear sight, which is adjustable for elevation and windage by means of a fine screw adjustment made with a screw-driver. Making both adjustments on the rear sight removes a possible cause for confusion when one adjustment is made on the rear sight and the other on the front sight, because the rear sight must be moved in the same direction as the desired change, whereas the front sight must be moved in the opposite direction.

The ejector on this gun is automatic. Once you open the breech the cartridge is thrown out with considerable force. The action of the automatic ejector is also shown in the X-ray sketch.

The description given above applies to the early models of this gun such as were produced early in 1931. There have, however, been numerous changes, as the company has constantly followed the performance of their guns among the shooters, and when any trouble or criticism has been encountered, there has been an earnest attempt to correct it, and many changes have been made since the original models were produced. Most of the changes actually do improve the gun, though in the author's opinion the older models were better in some respects.

For example, in the later H. & R. single shot pistols the hammer is made much larger and heavier, which makes it easier to get hold of, but also makes it slower and causes it to jar the gun more when it falls. This change was a mistake; the old hammer is preferable. In the later models the trigger is made straight, instead of curved. Theoretically this should be an advantage as it allows the finger to be placed low on the trigger so as to get more leverage and make the gun fire more easily; but in practice I like the old one better as the curve fits the finger and brings it to the same place every time.

The lockwork has been much improved as to durability by redesigning the hammer and trigger so that the rebound notch in the hammer rests on a special shoulder on the trigger, and not on the sear point that releases the hammer in shooting. Thus the heavy work of keeping the gun safe in case of a blow on the hammer as in letting the gun fall, etc., is taken away from the sear, which never has any work to do except to release the hammer in actual shooting.

One thing about this gun that sometimes causes trouble is the ejector. It is of the spring type, as has been described above, and is so arranged that when the gun is opened, the cartridge is thrown clear. Ordinarily this ejector works admirably, and when it is working well it is extremely convenient; but it sometimes happens that a cartridge will stick in the chamber of the gun too tightly for

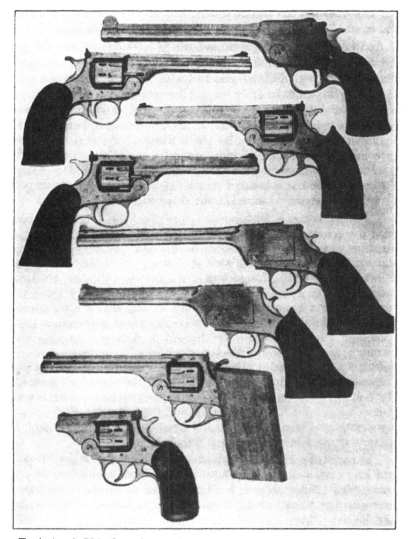

Harrington & Richardson pistols and revolvers with the interchangeable stocks furnished by the makers. From top to bottom, 10 inch pistol with No. 1 stock. Single action Sportsman Revolver with No. 2 stock. Double action Sportsman revolver with No. 3 grip. Single Action Sportsman with No. 4 stock, the best for this gun. 10 inch pistol with No. 5 stock. 8 inch pistol with No. 3-5 stock—the author's favorite combination for high scores. Double action Sportsman with rough wood block to be shaped by the purchaser. New Defender with modified No. 2 stock, the best for this model.

the spring to start it loose; and then when the gun is opened, nothing happens, and the gun is entirely out of action until a cleaning rod can be obtained with which to push out the empty shell.

Another thing that has caused me a considerable amount of trouble—in fact I should say more trouble than anything else, and the only real trouble I have ever had with the H. & R.—is the rear sight. In some of the early models the rear sight is made of very soft steel and after the sight is adjusted for elevation and the gun is all targeted in it is somewhat of an annoyance to have the adjustment entirely destroyed by the bending of the rear sight due to some slight pressure or blow against some other object. The later models have an improved rear sight, but again I do not like the improvement as much as I do the original and would rather put up with the bending than to use the shape that I do not like.

This Harrington & Richardson target pistol was originally made with a ten inch barrel; but in 1931 Walter Roper got to experimenting with shorter barrels, as he thought that they would be steadier when shooting in a wind outdoors. He made up an eight inch barrel model and found that it was not only steadier, but that the sights appeared clearer, as the eye can more easily focus on two sights that are close together than on two that are far apart. In addition he thought that the short barrel had a favorable psychological effect on the shooter because it does not magnify the tremor of the hand or any inaccuracies of holding quite as much as does the longer barrel. He wrote to me about this and asked my opinion, and in addition he sent me one of the eight inch guns to try out. It so happened that this gun arrived just before I was due to leave for England as Captain of the American Rifle Team competing at Bisley that year and as sort of an afterthought I threw the gun into my trunk and took it along.

The gun had a No. 5 grip which was the first of that type that I had ever seen as it had just been evolved from somewhere in the recesses of Walter Roper's head a week or so before. With this new grip and short barrel the gun seemed to balance exactly right and Ensign Harry Renshaw, the Coach of the Team, went with me when we tried it out on the range at Bisley and we both shot such good scores with it that we decided to target the gun in for twenty yards and enter the pistol match. To everybody's surprise including my own I was fortunate enough to win the match with a perfect score of one hundred and Harry won second place with a score of ninety-eight. The gun excited a great deal of interest and we allowed as many of the British to use it as wanted to and some of them shot very high scores with it in the match.

On my return to Camp Perry that year I used this gun in Match B of the U. S. R. A. and while I did not make a particularly high score in the full fifty shot match, I did have one ten shot target of ninety-seven, three shots being just barely outside the bottom edge of the ten ring. This was of course at fifty yards on the standard American target.

I have two ten inch Harrington & Richardson pistols, one of an earlier model made in 1931 and one of the latest models; and I repeatedly tried these guns out against the eight inch gun and my scores always run slightly higher with the eight inch barrel.

As a result of the success of the short barrel gun in this and other matches, Harrington & Richardson regularly supply a seven inch barrel model when desired. The reader will note that the gun that I used and still use is an eight inch gun whereas the model supplied commercially is of seven inch length. I do not place any importance on the difference of one inch; as far as I can tell the seven inch and the eight inch models shoot about alike. It is undoubtedly true that the longer barrel gives the theoretical advantage of a longer sighting radius and consequently closer sighting on the target; but quite evidently the clearer definition of the sights in the shorter model makes up for its lack of sighting radius.

From what has been said above the reader may be inclined to think that I would always recommend a seven inch or eight inch barrel as against the usual ten inch; but I am frank to say that many excellent shots, and perhaps the majority of them prefer the usual ten inch barrel and seem to get better results with it. However, as the target shooting world is learning that the shorter barrel has certain distinct advantages and capabilities of making the very highest scores, there is apparent a distinct trend towards short barrels and away from the long barrels formerly in vogue. For example, in 1934 the Colt Patent Firearms Manufacturing Company reduced the barrel length of their Camp Perry model to eight inches and of their Woodsman model automatic from $6\frac{1}{2}$ inches to $4\frac{1}{2}$ inches. As mentioned above, all of these Harrington & Richardson pistols are targeted at twenty yards in the factory using a machine rest; and no pistol is accepted unless all five shots cut a circle $\frac{1}{4}$ of an inch in diameter. The writer has spent quite a bit of time watching these machine rest tests at the H. & R. factory and can state from personal observation that the average pistol, just as it comes to the tester will more than meet the requirements. At fifty yards the average accuracy of twenty regular pistols taken from stock with all makes of ammunition was such that a circle .65 of an inch in diameter would pass through the centers of the most distant shot holes of the five-shot groups.

I have never asked the company what their standard bore and groove dimension is; but I did measure one of my own guns with very great accuracy and for my own information I compared the figures with the dimensions of the super-accurate Vickers match rifle and with those of a Springfield .22. The results are:—

	H & R	Vickers	Springfield
Groove Diam.	.2175	.221	.2230
Land Diam.	.2141	.2188	.2180
Depth. Groove	.0017	.0011	.0025
Width Groove	.0835	.0737	.0854
Width Land	.0304	.0420	.0897
Area of Bore	.0369	.0381	.0381

The weight of the gun is 31 ounces with ten inch, 28 ounces for the eight inch and 26½ oz. for the seven inch barrel.

The rear sight is adjustable for both windage and elevation. The shooter will be interested to know how much the shot group will move on the target for a half turn of the rear sight screw. This of course depends on the sight radius and the distance to the target as well as on the amount the sight moves when the screw is turned. The ten inch barrel gun has a sight radius of 9.2 inches, the eight inch barrel, has a sight radius of 7.2 inches, and the seven inch model has a sight radius of 6.2 inches. The elevation and windage screws have eighty threads per inch, but this does not mean that the sight moves only 1/80 of an inch for a turn of the screw because the sight screw acts with a leverage so that the sighting part of the rear sight moves more than the part where the screw is attached. Actual measurements on several models show that the sight moves side-ways .020 inches for each turn of the windage screw and raises .023 inches for each turn of the elevating screw. The table given below shows the amount in inches that the shot group will move on the target for each turn of the elevation and windage screws. These figures were obtained by calculation and checked by actual firing.

	10" Barrel		8" Barrel		7" Barrel	
	Eleva-	Wind-	Eleva-	Wind-	Eleva-	Wind-
Range	tion	age	tion	age	tion	age
25 feet	.69	.60	.88	.77	1.02	.89
10 yards	.84	.73	1.07	.93	1.24	1.07
15 yards	1.29	1.11	1.65	1.43	1.91	1.65
20 yards	1.74	1.51	2.22	1.94	2.56	2.25
25 yards	2.19	1.90	2.80	2.43	3.25	2.82
50 yards	4.44	3.85	5.65	4.95	6.56	5.74

In making up this table, the range used for the calculations was in each case two feet less than the nominal range. This was done to compensate for the fact that in target shooting the stated range is the distance from the feet of the firer to the target, and the sights of the gun are about two feet closer to the target. This is why, for example, the figure given for 20 yds. is not exactly twice the 10 yard figure.

The Webley & Scott Single Shot Target Pistol

This pistol has a ten inch barrel with fixed sights and a tip-up action operated by pulling down the trigger guard which serves as

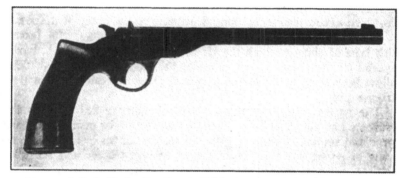

Webley and Scott Single shot Target Pistol given as First Prize in the Pistol Match at Bisley, England, in 1931. Won by the author, shooting an 8 inch barrel Harrington & Richardson.

a lever for opening the gun. The handle is very large and bulky and the barrel lies very low on the frame so as to be close to the line of the shooter's arm. There is a hole in the butt for the attachment of a skeleton stock which can be used with the pistol converted into a short rifle for accurate work up to 150 yards. This pistol is almost universally used for .22 caliber target shooting with the pistol in Great Britain. The photograph shows a gun of this type won by the author as a prize at Bisley in 1931. The gun is very comfortable to hold but seems hard to shoot after using our American pistols because of the rather heavy trigger pull which runs around six pounds on the sample that I have.

In view of the fact that the sights are not adjustable I was somewhat surprised on first using this pistol to make an actual score of ninety-three on the standard American target at 20 yards with my first ten shots. This score is better than my average with any gun and indicates that this Webley & Scott pistol is accurate and that the sights were properly adjusted at the factory for the average user. The weight of the pistol is 37 ounces.

FOREIGN FREE PISTOLS

It has been mentioned above that under our American shooting rules the length of all target pistols and revolvers is limited to not over ten inches. There is, however, one exception. In Europe shooting is done at fifty meters on a target with a ten ring which is smaller than that on our fifty yard target and the European match rules allow barrels up to 20 inches long and permit hair triggers.

The single shot pistols generally seen at the international matches are, therefore, fitted with set triggers and with barrels anywhere from ten to fourteen inches long depending on the fancy of the user.

In order to give opportunity to American shooters who favor this type of shooting both the U. S. R. A. and the N. R. A. have special matches at fifty meters under the international rules which allow barrels up to 20 inches long and place no restriction on the trigger pull.

The writer, who has attended several international matches in Europe, has naturally been interested in these free pistols and has procured several of them of different makes for his own use with a view to trying out the advantages of the set trigger and the unlimited sighting radius which is even longer than the length of barrel would indicate because in recent years the practice has arisen of mounting the sights on an extension which curves back over the hand so as to extend the sight radius.

On these pistols the fancy of the European gun makers has been given free rein in the matter of handles. Generally there is a shelf for the thumb on the left hand side and also a ledge or projection at the lower part of the grip on the right, to support the bottom of the hand. Frequently these grips are made full at all points, so that the gun maker can fit them to the hand of his individual customer. When you take hold of one of these guns with the grip properly fitted to your hand, you have only to extend your arm and the pistol very nearly holds itself.

The Buchel Pistols

Among the well known makers of these pistols are Ernst Friederich Büchel of Zella-Mehlis, Germany, who makes the Tell and Luna patterns. The Tell pattern has a handle that slopes back at quite an angle with the barrel, and with this pistol it is necessary to bend the wrist down sharply in order to aim at the target. Some marksmen prefer this shape because they think that the tension placed in the wrist by bending it down adds stiffness to the arm and takes away muscular tremor. Another school of marksmen prefer the grip at such an angle that the wrist can be in a natural position, so that there will be no strain whatever on the arm.

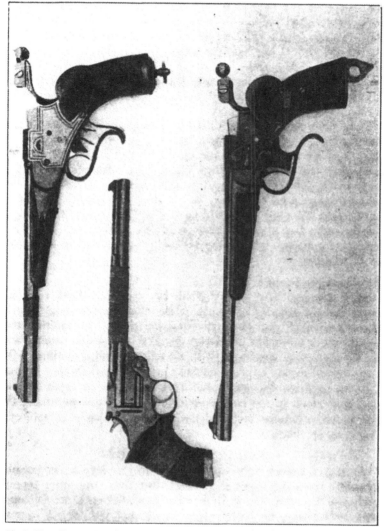

Single-Shot Target Pistols seen at the International Matches, St. Gall, 1925, by the author. Left: Stotzer Perfekt Pistole. Center: Author's S. & W. Single-Shot. Right: Author's Widmer Pistol (Buchel action).

These guns have a falling breech block, which is swung downward and into the frame of the gun by the action of a lever in order to expose the breech of the barrel for loading. The "Tell" pattern has a lever, lying along the back of the stock, which is lifted up to depress the breech block. The later improved model, called the "Luna," has a ring, in the bottom of the grip, which is pushed forward to open the action, thus making it unnecessary for the marksman to change his hold on the gun in order to reload. Both the "Tell" and "Luna" pistols weigh approximately forty ounces with twelve inch barrel.

There is another make of free pistol that is well known, called the Stotzer Perfekt Pistole. This gun operates by pushing down the trigger guard.

It is quite common for different European gunsmiths to buy these actions and fit their own barrels; and for this reason the quality of the free pistols found on the market is variable, as some gunsmiths will use a very high quality and accurate barrel carefully bored for the best American cartridges; whereas others will take a cheap barrel rifled for the .22 short and simply chamber it out to take the long rifle cartridge. For this reason it is wise in purchasing a free pistol of this type to be sure that you get it from a reliable gunsmith who makes his living by catering to marksmen of reputation.

The Stoeger Pistols

A. F. Stoeger, Inc., of 507 Fifth Avenue, New York City, imports foreign arms of all kinds. The "Tell" and "Luna" pistols, above described, can be purchased from them. In addition they always stock a number of foreign made target pistols usually with the tip-up action, sometimes with set triggers and sometimes without. These pistols are reasonable in price and satisfactory in quality. In addition Stoeger handles various foreign types of ammunition which cannot be obtained elsewhere in this country. The real pistol enthusiast will find the Stoeger catalog a valuable addition to his library.

TARGET REVOLVERS

As stated before, it is easier to obtain the very finest possible accuracy from the single shot pistol than from any other type of arm, and for that reason those who specialize in target shooting only, will always be found using single shot pistols. It is more difficult to get the finest accuracy with a revolver than it is with a single shot pistol because in the revolver the cartridge is exploded in a separate chamber in the cylinder and must pass from this chamber into a barrel before it encounters the rifling. In doing this it must move through a certain travel in the cylinder, which is not rifled; and then it must jump a gap into the barrel. In general, the less the travel of the bullet before it hits the rifling, the easier it is to obtain the finest accuracy; and the more perfectly the cylinder is lined up with the barrel the more accurately will the gun shoot. In constructing the revolver it requires the most meticulous care to insure that the chambers in the cylinder are in the same line as the barrel, and that successive chambers line up properly as the cylinder is turned. However, such is the perfection to which the manufacture of the revolver has been brought, that the modern .22 caliber revolver will now shoot with practically the same accuracy as can be obtained with the finest target pistols.

Up until a few years ago all .22 caliber revolvers were made on a very small frame. Fortunately in the last several years a number of the finest full sized target revolvers have been manufactured in .22 caliber so that the user of a large caliber revolver can attain proficiency with his arm by the use of the cheap and highly accurate .22 caliber long rifle cartridge in arms which are exact duplicates both as to size, weight and action of the regular military and target revolvers using expensive, high power cartridges.

The Smith & Wesson .22-.32 Heavy Frame
   Target Revolver

Back in 1908 Phil B. Bekeart, a gun dealer of San Francisco, persuaded Smith & Wesson to build a .22 caliber target revolver that would be large enough for the average man to shoot with comfort. In order to insure that the firm would not lose money on the deal, Mr. Bekeart guaranteed that he would buy one thousand of the new revolvers. The result was the production of a .22 caliber revolver on the frame of the regular .32 police model. While this gun was very much larger than any other .22 on the market at the time the handle was undesirably small for target use, and in order to overcome this disadvantage a larger size wooden grip was supplied to fit over the small .32 caliber frame.

While this gun was anything but a "heavy frame" model according to present day standards, it was so much larger than anything on the market at that time in the .22 caliber, that it met with an instant and most gratifying popularity. Moreover, the superb workmanship for which Smith & Wesson is justly famous was embodied in this gun in a very high degree, so that it has always been a gun that any revolver enthusiast might be justly proud to own. Today the average revolver shot will no doubt prefer the somewhat larger K-.22, but the .22-.32 will continue to hold its own as a wonderful gun for those who prefer a somewhat lighter weapon. For example, most women shooters will find the .22-.32 preferable to the larger models.

This gun was at first called the Bekeart model, and is still often referred to in that way. It was made a standard model by Smith & Wesson in 1911, with a six inch barrel, a cylinder holding six shots, and a rear sight adjustable for windage and elevation. Its accuracy is such that it has shot groups of 1½ inches in diameter at fifty yards from a machine rest. Weight 23 ounces.

The Colt Police Positive .22 Target Revolver

At about the same time that the Smith & Wesson firm brought out their Bekeart model, Colt produced a .22 caliber target revolver of similar size known as the Police Positive Target. This gun was very much of the same size and weight as the .22-.32, and was also made on the .32 frame. The handle is somewhat larger and longer than that of the corresponding Smith & Wesson gun. In this gun the rear sight is adjustable for windage and the front sight is adjustable for elevation.

The earlier guns of this model were made with a rather slender grip with rubber side pieces; of late years the grip has been made considerably larger and walnut stocks are used. The earlier guns weighed about 23 ounces and the later ones weigh about 26 ounces. The author obtained one of these guns in 1911 when he was stationed in Florida and used .22 caliber shorts in it for reasons of economy, purchasing them by the case. This gun gave superb service and showed conclusively the advantage of using cheap ammunition and doing plenty of shooting with it as a method of training for pistol proficiency.

This gun is made in .22 long rifle (using also the .22 short) ; .22 W. R. F.; and .32 Police Positive calibers. The barrel length is six inches. This is a first class .22 caliber target revolver which is highly recommended to those marksmen who prefer a gun somewhat lighter than the Officer's Model .22.

Smith & Wesson Military and Police

This is a full size Military Style .38 Special caliber revolver made with four, five or six inch barrels. For many years a Smith & Wesson revolver of this general type, chambered for the .38

long Colt cartridge, was one of the standard side arms of the United States Army, sharing this honor with a similar Colt model formerly called the Army Special and now known as the Official Police.

The Military and Police is made either with fixed sights as in the

Three outstanding target hand-guns. Top: The .22 Colt "Woodsman." Center: The .22 Colt Police Positive target revolver. Bottom: The .22 Colt single-shot "Camp Perry" Model; the original gun with 10 inch barrel and curved trigger.

Army guns above mentioned, or with adjustable target sights, in which case it is known as the Military and Police Target. In the fixed sight model it can be had with either the round or the square butt; and incidentally the round butt is preferable for almost every purpose.

This is a most admirable arm and one that has no superior in its class in the world. It is medium in size and weight, and yet with the powerful .38 special cartridge it is suitable for almost any use. The lockwork is as smooth as velvet and the accuracy is superb. With the round butt and four inch barrel this makes a wonderful self-defense arm well adapted to being carried in the shoulder holster or in the overcoat pocket. Weight of the gun with six inch barrel is 31 ounces. This model can also be had chambered for the .32 Winchester cartridge.

Smith & Wesson K-.22

For this gun, the first "Outdoorsman's" revolver, the pistol enthusiasts of America have to thank the foresight and inventive genius of Major Douglas B. Wesson of the great Smith & Wesson firm. Major Wesson is one of the most progressive arms manufacturers of the present day and is constantly working to produce new guns which will embody the greatest possible advantages for the shooter. In the K-.22 he has produced a masterpiece.

This gun was first designed when Remington brought out their Hi-Speed .22 caliber ammunition in 1930. This very greatly improved .22 caliber cartridge was sold with a caution against using it in pistols or revolvers where the head of the cartridge is unsupported and there might be danger of injury to the shooter from burst heads due to the very high pressure necessary to get the increased velocity. At this time Major Wesson had it in his mind to produce a full size .22 caliber revolver on a .38 frame to act as a companion gun to the .38 Military and Police above described; and at the same time he built this new gun specially for the recently designed high speed ammunition. The heat treated cylinders that Smith & Wesson had been using for sometime had of course more than ample strength for the cartridge; the only weak point was the rim. This point Major Wesson took care of by producing a countersunk cylinder with recesses for the cartridge heads, so that the rims of the cartridges are supported all around, and the danger that the fingers will be cut or burned by escaping gas, or that the adjacent cartridges in the cylinder will be prematurely exploded, is absolutely avoided. Moreover, the rifling in this new gun was especially adapted to obtain the highest accuracy with the new cartridges.

While the accuracy in the early K-.22 was up to the usual Smith & Wesson standards, and therefore was excellent, a further great improvement has been made since that time. This improvement

Upper: The Smith & Wesson K-.22.   An outdoorsman's revolver of the highest grade. It is built on the same frame as the famous Model K-.38, or Military and Police.
Lower: The Smith & Wesson .22-32 Heavy Frame Target Revolver. This gun, often called the Bekeart Model, was the favorite .22 caliber revolver until the advent of the K-.22 and the Officer's Model.

was accomplished by the invention by Major Wesson of a special machine rest for testing the revolver. Previous to the invention of this new machine rest it had been very difficult to make a rest of any kind that would hold the revolver satisfactorily enough for accuracy testing. However, the problem was finally solved, and with the new rest all variable factors in testing for accuracy were removed and the factory was put in a position to determine with absolute certainty the effect of any change in design that might be tried out. This new rest embodies certain novel features that have been kept secret by the company, although the author has had the pleasure of seeing this rest and working with it.

Another improvement embodied in this gun is the burnishing of the chambers. The chambers of all Smith & Wesson revolvers, including the K-.22, are reamed rather small and then burnished longitudinally to exact size, giving a perfectly smooth, mirror like surface, and insuring extremely easy extraction as well as freedom from rust.

This gun has a fully adjustable rear sight, with the screws so threaded that one turn of the adjusting screw will change the point of impact one inch for each ten yards of range. The front sight is of the square or "Patridge" shape with a gold bead inlet into the rear surface flush with the face of the sight. This is named the "Call" sight and is the most satisfactory sight for use either indoors as a target sight when the gold bead is not seen, or outdoors in the woods.

It has been stated above that the K-.22 has been made especially for the Hi-Speed ammunition, but naturally it will use the regular or low speed .22 ammunition equally as well.

This revolver is made only on the following specifications:

Caliber: .22.

Frame: .38 M. & P. Target.

Length of Barrel: 6 inches only.

Number of Shots: 6.

Sights: Call gold bead front, Patridge square notch rear, adjustable for windage and elevation. Other sights fitted on request.

Distance Between Sights: 7⅛ inches.

Trigger Pull: 3 to 4 pounds.

Finish: Smith & Wesson blue.

Stocks: Checked Circassian walnut with S. & W. monogram.

Straps and Trigger: Grooved to prevent slipping.

Weight: 35 ounces.

Cartridge: Any .22 Long Rifle.

Accuracy at 50 Yards: 1½ inch circle.

Accuracy Life: At least 100,000 rounds.

Colt's Officer's Model and Colt's Official Police

As mentioned above, for many years the standard side arm of the Army was the Colt .38 caliber revolver and a Smith & Wesson

.38 caliber revolver of similar size. These revolvers were chambered for the .38 long Colt cartridge. After the advent of the .38 special cartridge, the Colt gun of this type was called the "Army Special." It was a large size .38 caliber military type revolver with fixed sights and a cylinder holding six shots.

In response to the demand for a similar gun for the special use of target shots the Colt firm brought out a gun like the Army

Three guns for different purposes all on the same frame. Top, .38 Caliber Colt Officer's Model Target Revolver. Middle, Colt Camp Perry Model Single Shot Target pistol. Bottom, .22 caliber Officer's Model Target Revolver. The Single Shot Pistol is fitted with a Pachmayr Sure Grip Adapter. This is a fine battery of guns for the all-round target shot, as when he is used to one grip he is used to all. Fear the man who sticks to one type of gun.

Special except that it had adjustable sights, finely finished lockwork and every refinement that was known or could be suggested for target work. This superb weapon attained an enviable reputation as the Colt's Officer's Model Target Revolver and there is no finer gun made today. It is furnished with a 4½, 6 or 7½ inch barrel in .38 special caliber, and recently, much to the satisfaction of target shots who for years have been demanding a full size .22 caliber revolver on a .38 frame, this gun has been brought out in the .22 long rifle caliber with a six inch barrel only.

The gun formerly known as the Army Special is now called the "Official Police" and is also made in .22 caliber. It is the same as the Officer's model except that it has fixed sights and the lockwork is not as finely finished. Both of these guns as well as all other modern Colt revolvers embody a safety feature known as the "Colt Positive Lock," which is a block of metal resting between the hammer and the frame of the gun, except when the trigger is pulled, and thus positively preventing the cartridge from being exploded by a blow on the hammer or by dropping the gun. In the Officer's model the rear sight is adjusted for windage and the front sight for elevation.

The Official Police is furnished in .32 Winchester (.32-20) and in .38 Special with four, five or six inch barrels and in .22 caliber with six inch barrel only. Weight with six inch barrel 34 ounces for the .38 and 38 ounces for the .22 for both the Official Police and the Officer's model.

The Smith & Wesson ".44 Military" and ".44 Target"

For a military side arm of the largest size and greatest power Smith & Wesson produce a gun known as the ".44 Military" using the highly accurate and very powerful .44 S. & W. Special cartridge and also using in the same gun without change the .44 Russian cartridge. This gun is made with a five or 6½ inch barrel, fixed sights and a cylinder holding six cartridges.

A similar gun with adjustable sights suitable for the finest target work is called the ".44 Target."

It was the .44 Military rechambered for the automatic pistol cartridge and fitted with a special clip designed by Smith & Wesson that became the "model of 1917" Army revolver, together with the Colt's New Service also chambered for the automatic pistol cartridge.

Weight of both the .44 Military and the .44 Target is 38 ounces.

The Smith & Wesson .38/.44 Outdoorsman's Revolver

This is the .44 Target redesigned to shoot a .38 special cartridge which has been improved to give it 1100 foot-seconds velocity instead of 860 foot-seconds which is standard. The new cartridge, made especially for this .38 caliber revolver on a .44 frame, is called the .38/44. As was the case with the K-.22 this new Outdoorsman's revolver and the improved .38/.44 cartridge were originated by Major Douglas B. Wesson.

It will be appreciated by the experienced revolver shot that increasing the power of the .38 special cartridge by stepping up the velocity to 1100 feet will not only greatly increase the effectiveness of the cartridge but will also result in a very heavy recoil. It is specifically to take care of this heavy recoil that is the reason for using the heavy .44 frame for this .38 cartridge. The weight of this large size revolver, 41¾ ounces, is sufficient to absorb the recoil of the new high velocity cartridge with no more shock than is felt when the ordinary .38 special cartridge is used in the Military and Police revolver.

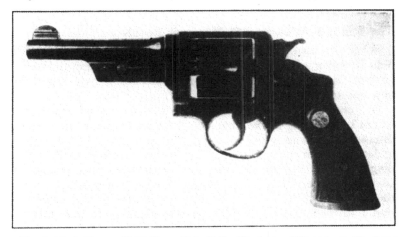

The Smith & Wesson .38/44 Heavy Duty Police Revolver. This gun, on the frame of the .44 Military, is chambered for the ultra-powerful .38/44 cartridge, which gives a muzzle energy of 425 foot pounds with 1100 feet per second velocity.

After much experimentation, 6½ inches was decided on as the proper barrel length for this gun to give it the most favorable balance; and it is furnished only in this length barrel. When desired a special patented filler piece can be obtained to take up part of the space behind the trigger guard. In the author's opinion this filler piece is an advantage and improves the use of the gun.

On account of the very high power of the new cartridge used in this gun an additional refinement has been added in the shape of a set screw in the rear sight, just forward of the adjusting screw, which serves to lock the adjustment in place so that it will not become deranged by the shock of shooting.

While this new gun is designed especially for the high power .38/.44 cartridge, the regular .38 special cartridge can be used in it as well, and when this is done it is an exceedingly pleasant shooting gun, as the weight absorbs almost all of the noticeable recoil. At twenty yards no readjustment of sight is required in changing from one cartridge to another but at longer ranges it will be found that decidedly less elevation is needed when using a .38/.44, due to its tremendous velocity.

There is another gun called the .38/.44 S. & W. Heavy Duty revolver, which is similar to the one described above except that it has fixed sights and a 5 inch barrel. This makes a superb heavy duty police gun, as the penetration is very great, so that it is suitable for stopping automobiles or any such duty.

The Smith & Wesson .357 Magnum Revolver

When this book leaves the press the Smith & Wesson .357 Magnum Revolver will be the very newest thing in the firearms world. In fact this book will carry the first announcement of this great new gun to the public.

In June, 1934, Major Douglas B. Wesson visited Annapolis, where I was living at the time and as we sat together one evening discussing firearms problems in general and the .38-44 Revolver and cartridge in particular, our conversation turned to the stopping power of bullets and the very remarkable effectiveness of some high speed loads which Major Wesson had developed using the 160 grain Keith bullet. During the course of this conversation I learned that Major Wesson was planning to take this remarkably effective bullet and build an entirely new cartridge around it. All previous standards or limitations as to pressure or recoil were to be disregarded and the entire object would be to make the most effective possible revolver cartridge. Ultra high velocity was to be obtained at any cost and then when the cartridge was perfected a gun would be built capable of handling it no matter what the pressure or recoil might be. Four months later I was shooting the first one of the new guns to leave the factory; and it came to me under the very suggestive name of the .357 Magnum. And truly a fitting name it is for this great gun—"the doggonedest hand cannon that has ever been produced" Major Wesson calls it.

It is built with the frame of the .44 Target as a basis. This is the same size as the frame of the Smith & Wesson .45 Model 1917 Army Revolver so that with a cylinder and frame of such large dimensions the gun would be amply heavy to take care of any recoil and amply strong to stand any reasonable pressure. But in addition to this large size frame, the gun has still greater size and weight because the barrel is 8¾ inches long and has a rib along the top for the full length from cylinder to muzzle.   With this 8¾ inch barrel the gun measures 14¼ inches long overall and weighs just three pounds when fitted with the Smith & Wesson grip adapter which is regular equipment on this model.   When the adapter is removed the gun weighs three ounces less.

The top of the rib, and the frame over the cylinder as well, are finely checked to prevent the reflection of light.   The usual Smith & Wesson target rear sight, adjustable for both elevation and deflection is fitted to this gun, and the rear sight, like that on the .38-44 Outdoorsman has an additional screw just in front of the elevation screw to lock the sight adjustment after it has been cor-

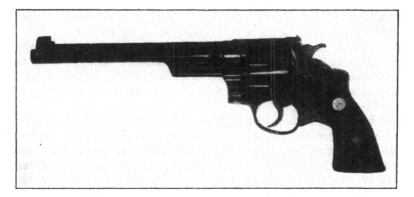

The Smith & Wesson .357 Magnum Revolver. This great gun is an ultra high-velocity weapon built on the frame of the .44 Target. The chambering for the new Smith & Wesson Magnum Cartridge is the same as for the regular .38/44 and .38 Special Cartridges, so that these cartridges also may be used in the same gun. The barrel length is 8 3/4 inches. The gun is a marvelous performer at any range, and has shown wonderful groups at 50 yards, but its real capabilities become apparent when long range shooting (200 to 300 yards) is attempted. At the time this book goes to press this is the newest thing in hand-guns, as the first shipments to the public will go forward in January, 1935.

rectly set.   The gun of course has the patent safety hammer block which makes it safe to carry a live cartridge under the hammer.

In spite of the name ".357," the gun is chambered so that it will handle the regular .38-44 and .38 Special as well as the new Smith & Wesson .357 Magnum cartridge.   As a matter of fact the bullet diameter of the Magnum cartridge is the same as that of the .38 Special, but in this new cartridge the name has been changed to show the real caliber.   Actually the .38 Special cartridge has always been made with a bullet diameter of .359 and barrels bored for the .38 Special cartridge have a land diameter of about .357.

Thus the new gun is correctly named for its caliber which is not the case with the older .38 Special guns. An excellent reason for the new name is to discourage careless individuals from confusing the ultra powerful .357 cartridge with the old style .38. With the new name for both the cartridge and gun there will be less danger of some user attempting to fire this powerful load in a gun which is not specially designed for it with the resultant possibility of accident.

Now a word as to the cartridge itself. It has a shell of the same dimensions as those of the .38 Special except that it is 1/10 of an inch longer. It is loaded with the 160 grain Keith bullet to as high a velocity as this bullet will stand without danger of stripping or of having the base fuzed by the heat. Of course this cartridge is brand new at this time and it is to be expected that some changes will be made in the ballistics as experience is gained; but there is no reason to anticipate any further changes in the gun. In order to handle this cartridge with absolute safety, the extra precaution has been taken of recessing the cylinder so that it completely surrounds the head of the cartridge the same as it does in the K-.22.

I have been fortunate enough to have been able to do quite a bit of shooting with the Magnum and in spite of its great barrel length the gun feels exceptionally well balanced when it is used with the grip adapter, which is regular equipment. This device can of course be removed in a few moments, but without it the gun feels muzzle heavy. There is something in the weight and balance of this gun, and in the way the grip adapter positions the hand, that makes the gun seem to want to lie steady in the hand when the trigger is pulled, without any particular effort on the part of the user to accomplish this steadiness.

I noticed this quiet balance when I first snapped the gun, and when I actually shot it at fifty yards I was amazed at the result, for four of my five shots were in a group 1½ inches in diameter and the other shot was about four inches to one side. Considering the fact that this shooting was done strictly off hand and under very poor weather conditions this group was truly remarkable and is much better than I am ordinarily able to do. Further shooting at 100 and 200 yards fully confirmed the 50 yard result and convinced me that this is a truly great slow fire, long range revolver. Smith & Wesson do not recommend this gun for the ordinary user, as they state that it is intended for men of large build and more than ordinarily powerful physique, but in spite of its great size I did not find it at all difficult to control. It points easily, and the rather heavy weight and long barrel absorb the recoil and jump of either the Magnum cartridge or the .38-44 until it is hardly noticeable at all.

The present plan of the company is to make this gun on special order only and not to carry it regularly in stock. As each gun is ordered specially, any barrel length from 3¾ inches to 8¾ inches will be furnished at the option of the user.

The Colt "New Service" and "New Service Target"

For years the ultra heavy military revolver has been the Colt .45. The current model of this gun is called the "New Service" and is chambered for the .38 Special, .38/40, .44/40, .44 Special, and .455 Eley as well as for the regular .45 Colt. This gun has 4½, 5½ or 7½ inch barrel and weighs 41 ounces with the 5½ inch barrel. It has fixed sights and a Colt positive lock. Chambered for the .45 Colt it was used in the United States Army under the name of Model of 1909 and chambered for the .45 Automatic cartridge it is known as the Model of 1917.

This same gun with the 7½ inch barrel and adjustable target sights and all lockwork hand finished for target use it is known as the "Colt New Service Target" and is an exceptionally fine heavy caliber target revolver. The world's record for the first perfect revolver score recorded under official match conditions at twenty yards was made with this gun. As is usual with the Colt arms the rear sight is adjustable for windage and the front sight for elevation.

The Colt Shooting Master

This is a .38 caliber target revolver of the very highest refinement built on the frame of the Colt New Service described above. It is frankly a specialized target revolver. In the design of this gun everything else was subordinated to producing an instrument that would give the very highest target scores capable of being obtained with a large caliber revolver.

The gun is built on the frame of the New Service Target but it differs somewhat in appearance from that gun as the shape of the handle has been changed so that it looks more like the handle of the famous Bisley Model. The grip is narrower in the fore and aft direction, especially at the bottom, and is thinner. The choice of dimensions seems to have been a happy one for it has sufficient length to fit a large hand and at the same time is thin and narrow enough to be comfortable for a shooter with a small hand.

The barrel is 6 inches long, with a special taper scientifically designed to damp out barrel vibrations and thus secure the highest possible accuracy.

The length and taper of the barrel have been coordinated with the frame in order to secure perfect balance and the result is that while the gun is heavier even than the New Service Target, its balance is such that the additional weight is not noticed. Nevertheless the weight is there and it aids materially in holding steadily under windy conditions and in addition, it gives this gun quite an advantage in rapid fire because the additional weight reduces the recoil of the .38 Special cartridge to a point where it is not disturbing in the least.

The weight of the "Shooting Master" is 44 ounces and that of the standard .38 target revolvers is in the neighborhood of 34 ounces. As the recoil energy with a given bullet weight varies inversely as the square of the weight of the gun, this means that the "Shooting Master" gives only 59% of the recoil felt with the standard .38 target revolvers.

In the .38 caliber this gun is now furnished, at the option of the purchaser, with a special heavy barrel which some marksmen find adds steadiness to the aim, damps out vibration and reduces the jump. The strong, powerful marksman of good physique will find the heavy barrel to be a distinct advantage, while the shot who does not employ sufficient practice to enable him to hold a heavy gun without fatigue will prefer the regular barrel.

The Iver Johnson "Supershot Sealed Eight"

This gun is called by the makers a sport revolver. It has a cylinder chambered for eight cartridges as the name indicates, and moreover, the heads of the cartridges are countersunk into the cylinder so as to prevent the escape of gas from burst heads which is likely to happen in case a defective cartridge is encountered, especially when using the high velocity cartridges.

The cylinder is made of high carbon alloy steel, heat treated to give the greatest possible strength and the factory states that each gun is targeted and tested with proof loads giving 10% greater breech pressure than any .22 caliber long rifle factory loaded cartridge. In the words of the maker, "This model is especially adapted for target practice, vacation sports, and camping, and will prove amazingly effective for game, especially for small animals and harmful pests. The length is 10¾ inches and the weight is 24 ounces."

An examination of this gun shows that it is a handsome, well balanced .22 caliber revolver, with gold finished front sight and adjustable rear sight of Patridge design. It has a six inch barrel

Upper: The Iver Johnson "Supershot Sealed Eight." An eight shot revolver with the cylinder counterbored to allow the use of high-speed .22 caliber cartridges, without danger from burst cartridge rims. A very satisfactory gun for a low price.
Lower: The Harrington & Richardson .22 Special. A suitable revolver to take on camping trips and outings. It is very inexpensive, but is capable of satisfactory accuracy.

with a top rib which is finished with a dull matte finish to prevent reflecting light.

The trigger is grooved vertically to prevent slippage of the finger. The walnut grip is amply large for any hand and is checked on the back to prevent slipping.

The earlier models of this gun had a grip with a projection, or lip at the top of the handle, to position the hand, but this lip had the disadvantage that it prevented the user from taking a high grip on the gun. This high grip is the best one for accuracy, and is the favorite with target shots. In 1932 the company adopted a new grip, called the Hi-Hold Grip, which, to my mind, is excellent, and gives just the right position of the hand for accurate shooting. In addition, in 1934 the Company added a very clever and convenient finger rest to the Supershot Sealed Eight. It consists of a spur of metal attached to the front of the frame between the wooden grips, so as to bridge over the space behind the trigger guard. This finger rest is adjustable as to position, as the screw holding it to the stock works in a slot, so that by loosening the screw the spur can be moved up or down to a limited amount.

This gun embodies the famous Iver Johnson "hammer the hammer" safety. This device comprises a lever operated by the trigger. When the trigger is pulled this lever rises and the hammer strikes it and transmits the blow through this hammer to the firing pin. However, when the trigger is not pulled, this lever is down out of the way and the hammer cannot strike the firing pin. Therefore, this gun is perfectly safe to carry with all chambers loaded and the hammer down as dropping the gun or striking the hammer cannot cause a discharge unless the trigger is pulled all the way back. In the same way, if the hammer slips out from under the thumb while cocking the gun, a discharge cannot occur. This is a valuable feature and has no doubt saved many lives.

An examination of the interior parts of the gun shows that the hammer, trigger and sear are well finished and are case hardened. The mainspring is a coil spring instead of the flat spring used in some other makes, and in fact, all the springs in the gun are coiled piano wire springs guaranteed by the makers not to lose their strength or break. The cylinder is fitted with an independent cylinder stop which registers and locks the cylinder in line with the barrel each time the hammer is cocked. When the hammer is down this cylinder stop prevents the cylinder from rotating which sometimes happens with makes which have a rachet cylinder stop instead of the positive stop.

The action is made on the tip-up system, which is excellent for a .22 caliber revolver, as it allows the easy removal of the cylinder for cleaning, and when the action is open and the cylinder removed, the breech of the barrel is readily accessible. The cylinder is held in place by the latch that serves also to open the gun for loading. To remove cylinder, simply lift up the latch and tip up the barrel as for loading, then, with the action open, lift up the latch and draw the cylinder off its axis.

The balance and hang of this gun are very comfortable, and it fits the hand well. Both the accuracy and durability are satisfactory. My average score with the "Supershot" on the Standard American Target at twenty yards runs between 87 and 90, and I have made scores as high as 93 on occasion. The trigger pull is rather hard, and naturally the lockwork does not have the smoothness of that on the high priced and beautifully finished Colt and Smith & Wesson guns, but it must be remembered that they cost about two and a half times as much. For the price this "Supershot" revolver is excellent value.

The Harrington and Richardson .22 Special

This gun is very similar to the Iver Johnson Supershot in size, shape, price, action, and performance. However, the H. & R. has a cylinder capacity of 9 shots, instead of eight and it does not have the "hammer the hammer" safety as this is a patented Iver Johnson feature. The gun does have a half-cock notch which to a certain extent takes the place of the "hammer the hammer" feature, as when the gun is placed on the half-cock, the hammer cannot fall and the gun will not go off if dropped. Moreover, if the hammer slips from under the thumb while cocking, a discharge cannot take place as the hammer will catch on the half-cock.

This H. & R. gun does not have the head of each cartridge sunk into the cylinder, but instead it has a recess to hold the heads of all the cartridges and a guard ring or raised portion outside the cartridge head to stop any gas from coming out and injuring the firer's hand should a burst head occur. Weight of the gun, 25 ounces.

Harrington & Richardson "Sportsman" .22 Cal. Revolver

This arm, which can be had in either Single Action or Double Action lockwork, is a highly accurate target revolver which has been placed on the market very recently by the Harrington & Richardson firm, in an endeavor to give the revolver shooter a gun with the same features that have made the H. & R. Single Shot pistol so eminently successful.

The Single action model is almost a duplicate of the U. S. R. A. Model Single Shot Target Pistol as regards shape, size, weight, and balance. Like the Single Shot, it has a frame that will take the five interchangeable grips that can be had for the pistol. It also has the same type of trigger guard, with a spur of metal extending back, to fill up the space behind the trigger guard, and give a rest for the middle finger. The lockwork is as nearly the same as it can be, with the addition of the necessary parts for turning and locking the cylinder.

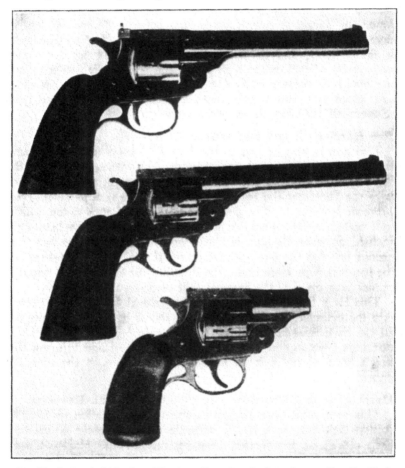

The Harrington & Richardson "Sportsman" revolver in three forms. Top, the Single Action Sportsman Revolver. Middle, the Double Action Sportsman Revolver. Bottom, the New Defender, which is nothing more or less than the double action Sportsman with the barrel cut off to 2 inches, and fitted with a modified No. 2 stock.

In designing this gun, Walter Roper had in mind the well deserved popularity of the old Single Action guns of frontier days, and he made the handle as nearly a duplicate of the old frontier grip as he could. It is the Harrington & Richardson No. 4, or

Frontier grip, and while any of the cther four standard H. & R. grips will fit the frame of the revolver, none of them are as good as this one. It seems to give just the right feel and balance. The cylinder holds nine shots, and embodies the H. & R. Safety Cylinder, with a steel ring surrounding the heads of the cartridges, to eliminate danger in the case the head cf a high speed cartridge should burst.

The rear sight is adjustable for windage, by means of two screws, one on each side, having 80 threads per inch. The front sight is adjustable for elevation by means of a screw in the end of the barrel, above the bore. Turning this screw in raises the sight, and one turn of the screw raises the sight blade ten one thousandths of an inch. The front sight screw is flattened on opposite sides, so that it moves by half turns, and as the front sight is pivoted, and held in its lowest position by a spring, it always rests on one of these flat sides, and thus acts to hold the adjusting screw from moving accidentally.

The distance between sights on both the single action and the double action models is 7¼ inches, and consequently a half turn of the elevation and windage screws will move the shot group the amounts indicated in the table below for the various ranges:

Range	Amount shot group moves for each ½ turn front sight elevation screw	Amount shot group moves for each ½ turn rear sight windage screws
25 feet	.21 inch	.26 inch
10 yards	.25 "	.31 "
15 yards	.37 "	.46 "
20 yards	.50 "	.62 "
25 yards	.62 "	.77 "
50 yards	1.25 "	1.55 "

These guns are of the hinged frame type, in which the barrel and cylinder tip up to eject and load. When the action is open, the cylinder can be instantly removed for cleaning by pressing a spring catch on the right side of the barrel. Removing the cylinder greatly facilitates cleaning the barrel, also, as it leaves the breech fully exposed.

A notable improvement in the lockwork of these guns is the double point trigger, which eliminates trouble with trigger pulls, such as having the pull change spontaneously with wear. In this new mechanism, there are two separate trigger points and hammer notches, one for the full cock position, in which a fine pull is required for actual shooting, and another for the half cock and rebound notch, which does the heavy work of keeping the mechanism safe from accidental discharge in case of dropping the arm, or a blow on the hammer. Previously, when the trigger pull has been made very light, there has been trouble with the half-cock notch striking on the point of the trigger and breaking the point, or changing the trigger pull. In this new mechanism there is no chance of the half-cock notch on the hammer ever striking the full-cock point of the trigger, for the hammer cannot fall far enough to bring the points together. Moreover, the half-cock point on the trigger and its notch on the hammer are placed further from the center than the full-cock point and its notch, so that when the trigger is pulled in firing, the half-cock point and its notch are widely separated, and there is no possibility of their striking. Mr.

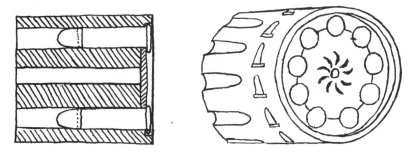

The new Harrington & Richardson Safety Cylinder, in which the cartridge heads are located in a recess in the end of the cylinder, and are surrounded by a raised portion, or guard ring, to prevent damage in case of burst cartridge heads, which may occur in using high velocity .22 caliber cartridges.

Harrington is justly proud of this device, and he tells me that since the change, the trouble that was formerly encountered with trigger pulls has entirely vanished. A study of the diagram shown on page 28 will make this clear.

Since the introduction of the Sportsman Single Action Revolver it has not only become prominent as a winner in the revolver matches, but has also made scores which are new high records, Dr. I. R. Calkins having made a new record of 280 x 300 in the "Slow, Time, and Rapid" match on Feb. 2, 1933, and Mr. G. W. Bassett having made a new high record score of 470 x 500 in Match K in the Indoor Championship Matches of 1933.

Both the Single Action and the Double Action Sportsman Revolvers are regularly furnished with 6 inch barrels, but the Double Action Model can also be had with a two inch barrel under the name of the New Defender; or with a three inch barrel for pocket use. Weight, with 6 inch barrel, 30 ounces.

The New Webley Mark IV .22 Target Revolver

This British revolver, of excellent design and workmanship, has a 5 inch or 6 inch barrel, as desired; is 10⅛ inches long over all, and weighs 30 ounces. It has a hinged frame and tip-up action, with the rugged stirrup lock for holding the action shut, which is a feature of the Webley line. Capacity of the cylinder, 6 shots.

In common with the other revolvers made by Messrs. Webley & Scott, this gun has a handle of excellent design and proportion. A notable feature is the very generous amount of space between the grip and the trigger guard. In this particular, as well as in the general slope and contour of the grip, this gun is ahead of its American contemporaries. As it comes from the factory this gun has a particularly light, clean trigger pull, weighing between two and three pounds, and shooting it is a pleasure. It has my full recommendation.

.22 CALIBER AUTOMATIC TARGET PISTOLS

There are a number of excellent and highly accurate .22 caliber automatic target pistols now on the market. They are invaluable as training weapons for the Military shot who must use the Automatic Pistol as his standard arm, or for the target shot who wishes to prepare himself to shoot the Service Automatic in the National Matches.

In these pistols the cartridges are loaded into a detachable magazine in the handle, and the first one is inserted into the chamber by drawing back the slide and then letting it go forward. This leaves the arm cocked. A pull on the trigger fires the shot, whereupon the arm automatically throws out the old cartridge and inserts a new one, remaining cocked ready to be fired again by another pull of the trigger. The trigger must be released and pulled again for each shot, as continued discharge will not result from one pull of the trigger. A thumb safety is provided to lock the gun against the danger of accidental discharge.

The Colt "Woodsman"

This pistol, designed by the late John M. Browning, of machine gun fame, is one of the best balanced hand arms ever manufactured, and has shown itself capable of the finest target accuracy. It is a first class arm to carry on hunting or camping trips. The fit and balance of the gun make it a fascinating arm to use and the fact that its shots can be followed up so fast quickly teaches rapid fire.

It is a most necessary hand gun for a well equipped pistol shooter's armory, and one that should be in the hands of every enthusiast who follows the game extensively, but the words of

Top: Colt "Woodsman" .22 Caliber Automatic Pistol with 4½ inch barrel. Note the improved shape of the fixed front sight. The rear sight is adjustable for deflection.

Bottom: The Hi-Standard .22 caliber automatic pistol, Model B. This gun is shown in the 4½ inch barrel style, but is also made with a 6¾ inch barrel.

warning which follow should be taken to heart and an attitude of great care should be cultivated in its handling and use.

This is not the gun for a beginner. Its automatic and hammerless action are confusing to the tyro, and he cannot tell from a casual look whether or not the gun is loaded. The large number of shots carried in the magazine prevents one from unconsciously counting the shots as they are fired and there is a tendency to lower the gun and snap it on what is supposed to be an empty chamber, when in reality there may be two or three shots left in the magazine.

The strictest of care should be used with this arm to prevent accidents, because after the first shot, it is always loaded and cocked and it only requires a slight pressure on the trigger to let off an additional shot. The fact it is of only .22 caliber also tends to encourage careless handling of this gun by persons who are not well versed in the use of firearms, as there are many ignorant people who consider a .22 to be more or less of a plaything, while as a matter of fact it is about as fatal as any cartridge and more so than many of them.

This is a gun that is best carried in the holster when it is not being held in the hand for actual firing. In fact, a proper holster is essential to this gun. It is a beautifully designed weapon and has a fatal attraction to on-lookers, and as they usually know nothing about its action or function there is grave danger of an accident if they are allowed to handle it. In the holster this is prevented. Moreover, this is no gun to carry about in the hand while loaded or to slip in and out of the pocket, for its shape is such that about the only way that it can be carried in the pocket is butt first and muzzle up; and as there is always the chance for the safety to work off, such a method of carrying the gun is highly undesirable. I have gotten into the habit of carrying my .22 automatic with the chamber empty at all times, as it takes only a second to slip back the breech block and have it ready to fire. This is also recommended even when the gun is carried in the holster, and on the firing line or in the company of others the gun should always be carried with the breech block locked back and the action left open.

The angle of the stock on this gun is such that when the gun is grasped and the arm extended, the barrel naturally points in a horizontal direction, which is the ideal condition. The distance from the back of the grip to the trigger is such that the trigger comes just at the first joint of the index finger of the average size hand, and thus gives the most favorable leverage for pulling the trigger. I have always found the Woodsman a remarkably easy gun with which to shoot good groups and I believe that these two features have a great deal to do with this inherent tendency to accurate shooting which seems to be built into this gun.

The gun is made to handle the ordinary .22 caliber long rifle cartridge, and has a magazine holding ten shots. The early models of this gun were not intended to handle the high speed .22 caliber cartridges, and after these new cartridges came on the market the company made a number of tests and found that when the gun was used with the high speed ammunition there was a tendency for the mainspring housing, which takes the impact of stopping the rearward motion of the breech block, to bend under the repeated heavy shocks. To overcome this difficulty a new heat treated

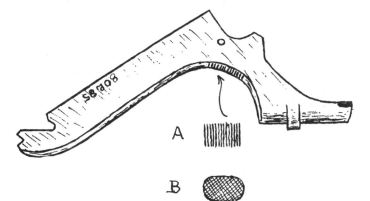

Mainspring Housing on the Colt Woodsman Pistol, showing how to tell whether or not the housing is specially heat treated for the use of high speed cartridges. Housings scored straight across as indicated at "A" are of the new type for use with high speed ammunition, while those with oval spot of knurling as shown in "B" are of the old type.

main spring housing was produced, and the present Woodsman pistols will handle the high speed ammunition with no difficulty. To tell whether or not the housing is the new heat treated type, look at the checking on the curved part under the back of the breech. The old checking is diagonal, while the new style housings are checked straight across in a rectangular pattern. See sketch. This change was made at gun No. 83,790, and to make any pistol with a lower serial number safe for use with the high speed ammunition, it should be fitted with one of the new heat treated mainspring housings, which can be obtained from the Company at a small cost.

The original Woodsman pistol has a 6½ inch barrel with the rear sight adjustable for windage and the front sight adjustable for elevation, and the sights 9 inches apart. Weight 29 ounces.

In the Spring of 1934 the Colt Company brought out a new

Sport Model Woodsman Pistol with a 4½ inch barrel, with the rear sight adjustable for windage and the front sight fixed, and of a special shape that will not catch in the pocket. The balance of this short barrel Woodsman Pistol is superb, and it is one of the finest shooting guns that it has ever been my pleasure to own. As far as I have been able to tell from an extended trial it shoots equally as well as the longer model, and it has the great advantage of fitting nicely in the pocket, which the other model will not do, as was stated above. The Sport Model Woodsman is one more embodiment of the recently growing tendency toward shorter barrels. This new gun is one of my favorite pistols, and no real pistol enthusiast should be without it. Weight 27 ounces.

Troubles and malfunctions with the Colt Woodsman pistol are very rare but when they do occur they are usually due to a worn or damaged magazine and usually the use of a new magazine will remedy the trouble.

The Woodsman is a gun that is very easy to clean because the breech block can be taken off very readily leaving the rear end of the barrel exposed so that the gun can be cleaned from the breech.

The "Hi-Standard" .22 Cal. Automatic

In outside appearance, balance, feel, etc., this gun very closely resembles the Colt Woodsman. The Hi-Standard pistol is, however, somewhat heavier, and differs from the Colt in several features of the construction, and particularly in the method of removing the breech block for cleaning.

Like the Woodsman, this pistol is made in two models, one with a 6¾ inch barrel and the other with a 4½ inch barrel. Both front and rear sights on both models are fixed. Rifling is right handed, with six grooves. The magazine holds ten shots, and so closely resembles the magazine of the Woodsman that magazines from one make will fit into the other. The barrel is somewhat heavier than that of the Colt, and this makes the gun weigh slightly more. With the long barrel the gun weighs 35 ounces, and with the short barrel it weighs 32 ounces.

On the left side of the gun there is a thumb safety which locks the slide and firing mechanism when it is pushed up, and makes the gun ready to fire when pressed down. Just back of the safety there is another serrated thumb piece which looks like another safety; this is the latch for removing the breech-block. Projecting from the rear end of the breech-block is a knurled stud, which is the end of the recoil spring guide. To remove the breech-block, press in this knurled stud, and at the same time, press down the corrugated latch on the left side. Holding the latch in the down position, draw the breech block to the rear. This leaves the breech of the barrel fully exposed for cleaning from the breech. To replace the breech block, hold down the latch as before, and slide the breech block on as far as it will go, which is about an inch. At this point the front of the breech block will strike against the top of the hammer, which in the cocked position lies almost concealed in the frame. Press down the hammer slightly, and slide the breech block all the way forward. Press in the knurled stud on the rear of the breech block, which will allow the latch to snap up into place. This take-down is extremely quick and convenient. The breech-block can be removed almost instantly, and can be replaced in a fraction of a second.

Obviously, the remarks as to danger, care in handling, etc., given under the description of the Woodsman apply with equal force to the Hi-Standard .22 Automatic, which is a weapon of the same general character.

The Colt Ace

The adoption of the Colt. .45 Automatic by the U. S. Government in 1911 immediately made this pistol of paramount interest to military target shots because the Government's adoption of the automatic meant that this gun would of necessity have to be used in all official military matches, such as the National Individual Match. The natural result was that the great body of military pistol shots who had previously been using the revolver started in to practice with the automatic pistol.

It was soon found that there was a need for a method of obtaining proficiency with the Government .45 that did not involve shooting the very expensive and powerful cartridge which was adapted to this arm. Of course a certain amount of skill in slow fire can be obtained by dry shooting; that is, by snapping the gun carefully at a target with no cartridge in the chamber. This will teach the user to hold the gun steadily and squeeze without deranging the aim, but it does not give him any chance to practice rapid fire. With a revolver rapid fire can be practiced without cartridges by cocking and snapping the gun against time in the same manner as it would have to be done in actual firing, but with the automatic, where the gun cocks itself, this is not practicable, or at least if it is done it does not give the kind of practice that is necessary. One of the common methods adopted among military pistol shots in an attempt to overcome this difficulty, is to tie a string to the hammer of the pistol and then holding the end of the string in the left hand, jerk the hammer back after each time it is snapped. This gives valuable practice but it is still quite different from being able to fire the gun rapidly against a time limit.

The need for a .22-45: These considerations soon led to the wish by users of the .45 Automatic that they could have a cheap way of actually firing the gun without using a cartridge worth from two to four cents each time the trigger is pulled.

This wish obviously pointed to the desirability of a gun similar to the .45 automatic that would fire with .22 caliber cartridges and it was not long after the adoption of the .45 that attempts were made to design such a gun.

An additional need for this sub-caliber arm for the .45 was found in the fact that it is much easier to train a novice in shooting a gun if the recoil, noise and other disturbances accompanying the shooting are reduced to a minimum. The .45 Colt Automatic Pistol, Government Model, is about the most powerful side arm in existence and when the trigger is pulled there is a noise and recoil that is rather startling to one who is not very well used to firearms anyway. As Al Woodworth, ballistic engineer at Springfield, used to say, when a novice with a .45 automatic pistol is trying to learn to shoot he frequently lets the noise and recoil disturb his aim to such an extent that he "shuts both eyes and takes both feet off the ground each time he pulls the trigger."

In other words, with a novice in the pistol shooting game the noise and recoil of a very heavy caliber gun frequently masks the errors of the shooter to such an extent that he cannot recognize the causes of any wild shots he may get. Even if he flinches violently the recoil will cover up this flinching and he will never know it. On the other hand, if you give him exactly the same kind of gun, which will function and fire in exactly the same manner, but which makes a very mild report and gives very little recoil, he will learn to shoot it without being afraid of the noise and the jump of the gun and, consequently, he is far less likely to acquire the bad habit of flinching than he would be if he tried at first to use the full-powered gun. Moreover, he will be able to recognize his faults in shooting and correct them. Then, too, the low price of the ammunition will enable unlimited shooting which will greatly increase his proficiency. The amount of shooting that can be done is further increased by the fact that the .22 is comparatively so low powered that it can be shot in many places where it would be impossible to shoot the .45.

It has been found by experience that when a man once acquires proficiency in aiming, holding and squeezing in actual firing with one caliber of cartridge, his proficiency will be retained when he changes to another caliber. If a man learns to shoot well with a .22 revolver he can usually shoot just about equally as well with a larger caliber.

All these considerations finally led the Government to undertake the development of a sub-caliber weapon for the .45 automatic as long as fifteen years ago. The .22 adapter to go on the .45 frame was constructed at Springfield Armory to shoot the .22 caliber shorts. This worked fairly well and soon after it was made the author, who at that time was in charge of the experimental department at Springfield, had occasion to show the gun to Mr. John Browning, the inventor of the .45 Automatic Pistol, who expressed himself as very much surprised that we had been able to get the gun to work with the shorts.

After playing with these models for several years and sending them out for test, it was decided that it was preferable to change over to the long rifle cartridge, as the .22 short, which had formerly been used for gallery practice by the Army, was being abandoned for that use and it was recognized that the use of the .22 long rifle would give a very much greater certainty of action in the .22-45.

Accordingly, a new .22 was constructed at Springfield on exactly the same pattern, but this time it was made for the long rifle cartridge. Twenty-five of these guns were made, and a number of them were sent out for service test. The model seemed to work fairly well in the factory, but in the service there was always difficulty in feeding from the magazines. The .45 automatic cartridge is a rimless cartridge made especially to feed out of the automatic pistol magazine, whereas the .22 long rifle cartridge has a rim, and it is very difficult to make it work successfully in a magazine that will fit into the handle of the .45 automatic pistol.

During the several years of trial and occasional redesigns of this .22-45 by the Government, the Colt's Patent Fire Arms Mfg. Company, of Hartford, Connecticut, had been an interested observer of the work. From time to time these designs were discussed with the officials of the Colt Company and they gave helpful suggestions. Finally the Colt Company decided to take a hand in this development themselves and they got out a design which differed radically from the one the Government had, though it accomplished the same object.

In the Government .22-45 the slide of the pistol was a solid forging with a hole bored in it to form the barrel and with a recess milled out in the back to take a sliding breech block. This adapter mounted on the .45 receiver made a .22 caliber automatic very much the same size and shape as the .45 and with the same handle, but differing considerably in appearance and also differing in action, in that the slide did not move back with each shot, the only moving part being the small breech block and the spring rod attached to it.

When the Colt Company took up this problem they attacked it in an entirely different way. They made the gun very much more like the automatic pistol in appearance and action. The Colt .22-45 was constructed with the same kind of slide, barrel, recoil spring, and other parts as are used in the .45 model, except that the moving parts were made lighter in order to operate with the comparatively low powered .22 long rifle cartridge.

This Colt adapter was a great improvement over the one made by Springfield and after numerous trials of this device by the Government, ten samples were ordered in 1927 and sent out to the various Army boards for test. As a result of these tests, many changes were found necessary and numerous recommendations were made. After these changes were made by Colt, the devices were again tested by the Army and further changes were found desirable. As a result of the various designs and redesigns made by Colt and of the extended test made by the Army, the .22-45 was finally perfected and when it reached the point where it was apparent that all the difficulties had been overcome, the Colt Company decided to place the gun on the market, and the result is the Ace Target Pistol.

From the above it will be seen that this new Colt gun is not an untried experiment but is the result of years of careful, expensive and painstaking development in which the engineering organization of the Colt Company has had the benefit of a large amount of actual shooting under service conditions in Government trials.

Details of the Ace: On examination the Ace will be found to be an automatic pistol almost exactly resembling the Government .45 or the Super .38 in outside appearance, weight and balance. On disassembling the gun numerous changes in construction will be found in the slide and parts attached to it and the barrel, and in the magazine; the receiver and the parts contained in it are the same as those used on the .45 Automatic. If you disassemble an Ace and a .45 Automatic at the same time, you will note just one difference in the receiver, and that is that in the Ace the ejector is not assembled to the receiver, as it is carried on the barrel. In the Ace receiver one of the little cross holes for pinning the ejector in place is omitted. This is the only change that I can find between the .45 receiver and the Ace receiver. The slide is the same in outside appearance as that of the .45 but it is cut away inside as much as possible in order to make it light enough to recoil under the action of the .22 cartridge. The locking lugs in the slide which hold the barrel and receiver locked together are omitted as they are not necessary in the .22 caliber gun.

The firing pin in the Ace has been specially constructed in two pieces instead of being in one piece as it is in the .45. This is made necessary in order to prevent the firing pin from striking the back end of the barrel when snapping the gun empty. Much of the accuracy of a .22 is dependent on the way in which the rim of the cartridge is struck, and after exhaustive experiments a certain form of wedge shape was found by the Colt Company to be best adapted to give accurate ignition and this form is used on the Ace firing pin. In order to insure that the wedge shaped point strikes the cartridge correctly a small lug is formed on the bottom of the firing pin to prevent it from rotating in its seat.

A most important improvement which is found in this gun and not found on its companions, the .45 Government Model and the .38 Super, is the provision of adjustable target sights of entirely new design.

On any pistol or revolver which is to be used for target practice of any kind or for general "outdoor use," adjustable target sights are almost a necessity. Without adjustable sights the usefulness of a gun for this purpose is severely limited. The variations in individual hold and eyesight are such that it is never possible to be sure that a gun which shoots center for one user will do the same for another. In target shooting with pistols and revolvers it is impossible to make the best scores unless your gun does shoot so that you can take the same definite point of aim each time. On a target you should be able to aim exactly at six o'clock and the gun whose sights are too high or too low so that the user must aim an indefinite amount above or below the six o'clock point, will always spread the group in elevation; and if the sights are off in deflection so that the user cannot aim exactly under the center of the bull's-eye, the chances are that the group will be ruined. When a revolver or pistol has fixed sights it is a matter of great difficulty to adjust the gun so that it will shoot properly with any one user for any one range and under one set of conditions; and when once it is so adjusted it will be incorrect for another user and for another range or set of conditions for the same user.

Only recently I was called on to shoot in a match without any previous notice and the only gun I had at hand was a .38 Special revolver with fixed sights that I had not shot for several years. As soon as I started in the match I found that the gun was shooting slightly low and to the left so that I had to correct the aim and hold off the bull's-eye. I found this to be handicap in the match and it undoubtedly resulted in quite a few points off my score even though I was using my own gun and one that I was fairly well used to.

There is no substitute for adjustable sights. The adjustable sight on the Ace is of an entirely new design which was produced by the Colt Company especially for this model. It has a lateral adjustment which is obtained by means of a cross screw and there is a clamping screw to hold the lateral adjustment after it is made very much the same as is used on the Woodsman, the Officer's Model and other Colt target guns at the present time.

Vertical adjustment on the Ace is not made on the front sight, however, as is the case on other Colt target guns. Instead, the central and rear part of the rear sight is dovetailed on the main part and slides up and down. The vertical movement is given by means of a screw in the top of the sight body and there is an index for reference to show just what adjustment is being used. There is no clamping screw on the elevation adjustment. Instead the elevation screw is split and spring-tempered and it has a snug spring fit in the hole so that the sight will retain its elevation adjustment at any point at which the elevation screw is set. As a safety precaution the elevating slide and elevating screw are so arranged that they cannot be removed entirely from the rear sight and there is no danger of losing them.

The rear sight has a movement of 1/10-inch in the vertical direction which is amply sufficient for any adjustment that may be required, with some to spare. The front sight is of the round form found on the .45 Automatic but is considerably higher in order to match the rear sight whose elevation adjustment brings it higher over the line of the slide than a fixed sight would be.

The front sight is 1/10-inch wide and when viewed through the rear sight notch it gives the effect of a square or Patridge type sight which is ideal for target shooting.

An examination of the inside works of the Ace Target Pistol reveals a surprising amount of painstaking work that the average user never sees. The sear, hammer, disconnector, sear spring, trigger, mainspring housing and grip safety are all hand-finished, giving the action of the Ace Pistol a velvety smoothness which cannot help appealing highly to the lovers of fine firearms and to those who admire fine workmanship. After the nose of the sear is made the exact thickness for the required trigger pull, the front and back of the sear and the slot for the disconnector are polished, and at assembly the corner and top of the sear nose are very carefully honed to give additional smoothness to the pull. The full-cock notch of the hammer is made dead smooth and just the proper depth for the required trigger pull, after which the circular section of the sides, as well as the lower outline including the half-cock notch are hand-polished and the hole for the hammer pin is burnished. At assembly the full-cock notch is honed to give an extremely smooth surface across which the nose of the sear swings. Even the sear spring is hand-polished all over. The inside surface of the grip safety on which the right leg of the sear spring operates is also hand-polished giving additional smoothness to the operation. As a result of the special care taken with these guns, the smoothness of the action is such that the trigger can be squeezed without the slightest tendency of the front sights to jerk or deviate from the line of aim.

One of the greatest problems in this gun was the design of the magazine. As mentioned before, the .22 caliber long rifle cartridge was never designed to be fed from a magazine which had to be fitted into the handle of the .45 Automatic Pistol, and magazine difficulties were one of the stumbling blocks that the Government encountered on its early designs of this nature. It would take up too much space here to tell of all the different expedients that were found necessary in order to get perfectly satisfactory, reliable, smooth operating feeding with the .22 caliber cartridges in the Ace, but just among other things it may be mentioned that the filler used in the back of the magazine is built on a scientifically constructed curve that guides the cartridges to the proper feeding angle in the magazine, and the under part of the breech block in the slide is also cut away at a certain slope which helps guide the cartridges up.

A most difficult problem was successfully accomplished when a way was found to make the follower on this magazine operate the slide stop on the pistol, a thing that was not done on the Government model .22 or the early Colt model .22's that the Government tested. The magazine has a pull-down to hold the follower for ease in loading and the top part of the magazine, including the magazine lip and the ears at the top which guide the cartridge in feeding, is made of sheet steel which is specially heat treated to withstand almost any conceivable rough use to which the magazine may be subjected. The capacity of the magazine is ten shots.

Accuracy: In attempting to obtain the very finest accuracy for this gun, the Colt Company made numerous experiments and finally developed what they term the "super precisioned barrel." There are six lands and grooves, with the rifling twice the width of the lands, left hand, one turn in fourteen inches.

It is absolutely certain that this barrel is highly accurate from a machine rest, but the question that the target shooter is most interested in is how accurate is the gun, including the barrel assembly, sights, grip, trigger, etc.; in other words, "What results can I get by shooting it?"

The fact that this gun has a 4¾ inch barrel and a 6¼ inch sight radius adds interest to the speculation regarding the practical results as to accuracy. There are many novices in the shooting game who think, the longer the barrel, the more accurate the gun. The barrel in itself is not so important in accuracy as many people think, for as soon as the bullet gets started in a given direction it will continue to go in that same direction until something disturbs its line of flight. It does not take a long barrel to start a bullet toward the target. A 4¾ in. barrel is plenty long enough to get a bullet started in the same direction and once the bullet starts in one direction it will keep right on going in that direction until something pushes it to one side or another.

A matter of much more importance than the barrel length is the sight radius. For a good many years the maximum sight radius used on American target pistols has been ten inches, but it has frequently been questioned that the long sight radius is always best. There are many shots who, much to their surprise, find that when they shoot with a short barrel gun, with six or eight inch barrel, they seem to make better scores than with the 10-inch barrel under certain conditions.

At first this may seem to be a puzzler, but on further consideration of this subject it was found that the further apart the sights are the harder it is to see both the front and rear sights clearly. Also, the further apart the sights are, the more apparent motion there is in the sights due to the failure of the user to hold perfectly. Shortening the sight radius not only clears up the sights to the vision, but it also makes the wabble seem less and therefore it makes the holding seem easier whether it is or not, and the result is that sometimes better scores are made with a short barrel and sight radius than with a longer barrel and sight radius under the same conditions.

As mentioned above, the barrel on the Ace Pistol is 4¾ inches long, whereas the barrel on the .45 Automatic is five inches long, and several correspondents have written to me to ask why the difference in barrel length. As explained to me by the Colt people, this is due to the fact that in order to get this gun to accommodate every kind of the many different makes and varieties of .22 long rifle cartridges on the market, it was necessary to have a certain minimum weight for the slide in order to insure certainty of functioning. After hollowing the slide out as much as possible it was found that it was desirable to make it still lighter and this was done by cutting off one-fourth of an inch at the front end.

One of the very frequent questions that I have received on the Ace is as to whether or not the slide and barrel can be purchased separately and placed on a .45 or Super .38 receiver.

The answer is that under present conditions this cannot be done. When the Colt Company first started to get out this gun the original idea was to get a .22 adapter, consisting of barrel, slide and magazine, to be placed on the frame of the .45. It was found, however, that in order to make this gun work with the comparatively low-powered and very variable .22 caliber ammunition, it was necessary to have the fitting done with extreme care. When the Colt .45 was first manufactured it was made by the Colt Company and by Springfield Armory, but with a slight difference in the dimensions of the guns made at the two places. Then when the World War came on a number of other factories were tooled up to make the Colt .45 and many of these ran into great difficulty in maintaining the very close dimensions that had been required on this job in the past and there was constant pressure brought to bear on the War Department to loosen up on the tolerances. The result is that there are many thousands of war-time Colt automatics now on the market whose dimensions are considerably beyond the limits required by the Colt Company. An attempt to fit the slide and barrel of the Colt Ace on one of these guns would undoubtedly result in frequent malfunctions. Moreover, in many of these guns there is a variation in the position of the magazine latch and if the magazine is not held snugly up to the proper place trouble will occur.

For all these reasons the Company foresaw an endless amount of trouble for themselves if they put on the market a .22 adapter, backed by their name and guarantee, that was likely to be used under all of these different conditions. In other words, they felt they did not want to risk their hard earned reputation of many years by a proposition that would almost certainly give trouble, and for that reason feel that they cannot guarantee performance with the Ace unless the receiver and slide are assembled and fitted together at the factory so that all of the very critical points can be taken care of correctly.

The weight of the Ace is 36 ounces which is just three ounces less than that of the .45 Automatic. The capacity of the magazine is ten shots.

A very important feature about the new pistol is that it is designed for the Remington Palma Hi-Speed and the Super-X as well as the ordinary .22 caliber long rifle cartridges.

From the description that has been given above of the tremendous amount of work and expense that both the Government and later the Colt Company put into the production of a satisfactory .22 on the frame of the .45 automatic, it will be seen that the problem was a very difficult one to solve; and although the Ace is a very satisfactory gun, it does not always function perfectly with every make and kind of .22 caliber cartridges. The principal reason for this is the fact that the gun had to be made of the same size and shape as the .45 and for this reason the work of operating the mechanism is just about all that can be accomplished with the .22 caliber long rifle cartridge. Part of the work accomplished by the recoil of the cartridge is cocking the hammer against the resistance of the main spring; and in order to insure greater certainty of operation it was necessary to use a weaker mainspring than that in the .45, so that the hammer would not be so hard to cock and, therefore, would not retard the mechanism so much. This rather weak mainspring means that if the primer of the .22 is not up to standard trouble is sometimes encountered with hangfires or misfires. Moreover, in spite of the weakened mainspring and the easing up of the action in every way possible, it sometimes happens that some makes of .22 caliber cartridges may not have quite power enough to operate the slide with certainty and occasionally the slide will fail to stay open when the last shot has been fired. Occasionally also failures to feed may occur from the same cause. The remedy, when conditions of this kind occur, is to try a different make of ammunition.

In spite of these occasional functioning difficulties the Ace is extremely valuable as an understudy or sub-caliber gun for the large size automatic and is a weapon that no serious user of the .45 automatic or .38 super-automatic can afford to be without. Moreover, to the user of such a gun the purchase of an Ace pistol is an economy as the saving in ammunition will pay for the gun in a few months if any reasonable amount of practice is indulged in.

CHAPTER 3

MILITARY REVOLVERS AND AUTOMATIC PISTOLS

MILITARY revolvers and automatic pistols are large caliber guns of .38 or larger bore, with fixed sights. While they are not as finely finished as are special target arms, they are capable of very satisfactory accuracy, and it is guns of this kind that are always used in the national pistol matches at Camp Perry, and in other military shooting events.

The Colt Single Action Army Revolver

This old gun, which was used in the Army from about 1876 until the time of the Spanish-American War, has been manufactured and sold for well over half a century and is still made and sold in large quantities. Because of its simple construction and its very comfortable grip and because of the great reputation it attained in the early frontier days it is still a favorite and no doubt will retain its popularity for years to come. The gun has a very simple mechanism, aptly described by the saying, "Almost as complicated as a monkey wrench."

To a casual inspection the gun as a whole seems bulky and rugged, and it is true that some of the parts such as the hammer and mainspring are extraordinarily heavy for the work they have to do, but the outside appearance of this gun gives a very false impression, for several of the parts inside are entirely inadequate in size and strength, and I know of no hand gun which breaks down easier or oftener.

The most common break is the cylinder stop spring. Next comes the pawl spring and after that the pawl itself and the mainspring breaks at times. The quarter and half cock notches seldom last long with this model, although their absence may be a benefit rather than otherwise. On continued firing the cylinder pin moves forward on many of these guns and will sometimes drop from place before this motion is detected.

Strange to say, notwithstanding its liability to breakage, it is possible to fire this gun irrespective of what part is broken and this feature is one point that endeared it to the old westerner and frontiersman. If the full cock notch on the hammer is broken off, or if the trigger nose is broken, it is only necessary to hold back the hammer with the thumb, slipping it off when aim is taken. If the pawl or cylinder lock is broken, it is possible to rotate the cylinder into place by hand.

Another reason for the long-continued popularity of this revolver in the West is due to its being safe for use on horesback. The average horse does not take kindly to the report of any firearm and even a mount which has learned to stand firing will sometimes start violently at a report and if he starts cutting up, you are lucky indeed not to let off more than one shot if you are using an automatic, and there is some danger of this even with a double-action revolver.

Another reason for its great popularity, is the fact than any old kind of ammunition will work, owing to the extremely heavy hammer and mainspring.

A number of years ago, out on the Rio Grande, I saw one of these guns fished up out of an irrigation ditch and though it had apparently been in the water some time, it went off when the hammer was cocked and the trigger was pulled, which speaks well not only for the gun, but for the ammunition which was in it.

This model is not designed for superaccurate shooting. I do not believe there is anyone who could do first-class match shooting with the single action, and moreover, I believe that anyone who can do fair shooting with this gun, could do better work with an automatic or double action. The long hammer travel, heavy blow, and height of bore above the hand all tend to mediocre shooting and I consider this to be one of the hardest guns to shoot, even fairly well. It has one outstanding feature though, this being the grip, which is without question the best fitting, most comfortable and natural grip on any revolver sold today.

This is the type of gun in which the hammer can be "fanned" by tying back or removing the trigger. "Fanning" is accomplished by holding the gun in the right hand and sweeping the left hand back over the spur of the hammer so as to push the hammer back to the limit of its motion and then release it. As the hammer is swept back by the left hand the cylinder rotates, and as the hand lets go of the hammer it falls and discharges the gun. One shot from the hip can be gotten off very quickly in this way and with ample accuracy for the purposes of a barroom fight or a shooting scrape over a game of cards which figured so often in the stories we hear of the old western frontier days, when this type of shooting was supposed to be in vogue.

This is the only type of revolver now made in which this can

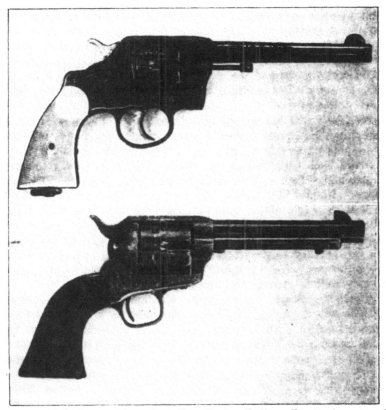

Two obsolete Army revolvers from the author's collection. Upper: An engraved and ivory stocked .38 Colt Double Action. Lower: A Single Action Army .45 with 5½ inch barrel.

be done, as the modern double action guns depend on the motion of the trigger to operate the mechanism which turns the cylinder, and if the trigger is held or tied back the cylinder will not rotate when the hammer is cocked. Recently the late John Newman of Seattle, Washington, and Elmer Keith of Weiser, Idaho, have given prominence to what is known as "slip shooting" with the .45 single action Army. The gun is converted into a "slip hammer" revolver by altering the hammer, taking off the hammer spur entirely and substituting for it a short peg projecting to the rear and lower down on the hammer than the conventional hammer spur. The trigger is preferably removed altogether and sometimes the trigger guard itself is also removed. A gun like this can be fired rapidly and accurately by simply drawing the hammer back with the right thumb and then, when it is ready to fire, allowing the handle of the "slip hammer" to escape from under the thumb. The speed with which this can be accomplished is shown by the fact that "Burro Puncher" John Newman has been known to throw a tin can into the air and put four shots into it with his "slip hammer" Colt before it hit the ground. However, the "slip gun" is not as fast as the modern double action. Mr. Ed. Mc-Givern, the well known exhibition shooter of Lewistown, Montana, has done a great deal of experimenting on this point and finds the double action gun much faster. Moreover, Mr. McGivern's experience well demonstrates the superior durability of the modern double action Colt and Smith & Wesson guns over the old single action. In Mr. McGivern's speed work he has a very hard time to keep a single action gun in repair for any length of time; whereas the modern Colt and Smith & Wesson guns require no repairs even after years of use. His experience also demonstrated the fact that the single action Army is not strong enough to stand being "fanned" for the speed with which the cylinder is rotated by this method causes it to break the cylinder stop.

When the Single Action Army was first designed, smokeless powder was unknown, hence the older samples of this model are intended only for black-powder use. After smokeless powder became popular, an improved grade of steel was used in the cylinders and other important parts of the Single Action Army and it was tested with a higher pressure than the early samples were. This change was made at No. 160,000, and all Single Action Army Colts with later numbers have been tested for smokeless powder and are intended for use with either black or smokeless.

A few years ago the Army sold many thousands of these revolvers, and at the present time they may be bought from some dealers in second-hand and Army supply goods. Such guns are not advised for the reason that they are often made up from miscellaneous parts and it is not likely that you will get one composed of the original pieces. In purchasing such a gun, look it over and see that all the parts carry the same serial number.

Some of these old assembled guns are fitted very poorly and

may be dangerous. In some of them the cylinders line up badly and you never know when one may have been reblued by heating until it is in no condition to stand the strain of modern cartridges or even heavy loads of black powder.

This gun must be loaded one cartridge at a time through a loading gate on the right-hand side. Cartridges are ejected by a sliding ejector rod under the barrel. Never load but five chambers of the cylinder and always leave the hammer DOWN on the empty one. Do not try to carry the hammer down between two loaded chambers, as it starts back too easily and the cylinder then works over until the primer is under the hammer. Do not attempt to carry it with the hammer on the quarter or safety notch; the heavy hammer will fire thin primers when snapped from this position, and it snaps easily. I know of a man who carried his Colt in this manner for years and finally in an argument to prove that it would not discharge the cartridge, shot off his left forefinger while demonstrating.

The following table of dimensions, etc., pertaining to the old Service Single Action Army Revolvers is taken from an old Ordnance manual describing these arms:

Total length	12.5 inches
Length of barrel	7.5 "
Length barrel, later reduced to	5.5 "
Grooves, number of	6
Grooves, width of along their middle lines	.2 inch, flat, tangent to the bore
Lands, width of	.03 to .033 inch.
Grooves, depth of, (uniform)	.005
Twist, uniform left handed, 1 turn in	16 inches.
Bore, diameter of	.445 inch.
Chambers, number of	6
Chambers, diameter of rear end	.485
Chambers, diameter of cone	.482
Chambers, diameter of front end	.450
Cylinder, length of	1.608
Cylinder, diameter of	.65
Height of front sight above axis of bore	.6225
Weight, with 7½ inch barrel	2.31 lbs.

The form of rifling in the modern Single Action Army Colt revolvers differs from that given above for the older guns, and is the same as that on their other .45 revolvers, given as follows in the Ordnance pamphlet on the 1917 revolver:

Bore, diameter of	.445
Rifling, diameter of	.452
Rifling, depth of	.0035
Grooves, width of	.156
Lands, width of	.073

The single-action Army is made in 4¾-, 5½- and 7½-inch barrels. The 5½-inch is the best length as it balances better than the other two. The gun weighs 37 ounces in the .45-caliber. It is made in the .32-20, .38-40, .38 Special, .44 Special, .44-40 and .45 Colt.

Colt and Smith & Wesson .38 Army Revolvers

During the many years that the Army was using the old single action Colt revolvers improvements were gradually being made in firearms sold for commercial purposes. For one thing the double action lockwork had been perfected; and more important, revolvers were arranged for simultaneous loading and ejection, using the swing-out cylinder. Finally in 1892 the Army decided to replace the slow loading .45 single action revolver with the more modern and up-to-date swing-out cylinder double action type, and a board which convened to consider this matter adopted the Colt and Smith & Wesson .38 caliber revolvers as standard. The first Colt model adopted by this board was known as the Model of 1894. There were also successive models known as the Model of 1896, the Model of 1901, and the Model of 1903. These models looked much alike but involved slight changes. The Smith & Wesson revolvers were of the same general type and looked like the Colt except they had a round butt. These Smith & Wessons did not have the front latch on the ejector rod which is a distinctive feature of modern Smith & Wesson guns.

These old Colt .38 caliber revolvers were really not very satisfactory arms. They had several weaknesses, the most serious of which was the frequent failure to line up the cylinder properly with the barrel. This resulted in shaving of lead and inaccuracy. Another trouble was the regularity with which the "hand-spring" became broken so that the cylinder would not rotate. This was usually due to faulty assembly of the side plate, as there is a pin on the side plate against which the hand-spring bears and if care is not taken to put this pin behind the spring in assembling the gun the spring will be broken off the first time the gun is cocked. Part of the trouble in shaving lead, etc. was due to the fact that the cylinder rotated to the left, so that the thrust of the "hand" or pawl which rotates the cylinder tends to push the cylinder away from the frame.

The Smith & Wesson .38 made for the Army were far superior to the Colt guns of that model and were really excellent revolvers. I have been told by Smith & Wesson that they protested against the left hand rotation of the cylinder, but were obliged to make the guns that way to conform with Government specifications. However, by means of superb workmanship and excellent fitting these Smith & Wesson guns were made so that the cylinder lined up satisfactorily and the shaving of lead was avoided.

The difficulty experienced with these old revolvers in having the thrust or rotation tend to push the cylinder away from the frame finally led Smith & Wesson to invent the front latch for the cylinder. Colt also overcame this difficulty in their later commercial models by changing the rotation of the cylinder so that the thrust of rotation tends to hold it against the frame instead of pushing it away.

The board which recommended the adoption of the .38 caliber realized that the stopping power was inferior to that of the .45 but concluded that it was probably sufficient, and stated that this point could not be definitely decided until actual experience was had with these revolvers in war. This experience came in the Philippine Campaign and the .38 caliber revolver was found not to have sufficient stopping power. This led to the adoption of the Colt New Service .45 as will be described next.

Many of these old Colt and Smith & Wesson revolvers were sold to civilian marksmen at a reduced price after they were declared obsolete by the Government and for that reason revolvers of that type will frequently be encountered.

The following dimensions, etc., pertaining to these old Colt .38 Caliber Army revolvers is taken from contemporary Ordnance pamphlets:

Weight of revolver	33	ounces
Total length	11.5	inches
Barrel length	6	inches
Diameter of bore, models 1894, 1896, and 1901	.363	inch
Diameter of bore, model 1903	.357	"
Number of grooves	6	
Width of grooves	.156	inch
Depth grooves	.003	inch
Twist, left hand, 1 turn in	16	inches
Lands, width	.034	inch
Length of cylinder	1.499	inch
Diameter of cylinder	1.52	"
Number of chambers	6	
Diameter of chambers	.3825	inch
Height of front sight above axis of bore	.6045	inch

After the adoption of the .45 by the Government both the Colt and the Smith & Wesson firms continued to manufacture a commercial model similar in size, weight and general appearance to the Army guns described above. These commercial guns were, however, vastly improved over the old Army models and are among the most popular and satisfactory military type arms that can be bought today. The Colt gun of this type is the Official Police and the Smith & Wesson is the Model K or Military and Police. These guns were described in the last chapter and are both arms of the highest excellence.

The Colt New Service Revolver. The U. S. Army Model of 1909

When, as has been mentioned before, the Philippine Campaigns developed the fact that the .38 did not have sufficient stopping power to put an end to the rushes of fanatical Moros the Army was engaged in an endeavor to find a suitable automatic pistol for adoption, and as a result of this experience it was decided that when an automatic pistol was finally adopted it should be of .45 caliber.

The automatic pistol was finally adopted in 1911, but in the meantime the Army had adopted the .45 caliber revolver for special use in the Philippine Islands. This revolver was the regular Colt New Service Military Model and as used in the Army was officially called The .45 Caliber Revolver Model of 1909. It was chambered for the powerful and highly effective Colt .45 cartridge which has a 255 grain lead bullet. The nose of this bullet is somewhat flattened and this adds to its stopping power. This cartridge is far more effective as to shock power and stopping ability than is the .45 automatic.

The Colt New Service Revolver is regularly chambered for the .38 Special, the .44 Special and Russian, the .38-40, .44-40, .45 Colt and .455 Ely cartridges. The gun can be had with 4½, 5½ or 7½ inch barrels and weighs 40 ounces. It is an extremely satisfactory, heavy caliber, military revolver, with high accuracy and very great ruggedness and durability.

The Smith & Wesson .44 Military

Before the World War, Smith & Wesson regularly produced a large frame, military type, double action revolver in the .44 S. & W. Special caliber. This gun called the "New Century" model had the ejector rod completely housed into a protecting rib built underneath the barrel and had an arrangement whereby the cylinder when closed was locked in position at the rear, and in addition the arm of the crane, or cylinder carrier, had a latch to lock it to the frame at the front end. Moreover, the ejector rod was also latched into place at the extreme front end of the housing under the barrel. Pushing forward the latch on the left side of the revolver frame unlocked the three catches above mentioned so that the cylinder could be swung out. This gun was often called the "Triple Lock" model.

However, at the beginning of the World War England and Canada both bought revolvers from Smith & Wesson chambered for the .455 British Service Cartridge and at this time the "New Century" was modified so as to omit the lock at the front end of the crane retaining only the lock at the rear of the cylinder and the front of the ejector rod. At the same time the housing under the barrel for the protection of the ejector rod was removed and only the locking lug under the barrel at the front end of the ejector rod was retained. These two changes were made to make the gun more serviceable by eliminating any possible difficulty in closing should the mud of the trenches get into the space between the crane and the frame or between the ejector rod and its housing. This modified gun was called the .44 Military and is now manufactured by Smith & Wesson under that name.

This is a gun of the highest workmanship and of superb accuracy which is still further enhanced by the fact that the gun is made especially for the highly accurate .44 S. & W. Special cartridge. It may be noted, however, that the somewhat less powerful .44 S. & W. Russian cartridge may be used when desired in any gun chambered for the .44 Special. This gun contains a sliding rebound block under the lower surface of the hammer which is designed to prevent the hammer from striking the cartridge except when the trigger is pulled this drawing the rebound block from its position. Thus the rebound block is intended to prevent accidental discharges should the hammer be struck by accident or by dropping the gun, or should the thumb slip from under the hammer in cocking. The gun is made in 5 or 6½ inch barrel and weighs 38 ounces.

This gun modified to take the .45 automatic cartridge and fitted with a 5½ inch barrel became the Model of 1917 revolver adopted by the U. S. Army during the World War, described below.

Model 1917 Colt and Smith & Wesson Revolvers

When the United States entered the World War the standard sidearm of the Army was the .45 Caliber Automatic Pistol, Model 1911, but it soon became evident that it would not be possible to obtain enough automatics to supply the demand. In this emer-

gency the firm of Smith & Wesson suggested using their .44
Military Revolver modified to take the .45 automatic pistol cartridge, using a clip that they had invented to facilitate the quick
loading of revolvers.

This clip was a crescent shaped piece of spring steel designed
to hold three automatic pistol cartridges. Two clips of three cartridges each could be quickly dropped into the cylinder of the re-

The Model 1917 Service Revolvers. Upper: The S. & W. .Lower: The Colt. Illustration shows very well the differences in the respective grips of each make. Note the
slightly greater depth and the different "set" of the Colt grip. Individual preference
for one or the other of these weapons is generally based upon the "fit" of these grips
to the shooter's hold and hand.

volver, thereby greatly reducing the time necessary to reload. This clip also facilitated the extraction of the rimless .45 caliber cartridge, which could not be extracted in the ordinary manner owing to the fact that the extractor would slip over the rim of the cartridge.

This modified Smith & Wesson revolver was tested out at Springfield Armory and found to be very satisfactory. Investigation showed that the Colt New Service Revolver could also be modified in the same way. The regular barrel length on the Smith & Wesson .44 was 6½ inches and that on the Colt New Service 5½ inches, so it was decided to have the barrel length on the modified Smith & Wesson 5½ inches, in order to make the two revolvers uniform in size. An order was then placed for the entire output of the Smith & Wesson factory in revolvers of this type, and a similar order was placed with the Colt Company.

These two revolvers became known as the U. S. Army Model 1917. This model is still manufactured and sold by Smith & Wesson, but at the close of the War the Colt Company discontinued the Model 1917 and returned to their regular New Service.

Whereas it was intended to use the clip with these revolvers for speedy loading and for extraction, it was soon found that the Smith & Wesson did not absolutely require the use of the clip as this gun was constructed with a shoulder at the front end of the chamber, the same as is found in the automatic pistol, and in placing the cartridges in the cylinder the square front edge of the cartridge case stopped against this shoulder so that the clip was not required to prevent the cartridge from going all the way in. It was found that the cartridges could merely be dropped into the cylinder one by one and would then fire in a perfectly satisfactory manner, but, of course, would not eject automatically by pushing the extractor rod as they would when the clip was used. It was found, however, that frequently if the gun was turned up-side-down the cartridges could be shaken out; or they could be pried out with the rim of another cartridge or pushed out with a short stick, or removed in some other manner.

It was found that in the early Colt guns there were no such shoulders, and the cartridges when dropped in would go all the way through, therefore a clip was necessary with the Colt. As soon as this was discovered a change was made in the Colt gun to make it have a shoulder the same as the Smith & Wesson. There were several hundred thousand Colts made, and the first fifty thousand did not have the shoulder, and with these the clip is necessary. With all the other Colts, except the first fifty thousand, and with all the Smith & Wessons, it is not necessary to use the clip except for speedy loading and ease of extraction.

Shortly after the war the Peters Cartridge Company put out a cartridge especially designed for the Model 1917, known as the "Auto Rim." This cartridge is made with both a jacketed bullet and a lead bullet, and is very similar in size to the .45 automatic pistol cartridge except that it has a rim which allows it to be extracted with the regular extractor.

The jacketed Auto Rim bullet weighs 230 grains and gives ballistics identical with those of the .45 automatic pistol cartridge. The lead bullet used with the Auto Rim weighs 255 grains and gives ballistics very similar to those obtained with the old style .45 Colt cartridge. Owing to the fact that a lead bullet is more effective than a jacketed bullet, the lead Auto Rim is the better cartridge of the two. The Remington Company also puts out an auto rim cartridge.

Many users of the Colt Model 1917 wish to change it over to take the .45 Colt Cartridge, and most of them think that this can be accomplished simply by purchasing a new cylinder, but it cannot be done so easily because there are quite a few differences between the Colt New Service .45 and the Colt Model 1917.

The Model 1917 was made on the New Service frame but the cylinder of the M 1917 is shorter than that of the New Service in order to give more headspace at the back of the cylinder. This is necessary because the thickness of the rim on the automatic pistol cartridge, plus the thickness of the steel clip, is considerably greater than the rim thickness of the old .45 Colt cartridge.

In the Colt revolver there is a raised surface on the side plate which holds the cylinder in place when it is swung out in the frame. This raised surface is made to correspond with the rear edge of the cylinder, and as the cylinder is shorter in the Model 1917 than it is in the .45 New Service, the top lug is located at a different point in order to take care of the shorter cylinder. When interchanging cylinders, therefore, it is necessary to have a new side plate. This involves a considerable amount of fitting, not only on the side plate but also on the crane, as each crane is fitted on an individual frame.

For this reason the changing of these cylinders is considered impracticable; besides, there is no good reason for making the change because the ballistics of the lead bulleted auto rim cartridge are almost equal to those of the .45 Colt cartridge, and there is not much to be gained by the change.

However, in response to the demand for changes of this nature, both Smith & Wesson and the Colt Company will furnish new cylinders, when ordered. The guns must be sent back to the factory to have these cylinders fitted. The length of the cylinder on the New Service .45 is 1.62″, on the Colt Model 1917 it is 1.59″, and on the Smith & Wesson it is 1.54″. The overall length of the .45 Colt cartridge is 1.57″, the rim thickness of the old style .45 Colt is 0.05″, whereas that on the .45 auto rim is 0.85″. Thickness of clip is .04.

Another question that sometimes comes up in connection with these revolvers is the desire of someone to use the Model 1917 cylinder in the New Service frame by sliding it onto the crane which is already fitted. The attempt to do this usually fails because the guide ribs on the ejector rods will not quite fit the slots in the cylinder. With a little gunsmithing this difficulty can be overcome, and the Model 1917 cylinder can be used in the 1909 frame by being careful each time that the cylinder is closed to guide it into place by hand, as the cylinder guide on the side plate is too short.

A comparison between the Colt and Smith & Wesson Model 1917 guns shows that they are very similar in general appearance and that they are about equal in accuracy. They both have 5½ inch barrels, but the Smith & Wesson is slightly lighter in weight and the handle of this gun is also smaller. The weight of the Smith & Wesson is 36¼ ounces and that of the Colt 40 ounces.

Numerous tests have been made to determine the relative velocities between the Model of 1917 revolver and the .45 Automatic pistol, both firing the same cartridges. In one test, the average results obtained by firing six guns of each kind showed the following comparative velocities:

Weapon Tested	Muzzle Velocity
.45 Cal. Automatic Pistol	800 foot seconds
.45 Colt M 1917 Revolver	813 " "
.45 Smith & Wesson M 1917 Revolver	785 " "

Ordnance Pamphlet No. 1918, describing these two arms, gives the following dimensions:

	Colt		Smith & Wesson	
Weight	2 lb. 8 oz.		2 lb. 4 oz.	
Total length	10.8	inches	10.79	inches
Barrel length	5.5	inches	5.5	inches
Diameter of bore	.445	inch	.445	inch
Diameter of rifling	.452	inch	.451	inch
Number of grooves	6		6	
Width of grooves	.156	inch	.157	inch

Depth of grooves	.0035	inch	.003	inch
Twist, 1 turn in	16	inches	14.659	inches
Width of lands	.073	inch	.075	inch
Cylinder length	1.595	inches	1.537	inches
Cylinder diameter	1.695	inches	1.708	inches
Chambers, number	6		6	
Chambers, diameter maximum	.4795	inch	.480	inch
Chambers, diameter minimum	.473	inch	.4795	inch
Front sight above axis of bore	.7325	inch	.794	inch

The Webley "Mark VI" Service Revolver, Caliber .455

This is the service sidearm of the British Army. It is a double action revolver of the hinged frame variety, in which the barrel tips up to eject the empty cartridges, and to reload. The latch which holds the action shut is made in the form of a heavy stirrup, which makes the closure very secure. This latch is somewhat on the principle of the one used on the .45 Schofield Model Smith

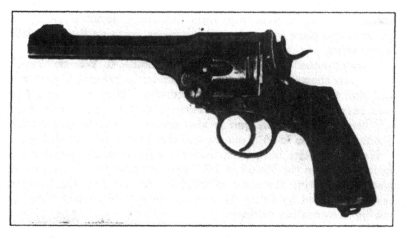

The Webley .455 Revolver, Mark VI, the service sidearm of the British Army.

& Wesson Army Revolver used in the Army years ago, but in the Webley, there is an extension, or thumb piece, on the left hand side of the revolver for operating the latch. Safety against firing the gun with the latch not fully fastened is provided by means of a projection on the hammer, which prevents the hammer nose from coming in contact with the primer unless the latch is fully in place.

The tip-up action offers the advantage that the cylinder can easily be removed for cleaning, and the breech of the barrel is accessible for the same purpose. Moreover, it makes it possible to convert the weapon into a .22 caliber single shot for practice. This is accomplished by removing the cylinder, and inserting a .22 caliber barrel, which fits inside of the regular barrel. This "aiming tube," as it is called, has an ejector of its own, operated the same as the regular ejector of the revolver, by the motion of tipping up the barrel to load. As the point of impact is different for the .22, the aiming tube carries its own sight, attached to a bracket on the tube, so as to slide into position on top of the frame when the tube is inserted in the barrel of the revolver.

Weight of the gun, 2 lbs. 6 ounces. It can be had in 6 inch or 4 inch barrel. It is an excellent heavy caliber military revolver.

The New Webley Mark IV .38 Caliber Military and Police Revolver

This is a weapon of the same general design and appearance as the .455, but is the latest Webley Pattern, and embodies a number of refinements and improvements. It was designed to meet the demand for a lighter gun than the .455 Service arm, which would combine perfect balance and great accuracy with exceptional stopping power.

This gun is notable for the excellence of its grip, which has a shape superior to that of any American revolver, and is exceedingly comfortable in the hand. In particular, the space behind the trigger guard is large enough to accommodate the second finger of the hand comfortably, which is not the case with any American gun except the Single Action Army Colt. Moreover, the slope of the bottom of the frame is such that this space behind the trigger guard is partly filled up by the metal of the frame, and thus affords a better support for the gun on the finger, without the necessity of using filler pieces, such as have become popular in this country on account of the defective design of our revolvers in this regard.

This excellent revolver, weighing 27 ounces, is chambered to shoot either the .38 S. & W. Cartridge, with 146 grain bullet, or the .38 Webley & Scott Special, with 200 grain bullet. As these bullets differ in point of impact, separate foresight blades are furnished, one to be used with the .38 S. & W., and the other for the .38 W. & S. Special. This model is supplied with 3 inch, 4 inch, or 5 inch barrel. It has an exceptionally light trigger pull. It can also be obtained in .32 caliber, for the .32 S. & W. long or .32 Colt New Police cartridges.

The Webley-Fosberry Automatic Revolver, Caliber .455

This gun stands in a class by itself as being the only automatic revolver in the world. It is a heavy frame military style large caliber revolver, made by Messers Webley & Scott, of Birmingham. In general design, it resembles the .455 Webley Mark VI, as the tip-up action, barrel latch, etc., are the same; but it has the additional feature, not shared by any other revolver, that the recoil

The .455 Webley-Fosberry Automatic Revolver. The cylinder and barrel are adapted to slide on the frame, and the force of recoil makes them move to the rear. When this motion takes place, the hammer is cocked and the cylinder is rotated, leaving the revolver ready for another shot by merely pulling the trigger.

is utilized to cock the hammer and rotate the cylinder after each shot, so that all the user has to do is to pull the trigger as desired.

The automatic action is accomplished by mounting the barrel and cylinder together on a piece arranged to slide to the rear, against the action of a spring, on a track located above the trigger guard and handle. A projecting lug in the track engages in cam grooves in the cylinder, so that the rearward motion turns the cylinder and brings the next cartridge into line with the barrel. At the same time, the rearward motion cocks the hammer. A safety lock is provided on the left side of the frame.

This gun can be fired with extreme rapidity; it is quite possible to fire all six shots in one second. It is chambered for the .455 service cartridge; has a six inch barrel, and weighs 42 ounces.

MILITARY AUTOMATIC PISTOLS

At the present time opinion is somewhat divided in military circles as to the relative advantages of the revolver and the automatic pistol as a service side arm. About the time that the United States Government adopted the automatic pistol it seemed as if the revolver was doomed to be replaced entirely by automatics; but twenty-five years have passed since that date and half the nations of the world still use the revolver and at this writing the situation seems somewhat stabilized.

In pocket automatic pistols using relatively low powered cartridges, the breech of the gun is generally kept shut merely by the strength of the recoil spring and the inertia of the moving parts; but in the high powered military automatics some method of locking the breech positively during the explosion, and then unlocking it later so as to allow the mechanism to open and throw out the empty shell, must be provided.

Colt Automatic Pistol, Government Model

This gun, known in the Army as the Model of 1911, is without doubt the finest heavy caliber automatic pistol in the world. It is simple, rugged, and reliable and is less subject to breakages than the average military revolver. Moreover, it is made so that it can be completely dismounted without the aid of tools, and all parts are readily interchangeable.

The Army Automatic is particularly compact, taking up much less space than a revolver of the same power. It is made in .45 caliber with a five inch barrel and has a magazine holding seven shots, in addition to which one can be placed in the chamber, making eight shots in all. The weight of the gun is 39 ounces and the length overall 8½ inches. The gun is so shaped that it fits the hand perfectly, and if the handle is grasped and the arm extended towards any object the pistol will naturally point directly at the object the same as pointing the finger.

An idea of the construction and mechanism of the gun can best be obtained by a reference to the sectional line drawings accompanying this description. The lower part of the gun, consisting of the handle into which the magazine fits is called the receiver, and contains the hammer, the safeties, and the firing mechanism. The upper part of the gun, containing the barrel is called the slide, and is arranged to move backward and forward on top of the receiver. Besides the barrel the slide contains the recoil spring and the firing pin and the extractor. The rearward part of the slide acts as a breech block and rests against the head of the cartridge when it is in the barrel.

The rear end of the barrel is pivoted by means of a link to the receiver; and on top of the barrel there are several ridges or locking shoulders which fit into corresponding grooves in the top of the slide. When the gun is fired, the head of the cartridge is pressed back by the powder pressure, and tends to separate the breech block from the barrel. However, the breech block, which

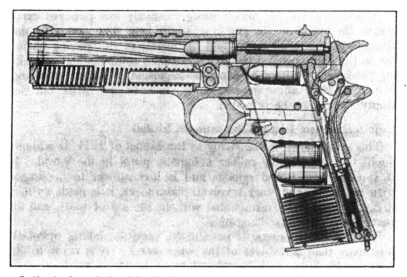

Sectional view of the Colt .45 Automatic Pistol, Government Model showing the mechanism as it appears in the safe carrying position with the hammer down and a loaded cartridge in the chamber. Note that the firing pin is too short to extend all the way through the breech block, so that a blow on the hammer or the dropping of the pistol cannot cause a discharge. This view also shows the relation of the parts at the instant of firing.

is part of the slide, is locked on to the barrel by means of the grooves above mentioned, and the powder pressure cannot separate the two parts. However, the pressure does cause the barrel and slide to recoil to the rear together at the same time that the bullet moves forward. As the barrel moves to the rear with the slide, the link pivoting its rear end to the receiver causes the rear of the barrel to swing downward, thus disengaging the locking shoulders on top of the barrel from those in the receiver. At this instant the barrel comes against a stop and cannot move any farther to the rear; but the slide now being unlocked from the barrel is free to continue to the rear.

As the slide moves to the rear it extracts and throws out the empty cartridge and also cocks the hammer.   It also pushes down a little plunger called the disconnector which disconnects the trigger from the hammer so that the gun will not fire again until the trigger is released and pulled once more.

When the slide reaches the end of its rearward motion, the recoil spring pushes it forward again, and as it goes forward it pushes the cartridge out of the magazine into the barrel and leaves

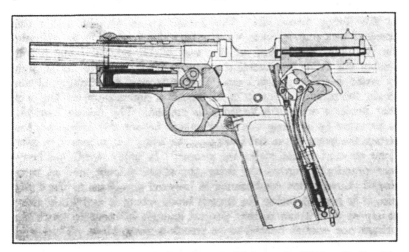

Sectional view of the .45 Cal. Government Model Automatic Pistol, with the slide fully retracted, and the magazine removed for reloading. Immediately on firing each shot, the slide recoils to the position shown, ejecting the empty cartridge and cocking the hammer, after which it instantly returns to the forward position, at the same time pushing a fresh cartridge into the chamber. When the magazine becomes empty, the mechanism remains locked open, in the position shewn.

the hammer cocked ready for the gun to be fired again by merely releasing and pressing the trigger.   When all seven shots have been fired the slide stays open.   If a catch on the left side of the gun is then pressed the empty magazine will fall out, and a new one can be inserted making seven more shots instantly available. After the insertion of the new magazine, a lever on the left side of the pistol just above the trigger guard, called the slide stop, is pressed down and this allows the slide to go shut, putting a cartridge in the chamber and leaving the gun cocked ready to continue firing.

On the left side of the gun there is a safety lock, arranged to be operated with the thumb.   When this safety lock is down, the gun can be fired, but when it is up, it locks the hammer in the cocked position. There is an additional safety on this gun consisting of a lever, called the grip safety, on the back of the handle. To fire the gun this grip safety must be pushed in at the same time that the trigger is pulled. This action is entirely automatic as the back of the hand will press the grip safety in whenever the butt is grasped and the trigger is pulled. The grip safety, however, prevents the gun from going off in case something catches on the trigger.

Another important safety feature in this gun is what is known as the flying firing pin. The firing pin is carried inside the breech block and is made shorter than the breech block. Should the hammer be lowered all the way down on the firing pin it pushes the firing pin inside the breech block, but not far enough to make it touch the primer. The only way the firing pin can touch the primer is for it to be struck a sharp blow on the part that projects when the hammer is cocked. The falling hammer is arrested by striking the breech block before the firing pin has struck the primer, but the inertia of the firing pin causes it to continue its motion and strike the primer. In other words the hammer practically throws the firing pin at the primer, and as mentioned above, when the hammer is lowered slowly on to the firing pin, it is pushed inside the breech block where it is housed away safely so that it can neither project enough in front to touch the primer nor enough behind to be struck a sharp blow. Thus with the hammer down and resting on the face of the breech and the loaded cartridge in the chamber, the .45 automatic is perfectly safe and the best way to carry it is with the hammer down on a loaded cartridge. Great care should be used, however, in lowering the hammer on to a live cartridge, and two hands should always be used for this job.

There are two other ways in which the automatic can be carried loaded. One way is with the hammer cocked and the safety on. This is the present regulation way of carrying the pistol in the Army. It has the advantage of avoiding the danger incident to lowering the hammer on a live cartridge, but also has the disadvantage that there is some chance of the safety working into the "off" position through motion of the gun in the holster, especially on horseback. The gun can, if desired, be carried with the hammer at half-cock; but this offers no advantage over carrying the hammer all the way down and is not as safe in case the gun is dropped, as a very sharp blow might conceivably break off the half-cock notch and discharge the gun.

It may be noted here that the gun is constructed so that it is possible to lower the hammer on a loaded cartridge to the half-cock notch with one hand. Many people do not know that this can be done, because it seems that with the finger on the trigger and the thumb on the hammer spur the grip safety will prevent the trigger from being pulled. However, if the hammer is pulled all the way back, the bottom of the hammer spur will strike on the rearward projection of the grip safety and release it, and if the trigger is then held back the hammer can be lowered. This should never be done, however, without pointing the gun in a safe direc-

The late Sgt. John M. Thomas, U. S. M. C., one of the finest pistol shots the author has ever known and a particularly good shot with the .45 Army Automatic.

tion, for if the thumb should slip from the hammer at this time, the gun will be discharged. It is better to use two hands, unless the left hand is engaged, as in holding the reins while on horse-back. It is the danger of accidental discharge when thus lowering the hammer with one hand while on horseback that caused the Army to change the regulations some years ago so as to require the automatic to be carried with the hammer cocked and the safety on.

With the Colt automatic pistol having the modern commercially made magazines in good condition, malfunctions are almost unknown. Six thousand consecutive shots were fired from one of these Colt automatic pistols in the final Government test without a jam or misfire or a broken part. Some feeding difficulties have, however, been reported with magazines of war time manufacture made under mass production methods. Prior to the war magazines were made by blanking out sheets of steel, bending them to the proper shape, and then welding. During the war, in order to facilitate production, drawn and welded tubes were substituted and the magazines were made of low carbon steel to facilitate the drawing process. The lips of these magazines were then hardened with cyanide in order to give them the requisite stiffness, and in some cases this made them so brittle that cracks developed. The commercial magazines made by the Colt Company at the present time are made of high carbon steel and are also slightly longer, which contributes to a more uniform and ready feeding of the cartridges.

As mentioned before, with the commercial magazines in good condition jams are almost unknown. Most troubles in feeding can be traced to some abuse or poor condition of the magazines of which the following are most common.

(1) Indentation of the side of the magazine from the pressure on the two snap-fasteners of the web magazine pocket in which spare magazines are carried on the belt.

(2) Deformation of the lips. This is difficult to detect by visual inspection when the deformation is slight.

(3) Dirt in the magazine, causing binding of the follower.

Troubles in feeding or functioning may also be caused by the excessive use of oil on the working parts of the gun in very cold climates or in very sandy locations such as in the desert. In such situations the gun should be wiped entirely dry of oil and it will function perfectly with no oil whatever, although, of course, the wear will be greater in this condition.

The .45 caliber automatic pistols manufactured commercially by the Colt Company are vastly superior in finish, workmanship, and fit of the parts to the guns that were turned out for the Army by various factories under rush conditions and by mass production methods during the World War. Guns purchased by the Government are marked "United States Property" on the right side of the receiver. The guns made and sold commercially by the Colt Company have the serial number preceded by the letter "C" and do not bear the Government mark described above.

Colt "Super .38" Automatic Pistol

This gun, the most powerful automatic pistol made, has the same design, mechanism, appearance, etc. as the .45 Government model automatic already described; but the Super .38 is chambered for the high velocity .38 automatic cartridge instead of for the .45. Like the .45 Army model, the gun weighs 39 ounces, has a five inch barrel, and an 8½ inch overall length. The capacity of the magazine is nine shots, which with one in the chamber, makes a total of ten at the command of the shooter. As the design and mechanism is exactly the same, the mechanical description, including safeties, method of loading, method of dismounting, etc. already given for the .45 automatic apply equally well to the .38 Super automatic.

In many ways the .38 automatic pistol cartridge which this gun uses is the finest high powered pistol cartridge made. It has a 130 grain bullet driven at 1200 foot seconds, and giving a muzzle energy of 417 foot pounds as against 340 foot pounds for the .45 automatic. But even more important than the high muzzle energy is the fact that this .38 automatic cartridge is notable for its very deep penetration, which makes it one of the few pistol cartridges that can be relied on to reach a vital spot when it is used for protection against very large animals. Moreover, it has speed enough in the bullet so that sure hits can be made on man-size targets at distances well over one hundred yards.

For years the small calibered but high velocity Mausers and Lugers have been the most popular guns when a pistol capable of very flat trajectory and high penetration was wanted. These German guns have several disadvantages, but they do have speed and penetration. Even at 200 yards they will shoot somewhere near the point of aim, and for this reason they retained sufficient popularity in this country to result in a respectable volume of sales in spite of the very high prices that must be charged for them as a result of our tariff. This popularity existed up until 1929, for until the advent of the Super .38 automatic in that year, we had no up-to-date American pistol that could equal these German guns in ballistics.

However, we have for years had an American pistol cartridge that is superior to either the Mauser or the Luger, and this is the .38 Automatic Colt Pistol Ctg., or ".38 A. C. P." This cartridge was developed for the first military automatic pistol ever made in this country, which was invented by John Browning and put out by Colt under the name of the .38 Military. The Army obtained a number of the then new Colt .38 automatics, as well as a number of nine millimeter Lugers for an extended service test. However, at that time the service side arm was the .38 caliber Colt or Smith

& Wesson revolver using the very low powered .38 Long Colt cartridge and this weak .38 failed to give a good account of itself in the Philippines, so that the Army decided that a larger caliber was necessary, and specified that the automatic to be adopted must be a .45 caliber.

In 1906 extensive tests were made of all available makes of automatic pistols, and the Colt design was selected as being the most promising, although it needed certain refinements. At that time the Colt was made in two calibers: .38 Military and .45 Military. Working with the Ordnance Department the Colt firm improved the .45 mechanically into what is now known as the Model of 1911; and this improved .45 was adopted by the Army. The .38 Military, which was very poor in size, balance, shape of grip, and angle at which the grip meets the body and which did not have the improved magazine catch, slide stop, grip safety, or thumb safety, remained on the market in its old form. The Army had set its stamp of approval on the .45 caliber, and it was only natural that the Colt Company should give all their attention to the new Army model, for it was assumed that any and all buyers of military automatics would want what the Army wanted and so the .38 automatic was left to die.

But it would not die. The ballistics of the cartridge were too good. People found that the new Army .45 fell short at long ranges at which the old .38 Military still held up, and that no pistol cartridge in the world equalled the .38 automatic in penetration. So it happened that there has always been a call for that excellent shooting gun from long range shooters and from people to whom deep penetration seems to be an essential feature. Thus the old .38 Military continued to have a good sale in spite of the fact that its mechanical features were twenty-five years old. It was clumsy and awkward, its grip was at the wrong angle but how it did shoot!

But the Luger is just as old, and even the old style Colt Military beat out the Luger in the early Army tests. Listen to what the board of 1906 said: "From a careful consideration of each weapon and of the tests made by the board, it is of the opinion that the Savage and the Colt automatic pistols possess sufficient merit to warrant their being given a further test under service conditions.

"The Luger automatic pistol, although it possesses manifest advantages in many particulars, is not recommended for a service test because its certainty of action, even with Luger ammunition, is not considered satisfactory."

It was generally recognized for years that the Colt .38 automatic cartridge is the best high powered pistol cartridge made and all that was holding it back was the fact that the weapon in which it was used had not kept pace with improvements in the art. This condition was remedied by the production of the .38 Super automatic in 1929. I received one of the first samples of these guns that the factory turned out and my first shot with it was over the water. My son, Bobby, and I took it to a little headland on the Chesapeake Bay and fired at a floating oil can about 200 yards off shore. The bullet seemed to be right there as soon as the trigger was pulled, and there was a vicious "crack" as the bullet struck the water just under the can. There was no ricochet. Then I fired with the same hold using an Army .45. There was an appreciable interval before the bullet dropped into the water with a dull "plup" about three-fourths of the way out, then ricocheted three times off to the left. A number of shots with both guns showed that the result described was no accident, for the same thing happened each time. Bobby said, "Say, Dad, that first gun you shot certainly lifts my hat when it goes off." The next thing that we did was to step down to the beach and fire into the wet sand. The .45 made a hole about big enough to put two fingers into. The Super .38 made a hole the size of my fist. Bobby regarded the results thoughtfully and remarked, "Gee, Dad, if a fellow got shot with that Super .38 it would be just too bad."

A very important feature of the .38 automatic cartridge is the extremely flat trajectory. The table gives the amount the bullet would drop at the various ranges if the gun were fired with the barrel held horizontal:

Name	Bullet Weight	Ballistic Coefficient	Drop of bullet in inches at					
			25 yds.	50 yds.	100 yds.	150 yds.	200 yds.	250 yds.
9 mm. Luger	121 gr.	.163	1.0	4.2	18	43	78	128
.38 A. C. P.	130 gr.	.172	.8	3.4	14.4	33	66	107
.45 A. C. P.	230 gr.	.189	1.5	6.8	28	68	122	203

It is apparent from these figures that the .38 Super automatic bullet drops just about half as much as the .45. This table shows how far the bullet would drop if the barrel were held firmly in a horizontal position when the gun is fired. However, this does not tell us how far above a given point the shooter must aim to hit that point, for the gun jumps considerably when fired; and, moreover, the line of sight does not coincide with the line of bore. As a matter of fact, the .38 and .45 automatic pistols are targeted at the factory to shoot into the center of a 2.72 inch bull's-eye at fifteen yards. That means that all the drop at that distance has been neutralized by the sighting, and that the bullet goes above the point of aim sufficiently to strike the center of the bull's-eye when aiming at the bottom. This upward direction in which the bullet starts neutralizes a considerable part of the drop at all ranges. Figured in this manner, the amount in inches that the shooter would have to hold over to hit an object at various distances would be as follows:

Name	100 Yards	150 Yards	200 Yards	250 Yards
.38 Super	3½"	16½"	44"	79"
.45 A. C. P.	15½"	50"	97"	171"

This shows for example, that at 150 yards if we aimed at a man's head with a Super automatic, we would hit him about in the pit of the stomach, whereas with a Government model .45 we would probably miss him entirely.

Differences Between the Super .38 and the .45: The fact that the Super automatic is built on the frame of the regular Army .45 has lead many users of the Army gun to ask if it would not be possible for them to have a double purpose gun by buying an extra Super .38 automatic slide and barrel and putting them on the .45 frame. The answer is, that it cannot be done. There are a number of reasons why some of the parts on the Super .38 automatic that are necessarily different from the corresponding parts on the .45. In the first place, the .38 caliber cartridge is considerably smaller in diameter than the .45 cartridge, although it is the same length. Moreover, the .45 is strictly rimless, whereas the Super .38 is not rimless but is what is known as a semi-rim cartridge. At a casual glance it looks like any rimless cartridge, but close examination reveals the fact that the head of the cartridge is just a little bit bigger in diameter than the body. On the other hand, the .45 is the same diameter from one end to the other, including the head. As there is no rim on the .45, and there must be some way to stop the cartridge in its proper place in the barrel so that it will be supported against the firing pin blow, the front end of the .45 cartridge case is left perfectly square and is not crimped into the bullet, and the chamber of the gun is so shaped that there is a sharp shoulder at the front end of the chamber for the cartridge case to rest on. On the other hand, the .38 automatic cartridge is crimped over at the front end, and there is no shoulder at the front end of the chamber. The cartridge is stopped in its position in the gun by a shoulder formed on the overhanging lip at the top of the barrel. The primer in the .38 cartridge is also much smaller than that in the .45.

On account of these various differences it is necessary to make quite a number of parts different. The receiver with all of its contained parts, such as the hammer, trigger, sear, etc., are the same, but there is one piece that goes on the receiver and in practice forms part of it, which is quite different, and that is the ejector. This is a little vertical piece of metal that fits on top of the receiver and is pinned to it, and works in a groove cut in the bottom of the slide. This ejector in the .45 is located at just the right place to strike the rim of the .45 cartridge; but because the .38 cartridge is considerably smaller, this .45 ejector would miss the .38 cartridge entirely. Therefore, in the Super .38 the ejector is made wide, so that it reaches closer in to the center of the gun. This wide ejector would prevent a .45 slide from being placed on a .38 frame; and also the narrow ejector used in the .45 would not work at all with a .38 slide and barrel assembly.

The barrel, of course, is quite different in the .38 from what it is in the .45, as it is smaller in bore and also smaller on the outside at the front end. The barrel bushing is different also. It is made smaller on the .38 so as to fit the reduced diameter of barrel.

The overhanging lip on the rear end of the barrel is longer on the .45 than it is on the .38, and the slide is also made different at this point to fit the barrel which belongs with it. The extractor well or hole in the .38 slide is closer to the center than it is in the .45. The firing pin hole is also different as the .38 uses a smaller firing pin to fit the smaller primer.

The magazine of the .38 differs from that of the .45 mainly in having a rib on each side so as to narrow down the inside space to fit the .38 caliber cartridges. However, the overall dimensions of the magazine are the same on both guns.

High velocity in a pistol cartridge has many important advantages and they are well utilized in the .38 Super automatic. This gun is extremely well thought of in countries where it may have to be used against very large animals. At close ranges the .45 is, no doubt, superior to the .38 Super automatic for most purposes; but it is certain that a man wearing one of the bullet proof vests which have recently become popular in certain quarters would have much more reason to be afraid of the Super .38 than of the .45. Another great advantage of the high speed bullet is that it shoots very close to the mark at reasonably long distances and still has plenty of energy at those ranges. For example, a good shot armed with a Super .38 would have small reason to fear a man 250 yards away armed with a Government .45 automatic.

The chances are that the man with the Super .38 could make the other man lay down his gun.

Luger Automatic Pistol

This gun, sometimes called the "Parabellum," is one of the most famous and popular military type automatic pistols in the world and is the service side arm of Germany, Switzerland, Holland, Portugal, Brazil and Bulgaria. The action, which is made on the same principle as that of the Maxim machine gun, was invented by an American named Borchardt who lived in Connecticut. The first models of this gun were called the Borchardt-Luger but the gun has been considerably simplified in the later models and the name has been shortened. The original makers of this gun were the Deutsche Waffen- und Munitionsfabriken, whose monogram "D. W. M." appears on top of the breech mechanism on all Lugers made by that firm. Guns that do not have this monogram are war-time Lugers made by other manufacturers.

The outstanding feature of the Luger is its neat appearance and excellent balance. It is rather light in weight for as powerful a gun as it is. The standard Luger weighs 30 ounces, which is approximately 9 ounces lighter than the Colt. All mechanism of the gun is contained in the part that lies directly above the hand and the barrel is comparatively light. For this reason the balance is exceptionally good. The gun is "muzzle-light" as compared with almost any other automatic pistol. It is the most "natural" pointing of any of the automatics. The angle of the grip to the barrel is very much greater than that of most automatic pistols, and this is one feature that adds to the natural pointing of the Luger. The gun is neat, compact, powerful, clean shooting, accurate and extremely well balanced. For these reasons it has been one of the most popular automatic pistols ever manufactured.

One very bad thing about the Luger pistol is the miserable trigger pull. This is due to the fact that the mechanism which pulls the trigger must work around several corners and for this reason the trigger pull is very hard to work over, to make it even passably good.

As for accuracy, the Luger is excellent, provided you get good ammunition and a good gun. The ordinary 4-inch barrel model generally shoots high and somewhat to the left as it is received from the factory. The longer barrel models—6-inch, 8-inch and 12-inch—generally are sighted so that they shoot about where they are pointed.

In general I have not found the Luger action to be as safe from jams as the Colt action. The main troubles are either failures to open entirely or failures to close entirely. Nearly every jam in the Luger can be traced to a variable quality of ammunition. The most important thing about this gun is to get good strong re-

The Luger Automatic Pistol. This weapon has enjoyed a very great popularity which is largely due to the very graceful shape and the excellent balance. It is a gun which can only be grasped in the right manner, as shown above.

liable ammunition. If you are sure of the quality of your ammunation, the gun will generally perform well mechanically.

An interesting and useful feature found on many Lugers is the indicator showing whether or not the gun is loaded. This indication is accomplished by means of the extractor, which remains in a raised position above the breech block when there is a cartridge in the barrel, and on the raised side of the extractor is the word "Loaded" or "Geladen." On guns intended for the American trade this marking was in English, and on guns intended for use in Germany it was in German.

There have been a great many different variations in the Luger model. Among the variations may be mentioned the following: In the earlier guns the action spring was a flat leaf spring made of several leaves fastened together. In the later guns it is a spiral spring. Some models have a catch on the right-hand side of the middle pivot of the breech block to hold the breech shut until the barrel has recoiled to the rear, thus preventing the breech from accidentally becoming partly opened. In the later models with the stronger action spring this has been omitted. Some models were made with a catch to hold the gun open after the last shot was fired. In others this catch is not incorporated. In some models the thumb safety pushes up to make the arm safe; in other models it pulls down to the safe position. Some models have a grip safety, others do not. In some models the markings for "safe" and "loaded" are in English; in others they are in German. Some models have an eagle stamped on the receiver just back of the barrel; others do not have it.

The genuine Lugers made today by D. W. M., and sold by A. F. Stoeger, as well as the pre-war Lugers, are of excellent workmanship and material and are in every respect high class arms. However, during the World War guns of the Luger pattern were manufactured under stress of necessity in many various factories under mass production methods and many of these are of very indifferent quality. Moreover, after the war this country was flooded with Lugers of the very poorest quality, many of which were miserable makeshifts apparently assembled from old components left in various factories when the war ended and most likely rejected as unsuitable for military use. It is, therefore important to be able to tell a war-time Luger from one made before or after the war. I have heard many rules quoted as to how to tell the war-time Lugers from the others, but I know of no rule that is infallible. For example, it is said that Lugers not made during the war had an eagle on the rear of the receiver, while the war period Lugers do not. This is not infallible as the only Lugers that had this eagle on them were those specifically manufactured for export to America. Again it is stated that the extractor indicator is marked "Geladen" on war-time guns and "Loaded" on the others. This also is not infallible. The "Loaded" sign was placed only on guns intended for export to

MILITARY MODELS 105

English speaking countries. Many excellent pre-war guns are marked "Geladen." It is said also that on the earlier guns the stocks are made of a dark colored American walnut while on the war-time ones they are made of a very much lighter colored wood. I have an excellent Luger which dates from 1910 which has no eagle on the receiver and has the right stock made of American walnut and the left one of Circassian walnut. It is also said that the war-time Lugers have the attachment on the butt for fastening on the holster stock while this is not on the pre-war ones. The Lugers made today do have this attachment and the ones made before the war generally do not whereas some war-time guns have the attachment and some do not have it.

Thus it will be seen that there is no reliable rule; the best indication is the general finish and workmanship of the gun. Guns that do not have the D. W. M. monogram on them or that have a date on the breech block or have a rough finish on the outside with a grayish appearance rather than the dull satiny black are probably of war-time manufacture and should be shunned.

At the present time the sole agent for the Luger pistol is A. F. Stoeger, Inc., 507 Fifth Avenue, New York. The guns sold by Stoeger today are of excellent quality. When the safety lever is "on" the word "Safe" appears. When there is a cartridge in the chamber the extractor projects above the breech block and shows the word "Loaded." On top of the breech block appears the monogram D. W. M. On the right side of the barrel extension appears the words "A. F. Stoeger, Inc., New York" and just above these words the marking "Germany" in small letters. On the right hand side of the receiver is the inscription "Genuine Luger—Registered U. S. Patent Office."

The Luger is made in both 7.65 millimeter, or .30 caliber, and in 9 millimeter or .38 caliber. Both Luger cartridges have very high velocity, flat trajectory and much penetration. The .30 caliber size is made with a metal jacketed bullet with a rounded point, having about 1200 foot seconds velocity and weighing 93 grains. The 9 mm. has 124 grain, flat pointed jacketed bullet with a standard velocity of 1050 foot seconds. Recently, however, an improved high velocity 9 mm. Luger pistol cartridge has been brought out by Remington which has a velocity of 1210 foot seconds. The 9 mm. bullet is in the shape of a truncated cone and its flat point adds greatly to the stopping effect.

The Lugers are made with four inch, six inch, and eight inch barrels in the 9 mm. caliber and with 3¾ inch, 4½ inch, and 6 inch barrels in the .30 caliber. The shorter barrels have a fixed rear sight at the back end of the breech toggle. The long barrel models have the rear sight, adjustable for range, located in front of the breech mechanism. The weight of the short barrel models is 31 ounces in both calibers.

Carbine barrels of 10, 12 and 16 inch length can also be obtained for these guns but the functioning of these longer barrels with ordinary ammunition is not reliable and they are principally suitable for single shot work although sometimes a special cartridge loaded to higher velocities especially for the Luger carbine can sometimes be obtained. These cartridges are distinguished by a black case instead of the ordinary brass colored one.

Modern Lugers have a fitting on the grip for the attachment of a wooden shoulder stock.

In common with the other high powered, military automatics, the Luger has a fully locked breech mechanism which opens only after the barrel has recoiled a short distance. Behind the breech block is a toggle joint, and the rear pin of this toggle is fastened in the barrel extension. The breech block and the two levers of the toggle are normally in a straight line. When the cartridge is fired the thrust of the recoil comes on the breech block and is transmitted through the toggle levers to the pin which holds them to the barrel extension; hence the barrel and breech block are forced to recoil together. After moving back approximately one-quarter inch the center part of the toggle joint strikes on the sloping part of the frame, which breaks the toggle, and as soon as the levers are out of line with each other the toggle is no longer locked and the breech opens.

.22 Caliber Attachment for Luger Pistol

A. F. Stoeger, Inc., the importers of the Luger pistol market a .22 caliber insert barrel, automatic breech block, and .22 caliber magazine which can be attached to the Luger pistol to convert it to a .22 caliber automatic. This attachment is very useful for target practice, small game shooting, etc. By the use of this relatively inexpensive attachment the user of the Luger pistol is enabled to obtain unlimited practice at small expense.

The Mauser Automatic Pistol

This is a very famous gun and has for years been used all over the world especially by explorers and those who live in the wilder and less civilized parts of the earth. One of its great advantages is that it uses the highest velocity cartridge made whose ballistics resemble those of a rifle more than those of any other pistol. Moreover, the holster in which this pistol is carried is made of wood and is so shaped as to form a rigid and efficient shoulder stock which can instantly be attached to the handle of the pistol, thereby converting it into a highly accurate carbine with which long range shooting can be done much more effectively than it can with any other hand gun.

The very great penetration of this pistol is shown by a recent test of armored vests conducted by the author. It is interesting to note that with no other pistol or revolver was penetration secured

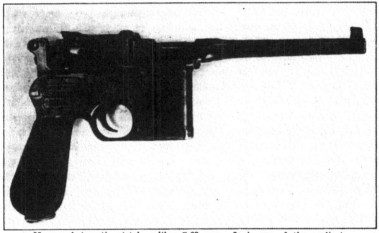

Mauser Automatic pistol, caliber 7.63 mm. It is one of the earliest automatics developed.

but in every instance in which the Mauser pistol was used the overlapping steel plates of the vest were entirely perforated. The only effect of the heavy .45 Colt revolver with lead bullet, and of the .45 automatic was to dent the plate. Even the Super .38 automatic failed to secure penetration.

The gun is twelve inches in length overall, has a 5¼ inch barrel, a magazine holding ten shots, a rear sight adjustable for elevation, and graduated from 50 meters up to 1,000 meters, an outside hammer and a thumb safety. Weight of the gun is 45 ounces.

When the gun is attached to the holster it is twenty-five inches overall; when placed in the holster the overall length is fourteen inches and the weight is 3 lbs. and 12 ounces.

The gun is made principally in 7.63 mm. or .30 caliber; but at one time it was made in 9 mm. for a 9 mm. Mauser cartridge.

During the war, however, a number of these 9 mm. Mausers were chambered for the Luger pistol cartridge and such pistols are distinguished by the figure "9" carved into the wooden stock and usually painted red. The gun is now made only in the .30 caliber. The 7.63 mm. Mauser cartridge has an 86 grain bullet with a velocity of 1323 foot seconds. An accurate range of 1,000 yards is claimed for this weapon with the shoulder stock.

The gun is characterized by an exceptionally clever design of mechanism with the total avoidance of pins or screws in the working parts and the workmanship is of the highest quality throughout.

The original Mauser pistol above described is known as the model of 1899, but recently some slight changes have been made, including a lever by which the gun can be made full automatic so that all shots are fired with one pull of the trigger. This new gun is called the 1932 model and is so arranged that a twenty shot magazine can be used in place of the regular ten shot magazine when desired. This gun, model 711, comes under the special restrictions governing the sale of machine guns which makes it a felony to keep for sale, offer or give a machine gun to any person except regularly constituted or appointed state or municipal police departments, sheriffs and policemen and other police officers and to state prisons, penitentiaries and county jails, and military and naval organizations. While this law at present applies only to the state of New York, the importers of the Mauser pistol, A. F. Stoeger, Inc., have extended these provisions to the whole of the United States and will sell this model 711 pistol with the automatic feature, only to constituted authorities. However, this pistol is also made without the automatic feature as model 712 and this model can be sold to any person who can legally purchase any other pistol or revolver.

The Mauser has a locked breech mechanism, consisting of a long sliding breech block in a barrel extension. The breech block is locked to the barrel extension by means of a locking bolt which engages in shoulders under the breech block and is held up in place by a cam on the frame.

When the gun is fired, the barrel, barrel extension and breech block move to the rear together for a short distance, when the locking bolt is pulled down by means of a cam, and the breech block then continues to the rear by itself. The gun remains open after the last shot and exposes the magazine ready to receive ten cartridges which are furnished in a clip. To load, these cartridges are stripped downward out of the clip into the magazine;

then when the clip is pulled out the breech block goes shut and the gun is loaded.

The .455 Webley Automatic

The official name of this gun, as it is written in Great Britain, is "Pistol Self-Loading, .455 Mark I." It is made by Webley & Scott, Ltd., of Birmingham. The most striking feature in the appearance of this gun is the generally square outline, and the fact that the handle sticks more nearly straight down than it does in our own Army automatic. The grip appears disproportionately long, and the gun seems short from front to rear, so that the impression as a whole is that of a stubby weapon with a very long handle. The grip safety is also very prominent, and sticks out fully half an inch in the rear of the handle, which is quite a bit thicker from side to side than that of our Model 1911 automatic.

The hammer has the same shape as that on the Mauser automatic, which is not bad, and certainly has the advantage of not biting the hand that holds the gun, as our automatic does at times.

While a glance would lead one to believe that the dimensions of the Webley & Scott are radically different from those of the U. S. Model 1911, this is something of an optical illusion, as the following measurements will show:

	W. & S. 2 lb. 7½ oz.	U. S. 2 lb. 7 oz.
Over-all length	8½ in.	8½ in.
Over-all depth	5½ in.	5⅜ in.
Capacity of magazine	7 shots	7 shots
Weight of bullet	220 grains	230 grains
Length sight radius	7¼ in.	6⅜ in.
Barrel length	5 in.	5 in.

A casual inspection of the outside of the British gun shows the following features: Front sight is square, a better shape for accuracy than our type, but more likely to catch in the clothes or holster, and therefore not so good for service. Rear sight is adjustable for windage, but not for elevation. Magazine release is under the butt; not so conveniently located as ours, and not adapted to ejecting the magazine with one hand. The slide remains back after the last shot, and is conveniently released by a large catch on the left side. The magazine is of a more sturdy construction than that in the U. S. Model 1911, and the lips at the mouth of the magazine look better able to stand service without deforming.

A grip safety is provided, but there is no hand-operated safety lock. The firing pin is made to operate by inertia, like the .45

Colt, and is shorter than its housing, so that the hammer may with safety be carried lowered with a cartridge in the chamber. The extractor is on top, and the ejection is straight up and forward, a marked improvement over the vicious backward ejection of the Army Model Colt automatic.

The rifling is six grooves right-handed and with a much sharper twist than that of the left-handed rifling in the Government Model Colt. The gun has a large comfortable grip, and feels pleasant to aim or shoot; but the angle of the grip is such that there is a natural tendency to point low. In this respect it is inferior to the Colt.

There are several novelties in the construction of this pistol. One that is stressed in the catalogue is the ability to use the pistol as a single-shot weapon, at the same time that the loaded magazine is in place and ready for instant use. This is made possible by having two retaining notches in the magazine, one above the other. When the magazine is pushed all the way in, the catch locks in the lower notch, and the gun is ready for rapid fire. On the other hand, if the magazine is pushed only part way in, so that the catch locks in the upper notch, the pistol can be loaded with single shots, and after each shot the slide will remain open ready for another cartridge to be inserted. The magazine remains in the handle, but down out of the way. If rapid fire is desired, an upward push on the magazine locks it in place for action.

An interesting feature is the extremely rapid take-down arrangement. The action is held shut by the tension of a flat spring which is inside the handle under the right-hand stock. The pressure of this spring is exerted against a hardened-steel pin, which extends transversely through the breech, called the "recoil lever bar and breech stop." On the right-hand side of the frame is a small stud with a milled head. This piece is called the "recoil lever stop," and its purpose is to lock the recoil spring out of action.

To disassemble the pistol, the breech is pulled about a quarter of an inch to the rear, and the recoil lever stop is pressed in, thus locking the spring out of action. The breech is then pushed forward again, and the breech stop (which is now loose, since the recoil spring is locked out of action) is pulled out as far as it will go. This removes it from the path of the shoulders on the frame against which it would normally strike, and at the same time it can not be pulled all the way out and lost because of a screw working in a groove provided for it. The displacement of the breech stop leaves the breech free to be drawn to the rear, which releases the barrel entirely, so that it can be lifted or shaken off. The breech can then be pushed forward off the frame.

The description makes this operation seem longer than it really is. It can be performed in about one second, and is the quickest take-down I have ever seen. It is very much quicker and easier than the corresponding operation on the Colt. In fact, this take-down operation can be done so quickly that it appears as if the operator had merely jerked back the slide and tossed the barrel off the frame. The very great ease with which the barrel can be removed is a strong point in favor of the gun, because it makes cleaning so easy that there is no temptation to shirk this duty.

Japanese 8 m/m Automatic Pistol, "Nambu" Pattern

This gun is not sold in America, but occasionally samples will be seen in the hands of travelers who have been in Japan. The gun resembles the Luger in appearance, size, and balance, which is excellent. It uses a cartridge which resembles the .30 caliber

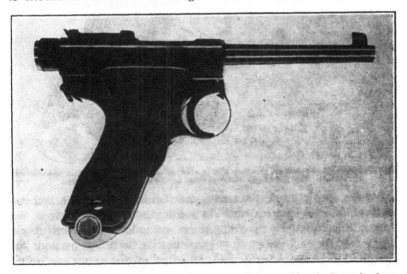

Japanese 8 m/m "Nambu" pistol. This weapon, which resembles the Luger in shape and outside appearance, has a mechanism of distinctive design which is entirely different from that of any other automatic.

Luger cartridge in appearance, but the size is slightly larger, being 8 mm., or .32 caliber, instead of 7.65 mm. as in the Luger. The bullet weighs 102 grains, smokeless powder charge 4 grains.

The pistol comes in a wooden holster stock, which attaches to the butt of the gun to form a carbine. The holster is made only long enough to carry the pistol, and as this does not make it long enough to serve as a satisfactory shoulder stock, it has a telescoping section, which pulls out to make the length correct for use as a stock. There is a grip safety on the front of the handle, under the trigger guard. Rear sight is adjustable for range.

While the gun resembles the Luger in appearance, the mechanism is very different in action. The breech block is locked firmly to the barrel extension by a locking bolt pivoted so that it can swing up to lock the parts, or down to unlock them. This down swing cannot be accomplished, however, unless the barrel and breech block have moved some distance to the rear. Therefore,

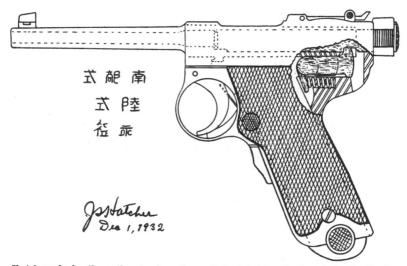

式 艦 南

式 陸

征 示

ﾉﾊｻtｃﾉﾟ
Dec 1, 1932

Sketch made by the author to show the method of locking the breech in the Nambu Pistol. The markings which appear on the gun are also shown.

when the gun is fired, the barrel, and the breech block, locked together, move to the rear until the locking bolt reaches a cut in the frame which allows it to swing down and unlock the breech block from the barrel. When this happens, the barrel stops and the breech block travels on to the rear, ejecting the empty cartridge. The spring then pushes the breech block forward, feeding another cartridge from the magazine into the chamber, and pushing the barrel forward to the position where the barrel and breech block are again locked. The entire mechanism can easily be dismounted with the hands, without the use of tools. The gun is very cleverly designed, and well put together, and is a good high-velocity small caliber military automatic.

CHAPTER 4

POCKET AND HOME DEFENSE HANDGUNS

UNDER this heading we include guns for the use of law officers and policemen, bankers, bank messengers, and others; guns for the protection of the home, and all pocket guns. It is rather difficult to draw any sharp line of distinction between the Military and target arms already described, and home defense guns. For example, any of the fine target arms will serve for home protection, and this protection will be unusually effective, because the owner of a target arm will be familiar with the sport of shooting, and therefore will know how to use the pistol safely and effectively. Then, again, the Military arms will be effective for home defense, banks, etc., and such guns as the S. & W. Military and Police or the Colt Official Police, when furnished with the 4 inch barrel make excellent and most effective pocket arms. These guns, which have already been described under the Military classification in the last chapter, also make the very best holster guns for policemen and law officers. The four inch barrel is the longest that should ever be used as a service arm by law officers. It is long enough to get almost the maximum power and accuracy out of the cartridge, and at the same time it is not so long as to be unhandy. It is a mistake for a police officer to use a gun with a six inch barrel. It adds nothing to the effectiveness, and it makes the gun slower to draw and to use.

With the understanding that many of the guns already described are excellent for the purposes we have in mind, we will now proceed to describe the smaller and shorter revolvers and automatic pistols, that are suitable only for these uses, and not for target or military use.

Smith & Wesson Safety Hammerless

Among the revolvers in the pocket class the place of honor certainly goes to the Smith & Wesson Safety Hammerless. This

113

gun has been on the market for forty-five years and is apparently just as popular today as when it was first introduced and is by no means obsolete.   In fact, for the average gun to keep around the house, I can think of no better revolver than this.   As its name indicates, it is hammerless and has no projections that can catch on the pocket or in any way cause accidental discharge.   It can not be discharged by dropping it or striking it in any way.   It has a double action with a rebounding lock, and unless the trigger

Two hammerless pocket revolvers.   Upper, the Smith & Wesson Safety Hammerless. Lower, the Iver-Johnson Hammerless.   The S. & W. is shown in the .38 caliber, and the Iver-Johnson in the .32, though both makes may be had in either caliber.

is pulled, the hammer, which is fully enclosed, is in the down position and the firing pin does not touch the cartridge. The trigger pull is purposely made long and fairly heavy, with a distinct pause just at the point where the hammer is cocked. This makes the gun very easy to shoot accurately. For quick work you simply point the gun at the object and pull the trigger all the way back, and the gun is fired. For deliberate work you point the gun at the object and draw the trigger back until a sudden decided resistance is encountered. At this point the hammer is fully cocked and then careful aim is taken and a little added pressure placed on the trigger, when the gun is discharged. After a little practice this gun can be fired almost as accurately as if the hammer could be cocked by hand.

This gun also has a grip safety, and this was the first arm on which the grip safety was used. An excellent feature about this arm is that it is physically impossible for a small child to fire it. This is on account of the fact that the hand must not only press the grip safety, but must also draw the fairly heavy trigger through quite a distance, something a child can not do. For a gun to be kept in a desk or bureau drawer around a house, I can think of nothing better. It can be thrown around or dropped on the floor and there is no danger of having it go off, and if small children should accidentally get hold of it they can do no harm. It is made in two calibers, the .32 S. & W. Short, and the .38 S. & W., shooting also the .38 Colt Police Positive. The .32-caliber has a 3-inch barrel and weighs 14¼ ounces. The .38 caliber has a 3¼- or 4-inch barrel and weighs 18¼ ounces. The gun has a tip-up action for loading and ejecting. The cylinder holds 5 shots.

Iver Johnson and Harrington & Richardson Revolvers

Both the Iver Johnson Arms and Cycle Company, and Harrington & Richardson also make .32 caliber and .38 caliber hammerless 5 shot pocket revolvers, and these firms also make hammer guns as well in the .32 and .38 pocket sizes, and the Iver Johnson has the famous "Hammer the Hammer" safety on it, which is, briefly, an arrangement whereby the hammer does not directly strike the cartridge, but strikes on a lever which is placed in front of the firing pin by the act of pulling the trigger. In this way there is no danger of accidental discharge if the gun should be dropped.

Smith & Wesson ".32 Hand Ejector"
Smith & Wesson "Regulation Police"

These guns are the same except for the shape of the butt, which is of the square, or military shape in the "Regulation Police," and the more desirable rounded shape in the ".32 Hand Ejector." They are both small counterparts of the large military revolvers made by this firm. They have the well-known solid frame, with swing-out cylinder, and simultaneous ejection by means of a hand operated ejector rod.

They are designed for the special requirements of policemen and law enforcement officers, and are arms of the highest ac-

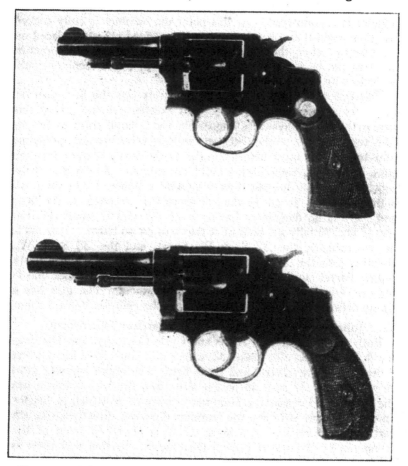

Upper: The Smith & Wesson .38 Caliber Regulation Police Revolver. The .32 Regulation Police is identical in appearance.

Lower: The Smith & Wesson Military & Police .38 with 4 inch barrel and round butt. This is a superb high powered pocket revolver. The round butt is preferable in nearly every way to the square style. The saving in bulk is especially noticeable when the gun is worn with a shoulder holster.

curacy, workmanship, and durability. This model in the .32 S. & W. Long caliber is about the "sweetest shooting" revolver at 50 yards that I have ever handled. The frame and handle of this model is small, the trigger action is light and smooth, and with the .32 caliber, the report and recoil is light. These features combined with the general overall small size and dainty proportions, make this gun perhaps the ideal home defense gun for women who are inclined to be nervous about handling the larger guns. The gun shoots either the .32 S. & W. Short, the .32 S. & W. Long, or the very effective .32 Colt New Police. This latter cartridge has a flat point, which nearly doubles its stopping power, and renders it practically as effective as the round nosed .38 S. & W. Cartridge.

These guns in .32 caliber may be had with 3¼, 4¼, or 6 inch barrel. Weight, with the 3¼ inch barrel, 18 ounces. The short barrel is preferable, unless the arm is to be used especially for target shooting. The round butt is to be preferred to the square or military shape, which has nothing to commend it except appearance, and has the disadvantage of being less convenient, and making the gun more bulky to carry.

These pocket guns have fixed sights, but the .32 "Regulation Police" may also be had in a target model, with adjustable target sights and a six inch barrel. The "Regulation Police" model is also made in .38 caliber, for the .38 S. & W. or the .38 Colt New Police Cartridges. It has a 4 inch barrel only, and the cylinder holds only 5 cartridges, instead of six, as do the .32 caliber guns of this size. Weight, 18 ounces. This is an excellent gun, which would be better if it had a 3 inch barrel and a round butt.

Colt "Pocket Positive" Revolver

This is a .32 caliber, solid frame, swing-out cylinder, pocket revolver, with a rounded butt to the handle. The name "Pocket Positive" comes from the fact that this revolver embodies the safety device known as the "Colt Positive Lock," which is a sliding piece of metal that lies between the hammer and the frame, thus positively preventing the hammer from striking the primer of the cartridge in case of an accidental blow, or a fall. When the trigger is pulled, this piece of metal is drawn out of the path of the hammer; but should the thumb slip while cocking the gun, the positive lock will return to its position ahead of the hammer and prevent an accident. Only when the trigger is held back during the hammer fall can the cartridge be exploded.

The Colt Pocket Positive Revolver. This is a .32 caliber revolver in which compactness and small size are the outstanding characteristics.

Colt's Police Positive Special Revolver. This is a Police Revolver of medium size, chambered for the powerful .38 Special Cartridge. It has been made as small and compact as a gun can be to handle this cartridge satisfactorily.

Length of barrel, 2½, 3½, or 6 inches. Weight, with 2½ inch barrel, 16 ounces. Caliber, .32, for the Colt New Police Cartridge, though the .32 S. & W. short or the .32 S. & W. long may also be used.

Colt "Police Positive" Revolver

This is a medium powered revolver of light weight and small size, made on military lines, with a solid frame and a swing-out cylinder, in .32 and .38 calibers. As the name would indicate, it embodies the Colt Positive Lock. It is made only with a square butt, which is undesirably bulky and thick at the bottom. Otherwise, this arm is almost ideal for personal or home protection, as well as for police use.

The .32 caliber is made in 2½, 4, 5, or 6 inch barrel, with fixed sights, and cylinder holding six shots. It will shoot the .32 Colt New Police, or the .32 S. & W. Short or Long Cartridges. Weight, with 4 inch barrel, 20 ounces.

The .38 caliber, with fixed sights, is made with 4, 5, or 6 inch barrel, and also, under the name of Banker's Special, with 2 inch barrel. It shoots the .38 Colt New Police or the .38 S. & W. Cartridge. Weight 20 ounces.

This gun is also made in a target model, already described in Chapter 2. It has a six inch barrel, and adjustable target sights, and can be had in .22 Long Rifle, .22 W. R. F., and .32 calibers.

Colt Banker's Special

This is the "Police Positive" with 2 inch barrel. It is made in .38 Colt New Police and in .22 Long Rifle calibers. The 2 inch barrel is surprisingly accurate, and the short barrel makes this a very compact gun for pocket use. This model is now made with the butt somewhat rounded, which is a decided improvement, as it makes the gun less bulky and less noticeable when carried in the pocket or in the shoulder holster.

This gun in the .38 Caliber is a wonderful gun for bank messengers, express or mail clerks, or others who must have a gun at all times. It was designed especially for the requirements of the railway mail service, and is now the standard gun of that service, many thousand of them having been purchased by the Government for arming the Railway Mail Clerks.

The .22 Caliber model is extremely valuable as a sub-caliber, or practice gun for users of pocket sized .38's. Guns for the protec-

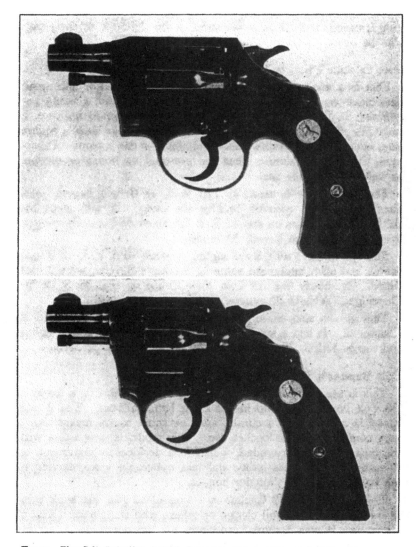

Upper: The Colt Detective Special Revolver, shown with round butt. The square butt can also be furnished if wanted, but is not desirable, as it is more bulky and not so pleasant to handle. This gun is chambered for the powerful .38 Special Cartridge.

Lower: Colt Banker's Special Revolver. This gun, chambered for the .38 Smith & Wesson or .38 Colt New Police, is furnished with either round or square butt at no extra cost. The round butt is much to be preferred, especially on a gun where every effort has been made to attain the maximum of compactness.

tion of valuables may have to be used at night or in other situations where the sights cannot be seen, and the only way to be able to use them effectively is to practice with them enough so that the pointing is instinctive. By the use of the .22 caliber of the same size and shape as the large gun, a sufficient amount of shooting may be done to make the user proficient, without a large expenditure for ammunition. In fact the saving on ammunition will often pay for the purchase of an additional gun in .22 caliber for practice.

The advent on the market of the High Speed .22 caliber Hollow Point Cartridges, and of the High Speed .22 Caliber Sharp Shoulder cartridges gives the user of such a gun as the .22 Banker's Special a .22 caliber cartridge that has quite a respectable shock power of its own, and loaded with these high powered .22's, the Banker's Special may be relied on as an effective home or personal defense gun.

The Colt "Police Positive Special" Revolver

This is a pocket revolver, of approximately the same size as the Police Positive, and weighing but 2 ounces more, but chambered for the powerful .38 Special, or the .32-20 (.32 Winchester) cartridge. It is made as light and small as a revolver can be to handle these heavy cartridges.

It has a solid frame, swing-out cylinder, fixed sights, and the Colt Positive Lock. Length of barrel, 4, 5, or 6 inches. Weight, with 4 inch barrel, 22 ounces. This gun is also made in the .38 Special Caliber, with 2 inch barrel, under the name of "Detective Special."

Harrington & Richardson "New Defender"

This newcomer to the field of pocket revolvers deserves special mention. It is the Harrington & Richardson "Sportsman" double action target revolver with 2 inch barrel, and rounded butt walnut stock.

It has adjustable sights, the front sight being adjustable for elevation, and the rear sight for deflection, the sights are low down on the barrel, so as to be suitable for pocket use, and the front sight is so shaped as not to catch in the clothing, and is fitted with an embedded gold ball sight, which can be quickly seen in all kinds of light.

Like all the recent Harrington and Richardson target arms, this gun has the standard frame, which will take any one of the 5 standard interchangeable stocks. However, the gun comes regularly equipped with the number two stock, shortened and rounded at the butt, and this stock is just right, and is the only one that does feel right.

The surprising thing about this little two-inch barrel gun is the accuracy that it gives on the target. The first time that I shot it my score was 90 on the Standard American Target at 20 yards, and my score, shot at the same time with a single shot target pistol was only 92. I could hardly believe that the little two-inch barrel was capable of such a result, but repeated trials showed that it had really remarkable accuracy. My average score on the Standard American Target at 20 yards over a period of months with this gun was 84.3, the lowest score being 80 and the highest being 94.

The Iver Johnson "Protector" Sealed Eight

Iver Johnson makes a light handy pocket revolver of .22 caliber with a 2½ inch barrel under the name of the "Protector" Sealed Eight. It is similar to the Supershot Sealed Eight except that the barrel is shortened 3½ inches, and the Hi-hold grip is modified somewhat, being smaller and thinner.

This little gun has fixed sights 3½ inches apart, and has the cylinders counterbored to receive the heads of the .22 cartridges, to make it safe for the high velocity ammunition. The author has fired one of these guns with every make of .22 ammunition available, and has not been able to produce a malfunction. It is a fine and handy little gun for those desiring a pocket revolver for the .22 caliber cartridge.

POCKET AUTOMATIC PISTOLS

For home and personal defense, as well as for military use, the automatic pistol has become very much used in late years. The problems involved in making an automatic pistol to shoot a small, low-powered cartridge, such as the .32 automatic, are much less difficult than in the case of high-powered automatics.

Automatics of military caliber must have a locked breech, but in small guns this is not necessary. The breech block is simply held against the base of the cartridge by a heavy spring, and when the gun goes off the bullet has left the barrel before the breech block can move very far. With the large military automatics there are only a few successful systems of locking the breech, therefore there are a limited number of types of these guns. With the small pocket automatic no such mechanism is necessary, therefore there is no limit to the number of different pocket automatics that can be made. All that is necessary is a frame containing a magazine of the ordinary kind and adapted to mount a short barrel, against which a breech block, enclosing the necessary firing pin, is held by means of a spring.

Pocket automatic pistols are made in three principal calibers, and they all use rimless cartridges with jacketed bullets. The calibers are: .25 automatic, which is known in Europe as 6.35 mm.; the .32 automatic, which is known in Europe as the 7.65 mm., and the .380, which is known in Europe as the 9 mm. Short. There is also the .38 automatic Colt cartridge, but there is no European cartridge that exactly corresponds to this, as the 9 mm. Long is not quite the same as the .38 Colt.

Automatic pocket pistols were made in Europe extensively before they were manufactured in this country, and those made there used the 6.35, 7.65, and 9 mm. cartridges. The earliest automatics made in America were the Colts, which were made on Browning's patent, and Browning already had a factory at Liège, Belgium. Therefore, the European models were closely followed in the first automatics made in this country and exactly the same cartridges were used, though they were given American names. For this reason the European automatic pistol cartridges can be used in American automatics with no trouble whatever. The most popular automatic pistols in this country are the Colts.

The Colt .25 Automatic

The smallest of these is the Pocket Model, Caliber .25, Hammerless. It carries 6 shots in the magazine and has a 2-inch barrel. The length over all is only 4½ inches and the weight is 13 ounces. This gun is small enough to be carried in the vest pocket, and that is its greatest recommendation. The cartridge is entirely too small to have stopping power, and while the gun is capable of inflicting a fatal injury, it does not impart enough shock to make a man feel sick as soon as he is hit. It is true that soft-point bullets are furnished for this gun, but this means nothing, as the bullet does not have enough speed to mushroom, and a soft-point bullet does no more harm than a jacketed one.

The gun has a distinct field, however, in spite of its lack of stopping power and the fact that it can only be moderately accurate on account of its short sight radius and short barrel. This field is in its enabling one to have a weapon under circumstances where a weapon could not otherwise be had. This gun is so small and light and insignificant that it can be carried without inconvenience or without any suspicion, and no one wants to be shot even with a .25. Therefore, this gun would often be just as effective as a larger caliber, because in many cases the purpose is served if a would-be assailant simply knows that you are armed. These little guns have a grip safety and also a thumb safety. The models after No. 141000 are provided with a magazine safety, so that when the magazine is taken out the gun can not be fired, which is an excellent thing indeed because it prevents accidents due to inexperienced persons who forget that another cartridge is in the gun when the magazine has been removed. An exact duplicate of this gun is made under the Browning patents by Fabrique Nationale d' Armes de Guerre, or "FN."

The Colt .32 and .380

Perhaps the most popular automatic pistol in this country is the Colt Pocket Model Hammerless, which is made in .32 and .380 calibers. This gun is built on Browning patents and, as its name indicates, is hammerless. It is fitted with both grip and thumb safeties. It carries 8 shots in the magazine in the .32-caliber and 7 shots in the .380 caliber.

This gun as now manufactured (the Caliber .32 from No. 468097 and the Caliber .380 from No. 92894) is equipped with a Safety Disconnector similar to that incorporated in the Caliber .25 as described under that model. Previous models do not contain the automatic magazine safety. An extreme source of danger with guns not so equipped is the fact that a cartridge remains in the chamber after the magazine has been removed and the gun is supposedly unloaded. One of the French catalogues that I have very aptly describes this remaining cartridge as "le malhereux dernier cartouche," or, "the unhappy last cartridge."

The Colt automatic pistol is powerful, accurate and very reliable in action. It has a 3¾-inch barrel and weighs 23 ounces. The .380-caliber is recommended as having the most stopping power.

The Smith & Wesson Automatic

Smith & Wesson have also for years manufactured a pocket automatic pistol. For a long time this was made in the so-called .35-caliber. It used a special cartridge designed by Smith & Wesson, which was supposed to represent quite an advance in automatic cartridge design. In this cartridge the front end of the bullet was jacketed in order to work through the magazine and mechanism without scarring up, while the back end of the bullet, which was inside the cartridge case, was somewhat larger in diameter and not jacketed. The idea of the manufacturer was that it was desirable to have the back part of the bullet made of soft metal, so that it could take the rifling better. While this was a very desirable cartridge, it was different from the ordinary .32 pistol cartridge, and for that reason it never did have much commercial success. People did not want to buy a gun and then later find that

Upper: The Colt Automatic Pistol Pocket Model, Caliber .32 or .380.
Lower: The Smith & Wesson Automatic Pistol. A notable feature of this gun is the ease of loading the first shot, as the breech block can be disconnected from the return spring by pushing in a catch before drawing back the breech block to load.

in some out-of-the-way part of the country perhaps they could not get the ammunition. Moreover, this so-called .35-caliber was not really .35 in diameter, but was simply named that to distinguish it from the regular .32. It was really the same diameter as the regular .32 Automatic pistol cartridge. The Company finally discontinued making the gun for this special .35 Caliber Cartridge, and now make it for the regular .32 A. C. P. (Automatic Colt Pistol) Cartridge.

It is a Hammerless pocket automatic with a magazine holding 7 shots. It has a grip safety located on the front of the grip, under the trigger guard. This gun has a feature which makes it easier to load than the usual automatic. This is an arrangement by means of which the action spring is disconnected from the slide during the operation of loading. Instead of pulling the slide back against the strong recoil spring, and then letting it slam forward, this gun is loaded by pressing in a catch on the left side, which holds the spring out of operation. The slide is then drawn back and pushed forward, placing a cartridge in the chamber, and in letting go of the slide, the catch is released, so that the spring holds the slide shut, ready for firing. This feature was placed on the gun to render easier its operation by women and others not having great strength.

The gun has a 3½ inch barrel and weighs 35 ounces.

The Savage Automatic Pistol

Though this gun is no longer manufactured, a description is included, as many thousand of these guns are still being used all over the world.

The Savage Arms Company made a pocket automatic pistol in .32 and .380 calibers which has a number of unique features. In the first place, this gun has a locking action for the barrel, something which is not common in the pocket automatics. In the second place, it has an extra large magazine capacity. The magazine of the .32 holds 10 cartridges and the .380 holds 9. About 1911 this gun was highly advertised in the magazines under the slogan of "Ten Shots—Quick!" The gun was invented by Major Searles, who formerly worked at Springfield Armory and was a major in the Ordnance Department during the World War. In 1917 the outward appearance of this pistol was changed somewhat by giving a greater slope to the back of the grip, so as to aid in natural pointing, and by putting a spur on the cocking lever or semi-hammer that was used on the earlier models.

The main feature of the mechanism is that when the breech block moves backward the barrel has to turn, and while the bullet is going through the barrel the work of spinning the bullet resists this rotation of the barrel; therefore, it helps to hold the breech locked. Another feature of the gun is the ease with which it can be completely dismounted for cleaning. The barrel comes out and is entirely separated from the rest of the mechanism without the aid of tools in just a few seconds. While this gun is what might be called a semi-hammerless, it has a thumb safety, and while this safety is on it positively holds the hammer back so that the arm can not be discharged even though the sear may be jarred off.

To clean the barrel, remove magazine, draw back bolt, and raise safety to hold it back. Insert brush or cloth saturated with good light oil, preferably a nitro-solvent, at muzzle, clean inside of barrel thoroughly, and leave a thin film of oil in the barrel afterwards. Then throw down safety, letting bolt snap forward, and insert magazine. Never use heavy oil or grease on the pistol. Occasionally dismount pistol enough to wipe off breech plug, sear-trip mechanism and inside of frame and bolt with an oily cloth.

The Remington Model 51 Automatic Pistol

Like the Savage, described above, this gun is no longer manufactured, which is to be regretted, as it had many extremely desirable features. It was invented by J. D. Pedersen, one of the greatest living designers of firearms in the world. He is also the inventor of the Remington pump action shotguns, the Remington trombone action rifles, the Semi-Automatic Military rifle made by Vickers, Ltd., and many other famous arms.

The Remington Automatic Pistol is a hammerless, locked breech, pocket automatic pistol, made in .32 and .380 calibers. The breech locking mechanism is very clever and ingenious.

The arm has a grip safety which also serves as an indicator to tell when the gun is cocked. When the hammer is snapped the grip safety stays in. The thumb safety also acts as an indicator because it can not be put in a safe position when the hammer is down. There is also a magazine safety, so that the gun can not be fired when the magazine is out of the gun. The magazine holds 7 shots. The length of the barrel is 3¼ inches. The weight of the gun unloaded is 21 ounces. In designing this gun the inventor gave the greatest care and attention to the features of balance, angle, and shape of the grip and sights. In designing the grip a

Upper: The Remington Model 51 Automatic Pistol. This excellent arm was formerly made in both .32 and .380 calibers, but has now been discontinued.

Lower: The .38 Colt Detective Special Revolver. This is really the Police Positive
Special with a 2 inch barrel.

frame representing the necessary shape of the magazine was covered with modeling clay until it was just right for the hands of various different-sized men and women. A number of these models were made, and finally all these models were compared and a grip was made up which was a compromise, so that it would best fit the average hand. The result is a grip that is more comfortable than that of any other automatic pistol that I know of. In addition, the curve at the back of the frame and the hole in the trigger guard were so located in relation to each other that the barrel lies in an exact parallel line with the index finger. The top of the slide was made flat and matted to avoid the reflection of light. The sights are low and close to the top of the slide, so that they will not catch in the pocket or clothing and are square, or Patridge, shape which is best adapted to accurate quick shooting.

Webley Automatic Pistols

Messrs. Webley & Scott, of Birmingham, manufacture pocket type automatic pistols in four calibers, namely, the 9 m/m Browning long, the .380 Automatic, the .32 Automatic, and the .25 Automatic. The name of the maker is a sufficient guarantee of workmanship and high quality material.

The "M.P." or Metropolitan Police Model

This is a pocket model automatic with an outside hammer. Capacity of magazine, 8 shots for the .32, and 7 shots for the .380. Weight, with magazine, .32 Caliber, 20 ounces.

This gun has been adopted by the London Metropolitan police force, as well as by the police forces of Cairo, Adelaide, and many other cities.

The ballistics are in every way similar to those of the corresponding Colt models.

Webley New Military & Police Automatic

This powerful pocket or holster automatic is chambered for the 9 m/m Browning Long cartridge, which is considerably more powerful than the 9 m/m short, known in this country as the .380. This pistol gives a muzzle velocity of about 1000 feet per second. Like the "M. P." model, it has an outside hammer. Weight of the gun with magazine empty, 32 ounces.

Webley .25 Caliber Automatic

This small pocket automatic is similar in size to the .25 Cal. Colt Automatic, and uses the same cartridge. It is made in two styles, one being hammerless, and the other having an outside hammer. The magazine holds six shots, and the gun, with magazine empty, weighs 12 ounces, (Hammer model.)

Walther Police Pistols, Models P.P. and P.P.K.

These German pocket automatics have a number of exclusive and unique features that demand special notice. They have an outside hammer, and a thumb safety, and if the safety is in the "Secure" position, indicated by a red circle, the pistol can be loaded, by drawing back and releasing the slide, without cocking the hammer. In this state, the pistol is loaded, yet is safe from accidental discharge, as the hammer is not cocked; yet the pistol can be discharged from this position with one hand by placing the safety lever in the "Ready" position, and then simply pulling the trigger; for the trigger has a double action arrangement by which the hammer is cocked and then discharged by a single pull. After the first shot, the gun cocks itself as usual, but in case of misfire, a second blow can be struck merely by pulling the trigger. When the safety is on, the hammer cannot strike the cartridge, even if the gun should be dropped.

There is an indicator pin that protrudes above the hammer whenever there is a cartridge in the chamber. This is furnished only on the center fire models, however, and not in the .22 rim fire.

There are two sizes, the P.P. (Polizei Pistole) and the short, or *kurz* model, P.P.K., which is three-quarters of an inch shorter.

These guns are made not only in the usual 7.65 m/m (.32 A.C.P.) and 9 m/m (.380 A.C.P.) calibers, but also in the .22 Long Rifle Rim Fire Caliber as well.

Dimensions of the .32 caliber are as follows:

	P.P	P.P.K.
Over all length	6⅟₁₆ inches	5⅞ inches
Barrel length	3⅞ inches	3¼ inches
Height	4¼ inches	4 inches
Thickness	⅞ inch	⅞ inch
Weight	1 lb., 7 oz.	1 lb., 3 oz.
Magazine capacity	8 shots	7 shots
Muzzle velocity	954 f.s.	924 f.s.

The Walther firm, of Zella-Mehlis, Germany, also make a 6.35 m/m (.25 A.C.P.) pocket automatic, and a .22 caliber rim fire target automatic.

Mauser Pocket Automatics

These guns, made by the famous firm of Waffenfabrik Mauser, of Oberndorf a/n ("On the Neckar") Germany, had attained a considerable degree of popularity in America before the World

War, and are now sold by the firm of A. F. Stoeger, Inc., New York, the sole importers.

They are made in two calibers, for the popular American .25 A.C.P. and .32 A.C.P. cartridges, known in Germany as the 6.35 m/m and the 7.65 m/m respectively. The two guns are alike in design. When the last shot has been fired, the slide remains open, and can be closed only by the insertion of a magazine, which causes the slide to close automatically, placing a cartridge in the chamber at the same time, in case the magazine be loaded. There is an indicator pin which protrudes from the breech whenever the mechanism is cocked.

There is a magazine safety, which prevents the firing pin from being released unless the magazine is in place. This prevents accidents resulting from the assumption that the gun has been unloaded by the removal of the magazine, while the cartridge in the chamber still remains. There is a thumb safety on the left side, near the trigger guard. Pressing this safety down makes the gun safe, and locks it so, as the safety cannot be pushed up again. The gun is made ready by pushing in a button located just under the safety, which releases the safety, and allows it to snap up to the ready position under the action of a spring.

The .25 Caliber model is considerably larger than the .25 Colt, and on account of the longer barrel, it is easy to shoot accurately.

The Mauser firm also make a vest pocket .25 Automatic, much like the Colt in appearance and size.

The Ortgies Automatics

Another pocket automatic pistol of German make that has been sold in this country in considerable quantities is the Ortgies, made in 6.35 and 7.65 caliber. An interesting thing about this gun is the fact that the safety is rather unique. It consists of a grip safety which, however, does not become operative unless a small button on the left hand side of the grip is pressed, when the grip safety springs out into position. Another interesting thing about this gun is the fact that it is very difficult to dismount without first being shown how, because, look all over the gun as you may, there is nothing apparent to show how it can be taken apart, and I have known some people to spend quite a time trying to find out how to get this gun taken down. It is really simplicity itself when you know how. Grasp the slide with the left hand and the handle with the right hand, pressing on the safety release button with the thumb. Push the slide back about a half inch and lift upward.

when it will come loose from the frame and the whole gun can be taken apart. However, once you have it apart it is almost impossible to put it together unless you know the trick of doing it, which is to lock the firing-pin spring out of action for the purpose of assembling. To do this, look in the top of the slide and inside you will see a small semicircular cut. By pushing the firing-pin spring in, the little stem which goes in the back end of the spring

Three pocket automatics often seen in this country. Top: The Mauser Pistol, caliber 7.65 mm., using the .32 A. C. P. cartridge. It is also made in 6.35 mm. (.25 A. C. P.) Caliber. Middle: Ortgies Automatic Pistol, 7.65 mm. Lower: Colt .25 Vest Pocket Model.

can be pushed down into this cut to lock the spring into place; then the slide can be assembled by reversing the operation of taking it off. If the spring is not locked in position as described, it is impossible to get the slide back on because the spring projects out the rear end.

There is one precaution to be followed in regard to assembling, however, and that is to remember that in putting back the slide you may disengage this spring from the little cut. In fact, this is quite likely to occur, and when it does the spring and the little rod on the end of it shoot out with violence, and if it is pointed toward your face it might put an eye out, so always hold it so if this comes out it will not do any harm and will not get lost.

Another tricky thing about this gun is the way in which the grips come off. There are no screws visible on the outside of the gun anywhere. To remove the grips, take out the magazine and with the end of a lead pencil press on the back of the frame inside the magazine space about half way up, when the grips will fall off, as they are held in place by a spring catch.

Belgian Automatics

Belgium is quite a center for the manufacture of firearms, and one of the most prominent of the Belgian factories is the Fabrique Nationale d'Armes de Guerre, located at Herstal near Liège. It

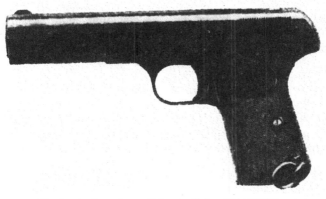

The 9 m/m Browning as it is manufactured in Belgium.

is this factory that makes the Browning pistols in Europe. The Colt Patent Fire Arms Company is licensed under the same patents to make automatic pistols in America, and under the patent agreement the Brownings are not allowed to be sold in this country, nor the Colts in Europe. For that reason the Browning automatic pistols are rarely seen here. These pistols are the invention of the late John M. Browning, of Ogden, Utah, who died in December, 1926.

Several years ago the millionth Browning pistol was manufactured at the Liège factory.

It was a Browning automatic pistol that fired the fatal shot at Sarejevo which assassinated the Archduke Francis Ferdinand, thus starting the World War.

The Browning factory makes pistols in the 6.35, 7.65 and 9 mm. short calibers. In fact, most of the automatic cartridges that you find are marked "For Browning or Dreyse."

The smallest of this line is the "Baby Hammerless," of which the .25 Colt is almost an exact duplicate. The 7.65 is very similar to the .32 Colt. The 9 mm. Browning pistol illustrated is marked on the left side, "Fabrique Nationale d'Armes de Guerre Herstal-Belgique, Brownings Patent Deposé." On the side of the barrel and frame it has three proof marks—an "E" with a star over it; a Lion over the letters "P.V.," which is the Belgian nitro-powder proof, and the little Belgian tower proof mark. On the barrel it also has the Crown over the letter "R," which is a proof mark for rifles, pistols and revolvers, and also the "ELG" in the oval with a crown on top.

In this gun the slide stays back on the last shot and is released by pulling back and letting go. To dismount, hook back the slide with the safety, turn the barrel one-quarter turn, release the safety and pull the barrel and slide forward.

The Bayard

Another well-known Belgian automatic is the Bayard. This arm is noted for its extreme compactness. It is made in 7.65 and 9 mm. calibers, and the barrel is bored in the front part of the frame just forward of the trigger guard. The Bayard is made by Anciens Etablissements Pieper, formerly the firm of H. Pieper.

The Clement

Another Belgian gun is the Clement, made in 6.35 and 7.65 caliber by Charles P. Clement of Liège. These pistols can be almost instantly opened for cleaning by pressing down on the trigger guard and tilting up the barrel.

The Pieper

The Pieper is made in 7.65 and 6.35 calibers by Nicolas Pieper of Liège. Some confusion is sometimes caused by the fact that the Bayard is also made by a Pieper firm in Liège, but it is a different company, as mentioned.

French Automatics

An interesting line of automatic pistols is made by the manufactory Francaise d'Armes et Cycles de Saint Etienne. One of the features of these automatics is that the lock mechanism is double action, not automatic. In other words, pulling the trigger cocks the hammer and then snaps it, the same as in the Smith & Wesson Safety Hammerless. This makes very greatly for safety because you do not have an automatic pistol with a cartridge in the chamber and the hammer cocked at all times, but at the same time you have an automatic that can be instantly fired merely by pulling strongly enough on the trigger. These little guns also have a magazine safety so they can not be fired when the magazine is out, and moreover, they are very easy to clean because the barrel tips up, by pressing a catch, so that the breech is fully exposed. They are made in 6.35 and 7.65 calibers.

Spanish Pistols and Revolvers

One of the two great European centers for the manufacture of inexpensive firearms is Belgium. The other is Spain. In both these countries there are cities where there are hundreds of small shops which either make complete firearms of nondescript patterns, or else make parts on a contract system for some larger establishment which does the assembling and marketing. Much of the work is largely done by hand, in the cheapest possible way. In Belgium, for example, there are many muzzle loading "trade guns" made in this way, intended for sale in Africa and other out of the way places where anything that looks like a gun will be welcomed by certain classes of natives. Perhaps the principal center of this type of manufacture in Belgium is Liège, while in Spain it is Eibar.

Spanish arms in general have obtained a bad reputation in America because just after the World War the American market was flooded with cheap and crudely made revolvers and automatic pistols of Spanish origin, which could be bought for ridiculously low prices, and many of these pot-metal weapons were almost exact copies of the more popular Colt and Smith & Wesson models. The unsuspecting buyer would see what was apparently a Smith & Wesson .38 Military & Police Revolver, for example, in a store window, and on the side of the barrel he would see, in big letters the name SMITH & WESSON. But if he purchased the gun, he would find that the workmanship and material was of the crudest, and if he looked more closely at the name, he would see that it read "for SMITH & WESSON ctg.," and that the name of the real maker was absent. Tucked away in some inconspicuous place he might find the word "Spain," or the statement, "Made in Spain."

The unfortunate situation that has been described above, which allows exact imitations of the American guns to be made as described, is due to certain complicated ramifications of the Patent and Trade-Mark laws in the two countries, with particular reference to the lack of reciprocal trade agreements, etc.

The Spanish authorities grant patents of which the duration depends largely on whether or not the article in question is manufactured in Spain. One pays an initial fee of moderate amount, and thereafter, for three years, a small annual fee, provided that the patented article is not manufactured in Spain during that time. If manufacture is started during the three-year period, the annual fee ceases, and no more fees have to be paid as long as the manu-

The "ATCSA" single shot target pistol, caliber 4 mm. To reload, the barrel swings on vertical pivots at the front end of the frame. The rear sight is adjustable for both elevation and windage.

facture continues; but if the three years are allowed to pass without any manufacture of the article in Spain, the patent lapses, and becomes public property. Several years ago the matter of a reciprocal agreement covering some of the points involved was taken up by the authorities of the two countries, and there was a lot of talking, but nothing was done, as the spokesmen for the United States were handicapped by a number of laws, customs, rules, etc., which affected the Spanish interests adversely, such as an American embargo on the importation of malaga grapes, the immigration laws, prohibition, etc., concerning which the United States either could not, or would not make any concessions.

However, there are reputable firms in Spain which do make arms of good quality and workmanship though these better examples of the Spanish gun making industry are not so often seen in America. Naturally the situation which we have described above has been distasteful to the better Spanish firms and to the authorities and effective steps have been taken to improve the general quality of Spanish arms so that it can confidently be said that the Spanish manufacture of pistols and revolvers has improved notably during the past ten years, and the improvement has been progressive. Much better steel is now used and one firm (ATCSA) even go so far as to make the cylinders of their revolvers of Poldi Anti-corro steel, though the manufacturers of Eibar do not, it is generally admitted among Spanish shooters, use as good steel as do Smith & Wesson and Colt; but the steel of the best Eibar manufacturers is considered very nearly as good and their arms are rugged and beautifully finished.

The number of Spanish makes has diminished with the improvement in quality and the innumerable firms which formerly turned out poor material have for the most part been driven from the market. Fifteen years ago one could buy a new so-called revolver in Spain for about $2.50; but it is hard to find such guns at the present time and the reputable arms made in Eibar cost about the equivalent of $15.00 at that place.

Revolvers

Perhaps the most popular revolver now made in Spain is called "El Tanque" and is manufactured at Eibar. The target model of this gun, with adjustable sights and a six inch barrel is chambered for the .38 special cartridge and combines features of both the Colt and Smith & Wesson revolvers. This gun is a very handsome weapon and of late years has won many matches in Spain where top notch shooters were competing. The Colt or Smith & Wesson revolvers still are considered in Spain as the most desirable target revolvers but by the time importation charges and customs duties are paid, they cost the Spanish buyer perhaps five times as much as El Tanque. One of my acquaintances who lives in Spain reports that he has seen charges of smokeless powder that can only be described as barbarous used in the Tanque by reckless hand loaders and he has never known one of these guns to burst.

Another Spanish make which deserves special mention is ATCSA of Barcelona. The name comes from the initials of the firm Armas de Tiro y Caza, S. A. These guns are of recent design and manufacture and cost in the neighborhood of $20.00 in Spain. They are notable for the fact that they use only the best material obtainable.   A feature of their revolvers is the fact that, though they have a solid frame and a swing out cylinder, there is a latch on the front of the crane by which the cylinder can quickly be removed.   This feature is made use of to allow the gun to be quickly

The "ATOSA" .38 Special Revolver, made in Barcelona. Note that the gun is fitted with interchangeable cylinders for speed in reloading. Note also that the extra cylinder has a spring-steel cover for holding the cartridges in the extra cylinder, and for protecting the primers.

reloaded, as an extra cylinder already charged can be carried in the pocket.   A quickly detachable spring steel cap fits over the heads of the cartridges in the additional cylinder and holds the cartridges in place until the cylinder is inserted in the revolver.

This firm also makes a single shot pistol in which the barrel swings to one side on a vertical pivot for reloading.   I have done a considerable amount of shooting with one of these gun in the 4 mm. caliber and find it to be highly accurate at short ranges.

This firm has thus far confined its sales efforts to the police and military authorities with whom they have had a considerable degree of success.

Other Spanish revolvers are the "Destroyer" which is made in a target model with six inch barrel chambered for the .38 special. As far as I know it has not won any big matches but it seems to be a glutton for punishment when it comes to withstanding heavy charges.

Other good revolvers are the Gaztañaga y Trocaola (made by the firm of this name in Eibar) and the "Alfa," made by a workers' guild in Eibar. They are made for the .22 long rifle, the .32 Smith & Wesson and the .38 Special, which is the most popular revolver cartridge in Spain.

Automatic Pistols

The improvements in automatics in Spain has been quite as marked as it has in regard to revolvers. The most popular cartridges are the 9 mm. Bergmann (same as the .38 Colt Super-Automatic except for a slightly longer cartridge case, and very powerful), the 9 mm. Browning Short (.380 A. C. P.), the 7.65 mm. automatic, (.32 A. C. P.), and the .25 automatic.

The largest Spanish manufacturer of automatics is Bonifacio Echeverría, of Eibar, whose make is the "Star." In the larger models the Star pistols are practically duplicates of the Colt. The smaller ones are more like the Browning except for the target model .22 which is similar to the Reising formerly made in America.

Echeverría manufactures the .45 caliber automatic pistol which looks just like the Colt .45 automatic as used in the United States Army. This gun is sold extensively in Mexico and South America and uses the regular .45 caliber A. C. P. cartridge.

His 9 mm. Bergmann (.38 caliber) has external lines and dimensions the same as the Colt Super Automatic though the barrel is a bit lighter.

His .22 caliber long rifle target pistol is an automatic with a six inch barrel and the ten shot magazine and retails in Spain for about $22.50. It appeared on the market only recently but has won several rapid fire matches and is very popular.

The Astra Automatic pistol is made in the .380 and 9 mm. Bergmann calibers. It is the regulation pistol for the crack Spanish Guardia Civil.

Only recently there appeared on the Spanish market a new automatic known as the "Llama" made in Eibar and in just one model chambered for the 9 mm. Bergmann cartridge. This gun is almost an exact duplicate of the Colt Super .38. Shortly after this gun appeared it was tested by the Barcelona police and military officials for accuracy, penetration, function, and etc. under all kinds of artificially adverse conditions in tests that lasted about six weeks. In these tests all kinds of reloads and many excessive charges were used with little or no difficulty and the gun created a very favorable impression. The authorities were making the tests for the purpose of deciding on the adoption of a gun which would be official for the police and "mozos de escuadra" (rural constabulary) throughout Cataluña.

The only other Spanish automatic that seems worthy of mention in this place is the "Bùfalo" made by the old and respected firm of Beristáin y Cia., of Eibar. This is a small pocket gun of 7.65 mm. and 25 caliber and sells for a low price.

There is no model or make of hand gun which is official with the Spanish Army, the officers of which buy their own guns as they like but they generally prefer automatics using the 9 mm. Bergmann cartridge, which as made in Spain is of excellent quality and not expensive. A census of hand guns among Spanish Army Officers would show that most of them use the "Star" or the "Astra" in the large 9 mm. models.

CHAPTER 5

TECHNICAL NOTES ON HANDGUNS

ALL THE arms discussed in this book, whether they be revolvers, automatics, or target pistols, have one object in common, and that is to project a bullet accurately in a desired direction and they all have a main feature of their construction in common, in that the most important part is a strong metal tube through which the ball is launched toward the spot to be hit. This tube is called the barrel, and in the first firearms it was merely a smooth cylinder, like the present day shotgun barrel. While such a tube will, it is true, launch a ball in the direction in which it is pointed, it is highly unsatisfactory for accuracy, for the ball will not continue in the direction in which it is started. Instead, it either shoots violently off in some unexpected direction, or more usually, curves away from its original direction.

This curve in the flight of a ball is familiar to everyone who has ever seen a baseball game. The pitcher, in throwing the ball, causes it to spin rapidly on its axis, and this spin, coupled with its forward motion through the air, causes the air which is compressed in front of the ball by its forward motion to be pushed to one side; and the resultant reaction causes the ball to deviate from its flight. The same thing causes the deviation of a ball when fired from a smooth-bore gun. Unless it fits the barrel very tightly, it bounces from side to side during its sudden passage through the bore, and as it strikes against the walls of the barrel, it acquires a rotation which causes it to curve in some undetermined direction, depending on which kind of rotation it happens to have imparted to it. Or if it doesn't bounce along, it rolls on the bottom of the bore, and acquires a rotation which makes it drop rapidly after leaving the muzzle.

If the ball fits the bore tightly enough so that it neither rolls nor bounces, the case is still worse, for then it emerges from the

141

muzzle with no rotation at all, and as it passes through the air it piles up a cone of compressed air in front of it, until, at some unknown instant, the point of this cone gets on one side or the other of the ball, and it shoots off in the opposite direction. This same effect is seen in baseball under the name of the spit-ball, where the pitcher avoids giving any rotation at all to the ball when he pitches it, and as a result, it "breaks" in some undetermined direction in some point in its flight, and so fools the batter.

Rifling

In modern firearms, these troubles are overcome by constructing the barrel so that the ball will receive a definite rotation in a given direction. In this case, it will curve, but the curve will always be the same, and can be taken into account in aiming.

In practice, this is accomplished by what is known as "rifling," which consists of making a number of spiral ribs on the inside walls of the barrel. These ribs, or "lands" as they are called in firearms parlance, bite into the bullet in its passage through the bore, and force it to turn as it passes along.

When a round ball is fired in a rifled gun it turns during its flight either to the right or to the left, depending on the direction of the rifling in the barrel. Some barrels are rifled with the lands making a clockwise spiral, and this is called right hand rifling. On the other hand some guns have a counter clockwise spiral, known as left hand rifling. There is no difference in the effectiveness of the two directions but there is a difference in the direction pursued by the ball after it leaves the muzzle. A ball fired from a right hand rifling curves to the right. This curve is called "drift." Left hand rifling gives a curve to the left or left hand drift.

When the round ball fired from right hand rifling rushes toward the target it is also falling toward the ground at the same time under the action of gravity. Naturally the air underneath the ball is somewhat compressed by this falling; and as the ball spins to the right it rolls on this layer of compressed air and hence drifts to the right. As a falling body falls faster and faster under the action of gravity so there is more and more compressed air under the bullet as it moves along, and this makes it drift faster and faster to the right. The drift during the first few yards of flight is so small that it can scarcely be detected, and for this reason drift is relatively unimportant for revolvers and pistols where the shooting is all done at relatively short ranges. The drift with the .38 Special is approximately 1 inch at 50 yards.

In the days when rifling was first invented, round balls were used exclusively; but the adoption of rifling had another effect besides merely stabilizing the flight of a round ball, for it enabled the use of oblong or cylindrical projectiles, because the spin keeps them end on in the same way that it makes a spinning top stand up. A cylindrical projectile is much more effective ballistically than is a round ball because for the same weight there is less surface presented to the air and thus the speed of the bullet is not retarded so quickly. Practically all modern rifle and pistol bullets are cylindrical, with a pointed nose.

In practice, rifling is put into gun barrels by the process of cutting spiral grooves in the bore. The ridges of metal that are left between the grooves form the "lands."

It is common to designate rifling by the number of inches of forward motion of the bullet for each complete rotation. Thus for example, the service Springfield rifle is said to have a rifling of one turn in ten inches because a bullet in passing through ten inches of the barrel makes one complete revolution.

With a round ball almost any twist of rifling that will keep the bullet spinning at all will be sufficient for accuracy; but with the modern, cylindrical bullet another factor enters, and that is stability. An oblong bullet tends to tumble in flight, and the longer the bullet, the more pronounced is this tendency and the faster must be the spin to keep it going point forward. For this reason a .22 short requires less spin than the .22 long rifle. The standard twist for rifles in the .22 short is one turn in twenty-four inches, while the .22 long rifle requires a twist of one turn in sixteen inches. Where two kinds of cartridges are to be used in the same gun it is made with the twist suitable for the longer bullet. In other words a rifle made to use both the .22 short and the .22 long rifle cartridges would have a twist of one turn in sixteen inches which is not so good for the short.

In general revolvers have rifling with faster twist than that used in rifles of the same caliber. This is because the bullet must spin a certain number of revolutions per second to give it gyroscopic stability and keep it end-on. In a revolver it has less velocity, and therefore goes less feet per second than it does in a rifle, and therefore the bullet must rotate more times per foot in a revolver to get the same number of rotations per second. An idea of the usual American practice in the matter of the twist of rifling may be obtained from the tabulation given on the following page.

TWIST OF RIFLING (INCHES PER TURN) IN AMERICAN HAND ARMS

Caliber	Colt Twist	H. & R. Twist	I. J. Twist	S. & W. Twist
.22 Revolvers	14	12	15.75	10
.22 Pistols	14	16	....	15
.32 S. & W. and Colt N. P.	16	12	23.33	18.75
.32 Winchester (.32-20)	16	20	....	12
.38 S. & W. and Colt N. P.	16	12	23.33	18.75
.38 Special	16	..	....	18.75
.38 Winchester (.38-40)	16	..	....	.20
.41 Colt	16	..	....	....
.44 Russian	16	..	....	20
.44 Special	16	..	....	20
.44 Winchester (.44-40)	16	..	....	20
.45 Colt	16	..	....	20
.455 Eley	16	..	....	20
.25 Automatic	16	..	....	....
.32 Automatic	16	12	....	12
.35 Automatic	..	..	....	12
,380 Automatic	16	..	....	12
.38 Automatic	16	..	....	....
.45 Automatic	16	..	....	14.6

The usual American practice is to make the rifling with a right-handed twist, and all American made arms except the Colt pistols and revolvers have right handed rifling. Colt guns, on the contrary all have the rifling left handed, which is the English practice. The reason for this is that after the failure of Col. Colt's first factory in America, he went to London and made his revolvers there for some years; and as the rifling machines in use there were adapted for a left handed twist, Colt used it, and the Colt guns have been made the same way ever since. Many English guns have left handed rifling, but those made by Webley & Scott, as well as most arms made on the continent of Europe are right handed.

The number of grooves in common use varies from four to eight. As an indication of current American practice the following may be noted:

Colt guns all have 6 lands and grooves.

Harrington & Richardson guns all have 6 lands and grooves.

Iver Johnson revolvers all have 5 lands and grooves.

Remington .32 and .380 Automatics have 7 lands and grooves.

Savage .32 and .380 Automatics have 6 grooves.

Smith & Wesson .32 and .35 caliber automatic pistols, .22 caliber revolvers and single shot pistols, and .45 revolver model of 1917 have 6 lands and grooves. All other Smith & Wesson arms have 5 lands and grooves.

In general the depth of the grooves is from three and a half to five thousandths of an inch, depending on the ideas and experience of the manufacturer concerned, and on other factors of the design, such as the relative width of the lands and grooves.

Rather complete particulars regarding the twist and depth of rifling, number and width of lands and grooves, dimensions of bore and rifling, and all other dimensions available is given in the tabulation in the appendix.

Usually the bore, which is the diameter of the barrel before it is rifled, and consequently is also the diameter across lands after rifling, is chosen so as to be about one or two thousandths of an inch smaller than the diameter of the bullet to be used in the gun. Some manufacturers use a smaller bore for the same bullet than do other makers. This does not necessarily mean that the bullet is a tighter fit, however, for the manufacturer with a small bore will usually be found to be using deeper grooves or wider grooves and narrower lands to compensate for the reduced diameter across the lands, and the ultimate fit will be about the same. When the gun is fired, and the bullet passes into the rifling, the excess metal displaced when the lands cut into the bullet goes to fill the grooves. If the fit is either too tight or too loose, the accuracy will suffer.

The differences in the barrel dimensions used by the different makers is well illustrated by the following measurements, taken from four highly accurate .22 pistols in the author's possession.

	Smith & Wesson Perfected	Harrington & Richardson U.S.R.A.	Buchel Free Pistol	Stotzer Free Pistol
Barrel length, inches	10	10	13⅜	12
Sight Radius, inches	10	9.2	15¾	14⅝
Twist of rifling, inches	15½	16	15⅝	14⅝
No. of lands and grooves	6	6	8	6
Width lands	.0496	.0304	.012	.027
Width grooves	.0635	.0835	.075	.085
Diameter lands	.216	.2141	.214	.214
Diameter grooves	.2232	.2175	.2230	.2231
Depth grooves	.0036	.0027	.0045	.0045

It will be noticed that the latest of these four pistols, the Harrington & Richardson, has the smallest barrel diameter. These measurements, taken from guns made several years ago, cannot be taken to be the present standards of these manufacturers, as changes in guns may be necessary from time to time to keep up with new types of ammunition, such as the high speed .22's, etc. In fact, one of the troubles of both the gun and ammunition makers is the lack of a real standard for either gun dimensions or ammunition sizes. For example, the .22 Caliber cartridge was originated by Smith & Wesson many years ago, with a bullet size of .226, but as the years went along and some makers reduced the sizes of their .22 caliber bullet, it became necessary for the gun makers to reduce the bore size of the gun to keep pace.

Major Douglas B. Wesson informs me that he has recently (1934) encountered .22 caliber cartridges with bullets only .217 inch in diameter, and has had to change the bore dimensions of the K-.22 to a slightly smaller size than was formerly used in order to maintain the maximum accuracy in machine rest tests.

In rifles and single shot and automatic pistols, where the chamber of the gun is continuous with the barrel, instead of being separate, as it is in revolvers, the rear end, or origin, of the rifling, comes right up to the point where the bullet lies when the cartridge is in the chamber, so that any forward motion of the bullet will make the rifling cut into the bullet metal. This part of the rifling is usually cut or chambered away in a cone shape, so that the bullet can enter the rifling easily. This coned part is called the bullet seat or "lead."

Frequently it may be desirable to see just what form the rifling has, or to make measurements of the width of the lands and grooves. The best way to accomplish this is to make a cast of the inside of the barrel. Take a lead bullet of the same caliber as the barrel, start it in from the breech, and drive it half way through the barrel with a rod. Then put another rod, as near the barrel diameter as may be available, into a vise, and slide the gun barrel onto this rod until the rod is in contact with the bullet. Insert another rod into the opposite end of the barrel, and take a hammer and drive against the bullet, so as to compress it between both rods. It will take the exact form of the lands and grooves. Push the lead slug out, and you will have an exact duplicate of the inside of the barrel, with lands and grooves in their correct size. It must be remembered, however, that the lands in the gun make grooves in the lead slug, so that the raised portions on the slug represent a reversed image of the grooves in the barrel.

Measurements across these raised portions with a micrometer caliper will give the exact diameter of the grooves in the gun. To get the bore diameter, take a knife and cut away the raised ribs on the slug which represent the grooves in the gun. Measure across the remaining surfaces and you will have the exact bore diameter. The width of the lands and grooves can be measured with a steel scale and a magnifying glass unless more exact instruments are available.

For obtaining an exact cast of the inside of the chamber of a gun so that measurements can be made, gunsmiths ordinarily use melted sulphur. Simply stop up the barrel just forward of the chamber with a cork or a piece of cotton waste, and pour melted sulphur into the chamber until it is full. When it has cooled it can be pushed out, and will retain its shape indefinitely. There is, however, a slight shrinkage of a fraction of a thousandth of an inch in the first 24 hours. This shrinkage can be reduced and the sulphur cast made to be a more nearly exact permanent record if it is first mixed with lampblack and camphor according to the following formula:

Powdered sulphur, 2 ounces.
Powdered lampblack, 3 grains.
Gum camphor dissolved in alcohol, 3 drops.

A material sometimes used for making casts is a metal alloy which is composed of:

26 parts lead
13 parts tin
12 parts cadmium
49 parts bismuth.

This mixture melts at the very low temperature of 158° Farenheit. It is, however, somewhat less convenient to use than the sulphur.

Barrel Length

Pistol barrels, as made today in America, range in length from ten inches, the longest barrel allowed in matches, except those shot under International Rules, down to the two inch barrel used on the Colt .25 Caliber Automatic Pistol, and on some of the pocket revolvers, such as the Banker's Special and others.

The possible effect of barrel length on accuracy is a question of much interest. Most people mistakenly believe that a long barrel is necessary for great accuracy; but this supposition has no foundation in fact. The function of the barrel on any firearm is to give the bullet its velocity, and to start it in the direction of the object to be hit. Now once a bullet starts in a given direction, it will continue in that direction until something acts on it to turn it from its path, and no matter how short a barrel is, a bullet leaving the muzzle will continue to travel in the direction imparted to it at that instant. The mere fact that it may have been going in the same direction for several feet, as it does in a long gun, before it reaches the muzzle and receives its final direction, is of no importance. On high powered rifles, a fairly long barrel is necessary in order to give space and time for the complete combustion of the powder charge, especially when progressive powders are used; and in any rifle, the barrel must be at least long enough to extend beyond the reach of the arm that supports the gun.

Experiments with .22 caliber arms has shown conclusively that little, if any, additional accuracy or velocity is to be gained by making the barrel longer than ten inches, and for years that length was the maximum allowed under match conditions in America. However, in Europe, under International Match Rules, any length up to 20 inches can be used, and in late years a few matches under these International Rules have been shot in America for the benefit

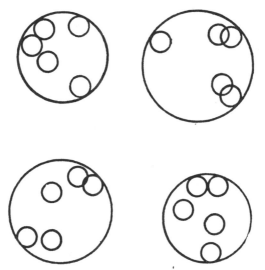

Four machine rest groups, (exact size) made with the 7 inch H. & R. single shot pistol at 50 yards, for comparison with similar groups made with the 10 inch H. & R. Pistol.

of those who desire to experiment with set triggers, etc. In the past, it has been customary for contenders in the "Any Pistol" class to take advantage of all the barrel length allowed, and the regular practice in the manufacture of single shot target pistols has been to make them with ten inch barrels; but recently, in the .22 caliber matches, shorter barrels, of seven and eight inches have been finding much favor, and have been demonstrated to be capable of making the highest scores.

The case for the shorter barrel in the .22 is very well put by Mr. Walter Roper of Harrington & Richardson in the following letter to Mr. F. C. Ness, of the *American Rifleman:*

"Since the appearance of the account of Major Hatcher's and

Ensign Renshaw's shooting in the Bisley matches with a new 7-inch barrel Single-Shot pistol, hundreds of shooters have asked about this new pistol, indicating that the possibilities of the gun are of real interest to handgun shooters.

"How this pistol happened to be made, how the accuracy compares with the usual 10-inch gun, the actual effect of the shorter sight radius upon sighting accuracy, and the type of shooter who can get better results with the short barrel pistol are the questions we want to answer here, in as brief a way as possible.

"As so often happens, the 7-inch Single-Shot was the result of

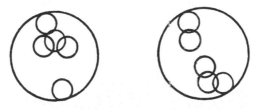

Four machine rest groups, exact size, made with the 10 inch H. & R. single shot pistol at 50 yards. Comparison with similar groups made with the 7 inch pistol. The 10 inch barrel makes only slightly better groups.

a question asked during an extensive series of 50-yard machine-rest tests of 10-inch barrel pistols. The tests had shown that the new barrel developed for the 10-inch gun was capable of making ½-inch groups at 50 yards, instead of the 1-inch groups so long considered finest 50-yard accuracy for a barrel of this length. Realizing that the modern smokeless .22 cartridge was a very different load, the question of how long a barrel was actually needed to obtain fine and consistent accuracy was a natural one.

"Some 6, 7, and 8-inch barrels bored and rifled like the 10-inch barrel, were therefore made, and accuracy tests carried out. A few of the 50-yard groups made with the 7-inch barrel are shown here full size, and for comparison, some average 50-yard groups made by the 10-inch barrel gun are also shown.

"It will be seen that the 7-inch barrel produces machine rest accuracy practically equal to that of the 10-inch gun.

"Having obtained this data, the 7-inch barrel was laid aside until some time later, when it was remembered that some shooters

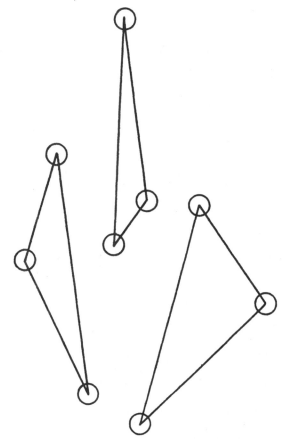

Sighting triangles, exact size, made with a 7 inch H. & R. Pistol by the same observer and under the same conditions as the similar set made with the 10 inch pistol. A comparison indicates that if there is any advantage, it lies with the shorter weapon.

are able to do decidedly better shooting with a revolver than they can with the long-barrel Single-Shot, regardless of the greater accuracy of the long-barreled gun, and the question arose as to what results such shooters would obtain from an arm of greater accuracy than the revolver, but having a similar weight, sight radius, and balance.

"Before asking expert revolver shots to make a test of this kind, we decided first to determine, by the use of the sighting triangle method of testing the accuracy of a shooter's sighting, just how the accuracy of sighting with the 7-inch barrel pistol compared

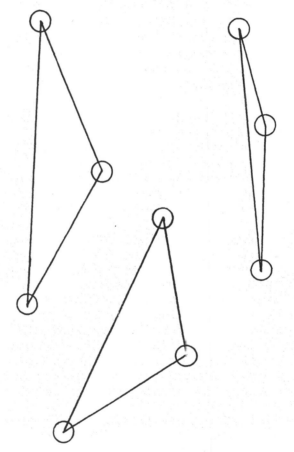

Sighting triangles made at 50 yards to investigate the relative merits of the 10 inch and the 7 inch barrels on the single shot pistol. These sighting triangles were made with the 10 inch H. & R. Pistol, and another set was made by the same person under the same conditions with a 7 inch pistol. Both sets are reproduced in exact size for comparison.

with that of the 10-inch barrel gun. Theoretically, it should be in the ratio of 6 to 9, or only two-thirds as accurate as the 10-inch barrel gun.

"Again a surprise awaited us, for as the sighting triangles shown here will indicate, the sighting with the 7-inch gun is almost exactly as accurate as with the 10-inch. This should not be considered, by any means, as indicating that a long sighting radius is not of value, however; but it does mean that the accuracy of sighting is not in direct proportion to the distance between sights, when the sights are as near together as they must be on a pistol.

"Later experiments indicate that the sights on a 7-inch barrel gun are much more sharply defined for many shooters, and probably this permits more than enough greater accuracy of sighting to make up for any disadvantage due to the shorter distance between sights.

"Knowing that the 7-inch gun, due to the heavy barrel, would balance as perfectly as the finest revolver, and shoot with almost exactly the same degree of accuracy as the 10-inch barrel, and also that the shorter sight radius did not affect the accuracy of sighting to any great extent, it was determined to manufacture a few of these guns, and obtain reports from expert shots with both Single-Shot pistols and revolvers on shooting at both 20 and 50 yards.

"The exceptionally fine shooting of Major Hatcher and Ensign Renshaw at Bisley with one of these 7-inch guns, and the work done by many other pistol marksmen, both at the National Matches and later, shows that for many shooters the short barrel Single-Shot has features which make it able to produce even better scores than the longer barrel gun.

"The experience of many experts now clearly shows that two classes of shooters can use the short barrel pistol to advantage. First, those who have averaged to do better shooting with a revolver than with a 10-inch gun, can make decidedly better scores with this extremely accurate short barrel gun; and second, those shooters who are troubled with "fuzzy sights," as the less widely spaced on the 7-inch gun stand out much more sharply and make sighting not only decidedly more accurate, but very much more pleasant.

"Many shooters have commented upon the greater ease of sighting with the 7-inch gun, reporting that because of the less movement of the sights, they are able to get the shot away during the best part of the hold. This feature is easily understood when it is remembered that being closer together, the same angular movement will cause less motion of the sights. It must be remembered, however, that while the shorter radius produces less movement of the sights, this less easily noticed misalignment affects the accuracy of sighting to a greater extent than it would with the 10-inch gun. However, due to the more clearly defined sights, errors of alignment are more easily noticed with the result that sighting is actually more accurate, and the group obtained most pleasing.

"The really expert shot with the 10-inch barrel pistol will find that his scores will be almost exactly as high with the 7-inch gun, but that he will shoot somewhat more quickly, due to the less movement of the sights, while the shooter who has done his best work with a revolver, or who has not been able to beat his revolver scores with the 10-inch pistol, will find that the 7-inch barrel Single-Shot will give him decidedly higher scores, because of the superior accuracy of the Single-Shot as compared with the revolver."

It will surprise many of our readers to learn how little is the real effect of additional barrel length on velocity, but actual tests with the .22 caliber long rifle cartridge, show that most of the velocity is acquired by the bullet in a ten inch barrel, and that after 16 inches, the velocity actually falls off with increased barrel length. This is because the powder gas expands as it follows the bullet down the barrel, and by the time it has reached 16 inches, it has little pressure left. Also, by this time the bullet is moving very fast, and the gas does little more than keep up with the bullet, without pushing very much, while all the time the bullet has to overcome the friction of the barrel.

This is very well illustrated by the accompanying graphs, made from a careful series of tests. This curve shows that with a four inch barrel, the velocity is 850 f.s., with a ten inch barrel the velocity is 1000 f.s., with a 16 inch barrel it is 1030 f.s., and with a 24 inch barrel it has again dropped back to 1000 f.s.

With revolvers, the effect is even more pronounced, as the cylinder, which is not counted in the barrel length, adds its effect, so that a two inch barrel on a revolver is about equal to a 3½ inch barrel on a pistol. The curve for the .38 Special revolver shows that with a 2 inch barrel we obtain 725 f.s., and only 75 feet more, or 800 f.s. with a four inch barrel, while adding two more inches to the barrel length and bringing it up to 6 inches adds only 30 feet more to the velocity.

An examination of the curves indicates that the difference in velocity between the six inch and the seven and a half inch barrels would be 20 foot seconds with No. 80 Powder, and 17 foot seconds with No. 5 powder: An actual test made by the author gave the following figures:

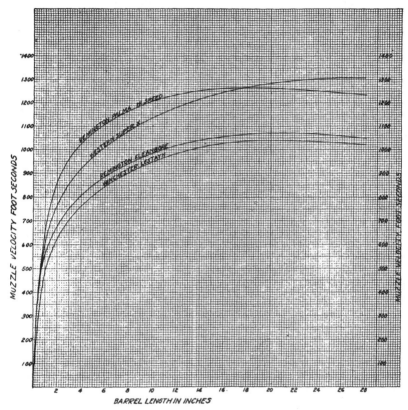

VELOCITY CURVE GRAPH

The effect of barrel length on velocity with four popular cartridges. Two of them are of the high speed type, and the other two are of the outdoor target type. See also the graphs with Chapter 8: Interior Ballistics.

The test was made with two separate revolvers, a S. & W. .38 Special Military & Police with 6 inch barrel, and a Colt Officer's Model Target with 7½-inch barrel. In addition to the regular factory loaded .38 special cartridge, with 158 grain bullet, the test included the Western .38 Special Super Police cartridge, with 200 grain bullet. The results were as follows:

	6 inch barrel length	7½ inch barrel length
.38 Special, Regular	850 f. s.	864 f. s.
.38 Special Super Police	705 f. s.	699 f. s.

This test shows that the regular .38 special cartridge gave 14 f.s. additional in the longer barrel, which agrees very well indeed with the figure of 17 feet taken from the curve, especially when it is realized that revolvers of two different makes were used, which may have given a slight difference even had the barrels been the same length.

The test also shows that in some cases a longer barrel may actually give less velocity than a shorter barrel. This is to be expected when a long, or very soft or very heavy bullet or a very small powder charge is used, for in this case the friction of the extra barrel length more than neutralizes the effect of the small remaining gas pressure. The test was actually made to prove a previous prediction that the Super Police load would give less velocity in a longer barrel.

A question more or less connected with barrel length is the difference in velocity between revolvers and automatic pistols. The .45 Automatic, model of 1911, has a barrel only 5 inches long, while the .45 Revolver, model of 1917 has a 5½ inch barrel in addition to the cylinder. In the revolver, of course, some gas escapes at the joint between the cylinder and the barrel; but tests have shown that generally the amount is too small to have any noticeable effect on the velocity, being usually not over 2 or 3 per cent.

A comparison of the velocities of the Automatic Pistol with the Colt and the Smith & Wesson revolvers using the same cartridge will no doubt be of interest. Five guns of each kind were used, and each gun was fired five times, using wartime ammunition, which was giving a velocity about 20 feet below the standard. The detailed results for each gun and the averages follow:

	.45 Auto. Pistol	.45 Colt 1917	.45 S. & W. 1917
Muzzle velocity, Gun No. 1	777.8	826.8	795.2
Gun No. 2	774.2	787.8	743.6
Gun No. 3	793.8	765.4	745.2
Gun No. 4	792.6	806.6	793.2
Gun No. 5	801.4	816.6	786.2
Average Muzzle velocity	787.9	800.6	772.6

While, as stated above, there has been a marked tendency toward the use of shorter barrels in the .22 caliber, the same arguments for shortening the barrel length lose much of their force when applied to heavier calibers, on account of the effect of barrel length on the recoil and jump of heavy caliber revolvers. About one-third of the recoil of the average revolver shot is caused by the reaction of the gas as it rushes out of the muzzle; and when the barrel is cut off to a shorter length, the gas is discharged into the air at a higher pressure, and the noise, blast, and recoil are all disagreeably increased.

However, there is another effect which is perhaps even more important, and that is a change in the radius of gyration of the gun, allowing it to jump more. This may be explained by stating that when the gun is fired, the gas pushes straight back in line with the barrel, while the forward reaction of the hand, in holding the gun against the thrust of recoil, is applied on the grip, which is considerably below the line of the barrel where the thrust occurs. The result is that the recoil tends to swing the muzzle upwards, and the longer and heavier the barrel is, the more will its weight and inertia resist this upward rotation, or "Jump"; and the metal at the muzzle of the barrel, having the most leverage, will have the greatest effect in resisting this upward jump. By cutting off the muzzle, we reduce the radius of gyration, or resistance to upward rotation, and the result is that revolvers with very short barrels and very heavy loads, such as the Detective Special, jump very unpleasantly. In the same way, revolvers with long barrels are quiet, easy shooting arms, which neutralize the recoil and jump to a large extent, and make possible accurate shooting with heavy loads.

Thus, with large caliber guns, a barrel at least six inches long is desirable for target practice, and lengths up to eight inches are desirable for the very heavy or high velocity loads, such as the .44 and .45 and the new .38/44. All the successful target revolvers follow this rule, as for example, the S. & W. Military and Police Target and the S. & W. .44 Target, with 6 inch barrel; the S. & W. .38/44 Outdoorsman, with 6½ inch barrel, the Colt Officers model .38 and the Colt New Service Target with 7½ inch barrel; and the new S. & W. .357 Magnum, with 8¾ inch barrel.

The question of the 6 inch barrel as against the 6½, 7½, or 8¾ inch barrel is largely one of the physique of the user. It takes a strong well trained man to hold the heavy Colt's New Service 7½ inch, or the new .357 Magnum at arm's length for any length of time. A strong and vigorous man who lives an outdoor life and keeps in training can do wonderful work with one of these arms, but the average man can no doubt do better with a gun such as the 6 inch barreled M. & P. or Officer's Model.

In late years, the ultra-short barrel length of two inches has become popular for pocket revolvers to be used by peace officers, mail clerks, bank messengers, etc., and two very popular Colt models, the Banker's Special, for the .38 Colt Police Positive

Cartridge, and the Detective Special, for the .38 Special Cartridge, are made with two inch barrels. These models originated when the U. S. Postoffice Department decided several years ago to arm the railway mail clerks with revolvers that could readily be carried in the pocket, and could still use a cartridge large enough to be decidedly effective in any emergency. As a result of a conference between government officials and the arms makers, several short

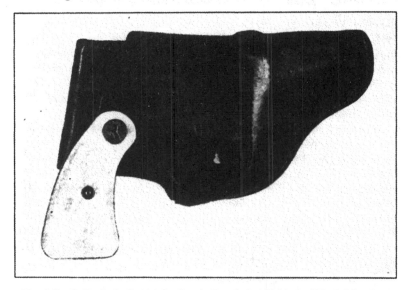

The Colt .22 Banker's Special in the Audley Spring Holster. This holster has a spring catch which engages with the trigger guard of the gun so that the gun is prevented from falling out or from leaving the holster at all unless the finger is placed in the trigger guard, when it comes in contact with the spring catch and releases the gun.

barreled models were submitted, and the one afterward known as the Banker's Special was the one that was finally purchased.

Recently the Banker's Special has been produced in .22 caliber, and is proving very popular as a means of providing a cheap means of obtaining proficiency with the larger gun by the use of the inexpensive .22 caliber cartridges for practice, instead of the more costly .38's. The first of these guns was made expressly to the author's order, and it is one of his favorite guns. Used with the high speed hollow point or sharp shoulder cartridges, it is itself a defensive weapon to be respected, and is capable of very satisfactory accuracy at full ranges. Another similar, though more recent arrival in the firearms world, is the Harrington &

Richardson New Defender, which is also a .22 with a two inch barrel. With it I have shot scores of over 90 on the Standard American Target at 20 yards.

While excellent shooting can on occasion, be done with these very short barreled guns, the sight radius is of course too short to allow them to compete seriously for target honors. A deviation of the front sight which is so small that it can hardly be noticed will give the shooter a six instead of a ten, and it requires the greatest of care to prevent these deviations from occurring. In fact, I am unable to do it. But in spite of that the accuracy is surprisingly good when the really very short barrel length is considered. With this little gun I averaged 84 on the standard American Target at 20 yards for several month's shooting, while with the same gun with a six inch barrel I averaged only four points higher, or 88.

Summing up the question of barrel length, it might be said that for target shooting with the single shot pistol, the ten inch length is perhaps the best for the average excellent shot, who sees the sights well, holds with extreme steadiness, and shoots promptly. However, for the many excellent shots who have trouble with blurring or fading of the sights, or who are inclined to be troubled by a tendency of the muzzle to wabble, or whose shooting temperament is such that they are inclined to hold too long before getting off the shot, the seven or eight inch length will be found to give definitely better results than the ten inch.

For target shooting with the revolver, the six or six and a half inch barrel length seems to be just about ideal, for the average man, though the unusually strong and well trained man will often prefer the 7½ inch or even the new 8¾ inch barreled guns.

For the law officer, the barrel should never be longer than four inches. The longer barrel adds nothing to the accuracy for short range work, and is much less convenient to carry and handle. Even if the gun is always carried in an outside holster on a belt, the short barrel is preferable, for it swings and handles more easily. Unless unusual compactness is desired, the three or four inch length is to be preferred to the two inch. The medium length barrels balance better, and feel better in the hand than the guns with extremely short barrels, and it is easier to sight accurately with a three or four inch barrel length than with a two inch. Moreover, the two inch barrel gives more recoil, on account of the fact that the gas escapes into the atmosphere under higher pressure, and hence the reaction of the gases on the air, which is responsible ordinarily for about a third of the recoil is increased, and as stated above, it jumps unpleasantly.

For prospectors, explorers and others in the wide open spaces of the world who may want to do long range shooting, (100 yards and over) with the revolver, the 7½ or eight inch length has important advantages. It will give about 25 foot seconds more velocity, on the average, than the six inch length, and it has a considerably longer sight radius, which is an important advantage when the revolver is shot from a steady position, using both hands, as is usual in practical long range work, when the rules of the target range do not apply, and the only object is to hit, using any available means to do so. For long range work, it is important also to choose a cartridge that has high velocity and small air resistance. The recently announced Smith & Wesson .357 Magnum with its 8¾ inch barrel and high velocity cartridge should be ideal for this work.

Weight

Modern hand firearms vary in weight from less than a pound to about two and a half pounds. The lower limit is represented by the .25 caliber automatics, weighing about 12 or 13 ounces, according to make, and such small guns as the S. & W. Safety Hammerless or the Colt Pocket Positive, weighing about a pound. On the other hand we find the large military models, weighing about 40 ounces, more or less, according to model or caliber.

Leaving out the question of recoil, a weight of about a pound and a half is a very pleasant weight for a target revolver. Certainly it is far less fatiguing to shoot with a light arm of about this weight, such as the S. & W. .22/32, or the Colt Woodsman, than it is with a heavier gun, such as the .22 Officer's Model, or the K-.22. On the other hand, when we consider other calibers than .22, we must take into consideration the question of recoil. The heavier the gun, the less will it recoil, and with very small and light revolvers which are made for heavy cartridges, such as the Police Positive Special, the punishment to the shooter's hand is sometimes rather severe, especially as the entire force of the recoil must be absorbed through a very small and narrow handle in these smaller guns.

Doubling the weight of the gun cuts the recoil in half; on the contrary, cutting the weight of the gun in half doubles the recoil. The serious part of it with these small guns is the fact that the recoil tends to turn the gun in the hand, so that the muzzle rises, and the grip is shaped so that it is very difficult for the shooter to prevent this turning, which may throw the edge of the hammer against the top of the hand with sufficient force to cause painful abrasions.

This is the reason for such heavy guns as the S. & W. .38/44, the Colt Shooting Master, and the new S. & W. Magnum. In these guns the weight and moment of inertia opposed to the recoil and turning effect of the cartridge makes a very pleasant-shooting arm.

This subject is treated at length in the section on Interior Ballistics, where the theory of recoil is stated, and a table of the actual recoil energy of the principal guns is given.

Accuracy

The accuracy of a revolver or pistol, which may be described as its ability to deliver its shots in a small group on the target, is dependent on many things, and may be affected or changed by many conditions. For example, a poor trigger pull may interfere seriously with accuracy. Other vital factors are the balance and weight of the gun, the kind of handle, the lock time, or speed of the hammer, the character of the firing pin blow, the sights, the precision with which the cylinder lines up with the barrel, the leading of the barrel, wear or erosion of the barrel, etc.

However, all of these things are more or less "accessories after the fact," for no accuracy can be obtained by the best of sights or trigger pulls unless the barrel has mechanical accuracy to start with, and is used with an accurate cartridge.

The first requisite is a barrel of the proper size, properly rifled, and having a smooth finish inside. Given such a barrel, the best accuracy is obtained when the barrel is so chambered for the cartridge to be used that when the cartridge is inserted in the chamber, the bullet rests on the beginning of the rifling. In the "Olympic" Smith & Wesson .22 pistols, the cartridge stops, with the bullet against the rifling, when it is about a sixteenth of an inch from being all the way in the chamber. Additional force must be applied to make it go the rest of the way, and this makes the rifling actually cut into the bullet, which is then all ready to start on its journey with the greatest possible uniformity and precision, and it starts to rotate at the same time that it starts forward.

On the other hand, in a revolver, the cartridge is in a cylinder which is separate from the barrel which has the rifling, so that the bullet cannot touch the rifling until it has been driven forward a half inch or more by the powder pressure. This first motion is in a straight forward direction, without any rotation at all, and when the bullet finally strikes the rifling, it is already moving very fast. At this instant it must pick up its rotation very suddenly, instead of acquiring the rotary motion gradually, in the same way that it obtained its forward speed. As a result, the bullet fails to follow the rifling at first, and the lands cut straight across the bullet until such time as a rotary motion can be imparted to it.

In the old cap and ball revolvers, in which round balls were often used, the bearing of the bullet on the rifling is very small, as only the narrow zone around the middle of the bullet touches the lands, and in order to allow the bullet to acquire its rotation gradually enough so that stripping would be avoided, the grooves were made straight in the back part of the barrel, with a gradually increasing twist. However, the modern bullets, with long cylindrical bearing do not strip so easily, and all modern revolvers are made with a uniform twist of rifling. This works very satisfactorily, but if bullet which has been fired from a revolver is examined carefully, it can be plainly seen that the bullet has moved forward against the rifling for a short distance before taking the rotation.

Perhaps even more important in its effect on accuracy is the fact that when the front end of the bullet is retarded by suddenly striking the rifling, the bullet has a tendency to tip over or turn sideways, and though of course it is restrained from doing this by its position in the cylinder it is not held as firmly in line as it would be if it were in the chamber of a single shot pistol and this tendency to turn sideways may frequently cause a considerable amount of deformation in the bullet, especially when the breech end of the barrel is eroded to a larger diameter than normal. For these reasons the single shot pistol is capable of higher accuracy than can be obtained with revolvers.

By this it must not be inferred however, that modern revolvers are inaccurate. Quite the contrary is true, for a great deal of ingenuity and engineering skill has been expended in bringing the accuracy of the revolver to the highest possible point, and the results have been extremely satisfactory. It is true that revolvers do not ordinarily place all of the shots in one hole, yet the good ones make groups that are very much smaller than the ten ring on the target and the dispersion given by the revolver is only a small fraction of that which is due to the errors of the shooter.

An index of what the revolver is capable of is shown by three consecutive groups of nine shots each (the capacity of the cylinder) fired from a machine rest at fifty yards. The largest of these groups was 1¼ inches in diameter and the smallest was slightly under an inch. All three of the groups could be placed in separate positions inside the ten ring so that no group would come within half an inch of any other group or within half an inch of the ten ring which is 3.39 inches in diameter. This shows that if the target shooter could hold as well as a machine rest and could see his sights perfectly, he would be capable of shooting possibles all day long. The errors of the shooter are so much greater than those of the average gun that barrel accuracy is very seldom a deciding factor in winning a match.

Among the factors which affect the accuracy of a revolver is the length of the cylinder and the distance the bullet has to jump before it hits the rifling. Most .22 caliber revolvers have a cylinder that is much longer than necessary. This is because most of them were designed to take a larger cartridge and when they are made for the .22 the chambers are simply made smaller without shortening the cylinder which could change the whole design of the gun and result in very great manufacturing expense. In modern, high grade revolvers chambered for the .22 caliber cartridge the cylinder is approximately ¾ of an inch longer than necessary for the .22 caliber long rifle cartridge. This could readily be changed merely by making the cylinder only as long as necessary leaving a gap in the frame in front of the cylinder; and extending the breech of the barrel back beyond the frame so as to meet the cylinder. Experimental models of this kind have been made but such a gun could not be sold because it looks awkward and the average public is more interested in looks than in very fine accuracy. Moreover, the accuracy already obtained is so good that the amount to be gained by such changes is not important enough to justify the trouble involved. It will be found, however, that some makers have decreased the forward end of the chamber in the cylinder so that it is a tight fit on the bullet.

Much more important than length of the cylinder is the precision with which it lines up with the barrel. If the cylinder is not exactly in line it can readily be seen that the bullet will strike more heavily on one side of the rifling than on the other, and will be deformed. Moreover, if the cylinder is considerably out of line, shaving of lead will result, with a considerable loss in accuracy and with possible injury to the shooter. The pieces of lead that are scraped off by the back of the barrel when the bullet enters are thrown out to the side and may strike the shooter on the hand or be thrown back into his face. This may be caused by a worn cylinder lock, or in cheaply or poorly constructed weapons, by faulty design. It is a dangerous and annoying defect.

The writer once owned a .44-40 single-action revolver which got to shaving lead, owing to wear of the hand cylinder and lock, and after the defect was corrected by replacement of the worn parts, the gun still could not be used with satisfaction due to a tendency to flinch caused by the memory of the particles of lead flying in the face at the time of the defect. As a result the gun was disposed of, although it was then working correctly.

Poorly made revolvers may not have the holes in the cylinders bored in perfect relation to each other and as a result the shaving of lead will occur. This defect is very rare in well-made weapons and is one of the reasons why cheap and poorly constructed revolvers of foreign make should be avoided.

In guns in which the cylinder swings out to eject and reload, as is the case with most modern American revolvers, the direction of rotation of the cylinder has an important bearing on the proper lining up of the chambers with the barrel, for if the rotation is to the right, or toward the frame of the revolver, the thrust of the "hand" or pawl that turns the cylinder, tends to push the crane and cylinder toward the frame of the gun, but if, on the other hand, the rotation is to the left, the thrust of the hand tends to push the crane and cylinder away from the frame of the gun, so that the cylinder would thus be slightly swung out from its proper position, and would not line up with the barrel.

Both the Colt and the Smith & Wesson .38 caliber Army revolvers which were used as the Service sidearm before the adoption of the automatic pistol had left hand rotation, which was undesirable. The Colt guns of this model often shaved lead very badly, but the Smith & Wessons were extremely well made, and I have never seen one of the old Army .38 S. & W.'s give this trouble. I have been told by members of the Smith & Wesson firm that they did not want to use the left hand rotation, but were forced to make their army revolvers that way to meet Government specifications of those days.

In their later revolvers, the Colt company changed the rotation to right-handed. Smith & Wesson retained the left hand rotation, but took steps to insure that the cylinder is always properly lined up with the barrel by the use of an additional cylinder latch made on a lug underneath the barrel, and arranged to engage the front of the ejector rod. This double latching is a feature of all modern Smith & Wesson revolvers having swing-out cylinders.

In inspecting guns at the factory they are tested for the precision with which the cylinders match the barrel, by using a testing plug called a "range rod" which is a steel rod that just fits inside of the barrel with a snug fit. In making this test the gun is snapped and the trigger held back and then this rod is pushed down through the muzzle until it enters the chamber in the cylinder. If it meets resistance in going into the chamber it shows that the cylinder is not properly lined up.

Even if the gun is properly constructed and meets this test it may become loose as a result of wear, so that the cylinder may not line up properly. For example, if the notches on the cylinder and the hand that engages in these notches to turn the cylinder become worn the cylinder may not turn far enough for the latch to drop into place; thus the cylinder would not be properly lined up with the barrel when the gun fired. In fact with old guns it is sometimes the practice of the user to touch the cylinder lightly with the forefinger in order to be sure that it is properly locked in place before pulling the trigger.

In buying a second hand gun it is a good plan to test it by holding back the cylinder with one hand and cocking the gun with the other so that if the parts that rotate the cylinder are worn, their defective condition can be detected. Then with the gun empty, cock the hammer and pull the trigger; and without releasing the pressure on the trigger rock the cylinder from side to side to see if there is any play. There should be very little, if any, motion in this position of the gun, that is, with the trigger pulled back all the way, because this is the position in which the gun is at the instant of firing and if there is any looseness of the cylinder it is likely to be on one side or the other of its proper position which will result in the shaving of lead and consequent inaccuracy.

Firing Pin Blow

Even though the gun should have excellent accuracy in the barrel and should be in good mechanical condition as regards the alignment of the cylinder there is still a chance for trouble if the firing pin blow is not correct, for if the blow is too weak hang-fires and inaccuracy will result. Of course if the blow is extremely weak the cartridge will not go off at all and there will be a misfire instead; but any weakening of the blow is bad for accuracy, even though the trouble may not be severe enough to result in actual misfires.

The .22 rimfire cartridge is particularly sensitive to variations in the firing pin blow. As an illustration of what may happen I will describe an incident that occurred a short time ago. A rifle club had some Springfield .22 caliber rifles and also some Winchester .22 caliber rifles. They also had two makes of .22 caliber ammunition in stock. The President of the Club came to me for advice stating that he was having great difficulty with one of the makes of ammunition. The accuracy was extremely poor and many of the bullets would not even reach the target at fifty feet. We went over to his club, took a brand new rifle out of the locker room and proceeded to fire fifty shots of both kinds of ammunition with excellent results. There was no trouble whatsoever and the Club President who had made the complaint was dumbfounded. I knew that he had undoubtedly been experiencing severe trouble, and I was puzzled to know why we did not get it in this test, so I questioned him further as to the rifles that had given the trouble. He then informed me that half of the rifles including the one we had just tried, were brand new ones which had never been used; while the remaining half had been in use for several years and were quite well worn. He said that all of the rifles that they had been shooting had given trouble. I then got one of the actual rifles that had been used and made a test with the result that ammunition "A" worked perfectly while ammunition "B," which was the one he complained of, gave about 25% of hang fires, squibbs, low reports, etc., and those shots that did reach the target were strung all the way from the bullseye to the bottom of the paper. A further test showed that both ammunition "A" and "B" gave perfect results in the new rifles while ammunition "A" gave perfect results in the old, worn rifles and ammunition "B" was the next thing to entirely useless in these old rifles. In the same way a brand new lot of ammunition purchased by the Government failed to function in .22 caliber automatic pistols although it had passed a perfect acceptance test just a few weeks before. A re-test of all this ammunition was made and again it passed a perfect retest, but these tests were made in rifles and not in pistols. Investigation showed that the firing pin blow in the pistol was very much lighter than in the rifle.

As a result of this test and of other similar experiences the Ordnance Department made up a testing device for measuring the firing pin blow in all types of weapons. In the .22 caliber weapons a cartridge made of solid copper is placed in the chamber of the gun and the firing pin was snapped on it. The depth of the indentation is then read by means of a dial indicator gauge. This gives a very accurate measure of the actual strength of the firing pin blow. For other types of guns steel cartridges are furnished with the outfit, one cartridge for each type of gun to be tested. Instead of a primer each one of these steel cartridges has a hole for the insertion of a little copper cylinder. To make the test, the copper cylinder is placed in the steel cartridge, which is then placed in the gun. The gun is then snapped and the depth of the indentation is measured as before.

During my experiments with this subject I made tests not only on fresh ammunition of different kinds but also on various old lots of ammunition that had been kept for some years and I found that with a light firing pin blow or in some cases even with a fairly heavy blow and some changes in the point of the firing pin that trouble would be experienced with many makes of ammunition. On the other hand with some other shapes of firing pin and sufficiently heavy blow even the old stale ammunition seemed to work very well. In the course of this investigation I tested the firing pin blow of a number of different guns in my possession with the results shown below:

Name of Gun	Depth of Blow (Inches)	Remarks
Fiala Combination	.005	Many misfires with this gun.
Colt Ace	.007	Hang and misfires with some makes.
Savage Rifle	.010	
Reising Auto. Pistol	.011	
Smith & Wesson Olympic	.011	Bad results with smokeless, excellent with Lesmok.
Winchester Single Shot	.013	
Colt Officer's Model	.0135	Single action.
Colt Officer's Model	.010	Double action.
H. & R. 10″	.014	
H. & R. 8″	.015	
Iver Johnson Sealed Eight	.014	Chisel shaped firing pin.
Iver Johnson Sealed Eight #2	.0085	Firing pin with egg shaped point.
H. & R. Sportsman	.015	
Winchester 52 with Speed Lock	.015	
S. & W. K-22	.015	Single action.
S. & W. K-22	.013	Double action.
Colt Woodsman	.016	
Webley Single Shot	.023	Excellent results with all ammunition.

As the result of these tests and of troubles encountered with some of the guns and certain makes of ammunition an extensive correspondence ensued between the author and several of the manufacturers concerned, with the result that some changes were made in firing pin shapes and blows, so that the table given above does not necessarily represent the present practice of the makers represented in the tabulation.

The uniformity and certainty of ignition, and consequently, the accuracy, is affected not only by the strength of the firing pin blow, but also by several other factors, such as the headspace, the character of the support for the rim of the cartridge, the shape of the firing pin point, the location of the blow as regards the edge of the rim, etc.

"Headspace" is the distance between the breech of the gun and the support for the cartridge rim; in other words, it is the space

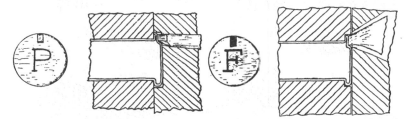

A STUDY OF FIRING PIN ACTION.
Left: The Colt Woodsman and the Colt Ace. The chisel shaped point of the firing pin strikes nearly across the rim; just slightly inside. The chisel shaped or rectangular point is probably somewhat better than the round shape, as the force of the blow is concentrated where it is most needed.
Right: The Colt Officer's Model Revolver. The point of the hammer nose, which is rectangular in shape, forms the firing pin, which strikes across the rim right to the edge. It gives excellent ignition.

occupied by the head of the cartridge when the gun is loaded. If it is too small, the gun cannot be closed after loading; this condition is not met in practice. If it is too large, ignition troubles may ensue from the fact that the cartridge is not held firmly against the breech of the gun, and may be so far away that the firing pin dents the primer only slightly; or the cartridge may rest against the breech, but may move forward when struck by the firing pin. Headspace should be no greater than necessary to allow loading the arm with all makes of cartridge. The more nearly the head of the cartridge fills the space between the barrel and the breech block, the better are the ignition conditions.

The character of the support for the head of the cartridge is important, especially in rim-fire cartridges, for if the rim is not firmly supported against the firing pin blow, the result will be unsatisfactory. In some single shot pistols especially, the part of the rim that receives the blow rests on the extractor, instead of the solid part of the barrel. This is not a desirable condition.

Most firing pins for center-fire cartridges have a rounded point, but there is a tremendous variation in the shapes used for rim-fire cartridges, hardly any two makers using exactly the same kind of point. Some firing pin points are round and flat on the end, like the end of a rod; others are round with a ball point; still others are chisel shaped or rectangular. In addition, there is a large variation in size. Some makes of gun have a large diameter firing pin, that covers a large area, while others have only a small point. Perhaps a mean between the two extremes is the most desirable, for too small a firing pin may strike a spot on the rim of the cartridge where there does not happen to be much priming, while too large a pin has to mash so much metal that the blow must be very heavy, and the jar on the mechanism is thus increased.

If a number of dummy .22 caliber cartridges are snapped in several makes of gun, it will be seen that there is also a large varia-

A STUDY OF FIRING PIN ACTION.

The author's old Smith & Wesson Perfected Single Shot Pistol. The small round end of the pivoted hammer nose acts as a firing pin. It strikes well inside of the rim, and does not give particularly good ignition with any but the most sensitive primers.

tion in the location of the impact as regards the edge of the rim of the cartridge. For example, one make may strike entirely inside of the rim, while another may strike half on the rim and half outside of it. . Obviously, a firing pin that strikes a rim-fire cartridge well inside the rim will give poor ignition, for best results are obtained only when the mixture is actually crushed between the front and back parts of the rim, and this means that the blow must fall on the rim, not inside of it.

The edges of the firing pin should be somewhat rounded, for sharp corners will have a tendency to puncture the thin, soft metal, with a resulting disagreeable or even dangerous escape of gas.

Another unfavorable condition is for the firing pin to strike too far toward the outside edge of the cartridge case, for then instead of smashing the hollow rim of the cartridge much of the energy of the blow will be wasted in trying to compress the outer wall of the cartridge head. These difficulties are most often seen in guns which have a round firing pin. In order to overcome troubles of this kind many guns have an oblong or chisel shape point to the firing pin which cuts right across the rim. This type of firing pin is very satisfactory but care must be taken that the corners are well rounded and that the firing pin is not wedge shape or sharp at the front, as otherwise it might cut through the thin metal and cause a ruptured head with an accompanying disagreeable escape of gas.

Firing pins on the Smith & Wesson straight line and K-.22 and on the Harrington & Richardson revolvers are round. The firing

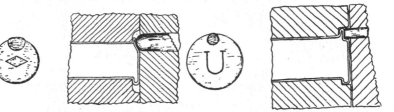

A STUDY OF FIRING PIN ACTION.

Left: The Stevens Conlin Model Target Pistol. The sketch shows a cross section through the chamber and breech of the gun, to give an idea of the manner in which the rim is crushed by the blow. The appearance of the cartridge head after firing is shown at the left. This gun has an exceptionally large firing pin with a rounded point, which not only covers the rim of the cartridge, but actually extends some distance beyond.

Right: The Smith & Wesson Model K-.22. The small round firing pin strikes squarely on the edge of the rim. This is where the blow should be struck for the best results.

pin on the Colt .22 caliber revolvers, the Camp Perry model, and the Woodsman and Ace pistols and on the Harrington & Richardson U. S. R. A. model pistols are rectangular in shape. An interesting firing pin or hammer nose is that on the Webley single shot target pistol which is similar in shape to the firing pin used on the Colt and H. & R. pistols as described above but has the striking surface rounded into a cylinder. This is probably made necessary by the very heavy blow which might cut through the metal if sharp edges were used on the rectangular face of the firing pin. This rounded surface together with the very heavy impact used is very effective and the ignition with this pistol seems to be excellent as it fires without trouble old and deteriorated cartridges which give misfires and hangfires in other guns.

Firing pin location is important in center fire cartridges as well as in .22's. Quite often revolvers and automatic pistols are seen in which the cartridge is not struck squarely in the center of the primer. In fact this is the rule rather than the exception even with many high grade arms. As long as the eccentricity of the firing pin blow is relatively small it does no harm; but if the blow is very far off center misfires are likely to occur.

Testing Guns for Accuracy

While a good shot can readily detect any *serious* lack of accuracy in a pistol or revolver by shooting it at a target, it is almost impossible to satisfactorily compare the accuracy of well made guns by this method, because the average high-grade arm will shoot much closer than even the best shot can hold. Even a champion shot cannot expect to make a group much less than six or eight inches in diameter at 50 yards, and yet groups of less than one inch in diameter at this distance are the rule in testing .22 caliber target pistols from a machine rest.

It would seem that the obvious solution would be to use a machine rest for testing the accuracy of all pistols and revolvers; but unfortunately this is not possible, because no satisfactory machine rest for heavy caliber hand guns has ever been devised. With rifles, the problem is comparatively simple. The gun is clamped by the barrel, receiver, and butt, or, preferably, by the receiver and butt alone, onto a heavy clamping device mounted on a massive concrete base. The strength of the parts is such that the gun cannot move between shots. It would seem that this should give a perfect test, but experience has shown that great care and skill are necessary in bedding the gun properly in the rest, and in clamping it so that no strain or distortion results. Even with a gun skillfully placed in the rest, the effect of heating between shots may destroy the accuracy of the test. In fact, so great are the difficulties involved, that for testing the accuracy of ammunition even this method is not good enough, and such tests are usually made by means of a testing device called the "Mann Rest," after the late Dr. F. W. Mann, who invented it during the course of an extensive series of tests on accuracy.

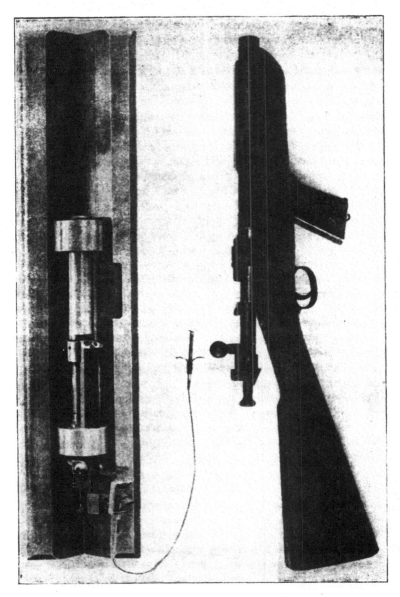

Left: Special Mann Barrel developed to test .45 Automatic Pistol Ammunition. Note the camera release used to pull the trigger without communicating a jar to the barrel. Right: A .45 caliber accuracy gun for use in a machine rest. The 5 inch .45 caliber barrel is fitted to the receiver of a Springfield Rifle.

The Mann Rest consists simply of a very heavy cylindrical barrel, rifled and chambered for the cartridge to be tested, and fitted with a breech action but no stock. A V-shaped trough of steel is mounted on a heavy concrete base, and is fitted with elevating and deflection screws. In preparing to use this rest, a telescope is first laid in the trough, and by means of the adjusting screws, the cross-hairs of the telescope are brought on the target. The adjusting screws are clamped so that the rest cannot move, the telescope is removed, and the heavy cylindrical barrel is laid in the trough. Obviously, this cylindrical barrel lying in the bottom of the V-shaped trough will point in the same direction as the telescope pointed when the adjustments were made, which is toward the target. The barrel is now loaded and fired. It will recoil and jump when the explosion takes place, but it will not move the rest, because it is simply lying in the trough, and is not fastened to the rest in any way. Every time the gun is loaded and put back in the rest it will always point in precisely the same direction as before, and thus firing it in this way will give a perfect test of the accuracy. Such Mann rests are constantly used in testing pistol ammunition; but these tests tell us the accuracy of the ammunition only, and do not help when we want to know whether or not revolver No. 1 or revolver No. 2 is the more accurate.

However, the Mann Rest has been adapted in a way to testing weapons; some years ago Col. Roy D. Jones of the Springfield Revolver club arranged a pair of steel rings to slip over the barrel of single shot target pistols and clamp in place, thus allowing the pistol to be tested in the V-shaped trough of the Mann Rest. This gave a very satisfactory test with .22 caliber arms, but did not work satisfactorily with the larger caliber guns, because they jump so violently when fired that the rings could not be clamped firmly enough to hold them from moving. No doubt, however, something of this kind could be worked out if enough effort were expended on it. Mr. A. L. Woodworth, of Springfield Armory devised a testing device for rifles which gives the best results of any method yet devised for testing the accuracy of individual rifles. The Woodworth Cradle, as it is called, consists of two large rings or cylinders of steel supporting a cradle into which a rifle can be clamped. The entire cradle, rifle and all is then laid in the Mann V-trough and fired. Undoubtedly a Woodworth Cradle could be made for revolvers.

For many years machine rests of one kind or another have been used in arms factories and in ballistic laboratories for holding revolvers for testing velocity, etc., where it is necessary that the gun point nearly in the same direction for each shot. These give much better accuracy than the average off-hand shot can secure, and are very satisfactory for making certain that the shot will strike a chronograph wire or screen, but they are not capable of showing the real accuracy of a revolver on a test.

Another method of testing is to use what is called the Six Point Rest. A V-shaped support is provided for the muzzle of the gun; another similar one for the breech end of the barrel; a stop to

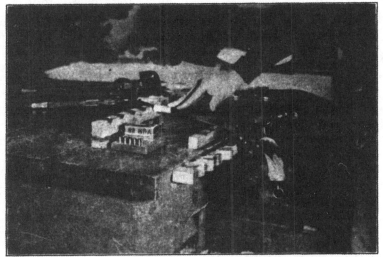

The "Six Point" rest and manner in which pistol is fitted into it.

come against the trigger guard, to limit the distance the gun is pushed forward in the Vs; and a stop to rest against one side of the butt to limit the position of the gun in a vertical plane. The gun is placed with the muzzle resting in the forward V, and the breech end of the barrel resting in the other. Then it is pushed forward until the trigger guard comes in contact with its stop, and is rotated until the handle comes against its stop. It is then fired. It will jump, but as it is not fastened in any way to the rest, the jump of the gun will not disturb the position of the rest. The gun is then loaded and again placed in the rest, when it will come to exactly the same position and will be pointing the same as before. It will be seen that there are six points of contact between the gun and the rest; namely, the two sides of the crotch which holds the muzzle; the two sides of the crotch which holds the breech; the stop for the front of the trigger guard; and the stop against which the stock rests when the gun is rotated as far as it can go.

Such a rest is very easily improvised by cutting a V-shaped notch in a piece of wood, and nailing it on a heavy wooden bench to act as a muzzle support; using a similar piece for a breech support; using the edge of the bench at the stop for the trigger guard; and nailing a block of wood on the edge of the bench to serve as a stop against rotation.   As there are no adjustments on this arrangement, the procedure in testing for groups with it is to

The "receiver-and-forearm" rest as used at Springfield Armory in targeting the .45
Automatic Pistols for National Match work.

first find where the shots are going by firing a trial shot, then hang the target where the first shot went and try for the group.

At the big revolver factories, expert shots are employed who target the guns by shooting them off-hand to test the sighting, and then fire from a forearm rest to test the size of the group.   The shooter stands or is seated behind a slanting table of the right height and slope so that when the gun is grasped with both hands and the forearms are rested on the table, the sights are at the right of the eyes. This gives a very firm support, which eliminates much of the personal error that otherwise might enter.

At Springfield Armory the thousands of Automatic Pistols specially selected for use at the National Matches are targeted by the use of an improvised rest made by taking a step-ladder of the right height to support the forearm of the targeter, and fastening to the top of it a piece of board with a V-shaped notch cut in it. This piece of board is adjustable up and down, and can be clamped in any position by means of a thumb-screw. This notched board is adjusted so that when the targeter's forearm rests on top of the step-ladder, the V-shaped notch will support the pistol by the receiver just forward of the trigger guard. This "receiver and forearm rest" is perhaps the most satisfactory method of testing heavy caliber revolvers for accuracy.

With .22 caliber arms, it is another story. They have such a light recoil that they can be successfully clamped in a fixed rest so that they will not change position during a string of shots. Harrington & Richardson use a machine rest to target every one of their target pistols and revolvers at the regulation distance of 20 yards. Every gun made is targeted as a part of the process of manufacture. Smith & Wesson have also developed an excellent fixed rest for their .22 caliber arms, which has enabled a constant check to be kept on the accuracy of their product, and has greatly facilitated studies of the effects of changes in construction designed to produce further advances in accuracy and to enable the arms to handle most efficiently all the various new types of .22 caliber ammunition that are constantly making their appearance.

Sights

Every gun must be provided with some accurate way of determining when it is correctly pointed at the target. This is accomplished by the use of "sights," consisting of a blade or post of some kind on the front end of the barrel, and a notch or groove or a peep-hole on the breech end. By holding the gun so that the post on the muzzle appears to be in line with the target when it is viewed through the notch or peep-hole on the breech end, the gun is lined up so that a hit will be made when the trigger is pulled.

The post or blade on the muzzle is the "front sight," and the notch or peep-hole on the breech is the "rear sight," and these two sights must be positioned in such a relation to the axis of the bore that when the sights point at the target, the axis of the bore points in such a direction that a bullet leaving the barrel will hit the target. The bore of the rifle when the gun is sighted points nearly at the target, but not exactly at it; for when the gun is fired, it jumps, and moreover, the bullet travels in a curve, and not in a straight line, so that when the gun is fired, the bullet never goes exactly where the barrel points.

The problem of sighting guns is complicated by the fact that as soon as a bullet leaves the muzzle it starts to drop. For example, the .45 Colt bullet drops about 7 inches at 50 yards, 30 inches at 100 yards, and 131 inches at 200 yards. The Springfield rifle bullet drops about 40 feet at 1000 yards. Thus if you fired directly at a man 1000 yards off, the bullet would go 40 feet below him.

To enable the shooter to hit accurately at different ranges and under different conditions, the sights on most rifles are made so that their position with relation to the line of the bore can be changed to meet different ranges, different powder charges, different wind conditions, etc.

With pistols and revolvers, where the range is always very short, it is not absolutely necessary to have adjustable sights, and most pocket or military type pistols and revolvers have what is called "fixed sights;" that is, the sights are lined up at the factory for the average shooter and average ranges, and are made a part of the frame and barrel of the gun. Usually the front sight is a vertical blade on top of the barrel near the muzzle, and the rear sight is a notch or groove in the frame. It is very important that the sights, and particularly the front sight, shall be shaped so that they cannot catch in the pocket or holster. For this reason, the front sight on most pocket revolvers is rounded, so that it looks like a half circle of metal sticking up on top of the barrel. This rounded form has the disadvantage that the light from the sky strikes it at different points under the different conditions, and thus makes it very difficult sometimes to see the sight clearly, or to tell just where the top of it is. To overcome this, some fixed front sights, such as those on the Colt New Service Revolver, are made with the back edge of the sight vertical, instead of rounded. This makes sighting easier, but has the disadvantage of being more likely to catch; but as this large military type gun is usually carried in a stiff holster, no trouble from this source is anticipated. The smaller Colt guns are all made with rounded sights.

An improved form of fixed front sight that will not catch, and at the same time does not suffer from irregular reflections is the sloping sight with corrugated rear surface used on the Mauser and Luger Pistols, and lately, on the Colt Ace and Woodsman automatics. The rear sight on the fixed sight model revolvers is simply a notch in the frame above the cylinder; but in late years even this simple notch has been greatly improved by making it practically square in outline, and by cutting into the frame just at the rear end of the notch, so that the edges of the notch are outlined sharply, and it looks the same in various kinds of light.

Sights differ considerably in the shape of the outline seen when

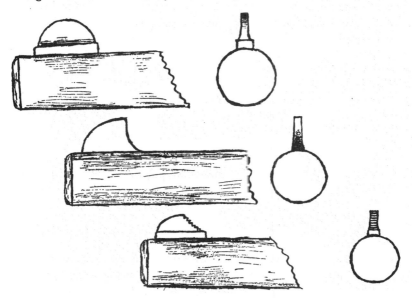

Different types of fixed front sight. Top, rounded sight as used on pocket models and on S. & W. Military. Middle, sight on Colt New Service Revolver. Bottom, slanting sight with corrugated rear face, as used on Colt Ace and Sport Model Woodsman. A similar sight is also used on the Luger and Mauser pistols.

sighting, and there has been a gradual style trend in this matter, the same as in many other things, so that while most target sights made some years ago were of one kind, those made today are all of a distinctly different and newer design. The earliest sights were of what is sometimes called the "barleycorn" type, consisting of a V rear notch, with a front sight which is wide at the base, and tapers to a narrow upper portion with a flat top.

Next there was "Paine" sight, named for Chevalier Ira A. Paine, a professional marksman who became very prominent about 1880. The front sight, when viewed from the rear, appears to be a little ball, or bead, supported on a stem, and the rear sight is a

U shaped notch. For many years practically no other sight was used by expert revolver shots, but finally a change in style came with the introduction of the "Patridge" sight, so called because it was first described in a letter to *Shooting and Fishing* by Mr. E. E. Patridge, dated January 13, 1898.

The Patridge sight is now almost universally used on target pistols and revolvers. It consists of a rectangular blade front sight with a vertical back surface, used in conjunction with a perfectly square or rectangular notch as a rear sight. In sighting, the top of the front sight blade is even with the top of the rear sight bar, and the blade is in the middle of the notch.

In late years the tendency has been toward wider sights. Formerly the idea was that fine sighting required fine and dainty sights; but this view has been proven by experience to be erroneous, for very small or fine sights are difficult to see, and the resultant eyestrain neutralizes all the advantages that they are supposed to give. Large sights, that can be plainly seen are easy on the eyes, and allow the sights to be seen plainly with a resultant increase in accuracy.

The present day Patridge sights on the best target arms range from .05 inch to $\frac{1}{8}$ inch in width, with 1/10 inch as the preferred size. The width of the rear sight notch depends on the barrel length, on how far the gun is held from the eye, and on the lighting conditions. The notch should be just wide enough to allow a plainly visible strip of light to be seen along both sides of the front sight. As the lighting of most indoor ranges illuminates the targets only, and as the brilliantly illuminated target has a tendency to form a glaring white background, a narrower strip of white is needed for indoor shooting than would be ideal for outdoor work. As an indication of the usual dimensions of the rear sight notch for good results, I might say that with a distance of $7\frac{1}{4}$ inches between sights, I find that with a 1/10 inch front sight a rear notch .09 wide is excellent for indoor work.

It is quite easy to experiment with Patridge sights of different sizes, for these sights are of such a form that anyone with a file and a few old scraps of metal can shape up a set in a few minutes. It is well, however, in doing work of this kind to remember that the best results are obtained if the shape of the front sight blade and of the rear sight notch are such that stray reflections are eliminated as far as possible. To prevent reflections from the top and sides of the front sight, the top should slope down toward the front, so that the tallest part is at the rear; and to prevent reflections from the sides, the sides should slope inward toward the front, so that the rear face is the widest part. As an added refinement, the rear surface of the front sight may be undercut, so that any backward reflection of light will be thrown down and will not reach the shooter's eyes.

In like manner, the rear sight notch should be shaped so that it is wider and deeper at the front than at the back, so that only a thin edge is actually used to sight with, thus giving the sharpest possible outline.

While sights of this kind are excellent for target practice, where the outline of the rear sight notch is sharply outlined against the white background of the target paper, they are not so good for use in the woods, for in certain lights it will be found that the sights cannot be seen at all, and even when the front sight can be seen plainly, the outlines of the rear sight notch will not be clear. For satisfaction in work of this kind, it is absolutely necessary to use a light colored bead, or a light colored facing of some kind on the

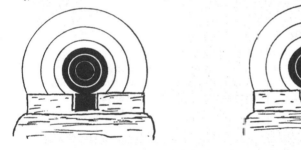

PATRIDGE   PAINE

The left. or Patr'dge sight is the favorite for target practice. The bead or Paine sight, formerly used almost exclusively for target shooting is still the best type for hunting and shooting in the woods. Besides showing the shape of these two kinds of sights, the author's sketch also shows the proper six o'clock hold for target shooting.

front sight. A flat faced ivory bead is very satisfactory, but a gold bead is even more easily seen in all kinds of light.

A bead that is rounded on the rear face is more easily seen than is a flat bead, but it will have high lights on one side or the other, depending on the direction from which the light comes, and it will tend to "shoot away from the light;" that is to say that if, for example, the light comes from the right, the gun will shoot further to the left than it should, and vice versa. This is because the part of the sight that is toward the light will have a bright spot or highlight on it, and this bright point is all that is seen when aiming.

This gives the same effect as if the front sight had been moved in that direction.

The best shape of sight for use in the woods is a fairly small bead, with a rather large U-shaped rear notch. The bead should not be too large, otherwise it will cover up the aiming mark entirely in many cases, for small objects such as the head of a snake, for example, are much smaller than a bullseye. It takes a round bead to get properly onto such a mark, because in game shooting the gun should be sighted to hold right on the mark; the practice of holding under is correct for the target range, where the sights can be more clearly defined against the white paper than against the bullseye, but it is not the best system for the woods, where everything is a dark color, and there is no chance to outline the sights against a white background. The sight must be placed just where the bullet is to go, because most of the time the mark will be moving off, and the sights must be held just in front of its head; and in the limited time for getting off the shot it is difficult to hold under and off at the same time. The ideal sight for this work would be a small round bead, with a center insert of gold or some bright material.

The rear sight for either a hunting handgun, or one for quick shooting should have a U notch of ample size; most of them are too small. There should be plenty of room around the bead when the arm is extended for sighting. In a poor light it is very hard to pick up the rear bead if it fits too closely to the sides of the rear notch. The Patridge sight with a rear notch that is right for use on the indoor target range is entirely too close to be of any use either in hunting or for quick defensive shooting. It is too hard to find, or to "notch" quickly, and you have to wobble the muzzle about to see where it is, as it may be right in the rear notch and yet block out so much light that it cannot be seen. The front sight also would be entirely too broad for hunting use, as it would block out too much of the mark; most of the time it would cover or block it out entirely. For both hunting and defensive work the shooter wants to be able to see around his sights and seem to see *through* them. The idea of blocking out all of the mark except what sticks up above the front sight is wrong except for bullseye or target work.

One way of improving a target sight so that it will work better in the woods, is to sink a circle of gold colored metal into the rear face of the ordinary Patridge front sight. This gives a sight having a gold bead which is perfectly flat and flush with the surface. It can be seen very well in most lights, and because it is flat, it does not shoot away from the light. When the sights are used on the indoor target range, the gold spot is on the dark side of the front sight and cannot be seen. For outdoor target work on the range, the front sight can be smoked, when the gold bead will disappear until the layer of smoke is rubbed off. This type of sight is described by the name of the "Call" sight, and is furnished regularly on many outdoorsman's revolvers, and can usually be obtained as optional equipment when desired.

Perhaps the most satisfactory sight for exclusive use outdoors is the King Ramp Red Bead Reflector sight. This is a front sight of a special red composition resembling ivory, which is mounted on a ramp containing a non-corrosive mirror of chromium which throws the light of the sky on the sight in such a manner as to make the red bead show up plainly under almost all conditions.

Peep Sights

By far the most successful iron sight for use on rifles is what is known as the peep sight. The rear sight, which is placed as close as possible to the eye, is a disc with a hole in it. In sighting, the shooter merely looks through this hole, and places the front sight on the target. He does not have to pay any attention to the rear sight; in fact, he does not even see it. It is a peculiarity of the human eye that in looking through a small hole the eye naturally centers itself in the middle of the aperture with great accuracy.

One of the greatest difficulties connected with sighting a weapon with open sights is the inability of the eye to focus sharply on three points at different distances, namely, the rear sight, the front sight, and the target. The eye can see sharply only one of these three things at a time; the other two will always be more or less blurred. In the actual operation of aiming, the eye is constantly changing its focus, so that first one, then the other of these three objects is clear. These changes take place with great rapidity, so that the mind is not conscious of them. The shooter sees all three points indifferently well because he is constantly shifting his attention, and at the same time his eyesight, from one point to the other. With a young man, whose eyes have excellent accommodation, this is fairly easy, but with older men, whose eyes have lost their flexibility, the matter of sighting becomes a very difficult problem. Many of the older rifle shooters have been forced to use telescopic or peep sights for this reason.

The use of a peep sight solves the rifleman's problem because he can neglect the rear sight entirely and concentrate on the front sight and the target. True, he now has to focus his eyes on two points at different distances, but this is not so hard, because both points are fairly distant from his eye. The closer to the eye one has to look, the harder it is. The focus of the eye is just the same for an object 50 feet away or a mile away; but it is tremendously different for an object a foot away or two feet away. It is when objects are placed within about a foot or two of the eye that they require a violent change in the curvature of the eyeball to enable them to be seen well. If the eye is focussed on a rear sight 18 inches from the eye, the bullseye will appear badly blurred; but if the eye is focussed on a front sight four feet from the eye, the bullseye will appear only slightly blurred; the eye is nearly right for it, too.

Because it is so hard to get clear definition of an object close to the eye, it is not possible to use an open rear sight satisfactorily if it is placed closer than about 15 inches from the eye; two feet is better. This is the reason why most open rear sights on rifles are placed well up toward the middle of the barrel. The further the sight is placed from the eye, the easier it is to see clearly. Moving the rear sight forward reduces the distance between the rear sight and the front sight, and gives a short sight radius; but the loss of sight radius is more than made up by the additional clearness of the rear sight.

With peep sights, on the other hand, the rear sight should be as close to the eye as possible, and if it is placed close enough, the eye will naturally look through the exact center of the hole, and the rear sight will not be seen. The eye can then concentrate on the front sight and the bullseye.

Besides removing the troublesome job of focusing on an object close to the eye, the peep sight helps in another way. It acts like a diaphragm stop on a camera, and sharpens up everything that the eye sees when looking through it. The lens of the eye has to collect all the divergent rays from every object seen, and draw them together into an image of what is seen. When looking through a very small opening, there are fewer divergent rays allowed to reach the eye, so that the eye has an easier task of collecting them and composing them into a picture.

This can be illustrated by drawing the curtains of a room, or putting a piece of paper over the windows so as to darken the room. Then if a small hole is punched in the curtain or paper, so as to let in a very fine ray of light, a picture of everything that is in view outside will be thrown on the opposite wall, or on a piece of paper held behind the hole. This is what is called a pin-hole camera. A metal disc or piece of black paper with a pin-hole in it can be used instead of a lens in a camera, and excellent pictures can be taken. The peep sight acts the same way. It throws a sharp image of everything in front of it into the eye, and very little accommodation is required in order to see well.

From what has been said about the peep sight, it would seem that such a sight would be ideal for pistol shooting, but actually we find that peep sights have never been used to amount to anything on pistols or revolvers. In fact the rules of the U. S. Revolver Association prohibited peep sights up until a year or so ago, when the rule was changed to allow them in some of the matches. The reason for this state of affairs is found very simply in the fact that when used on a pistol or revolver, peep sights are so far from the eye that most of their advantages disappear. It is possible to use a peep sight on a revolver or target pistol, but there seems to be very little advantage in it. Personally, I much prefer good open sights of the Patridge type.

Adjustable Sights and How to Use Them

Ordinarily the front sight consists merely of a rounded blade of metal fixed to the top of the barrel, and the rear sight consists simply of a notch or groove cut into the top of the frame. This is the case on most military or pocket revolvers. Such sights are called "fixed sights," and their location with respect to the axis of the bore is very carefully determined at the factory so that the gun will shoot into the bullseye with the average shot using the average ammunition. However, there are variations between different shooters in the method of sighting, the method of holding, etc., as well as in the kind of ammunition used, so that it quite frequently happens that a revolver with fixed sights will shoot too high or too low, or to one side or the other, with certain marksmen.

In order to allow such a condition to be remedied when it occurs, most target revolvers and pistols have sights which are arranged so that their position can be altered at will, usually by means of screws. They are called "adjustable sights," and are highly desirable, for they permit the sights to be changed to suit the individual marksman, or to compensate for differences in ammunition.

If the rear sight is moved to the right, the shot group on the target will also move to the right. In the same way, if the rear sight is raised or lowered, the group on the target will follow suit, and move in the same direction. On the contrary, the group moves in the opposite direction to any movement of the front sight.

On the Colt target pistols and revolvers, and the H. & R. Sportsman revolvers, the front sight is adjustable for elevation, and the rear sight is adjustable for deflection. Thus, if the gun shoots too low, the front sight is *lowered*. If it shoots too far to the right, the rear sight is moved to the left. The user must remember to move the rear sight in the direction that he wants the group to move, and to move the front sight opposite to the direction of the desired change.

On the other target pistols with adjustable sights, the front sight is fixed, and all of the changes are made on the rear sight, which can be moved up and down with one set of screws, and sideways with another set. The more desirable system is to have all the adjustments on the rear sight, which avoids the possible confusion incident to having to move the front sight in the opposite direction to that of the rear sight for any given correction.

In finding how much sights should be corrected, with either fixed or adjustable sights, always go by the results of the average location of a group of shots. Any one single shot may be affected by poor sighting, poor trigger pull, some inaccuracy in the cartridge, or one of several things. Usually if two shots are fired, they will be some distance apart. Obviously, it would be wrong to use either of them in this case. In the same way, if only one shot were fired, and the sights were judged by the result, the next shot might have gone in quite a different place without any sight change.

Instead of judging by the results of one shot, at least five, and preferably ten or more should be fired, and then the center of the group should be taken as the point to which the gun is shooting. To find the center of a group of shots, measure the vertical distance of each shot from the bottom of the target. Add all these vertical measurements, and divide by the number of shots. This will be the average vertical distance of the shots from the bottom. Draw a line across the target at this height from the bottom edge. The center will then lie somewhere on this line. Now measure the horizontal distance of each shot from the right hand edge of the target, add all these measurements, and divide by the number of shots, which will give the average distance of all shots from the right hand edge. Going in this far from the edge, draw a vertical line. The center of the group is where this line crosses the horizontal line already drawn.

Of course, in finding the center in this way, it is not at all necessary to use the edges of the target to measure from. If you prefer, you may draw a horizontal line across the target near the shot group, and use this as a base line to measure from; and you can draw a vertical line in any convenient place and use it instead of the right hand edge of the target.

A method of determining the approximate center of the group which is much quicker, but not quite as accurate, is to provide a sheet of celluloid or tracing paper with concentric scoring rings drawn on it like those on the target. Lay this transparent sheet over the group and shift it around until the highest score is obtained when the rings on the transparent sheet are used to score by. The center of the ten ring on the scoring sheet will indicate the practical center of the group. A hole should be provided in the center of the scoring sheet through which the center can be marked onto the target.

Having found the center of the group by one of these methods, take a foot rule and measure the amount that this center is above or below the center of the bullseye on the target, and also how much to the right or left it is. This will show one how many inches the group must be moved in both elevation and deflection by adjusting the sights. After this adjustment is made, the shooter should find his group centered on the bullseye when he aims at the bottom of the black.

The user of any target gun will naturally want to know how much he must move the adjustable sights on his gun to make a given change on the target. If, for example, he is shooting an inch too low, must he move the adjusting screw one turn, a half turn, or what? The amount that he must turn his sight adjusting screw to move his sight group an inch on the target depends on the following things:

1. The amount a turn of the screw actually moves the sight.

2. The distance between the front and rear sights; in other words, the "sight radius."

3. The distance from the gun to the target.

When all these things are known, the distance that the group will move on the target for each turn or half turn of the adjusting screw can be calculated by the rule of similar triangles, for the movement of the group on the target bears the same relation to the movement of the sight, in inches, as the range, in inches, bears to the sight radius in inches. This will be made clear by reference to the accompanying diagram.

The rule is, to find the amount that the shot group will move on the target for one turn of the adjusting screw, divide the range in inches by the sight radius, and multiply the result by the movement of the sight in inches corresponding to the turn of the screw.

For example, suppose that we are shooting an 8 inch barrel Camp Perry Model Pistol at 20 yards, and our group has gone one

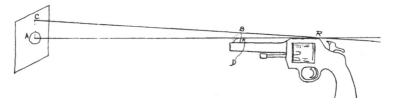

Effect of changing the height of front sight. With the high front sight the shot would drop too low and gun would have to be sighted at "C" to hit bull's-eye. The amount of sight to be removed may be calculated by similar triangles, thus BD is to AC as RD is to RA.

inch too far to the right. How much must we move the windage adjusting screws to bring the group to center? This gun has a 7½ inch sight radius, and the adjusting screws, acting directly on the rear sight, have 50 threads per inch, so that they move the sight .02 inch per turn. According to the rule given above, the range must be in inches, so we multiply our 20 yards by 36 and obtain 720 inches. Then dividing this by 7½ we obtain 97. Multiplying this in turn by the movement of the sight in inches for one turn of the screw, or .02, gives 1.94 inches that one turn of the screw will move the group on the target. But we want to move it only an inch, or approximately half this much, so that a half turn of the screw will be correct. We therefore slack off the left screw ½ turn, then tighten up the right screw. This will move the group .97 inch, which is very close to the figure desired.

Unfortunately, there is no universal rule as to the amount that the adjusting screws will move the group, as every manufacturer makes several different models with different barrel lengths, which use the same sight screws, and moreover, the screws do not always work directly on the sights. Usually they work through a leverage of some sort, so that the movement of the screw is multiplied by the time it reaches the sights.

An approximate rule, which is sufficiently close for all practical purposes, is that one turn of the adjusting screw will move the shot group one inch for every ten yards of range, except for the front sight adjustment on Colt guns, which moves the group three times this amount.

For those who are interested in the exact figures, the following tabulations covering sight radius, movement of the sights, and movement of the group on the target per turn of the screw have been prepared.

Sight Radius

A rough rule is that the sight radius is approximately ½ inch less than the barrel length on single shot pistols, and one inch greater than the barrel length on target revolvers. There are some exceptions, however, as will be seen.

Name of gun		Barrel length	Sight radius
Colt Ace		5¼ inches	6.3 inches
"	Camp Perry Model	8	7½
"	Camp Perry Model	10	9½
"	Woodsman	5½	9¾
"	Woodsman Sport Model	4½	7⅜
"	Police Positive Target	5	6.76
"	Officer's Model	5	7.05
"	Officer's Model	7½	8.55
"	Shooting Master	5	6.90
"	New Service Target	7½	8.60
Smith & Wesson .22-32		5	7.05
"	" Reg. Police Tar.	5	7.05
"	" K-22	6	7.15
"	" Mil. & Pol. Tar.	6	7.15
"	" .38/44	6½	7.65
"	" .44 Target	6½	7.65
"	" Straight Line	10	9.25
"	" Perfected Model	10	10.
Harrington & Richardson			
	U. S. R. A. Model	7	6.2
"	" " "	8	7.2
"	" " "	10	9.2
"	" Sportsman	6	7.25
"	" New Defender	2	3.37
Iver Johnson Sealed Eight		6	7.11
Webley Single Shot		10	9.

MOVEMENT OF SIGHTS IN INCHES PER TURN OF ADJUSTING SCREW

	Elevation adjustment		Windage adjustment	
	Threads per inch on screw	Movement of sight for 1 turn of screw	Threads per inch on screw	Movement of sight for 1 turn of screw
Colt Ace	50	.02	50	.02
" Woodsman	50	.07*	50	.02
" Camp Perry Model	50	.07*	50	.02
" Target Revolvers	50	.07*	50	.02
H. & R. U.S.R.S. Model	80	.023	80	.02
" Sportsman	80	.01*	80	.0125
" New Defender	80	.01*	80	.0125
S. & W. Perfected Model	64	.05	48	.021
" Straight Line	40	.027	40	.025
" .22-32 Revolver	48	.029	48	.021
" Regulation Police Target	48	.029	48	.021

	Elevation adjustment		Windage adjustment	
	Threads per inch on screw	Movement of sight for 1 turn of screw	Threads per inch on screw	Movement of sight for 1 turn of screw
S. & W. Model K, .38 & .22	44	.026	48	.021
" 38/44 & .44 Target	44	.026	48	.021
" .357 Magnum	44	.026	48	.021

*Elevation adjustment moves the front sight.

MOVEMENT IN INCHES OF SHOT GROUP ON TARGET AT TEN YARDS RANGE FOR 1 TURN OF ADJUSTING SCREW

Name of gun	Barrel length	Change in elevation for turn of screw	Change in deflection for 1 turn of screw
Colt Ace Pistol	5¼ inches	1.14 inches	1.14 inches
" Camp Perry Model	8	3.3	.96
" " " "	10	2.6	.75
" Woodsman	6½	2.7	.77
" " Sport Model	4½	..	1.00
" Police Positive Target	6	3.7	1.06
" Officer's Model	6	3.6	1.02
" " "	7½	2.9	.83
" Shooting Master	6	3.6	1.04
" New Service Target	7½	2.9	.83
Harrington & Richardson U. S. R. A. Model	7	1.33	1.15
" " "	8	1.15	1.00
" " "	10	.9	.78
" " Sportsman	6	.50	.62
" " N. Defender	2	1.0	1.30
Smith & Wesson Perfected Model	10	1.8	.75
" " Straight Line	10	1.05	.98
" " .22-32 Revolver	6	1.47	1.06
" " Regulation Police Target	6	1.47	1.06
" " Model K, .38 & .22	6	1.31	1.05
" " .38/44 & .44 Target	6½	1.22	.97
" " .357 Magnum	8½	.97	.78

Multiply these figures by 2 for 20 yard results; by 2½ for 25 yards, and by 5 for 50 yards. For finer changes, use half or quarter turns of the adjusting screw.

Sight Corrections on Fixed Sight Models

As mentioned above, most military and pocket type pistols and revolvers have fixed sights which cannot be adjusted to correct the location of the shot group in case the gun fails to shoot to the point of aim. Guns of this kind are sighted at the factory to shoot correctly for the average user, and in most cases will do very satisfactory work without any changes; but occasionally a fixed sight gun will be encountered that will not shoot anywhere near the aiming point.

In this case, the usual remedy is to aim to one side or the other, or high or low, as the case requires, a sufficient amount to make the shots go where they are wanted. Good shooting can be done in this way, but it is obvious that it is not as easy or convenient as to have the sights adjusted so that the shooter can aim directly at what he wants to hit. For this reason most skilled shots who have to use a gun of this kind for any length of time will want to change the sights in some way, even though they are not made to be adjusted.

The easiest defect to remedy is that of shooting too low, for all that has to be done is to file off the top of the front sight, and this will raise the group on the target. If, on the other hand, the gun shoots too high, it is sometimes possible to file off the top of the rear sight. This can be done in the case of guns like the Colt .45 Caliber Automatic pistol, where the rear sight is a separate piece. However, it is not possible on most revolvers, in which the rear sight consists of a notch or groove in the top of the frame of the gun. In this case, it is necessary to devise some means of raising the height of the front sight. Some times this can be done by peening or stretching the front sight by hammering it, so as to make it thinner and higher. Or a piece of metal may be brazed or soldered on top of it, and then filed down to the right height. If the owner is mechanically inclined, and has the tools available, it is usually easy to cut off the upper part of the front sight blade and slot the front sight base for a new blade which can be made as high as desirable, and then pinned in position.

If the gun shoots to one side or the other, the trouble can be overcome by driving the rear sight to one side or the other in the case of the .45 Automatic and other guns with rear sights which fit into a slot in the frame; but in the case of the ordinary revolver, in which the rear sight is formed in the top of the frame, this is not possible, and all changes must be made on the front sight. If the gun shoots to the right, the front sight must be moved to the right to correct the trouble; or if the gun shoots to the left, the front sight must be moved to the left. This change in position of the front sight can be accomplished either by bending the front sight to one side or the other, as the case requires, or by turning the barrel slightly in the frame. To turn the barrel, first make a clamp to hold it. This is accomplished by taking a block of oak wood about two inches square, and boring a hole in it. The hole should be of the same diameter as the outside of the barrel as nearly as is convenient. Then saw the block lengthwise through the axis of the hole. By placing one half of the block on one side of the barrel and the other on the opposite side, and then clamping the block firmly in a heavy vise, the barrel will be prevented from turning. The cylinder and crane should be removed, and a stout flat stick inserted through the cylinder opening in the frame will enable enough leverage to be exerted to move the frame with relation to the barrel.

This is possible because the barrel is screwed into the frame; of course a motion in one direction will tend to tighten the barrel in its seat, that is, will screw it tighter; while the opposite motion will loosen it. Usually the amount of motion necessary to correct the sighting is so slight that it can be obtained even if it means screwing the barrel in even more tightly; and if on the other hand, the correction is in the direction of loosening the barrel, the motion is not great enough to produce any noticeable loosening of the barrel.

This system of correcting the sights by rotating the barrel cannot be accomplished with the Smith & Wesson guns, because they have a lug under the barrel which is accurately lined up to latch the front end of the ejector rod, in order to maintain the accuracy of this position, the barrel is pinned so that it cannot be turned.

In the Colt guns, the rifling is left handed, so that the reaction of the bullet in taking the rifling tends to turn the barrel to the right. This makes it necessary to use a left hand thread on the breech end of the barrel where it fits into the frame, in order to prevent a tendency of the barrel to unscrew from the action of spinning the bullet. Thus if the gun shoots too far to the right, the sight correction by turning the barrel requires the barrel to be screwed more tightly into the frame; on the other hand, to correct a gun that shoots too far to the left requires the partial unscrewing of the barrel.

While fixed sights can be altered as described above to correct the sighting, it will be realized that the process is a rather difficult one, and once the change is made, it is very hard to go back to the original condition if a mistake has been made and the change was not needed after all. For this reason, no such changes should be made until a sufficient amount of shooting had been done to make it absolutely certain that a change is needed. Very often, in using a gun with adjustable sights, a change will seem to be needed, and will be made, and then in a few days another change back to the first sight setting will be required. Of course, with adjustable sights, this is a matter of no importance; changes can be made as desired. On the other hand, with fixed sights, it would be rather discouraging to file off the front sight because the gun is shooting too low, and then in a few days find that it is shooting too high. These changes in grouping do occur, however. They may be due to a change in the lighting conditions; a change in the hold or the sighting; a change from indoor to outdoor shooting or vice versa; a change in range from 20 to 50 yards, or from a variety of other causes. The moral of this is, go very slowly in making permanent changes in the sighting of your gun. Be sure that you have shot it enough to know just what to expect in the future. Of course, if a gun shoots badly off in a given direction every time you use it, a change is needed; but it is best to make just part of the change at first, and then use the gun for a while longer before making the rest of the change. In this way you will give yourself time to settle down to the use of the gun. Then when the final change is made, it should be just sufficient to correct the gun for *average* conditions.

If, for example, your gun groups a foot low the first time you use it, and something like a foot low the next few times, it would be safe to make a correction of something like 8 inches at once. It should now group 4 inches low. But maybe by several weeks more of shooting you will find that sometimes it actually groups 1 inch high, sometimes 2 inches low, and again occasionally it groups 3 inches low. Obviously, then, the average is halfway between these extremes of one inch too high and three inches too low. The halfway point is 1 inch low. By changing the sights to bring the group 1 inch higher, we will have done all that we can. We should then expect to find that on some days the center of our group will be as much as two inches high; on these days we must hold a little low to compensate for the error. Again, however, we might shoot under other conditions and find our group centered two inches low. Under most conditions, however, we should probably not be anywhere near these two extremes, but instead, would be very near the center of the target.

Trigger Pull

The ease of shooting with pistols and revolvers is very greatly affected by the amount of force required to pull the trigger. With a heavy trigger pull the muscular contraction required to make the gun go off is such that there is a considerable tendency to cause the bullet to deviate. This fact causes most target shots to favor a very light trigger pull.

The rules of the U. S. R. A. allow a minimum trigger pull of 2½ pounds for revolvers in the "Any Revolver" Match. For single-shot pistols the minimum pull is 2 pounds. For military revolvers and pistols, or pocket revolvers, the minimum trigger pull allowed 3½ pounds. There is also a special match based on the International rules, with no limit on trigger pull.

Revolvers, and especially automatic pistols, are somewhat safer to handle and use with a slightly higher trigger pull, generally between 5 and 6 pounds. This is about the amount of the trigger pull on revolvers and pistols as ordinarily received from the manufacturer. For practical shooting, it is recommended that a fairly heavy trigger pull be maintained.

The character of the trigger pull—that is, its smoothness—is really of more importance than the actual weight. A creepy, grating trigger pull is the very worst kind, and even though the actual force required to pull the trigger may not be excessive, good shooting can not be done with a trigger of this type. What is wanted is a smooth trigger pull, in which the trigger does not move as pressure is applied until finally it gives way all at once with no creeping or sliding at all.

In the matches of the U. S. R. A., or of the N. R. A., trigger pulls are always tested before the match by means of lead weights with a wire hook. In testing the trigger pull, the weight is applied at a point three-eighths of an inch from the end of the trigger, with the barrel held vertical.

Most users of target revolvers and pistols at some time or another want to smooth up their trigger pull or reduce it to a lower figure. In general this is a rather ticklish job and requires a great deal of care and practice to get good results. The character of the pull depends on the character of the rubbing surfaces on the nose of the sear, or the nose of the trigger, and the surface on the notch of the hammer. Another factor which influences the pull is the tension of the trigger or sear spring which is generally the rebound spring in revolvers, and on the strength of the mainspring.

I have frequently known revolver-shots to weaken the mainspring to get a lighter trigger pull. Sometimes they do this by turning out the strain screw on Smith & Wesson revolvers; sometimes by grinding off some of the back of the spring on Colt revolvers. I want to advise strongly against any such procedure because it is wrong in principle and results in a light blow on the primer, which will give hangfires and consequent inaccuracy. It may also give misfires.

One of the large revolver factories wrote to me and said that giving out full information to the public on changing trigger pulls is much like writing a popular treatise on how to perform an operation for appendicitis.

However, the amateur can learn to doctor up trigger pulls quite successfully if he is prepared to study the proposition and possibly spoil a few hammers or triggers before he gets through. The essentials are a couple of small fine oil stones and a watchmaker's glass. The first thing to do is to take off the side plate of your revolver and study the action of the trigger nose in the hammer notch very carefully. Then take out the hammer and trigger and examine the rubbing surfaces very carefully with your glass and you will see where they can be smoothed up. All file marks and roughness should be removed, so that there is a perfectly smooth surface. This will generally greatly improve the pull. Sometimes

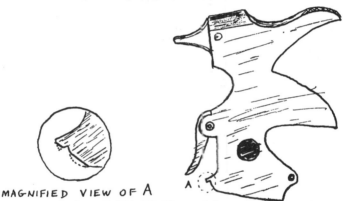

MAGNIFIED VIEW OF A

DOTTED LINES SHOW PARTS FILED AWAY.

Sketch of the hammer of the author's .38 Officer's Model revolver, showing how the factory had filed the notch in the hammer to produce a particularly clean, sweet pull. The careful and mechanically experienced shooter may accomplish the same thing, but if it is attempted by the unskilled owner, he may very quickly ruin the hammer.

the point of the trigger is very narrow, and the pull can often be improved by stoning it down until it is somewhat wider, and therefore has more of a bearing, taking care to preserve the angle correctly. Some experts reduce the depth of the hammer notch so that the trigger does not have so far to slide in being pulled out of the notch, but the factories generally advise against touching the hammer. Nevertheless, I have a Colt Officer's model with a very fine pull, and I note that as it came from the factory, the hammer notch had been reduced in depth with a file as per the accompanying sketch.

The factory experts, who make a living by tuning up trigger pulls generally work with a fine file. They have had so many years of experience that they can take just one glance at the hammer and trigger of a gun whose pull is not right, and then know exactly what to do. Often a single stroke with a fine file to reduce the depth of a notch, as described above, will do the trick. This is, of course, quite different from what I have advised above; but there is not one shooter in ten thousand that can have the experience at this work that is the lot of the factory man, and my advice to shooters who want to work on their own trigger pulls is to leave the file alone and stick to the oil stone.

The trigger pull on the .45 Automatic can not safely be reduced below 5 pounds, because if this is done there is danger of the

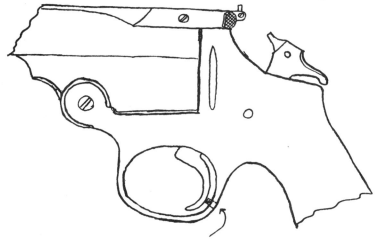

STOP-SCREW

Sketch of the author's S. & W. Single Shot Pistol, showing the stop screw fitted into the back of the trigger guard to prevent the trigger from jarring the gun by a sudden backward motion when the hammer is released. This screw was fitted at home, and the whole job required only a few minutes time.

jarring action of the mechanism causing the hammer to slip off the sear and follow the slide down with a resulting misfire. I have known these guns to have their trigger pulls reduced as low as 4 pounds and operate satisfactorily for some time; but just when least expected a malfunction is likely to occur.

If the trigger pull on the automatic has been reduced to a point where it is uncertain, this fact can often be discovered by a simple test. Be sure that the gun is unloaded; then take out the magazine, so that the slide will close when drawn back and released, and holding back the trigger, draw the slide back and let it snap shut as smartly as possible a number of times. If the hammer goes to half cock, it shows that the trigger pull is too light, and that the jar of closing the slide causes the hammer to fall. If the trigger pull is correct, the hammer will remain cocked until the trigger is released and pulled again.

Many target-shots use a stop to limit the motion of the trigger when it is pulled. The reason for this is obvious. When aiming at a target, the index finger rests on the trigger with a considerable amount of pressure until finally the trigger slips out of the notch. If the trigger moves a considerable distance after it slips out of the notch the resulting motion of the hand may deviate the aim enough to do quite a lot of harm. This motion of the trigger may be checked by wrapping a little adhesive tape around the trigger guard behind the trigger, so that when the trigger is pulled it strikes against this layer of tape. By adding layers, a point can be reached where the trigger can just be pulled enough to disengage from the notch but will move no farther. A neater way to accomplish the same result is to drill a hole in the back of the trigger guard and tap it for a small screw against which the trigger will strike when it is pulled. This screw may then be adjusted until the trigger can just be pulled enough to clear the notch.

Along the same lines is the practice sometimes encountered of placing a springy piece of live rubber behind the trigger. Once I had a pistol with a trigger that was difficult to let off without causing the muzzle of the pistol to dip at the instant of discharge. I blocked the trigger with rubber, and then when I pulled the trigger I felt my finger compressing the rubber more and more until finally there was a click as the hammer fell; but there was no difference in the feel of the trigger at this point, and the muzzle of the gun did not dip. Afterward I found that one of the members of the International Rifle Team of which I was captain had hit on the same device on his .22 caliber rifle.

One of the most annoying things that can happen to a match shooter who has worked on his gun until it has a fine trigger pull just above the minimum weight is to have the trigger or hammer wear just enough to make the gun fail to hold the weight when weighing in before some important match. Often this may be due simply to gradual wear; but more often it is due to the bad habit that some shooters have of absent mindedly grating the trigger and the sear notch over each other. Very often a shooter will pick up a gun and cock it, then pull the trigger just enough to ease the hammer down with his thumb, and as he talks, he will repeat this nervous mannerism, all the time grating the point of the trigger over the notch in the hammer and ruining the trigger pull more quickly than can be imagined. If you are going to let the hammer down, first hold the hammer well back with the thumb, then pull the trigger well back and hold it there while lowering the hammer. Then the trigger and sear notch cannot come in contact, and no harm will be done. Just grating the sear notch and trigger point once will do more harm to the surfaces than any amount of snapping empty or dry shooting.

If you ever do get caught so that your favorite pistol will not hold the weight by a very small margin, try in some way to strengthen the trigger spring. In the Smith & Wesson revolvers this can be accomplished by taking out the rebound block and placing behind the spring a thin disc of steel, brass, or fiber, sawed off the end of a rod of the right diameter, such as a piece of drill rod. Some modern guns, such as the Harrington & Richardson U.S.R.A. Model Single Shot Pistol, have a screw which compresses the trigger spring. Turning in this screw, which on the H. & R. is located just forward of the trigger guard, will make the trigger hold more weight.

Some of the older models of revolver, such as the Colt Single Action Army, have a half cock notch, and this, together with the rebound notch used on some modern guns is one of the worst enemies of fine trigger pulls. If the hammer slips out from under the thumb in cocking the gun, the half cock notch will strike the point of the trigger, usually with resultant damage to the trigger pull, which may even be so severe as to cause the trigger point or the notch to be broken. Then there is always the danger that when the trigger pull is very light, the half cock notch may rub or catch on the point of the trigger when they pass as the hammer falls. One remedy that is often used with the Single Action Army is to file off the half cock notch.

The modern Colt and Smith & Wesson revolvers and target pistols do not have a half cock notch or rebound notch. The rebounding hammer in these guns is operated by a sliding block or a lever under the heel of the hammer, operated by the trigger. When the trigger is released after the discharge of the arm, it moves forward under the action of the trigger spring, and it moves the rebound block forward under the heel of the hammer, locking the hammer in place.

However, the Harrington & Richardson U.S.R.A. Model does have a rebound notch on the hammer, and in the early models some trouble was experienced from the striking of the rebound notch of the hammer on the full cock point of the trigger. In the later models of this gun the difficulty has been entirely eliminated by a very clever design of the trigger, which uses a separate point for the rebound. This point is placed further from the trigger pivot than the full cock point, so that the half cock notch on the hammer never even approaches the full cock point.

Lock Time

Something that has a very intimate relation with the question of trigger pulls is what is called "lock time," or, in other words, the length of time it takes the lock-work of the gun to function, or the interval from the instant the trigger is pulled until the hammer actually strikes the primer of the cartridge.

Obviously, in fine target shooting, a very important factor is the time it takes for the bullet to leave the gun after the trigger is pulled. If the gun is waving around in the air, even one thousandth of a second may make a difference, because the gun may have moved considerably after the trigger was pulled and before the bullet starts on its way.

To cut down the lock time, the hammer travel must be short, and the mainspring must be very strong. This strong mainspring in turn causes a heavy pressure between the point of the trigger and the notch in the hammer, with resultant heavy trigger pull. This heavy pressure between the metal surfaces also has a tendency to cause rapid wear.

In modern target pistols with a very short hammer fall and a heavy mainspring, the designer has had to meet some very difficult problems in making a pull that will be light enough and at the same time will wear well. In the best designed guns this problem has been solved by wide surfaces on trigger and hammer notch, to reduce the unit pressure on the metal; by special steels and heat treatments to give great strength and durability; and fine workmanship and high polish on the surfaces involved.

A comparison between pistols made some ten or twelve years ago and those being sold today will reveal a marked change in the direction of a shorter hammer throw and heavier spring. For example, the latest Colt Camp Perry Model Target Pistols have a much shorter hammer throw and a much faster lock time than those made only a few years ago.

Set Triggers

In the International Matches there is no limitation as to trigger pull; it may be as light or as heavy as the fancy of the shooter directs. Consequently, most of the arms used in these matches are arranged for an extremely light trigger pull, often called a "hair trigger." This ultra-light trigger pull is obtained by means of a mechanism known as a "set trigger." This is an arrangement by means of which the trigger can be cocked or "set" so that it will discharge the piece with the lightest touch. Generally there are two triggers, one in front of the other. If the gun is cocked,

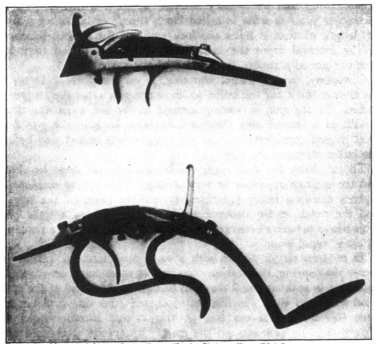

Top: Double set trigger from the author's Stotzer Free Pistol.
Bottom: Set trigger from the author's Buchel Free Pistol. In this model, the mechanism is "set" by depressing a side lever, instead of by pulling back the rear trigger, as is usual with double set triggers.

and the front trigger is pulled, it will discharge the piece, the same as will an ordinary trigger; but if the rear trigger is pulled, it does not discharge the piece, but "sets" the front trigger so that the slightest touch will cause the discharge of the gun. There are not always two triggers. Sometimes there is a lever on the side of the gun that will set the trigger, and again, there may be only one trigger, which may be set by pushing it forward.

The set trigger mechanism contains a striker or hammer of its own, which is cocked by the action of setting. Then, when the front trigger is pulled, this striker is released, and it flies up and strikes the regular sear, knocking it from its notch, and discharging the arm.

The pull of a set trigger is lighter than the pull of a regular trigger can be made, because the spring that cocks the striker in the set trigger is lighter than the regular mainspring of the gun, and there is a relatively light pressure between the set trigger and its own sear. Then, again, in the finer set triggers, the sear releases a lever, which in turn releases another lever, which in turn releases the striker of the set trigger. Each lever reduces the pressure, so that the pressure on the last notch, which is released when the trigger is touched, is very light indeed. Some fine Swiss and German set triggers have as many as five levers, and the pull is so light that the gun can easily be discharged by blowing on the front trigger after it is set.

While the set trigger gives a very light trigger pull, it does not improve the lock time. In fact, it is often very much slower than a plain trigger. When the plain trigger is pulled, the hammer starts to fall at once, but on the contrary, when the set trigger is pulled, the various levers must move before the striker can get started; and the striker must knock the sear out of engagement before the hammer can fall. Some of the European Free Pistols have an extremely short hammer fall and an extremely heavy mainspring, and their owners boast of the fast lock time, not realizing that the short throw and heavy spring no more than compensate for the set trigger delay.

Set triggers are almost always provided with an adjusting screw with which the amount of pressure necessary to discharge the front trigger can be varied to suit the user.

Shooting with a set trigger is quite different from ordinary pistol-shooting and requires a considerable amount of practice in order to excel in it. However, with set triggers it is very easy, after one has learned how to use them, to make much higher scores than can be made with the ordinary trigger. They are, however, quite dangerous to use, as accidental discharges are frequent.

In the International Matches each competitor stands in front of a long bench, and in loading his gun he rests the barrel on this bench or support so that the muzzle points downward toward the ground at an angle of about 45 degrees. Holding the gun in this position, he loads it, closes the breech and sets the trigger. If an accident occurs, so that the set trigger goes off prematurely, it is not charged against the shooter's score provided that the barrel of the gun is resting on the bench. If, however, the gun has been

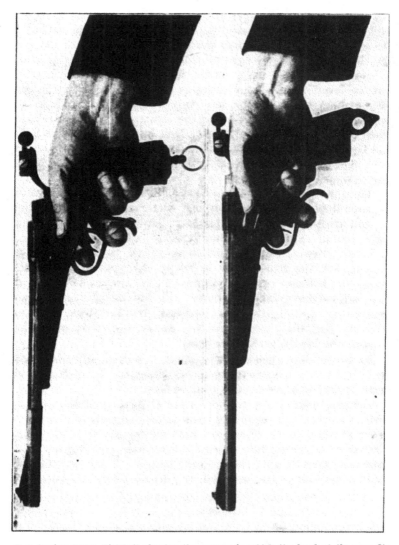

Two foreign "Free Pistols," showing the manner in which the hand of the user fits into the elaborate stocks with which such weapons are furnished.   Left: Stotzer Perfekt Pistole.   Right: Buchel pistol with barrel by Widmer.   Note that with the Buchel pistol, the line of the bore is much lower and more nearly in line with the arm, owing to the fact that the stock is so shaped that the hand and wrist are held in a higher position.   Both models are fitted with set triggers.

lifted off the bench and the set trigger goes off accidentally, it counts as a zero unless it actually makes a score on the target.

The method of using the set trigger requires a different action with the trigger finger from that of shooting with an ordinary trigger. The shooter does not put his finger in front of the trigger and then squeeze, as is ordinarily done with the plain trigger. Instead, he places the index finger carefully on the edge of the set trigger, pushing a little forward as he does so, so as not by any chance to pull the trigger. In aiming, all he does when he wants to make the gun go off is to relax the muscles slightly, so as to release the forward pressure on the edge of the set trigger, and if the trigger is set very fine this is about all that is needed to make it go off. The motion of the muscles in the hand is almost imperceptible. In fact, as some users express it, you more nearly "wish the trigger off" than pull it. Most good set-trigger pistols have a rest for the index finger which comes right down to the edge of the set trigger and prevents the natural wabbling of the finger from setting it off, as might otherwise occur.

The user of set triggers is cautioned that they are extremely dangerous even in the hands of an experienced user. Accidental discharges are of frequent occurrence whenever set triggers are used. Surprising as it may seem, accidental discharges are seen at the International Matches, where all the users have much experience in handling their arms. This is recognized in the rule above mentioned, which does not count an accidental discharge against the score provided the gun barrel has not left the bench when the discharge occurs.

The lesson in this is that the user should be supercareful to keep the barrel of a gun always pointed at the target after the triggers have been set. If for any reason the shot is not fired the action should be opened before the point of aim is changed, because the slightest jar to the gun may cause it to go off.

Grips

The handle or grip of a revolver is a very important part, and much depends on the shape of it in relation to the shooter's hand. In general, the revolvers of larger caliber have the larger handles, and in the very large calibers the Colt has a slightly larger handle than the Smith & Wesson. The old revolvers of thirty or forty years ago had more comfortable handles than those of the present day. In general these old handles were more rounded at the top than the later ones. On the modern revolver the handle rises straight up at the top, where it joins the frame, and has a sharp edge which tends to cut into the hand on heavy recoil. Also, on the later revolvers the space behind the trigger guard is narrower from front to back and longer from top to bottom than it was in the old-style guns, and the result is a very much poorer fit. The extreme comfort and excellence of its grip is the one reason why the old Single Action Colt still persists in popularity. In those days many other revolvers besides the Colt were made with similar grips, and these old guns are very comfortable to hold, even the smaller calibers.

The handle of the ordinary revolver is really very poor, and it is too bad that a conscientious effort is not made to intelligently design a grip which will give the greatest comfort and satisfaction in using the gun. It is interesting to note that the modern British revolvers, such as the Webley & Scott, have a much more comfortable grip than any modern American large caliber revolver.

One of the worst features of the modern revolver handle is the deep and narrow space behind the trigger guard, into which the middle finger must fit. In the human hand, the index finger naturally lies above the middle finger; but in grasping a revolver, the index finger must be brought down onto the same level with the middle finger in order to grasp the trigger. This results in a cramped and awkward position, which it is difficult to retain in rapid fire, as the repeated recoil impulses tend to move the gun about in the hand when it is grasped thus insecurely. In order to overcome as far as possible this difficulty, many shooters fill this space with a block of rubber or wood cut to fit the space and held in place with tire tape, or in some other way. This filler piece has come to be known to revolver shooters as a "gadget."

Recently the necessity for some change in this direction has been recognized by the arms makers. Walter Roper of Harrington & Richardson designed a trigger guard for the U.S.R.A. Pistol and the Sportsman Revolver with a spur of steel extending back so as to bridge over this space. This is a great help. Smith & Wesson make a filler which can be purchased as an extra. It consists of two steel plates which fit between the two grips and the frame. The top front portion of these plates extend forward beyond the grips to the trigger guard, bridging over the space behind the trigger guard. Between the portion of the plates which extends forward of the grips is a piece of rubber as a filler. Then the gunsmith Pachmayr of Los Angeles sells a rubber adapter or filler to fit any gun. It is held in place by two metal clips which slip under the edges of the wooden grips.

Perhaps the hardest men of all to satisfy in the matter of grips are the users of single shot target pistols. Formerly it was quite common for target shots to make their own grips by obtaining from the factory a piece of walnut of ample size milled out to fit over the frame of the gun. They fasten this walnut in place

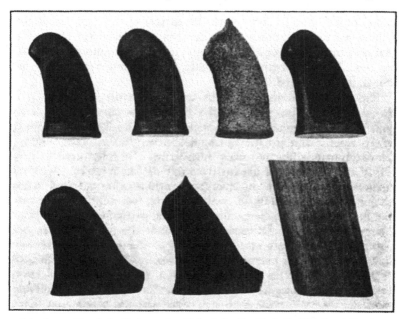

Interchangeable stocks that can be obtained for the H. & R. Pistol and Sportsman Revolver. Top, left, the No. 1 shape. Next, No. 2, which is somewhat fuller, especially near the top. No. 3 has the same shape as No. 2, except that there is an extra projection to keep the hand from slipping too high up on the grip. This particular sample is made of ground cork, moulded to shape. No. 4 is the Frontier Type, standard on the Sportsman Revolver, which gives the gun much the feel of the Old Colt Single Action. Bottom, left, No. 5 or free pistol style. Next, No. 3-5, which has the shape of No. 5 except that it also has the upward projection at the top as in No. 3. For the Single Shot Pistol with 7 or 8 inch barrel the author prefers this shape. Lower right, a rough block of walnut fitted to the gun and provided with a stock screw, intended to be whittled to any shape that suits the fancy of the purchaser.

like the handle, and then take hold of it and whittle it down wherever it feels too large, working on it a little at a time until it comes down to size and feels the best possible.

All this has now been rendered unnecessary by the manner in which the progressive firm of Harrington & Richardson have put the ideas of Walter Roper into practice. On the U.S.R.A. Model Single Shot Pistol and the Sportsman Revolver, five interchangeable grips of different shapes are furnished as options, and in addition, there is a big block of walnut milled out to fit, which can be obtained by the die-hard experimenter who insists on making his own.

The later automatic pistols have better grips than the modern revolvers. One of the most comfortable grips is that on the Luger automatic, and the Colt .22 automatic is very similar. Many of the earlier automatics were faulty, however, in having the grip at too nearly a right angle with the barrel, so that the barrel had a tendency to point down when the gun was held naturally. The best and most comfortable handle on any pocket automatic is that on the .380 Remington Automatic, which unfortunately is no longer manufactured.

This gun was designed by the celebrated arms inventor, J. D. Pedersen, who also designed the Remington pump action shotgun, the Remington trombone action rifles, the Pedersen Device, or Automatic Bolt for the Springfield Rifle, the Pedersen military semi-automatic rifle, and many other arms. In designing this grip Mr. Pedersen made an exhaustive study of the question. He first made a skeleton frame and then tried various different-sized hands around this frame, filling in with modeling clay until in each case the grip was the one best suited for that particular hand. After a large number of such models were made the final grip was designed to be a compromise between all of them in such a manner that it would fit the average hand the best. The curve at the back of the grip which fits over the junction of the thumb and forefinger, and the space in the trigger guard in which the first finger rests, are so proportioned to each other and the barrel that when the gun rests on the two places above mentioned the barrel points directly in line with the first finger.

A rather important item in regard to the handle on revolvers is the material of which it is made. The best material is one which will not slip when the hands are wet with perspiration or greasy. It is generally admitted that walnut makes the best grip, and it should preferably be checked to prevent slipping. Rubber or ivory make fair grips, though they have the disadvantage of becoming slippery when the hands are perspiring. Pearl is good looking, but it is not a desirable material from any other point of view, for it becomes slippery from perspiration, and it breaks easily. It is perhaps the least desirable material of all, but in spite of this, I have a pair of pearl grips for a Banker's special that I like better than I do any other handles for this gun, merely because these pearl grips are particularly well shaped. They are very thin near the bottom, and are well rounded, so that they feel extremely comfortable in the hand. Of course, walnut grips with the same shape would be preferable from a service point of view.

As mentioned above, the walnut grip should be checked to prevent slipping, and on most modern target arms, the trigger and the frame between the grips are usually checkered or grooved.

Sometimes the balance of a target pistol can be improved by filling the insides of the grip with lead or some other heavy material, or by putting a lead plate on the bottom. Still other target-shots like to weight the barrel of their target pistols by fastening steel rods on each side of the top rib. This is of some assistance in shooting in the wind as it prevents the gun from swaying so much. Pieces of ordinary drill rod serve very satisfactorily and can be bound on the gun with tire tape.

Safety Devices

In the construction of the modern revolver and automatic pistol, the makers have used all the ingenuity at their command in order to insure that there will not be an accidental discharge from any cause. In the old days of the simple six-shooter, it was the universal rule to carry the gun with an empty chamber under the hammer, so that if the gun should fall or be struck on the hammer, there would not be any danger of an explosion. Many fatal accidents are directly due to a failure to observe this rule.

With modern arms, conditions are changed considerably. For example, most small automatics are hammerless, so that there is no danger of striking them on the hammer and so causing a discharge; but they must be carried cocked at all times, with a cartridge under the firing pin, and a sharp blow or the dropping on the weapon may jar the sear out of engagement and allow the arm to go off. For this reason, all such arms are fitted with a safety lock operated by the thumb. Then, in addition, there are many hammerless revolvers. They actually do have a hammer, but it is concealed inside the frame. In these guns, the hammer is not cocked until the trigger is pulled, so that they are absolutely safe from discharge by being dropped.

Some automatic pistols and hammerless revolvers have a grip safety; that is, a piece of metal on either the front or the back of the grip, that must be pressed in when the trigger is pulled, in order to release the firing mechanism. The grip safety is always arranged so that it will be pressed in without any conscious effort on the part of the firer when the trigger is pulled; but if the trigger accidentally becomes caught on some object, the gun cannot go off, as the grip safety will not be pressed in unless the hand of the shooter is grasping the handle of the gun in the proper position for pulling the trigger.

In an effort to get away from the necessity of always carrying the chamber under the hammer empty, the later revolvers were designed with what is called the "rebounding lock." When the trigger is pulled the hammer falls all the way; but as soon as the trigger is released a block or lever, operated by a spring, pushes the hammer back a short distance, so that the firing pin no longer touches the primer, and then locks the hammer in that position. This was a step in the right direction; but the rebounding lock is not fully safe because the point of leverage where the hammer is held in a safe position is generally fairly close to the hammer pivot, and any play or looseness or spring of the parts might allow the primer to be struck in case of a heavy blow on the hammer.

Some years ago the Iver-Johnson Company added to their revolvers a safety device widely advertised under the slogan "Hammer the hammer." In this device there is a separate firing pin, which is mounted in the frame back of the primer, and the hammer is cut away so that it can not strike the firing pin. There is a lever attached to the trigger in such a manner that when the trigger is pulled this lever slides up and comes between the hammer and the firing pin, and the blow of the hammer is transmitted through this lever. In this way it is impossible for the cartridge to be struck unless the trigger is actually pulled. Owing to the very high advertising value of this safety device, it was not long before other companies followed suit. The Colt Company put into their revolvers a lever attached to the trigger in such a manner that when the trigger is at rest a block of metal is interposed between the face of the hammer and the frame of the gun in such a way that the firing pin can not strike the cartridge. When the trigger is pulled this block is drawn out of the way. This accomplishes the same result as the Iver-Johnson device and is known as the "Colt Positive Lock." Smith & Wesson have fitted a number of their models with a somewhat similar device, called the "New Patent Safety Hammer Block." This is found on the Regulation Police, on the .32-20, the .38 Military and Police, the .38/44 and the .357 Magnum, but is not found on the .44 Military or the .45 Model 1917. The company considers that owing to the large size of the hammer and rebound block, the second safety is not necessary on these larger guns. Unless the revolver is fitted with the Iver-Johnson "Hammer the hammer" safety, the Colt Positive Lock or the Smith & Wesson New Patent Safety Hammer Block, a cartridge should not be carried under the hammer. Hammerless revolvers, of course, are an exception.

Automatic pistols must be carried with a cartridge in the chamber, and consequently most automatics are fitted with a safety operated by the thumb in order to prevent the possibility of accidental discharge. In some types these safeties merely prevent the trigger from being pulled and offer no insurance to prevent the hammer being jarred off the sear. In other makes the safety actually blocks the firing mechanism, so that it could not be jarred off under any circumstances. It is well in getting an automatic pistol, to investigate this point and get one in which the safety is really safe.

The .45 Army automatic has a firing pin made shorter than the breech block in which it is housed, so that when the hammer is let all the way down on the firing pin the pin does not project through the front of the breech block and can not press the cartridge. The way this gun operates in firing is that normally the firing pin is held to the rear by the firing-pin spring in such a manner that a slight portion of it projects back behind the breech block. When the hammer falls it strikes this projecting portion and drives the firing pin forward with such force that its inertia carries it on until it strikes the primer though the hammer can not follow it up on account of striking the rear face of the breech block. This safety device was placed on the pistol by the designers to allow the gun to be safely carried loaded with the hammer down. It is quicker and easier to cock the pistol as it is drawn from the holster than it is to fumble for the safety with the thumb.

If the gun is carried with the hammer cocked and with the safety on, the rubbing of the pistol in the holster, especially when riding on horseback, may cause the safety to move enough to make an accident possible. For this reason it is preferable to carry the gun with the hammer down when loaded and in this condition it is absolutely safe from accidental discharge.

Many accidents have occurred with automatic pistols, owing to the fact that the user may consider the gun to be unloaded when the magazine has been removed, while there still remains one cartridge in the chamber. This has led to the incorporation of the "magazine safety" on many modern automatics. On these guns the trigger can not be pulled when the magazine is out of the pistol, thus rendering it impossible to cause an accident by forgetting that there still remains a cartridge in the chamber.

Silencers

The silencer is a device to muffle or eliminate the noise of discharge of a firearm. It consists of a cylinder about an inch in diameter screwed onto the end of the barrel. Inside there are a number of baffle plates, each with a hole in it to allow the passage of the bullet. The gas as it passes through the silencer expands into the space between the baffles, and then gradually escapes with little noise.

The great fault of silencers on high powered rifles is the fact that there are two distinct noises connected with the discharge of a fire arm; one is the noise of the escaping gas, and the other is the noise that the bullet makes as it passes through the air. The silencer will effectively eliminate the noise of the gun, but cannot have any effect on that made by the bullet after it leaves the gun.

It is a peculiarity of the bullet that when it is traveling faster than the velocity of sound in air, about 1080 feet per second, it will make a sharp report whenever it passes any object, such as a telegraph pole or a tree. The silencer has no effect whatever on this noise.

This is easily noticed with a .22 caliber rifle fitted with a silencer. When using low velocity ammunition, the gun will be almost absolutely silent. The velocity of this ammunition is about 900 feet per second, and is below the velocity of sound. On the other hand, if ammunition of the outdoor type, or the high velocity kind, giving 1200 feet per second or more is used, the gun makes almost as much noise with as without the silencer.

An explanation of this characteristic of bullets will often explain puzzling occurrences on the rifle range or elsewhere. For example my son Robert, shooting Marksman cartridges in his model 52 heavy barrel rifle on the small bore range was puzzled by the fact that while most of the time the report of the gun was a rather dull short "Blup" occasionally it would be very much louder; a piercing and long drawn out "Blarp." He applied to me for an explanation, as he was afraid that the ammunition might be bad, though the groups were all excellent. I told him that quite evidently the velocity of this ammunition was just about the velocity of sound. Those bullets that were just below this point, say, 1070 f.s. made no noise, and all that he heard was the escape of the gas from the muzzle. The other occasional loud shots were those with a velocity of say 1090 f.s., where the bullet made a sharp snap each time it passed a fence, a tree, or anything along the range.

In the same way, a .22 caliber rifle with silencer using the Winchester Staynless .22 short cartridge was quiet, and no report at all could be heard. On the other hand, when the .22 short Super X was used, there was the same loud "Blarp" that was heard before.

In detective fiction and on the stage we sometimes hear of silencers on revolvers, but in real life they are never encountered, simply because the silencer is not effective on a revolver. The escape of gas between the barrel and the cylinder makes such a loud noise that even if the muzzle noise is completely eliminated, the report still sounds very much the same.

There is nothing, however, to prevent the fitting of a silencer on single shot pistols, but when this is done, the result is a long clumsy weapon that would be hard to conceal. Silencers have also been used on specially altered .22 automatic pistols such as the Colt Woodsman, and are very effective in reducing the noise.

It is hardly advisable to experiment along this line, however, as in recent years the silencer has rather fallen into disrepute with the legal authorities. The recently enacted Federal Firearms Act of June, 1934, classes silencers or mufflers with machine guns and sawed off shotguns as weapons the possession of which must be reported to the Collector of Customs within 60 days after the passage of the act, and which are subject to rather stringent regulations as to shipment or sale.

Shot Cartridges in Revolvers

Metallic revolver cartridges loaded with shot are sold in all the popular revolver calibers from .22 up to .44/40. The smaller sizes, such as the .22 and the .32 are loaded with No. 10 or 11 shot, and the largest ones with No. 8. They are not very satisfactory, for the plain cylinder bore of the barrel, combined with the rifling, causes the shot to spread in too wide a pattern to be very effective.

Some gunsmiths convert large caliber revolvers for the use of shot cartridges by boring the barrel to a slightly larger diameter nearly to the muzzle, and then reaming the muzzle section to a choke. The following is abbreviated from an interesting article on this subject by Mr. Bud Dalrymple, of Scenic, South Dakota, in the April, 1930, issue of *The American Rifleman*.

"While hunting coyotes for the Government I decided that a fellow needed some kind of a scatter gun to hit the June and July pups, as we often ran them down and shot them from the saddle; and if anyone thinks a coyote pup at high speed is easy to hit from horseback, he had better try it.

"I tried a sawed off shot gun, and while it worked well at first, the horse soon began to object to having that young cannon fired so close to his ears; and thereafter as soon as I got close enough to the coyote pup to raise my gun, the horse decided that he had business in the other direction. As it requires two hands to work the pump gun, and I didn't have three, I sometimes hit the coyote pup and sometimes I hit where he was not.

"I tried shot in a .45 single action Colt revolver with the regular rifled barrel, but the twist in the rifling started the shot to whirling in a circle, and believe me, it was a large circle, too.

"Finally I decided to remove the rifling from that .45 Colt barrel and see what it would or would not do. I didn't have many gun tools along, but I did have a hand brace and a 15/32 inch twist drill; so I removed the barrel from the gun and proceeded to rebore it. I drilled almost the length of the barrel (from breech to muzzle), and then took the drill and honed the point to a longer taper and drilled on to the end of the barrel. This left a little choke. So far so good; but as the drill wasn't intended to bore a nice, smooth hole, nor polish the hole it made, that Colt barrel looked as if a bunch of rat-tail files had been revolving around in it, and I began to wonder if the shot could possibly travel through such a looking hole and not be all worn out. Fishing around in my ammunition tool box I found some emery cloth, and made a wooden rod that would pass through the Colt barrel loosely. Then I cut a slot through the end to fasten and hold a strip of emery cloth. Next I dressed the other end down to a square that would fit in the hand brace chuck, put the Colt barrel in the vise again, and proceeded to polish the inside of that terrible looking barrel. I turned the brace handle around I think, ten thousand times, and the hole in the barrel still looked like a horse radish grater and my arms were getting stiff and sore. So I decided to put the barrel back in the gun and shoot one load of shot through it and see how much shot would get clear through.

"I primed one of the regular .45 Colt shells and put in about seven grains of Ballistite powder. Then I cut some wads from a cardboard box, and with a stick seated four of them on top of the Ballistite powder. Then I took some No. 2 shot out of a twelve gauge shell and put in all the .45 shell would hold, which of course wasn't an eight gauge load. I used a thin cardboard wad over the shot, and with a shell resizing die I put a good heavy crimp on the brass. All was ready now, so I set up a board at 40 feet, the board measuring about 8 x 12". I could not help wondering if any of the No. 2 shot would hit it; but when I pulled the trigger the board was knocked clear off the rock I had set it on.

"I felt encouraged, and I certainly was surprised to find that a lot of those No. 2 shot had not only hit the board, but that most of them had gone right through it—and it was ⅞" pine! My arms were not nearly so stiff and sore now after seeing all those No. 2 shot holes in that board; so I took the barrel out of the gun again, and with that patent polishing tool proceeded to shine it up some more, and finally got it so that it looked quite respectable. And anyway a coyote pup wouldn't care whether it shone like a mirror or not and as long as it shot pretty well I was satisfied. This proved to be just the kind of a gun a fellow needed; and once I got up within fifty feet of a running coyote he was just the same as my coyote for I had six loads of shot to throw at him; and besides, I had one free hand to steer that fractious horse the way the coyote decided he wanted to go. And thus the gun was a complete success.

"Since retiring from Government work I have obtained some gun tools and put up a shop, and have converted a lot of Colt revolvers into shot arms. The .44/40 and .45 Single Action Colts make the best guns; and the .38/40 can be rechambered for the .44/40 shell and the barrel bored close enough so that it will shoot a .44 caliber round ball almost as accurately as a rifled barrel. I make the round balls for these guns of pure lead so they will not spoil the choke; and there you have a gun for both ball and shot. I have made several of these shot and ball barrels from the small ends of spoiled rifle barrels, and by using a barrel of caliber less than the revolver to be used, I can bore it close for round ball and shot. I like about a 7½" barrel on these shot revolvers as that length seems to pattern the shot better than the very short barrels, as a rule. But I have rebored and choked several 5½" barrels that shot splendidly. For reloading the shells—and they can be reloaded at least fifty or seventy-five times—I remake the regular Ideal or Winchester tools so that they will put a super-crimp on the shot cartridge and also seat the round ball properly.

"DuPont No. 5 Pistol Powder seems to work as well as any in these guns and I am using it largely. I find that one card wad, one thick, felt wad, and one more card is o.k. over the powder. Put in all the shot the shell will then hold, and put a thin card wad over the shot and crimp heavily. For the round ball I put a card and a felt wad over the powder leaving room so that the ball will rest snugly on the powder. Always use a smokeless primer, as the old black powder ones will cause hangfires, misfires and will also weaken the load.

"I forgot to mention that the abrupt shoulders in the revolver cylinder should be tapered off so that they will not cause the shot to jam; and the barrels must be choke bored or they will scatter too much.

"For those who like a double action revolver the Colt New Service makes a nice shot arm. There are many of these large caliber revolvers laid away, rusting out, since the free range and the cowboy gave place to the farms and the farmer; and these guns can be rebored to shoot shot and then are a very handy and useful arm. I have rebored a lot of them for bankers, doctors, policemen and tourists, and as a gun for self-protection they are just the thing as the .44/40 or the .45 can be loaded with sixteen pellets of BB shot, and at short range they will drive through 1¼" pine, and put the entire load in a would-be bad man's working parts. Such guns are much handier than the regular shot gun to carry in the automobile. I carry one in the auto all the time and pick up lots of game with it.

"While I was hunting predatory animals for the Government I needed my rifle on the saddle every day. There were lots of sage chickens, which are very fine eating when young but the young birds hide pretty close in the sage brush; and if a fellow did hit one with a high powered bullet the bird would be ruined. So I carried the Colt shot revolver and got all the small meat we needed for camp. It was real sport, too as I would scare the birds up and shoot them on the fly. I kept track one week of my hits and misses, and out of twenty-two sage chicks that I shot at on the wing, I killed twenty, using No. 8 shot. Dense smokeless powder must be used in these shot cartridges as bulk takes up too much room in the shell. Ballistite, Bull's-eye, Infallible, DuPont No. 5 and Oval are o.k. Be sure not to use too heavy a charge as these are very strong powders."

The above material, all of which is taken from Mr. Dalrymple's article is the best information I have yet seen in print on the subject of shot revolvers. I might add that he has been converting handguns to shoot shot for a number of years.

The Strength of Revolvers and Pistols

Occasionally we will hear of a revolver or a pistol being blown up from the use of an overcharge of powder, or from an obstruction in the barrel. Fortunately these accidents are rare, and moreover, they usually do not result in any injury to the shooter; in this respect revolvers and pistols are much safer than rifles or shotguns.

However, as stated above, accidents occasionally do occur, and every user of a pistol or revolver will no doubt be interested in learning about how and when such troubles occur, and how to avoid them. There are two principal causes of such damage. One, and it is the most usual, is the firing of the gun with an obstruction in the barrel. Sometimes a powder charge in a cartridge

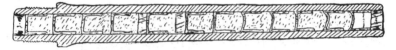

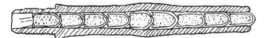

Two revolver barrels which were brought to the author for examination. They were sawn open as shown, and carefully sketched to show the exact condition. Top: .38 Special barrel with eleven bullets and one jacket lodged in it. Bottom: .32-20 barrel with nine bullets lodged in it.

may be weakened by the seepage of oil into the cartridge case, or in some other way, so that when the gun is fired, the bullet does not leave the barrel. Then if another shot is fired while the barrel is stopped up, a bulge will be produced, or the barrel may even be split open. This does not injure the user at all.

In large caliber high powered revolvers or pistols, such an accident always bulges the barrel, and often may split it as well. Many .45 Model of 1917 U. S. Army revolvers have been damaged in this way, on account of the deterioration of poor quality wartime ammunition.

In revolvers of small caliber, the barrel usually does not split, though it will generally show a bulge at the point where the obstruction was located in the barrel. I have seen a .38 Special barrel shot absolutely full of bullets from muzzle to breech, without showing even a bulge. This barrel had twelve bullets in it. A .32/20 barrel with nine bullets in it had a large bulge in the middle, which was the location of the first obstruction. The others merely piled up behind it and shoved it forward, until the whole barrel was full. The owner did not know that his barrel was obstructed, and kept on shooting. Both these two guns were brought to me to examine after these occurrences, and I had the barrels sawed open, and then took advantage of the occasion to make a very accurate sketch of the appearance of the barrels, which I include herewith. In both of these cases, as well as in practically every other one that I have ever seen, the bullet which stuck was metal jacketed. A metal jacketed bullet is much harder to force through a barrel than is a lead bullet, and therefore is more likely to stick.

Firing a gun with an obstruction in the barrel will never cause the breech of the gun to burst, unless the obstruction is right against the bullet when the gun is fired. In this case it may prevent the bullet from moving at all, and in this case the pressure in the chamber will rise so suddenly that the chamber may burst.

I have before me a 10-inch single-shot pistol that was stolen by a man who did not understand much about firearms. It was a new gun and the barrel was full of cosmoline. He loaded it with a .22 Long Rifle cartridge and fired it. Of course, the cosmoline

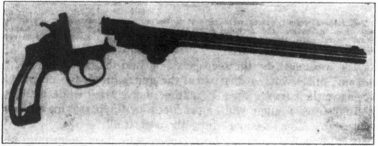

This Single Shot Target Pistol had the barrel split at the bottom near the breech, and the hinge of the frame broken as shown by being fired while the barrel was filled with cosmoline. The damage was caused by a .22 Long Rifle Cartridge loaded with Lesmok powder. The cartridge was not of the Hi-Speed or high velocity type, but was of the ordinary "Outdoor" type so popular for target practice.

in the barrel acted as an obstruction. The barrel split open along the bottom near the breech and blew away not only the lug on one side of the hinge, but also part of the frame, thereby wrecking the whole gun. It is amazing to think that this much power can be obtained in a .22-caliber cartridge.

Smokeless powder may either burn, explode, or detonate. It is a composition something like celluloid, and if it is ignited in small quantities in the open air, it burns something like celluloid does. On the other hand, if it is ignited in a confined space, as in the chamber of a gun, the heat and gas generated by the burning of the first part that is ignited cannot escape, and this intense heat and pressure will make the remaining portion of the powder burn more quickly. The smaller the space in the cartridge, and the more nearly it is filled with powder, the more quickly will the powder burn. In this case the burning is so rapid that it is called *exploding*. When a cartridge is fired, the powder explodes.

Another way in which explosives can act is to *detonate*. Take dynamite, for example. A stick of dynamite, which is only nitroglycerine dissolved in porous earth, may be cut in small pieces and the pieces thrown in the fire one by one, and they will burn quietly. But if a blasting cap is exploded in contact with the dynamite, a

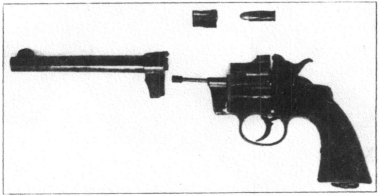

This gun was burst by using a double charge of smokeless powder. With most modern pistol cartridges, a double charge will come very close to bursting the gun.

sudden wave of chemical change will pass through the whole mass, and it will all turn into gas practically instantaneously. The action is so sudden that it will disrupt and wreck even the strongest materials. If it happens inside a gun barrel, it will break the barrel before the bullet has time to move. This extremely sudden change of an explosive into a gas all at one time is called a *detonation*.

Guncotton and nitroglycerine are both peculiarly sensitive to being detonated, and smokeless powders are all made either of guncotton, nitroglycerine, or both, or of some other nitrocompound resembling guncotton. It is true that they are treated chemically in such a manner as to remove nearly all chance of detonating them by any ordinary means; but if a very large charge of pistol powder is compressed into a very small space and exploded under conditions giving rise to very high pressures, a detonation will sometimes occur.

It is practically impossible to burst a modern high grade pistol or revolver merely by high pressure; but as the powder charge is increased and the pressure gets higher and higher, suddenly a point will be reached where the character of the explosion changes to that of a detonation. When this occurs, the gun will be wrecked,

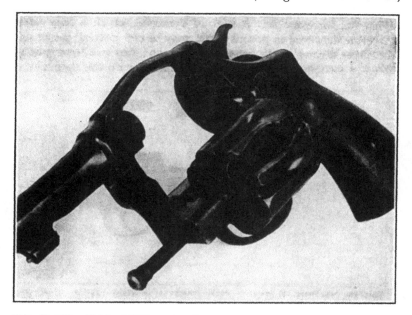

This .45 caliber Model of 1917 revolver damaged in a test, shows the result of using a double charge of smokeless powder.

no matter how good the material is or how thick the walls are made. When a detonation occurs, the nearest thing moves, no matter what it is.

Experience has shown that with high powered revolvers, a double charge of smokeless powder will sometimes burst the gun. This is of particular interest because a double charge is what would result if a cartridge were accidentally put under the powder measure twice in either hand or factory loading.

An exhaustive series of tests was once carried out with the .45 Colt cartridge, loaded with a 255 grain bullet and a standard factory charge of 5.9 grains of Bullseye No. 2. A number of cartridges were loaded with one extra grain, two extra grains, three extra grains, and four extra grains of powder. All these charges, running up to 9.9 grains of powder were fired with no damage to the weapon. However, when some charges of five grains extra, or a total of 10.9 grains, were tried, the revolver burst on the third shot. The test was then repeated, with another revolver, which burst on the 4th shot.

Some cartridges were then loaded with 6 grains extra, or 11.9 grains, which was just a little over a double charge. The revolver burst on the fourth shot. The test was repeated, and again the revolver burst, this time on the third shot.

A normal charge was then used, but two bullets were inserted, both resting together. The revolver burst when fired.

Occasionally, from some unknown cause, most likely an overload, a cartridge will detonate and burst a revolver. A theory was evolved that with cartridges loaded with nitro-glycerine powders, long exposure to prolonged heat might cause the nitro-glycerine to exude, and that as a result, the cartridge might detonate when fired. To test this possibility, cartridges were exposed to varying degrees of heat for varying lengths of time, and then fired. In no case was any dangerous pressure recorded, though in a number of cases hangfires and misfires occurred through having nitro-glycerine exude and deaden the primer. Likewise the exposure of cartridges to extreme cold did not cause any high pressures.

The most remarkable thing to my mind, is the tremendous amount of abuse that the modern revolver or automatic pistol of high quality will stand without giving way. Not long ago I saw an astonishing exhibit on the desk of Mr. Fred T. Moore, Vice President and General Manager of Colt's Patent Firearms Mfg. Co. It is quite easy to understand that with thousands of people all over the country experimenting with reloading cartridges, and especially with many of them trying to develop high speed loads, cases will occur where the experiment will result in the production of a load that no gun can stand, and a burst revolver will be the result. Most often the user will then write to the maker of the arm and state that the gun was defective, and demand its replacement free of charge.

Various are the excuses used in such a case. Sometimes the claim will be that the heat treatment in the cylinder is defective; or the claim may be that the design is too weak because the walls of the cylinder are not thick enough; or that the thin section of the cylinder wall where the chamber comes nearest to the outside wall is too thin.

When one man blew up a gun with a double load and then said that the heat treatment was defective, Mr. Moore took a cylinder and burnt it in the fire, so as to destroy all the heat treatment. The gun with this soft cylinder in it performed as usual.

When another man said that the walls of the cylinder were defective in design in that they were not thick enough, Mr. Moore took a cylinder of the same kind and shaved the walls down to a fraction of their original thickness. The revolver passed the proof tests and an exhaustive firing test without any trouble, thus proving that the cylinder walls are actually made much stronger than necessary.

When another man thought the design was defective in that the chambers approached too close to the cylinder walls, Mr. Moore took a cylinder and actually sawed through this thin section in each chamber. When the gun was fired, the walls of the cylinder bent over slightly, so as to open the crack a little wider, and close the crack on the adjacent cylinders; but that is all that happened.

In a revolver an overload of powder will never burst a barrel, but if it damages the gun it will damage the cylinder. In revolvers it is pretty safe to say that a damaged barrel is always caused by some obstruction and a damaged cylinder by an overcharge, or high pressure.

In the Government automatic an overcharge generally splits the barrel at the bottom between the two lugs, and the escaping gases bulge the projecting forward part of the receiver and generally also bulge out the slide. Usually the magazine is also blown out and the grips are split, which may injure the shooter's hand.

In all my own experience with hand firearms the only casualty I ever had was produced by experimenting with a Government automatic pistol with a special barrel to shoot blank cartridges, which I was attempting to develop at the time. The charge was 5 grains of EC blank-cartridge powder, which is quite a safe charge ordinarily when no bullet is used; but in this case there was a choke screwed into the barrel near the muzzle to furnish sufficient power to operate the mechanism, and somehow this choke became stopped up from one of the wads from one of the blank cartridges. On firing the succeeding cartridge, the whole top of the pistol was simply cleaned off the frame, leaving me holding just the receiver, much astonished, although not in the least harmed.

Mechanical Difficulties

With the advent of the modern high grade revolver and automatic pistol of good design, many of the mechanical difficulties formerly encountered have become a thing of the past. For example, in the old Colt .38 caliber revolvers formerly (1894 to 1911) used in the Army, a frequent cause of trouble was the breakage of the spring holding the hand or pawl which turned the cylinder. With this spring broken, the cylinder would not turn when the hammer was cocked, unless the muzzle of the gun was held pointing downward. In this case, the force of gravity dropped the pawl in place, and the cylinder would sometimes revolve.

With the modern revolver, the hammer nose or firing pin will occasionally break. This is usually due to faulty heat treatment of the part. Fortunately this accident is very rare with guns made at the present time. The accident puts the gun out of commission until another piece can be obtained and installed.

Occasionally a gun will be seen in which the firing pin hole in the standing part of the breech is too large, or is out of shape. This may cause a jam by allowing the soft metal of the primer to flow back into the hole under the pressure of the explosion. With high pressures and very soft primers, this difficulty may be experienced even with a well made and properly fitting firing pin and firing pin hole. The remedy in this case is to change to another make of ammunition.

Sometimes with automatic pistols, the thumb safety may become worn, or may not fit properly in the first place, so that when it is put in the "Safe" position, the gun can still be fired. The remedy is to replace the defective part with a new one.

In using single shot target pistols with a spring ejector, it frequently happens that when the gun is opened, the cartridge is not ejected. The only thing to do in this case is to push out the empty shell with a cleaning rod, taking care to keep the face and eyes out of line with the breech, for as soon as the cartridge is started from its seat, the spring will throw it out with a considerable amount of force. This failure of the ejector is usually due to the accumulation of lubricating grease from the cartridges. An occasional cleaning of the chamber of the gun with a light oil will usually prevent this trouble.

Even the hand ejector ordinarily found on revolvers is not free from its troubles, as it is quite easy for one or more of the empty cartridges to fall under the ejector and become caught so that it is somewhat troublesome to remove, and causes a considerable delay in reloading. The best way to avoid this is to hold the gun muzzle up when ejecting the empty shells. This will allow them to fall clear. In this connection it may be remarked that the useless flourish indulged in by some shooters who imitate wild west novels by swinging the revolver upward and backward when they cock it is said to have originated from the very practical necessity in the old days of the cap and ball muzzle loader of getting rid of the spent caps without getting them entangled with the mechanism. Before firing, the caps were a snug fit on the nipples of the cylinder; but when they exploded, they would split open and were ready to fall off and get in the works as soon as the hammer was cocked. Hence the practice of raising the gun over the right shoulder with the muzzle up when cocking the hammer, so that the spent cap could fall clear.

If the metal in the head of the rim fire cartridge happens to be weak or defective, or if the pressure happens to be excessive, the head of the cartridge may split when it is fired, and the result will be a disagreeable and dangerous escape of gas that may burn or cut the fingers of the revolver shooter. This accident is more likely to happen with the high speed .22 cartridges, which have a very high pressure, than it was with the old style low pressure cartridges. In order to allow the use of high speed cartridges with safety in revolvers, Smith & Wesson brought out their K-.22 with a cylinder having countersunk recesses to receive the heads of the rim fire cartridge, instead of merely allowing the head of the cartridge to lie in the space between the cylinder and the frame, as had formerly been the practice. This obvious but highly commendable improvement was so self evidently desirable that it was almost at once adopted by every other maker of importance.

There are on the market a number of revolvers chambered for long cartridges in which it is possible to use a similar cartridge of the same caliber but shorter in length. For example, .22 BB Caps, .22 CB Caps, .22 Short, .22 Long, and .22 Long Rifle cartridges may all be used in most .22 revolvers; the .38 Long Colt and the much longer and more powerful .38 special may be used in the same gun; and all guns chambered for the .44 S. & W. Special will also take the .44 S. & W. Russian, which is two tenths of an inch shorter.

The reader of firearms literature will often see warnings against this practice; but in general I see no objection to it. In fact I have personally fired many thousands of short cartridges in handguns chambered for longer ones, with no trouble.

It is true that the long continued use of short cartridges in long chambers may tend to cause corrosion or a slight burning or roughening of the chamber to take place just where the mouth of the short cartridge rests, so that when long cartridges are later used in the same chamber, this roughness may cause difficulties in extraction. However, this effect was much more likely to happen when the old fashioned corrosive primers were in use. With the modern non-corrosive primers there is little or no danger of any trouble from this cause, and anyway, the trouble at its worst was not serious. It merely meant a slight difficulty in extraction, or else the fitting of a new cylinder at a few dollars cost. For example, when living in Florida some years ago, I used to carry a .22 Colt Police Positive Target Revolver with me whenever I walked on the beach or in the woods; and I shot so much with this gun that I took to using the .22 shorts as a matter of economy. I used to buy them by the case of 10,000, and after using several cases I still found no difficulty with the gun, though I used it carefully and always cleaned it as soon as I had finished shooting. Anyway, the money I saved in ammunition would have paid for several new cylinders had it been necessary.

A more serious criticism of this practice of using short cartridges in long chambers is the statement sometimes heard that this practice will result in bulging or swelling the breech of the barrel where it is coned out to form a bullet seat. The theory is that the bullet gets to going with a considerable amount of velocity and then passes from the cylinder to the barrel, where it encounters the cone leading into the rifling. It is said that the sudden retardation of the rapidly moving bullet when it enters the coned rear section of the barrel will cause the barrel to bulge in time. This sounds reasonable; but before coming to any conclusion, it might be well to remember that every revolver bullet has to jump about half an inch before it comes to the rifling, so that we might with equal reason expect the same effect with the standard cartridge for which the gun was originally chambered, especially as the regular cartridge usually has a more powerful load than the short cartridge.

In fact, it is probable that this bulging of the rear end of the barrel from the impact of the bullet does sometimes occur, especially with long soft bullets and heavy powder charges; but I have never personally seen a case where this occurred from using short cartridges in long chambers; and I have had a lot of experience along this line, as for years I used thousands of .38 Long Colt Cartridges in my S. & W. .38 Military and Police and in my Officer's Model Target for rapid fire practice. At one time the Army had a large stock of these .38 Long Colt Cartridges, and they were issued to the competitors at Camp Perry in large quantities. One year as Ordnance Officer of the National Matches at that place I issued 20,000 of these cartridges, nearly all of which were shot by competitors in .38 Special revolvers, and there was no trouble reported. Consequently I never hesitate to use the .38 Long Colt in the .38 Special gun, or the .44 Russian in the .44 Special gun when it suits my purpose to do so.

Barrel Life

Naturally the user of a gun will consider that after he has used the gun for many thousands of shots, some wear will have taken place inside the barrel, and he will want to know how much this will affect the accuracy, and how much shooting can be done before the barrel must be replaced.

The answer depends on what kind of ammunition is used, and on what kind of care is given to the gun. Most barrels that have to be replaced have become unserviceable through rust and pitting caused by neglect and not by wear. In fact, it is very rare indeed for a revolver barrel to become worn out from shooting.

In high powered rifles using jacketed bullets, the case is different. The gases are under very high pressure and temperature, and the bullet seat or origin of the rifling rapidly becomes *eroded* with use. Moreover the jacketed bullets cause a very large amount of friction and barrel wear. Erosion and barrel wear will ruin a high powered rifle barrel in from three thousand to ten thousand shots, depending on the kind of powder used, etc.; but corrosion and pitting from rust and neglect may ruin any gun in a few days. It is well to bear in mind that erosion and corrosion, the two great enemies of gun barrels, are entirely different things, and operate in entirely different ways.

The principal cause of ruined barrels from corrosion is failure to clean them promptly and properly after using. This is less important now that non-corrosive primers are in use; but prompt and thorough cleaning is still the best gun insurance.

For years all small arms primers contained a chemical, potassium chlorate, which in firing the primer is changed into potassium chloride and deposited in the barrel. This potassium chloride has a very great affinity for moisture, and when wet chloride is in contact with steel an electrolytic action starts, which rapidly dissolves the steel. This is the cause of the corrosion which ruins so many gun barrels. The chloride must be removed before the gun is put away after firing. If it is allowed to stand even overnight in an ordinary atmosphere, the surface of the steel will be attacked and roughened; and once this has occurred, the matter of cleaning becomes increasingly difficult.

Fortunately the cartridge companies have all learned how to make primers containing no chlorate of potash, and these primers are non-corrosive. A gun fired with ammunition containing non-corrosive primers is no more liable to rust inside than outside, and immediate cleaning is not so important. But of course any piece of iron or steel will rust in time if it is left to stand without any oil on the surface, so that even with non-corrosive primers, a certain amount of care is necessary.

Moreover, not all cartridges are made with non-corrosive primers. The most popular cartridges for target use in the .22 caliber have long been those loaded with Lesmok powder, which is in effect a mixture of black and smokeless powders. Non-corrosive primers are not used with this powder, and moreover, the residue of the powder itself contains potassium salts which are corrosive. So the corrosion problem remains with us.

Recently a number of new steels called stainless have been coming more and more prominently into use for making cutlery, and for other purposes. These steels contain about twelve per cent or more of chromium, and will not rust or corrode. Numerous attempts have been made to produce rifle or pistol barrels from this material, so as to do away with all trouble from corrosion, but the stainless steels are very difficult to machine accurately, and the making of rifle barrels from it has proved to be an almost impossible task so far, though progress is always being made in improving the machinability of these materials, and it is possible that in the not too distant future stainless steel barrels may be the rule. Already a lot of 2000 stainless steel barrels for the .45 automatic pistol has been made by the Ordnance Department at Springfield Armory.

When a barrel becomes slightly rusted, the accuracy does not change at all, but the surface becomes roughened, and the barrel becomes more likely to suffer from leading if lead bullets are used. If the barrel is for an automatic pistol, where jacketed bullets are used exclusively, no difference in the performance of a slightly rusted barrel and a new barrel can be noticed.

When the corrosion progresses further, pits will develop in the metal. In other words, little depressions will be seen where the metal has been eaten away by rust. Small pits do no harm to the accuracy when jacketed bullets are used, but they cause leading and inaccuracy with lead bullets. When a pit is wide enough to extend from one land or groove to the next, and is a quarter of an inch or more in length, the barrel should be considered unserviceable.

Pistols and revolvers using lead bullets, properly lubricated, will practically never wear out from barrel wear. I am acquainted with several nationally known marksmen who are still shooting .38 Special revolvers that have been shot from 30,000 to 50,000 times, and these guns are still winning prizes the same as ever.

Major Douglas B. Wesson of Smith & Wesson writes me that some of the test revolvers in the ammunition factories have been fired over 300,000 times, and are still accurate. He further says, "I can state definitely that in 1912 or 1913 I personally inspected two .44 Russian Single Actions belonging to Ad Topperwein, and found the barrels in perfect shape inside, both by visual inspection and by gauging, and at that time one had been shot something over 250,000 rounds, and the other over 300,000 rounds, and he continued to use these same guns with the same barrels for years after that time."

Thus we can see that with lubricated lead bullets there is no reason to worry about wearing out a barrel from shooting. The life of the barrel is, for all practical purposes, indefinite.

It is quite another thing, however, with jacketed bullets. They are made of much harder material, and there is no lubrication to cut down the friction, so that barrel wear is rapid. I have personally conducted several tests which show that with the .45 automatic pistol or the .45 Model 1917 revolver using jacketed bullets, the barrel life is only about five thousand or six thousand rounds.

Improperly lubricated lead bullets will cause a rapid temporary loss of accuracy through what is called *leading*. Owing to the great heat and friction of the passage of the bullet through the barrel, a part of the lead from the bullet sometimes rubs off and sticks to the barrel. When this happens, the accuracy suffers until the offending particles of lead are removed from the barrel.

Some of the "dry" or unlubricated .22 caliber cartridges which have recently been placed on the market under various trade names are very bad offenders in regard to leading. When this book was in preparation I visited the publisher, Mr. T. G. Samworth, at his residence in North Carolina, and I took with me several new arms, and a quantity of various makes of ammunition. One morning was spent in trying a new .22 caliber revolver. During the fore-

noon, several boxes of these .22s were shot; not because I like
them, but merely to see what the result would be. At first the accuracy and performance of both gun and ammunition were all that
could be desired; but suddenly I noticed that I was missing an
unusually large number of easy shots at tin cans and other improvised targets, so we put up a regular target at 20 yards, and I fired
five shots, with not a single hit! I then went up to ten yards,
with the same result. Finally I did get a few shots on the bottom
of the paper, but they were all keyholes; that is, the bullets had
struck sideways.

We then took the gun inside and looked into the barrel and

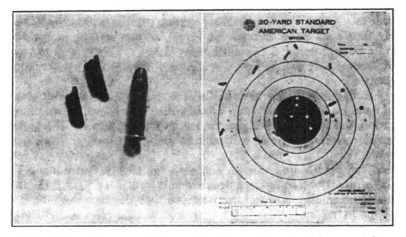

Left: Flakes of lead removed from a .22 caliber revolver after firing several boxes
of the unlubricated, or "dry" type of .22 caliber cartridges through it. The lead
formed a perfect cast of the bore for about three quarters of an inch near the breech.
Temporarily, the accuracy of the revolver was utterly destroyed, but it was fully re-
stored as soon as the leading had been removed.

Right: Effect of shooting about a hundred "dry" type .22 caliber cartridges of a
well known make in a revolver. The cleancut holes were made with Remington Sharp
Shoulder Cartridges fired from 20 yards. Then the gun was used for a while with
"dry" cartridges of another make. The keyholed shots were fired from 10 yards with
dry ammunition after the gun had begun to show signs of being leaded.

found that for over an inch forward of the breech the diameter
was reduced by fully one third. On pulling a brass brush through
the barrel a cylinder of lead was dislodged which formed a perfect
cast of the inside of the barrel. We scrubbed out the barrel with
the brass brush, and then again tried it at 20 yards. Result, ten
shots with all but one in the black, and that one was close.

This was the worst case of leading that I have ever seen, but I
have found that the same thing will happen every time if .22 cartridges of the dry type are fired rapidly. Owing to the rapidity with

which it is usually fired, this trouble will occur very readily in the Colt Woodsman or any other automatic, when using the dry cartridges; but it does not occur if proper greased cartridges are used. The moral is that the dry cartridges should not be used. The cartridge companies know perfectly well that the dry cartridges are liable to cause léading, but they have to make them and sell them because the great number of shooters who know very little about accuracy and want dry cartridges that can be carried loose in the pocket will buy this kind anyway, and if one company does not make them, its competitor will get the business.

Even with lubricated bullets, leading sometimes occurs. Occasionally in a match, the shooter who has been shooting for sometime may notice that the shots are getting hard to hold in the black. He then runs a rag through his barrel, and on looking at it carefully he will notice a few little shiny flakes. This is a mild case of leading. It will reduce the accuracy slightly until the lead is removed.

Leading in a fairly serious form is common among the users of hand loaded ammunition. Usually the cause is insufficient lubrication, too large a bullet size, or too soft a mixture for the bullet metal. A rough barrel will tend to aggravate leading from any cause.

lead can readily be removed, and then the steel barrel remains in
Fortunately, leading does not permanently harm a barrel, for the the same condition as before, provided that the lead was not left in the barrel long enough for corrosion to take place underneath. The easiest way to remove leading is with a brass cleaning brush. The brass is softer than the steel of the barrel and will not scratch the steel, but it loosens and removes the lead. In stubborn cases, the barrel may be corked and filled with metallic mercury, which will soften and dissolve the lead. Allow the mercury to remain in the barrel 12 hours, then pour it out and clean the barrel with good tight cloth patches, and all traces of the lead will be removed.

The condition of a gun barrel can be determined with sufficient accuracy for all practical purposes by visual inspection. In a new barrel the surface is smooth and bright and free from any spots or discolorations or irregularities and the edges of the lands and grooves are sharp and distinct.

If the barrel has suffered from excessive wear the edges of the lands especially towards the breech will be rounded over. Wear always shows up first at the breech end of the barrel and it is always advisable to examine the barrel from the breech rather than from the muzzle if this is possible. Even a considerably worn barrel will look good when viewed from the muzzle end.

If the surface of the metal instead of being uniformly bright and shiny has a dull or grayish appearance, or if it is covered with little fine, black specks, it has been allowed to rust slightly and the surface has become roughened. In an automatic pistol using jacketed bullets this will do no harm except to cause a slightly increased tendency to rust in the future.

If one or more little, oblong or irregular dark splotches are visible on the surface these are pits caused by the metal being more or less eaten away at the spot from rusting.

CARE AND CLEANING

The pistol or revolver, like any other object made of steel or iron, will rust unless it is kept oiled or greased. In fact a pistol is more subject to rusting than most objects of steel because it is liable to be handled in hot weather with moist hands and the film

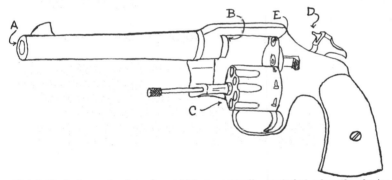

Sketch illustrates parts of revolver which are generally overlooked when the shooter is cleaning the arm. A, the end of the barrel; B, cylinder strap, right over barrel; C, front of cylinder; D, hammer nose and face of hammer; E, firing-pin channel and hammer cavity. Corrosive gases are prone to work into D and E.

of perspiration thus left on the surface has a chemical effect which will cause a rust in a very short time.

When any gun is first received from the factory the working parts will already have been oiled and the outside covered over with a light film of oil.

In order to preserve a gun from rust it is necessary to wipe the surface with a slightly oily cloth after the gun has been handled and before putting it away; otherwise finger prints and handprints will show up as rust streaks. After a gun has been fired additional care is necessary. The products of the powder combustion must be removed from the inside of the barrel and cylinder; and the smoke of powder gas must be removed from around the joint between the barrel and cylinder in a revolver and from the breech block and other working parts of an automatic pistol.

Immediately after shooting and before putting away the gun a dry canton flannel patch on a cleaning rod should be run through the barrel and each chamber of the cylinder, and this should be repeated with new patches until the patches come out clean and the barrel and cylinder look bright inside.

Then saturate a patch with nitro solvent or some gun cleaning oil and with this oily patch wipe out the interior of the barrel and cylinder thoroughly. Also clean off the front face of the cylinder and the frame of the gun wherever the powder gas has reached it. The firing pin or point of the hammer nose should be wiped off with this same oily patch. If the gun is to be used again in a few days it can be put away in this condition, but if on the other hand it is to be kept for sometime without shooting it again it is advisable to clean the barrel and cylinder out once more with a dry patch and then coat with a patch saturated with gun grease.

The outside of the gun and all places where the fingers have touched should be wiped off with an oily rag before the gun is put away. If the gun is to be kept for some time without using it again the outside should be gone over with a rag saturated with gun grease so as to leave a light coating of the grease on all parts exposed to the air. When the gun is laid away it should not be put in a leather holster or wrapped in a cloth or put in contact with pasteboard. These substances all attract moisture and are likely to cause rusting.

A gun treated as described above and laid away in a dry place will keep in good condition indefinitely without further attention.

In cleaning automatic pistols it simplifies matters and makes cleaning easier and more thorough if the breech block is removed so as to expose the breech of the barrel in guns such as the Woodsman; or if the barrel is taken out in pistols such as the Colt Automatic in which the barrel can easily be removed. The easiest revolvers to clean are those such as the Harrington & Richardson Sportsman and the Iver Johnson Supershot in which the frame is hinged so that the barrel can be tipped up. In both these guns the cylinder is easily and quickly removable. By tipping up the barrel and removing the cylinder both the barrel and the cylinder and those parts of the frame reached by the powder gas become easily accessible.

Two different kinds of cleaning material should be on hand; a nitro solvent or gun oil and a heavy gun grease similar in consistency to vaseline. There are a number of commercial preparations on the market in both classes. Most of the big arms companies make a gun grease sold in collapsible tubes like toothpaste. Any of these preparations put up by any of the big arms companies may be relied on to be free from acid and quite suitable for indefinitely preserving the gun from corrosion. Both the gun grease and the nitro solvent of various kinds may be found on sale at nearly all sporting goods stores.

One of the most famous and satisfactory nitro solvent oils that has ever been developed is the formula of the late Dr. Hudson. It is often made up in quantities by gun clubs for the use of their members and is very satisfactory. To make ½ gallon of this mixture use the following quantities of the materials given:

Amyl Acetate—90 c. c. or 6 parts
Acetone—285 c. c. or 19 parts
Spirits of Turpentine—285 c. c. or 19 parts
Sperm oil—870 c. c. or 58 parts
Pratt's Astral Oil—390 c. c. or 26 parts

Pratt's Astral Oil is simply a very highly refined, acid free kerosene, originally produced by Pratt & Company of Brooklyn. This was such a pure product that no one in the trade was able to duplicate it successfully and there was so much demand for it that the Standard Oil Company ultimately bought the plant and continued the manufacture. This product is still marketed by the Standard Oil Company and should be obtainable from any of their distributing centers. The price is usually somewhat higher than that of ordinary gasoline. If any difficulty is had in obtaining Pratt's Astral Oil a material about equally good for the purpose can be obtained from almost any oil concern by asking for double refined kerosene guaranteed to be neutral, that is free from either acid or alkali.

This Hudson's Cleaner is an extremely satisfactory material for both cleaning and preserving pistols and revolvers. Some of the large arms companies use it regularly and a number of years ago when I was a member of the Springfield Revolver Club a number of the members of this club used it exclusively. For some years the only care I ever gave any of my pistols or revolvers was to clean them thoroughly with this material just after shooting unless I was going to lay them away for a long time in which case I applied gun grease as described above. With this very simple treatment I have never suffered from having any of my guns rust.

Another excellent cleaner which can be obtained on the market is a sort of emulsion of oil and water known as Chloroil. This material was made especially to dissolve the salty residue of the primer combustion. The oily consistency of the cleaner also protects a gun from rust for a long time. At the present time when I am using a gun at frequent intervals I merely clean it out thoroughly with a bristle brush dipped in Chloroil and then put it in the rack still dripping with the Chloroil and leave it there until I get ready to shoot it again. Of course if a gun is to be left unused for any length of time it should be dried and lightly coated inside and out with grease as described above.

Besides mere cleaning, all firearms require a certain amount of lubrication to enable the mechanism to function smoothly and without friction. Several of the commercial nitro solvents have the consistency of a light oil, and will serve very well for lubrication. It is somewhat more desirable, however, to use a plain light lubricating oil, of good grade, such as sewing machine or typewriter oil for this purpose. The mechanism requires very little oil, and requires oiling only at long intervals. It is a mistake to have the mechanism reeking with oil, as oil is the greatest enemy of good ignition in cartridges, and if oil works into the cartridge or primer misfires or hangfires will result. Never put enough oil on the gun to make the cartridges oily.

Points which require most frequent oiling are the parts where the slide and frame rub together on automatic pistols, and the hub of the cylinder, especially at the forward end, in revolvers.

Oil should be used very sparingly in dusty or sandy climates, such as the desert, as otherwise it will tend to collect dust and this accumulation may cause malfunctions. In some very dry locations where dust storms are frequent, it is better to keep the gun entirely free from oil.

In the arctic regions and other very cold places it is advisable to wipe off all oil, as it may freeze and cause jams.

Many guns when they come from the factory may have the barrel nearly full of heavy grease. Naturally if the gun was fired before this grease was removed, great damage would be done. If there is enough grease or oil in the barrel to see, it is best to run a rag through the barrel to remove the grease or oil before firing.

Most guns will shoot in a slightly different spot when the barrel is oiled from what they will when it is dry. Hence in starting a string of shots in a match, it is well to fire a warming or fouling shot through the barrel before beginning the actual match.

When Lesmok powder is used, a considerable amount of residue will collect in the gun barrel, and it is desirable to run a dry patch through the barrel after each twenty or more shots. With smokeless powder this is not necessary.

One often hears the shooter advised always to clean the gun from the breech, and never from the muzzle, for fear of wearing the muzzle with the cleaning rod. Fortunately this is not very important, for the Colt and Smith & Wesson revolvers with swing-out cylinders cannot be cleaned from the breech. The objection to cleaning from the muzzle is the fear that the cleaning rod may wear or injure the rifling at the muzzle; but as mentioned above, this is not really important, for experience has shown that while erosion at the bullet seat and in the lands just forward of the bullet seat will cause inaccuracy, wear at the muzzle will not. Even very serious mutilation of the muzzle of a gun with a file will not appreciably change the size of the groups; but it will change their location; that is the group may be higher or lower, or to one side or the other. These changes can of course be compensated for by sight changes.

How to Select a Good Revolver or Pistol

It is of great practical value to know what points to check up when buying a revolver or pistol of any kind, and this is especially important when the arm to be purchased is a second hand one.

First clean out the bore and chambers, and examine their interior condition and appearance in a good light. The barrel should be examined from the breech if possible. In most automatic pistols the barrel can be removed, and this should be done, as it facilitates the examination greatly. Single shot target pistols can all be opened so that the barrel can be viewed from the breech end. In most revolvers of the hinged frame variety, the cylinder can readily be removed.

The bore should be bright throughout its entire length, with no pits or marks of corrosion, and the edges of the lands should be clear and sharp. There should be no nicks in the muzzle nor should it be worn or "belled" through the improper use of the cleaning rod. Each chamber of the cylinder should be clean and free of rust spots or pitting; look closely in the case of a .22 and see that the chamber has not been unduly eroded through the excessive use of .22 shorts.

Cock the hammer and hold the gun up sideways to the light while you examine the clearance between the face of the cylinder and the rear end of the barrel. There should be a minimum of light showing, and this clearance should be the same for each chamber when the cylinder is revolved by hand. The end of the barrel should be square and true from both sides. There should be no appreciable play back and forth when the cylinder is worked lengthwise with the fingers.

Cock the hammer and examine the sidewise play in the cylinder when it is locked in position for firing. This is a most important point for if there is much play when the cylinder is in the firing position the gun may go off when the chamber is not well lined up with the barrel and this will result in shaving of lead and consequent serious inaccuracy. It is well to bear in mind, however, that all revolvers have more or less play in the cylinder when the gun is in the position of rest; that is, with the hammer down and the trigger forward. When the hammer is cocked the hand or pawl rotates the cylinder until the cylinder latch drops in place and holds the cylinder from further rotation. At this point there should be very little play but there is usually some. Now when the trigger is further pulled to discharge the piece the remaining loose play of the cylinder between the pawl and the cylinder stop is taken out and the cylinder should be locked perfectly solid in line with the barrel. For this reason the sidewise play of the cylinder must be tested after cocking the hammer and pulling the trigger, while the trigger is still held all the way back. In this position there should be no play or rotation in the cylinder. The same test should be made for each chamber in the cylinder as it might be tight in one position and at the same time the notch for the cylinder lock might be worn or displaced when some other chamber was in line.

Test the gun for rotation of the cylinder by pointing muzzle upward and holding back the cylinder with the left hand while cocking the gun with the right. In some guns the breakage of the spring which operates the hand or pawl will allow this part to drop out of action when the muzzle is elevated and the cylinder will not revolve; while on the other hand with the muzzle pointed downward gravity makes the pawl drop into its notch and the cylinder will rotate just as though the spring was not broken.

Swing out the cylinder and test it for rigidity; neither cylinder nor crane should show loose play. Slide the ejector rod back and forth to test its fit and working qualities. It should slide back freely and be returned to place readily by its spring. Examine closely the ratchet on the end of ejector rod; it should have sharp edges and should not be worn or burred to any extent. The cylinder lock in the bottom of the frame should have sharp edges and be of full width; it should also work freely and positively. Depress it with the forefinger a few times and see that the spring still has life.

If the gun is a .22 caliber examine the edges of the chamber where the hammer nose or firing pin rests. It should not be burred or dented.

With the cylinder swung out snap the hammer and by holding the trigger down, test the firing pin for protrusion. It should project sufficiently to explode the primer and it should not show any deformation, rusting or pitting. Notice whether or not there is any wear or corroding away of the firing pin hole. It should not be enlarged to any extent. Examine the pawl or hand which rotates the cylinder. It should not be worn away on its upper end but should rotate each chamber completely to its locked position. Cock the hammer and notice the condition of the hammer nose. It should be clean, well formed and it should not show any corrosion or battering. The cavity into which it fits when down should not be rusted or eaten away with primer corrosion. In the case of a revolver having a separate firing pin it should work freely and be of sufficient length to function properly; the rear end should not be burred over and the firing pin should not be rusted or stuck. Examine the firing pin particularly to be sure it is not broken, as sometimes revolvers with separate firing pins will be found to have the firing pin broken in the middle so that the break is hardly noticeable. The front end of the firing pin protrudes through when it is struck by the hammer but it is not retracted when the rear end of the firing pin recedes when the hammer is cocked. If the hammer has a loose hammer nose which acts as a firing pin it should have a considerable amount of play on its pivot.

Snap the hammer a few times and notice its action. Percussion should be good and the trigger should snap back smoothly and quickly to its forward position. Test the double action pull which should work smoothly and allow the hammer to "break" cleanly from the notch when it falls. When at full cock the hammer should notch at the rear of its travel with but very little additional play.

The side plate should not be sprung away from the frame at any point but should fit flush all around. The screw which fastens it should not have burred heads or torn slots; if they do it is an indication of possible repairs in the past or at least that the arm has been disassembled by an unskillful person.

Grips should fit to the butt with no looseness and no signs of warping. Checkering should have clean, sharp diamonds which are not worn smooth. Sights should not be bent or dented and in the case of target guns there should be no lost motion in the sights.

In the case of an obsolete Army sidearm or a gun bought from any large stock of standard weapons such as discarded police models, etc., check up on the serial number found on the butt, frame, cylinders and barrel and make certain these are all the same, otherwise the gun is probably an assembled job made up by fitting together a lot of spare parts and if so you don't want it. The color on the bluing on all main parts should be of the same shade or show an equal amount of wear. If there is no serial number showing, or there is indication that they have been altered or ground off do not accept the gun under any condition. In many jurisdictions the mere possession of a gun with altered number is a presumption of illegal possession or violation of some of the various firearms laws.

If in your examination you find the words "Spain" tucked up under the trigger guard or "Made in Spain" in small type or the wording "for Smith & Wesson ctg." with only the Smith & Wesson part readable don't accept the gun as a gift. It is one of the notorious Spanish immitations of standard American arms and the quality is utterly undependable.

In the case of automatic pistols test the slide for looseness on the frame. If there is very much play the gun will most likely be in-accurate. See if the barrel has any loose motion in the barrel bushing when the slide is closed. It should be a snug fit. Snap the gun and holding back the trigger draw the slide to the rear and let it go forward again, then release the trigger and pull it and the mechanism should snap. If it does not then the disconnec-tor has failed to work and the hammer or firing pin has followed the slide down. If the gun is a .45 Government automatic or a Super .38 automatic test the disconnector as follows: Cock the piece and shove the slide one-quarter inch to the rear; hold the slide in that position and squeeze the trigger. Let the slide go forward, maintaining the pressure on the trigger. If the hammer falls, the disconnector is worn on top and must be replaced. Pull the slide all the way to the rear and engage the slide top. Squeeze the trigger and at the same time release the slide. The hammer should not fall. Release the pressure on the trigger and then squeeze it. The hammer should then fall. The disconnector pre-vents the release of the hammer unless the slide and barrel are in the forward position safely interlocked.

The first test indicates that the disconnector is sufficiently long to be forced, by the rear surface of the slide, from between the sear and trigger. With it in this position a release of the trigger is necessary to allow the disconnector to move upward into the intervening space between the sear and trigger. The slide prevents this until it is allowed to go forward, uncovering the nose of the disconnector.

The second test indicates that the disconnector is of sufficient length to be forced, by the forward surface of the slide, from between the sear and trigger allowing the sear to engage the hammer while the slide is going forward, thereby preventing a follow down. This test, when associated with the first test, indicates that the cam surface under the slide is proper to make a disconnector of proper length function throughout the travel of the slide. In so doing, the sear, disconnector, and trigger are given sufficient time interval to go through the natural cycle of action. In other words, if the first test fails the sear may not have sufficient time to move under the hammer, thereby producing a follow down.

Cock the hammer and then test the safety grip by pressing the trigger while allowing the grip safety to remain free. The hammer should not fall. If it does, the grip safety is defective.

Cock the hammer and put the thumb safety in the "safe" position, and then try to snap the hammer. If the hammer can be snapped with the safety on, or if the safety moves to the off position when the trigger is pulled, the safety is defective.

With the Government Model .45, the Super .38, the Ace .22, and other models in which the gun should remain open after the last shot is fired, put the empty magazine in place, draw the slide all the way to the rear, and release it. The gun should remain open. Press the slide stop downward. The slide should snap shut, and the gun should remain cocked.

Remove the magazine, grasp the gun firmly around the stock and grip safety with the right hand. Hold the trigger back, and with the left hand draw the slide back to the full extent of its rearward travel and let it snap forward smartly. Repeat this several times. The hammer should remain cocked until the trigger is released and again pulled. If the hammer follows the slide in this test, it shows that either the hammer or the sear is defective. This trouble is often caused by an attempt to reduce the trigger pull. If the trigger pull is reduced to too low a point, the hammer jars off when the slide slams shut.

Many pocket model automatic pistols are provided with what is called a magazine safety, which prevents a pull on the trigger from discharging the gun when the magazine is removed. This is to prevent accidents caused by the supposition of inexperienced persons that the removal of the magazine will unload the gun, when in reality a cartridge still remains in the magazine. Test for the presence and proper functioning of this safety by drawing back the slide and allowing it to go forward again, thus cocking the gun. Then remove the magazine and pull the trigger. The gun should not snap. Replace the magazine and again pull the trigger. This time the gun should snap.

Examine the lips of the magazine. They should appear well formed and in good order, without any cracks in the corners, or any signs of deformation.

It goes without saying that before starting to make any of the above described tests, the arm should be carefully examined to be sure that it is unloaded, and that all safety precautions should be observed. Particular care must be observed with automatics, where the magazine may be empty and an unsuspected cartridge may still be in the chamber.

All these tests will help greatly in giving the intending purchaser an idea of the condition of the gun, but the real proof of the pudding is in the eating, so try to get an opportunity to test the gun by actual firing with service ammunition if it is at all possible. This is particularly desirable in the case of an automatic pistol; malfunctions may be caused by things that are almost impossible to detect by visual examination, such as slight deformations of the magazine lips.

Proof Marks

Great Britain and many other countries prohibit the sale of firearms that have not been examined and tested by a recognized authority according to certain rules, and stamped with a mark to indicate that they are safe for sale and use by the public.

These proof marks form a very valuable indication as to the origin of an arm, because all arms made and sold in certain countries must be proved and stamped with the proof mark, even if the maker does not have confidence enough in his products to put his own name and address on them.

Apparently the practice of proving firearms started just about three hundred years ago, in 1637, when a royal charter was granted to the gunmakers guild of London, authorizing them to test and approve all firearms. This guild later became known as "The

Gunmakers Company," and at the present time continues to test and approve, under carefully drawn specifications and regulations, firearms intended to be sold in the British Empire, whether they be of British or of foreign make. A similar organization called "The Guardians" is located at Birmingham, which, like London, is an important arms making center.

All firearms are carefully inspected to see that the design of the mechanism is satisfactory, that the parts are of the proper tolerance and are assembled correctly, and that the mechanism will operate safely. This operation is called "viewing" and when a gun passes this test it is said to have been "viewed," and is marked with a cipher stamp and the letter "V." Then when the gun has been tested by actually firing heavy charges to test its strength, it is said to have been proved, and is marked with the letter "P." "V P" so often seen on arms either alone or in combination with other letters or symbols means "Viewed and Proved."

The United States does not require the proving of guns prior to sale, but as guns that are not proved according to specified regulations cannot be sold in some countries, nearly all American arms makers have a proof test conforming to the British regulations to which they submit all arms intended for export. Some makers, notably the Winchester Repeating Arms Company and the Colt's Patent Firearms Mfg. Co. prove all guns made. American guns when submitted to a proof test are marked by the maker with a stamp to indicate that a proof test has been made. There is no uniformity about these marks, as they are designed by each maker to suit his own ideas. This is quite different from the system prevailing in most foreign countries, where the marks to be used are often prescribed by law.

The proving of any firearm usually involves the firing of the gun with a much heavier charge of powder than that used in service, with the idea of being certain that the barrel is strong enough to stand the specified charge, and hence will be safe to use.

There are two main kinds of proof, Provisional Proof, and Definitive Proof. When gun barrels are first made up in the rough, they are clamped to a testing device and fired with a heavy charge of powder to see if they are strong enough to be finished and assembled into a gun. This is the "Provisional Proof," and a certain stamp is placed on barrels so tested. After the gun is finally completed, it is again fired with a heavy charge to insure that the finished barrel and its breech mechanism have a factor of safety to insure against accident. This is the "Definitive Proof," and guns passing this test are stamped with still another mark. In the early years of gunmaking all proving was done with black powder, but in later years, after the advent of smokeless powders, it became necessary to change the tests to include these more powerful propellants, and several of the proof houses adopted a spe-

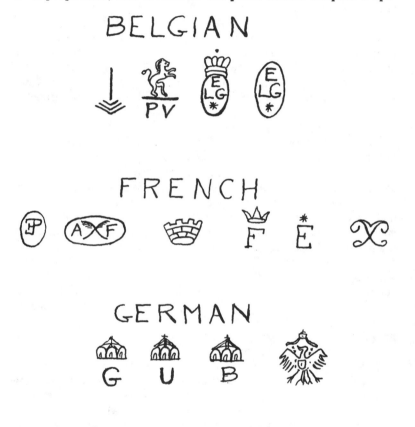

SOME PROOF-MARKS.

cial mark for the provisional and definitive proofs with smokeless, or, as it was often called, "nitro" powder.

Countries having established proof houses include Austria, Belgium, Czecho-Slovakia, France, Germany, Great Britain, Hungary, Italy, and Spain. Belgium is a great center for the manufacture of arms, and one of the most famous proof houses in the world is that of Liège, Belgium.

The common Belgian proof marks are an oval, containing the letters "ELG" and a star, or the same design surmounted by a crown; also the figure of the "perron" or monument of the city of Liège, an obelisk or tower on a terraced foundation, which, when roughly stamped on a gun, simply looks like a vertical line with three V-shaped marks under it. In the Belgian, French, and many other proof marks the letter "E," meaning "Epreuve," or proof, occurs, generally in combination with the initials of a town —as for example the E—LG mentioned above, meaning the proof of the city of Liège.

These Belgian proof marks are often found on guns that would not otherwise be suspected of being of Belgian manufacture. For example, I once had a man offer to sell me a supposed dueling pistol with a Damascus barrel, said to be of Italian origin. On close examination, the Damascus barrel seemed to be imitation, and on the breech of it was found the telltale oval with the letters "ELG," the Liège proof mark. This was apparently an imitation made up for the antique trade, but had to be proof-fired under the Belgian laws, and the proof mark remained there to tell the careful observer the origin of the gun. Again, I was once shown a large-size flint-lock pistol. The lock seemed too big for a pistol lock and looked more like a musket lock. It was marked "Royal Manufactury of St. Etienne." I looked on the breech of the barrel for proof marks and did not find any, so I took the barrel out of the stock and on the underneath part found two Belgian proof marks, also a slot for the rear sight. These supposed flint-lock pistols had simply been made up also for the antique trade by taking a number of old junk guns, removing the locks from some and barrels from others, cutting off the barrels and fitting the lock and barrel to a stock made of plain ordinary pine wood varnished over to look like walnut.

CHAPTER 6

ACCESSORIES

WHILE the pistol or revolver as purchased will shoot satisfactorily with no additional material other than the necessary ammunition, every owner of a hand arm will find that whether his gun is to be used for hunting, for target practice, or for home protection, there will be certain accessories that he will want in order that he may get the greatest satisfaction and benefit from the use of his gun, and in order that he may use it most conveniently.

Holsters

Perhaps the most important accessory of all is the holster, which is a leather scabbard used for the purpose of carrying the gun on the person.

Most holsters are worn on the belt; though a type of holster which is suspended from the shoulder has become increasingly popular in late years.

Although in some parts of the country the use of a belt holster for carrying a revolver or pistol may give the user a "Wild-West" appearance and make him feel that it is cause for comment from onlookers, it is by all means the safest and most sensible method of carrying a hand gun, either on the range or in the woods.

Any hand firearm is a dangerous weapon, and when not being fired should not be left lying around. Onlookers and strangers have a provoking habit of picking up pistols and aiming or manipulating them without the owner's consent. While a loaded pistol should never be laid down for a moment when others are about, it often happens that a shooter must stop his firing for a few minutes or is interrupted in his score and must leave the firing-point for some purpose. A loaded gun can be slipped into the holster and is absolutely safe as long as it remains there.

Not only is the safety of others taken care of with the holster, but the gun is properly guarded also, from scratches, dents and knocks. Even if the gun is carried in a hand bag to and from the range, it is an advantage to slip it in a holster, which keeps it from rubbing on other articles in the bag, such as screw drivers, cleaning rods, etc.

A well made belt holster is a good investment and tends toward safe handling of the gun. It is well to get one about ½ inch

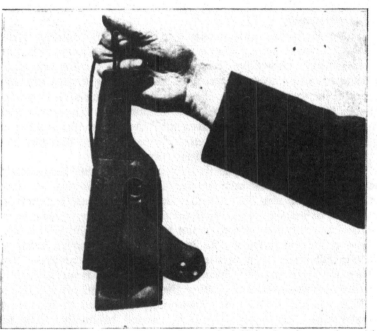

The Audley Spring Holster. The gun is securely held in place by a spring catch just inside the front of the trigger guard, yet it is easily and unconsciously released when the gun is grasped to withdraw it from the holster.

longer than the barrel and closed at the bottom. This keeps dirt from getting into the muzzle in case the holster comes in contact with the ground. There should, however, be a drain hole near the bottom to let the water out in case of rain.

It is best to get a holster without a lining. One disadvantage of a lining is that it will sometimes wear through and catch on sights, etc. Another disadvantage is that sometimes the lining will collect moisture and rust the gun. For the same reason it is a good plan to avoid cheap holsters, as the leather sometimes has chemicals in it that will cause a gun to rust badly.

For belt use, the holster should be of the type that is cut out around the trigger guard, so that the finger can get onto the trigger at once. There must be some method of keeping the gun from falling out of the holster. In the open-top holsters, which form the quickest ones to get into action, the gun is retained by simply fitting tight when shoved down into place. Some open-top holsters have a strap going down over the top to hold the gun from bouncing out. This must, of course, be unfastened before the gun can be drawn and is the source of quite a delay where a gun may be needed instantly.

There is on the market a holster called the "Audley Spring Holster," which has a flat retaining spring which snaps into place in the trigger guard and keeps the gun from coming out of the holsters. These holsters are open top, with the leather cut away around the trigger guard. You can hold them upside down and shake them, and the gun will not fall out, yet the minute your finger goes into the trigger guard at all the flat spring holding the gun is unconsciously pushed out of the way, and the gun then comes out as though it were absolutely free.

A special purpose open top holster called the Berns-Martin Range Holster, made only for the Government Model .45 Automatic, the Colt Ace .22, and the Super .38 automatic pistol has two ribs of leather on the inside of the front of the holster, so arranged as to form a protecting slot for the front sight, which keeps the gun from rubbing on the leather when the gun is being put into or taken out of the holster, or when it is being carried. Thus when the sight has been blacked for range use, it will remain in proper condition, without having the black rubbed off.

The type of holster with a flap on top to protect the gun is desirable when the weapon is to be carried habitually. The flap should be held down by a slot or buttonhole in it, which fits over a stud in the side of the holster. The holster should be well cut away around the trigger. Most holsters as they are now sold are not sufficiently cut away at this point, but the user can always cut them away for himself.

In making a quick draw the hand is swung up from below, striking the projecting lower part of the flap and disengaging it from the button; at the same time the last three fingers of the hand grasp the stock of the weapon and the forefinger goes on the trigger, with the thumb on the hammer, cocking the gun as it is withdrawn. It is remarkable how little extra time it takes to disengage the flap in this way when you have practiced at it and gotten the flap worked in so that it slips off the stud easily. Just one upward motion of the hand disengages the flap and brings the gun from the holster cocked.

A belt holster suspended from the belt, or worn loosely on the belt should always be tied down at the bottom, as otherwise the holster will follow when an attempt is made to lift the gun out, and a quick draw is impossible. Many holsters have rawhide or

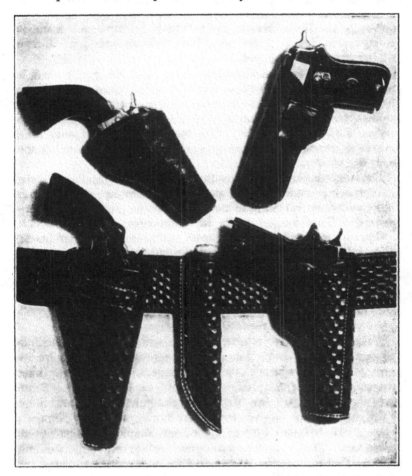

Upper Left: Slip Hammer Single Action Colt in Cross Stomach Holster. The trigger of this gun is removed, and the gun is fired by drawing back the hammer with the thumb as the gun is drawn from the holster, and then letting the hammer spur slip from under the thumb when ready to fire. For this reason the holster is not cut out around the trigger guard, as trigger is not used. Bottom: Berns-Martin Speed Holster, hunting knife in scabbard, Berns-Martin Range Holster.

buckskin thongs attached for this purpose. The regulation army holster has a strap to go around the leg and fasten with a buckle.

When a very stiff wide belt is worn, on which the holster fits tightly, it is not necessary to tie down the bottom, as the stiffness of the belt will keep the holster in place in making the draw.

An excellent holster, made for revolvers only, and especially designed for the fastest possible draw, which holds the gun securely under all conditions and at the same time gives it full protection is the Berns-Martin Speed holster invented and manufactured by two former Navy men, John E. Berns and J. H. Martin, of Bremerton, Washington.

This holster is open down the front, and the gun is held in place by a leather covered steel spring which clasps the cylinder. The top of the holster fits over the trigger guard, so that the gun cannot rise or be pulled straight up; it must be swung forward to release it from the holster. This feature is a good one, for it makes it impossible for anyone approaching from behind to disarm the wearer.

The material and workmanship on these Berns-Martin Holsters is of the very highest grade, and these holsters are made to order only, and fitted carefully to the particular gun for which they are ordered. They are not made for automatics.

Part of the outfit is the big wide stiff belt which just fits the slide in the holster, so that when the holster is on the belt, it is impossible to tip the holster or lift it up in making the draw. These holsters are made to be worn on the right side for a right hand draw; and they are made either for wear low on the right side of the leg or waist high just forward of the hip pocket. The high position is recommended as being the more practical.

When practicing at quick draw work with the speed holster, the beginner should, in his first attempts, draw slowly, grasping the butt of the gun with the last three fingers, extending the index finger downward and placing the thumb on the hammer. Avoid any tendency to lift upward. Pivot the gun forward and downward, allowing the muzzle to rest on its plug until the cylinder is clear of the retaining spring. The gun should be cocked at the same time. Then toss the gun upward while the thumb falls into place at the side of the frame and the index finger engages the trigger.

Those who from years of use of an ordinary open top holster have acquired the habit of lifting the gun during the draw, can overcome this tendency by exerting a definite downward pressure on grasping the gun. This downward pressure practiced with the tipping forward process described above will soon develop a smooth, clean draw. Speed will come in a surprisingly short time with intelligent practise, and when it has been attained, it will be found that both the downward pressure and the tipping forward or slight pivoting motion will be performed unconsciously and so swiftly that neither will be noticed.

Double action revolvers may, of course, be drawn and fired without cocking by the thumb if for any reason the double action method of shooting is preferred.

If desired, a safety strap is furnished with these holsters; but they are so carefully fitted to the gun they are to hold that the strap is entirely unnecessary, and should be left off. However, when it is fitted it is made with a generous extension of strap beyond the snap-fastener, so that it can be unsnapped very quickly with a sharp forward stroke of the hand.

The Berns-Martin Speed Holster was built primarily to be the fastest possible holster on the draw, but it has advantages even when the owner is not interested in exceptional speed. It is particularly practical for long barreled guns, as they can be drawn as quickly as very short guns. Sights do not come into contact with the leather, and so will not wear bright, and sights which have been blackened for use on the pistol range will not have the blackening rubbed off.

Shoulder holsters which hang from the left shoulder so that the gun is carried under the arm are very popular. They have the great advantage that the gun is entirely out of sight and not noticeable when the coat is worn.

There are two kinds of shoulder holster; the pouch holster in which the gun slides down in to the holster from the top, and comes out the same way; and the spring holster, which is open down the front and has a leather covered spring to clasp the cylinder of the revolver and hold it in place. To remove the gun from the holster, it is jerked downward and forward, pulling it from the grasp of the retaining spring.

The pouch shoulder holster is rather slow on the draw, as the gun must be raised very high to get it out. Otherwise, it is very satisfactory. The spring shoulder holster is very much quicker on the draw, but is not well adapted to carry automatic pistols, as the spring does not grasp the flat slide with the same security that it does the cylinder of a revolver. Many spring shoulder holsters for automatics are seen, but they are sold to those who have had no experience with them and do not realize how unsatisfactory they are. The design of a good shoulder holster is something that requires brains, knowledge, and experience in carrying a gun. Most shoulder holsters are poorly designed. Among the important points are the strength and shape of the retaining spring. It should fit the cylinder securely enough to prevent all danger of having the gun fall from the holster when the wearer stoops over, or in any other conceivable circumstance yet it should be flexible enough to release the gun easily when it is pulled smartly forward.

Most shoulder holsters seen in stores have too stiff a spring. In some that I have tried, it is almost impossible to pull the gun from the holster by a straight forward pull. Again, many of these holsters are made so that they carry the gun too high, so that it bulges out to one side. The holster should be of such length that the gun is carried with the cylinder resting right in the hollow of the waist, where there is most room for it to lie without pushing the coat out from the body. To give the best results, the spring shoulder holster should be designed and made specifically for a given model of revolver with a given barrel length, and these particulars should be required by the maker when the order is received. A very fine spring shoulder holster is the one designed by Mr. Wm. T. Smith, of the Police Department of Edw. K. Tryon & Co., 910 Chestnut St., Philadelphia, from whom these holsters may be ordered for a very reasonable price.

A good way to carry a small revolver unobtrusively, and at the same time in such a manner that it can be drawn with the maximum of speed, is in an open top belt holster worn in front of the abdomen on the opposite side from the hand with which the gun is to be drawn. The gun is thus concealed under the coat and vest, but can be drawn with lightning like rapidity by lifting up the edge of the vest with the left hand and at the same time grasping the gun with the right. This is called the "cross-stomach" draw.

Carrying Cases

The target shot will often have to carry his guns back and forth from his home to the range or club, which most often is located in a town or city, and obviously he must have some receptacle for his guns and ammunition during these trips, for a revolver or pistol cannot be carried in the hands through the streets.

Occasionally this problem may be solved at the time cf the purchase of the weapon by the fact that several makers furnish cases for certain of their target arms, usually at an extra cost. For example, the Smith & Wesson Straight Line Pistol comes in a pressed steel case with a cleaning rod and a screw driver. Harrington & Richardson furnish an excellent carrying case for their U. S. R. A. Model pistol at an extra cost. This is a little trunk with a carrying handle on top, containing space for the pistol and ammunition, and the cleaning rod and cleaning materials as well. The gun is held in place by a strap around the barrel so that the sights cannot touch anything. This not only protects the sights from injury, or from wearing bright, but also allows them to be smoked or blacked with the assurance that the blackening will not be rubbed off.

Recently, (1934) the Hartmann Trunk Company, in collaboration with the National Rifle Association of America, designed two pistol carrying cases of different sizes that are ideal for the target shot.

These N. R. A.-Hartmann pistol cases are constructed just like the standard luggage regularly made by the Hartmann Trunk Company for travellers. The body blocks and compartments are of basswood, with the corners dovetailed and strongly locked. A hard washable lining is used for the interior to promote cleanliness and minimize absorption. Holding blocks for the arms to be used are covered with handsome velour. The outside cover is a tough grained imitation leather, which is hide-glued permanently in place. There are two nickeled snap catches which may be locked with a key. Under the handle is a very handsome and distinctive N. R. A. name plate which bears a separate registration number for each case. It is a very attractive piece of equipment from a practical standpoint, and it is handsome no matter by what standard it may be judged.

The smaller sized case is 12¾ inches long, 9 inches high, and three inches thick. It has an ammunition compartment designed to fit a box of .45 or .38 special cartridges and several boxes of .22s. Another compartment contains two screw top bottles for small parts, cleaning oil, etc. There is also a compartment for any one of the three best Wollensak pistol telescopes in 15 power, 20 power, or 25 power. There are two sets of clips for cleaning rods, swabs, and brushes. The holding blocks are designed for two pistols and revolvers, one of them being held in an inverted position. This case will accommodate any standard revolver with 6½ inch barrel or the H. & R. 7-inch barrel single shot pistol.

The larger case is made expressly to carry a ten inch barrel target pistol together with a revolver with extra long barrel. It is made in the same way and with the same construction as the smaller case, but with slightly larger dimensions to agree with the greater capacity of the case. It is 15 inches long, 13 inches high and 3 inches thick. The telescope compartment is made expressly for the Bausch & Lomb N. R. A. Junior model draw-tube spotting scope. The ammunition compartment is also larger than the one in the smaller case.

In either of these cases, the guns and shooting equipment are all kept assembled together and securely protected, ready for a shoot or a trip at any time by merely picking up the case without having to remember to bring various articles from different places with the attendant risk of forgetting some of them.

For those shooters who do not desire to go to the trouble of providing themselves with a special pistol case, I want to call attention to the fact that the ordinary leather brief case will serve the same purpose fairly well. These cases are usually divided into three compartments by leather partitions; thus two or more guns may be carried in such a brief case without danger of their being marred from rubbing together. Targets, ammunition, cleaning rod and screw-driver may also be carried in the same case. While the brief case does very well, it has the disadvantage that everything gravitates to the bottom, and the guns are not held so that the sights are protected. On the other hand, an advantage is the fact that the brief case is not conspicuous, and no one would suppose that a gun was being carried, which is desirable, for a gun even in a case, always attracts notice and causes comment in the large cities.

Among the articles that should be carried in the shooting case are screwdrivers and cartridge blocks. A screwdriver to fit the screws of the adjustable sights on target pistols and revolvers is a necessity, and no user of a target pistol should go on the rifle range without the proper screwdriver for his gun, yet it is a fact that very often when a shooter finds it necessary to change his sights during a shoot, he holds up the entire proceedings and makes a nuisance of himself by going around from one to another of his fellow shooters trying to borrow a screwdriver, and as often as not finding that the one he can borrow is made to fit some other make of gun and will not go into the slots on the screws of his sights.

Cartridge blocks are simply pieces of wood with holes drilled in them for holding ten or twenty-five cartridges. In shooting a match with single shot pistols, the necessity of keeping a mental count of the number of shots fired is avoided by placing the correct number of cartridges in the block. Then when they are all gone, the right number has been fired. Some cartridge blocks made in the form of a little box of just the right size to hold two boxes of .22 caliber cartridges. The box has a sliding lid, with ten holes drilled in it, each hole being of the proper size to hold one .22 cartridge.

Another thing that should be in the shooting case of all pistol shooters who shoot outdoors is material for blackening the sights. The metal surface of the sights will shine in some lights, even if the metal is blued. This effect is particularly noticeable if the sights are oily, and is much worse when they have been worn shiny by rubbing on a holster, or from wear of any kind. In some lights it will be impossible to define the sights at all unless this shine is removed, and in any case, shooting outdoors is made much easier by taking away the glare and giving the sights a uniform dull black surface. This is ordinarily done by smoking the sights with a match, a candle, or a piece of camphor, which is excellent for giving a velvety black surface, or by painting them with a solution of lampblack in some very volatile fluid such as gasoline. Dealers in target shooting supplies sell sight blackening solution in a small bottle with a brush in the cork for a few cents. It is a very practical thing to carry such a bottle always in the shooting kit. Matches and a candle will give a better finish on the sights, but often on the range the wind will prevent their use, while the bottle of sight black will always work. It is not necessary to blacken the sights for indoor shooting, where nearly all the illumination comes from the target itself, for in this case the sights are like dark shadows silhouetted against a light background.

For indoor shooting with large caliber guns, some protection should always be provided for the ears, and while this protection is not essential outdoors, it is still desirable, for there is no use needlessly risking a permanent injury to the hearing. Ordinary absorbent cotton makes the best ear protector. There are a number of patent ear protectors on the market that work well, but they are no more effective than the cotton, and they are not as sanitary, as they are used over and over, while the cotton is used just once and then thrown away. A small roll of absorbent cotton which can be obtained from any druggist is all that is needed, and it should be in every shooting kit.

Cleaning Material

The most important single item of cleaning material is the cleaning rod, which is a steel, brass, or wooden rod used to carry a rag or cleaning patch with which the inside of the barrel is wiped out after shooting.

The cleaning rod must be of the proper size to fit the caliber of gun that it is to be used with. In other words, the .22 caliber cleaning rod is not suitable for cleaning the .38 or .45 caliber arms. However, when rods have detachable tips which screw on, a .32 or .38 caliber rod will do for cleaning larger caliber arms, provided the proper tip is used on the rod.

Every gun when sold has a cleaning rod of some kind packed with it, though usually these gift rods are next thing to useless. Generally they are simply a piece of wire with a slot in one end.

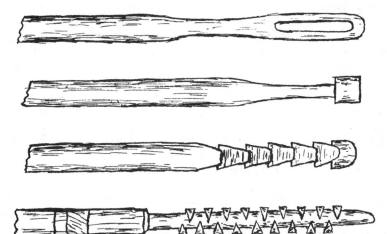

Common forms of cleaning rod. Top, the slotted rod, which is a poor shape for thorough cleaning, but is the most often seen because it is easy to use. Second, the button tipped rod. This is a good type, with much to commend it. Third, home-made rod constructed from No. 11 drill rod by filing four sets of teeth on the end. The teeth on two sides point back; these on the other two sides point forward. Bottom, the Parker Tru-form Jag, used with a special oblong patch which is rolled around the brass jag to form a tightly fitting cylinder of cloth which does an excellent job of cleaning.

A rag can be drawn through the slot and be used to swab out the barrel. Undoubtedly the use of a rag in a slotted cleaning rod is far better than no cleaning, for at least a coating of oil can be applied with it; but thorough and satisfactory cleaning can not be done with it. What is needed is a rod with a tip which nearly fits the barrel, and which will carry a canton flannel patch in such a manner that the patch will be pressed firmly against all parts of the bore as the tip of the rod passes through.

A common and very satisfactory form of cleaning rod is a steel or brass rod nearly as large as the bore, with a reduced diameter for a short space near the end, so that the end itself forms a button tip for holding a cloth patch. This and several other forms of cleaning rod are shown in the sketch.

With this button shaped tip, a round or square canton flannel or outing flannel patch is used, and the patch must be of such a size that it is just possible to force the rod into the barrel, with no difficulty when the tip of the rod is covered with the patch. It is most important to get the patch the right size, for if it is too loose, it will not wipe the bore clean, and if it is too tight, there will be too much friction, and the rod may pierce the patch and become jammed.

The main disadvantage of the button tipped rod is the likelihood of having the rod pierce the patch and jam in the bore. If the rod is of brass, it may be difficult to remove, but will not harm the barrel, but if it is of steel, an attempt to remove it may cause the cloth to pile up under one side of the rod and jam there more tightly than ever, thus forcing the sharp edge of the button against the other side of the barrel, so that it will have a tendency to scrape. I have seen a barrel badly marred by such an accident, so if a steel rod becomes jammed in your barrel, use great care to avoid forcing it unduly.

A very satisfactory home made cleaning rod that was much used in the Springfield Revolver Club at the time that I was a member of that organization consists of a piece of No. 11 drill rod, (which is .191 inch in diameter), with the end filed so as to make a number of saw-toothed notches, those on two sides pointing backwards, those on the other sides pointing forward. The extreme end is rounded. When an outing flannel patch one inch square is used with this rod, it is a snug fit, and will do an excellent job of cleaning. The saw teeth on the end of the rod hold the patch firmly in both directions, so that it can be scrubbed back and forth in the barrel as much as desired without coming off. The saw teeth cannot touch the rifling, for the rounded end of the rod in front of the teeth and the main body of the rod behind them are both higher than these teeth. The rod is fastened in a wooden handle, and is made just the right length so that it projects through the muzzle about a quarter of an inch when the handle strikes on the breech. Thus the rod cannot be pushed far enough through the barrel for the patch to come off, and with the barrel held firmly in a cleaning vise, the rod can be scrubbed back and forth through the entire length of the barrel without having to stop every time the rod goes through. I have bought most of the fancy cleaning rods on the market, but have never seen one any easier to use or more effective than this one.

Perhaps the best cleaning rods and attachments for them obtainable commercially are those made by A. G. Parker, Ltd., of Birmington, England. The rods are made in different calibers as desired, and are covered with a celluloid outer coating to prevent wear or injury to the barrel. The handles of the rods are made so that they can rotate, and are mounted on ball bearings so that the patch can follow the rifling when the rod is pushed through the barrel. Different styles of tip are furnished to screw on the end of the rod. A good style of tip is that known as Parker's Truform Jag. It is a brass rod with two sets of spiral grooves cut in it, the spirals being in opposite directions, so that the spaces between them form little raised diamonds of brass. To use this tip, specially made oblong patches of outing flannel sold by the makers of the rod are employed. When a patch is wrapped around the Truform Jag it makes a cylinder of cloth which just fills up the bore, and does an excellent job of cleaning. In the ordinary button tip rod, the patch is laid over the end of the rod, and then the outer portions or skirt of the patch have to fold over irregularly when the rod is pushed into the barrel. In this Parker Truform Jag the case is entirely different, for the patch does not go over the end of the rod at all but wraps around the jag in a neat cylinder which is just a tight fit in the bore.

Besides other styles of tip, there are various kinds of brush, of either bristle or brass wire that may be obtained to screw on to the Parker Rods. Wool mops or swabs for greasing may also be obtained. Altogether these Parker rods and their attachments are to be highly recommended, as everything needed for cleaning the gun, removing lead, oiling or greasing, etc., can be obtained in one outfit and at a very reasonable price.

As mentioned above, the size of the canton flannel or outing flannel patches used is very important, and when the Parker Rods and jags are used, it is extremely convenient to purchase the patches ready cut. These Parker accessories may be purchased from several large dealers in target practice material in this country, such as for example, P. J. O'Hare of Maplewood, N. J., who stocks nearly every shooting accessory that is used at all, whether it is made in America or abroad.

Besides ready cut patches for rods such as the Parker, it is well for the shooter to keep on hand a yard or so of outing flannel for use in making up patches when odd sizes are needed for special purposes. It is also very good to use for wiping cloths to remove perspiration. A small square of outing flannel into which a little light oil has been rubbed should be kept in a glass jar for use in wiping guns before laying them away. This will remove perspira-

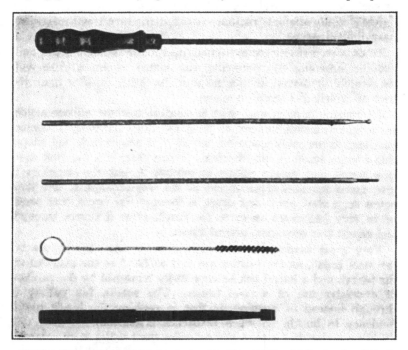

Cleaning Rods. Upper, Jointed rod for .22 rifle Middle, bristle brush, which is useful for hasty cleaning with nitro-solvent. Bottom, Bair cleaning rod made of walnut. This rod is excellent for thorough cleaning, when used with a patch of the proper size. It is made in various calibers, the one shown being for the .45 automatic. The length of the rod is such that the patch can be pushed just to the end of the barrel, but not all the way through. This makes it easy to clean thoroughly by scrubbing backwards and forwards.

tion and will deposit a film of oil on the guns which will preserve the finish and prevent rust.

In cutting patches from outing flannel or canton flannel, it is well to remember that the proper size for the patch to make it fit the cleaning rod correctly will depend on the thickness of the cloth. A thicker cloth will have to be cut into smaller patches, and if the cloth is thinner, the patches must be made larger.

Brushes of various kinds are indispensible for the proper and convenient care of firearms. Bristle brushes are useful for scrubbing out the barrel with nitro-solvent, chloroil, or the like, before using patches. They are also useful for applying grease to the inside of the barrel and cylinder, and to various corners such as the part of the frame just forward of the cylinder, where the rear end of the barrel projects through. There are little cracks at such points that are very difficult to be sure of reaching with a greasy cloth, whereas just one stroke of the brush will reach the most difficult parts.

Brass wire brushes are extremely useful for removing lead and also for loosening and removing rust spots. A brass brush will not scratch the barrel, for the metal of the brush is softer than the steel of which the barrel is made.

All gunsmiths have steel wire brushes of various calibers which are a tight fit inside the bore of the gun. They are used to remove rust, etc., from badly corroded barrels that are in such bad shape that a brass brush is not effective. When there is a bad rust spot in a barrel that resists efforts to remove it, put the barrel in a vise, run a threaded cleaning rod all the way through it, and then screw on a steel brush and draw in through the barrel just once, or in very bad cases unscrew the brush after it comes through and repeat this operation several times.

Very great moderation and care must be used in the use of the steel brush, as the bristles are just as hard as the material of the barrel, and a barrel can be very badly scratched by the careless or excessive use of a steel brush. The reason for pulling it through instead of pushing, is that in pushing the brush has a tendency to buckle up when resistence is encountered, and this buckling action has a tendency to make the bristles stick into the steel and thus scratch; whereas if the brush is pulled through, the bristles slant back in the direction from which they came and drag over the surface without any tendency to stick in. For the same reason, a steel brush should not be scrubbed back and forth, or used with a reciprocating motion, as the bristles which had slanted back due to the forward pull would catch in the metal and scratch as soon as the motion were reversed.

Shooting Glasses

Shooters with defective vision will naturally do better shooting if they are properly fitted with glasses by a qualified oculist; but quite aside from the question of defective eyesight, glasses of various kinds for protecting the eyes as well as for permitting the target to be more clearly seen in certain lights are very useful.

As for the question of protection, shooting glasses are a factor of safety in shooting any kind of weapon, but especially a high powered rifle, for occasionally the firing pin will puncture the primer and some gas under high pressure will escape to the rear, and this usually is very painful to the shooter's eye. Then again, in pistol shooting the head of a rim fire cartridge may burst and allow gas to escape in the same way. While this is not so dangerous with the pistol as it is with the rifle, because the pistol shooter's eyes are further away, protection to the eyes gives a very comfortable feeling of assurance, and sometimes results in bettering the scores through the removal of a possible cause of flinching.

This is even more important when a revolver is being used, and especially if others on the same firing line are also using revolvers, for if the cylinders do not line up correctly, shaving of lead may result from failure of the bullets to enter the barrel squarely. This shaving of lead may cause fine particles to fly back into the faces of shooters on the firing line. I have known a spectator at Camp Perry who was standing six feet back of the firing line to be quite sharply stung by particles thrown off by a newly designed model revolver which the manufacturer had brought to the range for a tryout.

Then there is the question of bright glaring light as found on some rifle and pistol ranges. Shooting in very glaring lights is hard on the eyes, as it causes the pupils to become contracted and renders it difficult to see the sights and the bull's-eye clearly and in detail. It may also give the shooter a headache.

For these reasons every shooter should be equipped with a pair of tinted glasses that will cut down the glare; and in order to furnish the maximum of protection from both the light and from foreign materials, these glasses should be of large size. There are a large number of different kinds of shooting glasses to choose from. King's "Rifleite" glasses may be mentioned as having very remarkable qualities. They have a brilliant yellow color that has the peculiarity of making the black of the bull's-eye seem even blacker and more clearly visible, while still protecting the eye from excessive glare. The reason for this is that the color in the glass cuts down the volume of the light that gets through; but at the same time what it does let through is the part of the spectrum to which the eye is most sensitive; in other words, in which the visibility is the greatest. It is a peculiar thing that if these glasses are put on in the deep dusk things are seen as easily as without them; they do not reduce the visibility. But approaching automobile headlights lose much of their glare when viewed through these glasses. For this reason I find them of even greater use for driving an automobile at night than for shooting.

These glasses may be obtained either plain or with a prescription ground into the lenses. It goes without saying that if the intending purchaser of a pair of these glasses has any defect of eyesight, he should have his own prescription ground into the lenses. Like the other accessories mentioned in this book, these glasses may be obtained from the dealers in shooter's supplies.

Orthoptic Discs

The orthoptic sight is the name given to the rear sight with a disc having a small hole in the center through which the sighting is done. In target shooting circles the name "orthoptic disc," "orthoptic spectacles," etc., is given to such discs worn on the spectacles or near the eye of the shooter, without being actually attached to the gun as is a peep sight.

Devices of this nature have been becoming more and more used in the last few years. They are based on the optical principle that it is much easier for the eye to accommodate itself to different distances if the field of view is restricted to a small pencil of rays where not much correction is needed, just the same as a camera has much sharper definition for different distances when a small stop or diaphragm is used.

When a pistol shooter aims at the target, he makes an effort to see three objects at the same time which are at different distances; namely, the rear sight, the front sight, and the bull's-eye. This is an impossibility, for when the eye is focussed properly for the bull's-eye twenty yards away, it cannot see the sights clearly; and when it is focussed for the front sight three feet from the eye, it will not be able to see clearly the rear sight ten inches closer, for as the distance from the eye diminishes, the accommodation required becomes increasingly difficult, so that there is almost as much change in focus between the rear sight and the front sight as there is between the front sight and the target.

What the eye actually does in this case is to focus first on one of these three points, then on another, so that the attention of the mind and the focus of the eyes is constantly shifting from one sight to the other and to the target, and then back again. These changes occur unconsciously and with such rapidity that the shooter thinks he sees all three points at the same time; but this is an illusion caused by the rapidity with which the action takes place.

As the eye ages, its ability for rapid changes in accommodation diminishes, and it gets harder and harder for the shooter to see the sights and the bull's-eye clearly; but by placing a diaphragm with a small hole in it in front of the eye so as to cut out all but a small pencil of rays, this condition is remedied, and both the bull's-eye and the sights can be seen more clearly, and the amount of accommodation required of the eye is reduced.

Devices for this purpose take various forms, to suit the ideas and personal convenience of the user, or of the designers or makers of such articles for sale. Some years ago Mr. Paul Van Asbroek of Holland, twice winner of the International Pistol Matches for the Championship of the World, who was at that time more than 60 years old, was using a disc with a pinhole in it suspended from his hatband so that it hung in front of his shoot-

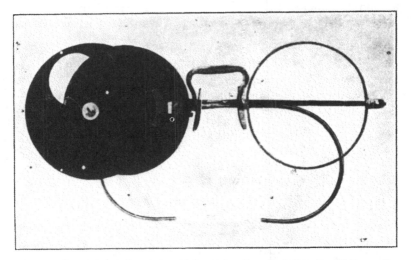

The Universal Aperture Spectacle. The revolving disc attached to the shield covering the right eye contains several small holes in different positions, to accommodate different positions of shooting. By sighting through one of these holes, marksmen with failing eyesight are enabled to see both the sights and the target clearly.

ing eye. Other well known shooters have suspended a disc from the hatband. At the Eastern Smallbore Tournament at Camp Ritchie, Maryland, in the summer of 1934, Mr. Ray Bracken of Columbus, Ohio, was using a very simple and effective device of this kind consisting of a small black celluloid disc about an inch in diameter with a clip to fit over the top of a spectacle frame. A hole about .05 inch in diameter is drilled in this disc, to coincide in location or align with the pupil of the sighting eye when aiming. Any optometrist or optician should be able to supply these optical shields from stock for a very small sum.

There is a very carefully designed and well made appliance of this nature on the market, which is sold by the designer, Henry P. Jones, M. E., of Burlington, Vermont. It consists of a pair of spectacle frames without glass, together with a blank metal disc which fastens on either right or left eye-frame by means of clips. This disc has a large aperture, ¾ of an inch in diameter in the center; mounted on this disc so that it can be rotated is a second disc, which has not only a ¾ inch aperture, like the first disc, but also several .05 inch holes in different locations. When the two large holes are together, the shooter can see as though he did not have the appliance on. It is worn this way for walking around the range, loading, scoring targets, etc.; but when the user is ready to commence shooting, a quarter of a turn of the

Wright's Eyesight Compensator. This device consists of a cup-shaped disc of sheet metal fitted with a spring clip to attach it to the rim of the user's spectacles. This small hole through which the sights are viewed acts like the diaphragm of a camera lens and clears up the image of the sights and bull's-eye.

overlapping disc brings one of the small holes over the pupil of the eye, and the only view that can be had is through this small hole, which sharpens up the images of both sights and of the bull's-eye until they can all be seen clearly. As remarked above, the overlapping disc has several of the small holes in it, in different locations for different uses. The one nearest the center is used for pistol shooting; but when shooting the rifle **prone, a** hole is brought into position which is near the edge of the frame, at the top. This appliance works very successfully, and is a wonderful help to the shooter whose eyes have lost part of their accommodation.

Another attachment to the eyeglasses for the same purpose is Wright's Eye-sight Compensator, made and sold by W. A. Wright of 1223 Lifur Ave., Los Angeles. It is a little cup-shaped disc of metal with a .05 inch hole in the center, and a clip on one side to fit over the edge of the eye-glass frame. This device does not take up the entire eye-glass lens, but covers only a part of it, so that the user can see quite well with it in place by looking around instead of through it. When both eyes are used in walking around, etc., the user is hardly aware that the device is on his glasses; but when he raises his gun to aim, it is in place, ready to use.

Telescopes

Another optical aid to the target shooter is the spotting telescope. During the progress of a match, the only way the shooter can know what he is doing and where his shots are going and how they are grouping is by inspecting his target from time to time by the aid of a range telescope.

A glass for this use must be of sufficient power and definition to clearly show .22 caliber bullet holes at 50 yards. A suitable telescope, magnifying objects twenty times, is the new Wollensak Spotting Telescope, which retails for the very reasonable sum of $10.50. The 15 power scope, which is also very satisfactory sells for $8.50.

Bausch & Lomb have designed a rifle range telescope called the N.R.A. Model, which gives excellent definition and a beautiful wide field of view. It is a prismatic telescope, which is made short and compact, as it does not draw out as do the non-prismatic glasses. It will give beautiful results on either the rifle range or the pistol range, but it is a better and more expensive glass than is necessary for pistol work alone. The rifleman who owns one of these glasses and happens to be a pistol shot also has in his equipment as fine a spotting telescope for either rifle or pistol work as could be desired.

A less expensive telescope by the same firm, which is amply satisfactory for any and all requirements of the pistol range is the Bausch & Lomb draw tube N.R.A. Junior Model.

Special Grips

The pistol shooter is never satisfied with the grip of his gun, and he has a good reason for his lack of satisfaction, for little or no care was given to the design of this most important item until very lately, when Walter Roper induced Harrington & Richardson not only to bring out a single shot pistol and a .22 Revolver with the best grip seen in years, but also to furnish a whole series of five different grips which are quickly interchangeable to fit the ideas and whims of any and every different type of shooter.

The universal search for a better grip is seen in the fact that there are at the present time several different gunsmiths and others who advertise and sell special grips for this and that arm, to overcome various and sundry difficulties of holding and shooting.

One of the greatest troubles with the modern revolver grip has been the deep and narrow space behind the trigger guard, into which the second finger is supposed to fit. If this space is partly filled up, the grip is steadier and more comfortable. For many years the shooters have been filling this space with wooden blocks, pieces of rubber, or other material, usually held on by adhesive tape wrapped around the grip and the filler, or "gadget," as it is often called.

Recently there have appeared on the market a number of first class well designed factory made filler pieces, that look well on a gun, as though they belonged on it to begin with, (which some of them do).

The Harrington & Richardson U.S.R.A. Model Single Shot Pistol and Sportsman Revolver both have the trigger guard constructed with a portion of it extending back in the form of a spur that bridges over the gap behind the trigger guard and forms a metal surface to rest on the middle finger and thus support the gun.

Smith & Wesson make a grip adapter for their .44, .45, and .38/44. It consists of two metal plates which fit between the frame and the walnut grips. The upper part of each of these plates extends beyond the grips and across to the trigger guard, so as to bridge the space behind the trigger guard. Between the two ends of the plates which extend across to the trigger guard there is a rubber filler plate held in place by a screw. This adapter greatly improves the handle of the large caliber Smith & Wesson revolvers.

The Iver Johnson firm has recently brought out a new finger rest in the form of a spur of blued steel fastened to the back strap of the grip frame by a screw. This spur extends forward and bridges the gap between the frame and the trigger guard.

The hole for the screw is slotted so that the spur may be moved up or down about a quarter of an inch to accommodate hands of different sizes.

Another filler for this space which is made for any Colt or Smith & Wesson Revolver or single shot target pistol except the Smith & Wesson Straight Line Pistol and the Safety Hammerless Revolver is the Sure Grip Adapter made by Frank Pachmayr of Los Angeles, and sold by most sporting goods dealers. It consists of a moulded soft rubber adapter curved to fit the space

The Pachmayr Adapter. This device, made in three sizes, as shown, is used to fill part of the space behind the trigger guard so that the hand can take a more natural and less cramped position on the handle of the revolver. It is a practical and very convenient accessory.

behind the trigger guard and in front of the grip, and held in place by two spring clips of metal moulded into the rubber. To attach the adapter, the grip screw is loosened, and the clips are slipped between the wooden grips and the frame of the gun, after which the grip screw is tightened, and the adapter is held firmly in place.

These adapters are made in a special individual shape for each of many Colt and Smith & Wesson guns on which they can be fitted. It is necessary therefore to specify what gun is to be fitted when ordering one of these adapters. For each gun there are three different sizes or thicknesses of adapter made, large, medium and small. For the average man the medium size will usually be the most desirable; while for very large hands the small size adapter will be the most comfortable, and for very small hands the large adapter is the most suitable.

Notes on Constructing Ranges

In constructing an outdoor pistol range great care must be used in two particulars. The first and most important one is to be sure that the range is located in a safe position, so that there will be no danger of stray bullets doing any damage. With a great many people shooting on a pistol range there is always a possibility that a wild shot may occur. One or two incidents in which a shot from a pistol club's range got away and did some damage would generally suffice to have the club closed up; therefore, it is of paramount importance that this should never happen. The very best way to insure this safety is to have the range where there is some natural obstacle that will stop any stray bullets. The best natural obstacle is, of course, a hill; next to this is an old abandoned quarry.

Another important consideration is light. On a pistol range the targets should be where the light is as steady as possible, and they should never be located so that the sun will shine directly on them if it can be avoided. The best location for a rifle range is in a north and south direction, with the targets at the north end of the range. At the firer's end of the range there should be a shelter constructed so that shooting can be done in rainy weather and also to prevent undue disturbance by wind. There should be a railing or fence extending along in front of the firing line with tables or shelves on which to lay the ammunition and guns.

The range should be carefully laid out and measured so that the fence or railing at the firing line is 50 yards from the point where the targets are hung, and in order to avoid the records ever being questioned an inch or two should be added to this measurement to make sure that there is no possibility of anyone ever claiming that the range is shorter than the standard.

As an example of the unexpected things that may happen in this regard, the following incident that happened in connection with the Dewar Match of 1931 is related. The author was the American witness of the British firing at the famous Ham and Petersham Rifle Range near London. Before firing the match, it is the duty of the witnesses to see that all the match conditions are correct, and to certify to that fact. This involves measuring the range with a steel tape; but as the firing was to be conducted on a regularly laid out range with everything permanently installed, this seemed entirely superfluous, the same as it would to measure the thousand yard range at Camp Perry with a tape measure before each match. But Lieut. General Sir Alfred Codrington, the British witness, with characteristic British thoroughness produced a steel tape and proceeded to measure the range for my verification, and to our utter astonishment, the range seemed to be short! We could not believe that we could be right, so that we repeated the measurement twice, and then got a different tape and tried again, but with the same result. The range was nearly two feet short. The explanation was that some new style target frames had just been installed, and they projected two feet further toward the firing point than the old ones.

At the target end it is highly desirable to have some stop for the bullets behind each target. Generally old boiler plates are available, and if these are placed behind the target, sloping downward and away from the target, all bullets will be deflected down toward the ground. This is better than putting them upright behind the targets, because heavy lead bullets striking the targets have a tendency to splatter and the pieces will cut the targets. Another very good form of backstop is a mass of wood built up behind the targets out of old railroad ties or similar beams, end-on to the line of fire. In any event, the backstop should extend far enough around the target so that there is no danger of a bullet striking on the edge of the backstop, as this might cause it to be deflected from the line of fire and go in some direction where it might do damage.

The most convenient thing at the target end is to have a deep target pit with target frames that can be lowered into the pit and new targets put on and raised again for firing, but this is generally too complicated for a local club, and usually the best that can be done is to construct a good safe backstop and put up clamps or other means of holding the targets in place. Then the shooters can walk down to the end of the 50-yard target range and examine the targets and put up new ones, or, in case of matches, this can be done by others to avoid the shooter performing this extra exertion between match strings.

Very much the same applies to an indoor pistol gallery; but the problem here is much easier because the range is shorter. A pistol gallery requires 20 yards between the firing point and the target.

Generally there is a partition put up at the firing point which should be an inch or so more than 20 yards from the target holders. This partition has holes or shooting windows put in it, and the contestants stand as near the partition as they desire and shoot through the windows or openings at the targets, which are hung at the distant end of the gallery. There should be a shelf on which to lay the pistol and ammunition, and it is highly desirable to have brackets on which the telescope can be laid for observing the targets between shots.

Most pistol galleries are arranged with traveling target carriers consisting of a cord going over a pair of wheels, one at the firing point and one at the distant end of the range. This cord carries a metal clamp for holding the target, and by turning the wheel at the firing point this clamp travels toward the shooter. When it is at the near end of the range, the old target is taken down and the new target hung in the clamp; then by turning the wheel the target is caused to travel down the range until it comes to a stop 20 yards from the firing point, and when it is against this stop it is also in the circle of illumination because, as stated above, the lighting in an indoor gallery, as in the U. S. R. A. rules, must be done by artificial light.

The far, or target end, of the pistol gallery should be lined with boiler plate sufficiently thick to stop a revolver bullet. It is also highly desirable that the ceiling and the walls of the range be bullet proof. This is very easily accomplished in many places by building the pistol gallery in the basement of a large building. In many of the large modern buildings the walls and ceiling of the basement are likely to be of heavy concrete which would turn a pistol bullet.

It is highly desirable at the firing point to have a boiler plate partition extending backward several feet between each firing point, so that if an accidental discharge should ever occur in loading a pistol, or otherwise, there would be no danger of one of the contestants accidentally injuring the one next to him.

Illumination in pistol galleries is best accomplished by placing a row of electric lights in front of and below the targets. The lights should have reflectors which will throw the light up onto the targets and should be placed behind a long narrow ledge of steel or of concrete which will serve the dual purpose of protecting the lights from stray shots and at the same time hide the lights from the shooter so that the range is in total darkness except for the light reflected from the targets themselves, which, being the only source of light in the range, stand out prominently and thus are most easily seen for aiming. There should, however, be provision for light at the firing points. Firing points are, according to the rules, to be either illuminated or left in darkness at the designation of the shooter. Some people get the best results in target shooting indoors by having no light at all except that which is reflected on the targets. Others like to have enough at the firing point to be able to see their sights. Under any circumstances there must be enough illumination at the firing point for the witnesses to be able to see that the rules are observed and that the shooting is done without any support of any kind.

Improvised Ranges

Besides the regular rifle ranges at organized clubs a great deal of shooting at targets is done by individuals on improvised ranges of their own. At one time when the author was living in Florida he measured off 25 yards from a large pine tree in the back yard, and every day he used to tack a target on this tree and shoot at it with various revolvers and pistols and often .22 rifles. The tree acted as a backstop for the bullets, and if anything missed the backstop there was no danger as there was nothing but a large forest extending for many miles around. After some months of shooting there was a hole in the tree behind the target about four or five inches in diameter and nearly a foot deep, with a mass of lead at the back and at the bottom of the tree quite a pile of lead that had dropped down.

Bullet Stops

A very useful accessory for those who have a cellar or basement with sufficient space for a pistol range is the combined target holder and bullet stop. This is a funnel shaped device of steel, with the mouth of the funnel large enough to extend beyond the edges of the twenty-yard pistol target. At the small end, the funnel curves, so as to deflect bullets entering it, and thus stop them. The K-B backstop is a rectangular funnel of steel that curves downward at the back so as to deflect the bullets down into vertical section. The X-Ring centrifugal bullet trap is a rectangular funnel with the small end curving around in a small spiral. The bullet in going around this spiral loses all of its velocity, and drops into a tin can which is fastened over a hole in the center. This makes it easy to remove the lead for re-melting.

There is a clip for holding a target, and also a bracket with a socket for an electric lamp to illuminate the target. The lamp and target clip are both protected by steel plates to deflect any wild shots. These bullet stops are made in several different sizes, to suit the various ranges and calibers with which they may be used.

Trigger Weights

Every club or range must be equipped with trigger weights, for the rules allow only a certain minimum trigger pull, and require that it be tested before each match. The minimum for single shot pistols under the U. S. Revolver Association Rules is 2 pounds; for "Any Revolver" it is 2½ pounds; and for military and pocket revolvers it is 3½ pounds. The trigger weights should be arranged to test these pulls, and it is well to have several additional pound and half pound weights that may be added to test heavier pulls.

The trigger weight is a lead weight with a steel rod attached to it, with a hook on the end of the rod. The rules require that in weighing the pull, the barrel of the weapon will be held vertical. The common method of measuring the pull is to rest the weight on the bench, and, with the pistol cocked and the barrel of it held in the hand in a vertical position, to hook the trigger under the hook on the weight, and then lift gently upward. If the weight can be lifted from the bench without causing the hammer to fall, the trigger weighs within the rules.

Ordinarily the steel lifting rod and hook are attached to a piece of lead of such a size that both the lead and the rod and hook attached to it weigh exactly 2 pounds. This is the basic trigger weight which is used for single shot pistols. An additional lead weight of ½ pound can be slipped on the rod for "Any Revolver," and still another of one pound for the "Military Revolver."

Sub-Caliber Adapters For Pistols and Revolvers

The greatest drawback to obtaining a sufficient amount of practice with the larger caliber pistols or revolvers is the cost of the ammunition. In order to be able to shoot the guns a reasonable amount without spending too much money, the marksman formerly had to depend on some kind of an auxiliary chamber or barrel liner of smaller caliber, which would enable the inexpensive .22 caliber ammunition to be used. The importance of such devices has declined somewhat in recent years, for many of the more popular large caliber guns have exact counterparts in .22 arms of the same size and pattern, such as for example, the Colt Officer's Model, the Smith & Wesson Model K-.22, the Colt Ace, and others. However, for the man who does not care to spend as much money as these arms cost, there are a number of adapters to be had, and some of them will be briefly described below.

The Webley "Aiming Tube," supplied for the .455 revolver is a .22 caliber barrel having its own extractor in an enlarged breech section. It fits into the barrel of the hinged-frame or tip-up action revolver after the cylinder is removed to make room for the attachment. As the hammer nose of the revolver is intended for center fire cartridges, it strikes directly in line with the center of the bore when the hammer is snapped. This introduces a difficulty, for the .22 cartridge used in the adapter must be struck on the edge; to accomplish this, it is necessary for the barrel of the adapter to be bored off-center, so that the edge of the .22 caliber cartridge will come in line with the striker on the hammer.

Another trouble in designing such an attachment is a tendency to shoot low, owing to the light recoil and the consequent absence of "jump" in the weapon at the instant of recoil. As the regular sights point the revolver low to compensate for the jump, the sub-caliber tube will shoot too low unless it has its own sights. The Webley adapter therefore has its own rear sight, which sits above that of the gun.

The Webley Aiming Tube converts the revolver into a single shot .22 caliber pistol. However, there is another attachment, made by A. G. Parker, Ltd., which has a barrel which goes inside of the barrel of the gun, and also has its own .22 caliber cylinder which goes onto the cylinder spindle in place of the .455 cylinder. This attachment converts the .455 into a six-shot .22 caliber revolver.

The importance of both these attachments is somewhat reduced by the fact that Messrs. Webley & Scott now supply a .22 caliber target revolver of the same size and general pattern of the Mark VI .455 Service revolver, and of the same weight when loaded, which of course forms the very best practice arm for the .455.

For automatic pistols of large caliber, it is quite easy to design a sub-caliber adapter, and several are on the market. Before the advent of the Colt Ace, the author made quite extensive use of a sub-caliber barrel for the .45 Automatic made by R. F. Sedgeley, of Philadelphia. This shot the .22 long rifle cartridge, and like the Webley adapter, it had to be bored off-center to bring the firing pin onto the edge of the cartridge rim. But no auxiliary sight is necessary, as the barrel is bored to compensate for the lack of recoil and jump. This device converts the .45 automatic into a single shot .22. It is designed so that the regular extractor of the .45 pulls out the empty .22 case as the slide is drawn back, but this feature does not always work, so that it is best to be armed with a ram-rod. Moreover, it is somewhat difficult to insert the .22 cartridge into the chamber of the device; but altogether it is very satisfactory, considering the low price.

Just before the advent of the Ace Pistol, A. F. Stoeger of New

York introduced an attachment to convert the .45 automatic into a convenient and accurate single shot .22 pistol. The device, called the "Stoeger .22 caliber attachment for the .45 Government Model or Super. 38" is made to replace the barrel and slide of the regular gun, which are removed to allow the attachment to be pinned onto the frame in their place. The device has a tip-up barrel, with an extractor that pushes out the empty .22 caliber case as the barrel is tipped up to load. It has its own sights as a matter of course, for the regular sights are removed with the slide preparatory to putting the device in place. It is convenient and pleasant to use, but allows single shots only, and quite naturally, the advent of the Ace pistol just after this device was marketed was a severe handicap to its popularity, as many prospective users of such a device would prefer to pay the extra amount and obtain the Ace pistol with which rapid fire practice can be had, and this is especially true as rapid fire is one of the most important features of any match with the automatic.

At the present time there is on the market at a reasonable price a .22 caliber "Insert Assembly and Accessories" for converting the Luger Automatic Pistol into a .22 caliber automatic. This consists of a separate barrel, breech block, and magazine. The .22 caliber barrel is inserted into the regular barrel, and the special .22 breech block and magazine replace the regular breech block and magazine. The new breech block carries its own sight. The attachment is supplied for either the .30 caliber or the 9 mm. Lugers.

While it is easy to produce a sub-caliber attachment for the automatic pistol or the tip-up barrel revolver, it is quite another matter to supply a satisfactory device of this kind for the solid-frame revolvers, such as the modern Colt and Smith & Wesson Arms. However, Mr. Albert Noel, of Barcelona, Spain, recently gave the author an opportunity to do some extensive shooting and experimenting with an adapter for the Colt Police Positive Special .38, and another of similar design for the .45 Colt New Service. These adapters are made for the tiny 4 mm. center fire cartridge, which is nothing more than a center-fire primer with a No. 1 shot (.16 inch diameter) attached. There is no powder charge.

These little cartridges look very much like a shotgun primer, being .373 long overall, by .187 in diameter, with the front part necked down to take the .16 diameter ball. There is no rim, and the fact that the rear part is larger stops the little cartridge from going all the way into the chamber. When it comes to extracting, the difficulty is that there is no rim, but a single shot pistol in this caliber has an extractor, which is simply the bottom part of the chamber that is pushed back by the extractor rod, and as the front part of the movable segment of the chamber fits the reduced diameter, pushing back the rod forces out the case. In Mr. Noel's adapters there is no extractor, and the empty is forced out with a rod.

The weight of this little cartridge was determined by trial as 15 grains complete, the ball weighing 7 grains.

These little cartridges are quite popular abroad, as they cost only a small fraction of the cost of the .22, and they are practically

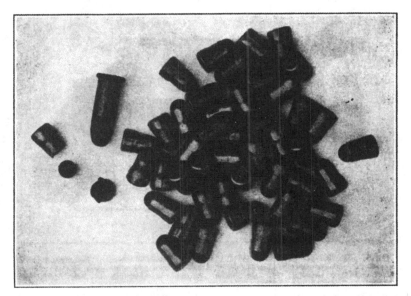

4 mm. center fire cartridges with a .22 short shown for comparison of size. Note that one 4 mm. ball has been pried out of its case and is shown together with its empty case at the left. These little cartridges have no powder, the primer furnishing all the power. They are nearly noiseless, but have speed enough to drive the shot through one-half inch of wood.

noiseless, so that they are well adapted for indoor practice. The report will not disturb a person in an adjoining room. However, in spite of the lack of noise, they have quite a respectable velocity, and will pierce a half inch of wood. They will easily pierce a tin can, break a bottle, kill a small rodent, etc. Mr. Noel's adapters are rifled with 14 fine lands and 14 grooves of the same width, with a twist of one turn in 11 inches. The maker of a single shot pistol of this caliber stated that the best barrel length is 25 centimeters (10 inches) as power is lost when the barrel is over this length. These 4 mm. cartridges are not made in America, but they may be obtained here, though the price is considerably higher than that of the .22, which is contrary to the situation abroad.

These cartridges have a great advantage for use in the sub-caliber arms, and that is that they are center-fire, and therefore do not require the bore to be off-set, as do the rim-fire cartridges.

Mr. Noel's adapter for the Colt Revolver has a barrel which fits inside the regular barrel, and at its rear end, this barrel is threaded into a breech block which fits into the place ordinarily

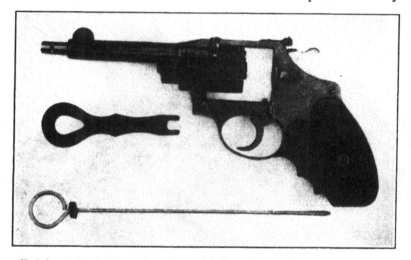

Noel 4 mm Adapter assembled to Colt Police Positive Revolver. The wrench shown is used for unscrewing the barrel, being fitted into the two slots near the muzzle end of the adapter barrel. The rod shown is used for ejecting the fired cartridges. Adapter is shown in the loading position.

occupied by the cylinder. This block will swing to the left using the barrel as an axis; though when firing it is locked against swinging by the regular cylinder latch.

To use the adapter in a Colt Revolver, the crane-lock screw in the right side of the revolver frame is partly turned out, the cylinder is swung open, and the crane is then pulled forward and out, carrying the cylinder with it. The sub-caliber barrel is now inserted into the barrel of the revolver, threaded end to the rear, and the breech block is held in the cylinder opening while the threaded end of the barrel is screwed into it until at the last thread, two index marks come into line. Then by pushing the breech-block to the rear and swinging it in, it is locked in the

firing position by means of the cylinder latch. After firing, the
cylinder latch is drawn to the rear, and the breech block is pushed
so as to swing the bottom part of it to the left, the barrel, which is
threaded into the top part forming an axis for this motion. When
the block has been swung to the left so that its bottom part clears
the frame, it can be pushed forward so as to leave space at the
rear end of the barrel for the ejection of the empty case and the
insertion of a new cartridge. I found this device to be extremely
accurate at 25 feet, but of only moderate accuracy at 20 yards.

Portion of the Military Pistol Range at Bisley showing the target arrangement and
the wooden stockade walls between sets of targets to prevent cross shooting. The
aiming mark, a black hemisphere, represents a steel helmet appearing over the enemy's
trench.

An improvised pistol range at Camp Perry. It was established to furnish contestants with a place to practice while the regular range was in use for matches. Strict firing line discipline is necessary with an arrangement of this nature, as the shooters walk up to the targets and do their own pasting at the conclusion of each score.

PART 2

AMMUNITION

CHAPTER 7

GENERAL INFORMATION ON AMMUNITION

THE object of this chapter is to give the reader a few elementary remarks about what ammunition is and how it is made. A more detailed and technical discussion of ammunition will be given in the chapters which follow.

Pistol ammunition consists of gunpowder, bullets, and primers or percussion caps for igniting the powder by means of the blow of a firing pin.

Previous to about seventy years ago, ammunition consisted of loose bullets and gunpowder, and percussion caps. To load a gun, the proper charge of powder was first measured out and put in the gun, after which a bullet was rammed down the barrel of the gun on top of the powder. The hammer of the gun was then cocked and a cap was placed on the nipple. Then if the gun was not to be fired at once, the hammer was lowered to half-cock, where it was securely held just clear of the cap. To fire, the hammer was cocked, the gun was aimed, and the trigger was pulled, allowing the hammer to fall on the cap, which exploded from the impact. The flash of fire from the cap passed through the nipple to the main powder charge, igniting it. The powder then exploded, driving the bullet from the barrel.

In modern ammunition, the powder, bullet, and percussion cap, or primer, are all contained in a brass holder called the cartridge case. The bullet projects from the front end of the cartridge case, and the primer is fastened in the rear end. This combination of bullet, powder, and primer in a brass case is called a cartridge. To fire a gun, the breech end of the barrel is opened, the cartridge is inserted with the bullet pointing forward, and the gun is closed, so that the cartridge is inside. Then the trigger is pulled, and a firing pin strikes the primer, which explodes from the impact. The flame from the primer is communicated to the gunpowder inside the cartridge case, which explodes and drives the bullet out through the gun barrel, leaving the cartridge case held firmly in place in the breech of the barrel. The gun is then opened and the empty cartridge case removed.

Naturally there are many different kinds of cartridges made for the various weapons in use, and these cartridges vary widely in size. In order to distinguish between the different sizes, they are named by the diameter of the bullet in hundredths of an inch or in millimeters. This is called the *Caliber* of the cartridge. Thus a .45 caliber cartridge has a bullet .45 hundredths of an inch in diameter, and an 8 m/m cartridge has a bullet 8 millimeters in diameter. But this system of naming is not sufficient, as there are many different kinds of cartridge of the same caliber; so additional descriptive matter is added to the cartridge name, as for example, the .45-70 cartridge. This means a .45 caliber cartridge with 70 grains of black powder. It is a rifle cartridge used in the old single shot Springfield Rifle. But there were .45-70 cartridges with bullets of different weights, as for example, the .45-70-405 with a bullet weighing 405 grains and the .45-70-500 with a bullet weighing 500 grains. Thus the first figure following the caliber of the cartridge described in this way is the weight of black powder in grains in the standard load, and the second figure is the weight of the bullet in grains. The figure describing the powder charge is for black powder only, as the smokeless powder charges vary widely depending on the kind of powder used. This system of nomenclature is no longer used for new cartridges, though several older pistol cartridges are described in this way, such as the .44-40, the .38-40, the .32-20, and the .22 Winchester Rim Fire, sometimes called the .22-7-45. Note, however, that the powder figure no longer tells how much powder is actually used in a modern cartridge of this type, loaded with smokeless powder. For example, the .44-40 cartridge, formerly loaded with 40 grains of black powder, now has perhaps only 4½ grains of Bull's-eye powder in it; or a similar charge of some other smokeless powder.

Most pistol cartridges are described by some such name as .45 Colt, .45 A.C.P. (Automatic Colt Pistol), .45 Auto-Rim, etc., or .38 S. & W., .38 Colt New Police, .38 S. & W. Special, .38 Long Colt, etc. In all cases, however, the caliber is given.

Calibers in ordinary use in this country for pistols and revolvers vary from the .22 short, with a bullet weighing 30 grains, to the .45 Colt, with a 255 grain bullet.

Rim-Fire and Center Fire Cartridges

In regard to the primers used, there are two principal varieties of cartridge made in America today, called rim-fire and center fire. The rim fire cartridge is made of thin copper, with a hollow rim around the head. This rim is filled with a percussion composition, and to fire the cartridge, the hammer or firing pin strikes the rim and dents it, thus mashing a portion of the ring of priming and causing it to ignite. The center fire cartridge is made of brass, and has a solid rim. In the center of the head of the cartridge is a circular depression, with a hole in the middle, which

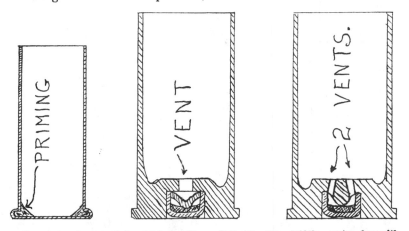

Types of primer used in pistol cartridges. Left, rim fire. Middle, center fire with separate anvil. All American center fire cartridges are made like this. Right, center fire with anvil integral with the case; called the Berdan primer. Used in all European center fire cartridges.

communicates with the inside of the cartridge. Into this depression a cap or primer is forced, with a tight sliding fit. When the cartridge is to be fired, the cap is struck by the firing pin, denting in the top of it and smashing the percussion composition which it contains against a pointed piece of brass inside called the anvil. The fire which results from the ignition of the primer flashes through the hole in the bottom of the primer cup and ignites the powder inside the cartridge.

Rim, Rimless, and Semi-Rim Types

As mentioned above, the center fire cartridge has a solid rim. Right here it might be well to state that most cartridges have a rim around the head of the case to stop the cartridge from going all the way into the gun, and to support it against the firing pin blow, as well as to give something for the extractor to hook onto when drawing the cartridge out after it is fired. However, the rim interferes with the feeding of the cartridges from the magazine of an automatic pistol, hence most automatic pistol cartridges are made in what is called the rimless type. The head of the cartridge is the same diameter as the body, and has a groove cut around it for the extractor to hook into. As there is no raised

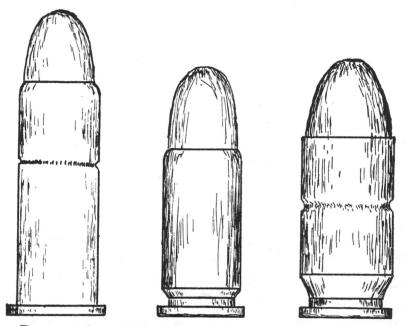

Three common types of center fire pistol cartridges. Left, the rim type. (.38 S. & W. Special). Middle, Semi-rim cartridge for automatic pistols. The rim projects only far enough beyond the body diameter to stop the cartridge from going all the way into the chamber, and to form a support for the cartridge against the firing pin blow. (Super .38 Automatic). Right, the rimless type. The front of the case is left square and abuts against a square shoulder at the front of the chamber. (.45 Automatic).

head or rim to stop the cartridge from going all the way into the barrel, the chamber is made slightly larger in diameter than the barrel and there is a shoulder at the front end of the chamber against which the front edge of the cartridge rests to support it against the firing pin blow.

There is still another type, used in some automatic pistols, such as the Super .38 Automatic, which looks like the rimless type at first glance, but is not strictly rimless, for the rim actually does project very slightly above the line of the body; and these cartridges use this projection of the rim to keep from going all the way into the gun, instead of having the front edge of the cartridge case strike against a shoulder in the barrel as do the rimless cases.

Black and Smokeless Powders

There are three principal kinds of powder used for loading the modern pistol cartridge. These are black powder, which was used exclusively up until about forty years ago; smokeless or nitro powder; and semi-smokeless powder, which is a mixture of the other two kinds. Black powder has a heavy recoil, gives off a large quantity of white smoke when fired, and fouls the gun barrel very badly. Smokeless powder gives off little or no smoke, does not foul the barrel appreciably, makes less report, and kicks less than black powder. On the other hand it must be loaded with great care, as it is more sensitive to overloads and other conditions, and from this viewpoint is not as safe as is black powder. The principal semi-smokeless found in commercially loaded pistol cartridges is Lesmok, with which many .22 caliber cartridges are loaded. It is extremely uniform in its action, and is a favorite for target shooting. More detail in regard to powders is given in another chapter.

Bullets

The bullet weights range from 30 grains for the .22 Short to 255 grains for the .45 Colt. Bullets are made usually of an alloy of lead and tin. The tin is used to harden the lead, so that it will not collect on the inside of the barrel—that is, "lead the barrel," as it is called. In general, a very soft lead bullet is more effective for stopping power than one that is hardened, but most pistol bullets are made of about one part of tin to fifteen parts of lead. Some pistol bullets are made with a jacket of harder metal covering the lead. These are called "jacketed" bullets, or "full-metal-patch" bullets.

For revolvers plain lead bullets are usually preferred, but for automatic pistols jacketed bullets are generally used to avoid battering in the magazine and to avoid jamming the cartridge in feeding. The full-metal-jacketed bullet does not have as good stopping power as the lead bullet. It has more of a tendency to glance when striking hard objects. A jacketed bullet has more accuracy in any pistol or revolver than a pure lead bullet in the same gun; but this slight increase in accuracy does not outweigh some other disadvantages of the jacketed bullet, which are its lack of stopping power and its tendency to glance or to be deflected easily from its path. A wound made with a jacketed bullet generally heals up more quickly than one made with a lead bullet.

Many rifle cartridges are made with a metal jacket, but with a soft lead point exposed. These are called "soft-point" or "mushroom" bullets, because they expand on striking an object, and therefore produce a much more serious shock and have correspondingly greater stopping power. This is true when they are used in rifles, but is not true when used in revolvers, because no revolver has enough velocity to cause a mushroom bullet to expand. Very soft lead bullets used in revolvers will expand somewhat on striking a bone, however.

The jacket of a metal-patch bullet is generally made either of cupro nickel or gilding metal. Cupro nickel is a combination of 60 per cent copper and 40 per cent nickel and is a white material like German silver. Gilding metal is a combination of copper and zinc. Years ago the Government pistol bullets were jacketed with gilding metal of 95 per cent copper and 5 per cent zinc. Now the mixture used is 90 per cent copper and 10 per cent zinc. Up until a few years ago the Government pistol bullets have been tinned lightly after manufacture in order to make them have a white appearance and avoid possible corrosion of the copper jacket. These jacketed bullets are the ones that are meant by newspaper reporters when they refer to "steel-jacketed" bullets. This term is not strictly correct, as steel is not used as a bullet-jacketed material in America at the present time, nor has it ever been except experimentally.

A good many foreign cartridges have steel jackets, however. Some of these foreign steel-jacketed bullets are covered with a thin coating of copper on top of the steel to prevent corrosion. This material is called "copper-clad steel." It is made by welding a sheet of copper onto a sheet of steel and then rolling it out thin. The copper spreads out as the steel is rolled, and no matter how thin it is, it always has a coating of copper on the outside. Cupro-nickel-covered steel is also used. Collectors and others who want to know what material bullet jackets are made of generally have, among their accessories, a magnet, as this is useful in detecting steel jackets.

All lead bullets must be lubricated to prevent the lead from sticking to the barrel inside and piling up in lumps. The metal-jacketed bullets, however, are not lubricated. The modern lead pistol bullet has from one to three grooves around it which, in the finished cartridge, are covered up by the neck of the case, and these grooves are full of a lubricant, usually Japan wax. A cartridge made like this is called "inside lubricated." Many of the older pistol cartridges, especially the rim-fire type, have grooves outside of the cartridge case which are filled with grease, and in some cases the whole bullet is dipped in grease so it is covered with a thin layer of lubricant. Such cartridges are called "outside lubricated." A common example is the ordinary .22 Long Rifle cartridge, which, as everyone knows, is covered over with a film of lubricant. A disadvantage of the outside lubrication system is if the cartridges are carried loose the bullets pick up foreign material which becomes embedded in the grease.

How Cartridges are Made

In the manufacture of a pistol cartridge a sheet of brass about ⅛ of an inch thick is fed into a punch press, which first cuts out a little disk of brass and then forms it into a cup shape. These little cups are fed through successive presses, in each of which

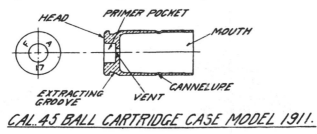

CAL. 45 BALL CARTRIDGE CASE MODEL 1911.

the cup is forced through a die by a steel punch in such a manner as to elongate the brass cup. When the cup is long enough to have the approximate shape of a cartridge case it is placed in another press, which flattens the head of it so as to form a rim around it and puts a cup-shaped depression in the head for the primer to fit into. The case is then nearly completed. It is afterwards trimmed to length, and the rim is turned to exact thickness and diameter on a machine similar to a lathe. A hole is also punched in the bottom of the primer pocket for the flash of the primer to go through. After being washed to free it from all oil and residue the case is ready to have the primer inserted.

It is interesting to note that the brass, when it first comes to the cartridge factory in strips, is very soft, but the work of forming it up into cups makes it become hard. Before it can be further drawn out it must be heated up to a red heat to soften it again, and this process is called "annealing." A cartridge goes through several of these annealing processes between the various draws it gets in changing from the form of a flat disk to that of a long thin cup. These annealing and drawing operations must be so adjusted that the cartridge has a certain hardness or temper after the last operation; otherwise it will not have enough strength in the head, and under heavy pressures the head would expand and allow the primer to fall out.

Manufacture of Bullets

If pure lead bullets were used they would be so soft that they wound tend to jump the rifling, or "strip," and would lead the barrel badly. By mixing certain hardening materials with the lead, such as antimony or tin, the tendency to lead is reduced and the bullet will hold its shape better.

The lead bullet for a pistol cartridge is manufactured by one of two processes. The process used at Frankford Arsenal consists of melting the proper mixture of lead and tin together and pouring it into a large ingot. This is then put into a high-pressure press, which forces the lead out in the form of wire about four-tenths of an inch in diameter. As it comes from the press this wire is wound on reels. This lead wire is afterwards taken to a swedging machine, which is entirely automatic in its action and which first cuts off a short section of the lead wire and then forces it into a hole the exact size of the bullet, under very heavy pressure, so as to form the bullet perfectly to shape except for the lubrication grooves. The bullets as they come from this swedging machine, if they are to be plain lead bullets such as those for the .38-caliber revolver, are then taken to a machine which rolls some grooves around them for the lubricant. They are then fed to a machine which forces lubricant into these grooves under pressure, and the bullet is then complete.

The other factory method of making bullets which is used in many ammunition factories in this country, is to cast the bullet mixture into little slugs, each containing the proper amount of lead for one bullet. This casting is done automatically in revolving moulds which operate very rapidly. The bullet slugs are then taken to a machine where they are swedged to final shape and then finished up as previously described.

When a jacketed bullet is to be made, the first part of the process is just the same. A slug is swedged to proper size and shape for the core of the bullet. The bullet jacket is then drawn up out of cupro nickel or gilding metal in just the same way that a cartridge case is drawn. The lead cores are then inserted inside of the jackets and the partly assembled bullet is placed in a die under a heavy press and a punch turns over the base of the jacket on the lead and presses the whole bullet together so that it is solid.

Primers

There are two sizes of primers commonly used in the center-fire cartridges of American make. The small size, used for the smaller cartridges, is .175 inch in diameter, while the larger one is .211 inch in diameter. Frankford Arsenal uses a special size primer for the .45 Colt, having a diameter of .204 inch. In America the center-fire primer has a separate anvil which is contained in the primer itself, while in the European cartridges the anvil is fitted

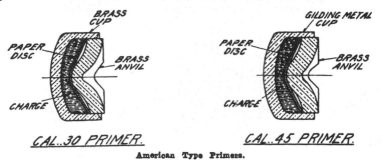

American Type Primers.

in the cartridge case and is not a part of the primer. This European style is known, after its inventor, as the "Berdan" type of primer, while the other is called the "Boxer" type. The rim-fire cartridges have their copper shell with a little priming mixture spread around in the rim.

Primer Compounds

The key to the primer composition is some material that will explode when it is crushed, as will the head of an ordinary "strike anywhere" match. The material most often used for this purpose in primers, until very recently has been Chlorate of Potash. If this substance is powdered very fine and mixed with almost any inflammable substance of granular texture, such as sulphur, it will explode from very moderate friction or crushing. In fact, I have known small boys to purchase this substance at drug stores, and mix it with powdered sulphur to make a fourth of July explosive that will go off violently when laid on street car tracks, etc.; or the experimentally inclined will mix it with sugar, forming a compound that will explode when a few drops of sulphuric acid is allowed to come in contact with it. However, I want to warn most emphatically against any such maneuvers, as the experimenter is likely to encounter unpleasant surprises. Chlorate of potash is very dangerous to handle. An attempt to powder it will often result in a violent explosion, which can easily have a fatal result, even when only a very small quantity is being handled.

In addition to the chlorate, some fuel is added; and the effectiveness and sensitivity is increased if the fuel is gritty in nature, so that the friction on the chlorate is increased. Antimony sulphide, or stibnite, as it is called in the native state, is the best known of such substances.

The primer used at the present time in the .45 caliber pistol cartridge as made at Frankford Arsenal has the following composition:

Potassium Chlorate .... 53 per cent
Antimony Sulphide .... 17 " "
Lead sulpho-cyanide .... 25 " "
Tri-nitro-toluol (T.N.T.) .... 5 " "

This mixture is moistened with gum water, which is a kind of thin mucilage, and then it is pressed into the primer cups and covered with a layer of shellacked paper. The anvils are then forced into the cups while the mixture is still wet, and the assembled primers are put into a drying house, where they are thoroughly dried out, which makes them very sensitive. After being dried, they are pressed into cartridge cases which have not been loaded with powder. After the priming of the cases has been successfully accomplished, they are ready to have the powder and bullet put in.

A typical rim-fire priming composition is the following, used in the United States Cartridge Company's N.R.A. Outdoor Type .22 Long Rifle Cartridge. This was obtained by chemical analysis of samples.

Potassium Chlorate .... 41.43 per cent
Antimony Sulphide .... 9.53 " "
Copper Sulphocyanide .... 4.70 " "
Ground Glass .... 44.23 " "

The average weight of the pellet of priming in this cartridge, (U.S.N.R.A.) was found to be 0.237 grain.

These compositions are both of the type which will cause corrosion unless the gun is promptly cleaned after shooting. The damage is done by the potassium chlorate, and consequently, a determined effort was made to get rid of this component, with the result that in 1928 the non-corrosive type of priming came into use by all the large American cartridge companies.

The following table gives the composition of the early non-corrosive priming compositions as used by several of the companies:

	Remington Kleanbore	Remington Palma	Western	Winchester Staynless	Peters Rustless
Mercuric fulminate ..	44.40	42.62	40.79	41.06	38.68
Barium Nitrate	30.54	27.40	22.23	26.03	9.95
Lead sulphocyanide ..	4.20	7.17	8.22	5.18	....
Ground Glass	20.66	22.13	28.43	26.66	24.90
Lead compound*	....	....	....	....	25.91
Gum, etc.	.20	.68	.33	.58	.56
	100 pct.	100 pct.	100 pct.	100 pct.	100 pct.

*Exact composition undetermined.

These primers were indeed non-corrosive, but they suffered from a tendency to become insenitive; and give hang-fires and misfires, through deterioration of the mercury fulminate which formed a large percentage of each mixture. Cartridges loaded with these mixtures, when kept on the shelf for a year or two, especially in warm and damp climates, became worthless.

In order to overcome this serious defect, it was found necessary to find a substitute for the mercury fulminate. This was finally accomplished, and the mixtures given above became obsolete. All the companies now make a non-mercuric non-corrosive primer composition.

Examples of a non-mercuric non-corrosive primer composition are given in U. S. Patent No. 1889116, by Edmund Ritter Von Herz and Hans Rathburg, assignors to Remington Arms Company, as follows:

COMPOSITION No. 1

Ingredient	Percentage		
Guanyl Nitro-amino-guanyl-tetracene	0.5	to	15.
Lead tri-nitro-resorcinate	20.	"	45.
Barium Nitrate	30.	"	50.
Antimony Sulphide and/or other fuel, as, e. g., Calcium Silicide	10.	"	30.

COMPOSITION No. 2

Ingredient	Percentage		
Guanyl Nitro-amino-guanyl-tetracene	0.5	to	2.0
Lead tri-nitro-resorcinate	35.	"	40.
Barium Nitrate	35.	"	42.
Lead peroxide	7.0	"	12.
Antimony Sulphide	0.	"	5.
Calcium Silicide	0.	"	12.
Glass	0.	"	3.

Priming and Loading the Cartridges

With the cartridge case, the primer, the bullets and the powder all at hand the next step is to prime the cartridge cases. They are sent to an automatic machine that inserts a primer into the primer pocket of each case, presses it home and places a little ring of waterproof and oilproof lacquer around the joint between the primer and the primer pocket.

The cartridges are now sent to the loading machine, which has three hoppers, one containing empty cases, one containing bullets, and the other having powder in it. The cases are fed down a long tube into a dial holder which carries them under a spout from the powder dome, where each cartridge receives an exact charge of powder. Next they go under another spout where a bullet is deposited on the mouth of the case, and a little further along a plunger seats the bullet to the proper depth in the mouth of the case. In the automatic pistol cartridges the bullet is held in place by friction, but in most of the others the brass is firmly crimped into the lead to hold the bullet securely in place.

Before, during, and after this loading operation, the cartridge cases, bullets, and primers are subjected to careful inspection to be sure that there are no defects, and the loading machine itself is fitted with a number of elaborate and delicate feelers and safety devices to insure that no cartridge will get by without a powder load, with an overload, without a primer, or with the primer upside down, etc.

With the large number of operations on a cartridge, and all the engineering skill, care and accuracy that goes into its construction, it seems remarkable that the finished product can be sold for such a relatively small price.

CHAPTER 8

INTERIOR BALLISTICS

INTERIOR ballistics is the study of what happens from the time the firing pin hits the primer until the bullet leaves the barrel. It deals chiefly with such things as powder pressures, muzzle velocity, recoil, etc.

Interior ballistics is a big subject, and is full of the most complicated and abstruse mathematics. Whole books have been written on this subject alone, so the reader will readily understand that this chapter does not in any sense of the word pretend to be a treatise on Interior Ballistics. It is merely a non-technical talk on some of the simpler phases of the subject, with particular reference to the interests of the pistol shot.

When the firing pin hits the primer, the priming composition ignites, and in turn sets the powder on fire. The powder burns very quickly in any case, but relatively there is a big difference in the speed of burning, depending on how closely it is confined. If you light a charge of smokeless powder in the open air, the unconfined powder will burn up in a few seconds, just like so much celluloid. But if it is slightly confined, the pressure and heat of the gases given off by the first particles to burn will add to the heat and pressure that is applied to the remaining particles, and will make them burn faster. In a revolver, the powder is confined in the very small space in the base of the cartridge behind the bullet; and the only way it can expand is to push the bullet along the barrel. The heavier the bullet, the more effective is the confinement of the gas, and the more quickly will the powder burn. The speed of burning depends also on how much empty space there is in the cartridge case. For example, if the case is only half full of powder, the vacant space in there is available for the gas to expand into at the beginning of the explosion, and the burning of the powder gets underway less rapidly than it would if the case were full of powder and there was no vacant space inside.

Cartridge Case Capacity

The following tabulation gives the powder capacity of various pistol and revolver cartridges in cubic inches. These figures are subject to a slight variation from time to time as manufacturing methods change, and moreover, they are not exactly the same for the different makers, but these typical examples, taken from measurements of cartridges of Winchester make will be found to be of value where it is desired to obtain an idea of the relative capacity of the different cartridges.

This is of importance, because the space for the charge has a lot to do with the way in which the powder burns. If the powder nearly fills the space, the pressure will be much higher than if the space is only partly filled.

Name of Cartridge	Volume of Powder Space, Cubic Inches
.25 A. C. P.	.013
.32 S. & W.	.026
.30 Mauser	.061
.30 Luger	.042
.32 S. & W. Long	.044
.32 Colt's New Police	.044
.32 A. C. P.	.019
.32 -20	.065
9 MM Luger	.033
.38 S. & W.	.043
.38 Colt New Police	.043
.38 Long Colt	.063
.38 S. & W. Special	.079
.38 A. C. P. (Super .38)	.049
.38 -40	.128
.41 Long Colt	.066
.44 S. & W. American	.089
.44 S. & W. Russian	.086
.44 S. & W. Special	.112
.44 -40	.129
.45 Colt	.125
.45 A. C. P.	.051

Pressure

When the powder burns, it all turns into gas, and there are many times the volume of gas produced as there were of the original powder. Yet when this gas is first produced, it is all confined inside the cartridge. That makes it have a very high pressure. This pressure exerts itself equally in all directions, on the sides of the cartridge case, on the back of the case, and on the bullet. The walls of the case are prevented from moving by the fact that they fit closely inside the chamber. However, the gas pressing on the base of the bullet and the inside of the cartridge head tends to separate these two surfaces and increase the distance between them.

The pressure in the chamber of the .45 Automatic Pistol is 14,000 pounds per square inch, and as the base of the bullet has an area of .159 square inch, that means that the total pressure in pounds on the base of the bullet is 2 225 pounds, or well over a ton. The pressure on the inside of the base of the cartridge is the same. This means that when the pistol is fired, there is a pressure of a ton pushing the bullet forward, and an equal pressure trying to push the pistol back.

As soon as this pressure is applied, the bullet starts to move forward, and the gun starts to move back. The bullet is much lighter than the gun, and can therefore get under way more quickly; but at the same time that the bullet moves toward the muzzle, the gun is moving back, and the speed of the gun's motion as compared to that of the bullet depends entirely on the relative weight of the gun and the bullet. The pressure works in all directions equally, and it moves the gun back as fast as the inertia of the gun will allow it to move. At the same time it moves the bullet forward as fast as the inertia of the bullet will allow it to move. The bullet has less inertia, so it moves faster.

It is this backward motion of the gun, as described above, that causes the recoil. The lighter the gun, the more easily it can move back, and the greater the recoil. Also, the lighter the bullet, the more quickly it can get out of the barrel and release the pressure, and the more quickly the powder gas will stop pushing the gun, and therefore a light bullet means a light recoil.

If the gun and bullet weighed the same, the gun would come back as fast as the bullet goes forward. It is the superior weight of the gun that protects the user of it from the pressure of over a ton that is pushing it back onto him. Another thing that saves him is the fact that the pressure lasts only a very small fraction of a second, and before the gun has moved very far, the pressure is gone, because the bullet has moved out of the barrel.

Time of Bullet in Barrel

It is really very easy to get a good close approximation to the length of time it takes a bullet to get out of a barrel. For example, take the .45 Automatic, with a five inch barrel. When the bullet leaves the barrel, it has a velocity of 810 feet per second.

It would move 1 foot in 1/810th of a second, and it would move 5 inches, the barrel length, in 5/12ths of 1/810th of a second, which is 1/1944th of a second. If the bullet started to move at this speed as soon as the powder was ignited, and moved at the same speed until it was out of the barrel, this is how much time it would take. But obviously, it does not do this, but takes longer, because it moves slowly at first, and gradually gets up speed, and while moving slowly at the first part of its path, it is losing time.

We might figure that at the beginning it had no speed at all, and when it left the barrel, it had a speed of 810 f. s., so that the average speed in the barrel is the average of 0 and 810, which is 405. Under this assumption, which is not so far from the truth, the bullet would take twice as long, or 1/972 of a second to traverse the barrel. However, this is not exactly correct, and if we want an even closer figure, we can get it by applying a little additional knowledge. The bullet starts from rest when the explosion occurs; and the pressure is highest at this instant, so that the most force is being applied to the bullet in the early part of its travel. As it moves along the barrel, the space for the gas to expand into is increased, so that the gas loses part of its pressure. The bullet continues to gain, but not so fast. The curve of velocity, if plotted out, resembles a parabola, where the average value of all the velocities is 2/3 of the final velocity. Thus the average velocity of the bullet in the barrel under this assumption would be 2/3 of 810, or 540 f. s., and the time required to traverse 5 inches at this speed is 1/1296th of a second, or, expressed in decimals, .00077 second. This is about three quarters of a thousandth of a second. It is merely because the pressure of a ton that you are holding at the end of your arm when you fire the automatic pushes against you for less than a thousandth of a second that it does you no harm. Even so, it causes a rather severe recoil.

Now that we have seen how to figure out how long the bullet takes to go through the barrel, we will go on and discuss the question of velocity. That means that we will have to leave the question of recoil, but later in this chapter we will discuss it and show it can be calculated, and what effect it has on the grouping of the bullets on the target.

Velocity

We have seen that in the .45 caliber automatic pistol there is a maximum powder pressure of about 14,000 pounds per square inch, and as the base of the bullet has an area of a little over one-sixth of a square inch, there is an actual push on the bullet of about 2225 pounds.

Naturally this push on the base of the bullet moves it, and as the bullet is very light, and the push is very large, the bullet moves very rapidly under the influence of this tremendous force.

According to the laws of physics, the velocity that will be caused by any force acting on a movable object for one second is equal to the force in pounds, divided by the mass of the object.   The mass is defined as the weight divided by the acceleration of gravity, 32.16, or in round numbers, 32.   The weight of the object must be in pounds.   If the force acts for two seconds, the velocity will be twice as great.   This is expressed by the formula $v = \dfrac{Ft}{m}$ where v represents the velocity, F the force in pounds, m the mass of the object, and t the time during which the force acts.   Also, if a force is allowed to act through a given distance instead of through a given length of time, the velocity that will be imparted to the object will be equal to the square root of two times the force multiplied by the distance through it acts, divided by the mass of the object, or, expressed as a mathematical formula $v = \dfrac{\sqrt{2FS}}{m}$, or $v^2 = \dfrac{2FS}{m}$ where S represents the space through which the force is allowed to act, and the other letters represent the same quantities as before.

Thus if we have a force of 2225 pounds pushing on the base of a bullet that weighs 230 grains until the bullet passes out of the 5 inch barrel of the automatic pistol, we can find out from the formula just what the velocity would be.   For F in the formula, substitute 2225; for S, substitute the barrel length of 5/12th of a foot; for m substitute the bullet weight *in pounds* divided by the gravitational constant 32.   To bring the bullet weight of 230 grains to pounds, divide by the number of grains in a pound, or 7000.   Thus m would be 230/7000 x 32, and we would get

$$v = \sqrt{\frac{2 \times 2225 \times 7000 \times 32 \times 5}{230 \times 12}} \text{ or } v = \sqrt{1,840,000} \text{ or } 1343 \text{ feet}$$

per second.

But we know that we do not get this much velocity in the pistol. The muzzle velocity is only 810 feet per second.   Why the difference?

The answer is simplicity itself.   Our powder pressure of 14,000 pounds per square inch does not remain at the same figure as the bullet moves along, for as more space is provided for the gas by the motion of the bullet along the barrel, the gas has more room to expand into, and naturally the pressure drops. When the powder is first ignited, it has only the powder space in the car-tridge case to hold all the gas. This space in the cartridge is only four-tenths of an inch long. By the time the bullet has moved a half inch along the bore, the powder has twice the space to expand into; and by the time the bullet has reached the end of the barrel, the gas will have expanded to 12½ times the volume of the powder space in the cartridge. At this point, the pressure will have dropped to a small fraction of the maximum of 14,000 pounds.

We can just as easily reverse our formula to find the average pressure if we know the muzzle velocity. For example, transpos-ing the formula we have $F = \dfrac{mv}{2S}$. Working this out for the

230 grain bullet with 810 f. s. velocity gives $F = \dfrac{230 \times 810 \times 810 \times 12}{2 \times 32 \times 7000 \times 5}$

or F = 810 lbs. which is the average push on the base of the bullet. As the base of the bullet is only .159 square inch this gives a pres-sure of $\dfrac{810}{.159}$ or 5,100 pounds per square inch average. Actually the pressure is a little higher than this, for some of it is used to overcome the friction of the bullet against the barrel; but the for-mula gives a very good idea of just what happens, and is per-fectly satisfactory for obtaining approximate results. More elab-orate formulae have been worked out, which take care of other factors, such as temperature, etc., but they would be out of place in a brief discussion such as this chapter.

The matter of powder gas expansion, discussed briefly above, is a very important factor in determining the barrel length that is necessary to use the powder properly. For example, the first .22 caliber Banker's Special with 2-inch barrel was made to order at my request. Some of my friends thought that I would get very little velocity with this gun; but actual tests showed a velocity of 1000 foot seconds with this 2-inch barreled revolver shooting the Remington high speed .22 cartridge. Almost everyone who has seen these figures has been astonished at this comparatively very high velocity, but if we go back to the fundamentals of interior ballistics and consider how many times its own volume gas in the cartridge is expanded before it leaves the barrel, we will see that this 2-inch barrel in the .22 corresponds to a 26-inch barrel in the

Springfield rifle. We arrive at this rather astonishing result in the following way:

The Springfield rifle has a bottle-neck cartridge that is much bigger in diameter than the barrel. The powder space in the Springfield cartridge is .251 cubic inches and it takes 3.4 inches of the caliber .30 Springfield barrel to have the same cubic capacity. This means that when the bullet in the Springfield has gone 3.4 inches the gas which originally filled the cartridge case has been expanded to twice its volume, and when the bullet has gone all the way to the end of the 24-inch barrel in the Springfield, the gas has been expanded seven times.

The caliber .22 long rifle cartridge on the other hand, is not a bottle-neck cartridge. The powder space in this cartridge is the same diameter as the inside of the barrel, and just .43 inch long, so that when the bullet has moved forward .43 inch, the gas has expanded to twice its volume. In this 2-inch barrel revolver the gas expands about 7.7 times its own volume which is more expansion than the gas in the Springfield rifle has. In figuring the barrel length of a revolver, it is necessary to add the length of the cylinder which in this case is 1.3 inches. Thus the 2-inch barrel revolver in this caliber may be considered as having a barrel 3-1/3 inches long. A revolver with a cylinder 1.3 inches and a barrel 1.8 inches long would correspond in barrel length with the Springfield rifle and should use the powder with about the same efficiency.

I do not know whether or not most of our readers are acquainted with this fact, but with the average .22 rifle the longer you make the barrel the less the velocity, because in these very long barrels the gas has expanded so much that the pressure has fallen too low to do any useful work in pushing the already fast moving bullet and hence the barrel friction retards the bullet more than this comparatively low gas pressure accelerates it.

Numerous experiments have shown that with a fast burning powder, such as du Pont No. 93, ordinarily used in smokeless caliber .22 cartridges, the maximum velocity is attained at about 14 to 16 inches. Any longer barrel length just slows the bullet down, though, of course, it is useful for giving increased sight radius. With a slower burning powder, such as Lesmoke, the maximum velocity is attained with about a 16 or 18-inch barrel.

Therefore, with a 2-inch barrel revolver having a cylinder 1.3" long, we might expect to get about 80% of the velocity that is in the powder, and with a 6-inch barrel revolver having a cylinder 1½" long we might expect to get about 95% of the velocity that

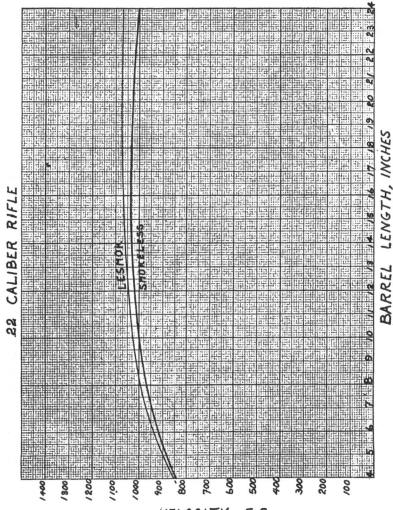

Curve No. 1. The relation of barrel length to velocity in the .22 caliber rifle. This curve shows that with smokeless powder the maximum velocity with the .22 long rifle cartridge is obtained with a 16 inch barrel, and that additional length reduces the velocity. It also shows that the velocity in a ten inch pistol would be the same as that in a rifle with 24 inch barrel.

is in the powder. This is including the effect of leakage through the joint between the barrel and the cylinder; but in actual practice this leakage has been found to have small effect owing to the law of physics which says that a fluid or gas moving rapidly past an orifice has difficulty getting out.

For those of our readers who may be interested in the details of this subject, Curve No. 1 is included which shows the actual velocities obtained from tests of both Lesmoke and smokeless caliber .22 cartridges in a rifle having a 24-inch barrel which was cut off two inches at a time and the velocity taken for each length. This curve shows at a glance the reason for the well known efficiency of the 10-inch barrel target pistol, as with the ordinary caliber .22 cartridges the 10-inch barrel pistol gives nearly all the velocity that can be obtained from a cartridge under any circumstances.

This question of the number of expansions in a barrel of a given length shows that the larger the powder space in the cartridge case, the longer the barrel must be to use the powder efficiently. Cartridge cases with very compact powder space such as the .45 automatic pistol cartridge, are very efficient and therefore require only a short barrel. The .45 automatic pistol cartridge has a powder space which corresponds almost exactly to that in the caliber .22. The powder will fill .4 inch of the barrel which means that the 5-inch barrel of the .45 automatic pistol gives 12½ expansions or the same that would be obtained in a Springfield rifle with a barrel 42 inches long. Actually the barrel of the .45 automatic pistol need only be 2.8 inches long to be equivalent to the present Springfield 24-inch barrel.

On the other hand, the old style caliber .45 Colt cartridge is less efficient for use with modern high potential smokeless powders than is the .45 automatic. In the old Colt it takes about 78/100 inch of travel in the barrel to expand the powder space to double its size, hence a 5½-inch barrel added to the 1½-inch cylinder gives 9 expansions, corresponding to a 30-inch Springfield barrel. The 4-inch barrel of this gun added to the 1½-inch cylinder would give the same efficiency as the present 24-inch Springfield barrel.

The .38 Police Positive cartridge which is used in the small Post Office guns or the Banker's Special, has a powder space which is about equal in length to that of the .22. In other words, it, like the .22, takes about 43/100 inch of the barrel to expand the gas once. Hence the figures we gave above for the .22 showing that

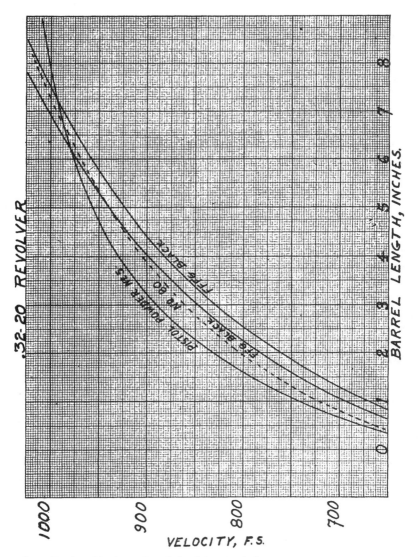

Curve No. 2. This shows the relation between velocity and barrel length with four different powders in the .32-20 revolver.

the 2-inch barrel expands the gas 7.7 times, apply equally well to the Banker's Special.

The .38 Special on the other hand, has a little over 50% more powder space in the cartridge. This space is necessary in order to get a high velocity with the heavy bullet used in the .38 Special. It also means that a longer barrel is necessary to use the powder with equal efficiency.

To equal the 2-inch barrel in the Banker's Special as far as powder burning efficiency is concerned, the .38 Detective Special would have to have a barrel 3¼ inches long.

In making the investigation of this subject, I considered not only smokeless powder and Lessmoke powder but also in the large caliber revolvers Pistol Powder No. 5, duPont No. 80, and Black Powder of two different granulations, FFG and FFFG.

I plotted a lot of curves on this subject to show just what happens when the barrel of the revolver is cut off inch by inch, and strange to say, there very much less difference between the black and the smokeless powders than the average reader would suspect. Our curves show that Pistol Powder No. 5 is a little quicker than either No. 80 or black powder. It also shows that the FFFG black is quicker than the FFG black which is an obvious fact as it has a smaller grain.

These curves, moreover, show very clearly the difference between a quick powder and a slow one. A quick powder gets more velocity in a short barrel than does a slow powder, but with a slow powder the ultimate speed when the barrel length is increased is greater.

There is included with this chapter curve No. 2 which shows velocity plotted against barrel length for .32/20 revolvers with four different powders. This curve shows that the speed of the powders is in the following order:

Pistol Powder No. 5
Sporting Rifle No. 80
FFFG Black
FFG Black

The caliber .32/20 is a revolver which has quite a large powder space, therefore it takes a long barrel to get all the velocity out of the cartridge. This curve shows plainly that with the 6-inch barrel in this caliber, there is still a considerable amount of velocity remaining, and a 7-inch barrel gives quite an increase.

Curve No. 3 shows the .38 Special loaded with No. 80. I plotted a curve for Pistol Powder No. 5 with the same gun and it

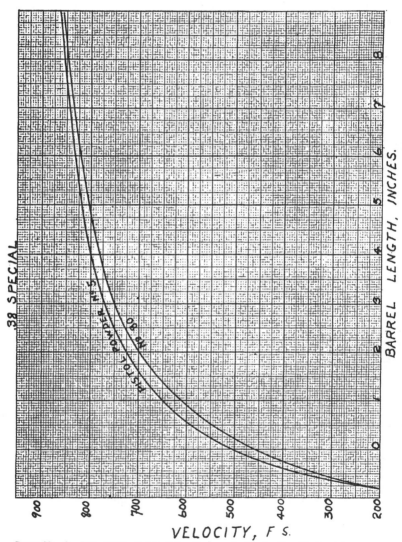

VELOCITY, F S.

Curve No. 3. The effect of barrel length on velocity in the .38 Special Revolver.

is almost the same except that the velocity for the 1", 2" and 3" barrels is a little higher and that for the 6", 7" and 8" barrels is about the same. In plotting these curves I have taken the origin of the curve as the base of the bullet.

In investigating the velocities obtained with the 2-inch caliber .22 barrel, we obtained over 1000 f. s. with the Remington Palma Hi-Speed as was mentioned above. One series of experiments included comparative firing between a 2-inch barrel revolver, a 6-inch barrel revolver and a rifle with 28-inch barrel.

The following tabulation shows the results obtained, all the velocities being at 25 feet from the muzzle:

Cartridge	Win. Lestayn	Rem. Kleanbore	Rem. HiSpeed Silvadry	Western Super-X	Rem. Palma HiSpeed
Powder	Lesmoke	DuP 93	Herc. 1300	Herc. 1300	DuP 93
Vel. in 28" Rifle	1022	1048	1216	1305	1244
Vel. in 6" Rev.	887	904	934	1058	1141
Vel. in 2" Rev.	740	780	762	879	997

In order to bring these results to muzzle velocities instead of instrumental velocities, it would be necessary to add about 25 feet.

It will readily be seen that there is very little difference in the performance between Lesmoke and the smokeless powder No. 93 which is ordinarily used in caliber .22 smokeless cartridges. It will be observed, however, that the more progressive burning powders used in the Remington Hi-Speed Silvadry and the Western Super-X are better adapted for use in a long barrel than they are in a short one. Their progressive quality which gives them high velocity in a rifle is a disadvantage when firing them in a short barrel gun.

I have taken the figures from this tabulation combined with previous figures obtained from firings in cut off rifle barrels and made them into a curve, No. 4 of those included with this chapter, which shows approximately the results and the relationship of these various powders. (Curve No. 4 is shown on page 154.)

It will be observed that in curve No. 1 the smokeless powder curve was below the Lesmoke curve, whereas in the No. 4 curve the smokeless powder is above the Lesmoke curve. This is merely due to the fact that in the first test the particular make of smokeless ammunition to be used happened to be loaded at a lower velocity than the Lesmoke, while the reverse was true in the ammunition used for the second test which was of a different make.

The important thing about these curves is not to show exactly how much velocity you will get, because this depends on what lot of ammunition you happen to use. The curves are intended to show the relation to velocity of one length of barrel to that of another.

All experience indicates that the best powder to use in a short barrel gun is the quickest powder, and in the caliber .22 this happens to be the ordinary smokeless and not the Lesmoke. In using Lesmoke with a short barrel Colt, there is a very noticeable flash and quite a loud report. In using the smokeless there is no flash noticeable and the report is mild.

Recoil and Jump

We saw at the beginning of our discussion of velocity that the maximum pressure in the .45 automatic pistol is about 14,000 pounds, and that the actual push on the base of the bullet, which has an area of about one sixth of a square inch, is in the order of one ton. We also saw that a similar pressure is exerted on the inside of the breech of the gun, for the gas presses equally in all directions, and not just on the bullet alone.

We also found how to calculate the velocity of the bullet from the formulae $v = \dfrac{Ft}{m}$ and $v = \dfrac{\sqrt{2FS}}{m}$. In the examples worked out, we were trying to find the velocity of the bullet, but these formulae give us the backward velocity of the gun also, if we use the mass, m, in the formula as that of the gun instead of the bullet. The gas moves the gun back at the same time that it moves the bullet forward, and the speed with which the gun recoils, or moves back, depends on the powder pressure and the weight of the gun. It also depends on the weight of the bullet, for if the bullet is very light, it gets away quickly, so that the pressure on the gun is released before the gun has had time to acquire much velocity. It is the very short time that the pressure lasts that keeps the recoil from being too great.

When you stop to consider that you are actually holding the pistol out there against a pressure of over a ton, you will realize how impossible it is for you to modify the recoil by holding against it. All that saves you from having the pistol torn from your grasp is the fact that the action lasts less than a thousandth of a second.

I once had an opportunity to fire some automatic pistols that had been converted to full automatic by a change in the sear.

This was at the beginning of the World War, when it was intended to mount these pistols in a fixed position in airplanes. The big surprise came when one of these guns was fired by hand. The gun operated so fast that the whole seven shots were gone in less than a second. In this case, the ton of pressure on the pistol was repeated seven times in rapid succession, and the result was that the pistol was swung violently upward, so that it finished the string of shots pointing almost straight up. A number of very strong men tried to fire it without letting it swing up in that manner, but it was impossible to modify the motion in any way.

As we have now made clear, there is a full ton of force exerted on the inside of the breech block, and as the hand which supports the gun, as well as the center of gravity of the gun itself, lies below the line of the barrel, the result of this strong force is not only to drive the gun backward, but to rotate the entire gun about a horizontal axis through the center of gravity, so that the muzzle tends to rise.

This is the explanation of something that has puzzled many of my correspondents. I have frequently been in receipt of questions of which the following is a sample: "My .38 Special Revolver is sighted for the factory loads, and when I shoot the 130 grain wad cutter bullet in my hand loads, my groups are all low. Please give me a load for this bullet that will make it group with the factory load." The answer to this problem, and all others like it is; "It can't be done."

And perhaps another correspondent will say: "In using the Western .38 Special Super Police cartridge, I find that it seems to group about five inches higher at 20 yards than the standard 158 grain load. What is wrong?" The answer is: "Nothing is wrong—except using bullets of two different weights in the same gun and expecting them to group together."

Now for the reason. We have seen above that the pressure of a ton or more on the inside of the breech of the gun, tending to push the gun suddenly backwards, operates in a line that lies above the center of gravity of the gun and therefore tends to rotate the gun around a horizontal axis through the center of gravity of the gun so that the barrel moves upward. Thus the bullet, while it is moving forward is moving through a barrel that at the same time is rising. This motion is equivalent to giving the bullet an upward flip in addition to its forward motion. Thus the bullet will strike a point on the target that is above the point toward which the barrel was pointed when the trigger was pulled.

In making revolvers at the factory, this fact is taken into account and the sights are adjusted so that they are directed above the line of bore just the right amount to correct for this jump of the gun when it is fired, so that the bullet hits the spot to which the *sights* were pointed, though not the spot to which the *bore* of the gun was pointed at discharge. If we want to go at all into the mathematics of the jump of revolvers, we must remember what was said above, namely, that the powder pressure pushes backward on the gun exactly as hard as it pushes forward on the bullet, and that the only thing that keeps the gun from coming back just as fast as the bullet goes forward is its superior weight. If the gun and bullet weighed the same, the gun would go back as fast as the bullet goes forward, and the gun would have as much energy imparted to it as the bullet would receive, so that the shooter would be injured as much as the object his bullet strikes. Fortunately the average revolver weighs over 100 times as much as the bullet, and the velocities imparted to the gun and bullet respectively are nearly in inverse proportion to their respective weights: that is, $WV = wv$ where W and V refer to the weight and velocity of the gun and w and v refer to the weight and velocity of the bullet. This relation is not exact because the weight of the powder has a small effect and the blast of gas leaving the muzzle also increases the velocity of the gun; and the shooter's hand holding the revolver adds weight to it and reduces the recoil.

However, if we take any given revolver used by the same shooter, the weight of gun plus hand remains constant and velocity of recoil varies directly with wv, the weight of bullet times the muzzle velocity. This is the velocity of recoil, and as the *energy* of recoil varies with the square of the recoil velocity, it follows that in the case of the same gun used by the same shooter the *energy* of recoil varies with the square of the bullet weight and also the square of the velocity, or w^2v^2. Thus if we double the weight of the bullet keeping the velocity the same, we make the recoil four times as great; or if we keep the bullet weight the same and double the velocity, the result is the same. With the same velocity, the 200 grain .38 Special bullet would give 75% more recoil than a 150 grain bullet in the same gun. With the .38 Special Super Police bullet, 200 grains at 725 f. s., the recoil is only 14 per cent greater than with the regular 158 grain .38 Special with 860 f. s., as the higher velocity of the regular load nearly compensates for the lighter bullet.

But in spite of the fact that the recoil is nearly the same, the slower 200 grain Super Police strikes 4½ inches higher at 20 yards. This is because it is not the total recoil that affects the position of the group on the target. It is only that part of the recoil that takes place before the bullet has left the barrel that displaces the groups, and as was mentioned before, this part of the recoil is independent of the velocity because the greater the velocity the greater the recoil, but at the same time, the sooner the bullet is gone.

On appealing to mathematics for an exact formula it is found that the part of the recoil that takes place before the bullet has left is proportional to the bullet weight and the barrel length and inversely proportional to the weight of the gun, or in other words is proportional to $\dfrac{wL}{W}$. But for any given gun the barrel length and the weight remain constant, so that the jump before the bullet leaves is proportional solely to the bullet weight w.

No doubt most shooters realize this, but what many do not know is what factors are responsible for the jump and what will change it. The general impression seems to be that if we put in a heavier charge of powder we will make the jump greater and thus make the bullet hit higher on the target, but this is not so. It is true that a higher velocity will neutralize some of the drop in trajectory, but it will not affect the jump. At 20 yards, the difference in the drop of the trajectory between the Western Super Police .38 Special with 200 grain bullet and 710 f. s. velocity and the factory load with 158 grain bullet and 860 f. s. is 4/10 inch, while the difference in point of impact due to jump is 4½ inches. The impossibility of making the 158 grain bullet strike as high as the 200 grain Super Police is further shown by the fact that the total trajectory drop of the 158 grain bullet at standard velocity at 20 yards is only 9/10 of an inch. Even if we raised the velocity to 2000 f. s. we should have raised the point of impact by only ¾ inch and the low velocity Super Police would still shoot nearly four inches higher.

Of course, raising the velocity of the 158 grain bullet would greatly increase the recoil of the gun, but on the other hand, at the higher velocity the bullet would get away much sooner, and a mathematical investigation will show that these two factors exactly balance each other and for a given bullet weight the amount the gun moves before the bullet leaves is exactly the same regardless of the velocity.

In trying to get an actual example to illustrate what has been said, I remembered shooting a number of hand loads with bullets of different weights several years ago, and a search through a notebook showed a record of ten shots each fired off-hand at 20 yards outdoors at the standard American 20-yard target, with .38 Special, .38 Special Super Police and .38 Long Colt factory loads; also with hand loads including four different bullet weights and three different powder charges for each.

The hand loads included the 154 grain Bond wad cutter, the 163 grain round point, the 177 grain flat point, and a 210 grain bullet shaped just like the Super Police. These were loaded with 4 grains of duPont No. 5, also with 4½ grains, and the 163 and 177 grain bullets were also tried with 5 grains, though this was too heavy a load to be safe for all conditions.

The firing was done with a Smith & Wesson Military & Police, 6-inch barrel, fixed sights. No range was available that day, so the targets were nailed up on a tree in the woods, and 20 yards measured off with a steel tape. The wind was blowing, the light was spotty (sunlight through trees), and the shooting was done off-hand, so the results could hardly be expected to be perfect, yet when the results were dug up two years later and the vertical location of the groups just as they stood in the notes, were plotted against bullet weights, the points fell almost exactly on a straight line, indicating complete agreement between the mathematical theory stated above and the results obtained through actual test.

The notebook data used was as follows:—

Height of Group in Inches Above Point of Aim
Factory Loads

.38 Long Colt	150 gr. bullet	— .08
.38 Special	158 gr. "	+ .20
.38 Super Police	200 gr. "	+4.50

Reloads

	4 Gr. #5	4½ Gr. #5	5 Gr. #5
154 Gr. Wad Cutter	+ .36	+ .22	
163 Gr. Round Point	+1.65	+1.54	+ .83
177 Gr. Flat Point	+2.26	+2.62	+2.96
210 Gr. Super Police	+6.07	+6.28	

Several years ago the late Capt. Philip P. Quayle, of the Peter's Cartridge Company made a study of the phenomena of jump by the aid of spark photographs of bullets coming out of the muzzles of the revolvers. The gun muzzle was rested on a wooden support and the photographs showed that in the case of the .38 Special, the muzzle had actually raised nearly 1/10 inch from the support, even when strenuous efforts were made to hold it from rising. In fact, a little consideration will show how futile any such attempt to *hold against* recoil would be; for if you were holding the muzzle of the gun pointed aloft and had the whole weight of an automobile, for example, dropped on the muzzle, you could do nothing toward holding it. In firing the revolver, of .45 caliber, a push equalling the weight of a small automobile is applied directly backwards, and keeps pushing for nearly a thousandth of a second. While this weight is operating, it will have its way, regardless of how hard you hold against it. Capt. Quayle found that the most strenuous efforts to hold the muzzle down on the support failed to keep it from rising enough to throw the bullet 14 inches above the line of bore at 20 yards; and the difference between holding as hard as possible and not holding at all was only a change of ½ an inch in the location of the bullet at 20 yards.

Theory of Recoil

When a gun is fired, the pressure of the gas acts backward on the gun equally as strongly as it acts forward on the bullet.

When a force acts on a movable body, the velocity that is given to the body in feet per second is equal to the force in pounds, multiplied by the time during which its acts, and divided by the mass of the body; or in other words, $v = \dfrac{Ft}{m}$. Where m is the mass of the movable body, F is the force in pounds, and t is the time during which it acts.

Now in a gun, it is quite obvious that the time during which the force acts on the gun is the same as the time during which it acts on the bullet; for when the bullet goes out of the barrel the gas stops acting on both the gun and the bullet at the same time. Also the force on the gun is the same as that on the bullet, for the gas pushes equally in all directions, backward as well as forward.

If we call the velocity of the bullet   v
the mass of the bullet   m
the velocity of the gun   V
the mass of the gun   M

Then the forward motion of the bullet will be $v = \dfrac{Ft}{m}$ or $Ft = vm$

and the backward motion of the gun will be $V = \dfrac{Ft}{M}$ or $Ft = VM$

Thus we see that Ft, or the powder pressure on the base of the bullet, multiplied by the time during which it acts, is equal to the bullet velocity multiplied by the bullet mass, and is also equal to the recoil velocity of the gun multiplied by the mass of the gun. This also tells us that VM = vm, or the velocity of the gun times its weight is equal to the velocity of the bullet times its weight. (Weight is proportional to mass; mass is the weight in pounds divided by the acceleration of gravity, 32.2). Also, moving M over to the other side of the equation, we have $V = \dfrac{vm}{M}$, or, in other words, the recoil velocity of the gun equals the bullet velocity times the bullet weight, divided by the weight of the gun.

Thus for example, if we have a .38 Special gun, weighing 2 pounds, and it shoots a bullet weighing 158 grains with a velocity of 860 feet per second, we would expect the gun to have a recoil velocity of 860 divided by the weight of the gun, and multiplied by the weight of the bullet in pounds. As there are 7000 grains in a pound, the bullet weighs 158/7000ths of a pound, hence the recoil velocity would be $\dfrac{860}{2}$ x $\dfrac{158}{7000}$, which works out to 9.7 foot seconds.

This is the *velocity* of recoil; but we are more interested in the *energy* of recoil than we are in the velocity. The weight of the gun, combined with the velocity is what makes it hard to hold. Velocity in itself does not mean much without weight. Thus a tennis ball coming very fast is easy to stop; it has velocity but not much weight. A baseball has more weight, and at the same velocity would obviously be much harder to stop.

The energy of the recoil of a gun is equal to one half the mass of the gun times the square of the recoil velocity, or $\frac{1}{2} MV^2$. The mass of the gun is the weight divided by the acceleration of gravity, or 2 pounds divided by 32.2; and the velocity squared is 9.7 multiplied by 9.7, or 94.09. Hence the recoil energy would be $\frac{1}{2}$ of $\dfrac{2}{32.2}$ 94.09, or 2.9 foot pounds.

However, in figuring recoil in this manner, there is something neglected, and that is the fact that the explosion not only drives out the bullet, but the powder charge as well. When the explosion started, the bullet was in the cylinder, and the powder charge was lying behind it in the cartridge; when the recoil has finished, the bullet and the powder charge have both gone out of the gun with extreme rapidity, and the work of driving out the powder is added to that of expelling the bullet, and has its effect in adding to the recoil. This could be taken care of by merely adding the weight of the powder charge to the weight of the bullet in our formula as given above; but the sudden expansion of the gas as it leaves the barrel has a reaction that is greater than is accounted for by the weight of the powder, so that a more nearly correct result is obtained by adding one and a half times the weight of the powder charge to the weight of the bullet in figuring the recoil.

In smokeless loads, where the weight of the powder is small in relation to that of the bullet, it makes relatively little difference whether or not the powder is figured in; in the .38 Special which we figured out above, the smokeless charge is only 3.6 grains, and adding one and a half times this weight, or 5½ grains to the bullet weight would make our recoil energy 3.15 foot pounds instead of 2.9, a difference of only about 8 percent. But in black powder loads, where the charge runs up to 30 or 40 grains, instead of from 3 to 5 as with smokeless, the difference in recoil is very considerable. This is the reason why black powder gives a much heavier recoil than smokeless. Very few shooters have realized the reason for this fact. As an example, take the .38 Special cartridge loaded with 22 grains of black powder. Adding one and a half times the weight of powder charge to the bullet weight would mean adding 33 grains to our 158 grain bullet, giving an equivalent bullet weight of 191 grains. This would give a recoil velocity of 11.7 f. s., and a recoil energy of 4.27 foot pounds, an increase of 36 percent over the recoil of the smokeless load.

By looking again at the formulae given above, it will be seen that the weight of the gun has an important bearing on the recoil. If instead of using a .38 Military and Police Revolver, weighing 2 pounds, we had used a .38 Police Positive Special, weighing only 22 ounces, the recoil with the smokeless load would be 4.7 pounds instead of 3.15 pounds. Thus every different load gives a different recoil, and the same load gives a different recoil in guns of different weights.

To understand just what the figures quoted above mean, it may be considered that a foot pound is the energy that is necessary to lift a pound one foot, or the energy that a pound weight will gain by falling from a height of one foot. Thus the recoil of the .38 Special, 3.15 foot pounds, should feel about the same to the hand as catching a one pound weight which has fallen from a height of 3.15 feet.

RECOIL TABLE

Name of Gun	Weight	Cartridge	Powder	Bullet weight	Velocity	Recoil energy
.45 Colt New Service	7½ inch 42 oz.	.45 Colt, Remington	40 grains	255 grains	910 f. s.	9.9 ft. lbs.
.45 Colt New Service	5½ " 39 "	same	same	same	same	10.7 "
same	5½ same	.45 Colt smokeless	4.6 grains	same	770 f. s.	5.32 "
.45 Colt Model 1917	5½ same	.45 A. C. P.	4.6 "	230 grains	810 "	4.8 "
.45 S. & W. 1917	5½ 36½ oz.	same	same	same	same	5.2 "
.45 Automatic	5 39 oz.	same	same	same	same	4.50 "
.44 S. & W.	6½ 38 oz.	.44 S. & W. Special	6.3 "	246 grains	770 f. s.	5.2 "
.38/44 Smith & Wesson	6½ 41.75 oz	.38 Special High Velocity	6 "	158 "	1100 "	4.0 "
same	same same	.38 Special	3.6 "		860 "	2.4 "
.38 Military & Police	6 inch 32 oz.	same	same	same	same	3.3 "
same	same same	.38 Special High Velocity	6 grains	same	1100 f. s.	5.4 "
.38 Officer's Model	same 34 oz.	same	same	same	same	5.1 "
same	same same	.38 Special	3.6 grains	same	860 f. s.	3.1 "
.38 Police Pos. Spl.	4 inch 22 oz.	same	same	same	same	4.7 "
same	same same	.38 Special High Velocity	6 grains	same	1100 f. s.	7.8 "
.38 Police Positive	same 20 oz.	.38 Colt New Police	2.4 "	150 grains	710 "	3.0 "
.38 Regulation Police	same 18 oz.	same	same	same	same	3.4 "
.32 Police Positive	same 20 "	.32 Colt New Police	2.1 grains	100 grains	760 "	1.6 "
.32 Hand Ejector	same 18 oz.	same	same	same	same	1.7 "
.22 Model K S. & W.	6 inch 35 "	.22 long rifle	2 grains	40 grains	938 f. s.	.2 "
9 MM Luger	4 " 31.3 oz.	9 MM Luger	4 "	125 "	1040 "	3.1 "
.30 Cal. Luger	4½ " 31.3 "	7.65 MM Luger	4 "	93 "	1180 "	2.2 "
.30 Caliber Mauser	5¼ " 45 oz.	7.63 MM Mauser	5 "	85 "	1323 "	1.7 "

CHAPTER 9

EXTERIOR BALLISTICS

THE subject of exterior ballistics is the study of the motions of bullets after they have left the gun. It is a very complicated subject, and requires many mathematical tables and formulae. In this chapter we will not make any attempt to go into that phase of the subject. There are books on it that are available for those who are interested. However, there are several things that almost anyone who is interested in shooting will want to know about his gun and the bullet it shoots, such as the velocity, the energy, the penetration, etc., and these all come under the general heading of exterior ballistics. In this chapter we will give some of the most pertinent data of that kind about the popular pistol bullets.

Velocity

One of the most important things to know about a gun is the velocity with which it shoots. This is measured by an instrument called a chronograph. There are several forms of chronograph; the most commonly known and used is the Boulongè chronograph. This consists of two metal rods held up by electro-magnets. The first rod, or registrar, is held by an electro-magnet energized by a current of electricity passing through a wire just in front of the muzzle of the gun. When the gun is fired, the wire is broken by the bullet, and the current stops, so that the magnet drops the rod. There is another rod or weight, held by a magnet energized by current passing through a wire that is connected to the target fifty feet (or some other measured distance) from the first wire. When the bullet hits this second wire, it drops the other rod, and it strikes the trigger of a knife that marks the first rod, which is still falling.

To get the zero mark, or disjunction, as it is called, both rods are dropped at once by pressing a key which opens both circuits.

Then the rods are hung up again, and the shot is fired. It hits the muzzle wire and the first rod starts to fall. An instant later the bullet strikes the second wire and the second rod falls and makes a mark on the first rod. When the rods fall together, the mark is at the zero point, but when one falls before the other, there is a difference between them that is the distance the first rod fell before the other one started. By measuring this distance the time it took the shot to pass from the first wire to the other is calculated, and as the distance between the wires is known, the velocity is easily found.

The velocities thus obtained are not muzzle velocities, however, for this procedure merely gives the average velocity over the distance from the muzzle wire to the target wire. If the wires are located with the first one three feet from the muzzle, and the other one fifty feet further along, as is often the practice, the velocity thus obtained will be correct for the point midway between the wires, or 28 feet from the muzzle. The reason for placing the first wire 3 feet in front of the muzzle is to get it out of the blast of the escaping gases.

A velocity obtained in this manner is called *instrumental* velocity, and is always lower than the muzzle velocity, for the bullet is slowed up to a certain extent by the air resistance in traveling over the space between the wires. The amount of this slowing up can be calculated by means of ballistic tables, and it depends on the muzzle velocity and the weight and shape of the bullet, so that it varies from one bullet to the next, but for most pistol bullets a very close approximation to the muzzle velocity can be obtained by adding three per cent to the instrumental velocity at 25 feet.

For rifles, the first and second wires are usually separated by 100 or 150 feet, giving instrumental velocities at 53 feet or at 78 feet. For pistols, the instrumental velocity is usually taken with the first wire right at the muzzle, and the second one 50 feet away, so that the velocity is correct for a distance of 25 feet from the muzzle.

The Trajectory

When a bullet leaves a gun, it does not move in a straight line, but in a curve, which is called the trajectory. See sketch.

The reason for the fact that the bullet moves in a curve is that while it has a forward motion given to it by the gun, it also has a falling motion imparted to it by the force of gravity.

Thus the curve of the trajectory results from the fact that as soon as the bullet leaves the gun, it starts to fall, the same as any other unsupported object. In the first second, it falls 16 feet, in the next one 64 feet, and so on, the amount of drop in feet for a bullet or any other falling body being equal to the square of the time in seconds, multiplied by one-half the acceleration of gravity, (approximately 32). This is expressed by the formula $h = \frac{1}{2} gt^2$, where h represents the distance the body falls, g represents the acceleration of gravity, and t the time in seconds that the body has been falling. As g is approximately 32, this formula reduces to $h = 16 t^2$. Thus a bullet dropped out of a window will drop

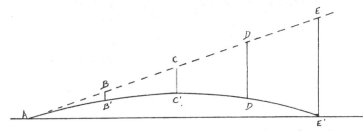

The trajectory of a bullet. In order to hit the point E', the bullet is fired in an upward direction along the dotted line A-E, and the angle, E-A-E' that this line makes with the horizontal, is the angle of departure. If E, C, D, and E are located at distances from A as indicated, the bullet will not pass through these points, but through other points located below them, the difference being due to the action of gravity during the time of flight to the points in question. The distance from A to E' is called the range.

16 feet in one second, 64 feet in two seconds, 144 feet in three second, etc.

Thus if a bullet is fired horizontally, it will have dropped 1 foot below the line of bore in one quarter of a second; four feet at the end of a half a second; 9 feet at the end of $\frac{3}{4}$ of a second; 16 feet in one second, and so on. It is this that limits the range of bullets. As soon as they get out of the gun, they begin to fall, and the problem is to move them as far as possible before they get to the ground.

This is partly solved by shooting the bullets slightly upward, instead of horizontally. For example, if we want to shoot a man who is 120 yards away with the .45 automatic pistol, it will take the bullet about $\frac{1}{2}$ second to get there. This will give the bullet time to drop 4 feet, so that we must point the pistol at a point four feet above him.

However, this is not all. The bullet slows up from the resistance of the air. Take for example the Super .38 Automatic, which has a muzzle velocity of 1200 feet per second. In one-fourth second it would go 100 yards if it didn't slow up, and we would expect the drop at 100 yards to be 12 inches. But actually, we find it to be 14 inches. Evidently the bullet takes longer than ¼ second to go 100 yards. And the drop at 200 yards, instead of being 4 feet, is found to be 66 inches. Working our equation for drop backwards, we find that the bullet took .27 seconds to go 100 yards, and .58 seconds to go 200 yards. That gives an *average* velocity over 100 yards of 1108 f.s. instead of 1200, and as the velocity at the start was 1200, we are forced to conclude that the final velocity on passing the 100 yard mark was 1030 f.s.

This loss of velocity, or slowing up, is caused by the resistance of the air on the front end of the bullet. There is a difference

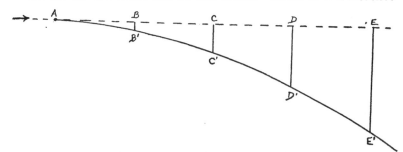

This diagram shows what happens when a bullet is fired horizontally. Suppose that a bullet is fired along the horizontal dotted line from A toward E. If the bullet has such a speed that without the action of gravity, it would reach the point B in ¼ second, it will actually pass one foot below that point, for a body which is dropped will fall 1 foot in the first quarter of a second. Thus the bullet will pass through B', one foot below B. Likewise, if A-C represents the distance corresponding to a time of flight of ½ second, A-D to ¾ second, and A-E to one second, the bullet will pass through C', D', and E', which are 4 feet, 9 feet, and 16 feet, respectively, below the corresponding points on the horizontal line. The drop for any range is equal to the distance that a body will fall in the time of flight, and this drop in feet equals 16 times the square of the time of flight in seconds.

in this resistance depending on the shape. A sharp pointed bullet will have less air resistance than one which is blunt or square across the front. In ballistics this difference in resistance due to shape is measured by a quantity called the "Form Factor," denoted in the ballistic formulae by "i".

Another important factor is the proportion of the diameter to the weight. The weight is what gives the bullet power to carry along its velocity, while the area with which it bores through the air causes its resistance.

Some bullets have more diameter in proportion to their weight than others. Thus, a .30 caliber Krag rifle bullet weighs 220 grains, or nearly as much as the 230 grain .45 caliber pistol bullet. But the area of the cross section of the Krag bullet is only .075 square inch, while that of the .45 automatic pistol bullet is .159, or over twice as much, so that the .45 pushes along more than twice as much air as the .30 caliber Krag, or any other .30 caliber bullet, for that matter; yet the Krag bullet has just about as much weight to use to do the pushing with. For this reason the air will slow the .45 caliber bullet more quickly than it will the .30.

As was said above, the force which causes the bullet to carry through against the air resistance is the weight, and the surface against which the air pressure pushes in holding it back is the cross-sectional area, which is proportional to the square of the diameter. Thus a measure of the ability of a bullet to hold its velocity is the "Sectional Density," which is the carrying power, or weight, divided by the retarding area, or the square of the diameter. To find the sectional density of any bullet, divide the weight (in pounds) by the square of the diameter in inches. Expressed as a ballistic formula, sectional density equals $\dfrac{w}{d^2}$.

However, the sectional density does not tell the whole story, for the shape of the point has its influence. The sectional density combined with the form factor "i" does tell the whole story, however. A bullet in which this quantity, (called the "Ballistic Coefficient," or "C") is larger than that of another bullet will hold its velocity better. "C" equals the sectional density divided by the form factor, or $\dfrac{w}{i\,d^2}$.

The table below gives the sectional density, form factor, and ballistic coefficient for several popular pistol cartridges.

Name of cartridge	Bullet weight grains	Bullet diameter inches	Sectional Density	Form Factor "i"	Ballistic Coefficient "C"
.25 A. C. P.	50	.250	114	1.10	.103
.32 S. & W.	85	.314	.1235	1.10	.112
.44-40	200	.426	.158	1.32	.120
.32 A. C. P.	74	.314	1085	.96	.123
.41 short	160	.400	.142	1.12	.127
.38-40	180	.400	.161	1.25	.128
.22 long rifle	40	.224	.115	.90	.129
.38 long Colt	150	.359	.167	1.26	.132
.32 Colt N. P.	100	.314	.145	1.04	.139
.38 S. & W.	145	.359	.161	1.10	.145
.41 Long	195	.388	.185	1.18	.157
9 MM Luger	125	.354	.142	.87	.163
.38 Super A. C. P.	130	.359	.144	.84	.172
.45 Colt	255	.455	.176	1.00	.177
.30 Mauser	86	.309	.129	.72	.179
.44 Special	246	.431	.184	.98	.188

Name of cartridge	Bullet weight grains	Bullet diameter inches	Sectional Density	Form Factor "i"	Ballistic Coefficient "C"
.45 Auto	230	.451	.162	.86	.180
.30 Luger	93	.309	.139	.72	.194
.38 Special	158	.359	.175	.89	.197

These figures are taken from actual ballistic tests, but should be considered only an approximation, as only a few firings in each cartridge were made, and exhaustive tests might indicate some changes. It will be noted that the cartridges are arranged in the order of the ballistic efficiency, the most efficient coming last.

For rifle bullets, these ballistic factors, such as the sectional density, the form factor, and the ballistic Coefficient "C" are very important, because rifles are used for long ranges of from three or four hundred yards up to a thousand yards or more, and it would be impossible to hit anything at these long ranges unless the ballistic data were known, so that the sights could be graduated correctly for the different ranges.

However, for revolvers, where the range usually does not exceed 50 yards, a knowledge of exterior ballistics is not so important. It is interesting, just the same, to see how much the various bullets will drop at ranges up to about two hundred yards, for many of the higher velocity revolvers, such as the .38/44 can do good work at ranges of 150 to 200 yards, and the owner of such a gun will find it useful to know how much he will have to aim above the target to make a hit.

The drop in feet for any range can very easily be calculated by the formula, drop in feet equals sixteen times the time of flight squared; and the drop in inches is twelve times this, or 192 times the square of the time of flight. If the bullet takes a half second to go 150 yards, the drop in inches will be 192 x $\frac{1}{2}$ x $\frac{1}{2}$, or 48 inches. This is the actual figure for the .38-40. Remember these two formulae:

Where t represents the time of flight in seconds,
Drop of the bullet in feet $= 16 t^2$
Drop of the bullet in inches $= 192 t^2$

It is interesting also to know that the time of flight can very easily be obtained from the height of the trajectory for any range, which is usually given in gun catalogs in the ballistic tables for the cartridges described in the catalog; for H, the height of trajectory *in feet* at its highest point equals 4 times the square of the time of flight. Thus the height for the 150 yard trajectory of the .38-40 cartridge is 4 T², or 4 x ½ x ½, or 1 foot. And note also, that the drop for any range is four times the maximum height of trajectory for that range. The drop for the .38-40 at 150 yards would thus be 4 feet, or 48 inches.

Most pistol bullets drop from about ½ inch to about 2 inches at 20 yards, and from 3 to 9 inches at 50 yards, depending on the muzzle velocity. The ballistic coefficient "C" has some little effect, but not much. Thus we can get a very close approximation to the drop by dividing the range in feet by the velocity, to

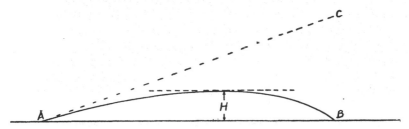

This diagram illustrates what is meant by the "height of the trajectory" for any range. This term is of frequent occurrence in gun catalogs in connection with tables giving the ballistics of cartridges. In the sketch, A is the point from which the gun is fired, and B is the target. A-B is the range. The dotted line A-C is the line of departure, or the direction in which the bullet must be started to hit the object B. H, the highest that the bullet rises above the ground in its flight to the target is the "height of the trajectory" for that range. The time of flight for the range A-B is equal to the square root of four times the height of trajectory in feet, and the drop of a bullet at any range if fired horizontally, is four times the height of the trajectory for that range.

get an approximate time of flight, and then by taking 192 times the square of this figure for the drop.

For example, take the .38-40. The velocity is 986 f.s., and if it did not slow down any, it would go 150 yards, or 450 feet in $\frac{450}{986}$ or .46 second.

The drop in inches would be 192 times .46 squared, or 41 inches. Actually it is 48, the difference being the amount that the drop increased owing to the slowing of the bullet by air resistance.

An even closer approximation, which is nearly enough correct for every practical purpose can be obtained by reducing the velocity used in this calculation fifty feet for every hundred yards of range. Thus for 150 yards we would reduce the velocity 75 feet, and use 911 instead of 986 feet. This would give a drop of 47 inches.

It is interesting to note that the way in which revolvers are sighted automatically neutralizes part of the drop. Most revolvers are sighted to shoot into the center of the bull's-eye at 20 yards when aiming at the bottom of the bull's-eye. The center is 1.36 inches above the bottom, so that the sights are adjusted to make the bullet go this much up the hill, so to speak, above the point aimed at. But this is not all. The front sight is about .6 of an inch above the line of bore, so that the bullet starts from this much below the line of sight and finishes 1.36 inch above it at 20 yards. But even this is not all, for the bullet drops .75 inch in going 20 yards, so that the total rise that the sights must give it to overcome all these factors is 2.71 inches. In other words it is started in such a direction that it would rise 2.71 inches in 20 yards if gravity and other factors did not neutralize part of the rise. If it were not for gravity, the bullet would rise 2½ times as far, or 6.75 inches at 50 yards, and ten times as far, or 27 inches at 200 yards.

The rise of 6.75 inches at 50 yards is partly neutralized at 50 yards by the drop, which is about 4 inches, on the average, so that the bullet will strike about 2½ or 3 inches above the bottom of the 8 inch bull, or nearly in the center.

At 100 yards, the rise will be about 13 inches, and the drop about 20, so that the average gun will shoot perhaps 7 inches low. At 200 yards, it will shoot over 6 feet low for the .38 Special, but only a little over 3 feet low for the .38/44.

Of course some of these factors vary a little for the various guns, and the differences as given above can be figured more closely for each individual gun, by taking the correct figures for that particular gun.

So that the reader may do any figuring along this line that he pleases, I have included here a table giving the ballistic coefficient, and the muzzle velocities and remaining velocities and drop in inches at 25, 50, 100, 150, and 200 yards for most of the leading pistol cartridges.

These figures are based on firings for retardation and drop at several ranges, and are approximately correct. However, it is only fair to state that there are slight differences even when the same cartridge is fired twice, so that a small variation from the figures given must be expected, as is usually the case with ballistic and other experimental data.

REMAINING VELOCITIES AND DROP IN INCHES FOR VARIOUS RANGES

Name of Cartridge	"O"	Remaining velocities in f.s.						Drop in inches				
		Muzzle Yds.	25 Yds.	50 Yds.	100 Yds.	150 Yds.	200 Yds.	25 Yds.	50 Yds.	100 Yds.	150 Yds.	200 Yds.
.30 Mauser	.18	1323	1256	1197	1105	1036	981	.65	2.75	12	29	55
Super .38 A.C.P.	.18	1190	1139	1096	1026	971	924	.78	3.37	14.4	33	66
.30 Luger	.194	1173	1130	1093	1031	981	939	.81	3.35	14.4	34	64
.38/44 Special	.16	1100	1060	1027	967	914	867	.94	3.8	16.6	37	69
9 mm. Luger	.168	1040	1008	979	930	885	844	1.0	4.2	17.8	43	77.5
.38-40	.128	986	958	923	867	817	773	1.15	4.7	20	48	92
.32 A.C.P.	.123	985	933	901	847	798	754	1.2	5.2	21	51	96
.32-20	.186	954	933	912	874	837	806	1.2	5.1	20.8	49	90
.22 Long Rifle	.129	950	920	892	840	794	752	1.2	5.1	21.6	52	97
.44-40	.120	918	888	859	808	762	719	1.3	5.5	23.5	56	103
.38 Special	.197	860	844	828	798	770	743	1.5	6.0	25	59	108
.45 A.C.P.	.18	810	794	778	750	720	693	1.7	7.1	26	64	123
.45 Colt	.177	790	775	759	729	701	674	1.76	7.2	30.8	70	131
.44 Special	.124	780	766	732	724	698	672	1.8	7.4	31.2	72	132
.25 A.C.P.	.103	745	720	696	650	607	537	2.0	8.3	35	86	166
.32 Colt N.P.	.139	730	712	694	660	628	597	2.1	8.6	36	85	158
.41 Long	.157	715	699	684	654	625	598	2.16	8.8	37	91	163
.38 Special Super Police	.177	710	696	682	656	630	606	2.16	8.85	37	90	161
.41 Short	.127	710	690	672	636	602	570	2.20	9.0	38	92	172
.32 S. & W.	.112	635	616	596	560	526	494	2.7	11.6	48	115	220
.38 S. & W.	.145	632	617	603	574	547	521	2.65	11.0	47.6	112	208

Bullet Energy

The power possessed by a moving bullet, or in other words, its ability to keep going when it meets an obstacle, and to do work on the obstacle is of immense importance, for obviously, the more power a bullet has, and the harder it is to stop, the more effective it can be as a weapon.

When any object is set in motion, it acquires what is called kinetic energy; that is, the energy of motion. A moving object tends to keep on moving, and the heavier it is, or the faster it moves, the harder it will be to stop. For example, a bullet that weighs 200 grains will be twice as hard to stop as one that weighs 100 grains, and is moving at the same speed. Thus the energy of bullets varies directly as the weights of the bullets.

Velocity, however, works differently; if two bullets have the same weight, and one is moving twice as fast as the other, it will be not twice as hard to stop, as might be expected, but four times as hard. And if a bullet is moving three times as fast as another of the same weight, it will be nine times as hard to stop. Thus the energy varies with the square of the velocity.

In order that the relative power of the different bullets may be known to the users, it is common for catalogs and ballistic tables to note for each bullet listed the Muzzle Energy, which is the kinetic energy possessed by the bullet when it leaves the muzzle. Like the velocity, the energy falls off as the bullet moves along its trajectory.

Energy is measured in foot pounds, and one foot pound means that amount of energy which would be capable of lifting a weight of one pound through a distance of one foot. Ten foot pounds would be capable either of lifting one pound ten feet, or ten pounds one foot. If a one pound weight is dropped ten feet, or a ten pound weight is dropped one foot, it will acquire such a velocity in falling that it will acquire ten foot pounds of energy.

Whenever an object has motion, it will keep on moving until some force stops it. If we had an object moving with an energy of ten foot pounds, and we applied a pressure of one pound against it to stop the motion, it would move ten feet before it came to a full stop. Moving against an opposing force is work, and the total amount of work done is equal in physics to the force in pounds multiplied by the distance in feet. A moving object which has a force resisting its motion will continue to move until the work it has done against the force is equal to the total energy it had.

Thus the air pressure on the nose of the .45 Automatic Pistol bullet over the first hundred yards of its flight is equal to about 2.46 ounces. During the 100 yards, or 300 feet, of its motion, this will take out 2.46 times 300, or 728 foot-*ounces* of energy, and dividing by 16 to bring this to pounds, we have 46 foot pounds of energy lost.

The same bullet will penetrate 10 inches, or 10/12th of a foot, of moist loam. The force on the nose of the bullet to stop it in this distance is the total energy divided by the distance in feet, or 337 divided by 10/12th, which equals 405 pounds. As the bullet has a cross-sectional area of only .159 inch, this force on the nose is equivalent to 2550 pounds per square inch.

Looking back into the last chapter, it will be found that we told how to find out the average push on the base of the bullet by figuring back from the muzzle velocity. Now if a bullet is moving 810 feet per second, or at any other velocity, and a force stops it in ten inches, the same force applied to a stationary bullet for ten inches will give it an equal velocity. Thus the force that will stop a bullet going 810 f. s. in ten inches, if applied to the base of the bullet in a ten inch barrel would give the bullet 810 f. s. muzzle velocity.

To check up on our mathematics, let us figure the matter out in that way and see if the pressure works out the same. We saw in the last chapter that the force on the base of a bullet equals mv divided by 2s, where m is the mass of the bullet, v is the muzzle velocity, and s is the barrel length in feet.

With a ten inch barrel, a 230 grain bullet, and a muzzle velocity of 810 f. s. we would have $F = \dfrac{230 \times 810 \times 810 \times 12}{2 \times 32 \times 7000 \times 10}$ or 405 pounds and dividing this by the area of the bullet cross-section to bring it to pounds per square inch, we get 2550, the same as before. This tells us that besides getting the average pressure on the base of the bullet by using the velocity, as we did in the last chapter, we can get it by simply dividing the muzzle energy by the length of the barrel in feet.

As we have already explained, the energy varies directly as the weight of the bullet and the square of the velocity. To find the energy in foot pounds, multiply the square of the velocity in feet per second by one-half the mass of the bullet. The mass is the weight in grains divided by the acceleration of gravity, or 32.16. The formula is thus $E = \dfrac{mv^2}{2}$. Thus the bullet of the .45 automatic pistol, weighing 230 grains and moving 810 feet per second, would have $\dfrac{230 \times 810 \times 810.}{2 \times 7000 \times 32.16}$ or 336 foot pounds energy.

Energy Factor

It will be noted that in the formula the weight of the bullet is divided by 7000 to bring it from grains to pounds, and by the gravitational constant 32.16 to give mass, instead of weight, and that the factor one-half also enters. As these are the same for all calculations of energy, time and trouble can be saved by multiplying these quantities together ahead of time and noting the value for future reference. It is 450,240. Thus to obtain the energy of any bullet, multiply the square of the velocity by the bullet weight in grains, and divide by 450,240. This divisor is called the energy factor.

Penetration

In catalogs and ballistic tables, the penetration of bullets is generally given in pine boards ⅞ inches thick, spaced 1 inch apart. This gives a certain amount of information as to the relative power of the various bullets. It is not, however, a good index of killing power, for the relative effect of bullets on flesh depends largely on the shape of the point, and the boards are so hard that they make all points about the same.

Moreover, there are several other factors that enter in the case of boards. If the velocity is high, there is a certain amount of mashing of the whole bullet, which reduces the penetration, and makes the bullet seem poor, but a mashed bullet would give more rather than less effect on flesh.

Then there is the effect of stability. A very well balanced bullet that has plenty of stability will penetrate more than a badly balanced one that will turn over when it hits; but the poorly balanced one will have more stopping power than the other one.

The driving power that forces a bullet through a resistance is the energy; and the force that holds it back is the pressure on the nose of the bullet. The larger in diameter the bullet is, the more surface it has for the pressure to work against. We might expect, therefore, that a big bullet would have less penetration than a small one of the same energy.

Then also, something depends on the hardness, or resistance of the material. Obviously it would be harder to penetrate a board than to penetrate mud, and harder to penetrate steel than to penetrate boards.

We might expect, therefore, that the factor which reduces the penetration would be the resistance of the material in question multiplied by the area of cross section of the bullet. As the energy is what drives it through, and the resistance times the area of the bullet is what stops it, we might expect the penetration to be expressed by some such formula as $P = \dfrac{E}{R A}$. Where P represents penetration, E represents striking energy, and A represents the cross-sectional area of the bullet. As this is proportional to the square of the diameter of the bullet, we could also write it $P = \dfrac{E}{R d^2}$ where d represents the bullet diameter.

From experiments, it seems to the author that the resistance of pine boards can be approximately represented by 350 in this formula.

Using these assumptions, the probable penetration of the principal pistol cartridges was figured out by the formula, and the result compared with the known penetrations of the bullets in question, as obtained from tests. The calculated results and the actual ones show a remarkable agreement, which leads to the conclusion that the author's formula for penetration must necessarily be correct. The principal use of this formula is to figure out the probable penetration of bullets of different weight and velocity than the standard, as in the case of hand loads, etc.

A table of calculated and actual penetrations follows.

Table of Penetration

Penetration is given in ⅞″ pine boards, and is the average of several tests. "Penetration factor" or the measure of the ability of a bullet to overcome a uniform resistance is obtained by dividing the striking energy by the cross sectional area of the bullet in square inches. From this figure the actual approximate penetration is obtained by dividing by a number that depends on the resistance of the material to be penetrated. For pine boards this number is found by the author to be somewhere in the neighborhood of 350. Naturally this can give only an approximation, as the actual penetration will depend on several things, such as the relative hardness of the wood, whether it is damp or well dried, whether the bullet is jacketed or not, how much the bullet deforms on impact, etc. A badly balanced bullet may turn over on impact, and the penetration will be poor, as in the case of the .32-20.

Name of Cartridge	Velocity f.s.	Energy ft. lbs.	Bullet area, sq. ins.	Pene-tration factor	Calculated pene-tration ⅞″ boards	Actual pene-tration ⅞″ boards
.30 Caliber Mauser	1323	329	.075	4390	12.5	11
.38/44 S. & W. Spl.	1100	425	.102	4170	11.8	11
Super .38 A.C.P.	1200	417	.102	4080	11.6	11
.30 Caliber Luger	1180	290	.075	3865	11.0	10
9 MM Luger	1075	320	.098	3260	9.3	9
.32-20	954	232	.076	2900	8.2	6
.38-40	950	360	.126	2859	8.1	7
.45 Colt, Western	910	460	.163	2825	8.0	8
.44-40	918	375	.143	2620	7.5	7
.38 Special	860	260	.102	2548	7.3	7
.38 Special Super Police	725	246	.102	2420	6.9	5
.44 S. & W. Special	770	320	.146	2260	6.5	7
.38 Long Colt	810	230	.102	2250	6.4	7
44 Russian	750	316	.146	2160	6.1	7
.45 Automatic Gov't	810	340	.159	2140	6.1	7
.45 Colt	770	320	.163	2023	5.7	5
.22 Long Rifle, Outdoor	930	77	.039	1975	5.6	5
.32 A. C. P.	950	140	.076	1840	5.2	5
.41 Long Colt	720	220	.129	1705	4.9	5
.38 S. & W.	730	170	.102	1675	4.8	5
.38 Colt New Police	710	170	.102	1675	4.8	5
.380 A. C. P.	900	170	.102	1670	4.8	5
.38 S. & W. Super Police	610	166	.102	1630	4.6	4

Name of Cartridge	Velocity f.s.	Energy ft. lbs.	Bullet area, sq. ins.	Penetration factor	Calculated penetration ⅞" boards	Actual penetration ⅞" boards
.32 S. & W. Long	750	124	.076	1630	4.6	4½
.32 Colt New Police	730	118	.076	1550	4.4	4
.32 S. & W.	725	99	.076	1305	3.7	3½
.22 Long Rifle	750	50	.039	1280	3.6	3½
.25 A. C. P.	745	62	.049	1265	3.5	3

Ballistic Tables

In this book are included several tables giving the ballistics of American and foreign pistol cartridges, and other exterior ballistic data of interest. In referring to these tables it should be borne in mind that there are numerous differences between the cartridges of the same caliber produced by different manufacturers. For this reason a ballistic table cannot be exact without going into great detail and listing every manufacturer separately. For example, take the case of bullet weights. The standard bullet weight for the .45 Colt is usually given as 255 grains, but some makers use a 250-grain bullet. Again, some makers use a different weight bullet in a given caliber for a smokeless load from the weight used for a black-powder load. Then some makers may test a cartridge, such as the .22 Long rifle, in a 10-inch single-shot pistol, while another maker may test the same cartridge in a revolver with a 6-inch barrel. It is quite obvious that the results would be different.

Another very important thing is that some makers load their black and smokeless powder cartridges to the same ballistics, while other makers load their black-powder cartridges to a higher velocity than their smokeless-powder cartridges. In other words, they consider it more desirable to crowd each individual type of a given caliber to the limit in velocity consistent with safety than to have the velocity uniform for the different kinds. For these reasons any ballistic table must be more or less of a compromise based on consideration of the various results obtained with cartridges of different manufacture.

CHAPTER 10

DETAILED INDIVIDUAL DESCRIPTION OF PISTOL AND REVOLVER CARTRIDGES

I T has been the aim of the author in compiling this chapter to gather together into one place as much detailed data and information as possible concerning each cartridge that the pistol or revolver shooter or the legal firearms expert is likely to encounter. It has been manifestly impossible to cover every make of every pistol or revolver cartridge in the world, but a sample of a representative make of every common American pistol cartridge has been carefully weighed, measured, and tested, and the results recorded here. In general, the lengths, diameters, etc., given are the results of actual measurements by the author of a number of samples of each cartridge. In using these measurements, the reader should bear in mind that there may be slight variations between different makes, and even between different samples of the same make; the aim has been to give a good average figure.

Factories do not like to make public the exact bullet diameter used, the exact charge of smokeless powder, or the pressure. However the author has endeavored to set down these figures for a representative factory load for each cartridge discussed, but in deference to the wishes of the makers, the name of the factory is omitted. Some time one make is used in the example quoted, sometimes the product of another manufacturer. Factory names are, however, quoted in connection with ballistics, that is bullet weight and muzzle velocity, as these figures are published by each factory. In many types of cartridge, the large American factories will all use the same bullet weight and load to the same velocity; but in other cases there will be slight differences in velocity, bullet weight, or both. Where all makers use the same standards, just one velocity and bullet weight is given in the tabulations; but where

323

there are marked differences in the standards used in one or more makers, separate figures are given for the makes concerned.

In many cases, recommended charges for hand loading are included. These have all been obtained from sources believed to be reliable, and the greatest care has been used in compiling them, so that they are believed to be perfectly safe to use under properly controlled conditions; but arms vary so in condition, and individuals differ so much in the skill and intelligence with which the reloading is performed, that neither the author nor the publisher can be responsible for any failure for these loads to work as expected, and all information of any kind included in this book is for the reader to use in any way that he may see fit at his own risk.

Cartridges described are listed by caliber, starting with the smallest first, so that the diameter of the bullet may serve as an index.

.22 CALIBER CARTRIDGES

There are no less than eight distinct types of .22 caliber rim-fire cartridges made in this country, of which six are regularly used in pistols and revolvers. There are also several center fire .22 caliber cartridges made, such as the .22 Winchester Center Fire, the .22 Hornet, and the .22 Savage High Power. As no revolvers are regularly made for the .22 Automatic Rim Fire, the .22 Remington Autoloading, or the .22 center fire cartridges, no detailed description of them will be given.

.22 B.B. Cap. (Bullet Breech Cap)

This is the smallest cartridge made or used in this country. It is a very short rim fire .22 caliber cartridge, with a lead bullet weighing only 20 grains. The cartridge case is made of copper, and is the same diameter as the .22 short and the other .22 rim fire cartridges, but is much shorter.

These cartridges were originally intended for use in Flobert Rifles, but they are found to be very accurate in revolvers and single shot pistols, and as they have very low power, and make scarcely any noise at all, they are very useful for indoor shooting. With an X-Ring Bullet Trap and a supply of B. B. Caps, the ordinary cellar makes a very satisfactory shooting gallery where much valuable and entertaining target practice may be had.

The bullet for the B. B. Cap is about as long as it is wide, and has a conical point with a rather abrupt shoulder where it joins the cylinder. This makes it tend to cut a clean hole in the paper, like the hole made by a wad-cutter.

The B. B. Caps may be obtained with copper clad, cadmium plated, or lubricated bullets. The lubricated type is slightly more messy to handle, but is less likely to lead the gun, though there is not so very much danger of leading unless a lot of shooting is done very rapidly.

Diameter of bullet	.224 inch
Weight of bullet	20 grains
Length of bullet	.25 inch
Diameter of case at head	.279 inch
" " " " mouth	.228 "
Length of case	.28 inch
Length of cartridge overall	.42 "
Muzzle velocity, rifle	875 feet per second (Federal Ctg. Co.)
" energy "	34 foot pounds
Muzzle velocity, 6 inch revolver	750 feet per second (Remington)
" energy, revolver	25 foot pounds

.22 C. B. Cap (Conical Ball Cap)

This cartridge has a case of the same size as that for the B. B. Cap, loaded with a larger bullet, which is the same as the bullet for the .22 Short cartridge. Like the B. B. cap, it makes very little noise, and is good for indoor practice. However I do not like it quite as well for this purpose as I do the B. B. Cap, for it is no more accurate, and has more power and more noise, both of which are undesirable for a cellar range. Moreover, it does not cut a sharp hole as does the B. B.

Bullet diameter	.224 inch
Bullet weight	29 grains
Bullet length	.36
Cartridge case dimensions	Same as for B. B. Cap.
Length of cartridge overall	.55 inch
Muzzle velocity, rifle	975 f. s. (Federal Ctg. Co.)
Muzzle energy, rifle	61 foot pounds.
Muzzle velocity, 6 inch revolver	780 foot seconds (Remington)
Muzzle energy, revolver	39 foot pounds.

.22 Short, Rim Fire

This cartridge, one of the most popular in the world, was designed by Smith & Wesson in 1854, and today, 80 years later, is used in almost the same form as it was then. It has a 29 or 30 grain bullet, with a diameter of .223 to .224, some makers using 29 grain bullets as standard, while others prefer the 30 grain weight. It is loaded with black, smokeless, or Lesmoke powder. The standard charge of black powder is 3 grains, and of smokeless about ¾ of a grain.

Previously the .22 short smokeless loads were very destructive to gun barrels because the powder charge was so small that the corrosive residue of the primer was not sufficiently diluted; but since the advent of the noncorrosive primer, the smokeless loads have largely superseded the others, and are recommended in preference to either the black or the Lesmoke.

This cartridge is extremely accurate, and is very useful for rifle work, but is not much used in revolvers and pistols because most target revolvers and pistols are built, at the present time, with special reference to the use of the Long Rifle cartridge. The .22 Short can be used in any gun that is chambered for the .22 Long Rifle. The twist required for the .22 Short is not quite as great as that required for the .22 Long Rifle because the shorter bullet is easier to stabilize.

In using a .22 short in a barrel chambered for the .22 Long Rifle, or in a cylinder chambered for a long-rifle cartridge, a roughness or burning of the metal just forward of the place where the mouth of the short cartridge comes will eventually take place. This does not harm the accuracy of the gun when it is used with the longer cartridge, because this rough or corroded spot is covered up by the neck of the cartridge, but the result is that it makes the long rifle cartridge harder to extract.

The .22 short is made in several different styles. The ordinary .22 short smokeless with the lubricated lead bullet, giving a muzzle velocity in rifles of about 925 to 950 feet per second, according to make, may be considered as standard. In addition, all the companies make a hollow point cartridge, with a cavity in the point, and a bullet 2 grains lighter than the solid ball. The hollow point gives greater game killing ability. Then in addition, all companies now make a high speed type of .22 short, under some such name as Hi-Speed, High Velocity, Super X, etc. This is made with both the solid and the hollow point bullets.

Then in order to cater to the desires of those marksmen who desire to carry the cartridges loose in the pocket, there are greaseless or unlubricated cartridges made by all the companies. An example of a trade name covering the dry type is the Remington "Silvadry" cartridge with a cadmium plated bullet. Many companies plate all their .22 bullets with copper or lubaloy, which probably has a tendency to reduce the tendency to leading, but will not take the place of adequate lubrication.

For gallery use there is a special lead bullet made of compressed lead dust to prevent the danger from particles of the bullet bouncing back from the iron target plates, which is called spatter back. When these bullets of compressed lead dust hit the iron plate they simply go to powder, so that there are no particles left to fly back. Each company has its own trade name, of which examples are "Spatterproof," "Spatterless," "Krumble Ball," etc.

Bullet diameter	.223 inch or .224 inch
Bullet weight	29 grains or 30 grains
Length of bullet	.36 inch
Diameter of case at head	.279 inch
" " " " mouth	.228 "
Length of case	.42 inch
Length of cartridge overall	.69 "
Factory Black Powder charge	2.6 grains FFFG
Velocity, 6 inch revolver	755 foot seconds
Factory Lesmok Load	1.7 Grains Lesmok A.
Pressure	10,000 pounds
Velocity, 6 inch revolver	755 foot seconds
Factory Smokeless load	.82 grains DuPont No. 92
Pressure	10,000 pounds per square inch
Velocity, 6 inch revolver	750 foot seconds
Penetration, ⅞ inch pine boards	2 boards
Name, Winchester	.22 short, staynless
Muzzle velocity, rifles	975 foot seconds
" energy, rifles	63 foot pounds
" velocity, 6 inch revolver	850 foot pounds
" energy, revolver	48 foot pounds
Name, Western Ctg. Co.'s	.22 short Super X
Powder charge	1.49 grains smokeless
Muzzle velocity, rifles	975 foot seconds
" energy, "	63 foot pounds
Muzzle velocity, 6 inch revolver	850 foot pounds
" energy "	48 foot pounds

.22 Long, Rim Fire

This is a mongrel cartridge, having the bullet of the .22 short and the cartridge case and powder charge of the .22 long rifle. It is not as accurate as either the short or the long rifle, and has nothing to recommend it. Like the short, it is made in the hollow point, dry, etc., as well as in the regular type.

Bullet weight	29 grains or 30 grains
Bullet diameter	.224 inch
Velocity in rifle	975 feet per second
Muzzle energy	63 foot pounds
Muzzle velocity, 6 in. revolver	870 foot seconds
Muzzle energy, revolver	50 foot pounds

.22 Caliber Long Rifle

This is one of the most accurate cartridges in the world and is the favorite with target shots. There are more .22-caliber Long Rifle cartridges sold than all other kinds for use in pistols and revolvers. The .22 Long Rifle cartridge has a 40-grain bullet with a diameter of from .223 to .226, depending on the make.

The cartridge case, made of copper or brass, is almost exactly like that of the .22 short, except that it is slightly longer so as to hold an increased powder charge.

For many years the .22 long rifle cartridge was loaded to a standard velocity of about 950 feet per second; but finally a so-called outdoor type was developed, with about from 1050 to 1100 foot seconds velocity. This cartridge was loaded with Lesmoke, the first of its kind being the United States Cartridge Company's N. R. A. cartridge. Other brands are Western Marksman, Remington Palma, Peter's Tackhole, and Winchester Precision. The next innovation was the production in 1929 of a Hi-Speed Cartridge by Remington, with a velocity nearly two hundred feet higher than any other .22 cartridge then on the market, or about

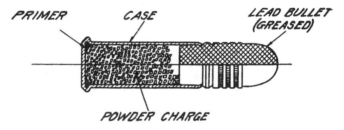

PRIMER   *CASE*   *LEAD BULLET (GREASED)*

POWDER CHARGE

CAL. 22 LONG RIFLE CARTRIDGE.

1275 feet per second. Western Cartridge Company in the latter part of 1930 produced a new line of ultra high speed .22 caliber cartridges known under the trade name of Super-X. The Super-X cartridges were claimed to have 1400 feet per seconds in the rifle, but samples received by me from the factory in December 1930 actually gave 1417 feet per second when tested. These cartridges were found to be loaded with 2.5 grains of smokeless powder, determined by breaking down and weighing a number of samples. At the present time all companies make high velocity .22 caliber long rifle cartridges.

For many years the .22 caliber outdoor type loaded with Lesmoke powder to give 1100 feet per second in rifles, and about 950 feet per second in revolvers or pistols was the standard load for target use; but in the last few years all the cartridge companies have developed satisfactory non-corrosive primers, so that the smokeless loads are now superseding the Lesmoke type. Names of popular smokeless target loads are: Remington Kleanbore, Winchester Staynless, Peter's Rustless, Western Super-Match.

.22 CAL. REVOLVERS

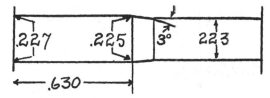

CAMP PERRY MODEL.

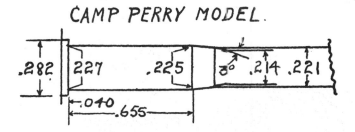

WOODSMAN PISTOL.

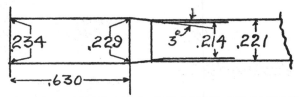

STANDARD CHAMBER DIMENSIONS OF COLT PISTOLS AND REVOLVERS
The upper chamber, accommodating .22 BB Caps, .22 C. B. Caps, .22 Short, .22 Long, and .22 Long Rifle Cartridges, is used in the Police Positive Target, the Official Police, and the Officer's Model Revolvers.

Name	.22 Long Rifle Rim Fire
Length overall	.995 inch
Length case	.613 inch
Bullet weight	40 grains
Bullet weight, Hollow point	37 grains
Charge, Smokeless powder	1.35 Dupont No. 93
Charge, Black powder	3.5 grains FFFG
Charge, Lesmok powder	2.5 Lesmok A
Pressure, smokeless load	11,000 lbs. per square inch
Muzzle velocity, rifle	950 foot seconds
Muzzle velocity, 6 inch barrel	750 foot seconds
Muzzle energy	50 foot lbs.
Penetration, ⅞ inch boards	3 boards
Name	.22 l. r. outdoor type
Powder charge	3 grains Lesmok A
Pressure	15,000 lbs. per square inch

Velocity, rifle	1100 foot seconds
Velocity at 100 yds. rifle	930 foot seconds
Muzzle energy, rifle	117 foot pounds
Muzzle velocity, 6 inch barrel	940 foot seconds
Muzzle energy, 6 inch barrel	78 foot lbs.
Penetration ⅞ inch boards	3 boards
Name	.22 Remington Kleanbore
Muzzle velocity, rifles	1070 foot seconds
Muzzle velocity, 6 inch barrel revolver	900 foot seconds
Name	.22 Hi-Speed Kleanbore
Velocity, rifles	1275 foot seconds
Velocity, 6 inch barrel revolver	1100 foot seconds
Muzzle energy	107 foot pounds
Name	.22 Super Match
Muzzle velocity, rifles	1215 foot seconds
Muzzle velocity, 6 inch barrel revolver	1015 foot seconds
Name	.22 Super-X Long Rifle
Powder charge	2.5 grains smokeless
Muzzle velocity, rifles	1400 foot seconds
Muzzle velocity, 6 inch barrel revolver	1075 foot seconds
Muzzle energy, revolver	102 foot pounds

.22 W.R.F. (Winchester Rim Fire)

This is a .22 caliber rim fire cartridge that is somewhat larger than the .22 long rifle. The old standard load for the long rifle cartridge was a 40 grain bullet and five grains of black powder, whereas the .22 W. R. F. has a 45 grain bullet and used to have seven grains of black powder, from which it is often called the .22-7-45.

.22 W.R.F. REVOLVER .

.246   .2435   3° .228

.935

The Colt Police Positive Target revolver can be obtained in this caliber, which formerly was more powerful than the .22 long rifle; and like it, is made in the high speed as well as the regular type.

Name	.22 Winchester Rim fire, Staynless
Bullet weight	45 grains
Bullet diameter	.228
Muzzle velocity, rifles	1010 foot seconds
Muzzle velocity, 6 inch revolvers	810 foot seconds
Muzzle energy, 6 inch revolver	66 foot pounds

Name	.22 W. R. F. Super-X
Muzzle velocity, rifles	1445 foot seconds
Name	.22 W. R. F. Kleanbore Hi-Speed
Muzzle velocity in rifles	1500 foot seconds

5.5 m/m Velo Dog

This is a very long cartridge of .22 caliber with a metal jacketed bullet weighing 45 grains. The cartridge is only adapted to a foreign gun called the Velo Dog, which is a high velocity Bull Dog type of revolver not often seen in America.

Name	5.5 m/m Velo Dog
Bullet weight	45 grains
Bullet length	.48 inch
Case length	1.12 "
Length loaded cartridge	1.35 "
Diameter of rim	.308 "
Thickness of rim	.047 "
Diameter case, rear,	.253 "
" " front,	.248 "
Muzzle velocity, 2 inch barrel	760 f. s.
Muzzle energy	56 ft. lbs.

.25 Caliber (6.35 m/m) Automatic Colt Pistol

This was first made for the Browning automatic pistol under the name of the 6.35 mm. and was primarily a European cartridge, but was afterwards introduced into this country extensively when

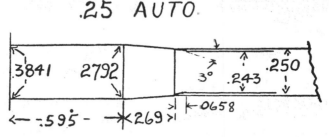

the Colt Patent Fire Arms Company took up the manufacture of the .25-caliber automatic. It is a very powerful cartridge for its size, having a 50-grain bullet with a velocity of 758 foot-seconds. It looks like a rimless cartridge, but is of the semi-rim type.

Overall length of cartridge	.905
Bullet weight	50 grains
Type of bullet used	Metal jacketed
Seating depth of bullet	.15 inch
Bullet diameter	.251
Bullet length	.46 inch
Diameter cartridge head	.298 "
" " mouth	.276 "

Length cartridge case	.62 "
Length loaded cartridge	.91 "
Type of cartridge	Semi-rim
Factory charge	1.65 grains Infallible
Pressure	10,000 lbs. per square inch
Velocity in 2 inch pistol	758 foot seconds
Energy	67 foot pounds
Penetration, ⅞ inch pine boards	3 boards
Charge for reloading	1.4 gr. Bullseye Powder
Velocity	751 foot seconds
Pressure	12,930 lbs. per square inch
Recommended by	Hercules Powder Co.
Charge for reloading	1.4 grains DuPont No. 5
Velocity	758 foot seconds
Pressure	15,000 lbs.
Recommended by	DuPont Powder Co.

6.5 mm. Bergmann Automatic

This is a very high powered, .26 caliber automatic with a rimless, bottle necked cartridge which looks something like the .30 caliber Luger cartridge. It contains a 76 grain, metal jacketed bullet with 2.2 grains of very fast burning smokeless powder.

Bullet weight	76 grains
Bullet diameter	.264 inch
Bullet length	.64 "
Diameter of cartridge head	.373 "
Diameter of cartridge body, rear	.367 "
Diameter of cartridge body, front	.324 "
Diameter of Cartridge Neck	.289 "
Length of case	.87 "
Length of Cartridge	1.23 "

7.5 mm. Nagant

The Nagant revolver used by the Russian, Norwegian, and other armies has a very distinctive action. The front part of each chamber in the cylinder is tapered and the rear end of the barrel is tapered to fit into this chamber. When the gun is cocked the cylinder is pushed forward so that the back end of the barrel enters the front part of the chamber, thus forming a seal to prevent the escape of gas between the barrel and the cylinder. In order to seal this gap more effectively the cartridge case is made longer than the bullet—that is, the bullet is sealed entirely inside the cartridge, and the front end of the cartridge case enters the barrel itself when the cylinder is pushed forward. The front end of the brass cartridge is tapered in toward the point of the bullet so as to facilitate its entering the barrel.

The Nagant cartridge shown in the photograph is loaded, but in the picture it looks like an empty case because the bullet is entirely

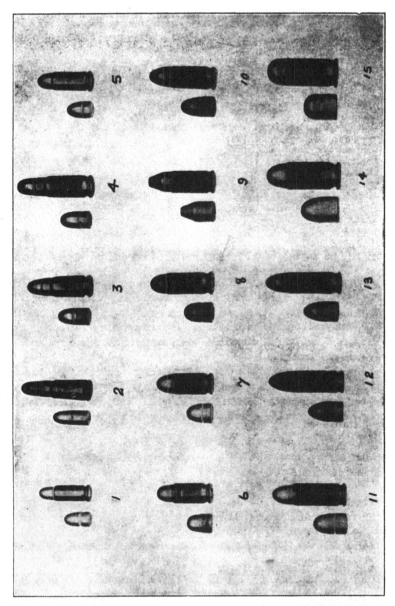

CARTRIDGES FOR AUTOMATIC PISTOLS

1. .25 (6.35) Automatic
2. .256 Bergmann Automatic
3. .30 (7.65) Luger
4. .30 (7.63) Mauser
5. .32 (7.65) Automatic

6. .35 S. & W. Automatic
7. .380 (9-mm Short) Automatic
8. 9-mm. Browning Long
9. 9-mm. Luger
10. 9-mm. Luger, Round-nose Bullet

11. .38 Automatic Colt
12. 9-mm. Steyr
13. 9-mm. Bayard
14. .45/230 Colt Auto.
15. .455 Webley Auto.

inside the cartridge case and does not project out where it can be seen.

This cartridge is too small in caliber and too low in velocity to have much stopping power or effectiveness.

Bullet weight	108 grains
Bullet diameter	2.95 inches
Diameter cartridge head	.388 "
Diameter cartridge body, rear	.355 "
Diameter cartridge over bullet	.330 "
Diameter cartridge case, front	.285 "
Length of cartridge case	1.53 "
Length of loaded cartridge	1.53 "
Powder charge, lead bullet	10 Grains black
Powder charge, M. C. bullet	5 " Smokeless
Velocity	725 f. s.
Energy	122 ft. lbs.

.30 (7.63 m/m) Mauser Automatic Pistol Cartridge

This is a rimless high-velocity, high-pressure cartridge. It has the highest velocity of any pistol cartridge, and the pressure runs up to around 30,000 pounds, over twice that of the ordinary revolver cartridge. It has an 85-grain bullet, and the velocity varies with different makes, from about 1,200 to about 1,325 foot-seconds. This is a European cartridge, and the foreign name of it is the 7.63-mm. Mauser.

The Mauser Company also makes a .32 pocket pistol, and that is called the 7.65-mm. The name is almost the same, but there is a big difference in the two cartridges. The .30-caliber Mauser cartridges are made either full metal-jacketed or soft point.

Bullet weight	85 grains
Bullet diameter	.309 inch
Bullet type	Metal cased or soft point
Length of bullet	.54 inch
Diameter cartridge head	.390 "
" " mouth	.332 "
Length cartridge case	1.04 "
Overall length of loaded cartridge	1.35 inch
Representative factory charge	7.0 grains Ballistite
Pressure	29,000 lbs.
Muzzle velocity, 5½ inch barrel	1323 feet per second
Muzzle energy	329 foot pounds
Penetration, ⅞ inch pine boards	11 boards
Remington velocity	1280 feet per second
Winchester velocity	1397 foot seconds
Western velocity	1323 feet per second

.30 Caliber (7.65 m/m) Luger

This is another rimless high-velocity pistol cartridge, but not as high as the Mauser. It has a velocity of around 1,200 foot-seconds, and the pressure is about 21,000 pounds. It has a 93-grain bullet made either soft point or full metal-jacketed. The name of this cartridge does not follow the same rule as that of the Mauser, because this is called 7.65-mm. Luger, whereas the Mauser is called 7.63, though the bullets are the same diameter, namely, .309. This bullet has great penetration, but not much shocking power because it is too small in caliber.

This 7.65 cartridge should not be confused with the other European 7.65's, which are the same as the .32 Automatic Colt.

Special cartridges are made by foreign makers for the Luger Carbine, which takes a more powerful cartridge to operate the heavier springs. The carbine cartridge is loaded with more pressure, and hence a higher velocity than the pistol cartridge, and is marked by being colored black. It gives a velocity in the 4½-inch barrel of 1363 against 1200 for the regular cartridge. The call for them is so small that they are not made in this country. The carbine may be used with satisfaction for single shots with the regular cartridges, which may even operate the mechanism at times.

The following ballistic data for the .30 Luger Pistol given in a German catalog may be of interest:

Distance	Group height	Group width	Height of 100 meter trajectory	Height of 200 meter trajectory
25 meters	2.4 inches	1.2 inches	5.9 inches	
50 "	4.3 "	2.7 "	9.4 "	17.3 inches
60 "			9.85 "	
75 "	7.1 "	4.7 "	8.3 "	
100 "	10. "	7.1 "		23.6 "
125 "				25.5 "
150 "	17.7 "	13. "		21.3 "

Name	.30 Caliber (7.65 mm) Luger
Make	German
Bullet weight	92.6 grains
Bullet diameter	.309
Bullet type	Full jacketed or soft point
Jacket material	Cupro-nickel coated steel
Bullet length	.58 inch
Diameter cartridge head	.390 "
" " mouth	.332 "
Length cartridge case	.85 inch
Length loaded cartridge	1.14 "
Powder charge	5.09 grains Rottweil flake
Pressure	28,798 lbs. per square inch
Velocity	1150 foot seconds
Name	.30 Caliber Luger
Make	American
Powder charge	4.7 grains Infallible

Velocity in 3¾ inch barrel	1207
Energy	300 foot pounds
Penetration, ⅞ inch pine boards	10 boards
Velocity, Remington make	1180. f. s.
Velocity, Peters make	1173 f. s.
Velocity, Western make	1173 f. s.
Velocity, Winchester make	1225 f. s.

.32 Rim Fire Cartridges

There are a great many old .32 rim fire revolvers still in existence, but the cartridges have long ago become obsolete, so that they can be found today only in the very large stores. These cartridges are of the same general construction as the .22 caliber rim fire cartridges, but are made larger. They have lead bullets, outside lubricated.

The .32 extra short has a 55 grain bullet. The .32 short has an 80 grain bullet and is loaded with 9 grains of black powder. The .32 long has a 90 grain bullet with 13 grains of black powder.

.32 Smith & Wesson

This is a standard size cartridge for small pocket revolvers. It was originally made with an 85-grain lead bullet and 9 grains of

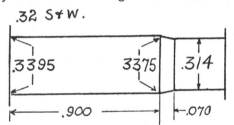

This chamber will accommodate the .32 S. & W., the .32 S. & W. Long, and the .32 Colt New Police cartridges, and is used in the Pocket Positive, Police Positive, and Police Positive Target revolvers.

black powder. It is now loaded with either black or smokeless powder, the average velocity being around 632 foot-seconds, though some makers load to higher velocities. It is a small, low-powered cartridge with little noise and practically no recoil, but capable of killing at short ranges. On account of the low velocity and small weight of the bullet, the stopping power is inferior.

Bullet weight	85 and 88 grains
Bullet diameter	.314
Bullet length	.54 inch
Diameter of cartridge head	.374 "
" " " mouth	.336 "
Length of case	.60 "
Length of loaded cartridge	.92 "
Representative factory charge	1.4 grains Bullseye

Pressure   8,000 pounds per square inch
Velocity   725 feet per second
Energy   99 foot pounds
Penetration ⅞ inch pine boards   3½ boards

There is some variation in the standards used by the different companies as follows:

Make	Bullet weight	Velocity
Peters	85 grains	635 foot seconds
Remington	88 "	710 " "
Western	85 "	725 " "
Winchester	85 "	700 " "

.32 Short Colt. .320 Revolver

These are old cartridges, designed years ago for arms that are now obsolete. The .32 short Colt was originally used in Colt revolvers, while the .320 Revolver Cartridge was a foreign cartridge made to fit the Webley, Tranter, and other European revolvers of this size. The .32 Short Colt will fit the revolvers chambered

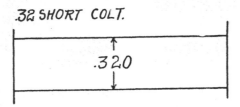

.32 SHORT COLT.

.320

This chamber is now obsolete, and is no longer made. It is found in the following arms which have been chambered for the .32 Short Colt cartridge: Pocket Positive, Police Positive, Police Positive Target, Single Action Army, Bisley Model, and Bisley Model Target.

for the .320, and the .320 can be used in the Colt revolvers of .32 Short caliber, so that these cartridges may be used interchangeably.

They are black powder cartridges, with outside lubricated lead bullets. The .32 Short Colt is loaded with black or smokeless powder; the .320 with black powder only. While these cartridges resemble the .32 Smith & Wesson, they will not interchange with it, as there are some differences in dimensions, as will be seen from an examination of the tabulated data.

Bullet diameter   .313 inch
Bullet weight   82 grains
Bullet length   .48 inch
Diameter cartridge head   .315 "
         "   mouth   .375 "
Length of case   .64 "
Length loaded cartridge   1.05 "

Factory charge, black powder   7.7 grains FFFG
    "   " smokeless powder   1.9 grains Bullseye
Pressure   8,000 lbs. per square inch
Velocity in 6 inch revolver   810 f. s.
Energy   116 foot pounds
Penetration, ⅞ inch pine boards   4 boards

For reloading, use an 82 grain lead bullet and 7 grains of King's Semi-smokeless FFG.

.32 Long Colt

Like the .32 short Colt, this is an obsolete cartridge, now made only to take care of the occasional demand from the owners of old guns of this caliber that are still in existence. The .32 Short Colt originally had an 80 grain outside lubricated bullet, and was loaded with 9 grains of black powder, while the .32 Long Colt had a 90 grain outside lubricated bullet and 12 grains of black powder. The diameter of the body of the bullet was .313, and the outside diameter of the case was the same; the bullet had a "heel" of reduced diameter, (.299 inch) to fit inside of the case. When the inside lubricated bullets of the same diameter both inside and outside the case came into use, the .32 S. & W. cartridge was produced, with a bullet the same in maximum diameter as the .32 short and long Colt, and with a cartridge case big enough to fit over the bullet of this diameter instead of fitting over a reduced diameter heel.

Thus the case of the .32 Long Colt is only .313 in diameter, while that of the .32 S. & W. is .336 in outside diameter. This explains why the two cartridges, which look much alike, will not interchange.

Lately the .32 Long Colt has been changed to inside lubrication. The bullet is made the same diameter outside of the case as inside, namely, .299, which is too small to fit the rifling, but a very deep hollow base is provided, so that the powder pressure will swell out the base to fit the rifling. This change reduced the weight of the bullet to 82 grains, which is now the standard.

Bullet weight   80 grains
Bullet diameter   .299 inch
Bullet length   .62   "
Diameter cartridge head   .374   "
Diameter cartridge body outside   .313   "
Length of case   .92   "
Length loaded cartridge   1.26   "
Typical factory charge   2.1 grains Bullseye
Pressure   8,000 pounds
Velocity, 4 inch barrel   770 f. s.

Energy		110 ft. lbs.	
Penetration, ⅞ inch pine boards		4 boards	

Reloading Data

Bullet name	Ideal 299155	Ideal 299155	Ideal 299155
Bullet weight	80 grains	80 grains	80 grains
Powder, kind	Pistol No. 5	S. R. No. 80	Bullseye
Powder, charge	3.1 grains	6.5 grains	2.0 grains
Velocity	830 f. s.	815 f. s.	765 f. s.
Recommended by	Ideal handbook	Ideal handbook	Ideal handbook

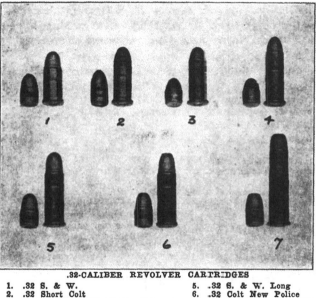

.32-CALIBER REVOLVER CARTRIDGES

1. .32 S. & W.
2. .32 Short Colt
3. .320 Revolver (Black Powder)
4. .32 Long Colt
5. .32 S. & W. Long
6. .32 Colt New Police
7. .32 Winchester (.32/20)

.32 Smith & Wesson Long
.32 Colt New Police (Police Positive)

These are more powerful cartridges for the small pocket size revolvers than was the original .32 Smith & Wesson. These two cartridges are interchangeable. The .32 Smith & Wesson Long has a 98-grain bullet, and the original black powder charge was 13 grains. The smokeless load is around 2 grains of Bull's-Eye. The velocity is 790 foot-seconds and the energy 140 foot-pounds. It is a very highly accurate cartridge.

The .32 Colt New Police, now known as the "Colt Police Positive," is an advanced design of .32-caliber cartridge, which is interchangeable with the .32 Smith & Wesson Long. It has a 100-

grain bullet with about 730 foot-seconds velocity and 120 foot-pounds of energy. The Colt New Police Cartridge differs from the Smith & Wesson Long mainly in that it has a flat point which gives it superior stopping power. A mid-range load is made for this cartridge with a 100-grain bullet and a reduced velocity.

All Colt and Smith & Wesson pistols and pocket arms in .32 caliber are now chambered for the .32 Smith & Wesson Long, and the .32 Colt Police Positive can be used in the same gun. An exception is the Smith & Wesson .32 Safety Hammerless, which is made only for the short cartridge—that is, the .32 Smith & Wesson. These firms also make revolvers chambered for the .32/20, but these are in the larger frame type.

Both the .32 Smith & Wesson Long and the .32 Colt New Police may be obtained in black and smokeless loads, and with lead or metal point bullets.

Name	.32 Smith & Wesson Long
Bullet weight	98 grains
Bullet diameter	.313 inch
Bullet length	.58 inch
Diameter of cartridge head	.374 "
Diameter of cartridge mouth	.336 "
Length of case	.92 "
Length loaded cartridge	1.27 "
Typical factory powder charge	2.1 grains Bullseye
Pressure	9,000 pounds per square inch
Velocity in 6 inch barrel	750 feet per second
Muzzle energy	124 foot pounds
Velocity, Peters make	720 feet per second
" Remington make	790 " " "
" Remington black powder load	820 " " "
" Western make	775 " " "
" Winchester make	810 " " "
Penetration 7/8 inch pine boards	4½ boards
Name	.32 Colt New Police
Bullet weight	100 grains
Bullet diameter	.3125 inch
Bullet length	.57 inch
Case dimensions	Same as for .32 S. & W. Long
Length loaded cartridge	1.26 inch
Typical factory charge	2.0 grains Bullseye
Pressure	8,500 pounds per square inch
Velocity, 4 inch barrel	730 foot seconds
Energy	120 foot pounds

Bullet weights and velocities vary as follows:

Make	Bullet weight	Velocity
Peters	100 grains	730 f. s.
Remington	100 grains	730 f. s.
Western	98 grains	750 f. s.
Winchester	98 grains	706 f. s.

Reloading Data

Bullet name	Ideal 313249	Ideal 313249	lead
Bullet weight	87 grains	87 grains	85 grains
Powder, kind	Pistol No. 5	DuPont No. 80	Bullseye
Powder, charge	2.5 grains	3.4 grains	1.5 grains
Velocity	625	625	696
Recommended by	DuPont	DuPont	Hercules

.32 Winchester

This cartridge, which is also called the .32/20, was originally intended to have a 20-grain charge of black powder, hence the name. ".32/20." It has a 115-grain bullet as ordinarily loaded, though some companies use a 100-grain bullet. The full factory load generally runs a little under 20 grains of black powder, usually about 16 grains of FFG, which gives a velocity of about 970 foot-seconds with the 115-grain bullet. It is primarily a rifle cartridge, intended for the old Winchester Model 1873 rifle and afterwards for the Winchester Model 1892, for the Marlin, Remington and Colt repeating rifles and for the many single-shot rifles.

Revolvers were chambered for this cartridge in order to give the user of the rifle of this caliber out on the frontier a hand arm

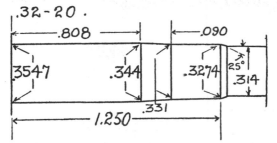

The above is the chamber for the .32-20 (.32 Winchester) cartridge, the Single Action Army, the Official Police, and the Police Positive Special are now made for this cartridge. This chamber was formerly used in the following arms, now obsolete; New Army, New Navy, Bisley Model; also in the Army Special, now known as the Official Police.

that would take the same cartridge, so that he would only have to carry one kind of ammunition. This worked out very well indeed in the old frontier days, when black powder was the only powder known, but when smokeless powders came into fashion a difficulty was met in that a smokeless powder that is well adapted for burning in a long rifle barrel will not burn well in a short revolver barrel, and vice versa. Accordingly, the .32/20, as it is now loaded, is more or less of a compromise intended primarily to give the best results in rifles, but loaded with the type of smokeless powder that will perform fairly well in revolvers. It is loaded usually with Sharpshooter powder, which is a nitroglycerin powder and is very erosive on gun barrels.

The .32/20 is the highest power .32 made for revolvers. It has a 115-grain bullet with nearly 1,000 foot-seconds velocity and a flat point that adds more shock power than the caliber would otherwise give. In spite of the disadvantage of not being primarily a revolver cartridge, it is quite a favorite, as is shown by the fact that Smith & Wesson make a gun called the "Winchester" for it.

This cartridge is quite accurate when properly loaded; but there is more variation between the different makes in this cartridge than in most calibers, and they do not all perform equally well in revolvers. It is therefore a good plan for the user of a .32/20 caliber revolver to experiment until he finds the make of .32/20 ammunition that performs best and then stick to it.

In recent years the cartridge companies have improved this cartridge for rifle use by loading it with a more powerful load, and these new cartridges are called "High-Speed" or "High-Velocity" cartridges, and have a pressure too high to be safe in revolvers. Before using .32/20 cartridges in revolvers, read the box label carefully. The High-Velocity type are marked "Not for use in revolvers," or something to that effect.

Bullet diameter	.312 inch
Bullet weight	115 grains or 100 grains
Bullet length	.54 inch
Diameter cartridge head	.405 "
" " mouth	.325 "
Length cartridge case	.131 "
Length loaded cartridge	1.60 "
Typical factory charge, black powder	16 grains F. F. G.
" " " smokeless powder	9.0 grains Sharpshooter
Pressure	17,000 pounds per square inch
Velocity, 6 inch revolver	954 foot seconds
Energy	230 foot pounds
Penetration, ⅞ inch pine boards	5 boards

Remington and Peters use a 100 grain bullet, while Western and Winchester use a 115 grain bullet; all four companies load to the same velocity, 954 f. s.

Reloading Data

Bullet name	Belding & Mull 31198	Belding & Mull 31198	Bond C311655
Bullet weight	103 grains	103 grains	115 grains
Powder, kind	DuPont No. 80	Pistol No. 5	Bullseye
Powder, weight	9.5 grains	4.5 grains	4.5 grains
Velocity	1000 f. s.	903 f. s.	1042 f. s.
Recommended by	DuPont	DuPont	Hercules
Pressure			17,240 lbs.

The King Powder Company recommends the use of 16½ grains King's Semi-smokeless, granulation FG.

It is interesting to note that in spite of the fact that the .32 S. & W. cartridge is both smaller in diameter and much shorter than the .32-20, it can still be shot in the .32-20 revolver with fair accuracy. There is some danger, however, of split cartridges, owing to the fact that the chamber is larger than the case, and thus allows quite a lot of expansion to take place.

.32 Caliber (7.65 m/m) Automatic Colt Pistol Cartridge

This is a semi-rim automatic pistol cartridge, loaded with smokeless powder only, and having a 73 grain metal jacketed bullet driven at a muzzle velocity of about 950 feet per second. It is very popular for pocket automatic pistols, and has a wide use in both Europe and America. It is the next above the .25 automatic in the Colt and Browning series. In America it is known as the .32 A.C.P., (Automatic Colt Pistol), and in Europe it is called the 7.65 m/m automatic. It is used in the Colt, Savage, Remington, Smith & Wesson, Harrington & Richardson, Webley, Browning, Mauser, Clement, Frommer, Steyr, Pieper, Schwarzlose, Walther, and many other pocket automatics.

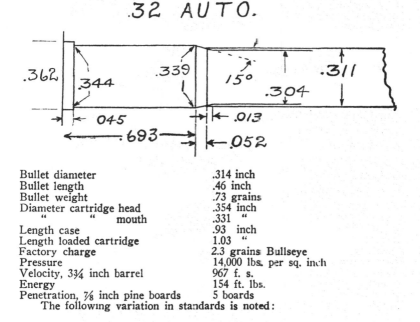

Bullet diameter	.314 inch
Bullet length	.46 inch
Bullet weight	.73 grains
Diameter cartridge head	.354 inch
" " mouth	.331 "
Length case	.93 inch
Length loaded cartridge	1.03 "
Factory charge	2.3 grains Bullseye
Pressure	14,000 lbs. per sq. inch
Velocity, 3¾ inch barrel	967 f. s.
Energy	154 ft. lbs.
Penetration, ⅞ inch pine boards	5 boards

The following variation in standards is noted:

Make	Bullet weight	Velocity
Peters	73 grains	965 feet per second
Remington	71 "	950 " " "
Western	74 "	950 " " "
Winchester	74 "	965 " " "

Reloading Data

Bullet name	Ideal 308252	Ideal 308252	Winchester full patch
Bullet weight	77 grains	77 grains	74 grains
Powder, kind	DuPont No. 80	Pistol No. 5	Bullseye
Powder, charge	4.5 grains	2.6 grains	2.1 grains
Velocity	950	950	829
Recommended by	DuPont	DuPont	Hercules

8 mm. Lebel

This cartridge which fits the French service revolver looks very much like our own .32-20. It is not often met with in this country. The bullet is copper jacketed, and the cartridge is loaded with black powder only.

Bullet weight	120 grains
Bullet diameter	.330 inch
Bullet length	.62 "
Diameter of cartridge head	.400 "
Diameter of cartridge body	.384 "
Length of case	1.06 "
Length of cartridge	1.45 "
Powder charge	11.5 grains fine black
Muzzle velocity	625 f. s.
Muzzle energy	104 ft. lbs.

8 mm. Nambu Cartridge

This is the cartridge used by the Japanese pistol of the same name. It is a bottle necked, rimless cartridge which at first glance looks very much like the .30 caliber Luger. I have never had an opportunity to make velocity or pressure tests on these cartridges as I have seen only a few samples which were brought to this country by persons who had purchased guns and ammunition of this kind while visiting in Japan. However, I have weighed and measured some samples with the following results:

Bullet weight	102 grains
Bullet diameter	.320 inch
Length of bullet	.60 "
Case length	.86 "
Length loaded cartridge	1.26 "
Diameter cartridge head	.413 "
Diameter cartridge case, rear	.408 "
Diameter cartridge case, neck	.388 "
Diameter cartridge case, mouth	.338 "
Powder charge	4 grains smokeless

.380 Revolver

This is a short, low powered .38 cartridge with outside lubricated bullet, intended for foreign .38 caliber revolvers of old models. It is almost exactly the same as the .38 short Colt, about the only difference being that the rim of the .380 is .005 smaller in diameter and somewhat thicker.

Bullet weight	125 grains
Bullet diameter	.375 inch
Bullet length	.56 "
Diameter of cartridge head	.426 "
Diameter of cartridge body, front	.377 "
Length of case	.69 "
Length of cartridge	1.10 "
Powder charge	10 grains F. F. F. G. Black
Muzzle velocity	650 f. s.
Energy	120 ft. lbs.

.38 Smith & Wesson
.38 Colt New Police (Colt Police Positive)

The .38 S. & W. and the .38 Colt New Police, (which is the same cartridge with a flat pointed bullet), have for a long time been by far the most popular cartridges for pocket revolvers. Their popularity is deserved, for they are accurate, well designed cartridges, which have much greater stopping power than the .32 caliber.

The standard load for the .38 S. & W. is a 146 grain bullet with 2.3 grains of bull's-eye, or 3.8 grains of Pistol Powder No.

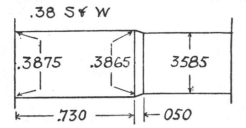

This chamber will accommodate either the .38 S. & W. cartridge or the .38 Colt New Police cartridge. It is used in the Police Positive and Banker's Special revolvers.

5, giving a muzzle velocity of about 730 feet per second and a muzzle energy of about 170 foot pounds.

The .38 Colt New Police has a flat point bullet of 150 grains weight, with about 710 foot seconds of velocity and 170 foot pounds energy. The flat pointed Colt New Police bullet is far superior to the round nosed .38 S. & W. in stopping power, and should always be used in preference to it.

Name	.38 Smith & Wesson
Bullet weight	146 grains
Bullet diameter	.359 inch
Bullet length	.67 "
Diameter of cartridge head	.433 "
Diameter of cartridge case	.383 "
Case length	.77 "
Length loaded cartridge	1.20 "
Powder charge	2.3 grains Bullseye
Pressure	8,000 pounds
Velocity	730 f. s.
Energy	170 foot pounds
Penetration ⅞ inch pine boards	5 boards
Name	.38 Colt New Police (Police Positive)
Bullet weight	150 grains
Bullet diameter	.359 inch
Bullet length	.65 "
Case dimensions	As above for ⁻38 S. & W.
Powder charge	2.1 grains Bullseye
Pressure	9,000 pounds
Velocity	710 foot seconds
Energy	170 foot pounds

Reloading Data

Bullet name	Ideal 358246	Ideal 358246	Ideal 358246
Bullet weight	147	147	147
Powder, kind	Pistol No. 5	S. R. No. 80	Bullseye
Powder, weight	3.8 grains	5.9 grains	2.0 grains
Velocity	796	816	710
Recommended by	Ideal Handbook	Ideal Handbook	Ideal Handbook

.38 S. & W. Super Police

This is a cartridge made by the Western Cartridge Company for the solid frame revolvers chambered for the .38 S. & W. cartridge. However, instead of having a 146 grain bullet, as is standard for the .38 S. & W., this cartridge has a 200 grain, soft lead bullet. On account of the additional bullet weight the muzzle velocity is quite low. Moreover, the additional weight in the bullet increases the jump of the gun when fired and thus causes the group to be several inches higher than that of the regular .38 S. & W. at a range of twenty yards. The slow velocity causes the bullet to drop somewhat faster than the ordinary bullet and this additional drop counteracts most of the tendency to group high at the longer ranges. The object of this design is to produce a bullet which will have superior stopping power. With this end in view the nose of the bullet has been made quite blunt which undoubtedly adds considerably to the stopping power.

A number of tests, made by the author to determine whether or not this low velocity, heavy bullet load has greater stopping power than the regular load were inconclusive. If anything these

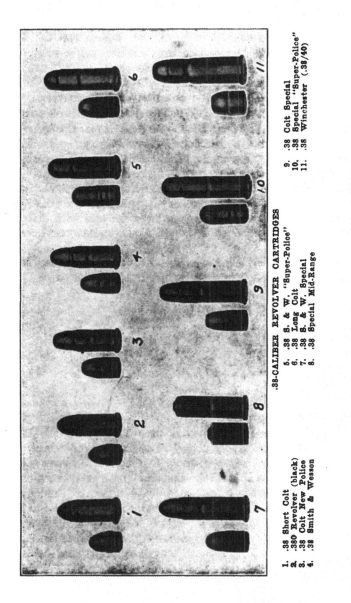

.38-CALIBER REVOLVER CARTRIDGES

1. .38 Short Colt
2. .380 Revolver (black)
3. .38 Colt New Police
4. .38 Smith & Wesson

5. .38 S. & W. "Super-Police"
6. .38 Long Colt
7. .38 S. & W. Special
8. .38 Special Mid-Range

9. .38 Colt Special
10. .38 Special "Super-Police"
11. .38 Winchester (.38/40)

tests seemed to indicate that the .38 Colt New Police cartridge has more stopping power than either the .38 S. & W. or the .38 Super Police. However, as stated before, the tests were not very conclusive as about the only way to make such a test that would be satisfactory would be to shoot live animals and even in this case no two animals are alike and no two shots would strike exactly the same.

The following is quoted from a letter received from the Western Cartridge Company: "A policeman shot a hold-up artist in East St. Louis the other day with this Super Police. Hit him square in the center of the back at 75 yards which was a darn good shot. When the coroner dug the bullet out of the crook he found it more than half way through him and flattened on the point to about the size of a quarter. This officer was certainly good. He had two hold-up artists, one of whom broke and ran. Without further ceremony he cracked one over the head with his revolver, took deliberate aim at the other and made a dead center bull's-eye on him."

The .38 Super Police cartridge is not recommended for use in jointed frame revolvers with tip-up action as the jar of the recoil has a tendency to unlatch the action.

Bullet weight	200 grains
Bullet diameter	.359 inch
Bullet length	.81 "
Cartridge case dimensions	Same as .38 S. & W.
Length of cartridge	1.24 inch
Weight of powder charge	2.5 grains Infallible
Velocity, 6″ barrel	610 f. s.
Energy	166 ft. lbs.
Penetration, ⅞″ pine boards	4 boards

.38 Short Colt

This is a cartridge adapted to the original Colt .38 Double Action revolver, and to other revolvers of this caliber, which are now obsolete. It will, however, shoot in the Colt .38 Army Revolvers chambered for the .38 Long Colt, and in all revolvers chambered for the .38 Special. It has an outside lubricated bullet weighing 125 grains in the Remington and Peters makes, and 130 grains in the Western and Winchester makes. The standard charge is 2.5 grains of Bull's-eye or 3.5 grains of Pistol powder No. 5.

Bullet weight	125 grains or 130 grains
Bullet diameter	.375 inch
Bullet length	.56 "
Diameter of cartridge head	.433 "
Diameter of cartridge mouth outside	.383 "
Case length	.69 "

Length loaded cartridge 1.10
Muzzle velocity, 6 inch barrel 775 f.s. (Western 130 gr.)
Muzzle energy 173 foot pounds
Penetration, ⅞ inch pine boards 5 Boards

Reloading Data

Bullet name	Cast lead	Cast lead	Ideal 358159
Bullet weight	130 grains	130 grains	125 grains
Powder kind	King's Semi-smokeless	Bullseye	Pistol No. 5
Powder charge	14 grains FFG	2.5 grains	2.7 grains
Velocity	765 f.s.	745 f.s.	700 f.s.
Recommended by	King Powder Co.	Hercules	DuPont

.38 Long Colt

This cartridge is of interest because it was for years the military cartridge of the United States Government. Thousands of Colt and Smith & Wesson revolvers, chambered for this gun, were issued to the Army and Navy and were the standard side arm for many years. Therefore, there are vast numbers of these guns

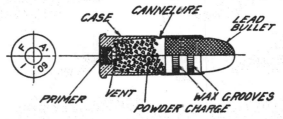

CAL.38 REVOLVER BALL CARTRIDGE

still in the hands of the public, and for this reason the .38 Long Colt cartridge will continue to be manufactured for years, though all the modern military .38's that are manufactured are chambered for the longer .38 Special, and none now manufactured are chambered for the long Colt.

This bullet as originally made was smaller than the diameter of the barrel and had a hollow base so that the powder pressure would expand the bullet and make it take the rifling.

On account of the fact that this was the standard military cartridge it has been thoroughly investigated by our Ordnance Department, and the data available on this cartridge are much more complete than on most other cartridges. Ordnance Pamphlet No. 1919 gives the following data on the .38 Long Colt Cartridge, which is very interesting in showing about how a revolver cartridge of .38 caliber will behave ballistically, because the results on the .38 Special will not be far different:

ACCURACY

Range, yards	Mean hor. dispersion, inches	Mean vert. dispersion, inches	Mean radius, inches
25	.668	.515	.903
50	.604	1.400	1.553
75	2.278	1.612	2.888
100	2.400	1.994	3.656
150	2.762	7.296	8.018
200	4.600	16.990	9.255

NOTE: The group diameter is about three times the mean radius.

DRIFT

Range, yards	Drift, inches
25	0.75
50	1.09
75	1.57
100	2.24
150	7.80

NOTE: This was obtained by having special guns made up with right and left-hand twist for use in this experiment.

PENETRATIONS IN WHITE PINE

Range, yards	Depth, inches
25	4.97
50	4.35
75	4.26
100	3.64
150	3.05
200	2.90

NOTE: One inch corresponds to a dangerous wound.

REMAINING VELOCITY WITH FORCE OF IMPACT

Range, yards	Velocity, feet per second	Force of impact, foot-pounds
25	689.9	155.2
50	671.9	147.2
75	654.5	139.7
100	637.5	132.5
125	620.9	125.7
150	604.8	119.3
175	589.09	113.2
200	573.8	107.4

Bullet weight   148 grains
Bullet diameter   357 inch
Bullet length   .72 "
Diameter cartridge head   .433 "
Outside diameter case mouth   .377 "
Length of case   1.03 "
Length loaded cartridge   1.32 "
Factory charge   3.0 grains Bullseye
Pressure   12,000 pounds
Velocity, 6 inch barrel   810 foot seconds
Energy   230 foot pounds
Penetration, ⅞ inch pine boards   7 boards

Reloading Data

Bullet name	Ideal 35870	Ideal 35870	Cast lead
Bullet weight	150 grains	150 grains	148 grains
Powder, kind	Pistol No. 5	S. R. No. 80	Bullseye
Powder, charge	3.6 grains	6.2 grains	3.0 grains
Velocity	815 f.s.	795 f.s.	810 f.s.
Recommended by	Ideal handbook	Ideal handbook	Hercules

.38 S. & W. Special. .38 Colt Special

This is an extremely accurate cartridge and is the most popular of all center fire revolver cartridges for target shooting. It has superb accuracy and is capable of making groups of less than 1½ inches in diameter at fifty yards.

The .38 Special has a very great popularity in almost every field of use, as it is large enough and powerful enough for military use and at the same time it is not too large for pocket revolvers. The most powerful pocket guns are chambered for this cartridge which is a favorite with Police Departments. There is also a line of military revolvers made for this cartridge which have become extremely popular as target arms; and our most popular special target revolvers are chambered for this cartridge. It is the cartridge that has been most hand loaded and there are a tremendous number of bullets furnished for it by the reloading company and a large variety of hand loads from which to choose.

It is regularly made and stocked by the cartridge companies not only in full loads but also in mid-range loads with square shouldered bullets, in special target loads which have a still further reduced weight of bullet and in a special gallery load with a round ball.

Recently this cartridge has been produced loaded to a very high velocity, especially for use in the new Smith & Wesson .38/44 revolver and other .38's on .44 or .45 frames. These new ultra powerful cartridges are the same in every respect except the velocity as the regular .38 Special and are sold under the name of .38/44 S. & W. Special, .38 S. & W. Special High Velocity or .38 Colt Special High Velocity.

The .38 Special cartridge is both accurate and powerful and has plenty of penetration, but does not have nearly as great stopping power as the .45 merely on account of the smaller diameter of the bullet.

The original .38 Special has a bullet with a rounded nose; in order to improve the stopping power of this cartridge the Colt Company induced the cartridge makers to make the same cartridge with a bullet having a flat space on the nose. This flat space adds greatly to the effectiveness of the bullet as regards stopping power. When this cartridge is being used for self-protection or any other purpose but target practice, the Colt Special rather than the Smith & Wesson Special should be obtained. An even more effective shape from the viewpoint of stopping power is the bullet designed

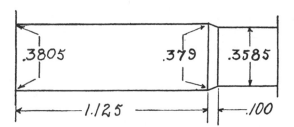

by Elmer Keith which has a flat point with a ledge around the body of the bullet just forward of the cartridge case.

Were it necessary for the average shooter to own and use but one revolver it should be a .38 Special.

Name	.38 S. & W. Special
Bullet weight	158 grains
Bullet diameter	.359 inch
Bullet length	.74 "
Diameter of cartridge head	.433 "
Diameter of cartridge body	.377 "
Length of case	1.16 "
Length of cartridge	1.55 "
Powder charge	3.6 grains Bullseye
Pressure	15,000 lbs.
Muzzle velocity, 6 inch barrel	860 f.s.
Muzzle energy	260 ft. lbs.
Penetration, ⅞ inch pine boards	7 boards
Name	.38 Colt Special
Bullet weight	158 grains
Bullet length	.71 inch
Length of cartridge	1.51 "
Other dimensions	Same as .38 S. & W. Special
Ballistics	Same as .38 S. & W. Special
Name	.38/44 S. & W. Special
Bullet and cartridge dimensions	Same as .38 S. & W. Special
Muzzle velocity	1100 f.s.
Muzzle energy	425 ft. lbs.
Name	.38 Colt Special, High Velocity
Bullet and cartridge dimensions	Same as .38 Colt Special
Ballistics	Same as .38/44 S. & W. Special

Reloading Data

Bullet name	Ideal 358311	Ideal 358311	Ideal 358311
Bullet weight	158 grains	158 grains	158 grains
Powder, kind	Pistol No. 5	Bullseye	King's S. S., FFG
Weight of charge	5.0 grains	3.0 grains	18 grains
Velocity	950 f.s.	790 f.s.	820 f.s.
Recommended by	Ideal Handbook	Ideal Handbook	King Powder Co.

The hand loads given above approximate the regular factory charge. The shooter interested in hand loading will find literally dozens of other hand loads both more and less powerful listed in the works on reloading and the hand books of the loading tool makers.

.38 Special Super Police

With the idea of increasing the stopping power of the .38 Special cartridge, the Western Cartridge Company sometime ago placed on the market a .38 S. & W. Special cartridge with a 200 grain, blunt nosed bullet instead of the standard 158 grain bullet. This is called the .38 Special Super Police. On account of the heavier bullet this cartridge has a lower velocity than the standard .38 Special; but the heavier bullet also causes more jump so that the group goes several inches higher at twenty yards with the .38 Special Super Police than it does with the regular .38 Special.

As the object of this bullet is increased shock power the author made numerous tests to determine whether or not this bullet has more stopping power than the regular .38 Special. While the tests were inconclusive the results seemed to indicate that perhaps the .38 Colt Special has more stopping power than either the .38 S. & W. Special or the .38 Special Super Police.

The following is quoted from a letter received from the Western Cartridge Company. "This 200 grain bullet of ours in the .38 Special Super Police is now being used in considerable quantity by the St. Louis Police Department. We, therefore, have an opportunity to watch its effectiveness. Three times this month it has proven instantly effective, that is, it has put the bandit flat on his back at the first crack. Each time penetration has been clear through. One shot struck just forward of the hip bone on the right side, ranged downward, smashed the pelvis and came out in the left hip. Second instance, shot struck at base of skull in the rear, ranged through and came out at bridge of nose. Third instance, shot struck in front of left ear, ranged through and came out the base of neck on the right hand side."

In a number of tests made by the makers of this bullet to determine the velocity and different barrel lengths, the results were as follows:

Barrel Length	Standard .38 Special	.38 Special Super Police
2"	723 f.s.	623 f.s.
6"	818 "	671 "
7½"	791 "	656 "

Bullet weight	200 grains
Bullet diameter	.355 inch
Bullet length	.81 "
Cartridge dimensions	Same as .38 S. & W. Special
Powder charge	4 grains Infallible
Velocity, 6 inch barrel	725 f.s.
Energy	246 ft. lbs.
Penetration, ⅞ inch pine boards	5 boards

.38 Winchester (.38-40)

Like the .32-20, this is a rifle cartridge, intended for the old-style Winchester rifles and for which revolvers were also chambered, so that the user could have both a rifle and a revolver and only one kind of ammunition. In common with the .32-20 and

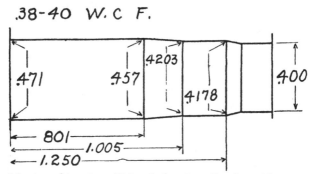

.44-40, this cartridge is still loaded primarily for rifle use with a compromise type of powder known as "Sharpshooter," which is a nitroglycerin powder and rather erosive. This cartridge has a 180-grain flat-point bullet with a muzzle velocity of 950 foot-seconds and a muzzle energy of 360 foot-pounds. Because of its comparatively light bullet weight and the square nose which adds to air resistance, this bullet does not carry up as well at long distances as the .44 Special and other advanced designs.

This cartridge is called ".38-40" because it was originally loaded with 40 grains of black powder.

The bullet diameter of this cartridge is .400; therefore this is really a .40 caliber. Owing to the large size of the bullet and the flat point, it has very good stopping power. Like the .32-20, this cartridge has been made recently in the high-speed or high-velocity types, which are too powerful for use in revolvers as they are likely to burst the cylinder.

Bullet weight	180 grains
Bullet diameter	.400 inch
Bullet length	.60 "
Diameter cartridge head	.545 "
Diameter cartridge body	.414 "
Length of case	1.31 "
Length of loaded cartridge	1.60 "
Powder charge	16.0 grains Sharpshooter
Pressure	14,000 lbs.
Velocity, 5.5 inch barrel	950 f.s.
Energy	360 ft. lbs.
Penetration, ⅞ inch pine boards	7 boards

Reloading Data

Bullet name	Ideal 40043	Ideal 40043	Ideal 40043
Bullet weight	180 grains	180 grains	180 grains
Powder, kind	S. R. No. 80	Bullseye	King's S. S., FG
Weight of charge	14.8 grains	4.0 grains	33 grains
Velocity	1030 f.s.	700 f.s.	850 f.s.
Recommended by	Ideal Handbook	Ideal Handbook	King Powder Co.

.38 A.C.P. (Automatic Colt Pistol)

This is a high velocity semi-rim type, automatic pistol cartridge resembling the 9 mm. Luger in size and general appearance. It

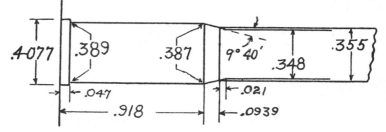

is however, somewhat more powerful than the Luger as it has a slightly heavier bullet and a somewhat higher velocity. It was designed for the first high powered Browning automatic pistol, which became the Colt .38 Military. This cartridge had excellent ballistics but for a good many years it did not become very popular on account of the fact that the arm which it fitted was designed as a military side arm in 1904 but was not adopted by the Government which took the .45 instead. The .45 caliber automatic, after its adoption by the Government, was greatly improved to meet the military requirements and to overcome the defects and disadvantages brought out by the test for adoption. Thus the .45 caliber automatic pistol became very much superior mechanically to the old .38 Military and shooters who otherwise would have liked to avail themselves of the excellent ballistics of this cartridge very frequently were restrained from doing so by the fact that no gun of up-to-date design was available for it.

However, the Colt Company several years ago brought out a thoroughly up-to-date automatic pistol, the Super .38, for this cartridge. At the same time the cartridge companies improved the ballistics of the cartridge somewhat by raising the velocity from 1126 foot seconds to 1200 foot seconds. This cartridge has more penetration and more energy than any other American pistol cartridge but it does not have the stopping power of the .45. An exception is that it is better than the .45 for use against very large animals in which the bullet will stop in spite of its great penetration. In such animals the Super .38 can be depended on to reach vital spots, and the deep penetration means that the energy of the bullet is distributed over a long track which increases the stopping power. This cartridge can be had in the hollow point style as well as the standard full metal jacket.

Bullet weight	130 grains
Bullet diameter	.359 inch
Bullet length	.58 "
Diameter of cartridge head	.403 "
Diameter of cartridge body	.382 "
Length cartridge case	.90 "
Length loaded cartridge	.127 "
Smokeless powder charge	4.6 grains Bullseye
Pressure	28,000 pounds
Muzzle velocity, 5 inch barrel	1200 f.s.
Energy	417 ft. lbs.
Penetration, ⅞ inch pine boards	11 boards

Reloading Data

Bullet name	Ideal 358422	Ideal 358422
Bullet weight	125 grains	125 grains
Powder, kind	Pistol No. 5	Bullseye
Weight of charge	5 grains	4 grains
Velocity	1100 f.s.	1100 f.s.

.380 Automatic (9 mm. Short)

This is a rimless, automatic pistol cartridge with a metal jacketed bullet, suitable for a medium size, pocket, automatic pistol such as the Colt, Remington, Savage, Browning, Bayard and many others. It is far superior to the .32 A.C.P. because its larger diameter gives it greater stopping power.

Bullet weight	95 grains
Bullet diameter	.356 inch
Bullet length	.46 "
Diameter of cartridge head	.372 "
Diameter of cartridge body	.372 "
Length of case	.68 "
Length of cartridge	.93 "
Powder charge	2.5 Bullseye
Muzzle velocity, 3.75 inch barrel	870 f.s.
Muzzle energy	160 ft. lbs.
Penetration, ⅞ inch pine boards	5 boards

380 AUTO.

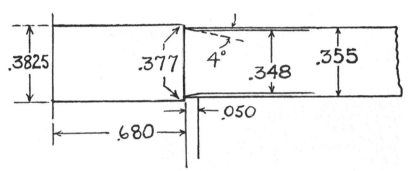

9 mm. Long

This is a semi-rim automatic pistol cartridge somewhat more powerful than the .380 and somewhat less powerful than the .38 A.C.P. It is used in the Webley, Browning and other European pistols. There is no American pistol made for this cartridge.

Bullet weight	110 grains
Bullet diameter	.355 inch
Bullet length	.51 "
Diameter cartridge head	.404 "
Diameter cartridge body	.384 "
Length of case	.80 "
Length of loaded cartridge	1.10 "
Powder charge	
Velocity, 5 inch barrel	1110 f.s.
Energy	300 ft. lbs.
Penetration, ⅞ inch pine boards	8 boards

9 mm. Luger

This is a German cartridge that has been very much used in this country. It is a high-velocity cartridge with a bullet weighing 125 grains. The standard bullet diameter is .355, and the velocity is around 1,040 foot-seconds. It is made in a metal-jacketed bullet with a square point. The bullet has a peculiar shape. It is conical; but the point is square, so that the actual shape of the front part of the bullet is that of a truncated cone. The square shape adds somewhat to the stopping power of the bullet and also partly prevents it from glancing.

These Luger cartridges are sometimes loaded with "double" or divided bullets with the idea of increasing the probability of hitting in the case of a poor marksman. During the World War a number of Mauser pistols were made in 9 mm. for this same cartridge, and the Luger cartridge was seen with the round nose instead of with the ordinary conical-shaped bullet.

The Remington Arms Company loads the Luger cartridge with a 124 grain bullet to a velocity of 1210 f.s. measured in the 8 inch barrel model. This gives 400 foot pounds of energy.

Bullet weight	125 grains
Bullet diameter	.354 inch
Bullet length	.61 "
Diameter cartridge head	.392 "
Diameter cartridge body	.377 "
Length of case	.76 "
Length of loaded cartridge	1.16 "
Powder charge	5.5 grains Smokeless
Pressure	24,000 pounds
Velocity, 4 inch barrel	1075 f.s.
Energy	320 ft. lbs.
Penetration, ⅞ inch pine boards	9 boards

Reloading Data

Bullet name	Ideal 356402	Ideal 356402
Bullet weight	123 grains	123 grains
Powder, kind	Pistol No. 5	Bullseye
Weight of charge	6 grains	4.8 grains
Velocity	1135 f.s.	1120 f.s.
Recommended by	Mattern	Mattern

9 mm. Bayard

The Bayard automatic pistol, model of 1910, is the standard of the Danish army. It was also much used by the Germans during the World War. The cartridge is very powerful and is similar to the .38 automatic Colt in size and shape. It is a rimless case and has a jacketed bullet. The case appears to be straight but measurements show that it has a considerable taper from front to rear to facilitate extraction.

Bullet weight	126 grains
Bullet diameter	.355 inch
Bullet length	.60 "
Diameter of cartridge head	.392 "
Diameter of cartridge body, rear	.390 "
Diameter of cartridge body, front	.375 "
Length of case	.90 "
Length of cartridge	.131 "

Powder charge 5.6 grains Smokeless
Muzzle velocity 1148 f.s.
Energy 365 ft. lbs.

9 mm. Steyr

This cartridge is almost exactly the same size and shape as the 9 mm. Bayard described above and comes in clips of eight. The bullets are steel jacketed and in spite of the fact that they are plated over with a protective coating they have quite a tendency to rust.

Bullet weight 116 grains
Bullet diameter .355 inch
Bullet length .60 "
Diameter of cartridge head .381 "
Diameter of cartridge body .381 "
Length of case .90 "
Length of cartridge .130 "
Powder charge 6.2 grains Smokeless
Muzzle velocity 1200 f.s.
Muzzle energy 370 ft. lbs.

.41 Short Colt

This cartridge is still manufactured for use in the .41 Colt revolvers still in the hands of the public although revolvers of this

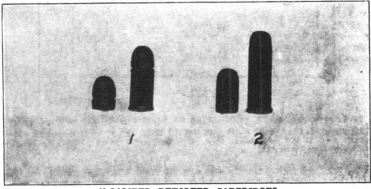

.41-CALIBER REVOLVER CARTRIDGES
1. .41 Short Colt   2. .41 Long Colt

caliber are no longer made. The .41 Short Colt has an outside lubricated bullet and was originally loaded only with black powder though at the present time smokeless loads are the rule.

Bullet weight 160 grains
Bullet diameter .406 inch
Bullet length .57 "
Diameter cartridge head .435 "

Diameter cartridge body   .404 "
Length of case   .65 "
Length of loaded cartridge   1.10 "
Powder charge   2.7 grains Bullseye
Pressure   12,000 lbs.
Velocity, 6 inch barrel   672 f.s.
Energy   160 ft. lbs.
Penetration, ⅞ inch pine boards   4 boards

Reloading Data

A satisfactory load for this cartridge as recommended by King's Powder Company is the 160 grain bullet and 15 grains of King's Semi-smokeless FFG.

.41 Long Colt

At one time the Colt .41 Revolver was a famous and popular arm out West and it is still much used in certain sections of the South though it is not made at the present time. Both the .41

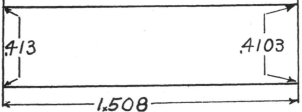

41 SHORT & LONG

.413   .4103

1.508

STANDARD CHAMBER DIMENSIONS OF COLT REVOLVERS AND PISTOLS
This chamber, for the .41 Short Colt and .41 Long Colt is no longer made. It was formerly used in the New Army, New Navy, Colt Army Special, Single Action Army, and Bisley Model revolvers.

Short and .41 Long cartridges can be used interchangeably in these guns.

The .41 Long Colt originally had an outside lubricated bullet with a heel of smaller diameter fitting into the neck of the cartridge case. However, it is now loaded as an inside lubricated cartridge and as a result the whole bullet is of the diameter of the former heel. To compensate for this the base of the bullet is made hollow so it will swell out from the powder pressure and thus fit the rifling.

FOREGN REVOLVER CARTRIDGES

1. .30 Nagant
2. 8-mm. French Revolver, Model of 1892
3. 11-mm. French Revolver, Model of 1873
4. 11-mm. German Revolver, Model of 1888
5. .455 Webley "Manstopper"
6. .476 Eley

CARTRIDGE -

SECTION OF BULLET.

WEBLEY MANSTOPPER
220 GR. BULLET WITH
HOLLOW POINT AND BASE.

TWO MODERN MAN-STOPPERS
LEFT, REMINGTON "RIOT" 45
RIGHT, MULTIPLE BALL FOR
THE LUGER 9 m/m CTG.

Bullet weight	195 grains
Bullet diameter	.388 inch
Bullet length	.73 "
Diameter cartridge head and body	Same as .41 Short Colt
Length of case	1.13 inch
Length of loaded cartridge	1.40 "
Powder charge	3.5 grains Bullseye
Pressure	14,000 lbs.
Velocity, 6 inch barrel	750 f.s.
Energy	255 ft. lbs.
Penetration, ⅞ inch pine boards	5 boards

Reloading Data

Bullet name	Ideal 386177	Ideal 386177	Ideal 386177
Bullet weight	196 grains	196 grains	196 grains
Powder, kind	Pistol No. 5	Bullseye	King's S. S., FG
Weight of charge	4.2 grains	3.0 grains	25 grains
Velocity	730 f.s.	700 f.s.	710 f.s.
Recommended by	Ideal Handbook	Ideal Handbook	King's Powder Co

11 mm. German Revolver Model 1888

This old German service revolver cartridge has very much the same appearance as the .41 Long Colt. It has a rather heavy load consisting of 262 grains bullet with 20½ grains of black powder.

Bullet weight	262 grains
Bullet diameter	.428 inch
Bullet length	.74 "
Diameter cartridge head	.504 "
Diameter cartridge body	.451 "
Length of case	.95 "
Length of loaded cartridge	1.21 "
Powder charge	20.5 grains black

11 mm. French Revolver Model 1873

In outside appearance this cartridge resembles the .44 Webley. This cartridge is hardly ever seen in America as arms chambered for it are rarely found in this country.

Bullet weight	176 grains
Bullet diameter	.454 inch
Bullet length	.60 "
Diameter cartridge head	.462 "
Diameter cartridge body	.448 "
Length of case	.68 "
Length of loaded cartridge	1.16 "
Powder charge	14 grains black
Velocity	700 f.s.
Energy	192 ft. lbs.

.44 Smith & Wesson American

This an old black powder cartridge, with outside lubricated bullet, which has been obsolete for many years, but is still made for the use of owners of the old .44 American Army revolver which was used in the service about 1871.

The name, .44 Smith & Wesson American was applied to this gun and cartridge to distinguish it from the .44 Russian model made by Smith & Wesson about the same period.

The cartridge is loaded principally with black powder, though both smokeless and semi-smokeless loads can also be obtained.

Bullet weight	218 grains
Bullet diameter	.434 inch
Bullet length	.70 "
Diameter of cartridge head	.502 "
Diameter of cartridge body	.437 "
Length of case	.90 "
Length of loaded cartridge	1.43 "
Powder charge	25 grains black
Velocity, 6 inch barrel	650 f.s.
Energy	200 ft. lbs.

Reloading Data

Bullet name	Ideal 414180	Ideal 414180	Cast lead
Bullet weight	200 grains	200 grains	205 grains
Powder, kind	Sport'g Rifle No. 80	Pistol No. 5	King's S. S., FFG
Weight of charge	12 grains	6.0 grains	20 grains
Velocity	800 f.s.	800 f.s.	650 f.s.
Recommended by	DuPont	DuPont	King Powder Co.

.44 Colt

Like the .44 Smith & Wesson American this is an old, black powder cartridge adapted to guns which are long ago obsolete. It has an outside lubricated bullet.

Bullet weight	210 grains
Bullet diameter	.444 inch
Bullet length	.66 "
Diameter of cartridge head	.483 "
Diameter of cartridge body	.451 "
Length of case	1.08 "
Length of cartridge	1.50 "
Muzzle velocity, 6 inch barrel	660 f.s.
Muzzle energy	200 ft. lbs.

.44 Bull Dog

This is an English cartridge adapted to pocket revolvers of that caliber and name. It has an outside lubricated bullet and is ordinarily loaded with black powder. However, smokeless loads can now be obtained.

Bullet weight	170 grains
Bullet diameter	.440 inch
Bullet length	.56 "
Diameter of cartridge head	.503 "
Diameter of cartridge body	.471 "
Length of case	.57 "
Length of cartridge	.95 "
Powder charge	15 grains black
Muzzle velocity, 4½ inch barrel	460 f.s.
Muzzle energy	80 ft. lbs.

.44 Webley

This cartridge, like the .44 Bull Dog, is an English cartridge made for pocket revolvers. It differs from the .44 Bull Dog principally in having a heavier bullet.

Bullet weight	200 grains
Bullet diameter	.436 inch
Bullet length	.64 "
Diameter of cartridge head	.503 "
Diameter of cartridge body	.471 "
Length of case	.69 "
Length of cartridge	1.11 "
Powder charge	18 grains black
Muzzle velocity, 4½ inch barrel	560 f.s.
Muzzle energy	140 ft. lbs.

For reloading use a 200 grain bullet and 15 grains of King's Semi-smokeless size FFG.

.44 Smith & Wesson Russian

This famous cartridge was designed by Smith & Wesson for their Russian model revolver which was the standard of the Russian Army at one time. It was the most accurate and popular cartridge for target shooting in the old black powder days. Such great marksmen as Chevalier Ira A. Paine and Mr. F. E. Bennett won their fame with this cartridge. A tremendous amount of experimental work was done with it and many special bullets were designed for it by hand loaders and many special loads were developed for it.

It has a small case which works exceptionally well with reduced smokeless powder loads for gallery shooting. Many marksmen prefer this caliber to the .22 or to the .38 for target work because the larger bullet hole is a decided advantage at short ranges where the targets are small, because very often the big bullet will cut the next higher ring where a smaller bullet will not.

The original bullet of this cartridge is the most accurate long range bullet that has ever been designed for revolver shooting. At 200 yards the cartridge is capable of making ten shot groups less than eight inches in diameter and good shooting can be done with this cartridge off hand up to ranges well over 300 yards.

Bullet weight	246 grains
Bullet diameter	.431 inch
Bullet length	.82 "
Diameter of cartridge head	.508 "
Diameter of cartridge body	.455 "
Length of case	1.02 "
Length of cartridge	1.43 "
Powder charge	23 grains black

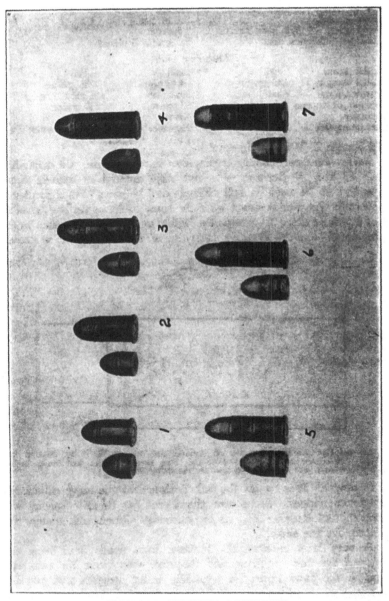

.44-CALIBER REVOLVER CARTRIDGES

1. .44 Bull Dog (black powder)
2. .44 Webley (black powder)
3. .44 S. & W. American (black powder)
4. .44 Colt (black powder)
5. .44 S. & W. Russian
6. .44 S. & W. Special
7. .44 Winchester (.44-40)

Muzzle velocity, 6 inch barrel   750 f.s.
Muzzle energy   316 ft. lbs.
Penetration, ⅞ inch pine boards   7 boards
Standard smokeless load   5.5 grains Bullseye

Reloading Data

Bullet name	Lead	Lead	Lead
Bullet weight	246 grains	246 grains	246 grains
Powder, kind	Pistol No. 5	Bullseye	King's S. S., FFG
Weight of charge	5.6 grains	5.5 grains	19 grains
Velocity	720 f.s.	674 f.s.	700 f.s.
Recommended by	DuPont	Hercules	King Powder Co.

.44 Smith & Wesson Special

When the first smokeless powders came into use, the cartridge case of the .44 Russian was not large enough to enable these powders to be used in full charges and to meet this difficulty a new cartridge was designed with the same bullet as the .44 Russian and a longer case. It retains the highly accurate .44 Russian bullet and equals the .44 Russian cartridge in accuracy while it excels

.44 S.+ W. SPL.

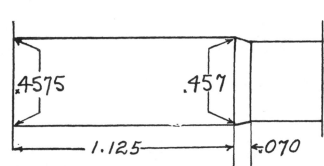

This chamber accommodates the .44 Russian and the .44 S. & W. Special cartridges. It is now used in the New Service, New Service Target, and Single Action Army Revolvers, and was formerly used in the Bisley Model.

it in power. It is by far the best designed of the large caliber revolver cartridges. Arms now chambered for the .44 Special will take the .44 Russian also, as the cartridge dimensions, except the length, are the same.

A very large number of excellent hand loads have been developed for this cartridge and the man who loads his own can find in the hand books on reloading bullet weights and powder charges which adapt this cartridge to every purpose from gallery shooting and small game hunting up to long range shooting and protection against savage tribesmen in the far parts of the earth.

Bullet weight and dimensions	Same as .44 Russian
Length of case	1.17 inch
Length of cartridge	1.60 "
Other cartridge dimensions	Same as .44 Russian
Powder charge, black	26 grains black
Muzzle velocity, 6 inch barrel	780 f.s.
Muzzle energy	330 ft. lbs.
Penetration, ⅞ inch pine boards	7 boards
Powder charge, smokeless	6.0 grains Pistol No. 5

Reloading Data

Bullet name	Ideal 429352	Lead	Ideal 429352
Bullet weight	245 grains	246 grains	245 grains
Powder, kind	Pistol No. 5	Bullseye	King's S. S., FFG
Weight of charge	7 grains	6.3 grains	22.5 grains
Velocity	900 f.s.	740 f.s.	730 f.s.
Recommended by	DuPont	Hercules	King Powder Co.

.44 Winchester (.44-40)

Like the .32-20 and the .38-40, this is primarily a rifle cartridge, for which revolvers were designed so that the user of a rifle of this caliber could also use the same ammunition in his six-shooter. In the old frontier days of black powder loads this was a highly prac-

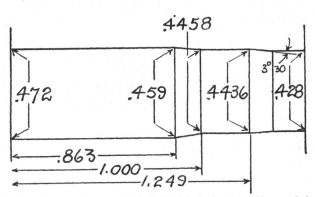

This is the chamber for the .44-40, (.44 Winchester) cartridge, and is used in the New Service and the Single Action Army revolvers. It was formerly used in the Bisley Model also.

tical idea. It meant that the ammunition supply was suitable for both the rifles and the handguns, and this was an item of importance to pioneers who might be located far from the nearest source of supply. However, with the advent of smokeless powders, it introduced complications, for the slow burning powders best suited to rifle use were not fast enough for revolvers. The result is that most of the .44-40 cartridges now on the market are loaded with a compromise type of powder, which does fairly well in both rifles and pistols, but not as well for either as certain other powders which are specially suited for either the rifle or the pistol, but not for both.

Even so, it is a powerful revolver cartridge, with its 200 grain bullet driven at 935 foot seconds, and giving 383 foot pounds of energy. Like the .38-40, it has a flat point, which increases the stopping power, and its large diameter also adds to its effectiveness. It is, however, inferior to the .44 Special and the .45 Colt in accuracy.

This cartridge was the original one for which the single action Colt, or "Peace Maker" was introduced in the far West in the old frontier days. For a time this idea proved very popular, and the .44-40 revolver was the standard large caliber gun in that part of the country. This popularity of the .44-40 suffered somewhat after the Army adopted the .45 caliber, as then everyone living near the Army posts wanted a .45 simply because the soldiers all had .45 caliber ammunition, and it became easier and cheaper to get.

But amongst plainsmen and prospectors the .44-40 "six gun" was standard equipment along with a Winchester rifle up until the coming of smokeless powder and more powerful, modern weapons.

The same caution applies to this cartridge as has been given in regard to the .32-20 and the .38-40—that is, the user should be careful to avoid the high-velocity or high-speed cartridges which are loaded to a high pressure and can not be used in revolvers without danger. In buying these cartridges for revolver use read the label on the box carefully. It will tell you if they are intended for rifles and revolvers, or for rifles only.

Bullet weight	200 grains
Bullet diameter	.426 inch
Bullet length	.59 "
Diameter cartridge head	.516 "
Diameter cartridge body, front	.441 "
Length case	1.31 "
Length loaded cartridge	1.60 "
Powder charge	16.8 grains Sharpshooter
Pressure	15,000 pounds per square inch
Muzzle velocity, 7½ inch barrel	935 feet per second
Energy	383 foot pounds
Penetration, ⅞ inch pine boards	7 boards

Reloading Data

Bullet name	Belding & Mull 425205	Metal cased	Lead
Bullet weight	195 grains	200 grains	200 grains
Powder, kind	Sport'g Rifle No. 80	Bullseye	King's S. S., FFG
Weight of charge	19.0 grains	7.0 grains	32 grains
Velocity	920 f.s.	920 f.s.	930 f.s.
Recommended by	DuPont	Hercules	King Powder Co.

.45 Smith & Wesson

This is another obsolete cartridge in the same category as the
.44 American. It is an old black-powder cartridge designed for
the .45 Schofield model Smith & Wesson Army revolver which

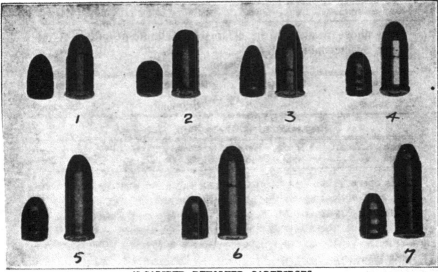

.45-CALIBER REVOLVER CARTRIDGES

1. .450 Revolver, black
2. .45 Webley, black
3. .455 Webley, Mark II
4. .45/230 Auto-Rim
5. .45 Smith & Wesson
6. .45 Colt
7. .45 Government Model of 1909

followed the .44 American as an Army service weapon. It
originally had a 230-grain lead bullet and was loaded with 28
grains of black powder, which gave 730 foot-seconds velocity.

After the Schofield Model Smith & Wesson revolver was in
use the Army began to buy the Colt single-action arm, known as
the "Peacemaker," and for many years both the Smith & Wesson
and the Colt .45 were in service. The Government, therefore,
continued to make the .45-caliber cartridge so it would fit both of
these revolvers, and this cartridge that the Government made for

so many years, though it was originally known as the .45 Smith & Wesson, afterwards became known as the .45 Colt Government, under which name it is listed in a recent Winchester catalogue.

The Ordnance Pamphlet on Army revolvers printed in 1898 gives the following data for this cartridge:

ACCURACY

Deviations	50 yds., inches	100 yds., inches	150 yds., inches	200 yds., inches	250 yds., inches	300 yds., inches
Mean horizontal ..	4.2	3.8	7	9.8	20	19
Mean vertical ·....	3.3	7.4	10.1	12.5	14.8	20.7
Mean absolute	5.3	8.3	12.3	15.9	24.9	28.7

The above results are the average of a limited number of targets of twelve shots each.

RECOIL

.Weight of revolver 2.31 pounds	Weight of powder 28 grains	Weight of ball 230 grains	Recoil (theoretical) 3.89 foot-pounds

PENETRATION IN WHITE PINE IN INCHES

Range	50 yds.	100 yds.	150 yds.	200 yds.	250 yds.	300 yds.
Inches	3¾	3½	3⅛	2¾	2½	2¼

As there is but one height of rear sight on this revolver—viz., that corresponding to 50 yards—the center of impact will fall lower and lower on the target as the range is increased. It will therefore be necessary in firing to raise the line of sight as much above the object as the trajectory passes below it. The following table gives the ordinates of points of the trajectory at 300 yards below the line of sight corresponding to 50 yards:

ORDINATES OF TRAJECTORY BELOW LINE OF SIGHT.
REGULAR SIGHT: 50 YARDS ELEVATION

Horizontal distance	50 yds.	100 yds.	150 yds.	200 yds.	250 yds.	300 yds.
Inches	0	16.2	48.6	99.9	165.1	256.4

This table is important, as it shows how far above one should aim in order to hit the object at the distances given. For instance, at 150 yards the point aimed at should be about 4 feet, and at 200 yards about 8 feet above the object.

All the early Colt and Smith & Wesson revolvers purchased by the Army were sighted for this cartridge (.45-230-28) and the

front sight was adjusted in height for a 50-yard range. Many of
these old Army Colt revolvers were later sold to the public through
the disposition of Army obsolete stores, and many people ask why
these guns always shoot about three inches high at twenty yards.
The reason is that they were sighted in for this old Smith &
Wesson cartridge and they are now being used with the regular
.45 Colt cartridge (.45-255-38) which gives a greater jump, owing
to the 25 grains additional bullet weight.

Most companies still load this old Smith & Wesson cartridge
with the original 230-grain ball and 28 grains of black powder,
but the Remington Company loads it with a 250-grain bullet which
gives a somewhat reduced velocity of 710 foot-seconds.

Bullet diameter	.454 inch
Bullet weight	230 grains
Bullet length	.72 inch
Diameter of cartridge head	.521 "
Diameter of case, front	.475 "
Case length	1.10 "
Length of loaded cartridge	.143 "
Powder charge	28 grains FFG black
Velocity	735 f. s.
Energy	266 foot pounds
Remington bullet weight	250 grains
Remington black powder velocity	710 f.s.
Energy	280 foot pounds

.45 Colt

This is one of the most famous and popular of all the .45-
caliber cartridges. It is the old Peacemaker cartridge which had
such a romantic history in the frontier days and is the cartridge
with which most of the civilization of the West was accomplished.

The Colt New Service revolver and the Colt single-action revolver are now made for this cartridge. It has a 255-grain lead
bullet with a muzzle velocity of about 770 foot-seconds and a
muzzle energy of 330 foot-pounds.

This cartridge was originally loaded with 40 grains of black
powder, which gave a higher velocity than the smokeless load
gives. Cartridge companies now generally load the black-powder
.45 Colt with around 34 grains of FFG Black, giving a little over
800 foot-seconds. However, the Remington Company uses a
somewhat lighter bullet, 250 grains, and loads the full 40 grains
of black powder behind it, giving a velocity of 910 foot-seconds
and a muzzle energy of 460 foot-pounds, which is the highest
muzzle energy of any revolver or pistol cartridge now sold.

Recently there has been much discussion and many lamentations from some of the old-timers out West who think that the Peacemaker has lost its wallop. They say that the .45-caliber Colt no longer has the punch that it had in the old frontier days. This, however, is not the true state of affairs as the present Remington load has more power behind it than any previous Peacemaker cartridge that has ever been put on the market. As a matter of fact, for years after the old Peacemaker was first introduced it was largely used with the .45-caliber Army cartridge

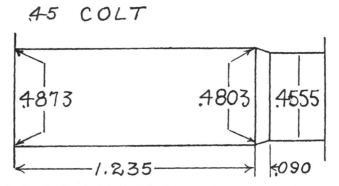

The chamber for the .45 Colt Cartridge is now used in the New Service, the New Service Target, and the Single Action Army revolvers. It was formerly used in the Bisley Model.

which was the same as the old .45 Smith & Wesson and had a 230-grain bullet with 28 grains of black powder. However, at the time this gun was introduced by the Colt Company they also introduced the present .45 Colt cartridge, originally loaded with 40 grains of black powder.

The fact that the Army had in service two kinds of .45-caliber revolvers, one of which was the Smith & Wesson which would not take the long Colt cartridge, gave rise to two types of .45 cartridges which were commonly used in the Peacemaker, one the original type, with the 255-grain bullet, and one, the Army type, with the 230-grain bullet, still manufactured under the name of ".45 Smith & Wesson."

In 1892 the Army abandoned the use of the .45 and adopted the .38 double action, using the .38 Long Colt cartridge. However, in the Philippine campaign it was found that the .38 cartridge did not have sufficient stopping power and the Army, in 1909, adopted the Colt New Service double-action revolver in .45 caliber for use in the Philippines.

The .45 Model of 1909

This revolver was chambered for the regular .45 Colt cartridge, but Frankford Arsenal proceeded to manufacture a .45 cartridge for this gun which differed somewhat from the old .45 Colt. This cartridge was the same size, except for the rim which was made larger to give more bearing on the extractor. The cylinder of the Colt New Service revolver is larger than the cylinder of the Colt Single Action, and this larger rim could be used in the Colt New Service revolver, but a considerable amount of confusion was created when this revolver was made obsolete by the Army, for many of these .45-caliber cartridges were sold to civilian marksmen by the Government in disposing of obsolete stores, and it was found that when an attempt was made to use them in the .45 single action, trouble was encountered because the rims of the cartridges would interfere with each other when two cartridges were placed in adjacent chambers. Only every other chamber could be loaded. Except for this difference in the rim, the .45-caliber cartridge Model of 1909 is the same as the ordinary .45 Colt. It had a 255-grain bullet and was loaded with 8.4 grains of RSQ powder to a velocity of 738 foot-seconds. Because this was a Government cartridge careful tests were made which give a very good index as to the ballistic performance of the .45-caliber Colt cartridge at the long ranges. These figures, taken from Ordnance Pamphlet No. 1927, are as follows for the .45 Colt with 255-grain bullet and 8.4 grains RSQ smokeless:

ACCURACY WITH FIXED REST

Range, yards	Mean radius, inches	Mean vertical deviation, inches
25	1.058	0.692
50	2.042	1.724
75	2.61	1.681

NOTE: The above figures represent the mean variations for a great number of targets. Targets with 50 per cent less variations have been made.

VELOCITY, WITH STRIKING ENERGY

Range, yards	Velocity, feet per second	Energy, foot-pounds
0	738.0	297.3
25	687.4	257.85
50	651.3	231.48
75	617.8	208.28
100	585.7	187.2

VELOCITY WITH STRIKING ENERGY (Continued)

Range, yards	Velocity, feet per second	Energy, foot-pounds
125	555.4	168.33
150	526.5	151.27
175	499.0	135.88
200	473.1	121.25

PENETRATION IN WHITE PINE

Range, yards	Depth, inches
25	3.45
50	3.38
75	3.22
100	3.15
150	3.00
200	2.18

The penetration in moist loam at 25 yards is 19.2 inches. The penetration in dry sand at 25 yards is 8.28 inches.

This pamphlet also says that the maximum ordinate for the 200-yard range is 4.16 feet, and that a close approximation to the maximum ordinate for any range may be obtained by multiplying the square of the range in yards by .000144, the result being the approximate ordinate in feet.

Bullet weight	255 grains (except Remington 250 grains)
Bullet diameter	.454 inch
Bullet length	.72 inch
Diameter cartridge head	.508 " (.536 for Model of 1909)
" " body	.477 "
" " mouth	.476 "
Length case	1.28 "
Overall length	1.60 "
Thickness rim	.054 "
Factory smokeless load	5.7 grains Bullseye
Pressure	14,000 pounds per square inch
Velocity, 5½ inch barrel revolver	770 foot seconds
Energy	335 foot pounds
Penetration, ⅞ inch pine boards	5 boards
Remington black powder load	40 grains
Velocity in revolver	910 foot seconds
Energy	460 foot pounds

Reloading Data

Name of bullet	Ideal 454190	Ideal 454190	Winchester
Weight of bullet	255 grains	255 grains	255 grains
Name of powder	No. 80	Pistol No. 5	Bullseye
Weight of charge	12 grains	8 grains	5.0 grains
Velocity	785	870	784
Recommended by	DuPont	DuPont	Hercules

Metal-Jacketed .45 Caliber Revolver Cartridge

In 1906 some Colt .45 double-action revolvers were issued for use in the Philippines, and Frankford Arsenal made, for use in these revolvers, a special .45-caliber cartridge with a bullet weighing 234 grains with a cupronickel jacket. The charge was 6.9 grains of RSQ powder.

This cartridge will interchange with the .45 Colt and the .45 Model of 1909 described above. However, this is only of academic interest, as only a few of these cartridges were made and they are never seen today except in collections.

.45 Automatic Colt

This is the largest caliber automatic pistol cartridge and is the present service cartridge. It is a highly modern smokeless-powder rimless cartridge with a full-jacketed bullet weighing 230 grains. Because this is a Government service cartridge it has a great deal of information available on the ballistics that is not available for an ordinary commercial cartridge. The following information is taken from Training Regulations No. 320-15.

ACCURACY WITH MUZZLE REST

Range, yards	Mean radius, inches	Mean vertical deviation, inches
25	0.855	0.619
50	1.356	0.910
75	2.244	1.422

The above figures represent the mean variations for several targets.

VELOCITY WITH STRIKING ENERGY

Range, yards	Velocity, feet per second	Energy, foot-pounds
0	802	329
25	788	317
50	773	305
75	758	294
100	744	283
125	730	272
150	717	262
175	704	253
200	691	244
225	678	235
250	666	226

PENETRATION IN WHITE PINE

Range, yards	Depth, inches
25	6.0
50	5.8
75	5.6
100	5.5
150	5.2
200	4.6
250	4.0

The penetration in moist loam at 25 yards is 9.95 inches. Penetration in dry sand at 25 yards is 7.8 inches.

The following table of angles of departure for the .45 A.C.P. Cartridge with 230 grain bullet and muzzle velocity of 800 feet per second may prove interesting.

Range	Angle of departure		
100 yards	0 degrees	19.2	minutes
200 "	0 "	44.7	"
300 "	1 "	14.2	"
400 "	1 "	50	"
500 "	2 "	34.7	"
600 "	3 "	26.3	"
700 "	4 "	27.5	"
800 "	5 "	33.5	"
900 "	6 "	47	"
1000 "	8 "	15.3	"
1100 "	9 "	55	"
1200 "	12 "	1	"
1300 "	14 "	50.5	"
1400 "	19 "	2	"

The maximum range is approximately 1600 yards at an angle of elevation of 30 degrees. The maximum ordinate, or greatest height of the 1600 yard trajectory is 2000 feet.

The accuracy figures given for this cartridge have been greatly improved since the tests quoted above. In the accuracy test at Sea Girt in 1919 the average mean radius at 50 yards was 1.81 inches and the average group diameter 5.59 inches. At the tests made at Sea Girt in 1920 for the acceptance of National Match ammunition the average mean radius at 50 yards was 1.14 inches and the average group diameter was 3.83 inches.

After this date a considerable amount of attention was given to the question of obtaining increased accuracy with the .45-caliber automatic ammunition, and changes were made in the diameter of the bullet and the dimensions of the barrel. The diameter of the bullet was changed from the old standard of .4505 to the present standard of .4515, and the standard bore diameter of the pistol was changed from .445 plus or minus .001, to .443 plus .001, minus nothing. A considerable increase in accuracy was at once apparent, the average mean radius of daily tests in May, 1924, at Frankford being .77, the average group diameter 1.92. Further improvement in accuracy was made as the result of certain changes in the jacket metal, and in 1925 an average of five targets fired in a daily test gave a group diameter of 1.75 at 50 yards. Groups of less than one inch at 50 yards are frequently obtained.

Formerly there were two distinct types of .45 Automatic cartridge; the Government standard, described above, loaded with

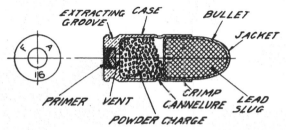

Caliber .45 Auto-Colt Pistol Cartridge.

a 230 grain bullet and a muzzle velocity of 810 feet per second, and the commercial type, loaded with a 200 grain bullet and a muzzle velocity of 910 feet per second. The muzzle energy of the Government type is 340 foot pounds, and that of the commercial type is 368 foot pounds. The manufacture of the 200 grain type has been discontinued.

A jacketed bullet generally does not have as great stopping power as a lead bullet and tends to glance more easily, and for that reason the .45 Automatic is not as effective as the .45 Colt, but it has a powerful knockdown blow and has been found highly satisfactory for military use.

Besides being used in the Automatic Pistol, this cartridge is used in the Model of 1917 Colt and Smith & Wesson Revolvers. When used in these revolvers it will not extract unless a special steel clip is used, which fits around the heads of the cartridges, which are of the rimless type. Without the clip the cartridges can be used in the revolvers but must be pushed out with a stick or lifted out with the rim of another cartridge after firing.

The .45 Automatic differs from the old .45 Colt in that it was originally designed for smokeless powder, and therefore the space in the shell was made only large enough to accommodate the proper charge. Thus there is no excess airspace, and the smokeless powder burns well and very efficiently. The .45 Colt, on the other hand, has a much larger case, originally intended to hold a large charge of black powder. When the dense smokeless powders

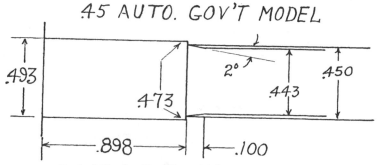

.45 AUTO. GOV'T MODEL

Standard Chamber Dimensions of Colt .45 Automatic Pistols.

came into use, it was found that the space in these cases, intended to hold 40 grains of black powder, were too large to work most efficiently with the small charges of perhaps 7 grains of smokeless. This is why the .45 Automatic, which appears to be much smaller than the .45 Colt, is nearly as powerful.

Many interesting experiments have been performed on the .45 Automatic Cartridge. For example, it was found that with a lot of Bullseye Powder which required 4.4 grains for a normal charge to give 800 f.s., a charge of 12 grains failed to burst an automatic pistol, though the head of the cartridge was blown out and the slide of the gun was bulged. However, fifteen grains split the barrel and blew out the side of the frame.

A charge of 1 grain of Bullseye drove the bullet halfway through the barrel; 1½ grains drove it 50 feet beyound the muzzle; 2 grains drove it into a sand butt 50 yards away, while 2½ grains functioned the mechanism.

Bullet weight	230 grains
Bullet diameter	.4515 inch
Bullet length	.662 "
Diameter of cartridge head	.471 "
Diameter of cartridge mouth	.471 "
Case length	.90 "
Length loaded cartridge	1.26 "
Factory charge, Bullseye	4.9 grains Bullseye powder
Pressure	14,170 lbs. per square inch
Velocity	821 foot seconds

Factory charge, Pistol No. 5	6.1 grains No. 5
Pressure	13,990 lbs. per square inch
Velocity	824 feet per second

Reloading Data

Name of bullet	Ideal 452374	Belding & Mull 452236	Factory made
Weight of bullet	220 grains	238 grains	230
Kind of powder	Pistol No. 5	No. 80	Bullseye
Weight of charge	5.6 grains	7.5 grains	4.6 grains
Velocity	880 f.s.	775	800 f.s.
Recommended by	DuPont	DuPont	Hercules

.45 Auto-Rim

After the war there were many thousands of Colt and Smith & Wesson Army revolvers, Model of 1917, sold to the public by the Government, and Smith & Wesson still manufacture and sell this model. This arm is chambered for the .45 Automatic Pistol cartridge, and it was intended that this cartridge should be used with a clip because it is a rimless cartridge and otherwise will not extract from revolvers. Just after the war the Peters Cartridge Company started to manufacture a cartridge specially designed for these Model of 1917 revolvers.

This cartridge is similar to the Automatic Pistol cartridge except that it has a rim. It is called the ".45 Auto-Rim." The Remington Arms Company soon followed suit and also manufactured the auto-rim cartridge. With the metal-jacketed bullet the auto-rim cartridge duplicates the ballistics of the .45 Automatic Pistol cartridge. However, this cartridge is now made also with a plain lead bullet.

The Auto-Rim lead cartridge made by the Peters Cartridge Company has a 255-grain bullet and gives ballistics very similar to those of the old .45 Colt.

Owing to the shape of the inside of the base, the .45 Auto-Rim cartridge has slightly more powder space than the .45 automatic.

Name	.45 Auto-rim, lead bullet
Bullet weight	.255 grains
Bullet diameter	.451 inch
Bullet length	.74 "
Diameter cartridge head	.512 "
Diameter case, rear	.475 "
Diameter case, mouth, outside	.472 "
Length case	.90 "
Length cartridge loaded	1.27 "
Thickness rim	.087 "
Muzzle velocity	740 feet per second
Energy	310 foot pounds

Name	.45 Auto-rim, jacketed bullet
Bullet weight	230 grains
Bullet dimensions	Same as for .45 A. C. P.
Case dimensions	Same as for .45 Auto-rim lead bullet
Powder charge	4.5 grains Bullseye
Pressure	14,000 pounds per square inch
Muzzle velocity	810 f.s.
Energy	340 foot pounds

Reloading Data

Name of bullet	Belding & Mull 452236	Belding & Mull 452236
Weight of bullet	236 grains	236 grains
Name of powder	Bullseye	Pistol No. 5
Weight of charge	4.0 grains	4.9 grains
Velocity	800 f.s.	780 f.s.

.450 Revolver

This is a black powder cartridge for foreign revolvers of that caliber. While it is not often seen in this country a few are

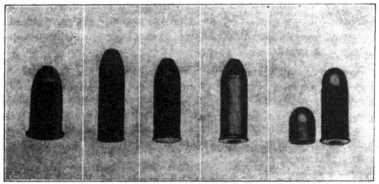

OLD-TIME CARTRIDGES IN THE AUTHOR'S COLLECTION

1. .50 Remington Navy.
2. .44 "Martin" cartridge made at Frankford Arsenal, 1871.
3. .45 cartridge made at Frankford Arsenal, 1878. Inside primer (central-fire) 28 grains powder and 230-grain bullet.
4. .45 cartridge made at Frankford Arsenal, 1891. 28 grains powder and 230-grain bullet.
5. .45 cartridge with metal jacketed bullet made at Frankford Arsenal in 1906.

manufactured to take care of the occasional demand. The sample described has a hollow base bullet.

Bullet weight	226 grains
Bullet diameter	.458 inch
Bullet length	.75 "
Diameter of cartridge head	.503 "
Diameter of cartridge body	.476 "
Length of case	.69 "
Length of cartridge	1.09 "
Powder charge	13 grains black
Muzzle velocity, 6 inch barrel	590 f.s.
Muzzle energy	170 ft. lbs.

.45 Webley

This is an English cartridge of moderate power that is largely used in target practice. It is manufactured in this country to supply the occasional demand.

Bullet weight	230 grains
Bullet diameter	.450 inch
Bullet length	.61 "
Diameter of cartridge head	.504 "
Diameter of cartridge body	.471 "
Length of case	.82 "
Length of cartridge	1.15 "
Muzzle velocity, 6½ inch barrel	550 f.s.
Muzzle energy	150 ft. lbs.

.455 Webley

This is the service revolver cartridge of the British Army. It follows the British idea of obtaining the maximum stopping power by means of a heavy bullet moving at low velocity. It has a heavy, conical bullet with a rather long, slender point with a weight of 255 grains. The powder space in the cartridge is very small.

Bullet weight	265 grains
Bullet diameter	.457 inch
Bullet length	.88 "
Diameter of cartridge head	.528 "
Diameter of cartridge body	.475 "
Length of case	.77 "
Length of cartridge	1.23 "
Powder charge	7 grains smokeless
Muzzle velocity, 6½ inch barrel	600 f.s.
Muzzle energy	220 ft. lbs.
Name	.455 Webley man-stopper
Bullet weight	220 grains
Bullet diameter	.455 inch
Bullet length	.72 "
Length of cartridge	1.11 "
Other dimensions	Same as .455 Webley

.455 Webley Self Loading Pistol

This cartridge is not made in America, but is interesting because it is the service cartridge of the British Royal Navy. It has a 220 grain, full jacketed bullet and a charge of seven grains of Cordite, giving a standard velocity of 750 foot-seconds.

The cartridge is very similar in appearance to the .45 Automatic Colt. The main differences are that the cartridge is of the semi-rim instead of the rimless type and the bullet is nearly flat on the point instead of being conical. The Colt bullet has an advantage of five grains in weight, but the Webley bullet is superior in stopping power on account of the very flat point.

Bullet weight	220 grains
Bullet diameter	.455 inch
Bullet length	.59 "
Diameter of cartridge head	.500 "
Diameter of cartridge body	.474 "
Length of case	.93 "
Length of cartridge	1.23 "
Powder charge	7 grains cordite
Muzzle velocity, 5 inch barrel	750 f.s.
Muzzle energy	270 ft. lbs.

.476 Eley

The only cartridges of this type that I have ever seen were those tried by the United States Government Board of Officers in 1904 when a bullet with more stopping power was found necessary for use in the Philippine Islands. This bullet was found to have more stopping power than any other bullet tried by the Board. It was tested in a Colt New Service revolver chambered specially for it. The bullet has a hollow base containing a clay plug which expands it into the rifling.

The data given below are taken from cartridges in the author's possession which were part of the lot originally obtained for the Board mentioned above.

Bullet weight	288 grains
Bullet diameter	.474 inch
Bullet length	.90 "
Diameter of cartridge head	.508 "
Diameter of cartridge body	.478 "
Length of case	.88 "
Length of cartridge	1.48 "
Powder charge	18 grains black

Old "Inside Primer" .45 Colt. Center fire Cartridge made at Frankford Arsenal in 1874. From the Author's collection. Box marked "12 Cartridges, for Colt's Revolver. Cal. .45. Powder, 30 grains. Bullet, 250 grains. Frankford Arsenal, February, 1874."

CHAPTER 11

TECHNICAL NOTES ON AMMUNITION

THE many uncertainties connected with nearly every phase of the manufacture, use, or study of ammunition are what make the subject so interesting. In making any ordinary mechanical object, such as, say, a knife or a wrench, the maker has only to use the correct material and make the material into the shape indicated on the drawing. If measurements show that he has done this, he knows that his production will be satisfactory, and will work as expected.

With ammunition, on the other hand, every precaution may be taken to make everything exactly to specifications, and the closest inspection may reveal that the product is as nearly perfect as the most delicate weighing and measuring instruments can detect, yet when the cartridge samples go on the testing range, the accuracy may be poor; and all the skill of the best engineers may be unable to detect the reason for the trouble. Again, another lot of ammunition made under exactly the same conditions may give superb accuracy.

Such small troubles as these are negligible, however, when compared to the feelings of the cartridge maker when a lot of ammunition that has been giving satisfaction in the hands of the shooters suddenly begins to go bad on the shelves of the dealers and in the hands of the public, as actually happened a year or so after the first introduction of the non-corrosive priming compound. One of the ingredients was subject to deterioration under conditions of storage in warm and humid places, and when this deterioration occurred, misfires and hang fires resulted, and the accuracy of the ammunition became very poor.

It is occurrences like this which discourage the cartridge maker from trying new things. Once he has a product which has stood the test of time in the hands of the shooting public, he feels safer to stick to it, even at the risk of being called non-progressive.

Even a time tried product may go bad when the conditions of manufacture are changed. The Government Non-Mecuric Primer which had been made at Frankford for years suddenly went bad and spoiled a large quantity of ammunition just at the beginning of the World War. There was not time to stop making ammunition and investigate the cause of the trouble so that the Ordnance Department took the drastic step of abandoning the standard primer formula and buying the needed primers from the commercial cartridge companies while they installed the process of making primers according to the formula of the Winchester Repeating Arms Company. It was later found that the cause of the trouble was the very speed with which ammunition had to be made. The haste to get large production made it necessary to rush the drying of the primers by artificial heat, and this caused the mixture to sour. This expression brings to mind the operation of making bread, and it is a fact that making an excellent lot of ammunition is something like making a cake; even when everything is done according to directions and experience, the result is better some times than at others.

Cartridge Life

Many times I have been asked how long cartridges will last; whether or not they will get stale; whether or not the powder will deteriorate so that they will get dangerous. The life of well made metallic small arms ammunition is perhaps ten years on the average. Some ammunition may lose some of its strength in five or six years, and other lots may last twenty years or more. Something depends on the conditions of storage. Damp, warm climates are the worst, but even there, the cartridges should last at least several years.

There is very little trouble from the deterioration of the modern smokeless powders. They have very much the same composition as celluloid, and will last just about as long, or longer. They do not deteriorate as fast as many common materials, such as silk, rubber, etc. And it is fortunate that when deterioration does take place, it always weakens the powder. There is no danger of the powder's getting stronger, so as to burst the gun. The only exceptions that need be made to this statement are to state that under different storage conditions, such as the presence or absence of steam heat, etc., the powder may absorb moisture or dry out slightly. When it dries, it will become moderately stronger until such time as it absorbs moisture again. Powder makers and cartridge companies endeavor to make their test firings for determination of charges with the powder having a moisture content that is about the average to be expected under conditions of storage and use. The changes from this cause are not serious, under any conditions. The other exception is in the case of black powder, which may become caked from moisture, so as to give high pressures.

Primer deterioration is unlikely with any well tried primer composition, though at times of radical change in methods, such as the introduction of the non-corrosive primer, which occurred several years ago, troubles may occur.

Occasionally cartridge cases will crack while in storage. This is due to a well known characteristic of brass, which has a tendency to separate or crack if it is strained from severe working and then allowed to stand without relieving the strains by heating. In the case of the small arms cartridge, it is not possible to anneal the metal and relieve the strains without making it so soft as to weaken it at the base of the cartridge and around the primer pocket, where the brass must be very strong and springy. A certain amount of annealing is done to relieve the strains and prevent season cracking, but the manufacturer is always working between the danger of over annealing and thus having blown primers and other troubles, or of under annealing, with the risk of having the ammunition split after a few years of storage.

Mercury and its compounds have the quality of causing brass to split very quickly if it is in a strained condition. In the cartridge factories a very weak solution of mercuric chloride, (corrosive sublimate), or mercurous nitrate is used as a test to see if the cartridges have a tendency to crack. A cartridge dipped in this solution will crack in a few seconds unless the brass is properly annealed.

For the reason that mercury is "poison" to brass, the early non-corrosive primers ruined the cartridges so that they could not be used for reloading. This was because the non-corrosive primer composition contained mercuric fulminate, a salt of mercury. During the explosion, mercury is deposited all over the inside of the case. The amount is small, but it is ample to make the cases too brittle for further use. Fortunately, the later non-corrosive mixtures are made without the mercury in most cases.

Cartridges will go bad very quickly if oil gets inside the case, for it will make the primer insensitive, and thus cause misfires, or if it does not reach the primer, it may cause the powder to burn slowly, so that the velocity is reduced. Many burst revolver barrels have been caused by the fact that oil, or grease from the bullet lubricant, has mixed with the powder to such an extent that the bullet would go only partway through the barrel. If the user fails to notice this trouble and fires another shot, the barrel will be bulged or burst.

In order to prevent the entrance of oil or moisture, it is common practice to varnish the mouth of the case before the insertion of the bullet, and to put a ring of waterproofing around the joint between the primer and the primer pocket. At the present time a substance much used for this purpose is what is called N.R.C. Compound. The name comes from "National Research Council," as the composition was developed by that body.

On account of the danger of misfires caused by oil on the cartridges, it is not a good thing for the peace officer or other gun user to keep his loaded revolver reeking with oil. On the other hand, when loading a gun it is desirable to wipe the cartridges over with a rag which has been moistened with the smallest possible quantity of oil, so as to leave an imperceptible film of oiliness on the surface. This will prevent the cartridges from corroding in the cylinder of a revolver if they should be left there for a long time.

Pressures

When any cartridge is fired, a very high pressure results inside the gun from the sudden explosion. In cartridge factories, constant tests are made of each day's production to insure that no cartridges are sent out that have a pressure so high as to be dangerous. The test is made by the use of a pressure gun. This consists of a gun with a hole bored into the chamber from the top. A piston with a copper cup on the end to prevent the escape of gas is fitted into the hole, and a copper cylinder is fitted on top of the piston, and held in place by a strong steel yoke. When the gun is fired, the gas pressure pushes upward on the piston, and this upward push crushes the copper cylinder. A number of exactly similar copper cylinders have previously been subjected to known amounts of weight, and the crushing that resulted from each weight has been entered onto a sheet called a tarage table. When the pressure gun is fired, the copper cylinder is taken out and measured with a micrometer caliper, and the resulting length is compared with the tarage table. The table shows what weight had to be applied to the copper to crush it that much.

In high-powered rifles, the pressures run as high as about 50,000 pounds per square inch, but in revolvers and pistols, it is usually not over about 15,000 pounds per square inch, and in most of them it is around 9,000 or 10,000 pounds per square inch. Exceptions are the Luger and Mauser cartridges, with pressures of 24,000 and 30,000 pounds per square inch respectively, and the Super .38 Automatic, with about 25,000 pounds per square inch.

A pressure gage for pistol cartridges. Inside the rectangular block near the funnel is a barrel chambered for the .45 automatic pistol cartridge. On top is a heavy yoke for holding a copper crusher cylinder on a steel piston communicating with the interior of the barrel. When the explosion takes place, the gas pressure, acting through the piston, compresses the copper cylinder, and the amount of this compression is afterwards measured to give the pressure. At the rear is seen the simple firing mechanism.

There are several factors which affect the pressure that a cartridge may give. The most obvious one is the amount of the charge; naturally, the more powder, the more pressure. Other factors which also have a bearing on the pressure are, the bullet weight, the bullet diameter, the air space in the cartridge case, and the temperature.

In general, for charges in the vicinity of the normal load, the pressure changes very uniformly with changes in the powder charge; but when a point is reached where all the air space in the cartridge is used up, or even with plenty of air space, when the pressures reach a certain point, small increases in charge may result in sudden and dangerous increases in pressure. This is why it is not advisable to experiment blindly with smokeless powder.

As an example of the changes that may be expected, take the case of the .45 Automatic Pistol Cartridge. With lot 101 Bull's-eye Powder, 5.1 grains were needed to obtain full velocity. A tenth of a grain more or less raised or lowered the velocity 20 feet per second, and raised or lowered the pressure 700 pounds per square inch. With Pistol Powder No. 5, lot 88, a charge of 6.0 grains gave the proper velocity, and a tenth of a grain more or less raised or lowered the velocity 15 feet per second and the pressure 700 pounds per square inch.

Hot weather raises the temperature, and cold weather lowers it. However, the changes in pressure in pistol cartridges due to weather changes are never sufficient to make any practical difference to the shooter. As an indication of how much the velocity and the pressure may be expected to change with high temperatures, the following tests are of great interest. A number of cartridges for the .45 automatic pistol were loaded with bull's-eye powder, and subjected to a temperature of 100 degrees Centigrade, (212 degrees F.), and were fired for velocity and pressure while they were at this temperature. The cartridges were retained at the high temperature for one hour before firing. The results follow:

Condition	Velocity	Mean Pressure
Normal cartridges not heated	830 f.s.	15,100 lbs.
Cartridges heated to 100°C	880 f.s.	16,600 "
Difference	50 f.s.	1,500 "

In another test, the cartridges, loaded with 4.9 grains of Bull's-eye, were frozen to 22 degrees below zero, F., and then fired. There was a loss of 32 f. s. in velocity and 2,600 pounds pressure. In another test, the ammunition was cooled to 79 degrees below zero, Centigrade, (110 degrees below zero F.) and fired at that temperature. A lot of cartridges loaded with 4.6 grains Pistol Powder No. 6 lost 41 feet in velocity, and 1,620 pounds pressure. A lot loaded with 4.7 grains Bull's-eye lost 56 feet velocity and 2,440 pounds pressure. A lot loaded with 5.8 grains of Pistol Powder No. 5 lost 111 feet velocity and 4,740 pounds pressure.

The high velocity tests did develop the fact that sometimes when nitro-glycerine powders are subjected to very high temperatures, some of the nitro-glycerine may be stewed out, and it may get into the primers and cause misfires. Otherwise, high temperatures do not seem to change ammunition that has been heated and then cooled again.

In making these tests, some of the ammunition was subjected to temperatures as high as 120 degrees centigrade, which is 248 degrees F. At this temperature several of the cartridges exploded from the heat. When left at this temperature 48 hours, 4 out of 5 exploded. When left at this temperature 8 hours, none exploded, but at 16 hours, 1 out of five, and at 18½ hours, 3 out of five had exploded. The explosions seemed weak, so that a loaded gun was subjected to the same temperature. The bullets on either side of the barrel did not clear the cylinder, being stopped by the frame. The bullet which was in line with the barrel passed out, but did not penetrate the side of the oven, which was made of two thicknesses of .035 galvanized steel. There was no damage to the weapon. Quite evidently where the powder is ignited very gradually in this manner, the explosion is extremely weak, and in no manner compares with the results when the powder is ignited all at once, as is the case when a primer flashes into the charge.

Conclusions from these tests are:

1. Caliber .45 cartridges, loaded with nitro-cellulose or nitro-glycerine powders, when subjected to temperatures in the order of the boiling point, for varying times up to 72 hours, after cooling to normal temperatures, may be fired with normal velocities and pressures.

2. Caliber .45 cartridges, loaded with nitro-glycerine powders, when subjected to temperatures ranging between 40 degrees C. (104 degrees F.) and 140 degrees C., (248 degrees F.) are subject to misfires, which increase in number generally with an increase in the temperature or the time during which they are subjected to high temperature. These misfires are due to the penetration of the primer, and its deadening by products of decomposition of the powder.

The three rifle cartridges that are used in revolvers—namely, .32-20, .38-40 and .44-40—are all old-timers. They were originally made with black powder for use in both the Winchester rifles and the Colt revolvers. As the years went by and rifle cartridges became improved these three cartridges were considered to be too low in velocity for modern conditions. As powders were improved the ammunition companies found they could increase the velocities of these old cartridges by using some of the later powders, and the result is what is known as the "high-velocity" type. In these the pressure runs way above what it did in the original cartridges, and they should never be used in revolvers. Many accidents have been caused by ignorance of this fact on the part of owners of revolvers of these calibers who would naturally just ask for the .38-40 cartridge, or whatever caliber they wanted, and take whatever the hardware dealer gave them. If this happened to be the improved high-velocity type they were in danger of bursting the cylinder of their revolvers. These high-velocity cartridges are marked on the box, "Not adapted to use in revolvers," but this caution is not always read. Of late years the cylinders of revolvers have been specially heat-treated to minimize the danger of accidents from this cause, but even if you have a late revolver with a heat-treated cylinder it is not advisable to use this high-pressure ammunition, it is a bit too strenuous for any handgun.

Velocity

Pistol and revolver bullets usually have velocities of around 800 feet per second. There are some, however, which have higher velocities, such as the Super .38 Automatic, with its velocity of 1200 feet per second, and the .30 Caliber Mauser, regularly listed at 1375 feet, which often runs above 1400. I personally tested a lot of wartime .30 Mauser cartridges brought from Germany after the war, which gave an average of 1425 feet per second.

Recently there has been a big increase in the standard velocities of a number of the more popular pistol cartridges. Notable is the case of the .22 long rifle, which in 1930 appeared in the Hi-Speed and Super X types, giving velocities of 1300 and 1400 feet per second respectively in rifles, and up to 1100 feet per second in revolvers. The attainment of these high velocities was naturally accompanied by an increase in pressure, and the fear that this might result in burst heads in the .22, with the consequent escape of gas and possible injury to the shooter led to a recommendation by the makers of the first of these high velocity .22s against their use in pistols or revolvers, or indeed, in anything except the very highest grade bolt action rifle. Shortly after these new cartridges appeared on the market, Major Douglas B. Wesson, of Smith & Wesson produced his K-.22 revolver, built especially for the Remington Hi-Speed cartridge. As a matter of protection in case of burst cartridge heads, or rather to keep them from bursting, the chambers of this gun are counterbored at the rear end so that the head of the cartridge can sink in flush with the surface. This idea was immediately followed by all the other makers of revolvers, and the high speed cartridges came into use in both revolvers and pistols.

Recently Major Wesson produced a .38 caliber revolver on the frame of the famous .44 Military. This gave a heavy gun, with a thick barrel and cylinder. In view of the additional strength and weight in this gun, it was thought that it would be advisable to make the .38 Special cartridge with higher velocity than standard especially for use in this heavy frame gun. This new cartridge has 1125 foot seconds velocity as against the standard velocity of 860 foot seconds. This new cartridge came out under the name of the .38-44. The .38 Colt Special, which is the same as the .38 Smith & Wesson Special with a blunt pointed bullet is also loaded to 1125 feet per second for use in this heavy frame gun, under the name of .38 Colt Special High Velocity. The regular .38 Special low velocity cartridges can of course, be shot in the .38-44 Outdoorsman's Revolver. The high velocity loads can also be shot in the regular .38 Military and Police or the Colt Official Police .38 if desired, but the recoil is rather heavy. Other heavy frame revolvers made in the .38 Special Caliber for which the .34-44 and .38 S. & W. Special High Velocity and .38 Colt Special High Velocity cartridges are especially suited are the Colt New Service, the Colt Shooting Master, and the Colt Single Action.

This recent tendency toward high velocities in revolver cartridges is further exemplified by the fact that for several years the Remington Arms Co. have made it a regular practice to load the .45 Colt cartridge with black powder to a considerably higher velocity than the 770 feet per second which has been the standard smokeless velocity for some years. The velocity of this Remington Black Powder load is 910 f. s. Recently the Western Cartridge Company changed their smokeless .45 from 770 f. s. to 910 f. s.

Range of Pistol Bullets

While the range at which the ordinary pistol and revolvers are supposed to be effective is only 50 or 75 yards, all of them will send their bullets much further than that, and are capable of inflicting fatal wounds at distances up to one mile, depending on the caliber.

Thus the .32 Automatic Colt Pistol, when discharged at an elevation of 26 degrees, will send its bullet over 1300 yards, and the .25 caliber elevated at an angle of 15 degrees will shoot 850 yards. The dispersion at these ranges is very great, and it would be difficult to hit an object the size of a large house, but stray shots discharged in the air may do serious damage a long way off. I know of a case where a boy was killed at a distance of 639 yards by a .22 short.

Moreover, bullets will bounce off many objects, and go in unexpected directions. A bullet fired so that it strikes the ground at a slight angle will usually bounce up at nearly the same angle, and continue its flight with plenty of speed remaining. Frequently an officer of the law has fired on the ground to frighten a fleeing person, and then has been surprised to see the fugitive fall. How many times have we seen in the papers that a boy who had been discovered in an orchard or melon patch was killed when the owner fired a shot on the ground "to frighten them."

A bullet fired straight up into the air would come back with the same velocity that it had when it started if it were not for the air resistance; but in practice, a bullet fired straight upward has little velocity remaining when it returns to earth. If you feel that you must fire a loaded gun to frighten someone, fire it straight down into the ground, so that it will not bounce, or straight up into the air.

Accuracy

The ordinary outdoor range for pistol-shooting is 50 yards in length, though some years ago the Army had a qualification course that went up to 75 yards.

Owing to the short sighting radius of a pistol or revolver, it is difficult to get accurate results offhand at distances greater than about 75 yards, though a good shot can place most of his bullets in an object the size of an ordinary barrel at a distance of 200 yards.

There is really not much known about the relative accuracy of different pistols and revolvers and their cartridges because it is so hard to get really satisfactory mechanical tests which will eliminate the human error of holding and pulling the trigger. In testing cartridges, it is difficult also to eliminate the variation in different guns, even of the same make, and in testing guns it is difficult to eliminate variations in ammunition. Therefore, for a long time all we had on the accuracy of pistols and revolvers and their ammunition was a sort of tradition, built up by a mass of accumulated experience of shooters with different types of arms. This information was, of course, far from exact and was often complicated and confusing. If a man happened to have a particularly good .44 revolver, for example, he would declare that the .44-caliber was the most accurate in the world. If, on a certain day, he happened to be holding particularly well, the make of ammunition he was using that day was probably considered by him to be the best make. The only indisputable facts that were developed in this way were that the .22-caliber Long Rifle and the .38 Smith & Wesson Special had extraordinarily good accuracy.

For a long time the author tabulated various opinions on this subject from well-known shots, and it was found that there was a very great variation between these authorities, but they all agreed in placing the .22 and the .38 Special ahead.

The following tabulation shows the relative accuracy of the different revolver cartridges fired by a good marksman from a muzzle rest. Such a rest eliminates most of the errors of holding, but still require the gun to be sighted by eye, so that the errors of eyesight remain. The range at which the firing was done was 50 yards in all cases. I consider these figures a reliable indication of the relative accuracy of the various cartridges.

AVERAGE GROUP DIAMETERS OF REVOLVER CARTRIDGES ACCORDING TO CHAUNCEY THOMAS; A. L. WOODWORTH, BALLISTIC ENGINEER OF SPRINGFIELD ARMORY; AND A. C. HULBERT, FORMERLY OF COLT'S PATENT FIRE ARMS COMPANY.

Cartridge	Figures of Mr. Thomas	Figures of Mr. Woodworth	Figures of Mr. Hulbert
.22 Long Rifle	1 in. to 2 in.	1 in. to 2½ in.	1 in. to 2½ in.
.32/20	2 in. to 3 in.		3 in. to 4 in.
.38 Special	2 in. to 3 in.	2 in. to 3½ in.	1½ in. to 2½ in.
.38/40	4 in. to 5 in.		3½ in. to 4 in.
.44 Special	3 in. to 4 in.	3 in. to 4 in.	2½ in. to 4 in.
.44/40	4 in. to 5 in.		3⅛ in. to 4 in.
.45 Colt	5 in. to 6 in.	4 in. to 5½ in.	2¼ in. to 4 in.

Many attempts were made to develop a machine rest for testing pistols, but it was found that when the arm was clamped in a machine rest, the recoil would gradually cause the group to spread, so that this method of testing did not get us anywhere. For a long time Frankford Arsenal, in testing the automatic pistol cartridges, used a short heavy barrel the same length as a pistol barrel screwed onto a Springfield rifle receiver and stock. Later on a special Mann barrel was developed for this test, consisting of a heavy barrel the same length as a pistol barrel, mounted on two concentric rings and sliding in a V block. With this apparatus all variables were eliminated except relative accuracy of the ammunition, and after this machine was developed the accuracy of the Frankford Arsenal .45-caliber pistol ammunition was rapidly improved.

In a test held at Sea Girt in 1919 to select ammunition for use in the National Matches, the average group diameter of the Frank-

An actual machine-rest target reproduced exact size of a 50-yard group made at Frankford Arsenal with .45-caliber, 1925 National Match Automatic Pistol Ammunition. Made on 50-yard Standard American target.

ford Arsenal Pistol Ammunition at 50 yards was 3.83 inches. In the daily tests at Frankford Arsenal in May, 1924, the group diameters averaged 1.92. An average of five targets fired in the daily tests in February, 1925, at Frankford Arsenal gave an average group diameter of 1.75 inches at 50 yards. Groups of less than 1 inch at 50 yards were frequently seen. One group noticed in making these tests was of such a size that all the shots would have touched a dime, the extreme group diameter being about three-fourths of an inch, but this, of course, was an exception. At the present time it is thought that the .45-caliber ammunition manufactured by the Government Arsenal at Frankford is, on the average, the most accurate pistol cartridge made.

Col. Jones, of the Springfield Revolver Club, constructed a pair of rings to clamp onto the barrel of the Smith & Wesson Single Shot Pistol, and with this device he obtained groups of around 1 inch at 50 yards with the .22 Long rifle cartridge. He made similar rings for different revolvers, and with the .22-32 revolver, using the .22 Long rifle cartridge, he reported groups of 1½ inches at 50 yards. With the larger revolvers, the rings clamped onto the barrel and frame did not work well, as there was too much jump.

Harrington and Richardson constructed a satisfactory machine rest into which a .22 caliber single shot pistol can be clamped. This rest worked very well indeed, and was of inestimable benefit in helping H. & R. to make their single shot pistols and Sportsman revolvers extremely accurate.

Major Douglas B. Wesson constructed a machine rest with which he was able to test the K-.22 Revolver and the Straight Line pistol. This rest has been most useful and satisfactory. However, both the H. & R. and the S. & W. machine rests will not work so well for any caliber larger than the .22.

Methods of Measuring Accuracy

While we are on the subject of accuracy, it is in order to say a word or two about the different methods of naming or describing the accuracy of a group of shot holes. The most practical way from the point of view of the user of a pistol is to measure the group diameter—that is, the actual size in inches of the group of shots. However, the Government has for years used a different system in measuring rifle accuracy, and this system makes use of what is known as the "mean radius."

First, the average center of the shot group is determined. Then the distance of each shot from this center is measured and all these distances are averaged up. Thus, the average distance of all the shots from the center of the group is obtained and this is known as the "mean radius." It is generally about one-third the size of the group diameter in inches. In other words, a group with a mean radius of 1 inch will probably have an over-all diameter of 3 inches or thereabout, though this varies, of course, with the characteristics of the group. The method of measuring a target to obtain the mean radius is to draw a horizontal line through the bottom shot hole and a vertical line through the left-hand shot hole. Then the vertical distance of each of the shots in the group from this horizontal line is measured, and the average taken and this gives the height of the center of the group. The horizontal distance of each shot from the vertical line is then taken, and the average gives the horizontal location of the center of the group.

These two figures used in arriving at the vertical and horizontal positions of the shot group are called the "mean vertical" and the "mean horizontal" deviations and will be found in ordnance pamphlets describing the accuracy of ammunition. It has been found that the mean-radius system is not a very good one when very small groups are encountered because it is difficult to distinguish the shots. For this reason, in measuring small groups, the Ordnance Department has adopted a system called the "figure of merit." The maximum horizontal width of the group and the maximum vertical width are measured and averaged, and this average is the figure of merit, which is very close to the group diameter.

Blank Cartridges

Blank cartridges are made in most revolver calibers. They are loaded with an extremely quick powder which does not require the pressure of a bullet to make it go off with a bang. This powder

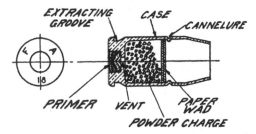

CAL. 45 BLANK CARTRIDGE MODEL 1918.

is called "EC Blank Cartridge Powder," the letters "EC" standing for "Explosives Company," the English firm that first made this powder. It consists of virtually all guncotton, mixed with some adhesive substance, such as gum water or very thin mucilage and made into little grains by the adhesiveness of the binder. It is, therefore, extremely rapid in its action and can not be used for loading any kind of ammunition that has a bullet, as the pressure would be too high. This is a little confusing, because there is another "EC" powder that is used for shotgun shells, and in two cases I have known the owners of shotguns to reload shells, using the EC Blank powder instead of the EC Shotgun powder, and in both instances this has resulted in the destruction of the gun with extreme danger to the user.

Blank cartridges should never be fired directly at any person because they all have a cardboard wad, and little pieces of the cardboard will fly for ten or fifteen feet and may pierce the skin. This would be particularly disastrous if one of these pieces should strike the eyes. Many cases of lockjaw have resulted from Fourth of July celebrations with blank cartridges in which they were fired directly at people at short range. The little pieces of cardboard being blown into the skin with violence usually carry germs with them.

Blank cartridges are not generally used with automatic pistols because they will not operate the mechanism satisfactorily; but recently some that will do this have been designed. They are made in Belgium for the pocket size automatics, and they have a bullet made of some paper composition which breaks up when the gun is fired. The bullet is hollow and is filled with powder. The powder charge is very large and fills, not only the whole cartridge case, but also the hollow paper bullet. This powder inside the bullet is what causes it to break up in small fragments. The powder used in these Belgian cartridges is not the EC Blank, but another kind.

At one time the Springfield Armory experimented extensively to make a blank firing attachment for the .45 automatic pistol. In this a special barrel was used with a choke screwed into the front of it and the chamber so shaped that an ordinary ball cartridge could not get in by accident. The device was only fairly satisfactory and has been discontinued.

Bullets

There are many different varieties and kinds and shapes of bullets used in modern ammunition. The earliest lead bullets were simply round balls, but the modern bullets are almost without exception elongated, and the most of them are rounded or pointed on the front end.

The pointed shape gives an advantage when it comes to getting through the air easily, but it is not quite so good when it comes to target shooting at short ranges as is a square shape. The pointed bullet goes through the target paper in such a manner that the resultant hole is much smaller than the bullet, and it is often difficult to tell just where the edge is. As the shot counts the next higher value if the edge touches the next ring, it is very convenient in scoring to be able to see plainly just where the edge comes on the target. In order to accomplish this, bullets with the front square instead of pointed are often used. These are called "wad-cutter" bullets.

Wad-cutters may be obtained in factory loads for the popular .38 Special cartridge, but if the target shot wants to use them for other calibers, he will usually have to purchase a bullet mould or some bullets of that type from one of the makers of reloading supplies, and load his own.

In 1934, the Remington Arms Company introduced a high speed .22 caliber long rifle cartridge with a wad-cutter bullet, called the Sharp-shoulder bullet. It is recommended for target practice up to 50 yards in rifles only, as it does not always feed perfectly in automatic pistols, and sometimes fails to pattern correctly in revolvers. In my experience with it, I have found that it shoots beautifully in single shot pistols.

Wad cutter or flat pointed bullets give more stopping power than round nosed ones. For that reason the .32 Smith & Wesson Long, the .38 Smith & Wesson, and the .38 Special are duplicated in cartridges called respectively, the .32 and .38 Colt New Police, and the .38 Colt Special, which have a rounded point with a flat end to it. These bullets are more effective in stopping power and ability to disable than the corresponding round nosed ones.

The .22 Caliber, .32-20, .38-40, and the .44-40 cartridges are made with bullets having a hollow point. Such bullets are also sometimes called "Express" bullets. When fired with rifle velocities, they tend to open up at the point, and make a much more deadly wound. However, when fired with pistol velocities against flesh, they fail to open or expand, and are of about the same effectiveness as plain lead bullets with a flat point, such as the regular .32-20, etc.

Jacketed Bullets

Most revolver bullets are made of plain lead alloy, with no hard covering. However, cartridges for automatic pistols usually have the bullets covered with a jacket of a harder metal, very often gilding metal, (90 parts copper, 10 parts zinc), or cupro-nickel (60 parts copper, 40 parts nickel), or in Europe and other foreign countries, steel coated with copper or cupro-nickel. Lubaloy, (from "lubricating alloy") the jacket material used by Western Cartridge Company, is similar in composition to gilding metal, with the addition of a small percentage of tin. Nobeloy, used by Nobel in Great Britain is understood to be practically the same thing.

This is done in the case of automatic pistols to prevent the bullets from becoming marred in feeding from the magazine. Bullets for high velocity rifle cartridges must be jacketed to keep the lead from melting from the intense heat of the powder gases under high pressure and the friction of passing through the barrel at high speed.

A jacketed bullet with the lead uncovered at the point of the bullet is called a soft-point bullet. When fired from a high velocity rifle, such a bullet will expand on striking flesh until it looks like a mushroom, hence they are often called mushroom bullets. Some times they are called Dum-dum bullets, from the fact that bullets intended to expand on striking were once produced at the British Government Arsenal at Dum-dum in India. Such bullets are of little more effect than a full jacketed bullet in revolvers or automatic pistols, because the velocity is too low to cause the bullet to expand.

Lead bullets must be lubricated, else the friction of the passage through the barrel will cause the metal to solder itself to the steel of the barrel in lumps or layers that will interfere seriously with the accuracy. This action is called "leading." Most lead bullets are what is called inside lubricated; that is, there are several grooves around the bullet inside the neck of the cartridge, and these grooves are filled with a lubricating grease or wax.

In the old days, however, the grease was put on the outside of the bullet. Generally the bullet was made the same size as the outside of the cartridge case, and 'the rear end, or heel, of the bullet was reduced in diameter so as to fit into the inside of the cartridge neck. Then the part of the bullet that projected outside of the case was dipped into melted lubricant, or had grooves around it filled with lubricant. Thus the grease was exposed, and whenever the cartridge was handled, grease would get smeared around. If the cartridge should be dropped, dirt or sand would adhere to it. Thus the outside lubricated bullet was messy and inconvenient, and has nearly been superseded for center fire cartridges, as all modern cartridges are inside lubricated, and the only outside lubricated ones now made are those whose design is old. However, one of the most popular cartridges of all comes in this class, and this is the .22 long rifle,

In order to make a cartridge of this kind that will be clean and convenient to handle, many expedients have been tried. One is to plate the bullet with a thin layer of copper or lubaloy. This does not rub off as easily as lead, and the danger of leading is thus reduced. Another way is to plate the bullets with cadmium. Remington puts out such a bullet under the name of Silvadry. These dry bullets are very convenient, but when fired rapidly in automatic pistols or other repeating arms, they will often cause bad leading. Moreover, they are not to be recommended for target matches, because the user never knows when the leading may start, and thus give him a poor score.

Recently the Peters Cartridge Company has placed on the market a .22 with an invisible lubrication called "Filmkote" which seems to do very well. The author has not examined any of these cartridges closely, and has not been told how they are made, but if required to hazard a supposition as to what it is, would as a first try at it say that it is very likely similar to the lubrication that J. D. Pedersen, the eminent gun designer used on the cartridges for his semi-automatic rifle. This consisted of a mineral wax dissolved in carbon tetrachloride (which is the same thing as Carbona or Pyrene). The cartridges were dipped in the solution, and when they dried, a thin film of wax was left on the metal. This was so hard that it would not pick up dirt, and could not be noticed in handling, but it provided sufficient lubrication for the purpose.

Cartridge Case Material

Center fire cartridge cases are today practically always made of brass. Rim fire cases are usually made of copper, but lately the advent of the Hi-Speed .22 brought with it a brass case for these particular cartridges, though the others are still made of copper. Cartridge cases of either brass or copper may be tinned or nickeled and thus may look like some other metal. Many of the old black powder cartridges had a white case, which was simply a brass case tinned.

It is useful to know that it is a common practice to make the modern smokeless cartridges with an indented ring or cannelure around the case, to give a ready means of telling them from the black powder loads, which are in plain cases with no ring around.

CHAPTER 12

BULLET EFFECT AND SHOCK POWER

BECAUSE pistols and revolvers exist primarily for personal defense, everyone who depends on them at any time for his safety should be interested in knowing just how effective a shot will be in instantly rendering an adversary incapable of further aggression.

Almost any pistol or revolver, of whatever caliber it may be, is fully capable of inflicting a fatal wound; but many of the smaller and less powerful hand firearms do not possess stopping power; that is, the ability to put an adversary out of the fight instantly, even though the blow may not be in a vital spot. There are pistols with which a man may be fatally wounded and yet not feel it at the time, whereas there are others with which he may be practically paralyzed for the time being, though he may afterward recover.

If the time ever comes when it is necessary to use a pistol to save your life, you do not want an arm that will merely enrage your adversary; you want one that will put him down and out at once.

A very good illustration of the lack of stopping power which characterizes some of the smaller calibers was furnished several years ago in one of our Eastern cities when a member of the police force was called on to kill an old stag in the park who had outlived his usefulness. The officer placed the muzzle of his .32-caliber revolver a few inches from the deer's head, and shot him near the base of the horns. The old fellow shook his head a couple of times, as though a fly had bitten him and he wanted to scratch the place; and then he went on eating grass. After awhile a rifle was found and he was killed, but the revolver shot had apparently not inconvenienced him at all. Of course, he could have been killed with the revolver if he had been shot somewhere else besides the thick part of the skull; but even if he had been shot in this manner with a .45 he would have been knocked flat.

This shows very well how useless this small-caliber arm would be to a hunter as an auxiliary to his rifle. If any large beast charged him and he shot it with this gun he would be gored or trampled to death before the wounded animal found out that it was hurt.

I have had a very clear illustration of this lack of shock power on the part of the .32-caliber revolver because I was once shot with one of these arms at a distance of about two feet. I was looking right into the muzzle of the gun and saw a number of bright sparks coming out of the muzzle apparently right into my face, and at the same time I felt a slight sensation of numbness in my right arm; and though the bullet had passed through the third finger of my right hand, through the handle of the revolver which I held and embedded itself into my wrist, it did not inconvenience me in the slightest nor put my arm out of action. There was no pain whatever, only a slight numbness, and later I washed my hand merely because the wound was bleeding slightly and walked some distance to a doctor's office and had the bullet taken out.

If the gun with which I had been shot had been a .45 instead of a .32, it would not only have paralyzed my right arm but would have passed entirely through my wrist and entered my body, inflicting a fatal wound.

The gun with the greatest shock power is not necessarily the most fatal one, however. A gun which delivers a very heavy paralyzing blow may simply knock a man out for a while and he may then recover, while a bullet of smaller caliber which lacks shock power may penetrate to a vital part of the body, such as the intestines, and cause a wound which is not felt at the time but which will cause death several days later.

It is a peculiar fact that the .22 caliber, while almost entirely lacking in shock power, is one of the most fatal cartridges. I knew a doctor out in a small Mexican border town where I was once stationed that said he was most afraid of a .22-caliber gun because he performed more autopsies on people killed with .22-caliber arms than with any other kind. He said he had seen lots of shooting with the jacketed .45's and that the victims frequently recovered. One reason is that the small outside lubricated .22-caliber bullet is a great carrier of germs which set up blood poison, and these little lead bullets usually lodge in the body, where they remain to start the infection, while the clean jacketed bullets of the automatic pistols do not easily carry dirt and, moreover, they frequently pass entirely through the body.

I once knew of a case of a boy who was shot with a .22 short at a distance of 639 yards—nearly half a mile—and he died the next day. The bullet pierced his abdomen. The stopping power in this case was negligible. The boy was not knocked off his feet, or made unconscious, but he was fatally hurt.

A case that is exactly the reverse of this happened in a small border town where I was stationed many years ago. Smuggling of arms had been going on, and a River guard was after a certain gun-runner and traced him to a certain saloon. The River guard entered with his Army automatic in his hand, and as he did so both he and the gun-runner fired at each other simultaneously. The heavy lead bullet from the gun smuggler's .45 Colt struck the River guard in the chest and passed completely through him. The two shots that the River guard fired both struck the gun smuggler in the head, the first striking him near the top of the forehead and the second in the mouth.

Both men went down in a heap, and when the doctor was called he said it was a case for the undertaker, not for the doctor; that they were not dead but would be in a few minutes. However, neither one of these men died. The smuggler was hit once in the forehead with a .45 Automatic bullet which glanced on his sloping forehead and passed around under the scalp. The other bullet entered his mouth and lodged in the solid mass of bone at the base of the skull; and he made a prompt recovery in about three weeks. The River guard was more seriously injured, the bullet having passed through his lung, but he recovered in about six weeks. In this case the stopping power was perfect; both men were put out of action instantly. But neither was fatally hurt. So it should be clearly understood that stopping power is not necessarily the same thing as killing power.

And while the .22 was described above as lacking in stopping power, it should also be borne in mind that this refers to shots which do not strike a vital spot. There are some parts of the body, such as the brain, where all shots, of whatever caliber or power, are practically equal. A young man shot himself in the head with a .22 which pierced the skull and traversed part of the brain. He became unconscious instantly and was pronounced dead in three minutes. A .45 would have had no more stopping power in this case.

There has always been much speculation as to just how a bullet delivers shock, and as to just which qualities are the important ones in this regard. This question has been the subject of much experiment and investigation, but at the present writing it is still unsolved. Some of the important qualities of any bullet as regards stopping power are:

1. Its weight.
2. Its velocity.
3. Its energy, which depends on the weight and velocity.
4. Its diameter, or caliber.
5. The shape of its point.
6. Its balance and gyro-static stability.

Effect of Bullet Weight

Obviously mere weight is of no account without velocity. Even a cannon ball will not hurt you when it is standing still. On the other hand, velocity will not be of any effect without weight to carry it through. Recently I read an article written in Europe in which the stopping power of bullets was said to be entirely independent of the weight of the bullet, but to depend only on the diameter of the bullet and its velocity.

The fact that this view of the matter is not the correct one may readily be realized by considering the difference between being struck by a .45 caliber pistol bullet weighing 230 grains, and moving at a velocity of 810 f. s., and being struck by a paper target paster of the same diameter moving at the same speed. A large animal would be stopped by the .45 caliber bullet; but he would not even notice the paper disc. Another illustration of the same thing is the difference between being struck by a paddle and a sledge hammer. The paddle has a very wide surface, and a relatively high velocity, but it lacks weight, and its effects are expended on the surface. It stings, but does not cause much injury. On the other hand, the sledge hammer has less velocity, but it has weight to carry the velocity through, and it will cause a deep and serious injury.

The statement is often seen in some of the older ordnance manuals describing the various weapons that a penetration of one inch in pine corresponds to a dangerous wound. However, penetration is not the only criterion, as is indicated by the following statement of a board of officers in considering a divided pistol bullet intended to increase the likelihood of hitting, as given in the report of the Chief of Ordnance in 1890: "It is generally considered that a dangerous wound from a small arm would be caused by a penetration corresponding to one inch in white pine; but this is dependent upon the supposition that a shock to the whole system is also given and which requires for its fulfillment some considerable weight in the projectile. The revolver bullet weighs 230 grains, and it is not likely that a ball of materially less weight would have a dangerous effect if capable of penetrating only an inch in pine. These fragments weigh about 55 grains, and their average penetration at 10 yards is but very slightly more than half an inch, and at 20 yards only a quarter of an inch. It would therefore appear as if a hit, even if made, could have but very little if any effect, certainly not immediately, and would be entirely unavailing to stop a bayonet charge and still more useless against advancing cavalry."

Effect of Bullet Velocity

But if we will suppose that the bullets under consideration all have a reasonable amount of energy and weight, what then is the relative effect of velocity on stopping power? Is it better to obtain your energy by means of a light weight and a high velocity, or a heavy weight and a slow velocity? Take a .38 Super Police bullet, weighing 200 grains, and having 725 f. s. velocity. It will have about 232 foot pounds of energy. The regular 158 grain .38 Special would have the same energy with a velocity of 815 f. s.

Which would be better?

The answer, as far as it can be given from the experimental work that has been done to date is that there is little difference whether the energy is obtained higher velocity and lower weight, or the reverse. In other words, in the range of velocities common in pistols and revolvers, that is about from 500 foot seconds to 1200 foot seconds, mere velocity itself seems to be of little moment. In connection with rifle bullets we hear a lot about the explosive effects of high velocities; and it is true that such effects are observed when the bullet strikes cavities filled with fluid; but these explosive effects do not take place until velocities well above 2000 feet per second are reached, and this is way above the range of velocities under discussion. Velocity seems to have relatively small effect on stopping power with pistols or revolvers, as long as the bullet does not strike bone. When bones are struck, however, the resultant damage is much greater with bullets having velocities of 1200 feet or the like, than with those in the neighborhood of 750 or 800 feet per second.

Right here it is only fair to say that the opinion is widely held that low velocities are actually more effective than high velocities for pistol bullets. The following is quoted from the British Text Book of Small Arms, 1929: "The value of the caliber of self-loading pistols and revolvers has been much obscured by theory, but the practice of recent years has amply proved that small caliber plus high velocity, although developing many foot pounds of energy, yet lacks stopping or shocking value. There have been many attempts to substitute a high velocity cartridge of .38 caliber, as a Service equivalent to the traditional .455. In practice it has been found that the small caliber sometimes fails to stop its man, and that the large diameter leaden plug of the .455, moving even 300 or 400 feet a second slower than the high-velocity, small caliber projectile, is yet far more effective. Recent experiment has, however, developed a new experimental .38 cartridge whose efficiency is, so far as ballistic tests can ascertain, not less than that of the .455 (Note—this cartridge resembles the .38 S. & W. Super Police in size, bullet weight, and ballistics—Author). A hit with a .455 anywhere literally knocks an adversary over. The quality of efficiency depends to some extent on the massive soft lead bullet and the relatively low velocity rather than on any inherent magic in the caliber, for the .455 or .45 self-loading pistol firing a lighter nickel covered bullet at a higher velocity cannot be depended on to produce equal shock effect. The efficiency of the .455 revolver cartridge is due to the combination of the large caliber with the soft material, the mass, and the relatively low velocity of the projectile. These combine so that the adversary experiences in his body the maximum of shocking as distinct from penetrative effect. This is just what is wanted in an active service revolver."

It seems difficult to believe that the low velocity adds anything to the effect. The author believes that the reason that large, low velocity bullets show satisfactory effectiveness, is that the low velocity allows the use of a large bullet, rather than that there is any inherent virtue in the low velocity itself. It is of course true that with very brittle materials, like glass, low velocities produce quite different effect from high velocities, and may cause more damage, as is seen when a bullet passes through a window pane and leaves a relatively small hole, whereas the entire pane is shattered by a rock tossed with relatively low velocity; but this is a very special case, which depends on the peculiar brittleness of glass, which cannot be penetrated at all, but fails always by breaking.

There is also more or less talk of the victim being "literally bowled over" by large and heavy bullets going at low speeds; and of their having knock-down rather than wounding power. It is true that the power of any bullet to put motion into its victim, so as to tend to knock him over depends more on the weight of the bullet than on the energy, and that a slow heavy bullet will communicate more motion to the victim than will a fast small one with more energy; but calculations and tests show that the actual push delivered by any bullet is too small to account for the knocking down of the victim. In fact, experience shows that men who are shot have a strong tendency to fall *toward* the gun.

When a bullet is entirely stopped in the body of the person shot, its power of giving him motion is measured by the bullet weight times the velocity, or the momentum, and is equal to the energy of the bullet divided by the velocity, (since energy is proportional to weight times velocity squared). Numerically, the motion given to an object when a bullet stops in the object is equal to the velocity of the bullet multiplied by the weight of the bullet, divided by the combined weights of the bullet and the object.

Thus suppose that the .45 automatic pistol bullet, weighing 230 grains, or 1/33rd of a pound, and moving at 800 f. s., should strike a man weighing 150 pounds, and stop inside him. The velocity that he would acquire would be 800 x 1/33 divided by 180.03. This works out to about one seventh of a foot per second. When it is realized that a man walking moves about seven feet per second, or nearly fifty times as fast, it will be seen that the actual motion impressed on a man when he is struck by a bullet is insignificant, and that he is never "literally bowled over" by a pistol bullet. The reason for this may be more clearly seen when it is considered how very quickly a bullet stops when it hits. The push that it gives does not have time to transmit any great amount of velocity, because it lasts such a short time. Consider what would happen if you threw a baseball against a heavy safe door that happened to be standing open. It would not move. Even if you threw your whole weight suddenly against the heavy safe door, it would hardly move. To shut it, you have to apply a push for a considerable interval of time. In striking a heavy body like a man, the bullet does not have time to put it into motion.

Quite another thing, however, is the nervous and muscular reflex set up by the impact of the bullet. It may cause the victim to move violently, to leap into the air, or to fall. It does not, however, depend on the bullet weight, but rather on the damage or shock transmitted to certain nervous centers.

But even if it does not knock the victim over, the heavy large caliber bullet is the one that is generally credited with being the most effective, and the velocity seems to make little difference, so long as it is sufficient to secure adequate penetration.

Effect of Bullet Energy

The striking energy of a bullet is a much better measure of its stopping power than is either weight or velocity, but even the energy is not a satisfactory criterion, for the amount of energy possessed by a bullet may bear little relation to the amount it delivers to the object it strikes. For example, a small calibered jacketed bullet may go all the way through a man without losing much of its velocity, and thus carry most of its energy away with it; while

The relative disruptive effect of bullets on plastic materials, as tested by firing into clay. These pictures of the entrance side of the clay cylinders indicate that increasing the velocity of the .45 automatic pistol bullet from 800 f. s. to 1050 f. s. causes it to make a hole with approximately twice the diameter. However, the square pointed .38 Keith bullet makes a hole nearly twice as large as the high speed .45. While the bullet making the larger hole in clay may be expected to have somewhat more effect in flesh than one making a small hole in clay, the relative effects of these three bullets in flesh are nothing like the results in clay. This is because the clay is soft and plastic, without strength, and thus is thrown in all directions with violence by a high velocity or a square point, while flesh is tough and fibrous, and cannot be thrown aside as is the clay.

a large calibered lead ball with a blunt point may expend most of its energy in forcing its larger diameter through the flesh, and very often it may stop in the body, in which case it has delivered all of its energy to the object struck.

And moreover, if two bullets deliver equal amounts of energy to the body, the wound produced may be much more serious in one case than in another. Thus the amount of energy actually expended by the bullet in the body does not measure either the killing effect or the stopping power. A thrust with a dagger, which may kill in a few minutes, will deliver far less energy than a blow from the fist. When a 6 foot man weighing 180 pounds trips and falls, the impact with the floor delivers 540 foot pounds of energy to his body, but this would probably not even injure him, though it is about double the total energy possessed by most pistol bullets.

But the energy possessed by a bullet is a most important factor in its ability to create shock, for large diameter and flat point will have little effect unless there is enough energy behind them to drive them through the tissues.

Effect of Bullet Diameter and Shape

As to diameter, it should be noted that the area of the hole that a bullet must punch through tissue is proportional to the *square*

The relative disruptive effects of different velocities and bullet shapes on clay. Exit side of clay cylinders shot at with .45 Automatic Pistol bullet, 800 f. s., (left), and 1050 f. s. (center), compared with the effects of a .38 caliber Keith bullet, which has a square point and a ledge around the bullet. The results on clay do not in any degree indicate the effect on flesh, which is tough and fibrous, and does not react in the same way as a plastic material.

of the diameter. Thus a .45 caliber bullet makes a hole with over four times the area of that made by a .22. Thus with the same energy in both a .22 and a .45, the larger bullet might be expected to deliver four times the damage to tissue. But actually, the .45 has much more energy than the .22, on account of the greater weight, and therefore its ability to cause damage is much more than 4 times that of the .22.

The shape of the point is a very important factor in stopping power. A square or blunt point offers greater resistance to penetration than does a sharp point; hence more work is done on the flesh by the blunt bullet in penetrating. Suppose, by way of illustration, that a truck is carrying a load of iron rods down the street at high speed, and a man who steps into the street at the wrong instant is struck and run through by a rod which projects in front of the load. If the rod has a sharp point, the damage will obviously be less severe than if the rod is square across the end. If, however, instead of a rod of iron, the projecting object which struck the man had been a telephone pole or a beam of wood, the man would be bowled over, but not penetrated at all.

While it is difficult to obtain a true measure of the relative effects of differently shaped points on bullets of the same caliber and velocity, an indication that there is a decided difference under some conditions may be obtained by firing into clay. However, the results cannot be taken as indicative of what happens in flesh, for the clay is soft and plastic, and has no strength, and is thrown in all directions by a sudden impact, or by having a blunt pointed bullet shot through it, while flesh is tough and fibrous, and does not act in at all the same manner. Nevertheless, the results in clay are interesting.

There are therefore included herewith photographs showing the front and back views of several cylinders of clay which have been

1 2 3 4 5 6

Bullet shapes with their relative disruptive power when fired against clay. These bullets are all for the .38 special cartridge, and when fired with the same velocity against a three inch thickness of clay showed the following relative disruptive power as measured by the energy left in the clay and the size of the cavity formed:

1. Regular .38 S. & W. Special shape. Disruptive factor   1.00
2. Western Super Police shape. Disruptive factor   1.25
3. Luger Shape. Disruptive factor   1.40
4. .38 Colt Special shape. Disruptive factor   1.50
5. Bullet designed by Elmer Keith. Disruptive factor   3.00
6. Wad cutter shape. Disruptive factor   3.50

It does not follow that the efficiency on flesh or bone follow these ratios, as clay is much more plastic than flesh.

fired at by the .45 caliber automatic pistol bullet at 800 f.s.; by the .45 caliber automatic bullet at 1050 f.s., and by the .38 Keith bullet at a velocity of 1100 f.s.

The first hole by the automatic is about twice the diameter of the bullet; the higher velocity one is nearly twice the diameter of the first; and the hole made by the smaller Keith .38 is nearly four times as large as the first and nearly twice as large as the second .45 caliber hole. This is due to the fact that the Keith bullet has a flat nose and a ledge around the large diameter of the bullet; these throw the clay outward with violence as the bullet plows its way through the soft plastic mass.

There is also a rough sketch by the author showing six different shapes of .38 bullets that were fired through clay. There was a tremendous difference in the energy left in the clay by the different shapes. The regular .38 Special shape, which is about the same as the .45 Automatic, was by far the least efficient in clay. The round nose, as used on the .38 Western Super Police, was about 25 per cent more efficient; the Luger shape, a truncated cone, with flat point, showed forty per cent more efficiency, the .38 Colt Special showed fifty per cent more efficiency while the .38 Keith bullet delivered fully three times as much energy and the wad-cutter three and one-half times as much as the regular shape when fired through three inches of clay. Somewhat surprisingly the hollow nose man stopper gave just the same results as the wad-cutter. This was no doubt due to the fact that the bullets did not distort or change their shape greatly on striking the clay.

If these same proportions held good for flesh we could use them in our calculations of stopping power, but unfortunately clay does not give us a true picture of the results obtained when a bullet strikes actual flesh. The reason is that while clay has mass, weight, and consistency that are reasonably comparable with those of flesh it has no strength. When a bullet plows through clay with high velocity, it throws the particles in all directions and makes a large hole. But when it plows through flesh the bullet cannot throw the particles freely to the sides, for the flesh is tough, fibrous and strong. You can poke your finger into clay, but not into flesh. Flesh acts to the bullet more like the rubber of a tire, with cotton cords vulcanized into it.

An important consideration in connection with shape of the point, is the fact that as soon as it hits a bone the point becomes flattened, no matter what shape it was previously. Thus the relative effect of the shape of the point applies more particularly when only flesh is traversed.

Then again a very important factor is the presence or absence of a jacket on a bullet. Bullets which are jacketed with gilding metal, cupro-nickel, or steel do not change their shape as much or break up as easily on contact with bone as do lead bullets. Moreover these jacketed bullets will glance off a bone unless the impact is nearly at right angles. When they do penetrate a bone near the edge they just make a small gutter through it, whereas lead bullets have a tendency to bite in and turn over, causing a much more serious fracture. For this reason jacketed bullets are less efficient in killing power than plain lead bullets.

Effect of Bullet Stability

A most important factor in stopping power, more especially in rifle bullets is the balance and gyrostatic stability of the bullet. Rifle bullets are generally very long in relation to their diameter; and when they strike fairly solid objects such as flesh or bone they tend to upset or turn end over end, thus creating very serious wounds. This tendency is particularly noticeable in some of the modern military bullets of small caliber, such as the 6.5 mm. used by several nations. These bullets are so small in diameter that they do not have much radius of gyration and they upset or turn end for end when striking flesh.

In the old days about 1870 and 1880 military rifle bullets were usually of .45 caliber or larger and made of plain lead with velocities of about 1300 foot seconds more or less. They had very satisfactory stopping power. Somewhat later they were superseded by small caliber, jacketed bullets with velocities of about 2,000 feet per second such as the Krag. These bullets had relatively good stability and possessed very little stopping power except for head shots or other vital wounds. Later about 1906 the velocity was stepped up further to about 2500 or 2800 feet per second, and many of the nations adopted small calibers such as 6.5 mm., (.256 inch). These bullets again showed stopping power and this change was due to two things. First the relatively low stability of pointed bullets and second the explosive effect encountered when bullets of velocities of 2400 foot seconds and over struck cavities containing fluid such as, for example, the skull with the brain in it which as in this case acts as a semi fluid.

The effect of bullet stability is not of great importance in connection with the study of the stopping power of pistol bullets because most pistol bullets are short in relation to their diameter so that they would not make much more of a wound going side ways than they would going point on; and moreover their stability is usually sufficiently high so that they have no great tendency to turn over unless a bone should be struck.

There are perhaps, one or two exceptions to this rule. The .38 Super Police is very long in relation to its diameter and would do a considerable amount of damage if it turned over. Another case is that of the .455 Webley Mark II which has a long rather sharply pointed lead bullet. Very likely this bullet also depends somewhat on its tendency to tip over when striking for its very satisfactory effectiveness.

Effect of Location of the Shot

Of far more importance as regards stopping effect than any of the factors mentioned above is the location of the shot or whether or not it strikes large bones. Even a small caliber, low powered bullet such as the .22 will render a victim instantly unconscious and cause death in a few moments if it pierces the brain. Any pistol bullet of moderate energy will have 100% stopping power if it pierces the bones of the legs or if it strikes the heart or one of the large nerve centers. However, even a very large caliber bullet with high striking energy and very great theoretical stopping power may be entirely ineffective if it fails to strike any of these points and traverses only flesh, or perchance after traversing flesh strikes an unimportant bone as it leaves the body.

An often quoted instance is the case of Antonio Caspi reported in Colonel La Garde's book *Gunshot Injuries*. The circumstances were as follows: "Antonio Caspi, a prisoner on the island of Samar, in attempting to escape on October 26, 1905, engaged in a hand-to-hand encounter with a guard, during which he was shot four times with a .38 caliber revolver loaded with Government ammunition. Apparently uninjured by the shots, he continued to fight until he was stunned by a blow on the forehead by the butt of a carbine. When he was examined in the hospital, it was found that the first bullet had entered his chest near the right nipple, ranged upward, backward and outward, perforating a lung, and escaping by passing through the edge of the right shoulder blade. Bullet No. 2 entered the chest near the left nipple, passed upward, backward, and inward, perforating the left lung, and lodging in the tissues under the skin of the back; the third entered the chest near the left shoulder, and passed downward and backward, perforating the lung and lodging in the back; while the fourth entered the palm of the left hand and escaped through a wound in the front surface of the forearm."

Three of these bullets perforated the lungs, and two of them, carrying 220 foot pounds of energy, stopped in his body. Any one of these three might have been expected to have stopped Caspi at once; yet a blow on the forehead by the butt of a carbine, carrying only a fraction of the energy delivered by the bullets stopped him where the bullets had utterly failed to do so. In three weeks he was discharged from the hospital cured. The significant thing about this case is that none of the bullets damaged any important bone, or traversed anything but soft tissue, with the exception of the one that chipped a small piece from the shoulder blade in passing out. Had any of the bullets struck the brain, spinal cord, or bones of the leg, he would have stopped at once.

An even more remarkable case was told the author by Col. Edwin Butcher, of the Army, who described an incident that happened while he was stationed at Fort Duquesne, Wyoming. The State at one time ceded the land of the Fort to the Federal Government and when the survey was made there was a discrepancy between the State and Government Surveys that left a small strip of land outside of the Fort which was disclaimed by either State or Government. Finally a civilian found this out and established a saloon there and as he was on neither Government nor State land, he was not bothered by anyone and a number of questionable characters soon began to congregate in his place.

One day a half-breed Indian and a tough white man, whom we will designate as Smith, though that was not his real name, held up a judge in Laramie, and brought their spoils from this holdup to the saloon in question, where they began to divide the loot. They quarreled over the division, and as the saloon keeper knew that they were both desperate characters, he told them that if they were going to quarrel they would have to do it outside. At this, both left the saloon, the Indian going first. As he descended the steps from the front door, Smith placed a .45 Caliber Single Action Colt against the back of his neck and fired. The bullet just missed his spinal column, and carried away part of his jaw. The Indian then reached for his gun, and as he turned around, Smith placed his revolver against the Indian's right arm and fired again. The bullet just missed the bone and went through the flesh of the arm into his chest, carrying away a large portion of the breast-bone. The Indian then fired five shots at Smith, all of them piercing his heart. He then rode some miles into the desert where he was later found lying beside his horse, exhausted from loss of blood. He was put in a buckboard, brought back to the Post and the wounds were washed out with a solution.

Colonel Butcher saw this done. These were terrible wounds as the muzzle of the gun was right against the man in both cases. The flesh was badly burned and very badly torn. When the wounds were washed out with solution, large chunks of bone floated out especially from the chest wound where the breastbone was shot to pieces. After these wounds were dressed, the Indian was placed on a mattress on the guardhouse floor. In a few weeks he was entirely recovered and was tried for the murder of Smith for which he was acquitted, and for the holdup of the judge for which he received twenty years in the penitentiary.

Note also in this case, that the bullets struck neither the spinal column, the brain, or the arm bones. If they had, the Indian would have been unable to shoot. Smith lost his life because he did not realize that stopping power depends very largely on the location of the shot. Had he shot the Indian in the back of the head, instead of the neck, the fight would have ended at once.

Tests of Stopping Power

There has always been a great deal of curiosity as to the relative stopping power of pistol and revolver bullets, and many incidents similar to those recounted above have been collected, but this evidence is not very satisfactory from a scientific point of view, as too many variables always enter. Much depends on just how the shots were placed, what organs they struck, the physical condition of the person shot, and many other factors. Moreover, these cases generally do not furnish any good basis for comparison of the relative effectiveness of the different calibers, velocities, bullet shapes, etc.

To get away from these uncertainties, and obtain a real comparison of stopping power that is based on scientific tests and will stand analysis is very difficult. In the first place, no satisfactory substance is available as an object to shoot at which we can be sure will act the same as living flesh does under the bullet impact. Clay has often been tried, but it lacks the necessary toughness and fibrosity of flesh, and is too easily thrown outward by the bullet as it plows through at high velocity.

Yellow laundry soap has often been tried for the same purpose, as it is of very much the same order of density as flesh; but it, too, like the clay, is much more plastic than flesh, and probably gives a highly exaggerated idea of what may happen.

Lead seems very dense and tough; but under the impact of bullets moving at high velocities, it also becomes quite plastic, and behaves something like the clay and the soap; with the difference that it stops the bullets very quickly. Mr. L. Cloud Newman of Washington, D. C., made an interesting series of firings against a lead plate with various pistol bullets. A photograph of this plate, with a description of the results is included here.

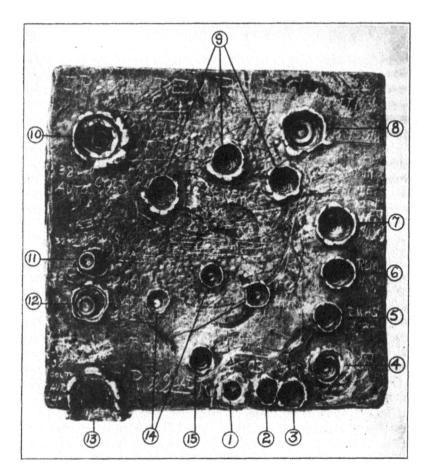

A lead plate an inch and a half thick against which various pistol bullets were fired by Mr. Newman. Nos. 1 to 7 were fired from a rifle with 20 inch barrel; the others from revolvers or pistols.

No. 1, .22 BB Cap, fired from rifle. No. 2, .22 CB Cap, fired from rifle. No. 3, .22 Short, fired from rifle. No. 4, .22 Long Rifle, fired from rifle. No. 5, .22 Remington Hi-speed hollow point, fired from rifle. No. 6, .22 Remington Hi-speed, fired from rifle. No. 7, .22 Western Super X, fired from rifle. No. 8, .45 Colt, from New Service Revolver 5½ inch barrel. No. 9, .22 Remington Plama Hi-speed from 6 inch revolver. No. 10, Super .38 A. C. P., from 4 inch barrel. No. 11, .38 S. & W. Spl, from 6 inch revolver. No. 12, .38 S. & W. Spl. Super police, 200 grain, from 6 inch revolver. No. 13, Super .38 Automatic from 4 inch barrel, same as No. 10. No. 14, .22 Long Rifle in 6 inch revolver. No. 15, .22 Remington Hi-speed hollow point in 6 inch revolver. The following data were obtained from measurements of this plate:

Number	Caliber	Diameter of hole	Depth of hole	Volume of hole, cu. ins.	Weight of lead displaced, grains
1	.22 BB	.32	.15	.012	34
2	.22 CB	.38	.18	.018	53
3	.22 Sht.	.44	.30	.046	130
4	.22 L. R.	.50	.38	.075	215
5	.22 H. S. H. P.	.50	.42	.083	237
6	.22 H. S.	.55	.50	.118	339
7	.22 Super X	.60	.55	.155	445
8	.45 Colt	.72	.35	.142	408
9	.22 H. S.	.50	.40	.079	226
10	Super .38	.80	.95	.326	935
14	.22 L. R.	.40	.23	.029	83
15	.22 H. S. H. P.	.40	.38	.048	137

Note—11, 12, and 13 could not be measured.

Some years ago a number of tests were carried on by shooting into human cadavers, and still other tests were made by shooting live animals on the killing floor of an abattoir. These tests are described in Col. La Garde's book, *Gunshot Injuries*, previously mentioned.

The results of shooting against cadavers do not give a close comparison with what happens when a live animal is shot, for after a man or animal dies, the flesh coagulates more or less as rigor mortis sets in, and this change and hardening of the tissues is rendered more pronounced by the pickling of the body in preserving fluids. About all that such tests tell is the relative action of the different bullets on bones, and even here, there is much that is unsatisfactory, because bones differ greatly in brittleness, according to the age and condition of the subject, and moreover, it is difficult or impossible to insure that all shots strike in the same manner. Then again, the effect of a bullet on dead meat, where the blood has all drained out of the vessels and the tissues have lost their natural fluids as well as their elasticity, might be expected to be entirely different from the effect of the same bullet on a live animal, where the natural fluids are present to transmit the shock, and the tissues are in their normal condition, so that the effects on the various layers of tissue and the blood vessels, etc., can be observed.

But even were live animals available for such tests, the matter would be far from simple, for any two animals differ from each other, and it would be difficult to compare two different bullets when the objects shot with them differ even more perhaps, than the bullets themselves. Then, too, there is the difficulty of insuring that all the shots strike the same kind of tissue. When a bullet strikes a bone, it may turn over, or glance in almost any direction, with widely varying results for nearly similar shots.

However, the tests described in Col. La Garde's book are far more comprehensive and complete than any other such investigation of which we have any published description, and a study of the results gives the best basis for forming an opinion as to the relative effectiveness of the different calibers that is available today.

Tests Described By Col. La Garde

Because the stopping power of the Army .38 caliber revolvers had shown itself unsatisfactory on numerous occasions in the Philippines and elsewhere, the War Department in 1904 constituted a board, consisting of Col. John T. Thompson, Ordnance Department, (The inventor of the Thompson Sub-machine Gun), and Col. Louis A. La Garde, to conduct a series of tests with bullets of different sizes, weights, and other characteristics, to determine which of the bullets then in existence had the stopping power and shock effect at short ranges that had been found by experience to be necessary for a pistol in the military service.

Caliber	Weapon	Bullet type	Bullet weight grains	Velocity foot secs.	Energy foot pounds
.30 (7.65 MM)	Luger Automatic Pistol	Jacketed	92.6	1420	415
.38 (9 MM)	" " "	"	123.5	1048	301
.38	Colt Army Revolver	Lead	148	763	191
.38	Colt Automatic Pistol	Jacketed	130	1107	354
.38	" " "	Soft Pt.	120	1048	293
.45	Colt New Service Revolver	Lead	250	720	288
.45	" " " "	Hollow Pt.	220	700	239
.455	" " " "	Man Stopper	218.5	801	288
.476	" " " " .	Lead	288	729	340

The Luger pistols used in these tests were practically identical with those in use today. The 9 MM bullet had the same weight, shape, and velocity as the present conical flat pointed bullet. The .30 Luger had a slightly higher velocity than the present cartridge of that caliber, and had a bullet shaped like a truncated cone, with a flat point, the same as the 9 MM, instead of a round nosed bullet, as does the present .30 Cal. Luger.

The .38 Army Revolver used the .38 Long Colt Cartidge, at that time the Army standard.

The Colt Automatic Pistol, Caliber .38, Military Model 1902, was the progenitor of the Super .38 Automatic of today, and had the same cartridge and bullet. However, the velocity, 1107 f.s., was about 85 f.s. lower than the average velocity of the same cartridge today. Note that in addition to the regular jacketed bullet, a soft pointed one was furnished.

The .45 Caliber Colt New Service Revolver was chambered for the old .45 Colt Cartridge, which in the tests fully justified its reputation as a powerful hand gun load. A hollow point, or express type bullet was also furnished, but apparently was not particularly more effective.

The .455 Caliber Colt New Service Revolver was used with the Man-stopper bullet, which has a square point with a cup-shaped depression in it.

The .476 New Service Revolver was furnished with a cartridge having a round nosed lead bullet weighing 288 grains, and driven at a moderate velocity. It proved to be the most effective of all. The author has one of the original .476 cartridges that comprised the lot used for this test.

These tests were of greater interest, because they included both the old style .45 Colt, with its massive, slow bullet of large caliber, and the then ultra-new automatic pistols with high velocity small caliber jacketed bullets having very high muzzle energy. The

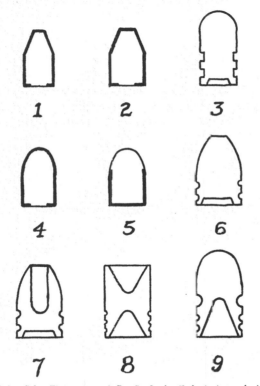

Bullets used by Cols. Thompson and La Garde in their tests against cadavers and live animals in 1904. The bullets are arranged by caliber, and their relative stopping power was found to be about in the same order.

1. .30 cal. Luger, jacketed. Weight 92.5 gr., 1420 f. s., 415 ft. lbs.
2. 9 mm Luger, jacketed. 123.5 grains, 1048 f. s., 301 ft. lbs.
3. .38 Long Colt, Lead. 148 gr., 723 f. s., 191 ft. lbs.
4. .38 A. C. P., jacketed. 130 gr., 1107 f. s., 354 ft. lbs.
5. .38 A. C. P. soft point. 120 gr., 1048 f. s , 293 ft. lbs.
6. .45 Colt, lead. 250 gr., 720 f. s., 288 ft. lbs.
7. .45 Colt, hollow point. 220 gr., 700 f. s., 239 ft. lbs.
8. .455 man-stopper. 218.5 grains, 801 f. s., 288 ft. lbs.
9. .476 lead. 288 gr., 729 f. s., 340 ft. lbs.

results should be read with interest today, for we still have with us the argument of the Super .38 Automatic *vs.* the .45.

As revolvers are essentially short range weapons, it was decided that 75 yards would be the extreme range, 37½ yards the medium range, and close to the muzzle the short range. Simulated velocities were used for the first two; that is, the cartridges were loaded to a reduced velocity corresponding to 75 yards and 37½ yards respectively, and the shooting was done from a short distance.

The board in its tests fired into ten cadavers, sixteen beeves, and two horses. The shock on the cadavers was estimated by the amount of disturbance which appeared in a limb when the body was fired at when suspended by the neck. Col. La Garde states, "We found that the amount of shock as measured by this method was always proportional to (1) the sectional area of the bullet, (2) the resistance which the bullet encountered on impact, and (3) that it was proportional also to the amount of tissue destroyed. The diaphyses (shafts) of the long bones showed the greatest amount of resistance, and consequently the greatest amount of destruction, and the two latter—viz., resistance and destruction of tissue, which are so intimately associated with shock effects— were invariably greater when a larger caliber bullet was used.

"In attempting to define shock effects or stopping power in living animals we had to consider shots against—

1. Vital parts.
2. Non-vital parts.
3. The anatomy necessary to locomotion, or parts essential to activity.

(a)   As one might suppose, all shots against vital parts from whatever arm showed immediate and complete stopping power.

(b)   For shots in non-vital parts like the lungs, liver, intestines, etc., exclusive of large vessels, the shock or stopping power increased with the sectional area of the missile, and it was notably less with the smaller sectional area projectiles, although they possessed far more energy."

In an article in *Arms and the Man* some years ago, Stephen Trask discusses these tests rather more in detail than they are discussed in Col. La Garde's book. The following is quoted from Mr. Trask's article.

"Ten human bodies were the gruesome subjects for the first of the pistol and revolver caliber and velocity tests of 1904. They were cadavers which had been sent for dissection to the Philadelphia Polyclinic and to one of the large New York medical schools.

"In undertaking to fix the relative military value of different cartridges, and to discover which among those available were best adapted for use in short-range, rapid firing weapons of defense, Colonel Thompson and Colonel La Garde desired data for comparative study along several different lnes. First, they wished to ascertain the nature of wounds inflicted when the bullets of different caliber encountered parts of the bony structure, including the head; second, they desired to know the character of injury inflicted by each of the hand-gun projectiles in the soft parts of the human body; third, they wished to fix beyond all doubt the relative shock effect exerted by the missiles in question.

"The wounds made by the bullets would, of course, speak for themselves if the channels were traced by dissection in the softer tissues and if the fractures of the bony structure were photographed. It was further agreed that so far as man-stopping was concerned, a shot upon an inanimate subject would be considered positive whenever one of the long bones was fractured.

"In the cadaver tests the bodies were suspended by the neck and permitted to swing, so that the oscillation caused by the impact of the bullets might be noted and considered in forming conclusions as to shock effects. In these tests Colonel Thompson did the shooting and Colonel La Garde made the examination of the wounds.

"During the tests upon the cadavers it was consistently demonstrated that the amount of oscillation, and consequently the shock effect, was always greater with the larger-caliber bullets. For instance, when the small-caliber projectiles struck the bone of an arm, or ploughed transversely across the small bones of the hand, the amount of swaying caused by the impact of the bullet was very small—more like a tremor than an actual oscillation—but when large-caliber bullets were used the oscillation was quite marked.

"The actual wounds were scrutinized both by the use of X-rays and by dissection. With these aids it was found that the channel of the wound generally corresponded in diameter to the caliber of the bullet, the wound of exit being slightly larger than that of entrance. Shooting into the joint ends of the bony structures, the evidence brought out was that when high-velocity, jacketed bullets were used, the tendency was toward clean perforation without fracture. When unjacketed lead bullets of lower velocity were used, fissures and fractures were almost invariably found in the joint ends, with only occasionally what appeared to be a clean-cut perforation.

"In the long bones, away from the joints, where the bony tissue is compact and very resistant, the tendency of the jacketed bullets was to make fractures at the area of impact, with occasional splitting and fissuring into the bone above and below the spot where the bullet struck. Sometimes the injury assumed the character of what is known as the 'butterfly fracture,' consisting of decided fragmentation in the center of impact with fissures extending on each side upward and downward externally to the surface of the bone, roughly forming an outline similar to that of the wings of the insect after which it is named.

"All of the perforations and fractures made by the jacketed, high-velocity projectiles, especially those of the 'butterfly type,' were observed to be of a character very easily healed.

"With the fractures made by the larger-caliber lead bullets, fired at much lower velocities, the reverse was generally true. In the compact substance of the long bones, they caused extreme fragmentation and usually lodged at the point of impact, splintering off bits of bone varying in size and causing long fissures in the bone shaft above and below the point of impact.

"Injuries to the head were productive of vastly different conclusions. A jacketed bullet of high velocity, fired through the brain, involved a tremendous amount of fragmentation in the skull cap. Such a wound would show a small orifice of entry with clean penetration, but a large area of fracture around the orifice of exit. For instance, when the bullet left the skull through the temporal bone, where the tissue is brittle, the exit was marked by many fragments completely isolated by fracture, and this extreme fragmentation even extended into the bones of the face in the case of bullets which passed from forehead to occiput, showing that the amount of energy delivered in the head as a whole was terriffic.

"A similar wound made by a lead bullet from a .38- or .45-caliber Colt was marked by an orifice of entrance accompanied by very slight fissuring; also, unlike the jacketed high-velocity bullet, which invariably passed entirely through the head, the lead bullet was apt to lodge against the opposite wall of the skull, making no orifice of exit and occasioning no fracture. This lodgment of the bullet was deemed probably due to the fact that the resistance of the skull at the point of first impact caused the bullet to flatten, increasing its sectional area, with a consequent limiting of its powers of penetration.

"From the tests on the cadavers, then these conclusions were established:

"First. That in wounds involving the skull, greater explosive force was apparent in the impact of a high-velocity, steel-jacketed bullet than in the impact of a large-caliber lead bullet at lower speed. This fact, however, could not be regarded as in any way disposing of the question in hand, since regardless of fragmentation or other explosive effect, the lead bullets which flattened and lodged inside of the brain pan killed just as quickly and just as surely as the Luger bullet, which literally blew out the back of the skull in making its exit.

"Second. That in all bony structures, except the head, the fractures made by the unjacketed lead bullets of low velocity were much more serious injuries than the clean perforations or the easily healed 'butterfly' breaks from the Luger bullets.

"Third. That measured by the amount of swaying apparent, the large-caliber, lead, blunt-nose bullets exerted a greater smashing power upon impact than the high-velocity, jacketed projectiles. In this connection it was found that the jacketed projectiles, being longer in proportion to their diameters than the lead bullets, would fly straight and in most cases make a nose impact. On the other hand, the lead bullets would frequently turn in their flight, making a sidewise, or what is known to the rifleman as a 'keyhole' impact, and that they invariably turned after entering the body, gaining thereby in stopping power by virtue of added sectional area; also, the penetration of the lead bullets was so greatly reduced by the impact that they almost uniformly lodged in the body.

"Fourth. As to deformation in the different bullets, very little was apparent in the lead bullets, and none at all in the jacketed bullets. This finding coincides with the testimony of other surgeons who have studied the small-arms projectiles from a medico-military standpoint. The investigators in the tests of 1904 concluded that there is nothing in the way of resistance in the human body which tends to deform a jacketed pistol projectile.

"Now, while the tests upon the cadavers had established several facts of interest, the most important phase of the question—that concerning the actual man-stopping power exerted by the different bullets when fired into live tissue—remained unsettled, the degrees of oscillation evidenced in the swaying of dead bodies being no more than an indication of what was sought.

"The means of carrying out tests on living tissue, and at the same time occasioning a minimum amount of suffering, was found on the Nelson Morris killing floor in the Chicago stockyards. There arrangements were made for a series of quick-firing experiments in which a noncommissioned officer of the Army who was an expert with the pistol was directed to pump shots in the shortest possible time into steers about to be slaughtered. As soon as the effects of the shots had been noted, the animals were dispatched in the usual manner in vogue on the killing floor and without loss of time.

"The conditions under which the tests were made were these: The firing commenced with the smaller-calibered weapons, those of larger caliber following. The muzzles of the pistols were two or three feet from the animal. No shots were fired into vital parts, into areas traversed by the large blood vessels or into locomotor centers. It was agreed that if any animal failed to drop after ten shots in the lungs or intestines, the firing should cease and the animal should be dispatched.

"In commencing firing with the Luger, the animals were apparently not disturbed either by pain or shock. They evinced no alarm, simply turning their heads at the crack of the weapon and looking at the sergeant inquiringly. It was only after eight, nine or ten shots had been fired that they commenced to show any distress. In no instance with the .30-caliber Luger did any animal drop at the tenth shot.

"As the investigators worked up in the scale of calibers, it was found that the steers shot with the Colt .38-caliber automatic and the revolver of similar size showed greater distress, and that by the time six or seven shots had been fired they gave evidence of shock and exhaustion and dropped.

"With the .45-caliber Colt revolver the steers showed shock and distress after the fourth or fifth shots and then dropped.

"With the .455 and the .476, they dropped after the third or the fourth shot, and with the impact of the first bullet the shock effect was apparent in strong tremors through the entire body.

"In addition, the shock of the smaller-caliber pistols was not accompanied by hemorrhage; on the other hand, at the first or second shot from a .45 caliber weapon the animal would begin to bleed from the mouth and nose."

Several further quotations from Col. La Garde's book are given here, as they have an important bearing on the relative importance of energy, velocity, penetration, bullet diameter, shape and weight, on stopping power.

He says in part--"For the quick firing experiments (against

live animals) we used the following calibers: .476, .455, and .45 from Colt's Revolvers; the .38-cal. Colt's automatic and the .30 Luger pistol which employed the metal-clad bullets. All of the bullets used in the experiments lodged in the body, so that every particle of energy was delivered with each bullet. The animals invariably dropped to the ground when shot from three to five times with the larger caliber Colt's revolver bullets, and they failed in every instance to drop when as many as ten shots of the smaller jacketed bullets from the Colt's automatic and Luger pistol had been delivered against the lungs or abdomen. This failure on the part of the automatic pistols of small caliber (and high velocity and energy) set at rest at once the claims of the makers that the superior energy and velocity of their weapons was a controlling factor in stopping power. The Board was of the opinion that a bullet which will have the shock effect and stopping power at short ranges necessary for a military pistol or revolver should have a caliber not less than .45.

"The tests showed that the .476 caliber lead bullet has the greatest stopping power. Its weight is 288 grains, muzzle velocity 729 f.s., muzzle energy 340 foot pounds. The .45 caliber lead bullet with slightly blunt point was next in stopping power. It weighs 250 grains with a muzzle velocity of 720 f.s., and muzzle energy of 288 foot pounds. A slightly blunt point has the advantage of making a bullet bite better in striking hard bone at an angle, or in clipping the edge of a vessel. All things considered, such a bullet is best suited for the military service in close combat.

"The board considered that cup shaped bullets, such as the 'man-stopper' might be issued to troops fighting savage tribes, and fanatics in the brush or jungle. This bullet showed great execution on live animals. It weighs 218.5 grains, and has a muzzle velocity of 801 f.s. and a muzzle energy of 288 ft. lbs. The edge of the cup mushrooms readily upon striking cartilege and joint ends of bones thereby adding to its sectional area and stopping power.

"None of the full jacketed or metal-patch* bullets (all of which were less than cal. .45) showed the necessary shock effect or stopping power for a service weapon. They failed especially in the joint ends of bones and non-vital parts which comprise the larger part of the target area presented by the human or anical body.

"Shock effect depends upon the sectional area of a bullet and the amount of energy which it delivers at the point of impact. A

---

* Note—Apparently when Col. La Garde refers to "metal patch" bullets he means a bullet with a metal jacket around the core, and a soft-point.

full jacketed bullet which makes a clean fracture in bone and then leaves, takes the greater part of its energy in flight. When the bone is very resistant, or the jacket is marred, the bullet may disintegrate. Its sectional area is then increased, and it leaves energy in the body in proportion to the amount of metal which it deposits in the foyer of the fracture. When it lodges entirely, it parts with all of its remaining energy.

"We are not acquainted with any bullet fired from a hand weapon that will stop a determined enemy when the projectile traverses soft parts alone. The requirements of such a bullet would need to have a sectional area like that of a 3-inch solid shot the recoil from which when used in hand weapons would be prohibitive."

Points that are particularly interesting are that the .30 Luger bullet, which had the highest velocity, energy, and penetration of any of the bullets used in the tests showed by far the least stopping power of any bullet used, even though it delivered all its energy by stopping in the animal for every shot. This disposes of the idea that energy delivered is a criterion of stopping power.

Moreover, note that the .38 automatic pistol which also failed to knock down any animal with ten shots is practically the same as the Super .38 automatic of today as far as ballistics are concerned. It is true that particular cartridges used in the tests gave a muzzle velocity of 1107 f.s., and that the Super .38 of today gives from 80 to 90 more feet per second, but this difference is insignificant, so that these tests can be taken as fairly representing the performance to be expected from the Super .38 under the same conditions. Ten shots from the .38 failed in every instance to knock down an animal, and four shots from the .45 Colt were the average required.

This result compares very favorably with the report of a correspondent who wrote to the author in regard to some experiences he had had in killing outlaw horses out west. He used the .38 Special, the .38 Super Automatic and the .45 Colt Automatic. He says, "I absolutely discarded the .38 Special. Even the 200 grain Western load didn't seem any better than the regular cartridge. The .38 Special cartridge has penetration, but lacks shock power, and that is what is necessary when the first shot counts. The Super .38 Automatic disappointed me very much. Give me the .45 Automatic every time. It hasn't the velocity or penetration, but the first shot drops them, for either head, body or shoulder shots."

In Col. La Garde's tests, note further that the soft point bullet with the .38 automatic gave no very different results from the jacketed bullet. The destruction on hard bone was somewhat greater, but in flesh the results were very much the same.

As to the effect of the shape of the point, note that the .455 man-stopper, which had the same energy and diameter as the .45 Colt had noticeably more stopping power, but the .476, which had a round point and a sectional area only about 9 per cent greater than that of the man-stopper had more stopping power. However, the .476 had about one-third more weight, which no doubt had its effect, especially as it was a long bullet of the kind that might greatly increase its sectional area if it turns over during penetration.

The tests reported by Col. La Garde give an important indication as to the probable answers to some of the questions regarding relative stopping power under the following headings:

1. *Relative effect of bullet velocity.* The tests indicate that within the range of velocities found in pistols, there is no marked difference in the results obtained with the highest and the lowest velocities available. Naturally, there is more penetration with the higher velocities, and especially with blunt pointed bullets, there is more smashing of bone, but there is no marked difference in the effects on flesh.

2. *Relative effect of bullet material.* On flesh there is little difference between the effect of a full jacketed bullet and of a lead one, or of a soft point bullet, or of a jacketed bullet with the metal of the nose cut so as to encourage mushrooming. None of these bullets will change their shape when traversing soft tissues. If a bone is struck, however, the lead or soft point bullet is distinctly more effective, for it will be flattened or distorted so as to increase its sectional area.

3. *Relative effect of bullet shape.* In flesh there seems to be little difference between the effect of a round nosed or a sharp pointed bullet and a square pointed one. However, the square or partly flat pointed shapes are much more effective in oblique or grazing shots on bones, where the round nosed types would have a tendency to glance, and the square nosed ones would bite in. Moreover, in passing close to blood vessels, the round nosed bullets may push them out of the way, while the square pointed ones will clip them. Thus the blunt pointed or flat nosed bullets are undoubtedly more effective.

4. *Bullet weight.* A bullet must have enough weight to insure

adequate penetration and shock to bones; but otherwise weight does not seem nearly so important as caliber. It will be noted, however, that the most effective bullets, namely, those of largest caliber, were also the heaviest, as large size naturally goes with large weight. But various tests and considerations indicate that the real factor in the effectiveness of the larger bullets is their increased sectional area rather than their increased weight.

5. *Relative effect of bullet diameter.* All the tests of which the author has any knowledge, as well as nearly all the scattered reports received from various sources, indicate that caliber is by far the most important factor in the stopping power of any bullet that has adequate energy to carry it well into a body. The nature of flesh is such that a bullet will not cause much destruction outside of a narrow path including the actual bullet track; and the width of this track, and of the consequent area of destruction of tissue, nerve material, and blood vessels varies with the square of the diameter of the bullets concerned, unless a bone is struck and the bullet thus distorted.

The Moral Effect of a Bullet Wound

We have stated above that the actual stopping power of any shot depends not only on the energy and other characteristics of the bullet, but also very largely on the location of the wound; that is, on whether or not the bullet reaches the heart or one of the large nerve centers, or shatters an important bone. Another factor of perhaps equal importance is the mental attitude and condition of the victim. A man of courage and determination, who is keyed up for something desperate will obviously be harder to stop than one who has no stomach for a fight, or who has no expectation of trouble and is taken by surprise.

The person who lacks "intestinal fortitude," if I may be pardoned for using this recently popularized euphemism instead of its shorter and more expressive, but less refined synonym, is likely to "fold up like a jack knife" and quit at the first sign of trouble, and any wound, however slight will put him out of the fight.

Once I heard a shot and the sound of a fall in an adjoining room, and my investigation disclosed a young man lying on the floor with a still smoking .32 caliber revolver beside him, and a flesh wound in the upper part of the left chest. He had attempted suicide, and though he had used the smallest and least powerful center-fire cartridge to be obtained, and the bullet had not reached a vital spot, he had dropped like a log at the shot, and lay there prostrated until he was wheeled off to the hospital to recover in a few days. Compare this case with that of Antonio Caspi who paid no attention whatever to three shots through the chest and lungs with a service revolver, and continued to fight savagely until he was pole-axed with a musket; or with the conduct of the Indian who killed his opponent and then rode his horse several miles after being shot through the neck and chest at close range with a .45 Colt!

Undoubtedly surprise is a big factor, and the easiest person to stop with any bullet is the man who has no expectation of being shot. In this class come hold-up victims who are suddenly confronted by a vicious killer and shot down in their tracks; pedestrians who are walking in some public place and unexpectedly come into contact with a gun-fight and are struck by a stray bullet; and murder victims who are shot without any preliminary warning as to their fate. Usually such persons immediately give up or drop, and undoubtedly the sudden emotional shock to the nervous system is a very important contributing factor; often such unsuspecting victims will go off their feet and down from such trivial causes as, for example, a .22 caliber bullet through the fleshy part of the arm. In fact, such persons are very apt to faint away instead of being knocked down.

More difficult to stop are the participants in some gun fight or shooting scrape where the bullets are flying, and the individuals concerned are aware of the danger. They are keyed up with excitement and intention, and when hit with a bullet are very hard to put off their feet; in fact, they are apt to treat with indifference any but a serious wound. Soldiers in the early stages of a conflict or escaping criminals who are determined to get away in spite of a barrage of fire from pursuing peace officers come in this class. They have something more important on their minds than worrying over a bullet wound, and in many cases after being hit they will continue to fight or run off as the case may be.

Finally we have the third and last class of individuals who are the most difficult of all to stop. These are the ones who are in a frenzy of rage at someone and out with the intention to kill and in the mood to kill or escape at any cost. The cases of Antonio Caspi and of Smith and the Indian, related earlier in this chapter are exact instances of what is meant. Here we have individuals with but one thought uppermost in their minds, namely, to kill or fight clear; every nerve in their bodies is on fire and they are edged up to meet and oppose anything in their paths, no matter what it may be. They do not even know they are shot until they see the blood coming from their wounds after the fight is over. The Philippine native who has gone Hourimantado, the tribesman who has run amuck, the Dillinger who has been chased for weeks, or the desperate convict under the death sentence who has determined to make a break for liberty all fit in this class. Here also belongs the soldier who has come through the early stages of a conflict, and is at last in a bloody hand-to-hand fight with the enemy. He has seen his friends and comrades shot down and done to death beside him, and he is intoxicated with excitement and rage. All these chaps have become so keyed up and desperate that they have made up their minds to die if necessary, but to do as much harm to the other fellow as possible before that occurs; and it is these individuals who require a .45 caliber bullet in a vital spot to stop them. Wild animals at bay also come in this class.

Tables of Stopping Power

In *Pistols and Revolvers and Their Use,* written by the author in 1927, the opinion was expressed that an approximation to the relative stopping power of various revolver bullets could best be obtained by a comparison of the striking energy of each bullet multiplied by the area in square inches of the hole that it makes, or in other words, the sectional area. It was also stated in that book that "there are other factors besides those quoted above which affect the stopping power of bullets. One of these is the shape of the point. A flat pointed bullet has much greater stopping power than a sharp- or round-pointed one. Another factor is the presence or absence of a jacket. The jacketed bullet seems to have less stopping power than one made of plain lead."

Ever since that was written the author has been trying to find out how much the table of stopping power should be modified for a bullet having a jacket, or for one having a square point. Numerous experiments have been made, but a clear cut answer to all these problems has not yet been obtained. However, pending the acquisition of further information, it is thought that the tables of relative stopping power would more nearly represent the actual capabilities of the various bullets if the figures for the jacketed bullets are reduced by ten per cent, and if the figures for the lead bullets are increased by ten per cent for those like the .38 Colt Special, which have a partly flat point, and by twenty-five per cent for wad-cutter bullets, or those with the Keith shape. Those figures have been introduced as a shape factor in the table of stopping power

TABLE I. FACTORS USED TO COMPENSATE FOR THE PRESENCE OR ABSENCE OF
A METAL JACKET AND FOR THE SHAPE OF THE POINT IN COMPUTING
THE STOPPING POWER OF BULLETS

Jacketed Bullets with rounded nose.
.25 (6.35 MM) A. C. P. .... .90
.32 (7.65 MM) A. C. P. .... .90
.380 (9 MM Short) A. C. P. .... .90
.38 (Super .38 Automatic) A. C. P. .... .90
.45 A. C. P. .... .90
.30 (7.65 MM) Luger .... .90
.30 (7.63 MM) Mauser .... .90
Jacketed Bullet with Flat Point.
9 MM Luger 1.00
Lead Bullets with rounded nose.
.22 Long Rifle 1.00
.32 Smith & Wesson 1.00
.32 Smith & Wesson Long 1.00
.38 Smith & Wesson 1.00
.38 Long Colt 1.00
.38 Smith & Wesson Special 1.00
.44 Smith & Wesson Special 1.00
Lead Bullets with blunt rounded point, or with small flat on point.
.38 S. & W. Super Police 1.05
.38 S. & W. Special Super Police 1.05
.41 Long Colt 1.05
.45 Colt 1.05
Lead Bullets with Large Flat on point.
.32 Colt New Police 1.10
.32-20 (.32 Winchester) 1.10
.38 Colt New Police 1.10
.38-40 (.38 Winchester) 1.10
.38 Colt Special 1.10
.44-40 (.44 Winchester) 1.10
Lead Bullets with square point or the equivalent.
.22 Hi-Speed Sharp Shoulder 1.25
.38/44 Special with Keith Bullet 1.25
.455 Man-stopper 1.25

TABLE II. THE CROSS SECTIONAL AREA OF BULLETS IN SQUARE INCHES

Caliber	Bullet diameter, inches	Sectional area, square inches
.22	.223	.039
.25	.250	.049
.30	.309	.075
.32	.314	.076
9-mm. Luger	.354	.099
.38	.359	.102
.38/40	.400	.126
.41	.406	.129
.44/40	.426	.143
.44 Russian	.431	.146
.44 Special	.431	.146
.45 Automatic	.450	.159
.45 Colt	.455	.163

Using the figures given in the two tables above, the estimated shock power according to the formula in *Pistols and Revolvers and Their Use* can very easily be computed for any pistol cartridge by multiplying the muzzle energy as given in the ballistic tables by the shape factor and the area of the bullet as shown in Table II for each caliber. Such a table is given below, only for the purpose of comparison, as it has been superseded by one which follows, computed on a formula which uses momentum instead of energy.

TABLE III. THE ESTIMATED STOPPING POWER OF POPULAR PISTOL AND REVOLVER CARTRIDGES

(Sectional area of bullet in square inches times muzzle energy times a shape factor.) From Formula given by the present author in Pistols and Revolvers and Their Use, 1927. Now superseded by the momentum formula.

Cartridge	Muzzle energy, foot pounds.	Sectional area of bullet, sq. ins.	Shape factor.	Relative stopping power.
.22 Long Rifle, outdoor type	77	.039	1.00	3.0
.22 Long Rifle, Hi-Speed	107	.039	1.00	4.2
.22 Long Rifle, Hi-Speed Sharp Shoulder		.039	1.25	5.2
.25 (6.35 MM) A. C. P.	62	.049	.90	2.7
.30 (7.65 MM) Luger	290	.075	.90	19.6
.30 (7.63 MM) Mauser	329	.075	.90	22.3
.32 (7.65 MM) A. C. P.	140	.076	.90	9.5
.32 Smith & Wesson	75	.076	1.00	5.7
.32 Smith & Wesson Long	124	.075	1.00	9.3
.32 Colt New Police	120	.076	1.10	10.0
.32-20 (.32 Winchester)	232	.076	1.10	19.3
.38 Smith & Wesson	170	.102	1.00	17.3
.38 Colt New Police	170	.102	1.10	18.7
.38 Smith & Wesson Super Police	166	.102	1.10	18.7
.38 Long Colt	220	.102	1.00	22.5
.38 Smith & Wesson Special	260	.102	1.00	26.5
.38 Colt Special	260	.102	1.10	29.3
.38 Special Super Police	246	.102	1.10	27.5
.38/44 S. & W. Special	425	.102	1.00	43.4
.38/44 Special, Keith bullet	425	.102	1.25	53.2
.38 A. C. P. (Super .38)	417	.102	.90	38.3
.380 A. C. P. (9 MM Short)	150	.102	.90	13.5
.38-40 (.38 Winchester)	360	.126	1.10	50.0
9 MM Luger	300	.099	1.00	29.7
.41 Long Colt	220	.129	1.05	30.0
.44 S. & W. Special	320	.146	1.00	46.8
.44-40 (.44 Winchester)	375	.143	1.10	59.2
.45 A. C. P.	340	.159	.90	48.6
.45 Colt, 770 f. s.	330	.163	1.05	56.6
.45 Colt, 910 f. s.	460	.163	1.05	79.0

The author thinks that this table probably gives a closer comparison of the relative shock power of the various cartridges than can be obtained without some such compilation, and experience gained in many tests conducted since it was worked out indicate a fair agreement with experimental results; but for some time a feeling has been growing that the table gives too much weight to the velocity factor, and therefore places such cartridges as the .30 Luger and .30 Mauser with their high velocity and low bullet weight and small diameter too high in the list.

Much of the shock effect of any bullet is due to the throwing of particles of bone, flesh, body fluids, etc., to one side and the other as the bullet plows through the body. The factor that permits the transmission of velocity to other particles is not energy, but momentum, which is mass multiplied by velocity.

The use of momentum instead of energy in the formula would give a truer picture of the relative power of the different bullets to put into motion the particles with which they come into contact. Moreover, it would give the factor of bullet weight more importance. Perhaps the crushing and rending effect of a bullet of large mass on a bone is more serious than the effect of a small bullet at higher speed, which passes through so fast that there is scant time to communicate the effects to any structures that are not in immediate contact with the bullet.

To compute the relative stopping power by this method, first obtain the momentum of the bullet in pounds-feet, by multiplying the mass of the bullet by the velocity. The mass is obtained by dividing the weight *in pounds* by the constant of gravity, 32.16. To bring the bullet weight to pounds, divide the weight in grains by 7000, the number of grains in a pound. (Note—If the energy and velocity of the bullet are known, the momentum is obtained by dividing the energy by the velocity.)

After obtaining the momentum, multiply it by the sectional area of the bullet in square inches, and by the shape factor. The result will be the relative stopping power. This comes out as a decimal with three places, and to bring the results to whole numbers, which does not change the comparative values in the least, but looks less confusing, it is well to use the shape factor as 1000 for the standard bullet instead of 1.0. This would make the other shape factors 900, 1100, and 1250 instead of .9, 1.1, and 1.25 respectively.

It is interesting to plot the relative stopping power of the bullets used by Thompson and La Garde by both these methods and see which comes nearest to the results actually found by test. Bullets

are arranged in the order of the relative effectiveness as reported
in La Garde's book.

Bullet	Weight grains	Velocity foot seconds	Energy foot pounds.	Relative stopping power, energy formula	Relative stopping power, momentum formula.
.30 Luger	92.6	1420	415	31	22
9 MM Luger	123.5	1048	301	29.7	28.4
.38 Long Colt	148	763	191	20.5	27.0
.38 A. C. P.	130	1107	354	32.5	29.5
.45 Colt	250	720	288	49.5	68.4
.455 Man-stopper	218.5	801	288	58.8	73
.476	288	729	340	60.0	83

It will be seen that by the momentum formula, the figures are
in substantial agreement with the results given in La Garde's book,
where the .30 failed to down any animal after ten shots, while the
.38 downed them after say seven shots, the .45 after say four, and
the .455 and .476 after three.

While any formula of this kind is only an approximation at
best, the author now offers the following momentum—sectional
area—shape factor formula as the best method known by him at
present for estimating the relative stopping power of pistol bullets,
and as giving results that seem to be reasonably close to all the
experimental data that have been gathered so far. This method
is not fully applicable to rifle bullets because their stopping power
often depends largely on "yaw" and the consequent tipping or
upsetting of the bullet on impact.

TABLE IV. THE ESTIMATED STOPPING POWER OF POPULAR PISTOL AND REVOLVER CARTRIDGES

(Based on the momentum of the bullet times the sectional area times a factor to compensate for shape and bullet material.)

Cartridge	Momentum, pounds— feet per second	Sectional area of bullet, sq. ins.	Factor for shape and material.	Relative stopping power.
.22 Long Rifle Outdoor type	.083	.039	1000	3.3
.22 Long Rifle Hi-Speed	.097	.039	1000	3.8
.22 L. R. Hi-Speed Sharp Shoulder	.097	.039	1250	4.7
.25 (6.35 MM) A. C. P.	.083	.049	900	3.7
.30 (7.65 MM) Luger	.246	.075	900	16.6
.30 (7.63 MM) Mauser	.249	.075	900	16.8
.32 (7.65 MM) A. C. P.	.147	.076	900	10.0
.32 Smith & Wesson	.118	.076	1000	9.0
.32 Smith & Wesson Long	.165	.076	1000	12.5
.32 Colt New Police	.164	.076	1100	13.7
.32-20 (.32 Winchester)	.244	.076	1100	20.3
.380 A. C. P. (9 MM short)	.177	.102	900	16.2
.38 A. C. P. (Super .38 automatic)	.347	.102	900	31.8
.38 (9 MM) Luger	.288	.102	1000	29.4
.38 Smith & Wesson	.233	.102	1000	23.8
.38 Colt New Police	.240	.102	1100	27.0
.38 S. & W. Super Police	.273	.102	1050	29.2
.38 Long Colt	.272	.102	1000	27.7
.38 S. & W. Special	.302	.102	1000	30.8
.38 Colt Special	.302	.102	1100	33.3
.38 Special Super Police	.338	.102	1050	36.3
.38/44 S. & W. Special	.386	.102	1000	39.4
.38 Colt Spl. High Velocity	.386	.102	1100	43.3
.38/44 Spl., Keith bullet	.386	.102	1250	49.2
.38-40 (.38 Winchester)	.380	.126	1100	52.6
.41 Long Colt	.305	.129	1050	41.8
.44 S. & W. Special	.416	.146	1000	60.6
.44-40 (44 Winchester)	.408	.143	1100	64.2
.45 A. C. P.	.420	.159	900	60.0
.45 Colt, 770 f. s. velocity	.428	.153	1050	73.6
.45 Colt, 910 f. s. velocity	.505	.153	1100	87.4

A section of the pistol range at Camp Perry, Ohio, snowing a few of the competitors shooting in one of the rapid-fire matches.

PART 3

SHOOTING

CHAPTER 13

LEARNING TO SHOOT

IF the average man who has never fired a pistol has one placed in his hand and is asked to try his skill with it, he will usually make a very sorry exhibition. Really there is nothing very strange about this.

If you should give a pen to a man who had never learned to write, he would not do well with his handwriting until after quite a bit of practice; and even after he learned to write rapidly he would find that his pen felt strangely wobbly and insecure if he took it in his left hand instead of his right. The reader can test this for himself. If he takes a pen or pencil in his left hand he cannot write well with it; he lacks control, his hand feels wobbly.

A pistol feels just the same way when it is first grasped by a man who has never handled one before. It takes practice in aiming and snapping the gun to make it feel natural, and a large amount of aiming and snapping with the empty gun should be performed by every aspiring pistol shot before he tries to shoot live cartridges.

After handling a revolver a few times the average man can aim and snap it at a target in such a manner that the target would be hit if the gun happened to be loaded and the user did not know it. However, if he did know that there was a cartridge in the gun he would be expecting a tremendous flash, noise and kick, and as a result he would tense all of his muscles just before firing, or as Mr. Woodworth of Springfield Armory describes it, he has a tendency to "shut both eyes and take both feet off the ground when he pulls the trigger." The result is that a shot would probably hit the ground about half way to the target. If the gun made no noise and had no smoke or recoil, it would not take the average person very long to be a good shot with it.

On this principle, it is best when learning to shoot to select a

gun in which the noise and recoil are a minimum; that means the
.22 caliber. Other advantages of the .22 caliber are the cheapness
of the ammunition, which allows a great deal of practice for very
little money, and the fact that the comparatively low power of the
cartridge enables target practice to be done in places where it could
not be done with a gun of larger size.

Several years ago there was one disadvantage to using the .22
caliber, and that was the fact that all .22 caliber guns were made
small, as if they were intended for a child or very small woman;
in other words, the size of the gun seemed to be controlled by the
size of the bullet it shot more than by the size of the hand in
which it was to be used.

However, it is fortunate that in the last few years a number
of excellent .22 caliber pistols and revolvers have been produced which are the same size as a .38 or .45 caliber weapon,
so that now after learning to shoot with a .22 the marksman
will not find the larger gun strange or awkward.

Problems to be Solved

When the average man starts in to learn to shoot a pistol or
revolver, he will at once be confronted by several problems, one
of which will be to find a place to shoot. If he lives in a city or
settled neighborhood this may be a very serious question. This
phase of the matter will be discussed later, but it may be said at
this point that a man may become really very well grounded in the
principles of revolver shooting before having fired a single shot
and even if the opportunities for actual shooting should be few,
this should not deter the intending marksman from proceeding
with the ground work of instruction.

This will at once bring out another problem, and that is the se-
lection of a gun with which to begin practice.

Selecting a Gun

We have already said that the first gun should be a .22 caliber;
but this still leaves quite a wide latitude, because .22 caliber guns
are made in three distinct types. These are the single shot target
pistol, the target revolver and the automatic pistol.

The choice of a type of gun will depend to a considerable extent
on the kind of shooting which is intended to follow and the
reasons for learning to shoot. It may be that the motive is merely
a desire to become proficient in the use of hand firearms so that
the knowledge of how to use them will be available should the
necessity for their use for self-protection or other emergency arise.

On the other hand, the motive may be a wish to practice .22 caliber target shooting as conducted in the U. S. R. A. and N. R. A. clubs. Again, it may be that the marksman is interested only in military target shooting with large caliber revolvers. In each case a different type of gun may be the best.

If funds are not a serious object there is much to be said for the plan of starting in with a single shot target pistol in any case. This is the most accurate hand firearm of all and is by far the safest. Moreover, if you get really interested in pistol marks-

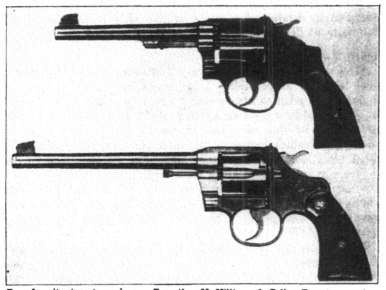

Two favorite target revolvers. Top, the .38 Military & Police Target, sometimes known as the Model K, with 6 inch barrel. Bottom, Colt Officer's Model Target Revolver, with 7½ inch barrel.

manship, you will undoubtedly at some time want to enter some of the matches and you can never expect to get the very highest scores unless you shoot with a single shot target pistol.

On the other hand, if you are only interested in learning to shoot from a practical viewpoint so as to know how to use a revolver or automatic pistol on hunting and camping trips and the like, and you are perfectly sure that you are never going in for target practice, then you would save money by getting the kind of gun best suited for the shooting you eventually intend to do.

Of course, practical shooting can be done with the single shot target pistols, but most people prefer the convenience of a revolver or automatic pistol which does not have to be reloaded after every shot.

If you are practicing up to learn to be a military shot, you would probably want to get a gun which simulates as closely as possible the action of the Government .45 automatic pistol. The Colt Ace automatic pistol is like the Government automatic pistol in size, shape and appearance but uses the .22 caliber cartridge instead of the .45, and as an understudy for the Government pistol this should be your choice.

In chapter 2 you will find all of the .22 caliber target weapons described in detail and a study of this chapter may assist you materially in determining what gun you desire to use.

Learn Your Gun

After getting your gun, the very first thing to do is to learn as much about it as possible. You should learn how to load and unload it and what safety devices it has, if any, also how to adjust the sights and how to clean and care for the gun. Much valuable information of this kind can frequently be obtained from the catalogs or leaflets issued by the manufacturer. If you buy the gun from a local sporting goods dealer, the salesman will be glad to give you information along these lines.

In any event, be sure to learn when you get the gun how to tell whether or not it is unloaded; and every time you pick it up always verify this point. This is one of the most important of safety precautions.

Just to illustrate what may happen, I will tell you that once I knew of a case where a man received a rifle all packed in grease and wrapped in oiled paper just as it came from the factory. The first thing he did was cock the hammer and snap the gun, and to his amazement it went off, but fortunately no damage was done. When the gun left the factory a live cartridge was left in the chamber through some mistake and naturally the purchaser did not think the gun could be loaded under these circumstances and so did not look. The same thing might happen with a revolver.

Safety Precautions

Make it a matter of pride as well as of insurance against accident to study the safety precautions for the proper handling of firearms and observe them on every occasion. Remember that if you do not use the recognized safety precautions that are generally known and observed among those expert with firearms, you will be looked upon as ignorant and inexperienced. The first thing a man who knows about guns looks for in a newcomer on the range is the way he handles his weapon. A man who flourishes his gun around or handles it in an ostentatious manner, brands himself as ignorant of firearms and is a dangerous man to have in a club or on a pistol range.

It is also well to realize that accidents are much more likely to happen with pistols and revolvers than they are with rifles unless proper care is used. This is because a pistol or revolver is so short and easy to handle that it can swing around in any direction with extreme facility. If you have a rifle in your hand, for example, you are not likely to point it at yourself, but a revolver swings around so easily that it may be pointed in any direction, therefore the need for the utmost care.

While the revolver is potentially dangerous, all chance of accidents can be eliminated if each user will observe a few simple safety precautions, and it is a matter for congratulation that among the pistol and revolver clubs and at the National Matches where guns are being used constantly, there is practically never an accident. It is the man who is untrained and unfamiliar with firearms who causes the "didn't know it was loaded" accidents with which we are all so familiar in the daily papers.

The strict observance of the following precautions are absolutely essential:

1. Never point a pistol or revolver at anyone unless you want to shoot him, and never allow anyone to point a gun at you. In general, never point a gun whether loaded or not in any direction where it could do harm if it went off.

2. If you hand a gun to another or if a gun is handed to you, always open and examine it to see if it is loaded, first removing and examining the magazine.

3. At matches or competitions always keep the cylinder swung out or if an automatic pistol, keep the slide latched back (except when actually on the firing line). Never aim or snap a gun back of the firing line. Army rules require these precautions and violations may result in the barring of the offender from the range.

4. Remember that with an automatic pistol taking the cartridge out of the chamber does not necessarily make it safe. There may be one or more cartridges in the magazine and when you shut the gun it is loaded again. Merely taking the loaded magazine out of the gun does not make it safe; a cartridge may remain in the chamber. Many fatal accidents have happened by neglect of these points. When you want to unload an automatic, **always**

remove the magazine first and after removing the magazine, look to see that there is no cartridge left in the chamber. Then work the action a time or two without snapping the arm.

5. In carrying a revolver loaded, always have an empty chamber under the hammer except in the case of hammerless guns or those having a positive hammer block operated by the trigger, such as the Smith & Wesson Patent Safety Hammer Block, the Colt Positive Lock, or the Iver Johnson Hammer-the-Hammer Safety.

Always take the precaution before shooting a gun to clean out any grease that may be in the barrel or cylinder. Sometimes

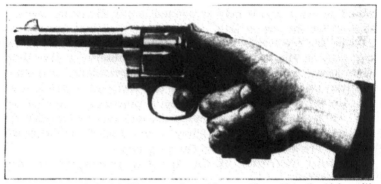

The preferred method of holding a revolver of large caliber. Note the high position of the hand on the grip, and the manner in which the thumb is held. The gun illustrated is the .45 Colt New Service.

grease is put in at the factory to keep the gun from rusting and there may be enough in the barrel to cause trouble if you fire without taking it out.

It is a very wise precaution to wear glasses when shooting either rifles or pistols, as sometimes the primers or head of the cartridge may leak and allow some gas to escape, with the risk of injury to the eyes.

In using heavy caliber guns, especially indoors, it is a very wise precaution to use cotton in the ears as continued firing will have a tendency to impair the acuteness of hearing unless this is done.

Immediately after shooting, always clean the gun and oil it with light oil if it is to be used again soon, or coat lightly inside and out with a rust preventive grease if it is to be put away for some time. A rag saturated with rust preventive grease pushed back and forth through the bore several times, will leave a thin film which will not interfere with shooting but which will stop the bore from rusting.

Holding the Gun

After you have learned all you can about the mechanism of your gun and about the safety precautions, the next thing is to practice aiming and snapping it until familiarity is obtained and until the trigger can be squeezed with such smoothness and coordination that the sights do not move when the hammer falls. Before you can start with this practice, you must know the proper method of

Some shooters with a large hand find no difficulty in grasping the gun so the middle finger fills the space in rear of trigger guard. Above is such a "grip" with the thumb bent down towards the trigger.

holding the gun and the proper position in which to stand while shooting. Much can be learned from a study of the illustrations which accompany this chapter.

Of course, before you begin your snapping practice you must first take the proper standing position. In the practical use of a pistol you may have to fire in almost any direction and from a standing, sitting or prone position. However, you are generally standing and facing the object that you are shooting at.

In target shooting you do not have any such limitations of time or circumstances and, therefore, you can take the most ideal position, and this is with the target to the right front of the shooter, right foot pointing toward the target, left foot about 12 to 20 inches to the rear of the right foot and pointing to the left at an angle of about sixty degrees to the right foot. This position of the feet braces the body against swaying either forward or backward or from side to side.

The pistol is held in the right hand at the level of the eyes with the arm fully extended toward the target. The body assumes as comfortable a position as possible to balance the weight of the extended arm and the revolver, and this generally means that the shooter leans back slightly. It helps a great deal if the belt is grasped with the left hand, as this steadies the body remarkably.

The method of holding the pistol or revolver is a most important point in learning to shoot accurately. While a great many hints can be given which will aid the beginner in eventually learning the proper grip, it must be understood that at first the gun will feel awkward, the same as a pen does to a person just learning to write. However, practice will bring familiarity and the proper grasp will come with experience.

Some shooters find this an excellent, way to hold a revolver that is not fitted with a grip adapter. Note that the back of the trigger guard rests on the second finger, and it in turn rests on the third, thus giving steadiness to the hold and supporting the gun in a vertical plane. This method of holding works well for either slow or rapid fire.

It should be realized at the outset that the exact method of holding the gun will vary according to the caliber of the gun and the amount it recoils, and also according to the type of weapon used. Obviously a .22 in which the recoil is negligible, can be grasped much more loosely than a .45 in which the recoil is considerable. Moreover, it is also quite obvious that the automatic pistol with its straight, flat stock must be grasped in a different way than a revolver with its curved handle.

No matter what kind of weapon is used or what method of holding is adopted, there are general observations that should be borne in mind. The most important of these is that while shooting can be done in several different ways, using various kinds of grasps, a change in the method of holding the gun will change the place where the bullets hit even when using the same sighting, hence it is best to learn a good method and stick to it so that your grouping will always be in the same place with regard to the line of sight. In other words, try to find the right grip as early as you can and avoid as far as possible changing from one method of holding to another from time to time, because this will delay your obtaining proficiency in marksmanship.

Long experience has shown that the best results are obtained if the butt is grasped as high up as the hand will go, so that the recoil will be more nearly in line with the arm than it would be if the gun were grasped lower down on the butt. Moreover, as most of the hand is on the right-hand side of the grip, the gun is supported more on that side than on the left, and consequently, the recoil has a tendency to turn the gun to the left. In order to overcome this difficulty, I prefer to place the thumb high on the frame of the revolver alongside the hammer, as this steadies the left side of the weapon more; but some well known shots prefer to cross the thumb down toward the trigger guard, and recommend that position.

Because the gun is supported only by the hand and because with all but the .22 caliber arms the recoil is considerable, it will be found that the method of holding will have a noticeable effect on the way the gun shoots. If held high it will shoot lower than if held with the hand low down on the grip. If held with the thumb laid alongside the frame as described, it will generally shoot where it is aimed; but if held with the thumb pointed downward and crossed over the frame toward the trigger guard, the gun will have a tendency to shoot higher and more to the left.

In general, no matter what type of weapon you are using, you should take hold of the gun in the most natural manner possible, and hold it fairly firmly, but do not grip it tightly, as this will cause trembling and will put the muscles under such a strain that twitching or flinching will most likely result.

With automatic pistols there is just about one position the hand can take, because the trigger guard rests on top of the middle finger and the curve of the grip at the back just below the hammer rests on top of the thumb. Hence, in general, the manner in which the modern automatic pistol is held is much more natural than the holding of a revolver, because in the automatic pistol there is no space behind the trigger guard for the middle finger to get into. The first finger goes into the trigger guard and the middle finger just below it in a natural position, so that the first finger does not have to be bent down in an acute angle in a strained position to reach the trigger as it does on a revolver. Moreover in the automatic pistol it is not possible to have the hand high on the grip one time and low the next.   Also, the thumb projects straight forward along the left side and the user does not have to worry whether to cross the thumb over, as described above, or lay it alongside the frame.

With revolvers, however, the case is different.   The average revolver is not well shaped for holding, and most marksmen are

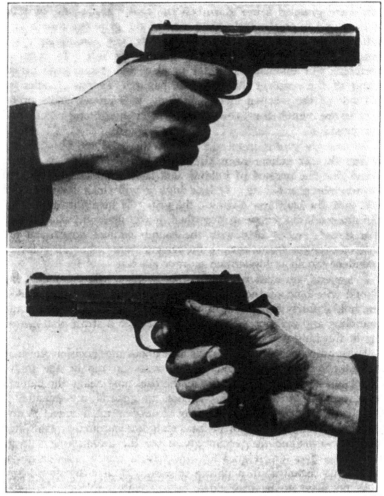

The proper grip for the .45 caliber automatic pistol.   This is an easy gun to hold properly, as the shape of the handle prevents the gun from being held in any other way, constantly struggling to find a comfortable and natural method of handling the gun. It is possible to hold it with either a high grip, that is, with the hand way up nearly in line with the barrel, or with a low grip, that is, with the hand well down on the butt the same as if you were grasping the handle of a saw. Moreover, the thumb may either be placed high along the side of the frame as shown in the illustration, or may be crossed over so that it comes down toward the top of the index finger as it rests on the trigger.

In most revolvers the space behind the trigger guard goes too high up, so that if the middle finger is placed in this space it is difficult for the first finger to get down onto the trigger without being bent out to an unnatural angle with the other fingers. A great many revolver shots fill up this space with a piece of rubber

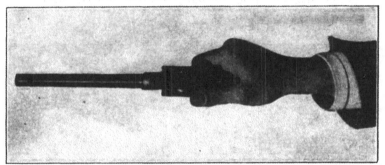

Grip the revolver so the line of sight will be in prolongation of the wrist and arm. This "beds" the weapon against the palm of the hand and the recoil is taken up squarely. Beginners invariably grasp the butt too low and too much to the right with the result that the line of bore (and recoil) is high above the hand; upon firing the recoil throws the barrel up and to the left.

or wood cut to the proper shape and then bound onto the grip with tire tape. Such filler pieces have acquired the name of "gadgets" among target shooters with the pistol. Thus when, at the annual meeting of the Association, there was a discussion of the advisability of allowing the use of the "gadget" in certain matches, this filler piece was what was meant. Several of the later models of pistol or revolver have such a filler piece built in as a part of the trigger guard or frame, and it is expected that this tendency will become more pronounced in the future. Several such devices are described in chapter 6.

All these attachments are a very great help in forcing the user to take the same grip every time. However, some shooters prefer to dispense with the gadget and instead curl up the middle finger and let it project slightly forward and allow it to support the bottom of the trigger guard instead of getting up into the space behind it.

It is desirable, of course, to avoid alterations or adjustments to your gun, such as the changes above mentioned, if you can do without them, but in any event you should be sure that you learn to take hold of the gun in such a manner that you can always quickly reach for it and have the same grip when it comes up to the firing position.

The smaller Colt revolvers (especially in the earlier models), such as the Police Positive Target, have a rather narrow oval shape to the bottom of the grip and the edge is well rounded.

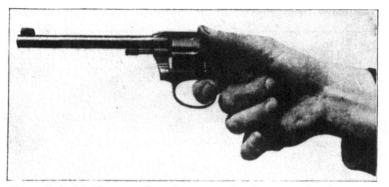

This method of holding a small revolver, or one that has a grip that is narrow at the bottom is especially good for rapid fire. The little finger is hooked under the bottom of the grip, thus preventing the hand from slipping to a new position from the jump of the gun on recoil.

With these guns it will be found quite comfortable to place the little finger under the bottom of the butt, which completely overcomes the difficulty above mentioned, as it prevents the hand from slipping up to a new position on recoil. If the gun has a fairly large handle, however, this method of holding means that a low position must be taken. In other words, it must be gripped fairly down toward the end of the butt.

We now come to the question of the single shot pistol, and here is where we find the widest variation in the kinds of grips that are allowed and recommended. In both the automatic pistol and the revolver, the method of holding the weapon is influenced to some extent by the heavy recoil experienced in the guns of larger caliber. However, as all modern single shot target pistols are made in .22 caliber only, recoil does not enter as a factor to be considered. There are some single shot target pistols such as the

Smith & Wesson Straight Line and the Stevens No. 10, that are shaped just like an automatic pistol. With these guns there can be only one method of grasping, as described above for automatic pistols.

Then there are other single shot target pistols that are made on the frame of a revolver. Examples are the Smith & Wesson Perfected Model and the Colt Camp Perry Model. These may be

Typical British shooting position as seen on the small bore pistol range at Bisley. Mr. B. Cooper, of the Imperial College Rifle Club, London, shooting his Webley Target Pistol.

grasped either high on the stock behind the hammer, or low; the thumb may either be laid alongside the frame or crossed down toward the trigger finger; a gadget may be used or not according to the fancy of the user. But in general, the method of holding these guns is the same as that of holding the revolver.

There are, however, several other single shot target pistols which are shaped entirely differently from either the automatic pistol or the revolver. Among these may be mentioned the Stevens Off-Hand Model and the Webley, which have curved handles somewhat like those of a revolver; the free pistol such as the Tell and Widmer Models which have massive grips especially shaped for some special method of holding; and the Harrington & Richardson Single Shot Pistol which is shaped very much like a revolver but has some important differences which render a distinctive method of holding possible.

In connection with the matter of gripping a single shot pistol, we have two distinct schools of thought; one which favors having the hand and wrist in a neutral position when shooting as is always the case when shooting an automatic pistol; and the other which believes in using a nearly straight grip, so that the wrist may be bent down sharply and put in a tense position while shooting.

The advocates of this latter position claim that the use of the neutral or automatic pistol position of the wrist is conducive to tremors. The wrist is a free universal joint which can be moved in any direction, and the only thing that holds it in one position is the balanced tension of the different sets of muscles. When grasping a pistol and pointing at the target with the wrist in the neutral position, especially if the pistol is balanced about the center of the hand, there is one set of muscles on top of the arm which pulls with certain tension to keep the muzzle of the pistol high enough, while the other set of muscles underneath the arm pulls at certain tension to keep the muzzle of the pistol low enough. Holding a pistol of this kind pointed at the target means a constant fight between these two sets of muscles to keep up an equal tension on the top and bottom of the arm, and in practice it is found that sometimes one set will strengthen up a little and the other will weaken slightly; then in a few seconds the condition will be reversed and cause slight, almost imperceptible tremors, which will have their effect on the grouping.

This fact is recognized by the makers of the Tell pistol, who arrange their gun with the grip nearly in line with the barrel, so that when the hand is held in the neutral position, the barrel points high in the air. To point the gun in a horizontal direction, as is done in aiming at a target, the wrist must be bent sharply downward, thus putting the muscles on top of the arm in a stretched position, keeping them under tension, and doing away with the balanced condition mentioned above as the possible cause of trembling.

This system has met with a considerable amount of success, but nevertheless it seems to be a strained and uncomfortable position, and is more or less tiring.

A good shooting position and an excellent method of holding the single shot pistol. Lieut. N. D. Sillin, U. S. Army, with 10 inch barrel Harrington & Richardson U. S. R. A. Model Single Shot Pistol.

After reviewing all of these different facts, the makers of the H. & R. pistol came to the conclusion that the most accurate and least tiring position for the hand and wrist for holding a pistol, could be obtained by making the shape of the grip such that the hand slopes down when the pistol is pointed at the target just exactly as much as the hand will normally droop when the arm and hand are extended straight out with the fingers open and the palm of the hand in a vertical plane and the fingers allowed to droop toward the floor as much as they will by action of gravity, still keeping the fingers open and the hand flat. This takes up all the motion of the wrist in an easy and normal manner, and there is no tendency to tremble, as the wrist joint just droops down as far as it will naturally.

Then, if we grasp in this hand a gun, the weight of the muzzle of the gun will add its effect in holding this gun in this position without any effort on the part of the shooter and without any tendency for tremors to arise.

It was on this principle that the grip and balance of the H. & R. pistol were first developed. Then later a number of different interchangeable grips were furnished to suit almost any style of holding, but with the original or No. 1 type of grip the recommended method of holding the gun is as follows: In grasping this gun, extend the hand flat and let the gun rest on the middle finger. The gun, being muzzle heavy, will tend to rotate in the hand, until the rounded part of the grip at the top strikes against the ball of the thumb. If the gun is grasped in this way, it will be found that the hand rides very high on the frame. In fact, the thumb is just behind the hammer of this gun when the hammer is cocked. It is impossible to take the same grip on any other gun on the market, because with most other single shot pistols the hammer comes back so far that it interferes and prevents the hand from riding up to this high position. With the H. & R., the hammer moves back only a small distance when cocked, and is entirely out of the way.

If one of these guns is taken and balanced on the middle finger as suggested, it is surprising how steadily it can be pointed. However, with a grip like this, where the gun is just held between the thumb and middle finger, there is nothing to stop any lateral deviations, but when the first finger is placed on the trigger, part of this finger lies along the frame on the right-hand side, and with the thumb on the left-hand side, we have all that is necessary to shoot the gun accurately. When shooting in this way, only the

Left: On the firing line at Camp Perry. 1931. Mr. George H. Keyes, of Boston, an outstanding pistol shot of today is seen in the foreground.
Right: A good shooting position. Posed by Mr. R. C. Bracken, of Columbus, Ohio, an excellent pistol and revolver shot.

first and second fingers and thumb are used; the other fingers can be allowed to rest lightly against the stock, and this forms an extremely comfortable and steady hold.

Moreover, the advocates of allowing the joints to do the work instead of balancing one muscle against another, also utilize the elbow by first turning the arm with the palm of the hand upward, which brings the elbow down. Then by straining the arm out as straight as it will go, it will be found that the elbow will lock; that is, the joints will come together and cannot be bent any farther in that direction. Holding the arm like that, turn just the hand over until the thumb is on top, then you will have both the elbow and wrist locked in a rather immovable position, not depending on muscular effort to keep them from bending farther.

The proponents of this position go still further. They face a good deal farther to the left so that the shoulder is thrown around as far to the right as it will go. This also has a tendency to lock the shoulder joints. The advocates of this position claim that the human shoulder and elbow are like the center joint and one of the end joints respectively of a folding two-foot rule which can just be bent only so far to the right and so far downward until they come to a locked position.

While a study of the orthodox position will repay the beginner, it is well for him to remember that there are many positions which have their strong advocates.

At the International Matches in Antwerp, Belgium, in 1930, everyone observed one particular shooter who had a very striking position. He held the gun with his arm very much bent so that the butt of the gun was just about a foot from his eyes. I heard several people remark that he used such a peculiar position that he undoubtedly did not know much about shooting. When the matches were over, however, he was the champion of the world, having won first place with apparent ease. This shooter turned out to be Mr. Revilliod De Budè, of Geneva.

It is quite possible to get most excellent results with these extreme positions, but I believe that the easiest and most natural way for the beginner is to take such a position that the pistol can be aimed at the target in the easiest and most natural manner possible. Moreover, the straight arm position has an advantage over the bent arm position in that the farther from the eye the pistol is held, the clearer will be the definition of both sights and the bull's-eye when they are viewed at the same time.

The eye really has quite a job to focus on those three widely separated points, that is, the rear sight, front sight, and bull's-eye, and still get them so that they all appear clear. In many cases it is not possible to do this when the shooter is advanced in years

Shooting position of Monsieur A. Revilliod de Bude, of Switzerland, who won the Pistol Championship of the World at Antwerp in 1930. The author, who was present on that occasion was much interested in the unusual weapon, grip and shooting position of M. Revilliod, and with his kind permission took several photographs.

and the power of accommodation of the eye has weakened somewhat.

The optical difficulty will bother some shooters but experience has shown that if this apparent blurring of the sights is ignored as much as possible, the best results will be obtained as the eye will automatically tend to center the sights even if they appear slightly blurred.

Sighting

After learning to stand correctly and to hold the gun properly, the next thing to do is to learn how to use the sights.

Appearance of sights and bull's-eye when aiming at the Standard American Target at 20 yards. This sketch was made with great care to show the actual relative size of the target and the sights. Gun is the Smith & Wesson .38/44 Outdoorsman's Revolver.

Pistols and revolvers all have open sights. The rear sight consists of a bar with a notch in it, and the front sight consists of a blade or bead. In target shooting, the front sight should be brought into the center of the notch in the rear sight, and the top of the blade or bead should be just level with the top surface of the rear sight, and should be brought exactly under the bull's-eye, so that the top of the front sight appears to just touch the bottom of the bull's-eye. This is what is called a "six o'clock" hold, because it is pointing just at the place where the six o'clock figure is located on the dial of a clock.

Most beginners think that it would be better to point right in the middle of the bull's-eye, but this is not so, because the bull's-eye is black and the front sight appears black when it is looked at at arms length and if you put it in the middle of the bull's-eye, you cannot tell just where it is pointing or whether it is in the middle of the notch in the rear sight.

However, if you point under the bull's-eye, the white paper makes a background for the sights and you can readily see that you have the front sight pointed in the right relation to the rear sight, and moreover, you have both sights properly aligned in relation to the bull's-eye itself.

Most beginners think that if you aim at the bottom of the bull's-eye, the bullet will hit at the bottom, but with adjustable sights a correction will be made so that shooting at the bottom will cause the bullet to go in the middle.

Most people think that in aiming a gun they must shut one eye and keep the other open. It is quite true that one eye does do all of the sighting but it is best if the shooter can accustom himself to it, to shoot with both eyes open, as this will help a great deal in avoiding eye strain. If the shooter cannot do this at first he can learn to do it by wearing a pair of glasses and hanging a cloth over the left eye until he becomes used to keeping this eye open also. Shutting one eye while keeping the other open causes squinting which puts a strain on the muscles and is hard to keep up for a long time as in a match, and it will be found perfectly easy and natural after a little practice to shoot with both eyes open.

You do this in a way when you point your finger at any object. There are really two images of your finger but mentally you disregard one of the images. Just try this some time : Point your finger at some object, then close first one eye and then the other and you will see that there are really two fingers apparently pointing in two directions but you have only taken mental note of one of them, and it is the same when sighting with both eyes open.

Some people want to sight with the left eye and some with the right eye. There is one eye that unconsciously dominates the other. This is called the master eye. You can quickly find out whether your right eye or left eye is the master eye by the experiment described above, by pointing a finger at some object and first closing one eye and then the other. The eye which sees the finger pointing at the object is the master eye and the eye that sees the finger apparently pointing somewhere else is the subject eye.

A very good exercise which would teach the proper methods of sighting and at the same time eliminate, as far as possible, the errors which arise in this way, is the making of sighting triangles. To do this the gun is rested on a bag of sand or sawdust on top of a tripod or step-ladder at a convenient height for the shooter's eye, and is aimed at a movable black disk, which represents a bull's-eye. Once the gun is aligned it is left without changing its position, and the man who is helping you goes to the target point and takes hold of the handle of the black disk above mentioned. This disk is generally cut out of tin, painted black, and is the same size as a bull's-eye and has a hole in the center of it just big enough to admit the point of a pencil. A white sheet of paper is pinned over the target, and the man who is practicing aims without touching the gun, at the same time motioning to the one who is helping at the target, indicating to him the direction in which he ought to move the black disk.

When the assistant has the disk in exactly the proper position so it appears just right to the marksman when he is looking over the sights, he calls out "mark," and the assistant then marks through the hole in the center of the black disk, making a dot on the paper. He then moves the disk away and the process starts over again. Of course, if the marksman were absolutely accurate and had perfect eyesight the two marks would be on top of each other, but in practice this is never so, as there is always a slight error in the aiming and the marks fall a short distance apart.

When three of these marks are made they are joined by lines and form a little triangle, which gives an indication of the error the marksman has made in getting the bull's-eye lined up with the sights. This error varies with the eyesight and judgment of the marksman, with the lighting conditions and with the kind of sights used.

This exercise is an excellent one to teach a shooter what kind of sights are best suited to his eyes. It is perfectly obvious that if his successive positions with the sighting disk are, for example, three inches apart, he cannot expect to get a half-inch group when he starts shooting, even if the gun were absolutely accurate.

Another thing to do about sights is to study the adjusting of them, learn which way to move the sights to make the bullet move the way you want it to go. This has been described in another chapter under the heading of sights.

Snapping Practice

The next step after learning how to sight is to practice snapping and aiming at the target without any cartridges in the gun. This practice can very well be carried out in your bedroom, cellar, or almost any place where there is proper light. It is not necessary to have a regular pistol range, nor is it necessary to have a regular target. Any round black spot on a white sheet of paper will do as an aiming point.

Some effort should, however, be made to get the same relative size as the bull's-eye of the target would be if you were aiming on a regular pistol range. Bear in mind that the bull's-eye is 2.72 inches in diameter at 60 feet. You can easily make an aiming mark that will be the proper size to use at 10 feet or any other desired distance.

When you are ready to start this practice, always examine the gun to be sure that it is empty. Then take the proper standing position, cock the gun, point it toward the target and squeeze the trigger carefully until the hammer falls. At the same time watch the sights carefully to see if they move on the target at the moment the hammer falls. If the sights do move when the trigger is squeezed, it shows that the shot would not have gone true.

With some guns it will require a considerable amount of practice and quite a bit of experimenting with different holds and grips before proficiency can be obtained in this "dry shooting." It is an interesting test of steadiness to balance a dime on the barrel of the gun just behind the front sight and see if it has a tendency to fall off when the hammer is snapped.

Quite a bit of practice may be necessary before the marksman learns to hold the gun absolutely steady when he lets the hammer drop. When this point has been attained, the marksman has reached such a stage that he would be able to hit the bull's-eye if a cartridge were in the gun when he pulls the trigger.

Here it may be stated that no properly made, modern weapon is injured by snapping without cartridges in it. Some cheap .22 caliber rifles are made so that the striker hits the metal of the barrel when snapped without a cartridge, but long ago American gun makers recognized the fact that a real gun enthusiast will wish to snap his weapon for dry practice, and accordingly all the better guns are made so that the striker does not hit the metal of the barrel when snapped.

The beginner may wonder why we start to learn to shoot without using cartridges. The reason is simple. The first thing to do is to learn to snap the gun in such a fashion that the aim is not disturbed. It might be thought that this could best be accomplished by actually shooting at a target and seeing if the bullet hits the point aimed at, the assumption being that if the bullet does not hit the point aimed at, the shooter did not snap the gun in such a careful manner as to avoid disturbing the point of aim.

This is the way many shooters first learn to shoot, but it has the very serious disadvantage that when a gun is actually fired there is recoil, noise, and flash, each of which produces something of a shock to the nervous system, especially when the nerves are not accustomed to these effects of firearms. A new shooter just starting to learn, who is trying to pull the trigger carefully, cannot put his mind at ease and concentrate on the trigger squeeze if he knows that the moment he squeezes hard enough to make the gun go off there will be a tremendous report and big kick; his nervous system will be all on edge waiting for the noise and the kick. The result is that he is likely to make up his mind and then suddenly jerk the trigger, or flinch. When he does this he actually makes the gun go off and the kick of the gun masks or hides the flinching and he never knows that he has done anything wrong. Under these conditions the shots may go in the most unaccountable places for no apparent reason.

If the gun could actually shoot a bullet without making any noise or recoil, it would be an advantage to use the target and shoot at it even in the first practice.

The Bull's-Eye Pistol

There is a gun on the market that does shoot a bullet very accurately without making any noise and without having any recoil. It is a toy called the Bull's-eye Pistol, which is made in the same shape as an automatic and shoots a No. 6 chilled shot by the aid of a rubber band.

This gun is extremely accurate at ranges of not over ten or fifteen feet. In the outfit with it are several small celluloid birds of the ordinary ten-cent store variety, and some wire perches for these birds arranged to clamp on the front edge of the box. The user is supposed to set these up at a distance of ten feet or so and then try to knock them down by shooting at them. The back of the box catches the shot that miss the birds.

While the Bull's-eye Pistol shoots hard enough to knock down these birds or make a small mark on the pasteboard target, or to kill a fly, it does not shoot hard enough to break an electric light bulb or to put out an eye, though it is certainly advisable to use every care not to point the pistol at anyone because it would, of course, be far from pleasant to be shot in the eye with it even though the bullet would not have enough velocity to penetrate.

A few years ago I gave one of these pistols to my two young sons, and without giving them any instructions except in safety

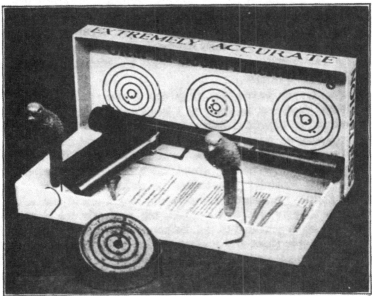

The Bull's-eye Pistol with complete outfit of targets and "gallery"

precautions, let them practice with it a week or two. They soon became very proficient in knocking down the birds and naturally there was no tendency to learn the flinching habit because nothing startling happened when the trigger was pulled; the only thing that happened was that sometimes the birds fell down and sometimes they did not. After a week or so the boys got so they could hit the birds every time with this pistol, and just for the sake of an experiment I took them for a walk and let them try my 10-inch target pistol with regular .22 caliber cartridges. Various targets were used, bottles, tin cans, etc., and a miss was a very rare thing indeed. Firing at the Standard American Target at the regular distance, they made fair groups.

A week later an impromptu target competition with automatic pistols was held at the request of a group of Army Reserve officers who were on fifteen days' annual duty. Among this group there were several men who were well qualified in pistol-shooting, and they suggested that the target be placed at half the regular distance, so that those members who were not familiar with shooting would not be utterly discouraged by missing the target 100 per cent.

In spite of this arrangement a large percentage of the shots fired by this group of officers (with exception of the two mentioned) missed the target entirely.

The reason that the half-grown boys did so much better than these officers was because they had been allowed to learn to shoot in such a way that they did not anticipate a disturbance every time they pulled the trigger.

Another very interesting thing that I observed in using this Bull's-eye pistol was its effect on a large and very intelligent police dog which had a decided dislike for the report of a gun. One day an acquaintance who was visiting me picked up this Bull's-eye pistol and began shooting at the birds, and I noticed that each time he aimed at a bird the dog would watch him very attentively and would start violently just before he pulled the trigger. After noticing this, I watched very carefully and I could not tell just when the trigger was to be pulled, but evidently the dog could. The dog, being sensitive to the discharge of firearms had evidently watched people shoot and learned to detect the moment when the shooter had made up his mind to pull the trigger.

If it requires such a nervous effort on the part of a marksman to bring himself to the point of actually pulling the trigger that this effort is visible to a dog, it is quite apparent that the tensing of the muscles which results from this nervous effort will have an effect on the marksmanship. This can be very well observed in target-shooting by loading one chamber of a revolver with an empty cartridge and the others with loaded ones, unknown to the firer. If he is flinching you may not be able to detect it, and he may not be able to detect it when a cartridge goes off, because the motion of the flinch is masked by the recoil of the gun, but when he comes to the empty cartridge he will flinch just the same, and then it will show up in a ridiculous manner, which will generally cause him to make a conscientious effort to overcome the trouble.

Frequently I have had a man complain that the gun was inaccurate or was improperly sighted, or state that he had to aim at the top right-hand corner of the target to hit the bull's-eye, and almost always these claims can be traced back to this flinching habit, and you can always show it up in the manner above described.

It does not always pay you to do so, however, as sometimes the man who asks your help in overcoming such a trouble may get angry when he is caught in the act.

Once on a rifle range at Guantanamo, Cuba, I had a lieutenant commander in the Navy ask me to see if I could find out what was wrong with his shooting. I told him that I thought he was flinching, and after watching him a while I asked permission to fire a few shots with his gun and then handed it back to him with one chamber empty. He fired two shots, missing the target with each, and on the third he came to the empty cylinder. He took careful aim and finally pulled the trigger, at the same time giving a violent convulsive twitch which caused the gun to point downward at a perceptible angle, so that the shot would have hit the ground in front of the target.

I told him that I had left an empty chamber in the gun to see if he was flinching; but instead of being glad to find it out he at once became very angry and walked off in a huff.

The foregoing discussion leads to the conclusion that the best way to learn to be any kind of a shot, whether a target shot or a practical shot, is to start at the beginning and learn to use a gun without flinching and get enough practice at it so that the muscles are sufficiently co-ordinated to be able to pull the trigger fast or slow without deranging the aim.

Slow Fire Shooting

After learning to use the pistol in dry shooting so that the trigger can be squeezed repeatedly without disturbing the aim, or after learning to use the Bull's-eye pistol so that accuracy has been attained, the next thing is to try some actual shooting with live cartridges.

Here we come squarely up against the problem of a place to shoot. Pistol shooting cannot be done in settled localities unless there is an adequate backstop which will be certain to prevent the bullets from going wild. While pistols are used only on short ranges, say up to fifty or seventy-five yards, nevertheless bullets will travel much farther than this. Bullets from a heavy revolver, such as the .45 or .38-40, are easily capable of killing a man at 1200 yards, and bullets from a .22 long rifle will kill at 1000 yards under some circumstances. A case is on record where a boy was killed with a .22 caliber short at a range of 639 yards, the bullet having struck him in the abdomen.

A revolver requires a much wider backstop than does a rifle because the very nature of a revolver is such that a slight twitch may deviate the bullet from the line of fire. This means that whatever place is selected for shooting must be of such a nature that it would be impossible for the bullet to go wild. However, this is not quite as bad as it sounds because the penetration of all

The Olympic Matches at Los Angeles, 1932. Col. Roy D. Jones, Secretary of the U. S. Revolver Association, (center), and M. E. Frank, coach, watching Tippins of the U. S. Team at practice.

revolvers and pistols is comparatively low, and whereas a back-stop or protection must cover a considerable amount of space in front of the shooter, it does not have to be of such a nature as to withstand a great amount of penetration.

Much shooting is done with .22's and it is frequently found that a range can be fitted up in the cellar, which is entirely safe because no matter which way the bullet goes it will strike something which is capable of stopping a .22. For larger caliber weapons the blank side of a brick building forms a good place to erect a target backstop. Of course, something must be placed behind the target that will stop the bullets before they hit the wall, as they would chip the bricks and eventually do a great deal of damage by having a number of bullets hit in the same place. The advantage of having the wall there is if a bullet should accidentally miss the backstop behind the target, the wall would prevent it from going where it would do any great harm.

Never make the mistake of tacking a target onto the wall of a wooden building, and then shooting with the expectation that the wall will hold the bullets. I once knew of a man who purchased a .22 caliber rifle and decided to do some target practice. He knew nothing whatever about shooting or the properties of firearms, so he tacked a target on his neighbor's garage and fired quite a few shots at it. When he took the target down he found a series of holes in the door where the target had been tacked, and then he began to wonder just how far the bullets had gone, so he looked inside and discovered that they had gone through the door and had penetrated the back of a sedan car which was sitting inside. The neighbor happened to be away, so this man without saying a word about it, had the automobile taken out of the garage, repaired and put back in the garage before the owner reappeared. The neighbor never would have known what happened had not the shooter gone to him and told him what he had done. This is one case where a lack of even a little knowledge of the precautions necessary with firearms cost the shooter a great deal of money.

In the less settled parts of the country it is usually easy to find a safe place to practice, and while the problem is more serious for city dwellers, there is usually available in or near the larger towns and cities a club affiliated with the U. S. Revolver Association or with the National Rifle Association, and these clubs will have the necessary facilities for safe target practice. The beginner can do no better than to join one of these clubs where he will find not only a place to practice, but also people able and willing to give advice and information.

The first actual shooting is best done at a target rather than at some object selected as a mark to shoot at. The reason is that the target provides a clearly defined objective to aim at and makes it easy to take the same aim every time. Thus any errors may be most easily detected and overcome by using the target. Moreover, it is advisable to stick as closely as possible to the targets and distances which are authorized in the regular target shooting rules, because sooner or later you may want to enter a target competition even though that is not your object in learning to shoot pistols and revolvers.

In an American target competition there are two types of shooting; outdoor and indoor. The outdoor shooting is done at fifty yards on the Standard American Target which will be described here briefly. This target has a black bull's-eye, eight inches in diameter, with rings both inside and outside of it for counting the score. Indoor shooting is always done at twenty yards and by artificial light. The target for indoor shooting is the same as that used for outdoors except that the rings are reduced in size, the bull's-eye being 2.72 inches in diameter.

The author shooting his 8 inch barrel Harrington & Richardson in 1931 at Bisley, England, where he was winner of the Webley & Scott Pistol match with a perfect score of 100. A perfect score has been made on one previous occasion, which was some years ago, and the author's winning score thus ties the British Empire Record for this ten shot match at 20 yards outdoors.

When the shooter has at last reached the stage of placing himself in front of a target on a safe range in preparation for shooting with actual cartridges, it is preferable at first to load the gun with only one cartridge at a time whether using an automatic, a revolver, or a single-shot pistol. Thus, each time the gun is fired it will be perfectly safe because the only cartridge in it will have gone off and the inexperienced shooter will not have to think about having a loaded gun in his hand. He should use just the same precaution as though the gun were loaded to its full capacity but the chances of accidents will be greatly minimized.

After loading extend the arm toward the target and sight under the bull's-eye in exactly the same way as is done in dry shooting. Each time the sights come in line with the required point at six o'clock, tighten the squeeze on the trigger slowly, increasing the pressure as long as the sights remain in the proper place; but as soon as you swing away from this place do not put any additional pressure on until you bring the gun back in line again. In this way you will tighten up the pressure on the trigger whenever the gun is properly lined up and you will never know just when it is going off, because you only tighten it up a very little bit at a time. If you never tighten up your squeeze except when you are lined up properly, it stands to reason that the gun will never go off except when lined up properly. Also, what is more important, if you never tighten up your squeeze enough at any time to be sure you are going to make the gun go off at that instant, you will never flinch, because you cannot flinch without knowing just when the gun is going off.

In firing this way, always keep the eyes open when the shot goes off and try to observe exactly where the sights are on the target at the moment that the discharge occurs. This, in itself, is a great help against flinching, as the man who flinches closes his eyes at the discharge and has no idea where the muzzle of the gun was pointing.

In the first practice always keep the same point of aim. If the shot strikes high do not aim low, so as to correct it. The first thing to do is to learn to make a good group. Always aim just the same and then you can see how good your group is. If the group is not on the bull's-eye it can be brought there later by adjusting the sights or changing them if they are not adjustable. When you have learned to make a really small group on the target, you have mastered nine-tenths of all the difficult part of shooting.

At first, it is better if the shooter does not see where his shots are going, because in that way any tendency to correct the point of aim in accordance with where the last shot went will be overcome. Simply fire five shots; then go down to the target and see if they made a good group, and strive constantly to improve this group until you get it as nearly perfectly as possible.

After shooting a few shots with actual cartridges, it is well to again try the snapping exercises to see if you can still hold on the bull's-eye and snap the gun without making the sights move when the hammer falls.

Changing the Sights

After having learned to group your shots satisfactorily, the next thing to do is to change your sights so as to bring the group onto the bull's-eye.

Most of the heavy caliber weapons with fixed sights are targeted at the factory, and the sights are made to gauge in such a way that when the average shooter, holding the gun correctly, fires it with a six-o'clock hold the bullet will go in the bull's-eye. Not every gun is actually fired in the factory to see if this is so, but one out of every so many guns is actually fired in the hand without any rest, by an experienced targeter, and gauges are made which will insure the front sight always being of such a height and of such relation to the rear sight that the shots go in the right place.

You hear of many people who say that a gun will not shoot into the bull's-eye with them and they have to change the sights in one way or another, but it is a fact that the longer a man shoots a revolver the more he will find that any time he picks up a Colt or Smith & Wesson revolver and shoots it he will find it is targeted just about correctly.

With target weapons which have adjustable sights, it is easy to experiment with sight changes and with placing your shots on the bull's-eye.

To move the shots on the target move the rear sight in the direction in which you want the shots to go. Smith & Wesson target guns have a rear sight movable for both elevation and windage, whereas the Colt guns have the rear sight movable for windage and the front sight movable for elevation.

The front sight must be moved opposite from the direction you want the shots to move on the target; that is, if you want the shots to go up, you must lower the front sight, and vice versa. You can readily figure out from the length of your barrel and the distance to the target how much you will have to move your sight to make any given correction in inches on the target. For example, if the distance from the rear sight to the front sight is 6 inches or ½ foot, and the distance to the target is 20 yards, which is 60 feet, the shot will move 120 times as far on the target as you move the sight. Moving the sight .001 inch would move your group on the target one-eighth inch.

In chapter 5, under the heading of "Sights," some figures on the various weapons are given to which the reader is referred for details.

It is very helpful in adjusting sights to make a duplicate of the 20-yard target out of celluloid, drawing in the rings with India ink. After shooting a group on the target this celluloid transparent target is laid over the real one and shifted about until it comes as near as possible over the center of the group. Then measuring with a rule both vertically and horizontally from the center of the transparent target to the center of the real one will give you the amount the shot group must be shifted in inches to be centered on the real target.

With guns which do not have adjustable sights, the only way to change the point of grouping is by changing the location of the front sight either by bending it to one side or the other slightly, or by filing it off. If the groups go too low, filing the top of the front sight will raise them. If they go to the right, bending the front sight to the right will shift them to the left, and vice versa. This changing of fixed sights should never be done until you have enough experience in shooting to know that your point of grouping is not going to change.

You will note that I have not explained how to make the sight group go lower. This is, of course, more difficult than filing the sight off to make it go higher, because you must in some way put metal onto the top of the front sight. Sometimes this is done by laying the front sight flat on a hard surface and peening or pounding it with a hammer until it gets higher on account of spreading out from the hammering. This has the disadvantage of making the sight thinner at the same time, and unless you are skilled in using the hammer you are likely to make a messy job of it. A method that is superior to this is to file the front sight down to a fraction of its height and then make a new front sight, which is slotted at the bottom and pinned on over the old front sight.

It may occur to the reader that the most logical way to make the shots go lower would be to file down the rear sight. Unfortunately, this cannot be done on most revolvers, because generally the rear sight is a groove in the frame of the revolver, and the frame cannot be filed down. I have known shooters to attempt to lower the shot group by merely deepening the notch in the rear sight. This is, of course, not effective if the sighting is done in the proper way, by lining up the top of the front sight with the upper line of metal of the rear sight. If, however, the user takes what is called a "fine" sight, where the tip of the bead is just barely visible in the rear sight notch, deepening the rear sight notch will help.

One thing to remember about sighting-in a revolver is that this is a job that you must do for yourself. No one else can satisfactorily do it for you because no two people hold the gun exactly alike and there is bound to be some difference in the way it groups when fired by another marksman whose hold and eyesight differ.

Another thing that you must remember in changing sights is that there is a difference in the way the gun shoots in artificial light and in natural light. Generally a gun sighted-in in a shooting-gallery in artificial light will shoot higher when taken outdoors, though sometimes the reverse is true, depending on how the lighting is arranged in the gallery. Bearing this in mind, you will sight-in any target guns that you intend to use for indoor shooting under the actual conditions that you intend to shoot under, and, of course, if in the future you use the gun outdoors, it is an easy matter with target sights to change back. However, with guns having fixed sights, it is another matter entirely and you must make up your mind how you are going to use the gun before you alter these sights.

In slow-fire matches, it is the practice to have a telescope on the stand near the shooter, and after each shot he will want to look through the telescope to see where the last shot went, and if several shots, for any reason, are going in one direction and not in the bull's-eye he will probably want to change his sights. It should be noted, however, that it is almost fatal to match accuracy to change the sights for each shot, for if anything happens to disturb your aim and make the shot go, for example, to the right and then you change the sights to bring it back again, it will go to the left because the accident that made it go to the right before is not present.

An experienced target shot knows that after getting his sights once adjusted so that the bullets are going into the bull's-eye, he should be very slow indeed to change it. This is especially true of those shots who are at all inclined to be nervous in entering matches, or, in other words, who get what is called the "buck fever." A man like this may shoot for weeks and group into the bull's-eye perfectly, but the first shot or two of the match will be fired under a nervous strain and he may throw his shots one way or the other until he steadies down. If he uses the telescope and changes his sights for every shot he will become hopelessly confused.

The same thing applies to shooting in the wind. When you first go to shoot outdoors in a puffy wind, you will find that it will bother you quite a little, as your gun seems to sway all over the target; but if you will tighten up on the trigger only when your gun swings under the bull's-eye you will find that your scores will be pretty good.

For shooting in a wind, it sometimes helps to face the target more than you normally would, as it prevents the body from swaying so much.

After having learned to shoot satisfactorily with a .22-caliber weapon the next thing to do is to change to larger calibers. It will be found that there is very little difference, and if you do not let the expected heavier recoil make you flinch you will get just as good results with the larger calibers as you did with the .22.

In fact, in target-shooting, the same degree of holding will give a larger score with big calibers than it will with the .22, because the large-caliber hole covers more territory on the target and therefore will frequently cut into a ring of higher count that would not be touched by a .22 whose center was in the same spot.

Rapid Fire

It will be found that after the principles of slow fire have been mastered, as described above, it is not very difficult to increase the speed at which the shots can be let off, at the same time squeezing the trigger only when the sights are lined up with the target.

Really excellent scores with rapid fire require a great deal of practice to get the gun lined up quickly and at the same time squeeze the trigger with sufficient force and not cause the gun to deviate; but the principles are exactly the same as described under slow fire.

The best way to accomplish rapid fire is to cock the gun for each shot and not attempt to use double action, though some skilled shots have made excellent scores with the double-action method. At first it seems hard to cock the gun and shoot it five times in 15 seconds, but with a little practice without cartridges in the gun it is surprising how quickly speed can be acquired.

A great many years ago, when I first entered the Army qualification matches with the old .38 revolver, I found difficulty in shooting five shots in 10 seconds, as was required under the rules. I took a gun to my room and made a small duplicate of the target, the exact corresponding size, and hung it up on the wall across the room and got someone to help me with a stop watch, calling "com-

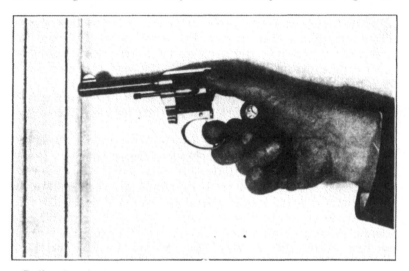

Testing the grip to see if it is firm enough to prevent the gun from slipping when executing rapid fire. This is done by taking the grip that will be used, cocking the revolver, and placing the muzzle against a firm wooden upright, as for example, a door frame, as shown. Then pull the trigger as in firing, and at the same time push forward sharply, so that the pressure of the gun against the door frame tends to displace the grip, the same as the recoil would in actual firing. If the gun does not slip in the hand, the grip is satisfactory. Note the position of the author's middle finger in this photo. It shows a good way to grip a gun with a small handle.

mence firing" and "cease firing." I practiced consistently at this about 15 minutes a day for a period of two weeks and then went into the qualification course and fired my two strings of ten shots in 5 1/5 seconds apiece with no difficulty at all, whereas I could not very well do it in 10 seconds before.

This shows how speed can be acquired; but though I got a good score in that practice and got the qualification of revolver expert, it was not as well done as it might have been, as I made the mistake of getting up too much speed.

In competitions the shooter should take advantage of all time allowed and not shoot his score off in half the time, losing all the rest, because the grouping is bound to be somewhat poorer than it would be if advantage is taken of every second.

There is one thing that the shooter will notice, and that is that shooting five actual shots in 15 seconds is different from merely aiming and snapping the revolver five times in 15 seconds. This is because the recoil is quite an important factor in rapid fire. It slows you up a lot and, moreover, unless you have a good method of holding your revolver, it will cause the gun to slip in your hand,

Testing the grip on the gun to see if it is firm enough to prevent the gun from slipping in the hand when executing rapid fire. This is done by pressing against a door frame or other upright piece of wood to simulate the reaction of the recoil. If the gun does not slip, the grip is satisfactory. In this case the grip did slip. Compare with previous picture showing a better grip being tested the same way.

so that your grip is not the same for the last shots as it is for the first ones of a string.

It is particularly important for a gun that is to be used for rapid fire, either for practical shooting or for competitions, to have the grip so arranged that you are bound to get hold of it the same each time and so that your hand will not slip to a new position when the shock of recoil comes. Building out the grip behind the trigger guard with a little piece of rubber or wood and some tire tape is a wonderful help in preventing this changing of the hold.

Of course, what I have said in regard to both the grip and the cocking of the gun for each shot does not apply in the case of automatic pistols. These guns do their own cocking, and the grip is such that it does not change in your hand the way that of a revolver does. It is naturally much easier to execute rapid fire with an automatic than it is with a revolver. However, with the Army automatic the recoil is a factor that must have serious consideration, for it will throw the arm 20 or 30 degrees off the line of fire if the gun is loosely held, and this, of course, will necessitate the use of valuable time to bring the gun back in line with the target. The most successful military rapid-fire shots straighten the arm out fully and hold the gun very hard against recoil, so that it does not move much from the line of fire.

In order to prevent the grip from changing in rapid fire, it is

One method of holding and cocking a revolver for rapid fire. Note that the little finger is hooked under the bottom of the butt to keep the hand from changing position during the firing of the string. This method of holding is best adapted for small revolvers, and cannot be used on very large guns, or on those which have a butt which is thick and has sharp edges at the bottom.

necessary to hold the gun much more firmly in this class of shooting than in slow fire.

In the U. S. R. A. Matches the time allowed for rapid-fire strings is 15 seconds.

At the beginning of the string the gun is loaded with five cartridges. The competitor stands at the firing-point with the arm loaded, not cocked, and the barrel pointing in a direction not less than 45 degrees from the target and notifies the scorer when he is ready to begin his string. The scorer, stop watch in hand, gives the command "Fire," after which the competitor may cock and aim his weapon and shoot his string. At the expiration of the time limit the scorer announces "Time," and no shot may be fired after this announcement. If any shot is fired after time is called, the shot of highest value will be deducted from the score.

What Constitutes Good Shooting

In the course of an extensive correspondence on shooting, the author has received many letters asking what scores a pistol or revolver shot must make to be considered a good marksman. A very good indication can be obtained from the scores made at Camp Perry each year. In the N.R.A. matches held at that place, the high score in each match receives a gold medal and the next a silver medal and the next eight bronze medals so that the first ten scores are considered as medal scores.

In the last National Matches, which were held in 1931, the medal scores in the single entry matches averaged as follows:

Slow Fire .22 Caliber Pistol Match:
(20 shots at 50 yds., 1 min. per shot)

Winner: C. E. Ward, Los Angeles Police:	187
No. 10: Major J. S. Hatcher:	182
Average Medal Score:	184.9 or 92.4%

Slow Fire Revolver or Automatic Pistol Match:
(20 shots at 50 yds., 1 min. per shot)

Winner: J. J. Engbrecht, Los Angeles Police:	184
No. 10: Clyde J. Sayers, Detroit Police:	177
Average Medal Score:	180.5 or 90.2%

Timed Fire Pistol or Revolver Match:
(4 scores of 5 shots each in 20 seconds per score—Standard American 50 Yd. Target at 25 yards)

Winner: J. J. Engbrecht, Los Angeles Police:	192
No. 10: 1st Lieut. Clyde A. Burchan, U. S. Cavalry:	184
Average Medal Score:	186.9 or 93.4%

Rapid Fire Pistol or Revolver Match:
(4 scores of 5 shots each, in 10 seconds per score—Standard American 50 Yd. Target at 25 yards)

Winner: Sgt. J. B. Jensen, U. S. Cavalry:	188
No. 10: R. J. Nowka, Los Angeles Police:	174
Average Medal Score:	178.5 or 89.2%

In the National Individual Pistol Match of 1931 there were 637 entries. The first 12 received gold medals; the next 24, silver medals; and the next 36, bronze medals. This match is fired with the Government model .45 Automatic Pistol in three stages; 50 yards slow fire, 10 shots at the Standard American target; 25 yards timed fire, two strings of 5 shots in 20 seconds each; 25 yards rapid fire, two strings of 5 shots in 10 seconds each. The target used at 25 yards is the 50 yard Standard American with only the nine and ten rings black.

The average scores received were as follows:

	Slow fire	Timed fire	Rapid fire
The 12 gold medallists	79.7	92.7	89.8
The 24 silver medallists	81.8	89.4	84.1
The 36 bronze medallists	77.0	87.1	81.2
Average of all 72 medallists	78.9	88.8	83.3

The following results of the U.S.R.A. National Championship for 1931 are of interest, as they show not only the scores made by medalists (the first five high men in each classification), but also the type of gun and the make of ammunition used.

MATCH A—REVOLVER—50 SHOTS AT 50 YARDS
STANDARD AMERICAN TARGET, SLOW FIRE

Place	Name	Arm Used	Ammunition	Score	Percentage
Champion	R. G. Pickrell	S&W .38/44	Dominion	470	94.8
2nd	R. C. Bracken	Colt Off. Model 38	U. S. Ctg.	464	92.8
3rd	W. F. Riedell	S&W .38 Spl.	Remington	455	91.0
4th	S. J. Jorgensen	Colt Off. Model 38	Peters	453	90.6
5th	M. H. Barnes	Colt Off. Model 22	Western	453	90.6
Average				459	91.8

MATCH B—PISTOL—50 SHOTS AT 50 YARDS
STANDARD AMERICAN TARGET, SLOW FIRE

Place	Name	Arm Used	Ammunition	Score	Percentage
Champion	E. S. Carpenter	S&W Olympic	Kleanbore	471	94.2
2nd	R. C. Bracken	Har. & Rich.	Peters	468	93.6
3rd	Dr. I. R. Calkins	Har. & Rich.	Western	467	93.4
4th	Cpl. J. E. Young	S&W Olympic	Western	464	92.8
5th	Milford Baker	H&R 7-inch	Remington	462	92.4
Average				466.4	93.3

MATCH G—NOVICE—25 SHOTS AT 50 YARDS
STANDARD AMERICAN TARGET, SLOW FIRE

Place	Name	Arm Used	Ammunition	Score	Percentage
Champion	C. P. Gustin	S&W Olympic	Winchester	232	92.8
2nd	R. J. Dunbar	Har. & Rich.	Kleanbore	232	92.8
3rd	R. S. Furst	Har. & Rich.	Peters	232	92.8
4th	L. K. Roberts	S&W St. Line	Kleanbore	232	92.8
5th	W. C. Schwab	S&W Olympic	U. S. Ctg.	227	90.8
Average				231	92.4

MATCH I—FREE PISTOL—60 SHOTS AT 50 METERS
INTERNATIONAL TARGET, SLOW FIRE

Place	Name	Arm Used	Ammunition	Score	Percentage
Champion	Dr. I. R. Calkins	Har. & Rich.	Western	515	85.8
2nd	L. K. Roberts	S&W St. Line	Western	502	83.6
3rd	Paul Pale	S&W Olympic	Peters	500	83.3
4th	G. M. Upshaw	Tell	Winchester	498	83.0
5th	F. L. From	S&W Olympic	Peters	497	82.8
Average				502.4	83.7

CHAPTER 14

PRACTICAL SHOOTING

T HE real purpose of target shooting with any kind of weapon
is to build up an ability to use the weapon correctly and to
hit actual objects when we shoot at them. Shooting at a white
paper with a black bull's-eye in the middle teaches the proper
method of holding, of aiming, of squeezing the trigger, etc., and
also shows the shooter where his shots go and just what accuracy
can be expected.

Unless we are going to follow target shooting as a sport, to the
exclusion of all other kinds of shooting, the next thing to do after
we have learned to shoot so that we can hit the target every time,
and have acquired a fair degree of accuracy and confidence, is to
learn to use our pistol or revolver for what is known as "Practical
Shooting" as distinguished from target work. Practical shooting
is using the weapon as we would on a hunting or camping trip, or
as we would in a wild country where the object of owning a gun
is utility and not target practice.

In several ways, practical shooting differs very greatly from
slow fire target practice, but learning to shoot accurately at a target
is the foundation of good shooting of any kind. Many practical
users of pistols or revolvers are fond of making fun of target
shooting, and of the advice given on how to learn this branch of
the sport. Such an attitude is well understood by the psychologist.
It is founded in the unconscious jealousy and feeling of inferiority
that the poor shot feels when he sees a well trained marksman
making scores out of his power to equal. Unconsciously he will
try to belittle that accomplishment that he does not possess, so that
he will seem to his audience to be just as important and well
equipped as the good marksman whom he ridicules.

It is very true that practical shooting differs very greatly from
target shooting in several important particulars, and that a target

shot who has never had any experience or training except slow fire at a bull's-eye is apt to give an ordinary account of himself in a gun-fight; but just the same, instruction and practice in accurate target shooting is the foundation of all success in practical shooting as well as in target work.

As a matter of fact, what instruction and practice in slow-fire target-shooting and then in rapid-fire target-shooting does is to drill thoroughly into the marksman's physical make-up an ability to contract the muscles of the hand easily and smoothly, so as to let off a shot without twitching the pistol in one direction or another. The trigger squeeze is only the first foundation of this later acquired smoothness of muscular contraction. Anyone who makes good scores with a pistol or revolver, whether at target-shooting or at practical shooting, does learn in time to do exactly this, and the quickest way to learn it is in the manner outlined in the preceding chapter.

The practical shot who has learned to shoot without any target practice is likely to possess only a very sketchy degree of accuracy. Most likely he will be what is sometimes described as a "trigger snatcher," able to register a large percentage of hits on a man-sized target at ten feet, but likely to make as many misses on the same target at twice the distance.

On the other hand, the target shooter who has graduated to the "practical" stage is likely to be a first-class marksman at either slow or rapid fire target shooting, or at standing or moving objects of any kind. I know several excellent target shots who can toss a half a brick into the air and hit it once, or even twice with a revolver before it hits the ground. Moreover, these men, even the best and fastest of them, use the sights for such shots.

Again, the "practical shot" who has no knowledge or experience of accurate target shooting with a revolver may find himself at the mercy of a good target shot, regardless of what that target shot knows or does not know about practical shooting. Thus some years ago on the Mexican border a tough two-gun man who had successfully defied the local authorities was arrested by an army captain, an acquaintance of the writer, who had acquired a reputation in that vicinity for long range marksmanship with a revolver. This capture was accomplished with amazing simplicity and ease. The "bad man" was utterly reckless, and was a quick and deadly shot with his revolvers at ranges under ten yards, but was unable to score a hit on a man with certainty at ranges beyond that distance. Fifty yards away the officer drew his revolver and ordered the other to halt, take out his guns, drop them on the ground, and walk away from them. The "tough hombre" meekly did exactly as he was ordered, for he knew that the officer could hit him at 50 yards or at 75. He knew that if he started to run, he would be a dead man, so that there was nothing for him to do but drop the guns as ordered, for even though he had two of them, he was fully aware that he could not shoot accurately enough to come anywhere near hitting the officer that far away.

There are several ways in which practical shooting differs from bull's-eye shooting. One is the difference in aiming, and in the way the sights show up. Another is the fact that practical shooting frequently requires the exercise of great speed. This speed may be necessary for hitting an object quickly when the gun is already in the hand, or, what is even more difficult, it may involve getting the gun quickly into action from the holster or pocket, and then hitting the object. Again, in practical shooting, situations frequently arise where the sights cannot be seen, and the shooting must be done by using the sense of direction only, as in pointing the finger at an object.

As for the question of sighting, the user of any gun will quickly find that aiming at an object in the woods or on the ground is very different from aiming at a black bull's-eye on a white paper, where the sights are clearly outlined against the white background. The sights that are best adapted to shooting at targets are the hardest to see and the poorest for use in the woods. On the target range, the sights are seen against the white paper, and they should be black, without any bright or shiny spots on them. In the woods, such sights often cannot be seen at all, and if they are seen, it cannot be told whether or not the front sight is in the middle of the rear sight notch. Therefore, for use in the woods, the sights should have the visibility increased in some way, which is usually accomplished by the use of a gold or ivory bead on the front sight. Sometimes also, the rear sight notch is outlined with white lines inlaid in the metal by making a groove around the notch and filling it with white enamel. Some of the King rear sights are made this way, and are excellent when used in connection with the King Ramp—Red Bead—Reflector sight, which has a red bead front sight with a chromium mirror let into the ramp under it, to reflect the light of the sky onto the bead.

In target shooting, it is common to use a wide rectangular front sight, with which aim is taken just under the bull's-eye. This works beautifully when the bull's-eye is always of the same size, and outlined clearly in black against the white paper; but it does not work so well when the aim may be at any one of a large variety of different objects with different colors, sizes, shapes, and backgrounds; and when the object may be moving or a wind may be blowing. In such a case, what is wanted is a small bead front sight, used with a U rear notch. Aim is taken directly at the point which it is desired to hit, with the bead held high for longer ranges, to compensate for the drop of the bullet. If the object is moving, the aim is shifted slightly to the direction of motion; or if the wind is blowing, the aim is shifted against the wind. In all these cases, it is better to have the gun sighted so that the bullet will hit when the sighting is right on the object at medium ranges. Then at longer or shorter ranges, the bead can be elevated or lowered in the notch, an amount for each range that will quickly be learned by experience. Sighting right on is better than sighting under when an allowance for motion or windage may have to be made by holding off. It is hard to hold off a certain amount when holding under at the same time.

As for the matter of speed, it is quite natural that in shooting at small game, etc., there would be more need for quickness in drawing the gun and in getting off the shot than there is in the case of a target, which will not move off at once, but will stay in position indefinitely. The question of speed shooting will be taken up in detail presently.

How To Learn Practical Shooting

After a satisfactory degree of proficiency in accurate shooting has been learned by target practice, and the shooter has confidence in the accuracy of his weapon, and in his own ability to use it so to place his shot close to the place desired, he is ready to learn practical shooting.

For this purpose a .22 caliber gun is best. The recoil and noise are so slight that there is little or no tendency for them to hide the errors of holding that may occur, as is the case with the .38 or the .45. Moreover, there is little tendency to flinch where the disturbance that accompanies the pulling of the trigger is reduced to a minimum. But perhaps the greatest advantage of all is the reasonable cost of the ammunition. With the inexpensive .22 caliber cartridge, an almost unlimited amount of shooting can be done at very little expense, whereas there are very few marksmen who can afford to blaze away at random with the .38 or .45 caliber cartridges at a cost of several cents a shot. And after all, practice is what counts.

In the woods, on the mountains, on the beach, or around the fields of the farm there are always hundreds of objects which make safe and interesting targets. Among the best targets are tin cans, bottles, floating objects, etc.; in short, anything that gives a visible reaction to a hit.

If the man who desires to become a proficient practical pistol shot will simply carry a .22 caliber revolver or pistol with him on his trips into the outdoors, and will take advantage of the opportunities that occur to shoot at safe and interesting targets as they present themselves, he will not only have a tremendous amount of exhilarating sport, but he will also rapidly become a good practical marksman.

Shooting on the water is excellent, for the splash of the bullets tells where the shot has gone, and the misses as well as the hits thus become instructive and interesting. It is practical to stand on a beach or a pier, and shoot at different objects in the water or on the beach which are at various distances from the gun. This teaches the estimation of ranges as well as the art of shooting. Moreover, it teaches how much the shooter must hold over for the longer ranges. Objects from ten to two hundred yards away may be used.

The publisher of this book, T. G. Samworth, is a formidable pistol shot. Recently I visited him in North Carolina, and together we stood on the end of a private pier and practiced shooting as above described. The location was far enough from any other habitation so that there was no danger in firing a .22 in any direction; and the irregular shore line, with objects jutting into the water at various distances, together with stakes driven into the water to mark sand bars, etc., gave us an abundance of targets. In addition, there were several floating objects in sight.

Together we stood on the end of the pier and fired in turn, emptying our .22 caliber revolvers at the various likely targets. The rule was that the shooter could choose any object he desired, but it must always be at a considerable angle from the last target, and at a different distance. This makes a sort of competition of it. Shooting this way, at objects up to 150 yards away, there will be many misses; but the relative ability of the rival marksmen in placing their shots will soon be apparent.

On a high bluff overlooking a wide body of water, with the wind blowing away from shore, there is opportunity for friendly rivalry and good practice. Tin cans, bottles, or old burnt out light bulbs make good targets. One such object is thrown into the water, and as it floats on the surface and is carried out from the shore by the wind, the marksmen fire at it in turn. Quite often, even with good marksmen, there is danger of having such an object get clear away; for as it is blown away from the shore by the wind, each shot is at a greater range, and is therefore harder than the last. It is very useful to have a .22 rifle near by to use when the target gets beyond pistol range.

Another splendid and most practical method of accumulating a combination of both speed and accuracy in hand-gun shooting is a procedure I have seen and tried, aptly called by its originator "Battle Practice." All that one needs for this game is a safe place to shoot and a supply of readily improvized targets. Small empty tin cans make the best marks, but blocks of wood will do also. Bottles are also interesting, but have the double disadvantage of being available for use but once and of littering the place with broken glass.

First, erect some sort of a rail or plank on two supports, so that it forms a shelf about twelve feet long and about four feet above the ground. Then place on it a row of the tin cans at intervals of a foot or so apart; if you are using revolvers six cans will be enough but if automatics are in use even ten or eleven targets may be used; with a pair of skilled shots a target for each cartridge in the gun will prove none to many in the end. The targets must be arranged so they will readily fall from the shelf when hit.

The procedure is for two shooters to engage, one against the other with both contestants standing side by side and about 15 yards from the targets. When the word is given each shooter commences firing at will, both firing at the same can, the one on the left. As soon as it is hit, it will fall off, and then both contestants shift to the can next in line. Under no circumstances must either contestant "jump ahead" a can or so, which a slow shot may be tempted to do when he finds he is outclassed. The object is for one shot to knock down each and every can in the line before his opponent can hit it. As soon as one can is down, each shooter turns his attention to the next one and no shooting shall be done at any others until the can on the left of the line is down. This practice is a splendid way to teach speed of fire with accuracy. In effect both shots are firing.against but not directly at each other and it is a most practical method to learn to shoot rapidly. At times, particularly with a pair of equally matched shots, it will be difficult to keep an accurate score, but the object of the game is more instructive than competitive and it is one of the most appealing and interesting forms of practical shooting which has come to my attention.

This game will improve the combined speed and accuracy of your pistol shooting more quickly than anything else that I know of. As one's skill improves it is merely necessary to step back a few yards further from the targets. Also, it is possible to use this same general scheme of shooting with other forms of practice; for instance a couple of "quick-draw" enthusiasts can start off with their guns in the holsters and draw and fire shot for shot at the marks. In case this is tried I would advise extreme caution at first and until great skill has been attained by both contestants, as one shooter might accidentally wound the other through having his gun go off in the act of being drawn.

Speed Work

The type of shooting described above will noticeably increase the speed with which the pistol or revolver is handled. Further increases in speed will result from shooting rapidly at moving objects, such as a block of wood floating downstream in a swift current, or a swinging target made by suspending a weight by a piece of string.

A type of shooting requiring speed and a knack of knowing just how to aim and when to pull the trigger is the shooting at objects thrown into the air. This is made harder when the object is thrown with the gun hand, and the gun is then removed from the holster and used to hit the object. If two or more objects are thrown at the same time, even greater speed is required.

Again, speed work is sometimes done at plain targets, the object being to see how quickly the gun can be drawn and the six shots be delivered onto a given area of the target.

When a really excellent super speed shot reaches for the gun in the holster, his first finger goes into the trigger guard, his thumb on the hammer, and the other three fingers surround the grip. As the gun comes away from the holster, he cocks it, and extends it in the quickest direction toward the object to be shot at, and as the gun lines up, he contracts the hand all over, which causes the trigger to be pulled without jerking the gun one way or the other or disturbing the aim.

Much practice in this with the pistol unloaded is of great value in acquiring speed of draw and let-off, but a loaded gun will always be found to be slower than an empty one. This is due to the psychological effect of the greater care necessary with the loaded gun.

To give an idea of just what speed can be accomplished after long and arduous practice, the following figures are given. These are from the experience of Mr. Ed. McGivern, of Lewistown, Montana, who is undoubtedly one of the fastest pistol shots in the world.

To draw from the holster and fire one shot, making a sure hit on a man target at 10 yards, ¼ to 3/5 second.

To draw from the holster and fire five shots with sure hits from double action revolver, 1¼ seconds.

Same with the single action gun, with slip hammer, using two hands, 1-3/5 to 1-4/5 seconds.

Same with single action gun, "fanning" the hammer, using two hands, from 1-3/5 to 2 seconds.

Good groups of five shots with double action revolver without the draw, using one hand, 3/5 to 9/10 second.

Good six shot groups, double action, using one hand, 4/5 to 1 second, giving groups not larger than a man's hand.

Shooting 5 targets, (clay pigeons) tossed into the air by two throwers at approximately the same time, using double action revolver, 1-4/5 to 2-4/5 seconds.

Shooting a tin can tossed into the air, 5 shots and 5 hits, with double action revolver, 1-3/5 seconds.

Throwing a target into the air with right hand, then drawing the gun with the same hand and breaking target, from 3/5 second to 1 second.

Mr. McGivern finds that getting off the first shot averages about the same time from either a single action or a double action revolver; but that the remaining shots cannot be delivered nearly as fast with the single action. Moreover, the double action guns are much more durable and reliable. Therefore he uses the double action guns, *and shoots them double action* in his stunts. Moreover, he uses the sights. His guns are all fitted with gold bead front sights, and he says "I'm often asked if I really do use, and really do see, the gold bead front sight when shooting aerial targets in a hurry. Yes, I certainly do! I've grown used to having them on my guns. I need them for my kind of shooting. And I use them! Just the instant one of the front sights is injured in any way, or changed at all, I notice it. Revolvers or pistols with the sights filed off or otherwise destroyed, are good for just one thing, and that is killing or maiming men at very short range, which was exactly the purpose for which they were used if and when they were used."

Instinctive Pointing

While I agree fully with the ideas of Mr. McGivern about the necessity of sights, I consider it important for the practical pistol shot to know how to get fairly good results without using the sights at all, but rather, pointing the gun entirely by instinct, as the finger is pointed in indicating an object. This is really very important, because any shooting that may be done at night will have to be this kind. Also pistol-shooting on the battle field or in holdups is more likely to be at night than at any other time.

You will find that if you will suddenly extend your arm and point your finger at any object near you, the finger is pointing pretty closely in the direction of the object in question. In the same way a pistol or revolver can be pointed without looking at the sights. One thing that makes it hard, however, is the fact that pistols and revolvers are of so many different shapes and that most of them do not point in the same direction that the finger would without considerable practice.

The Remington Model 51 automatic pistol was carefully designed after months of study, with the object of having it point just where the finger would point if it were not on the trigger. Many other pocket automatics point in the same way, and the Colt Woodsman and the Luger are among the best in this respect. The .45 Government Model Automatic also closely approaches this ideal, especially with the improved mainspring housing adopted about ten years ago.

While revolvers do not point in line with the first finger, nevertheless, if you use one type of revolver and stick to it, you can easily learn to point the barrel accurately without using the sights.

A very good way, indeed, to practice instinctive pointing is to fix the gaze on some object, and then close the eyes and point the gun at this object with the eyes closed. Open the eyes and see how near you are pointing to it.

Another way is to point into the mirror. Standing about 10 feet from a mirror, point the pistol suddenly at your own eyes and by looking at the reflection you will see whether or not it is actually aimed right. If so, you will be looking exactly into the muzzle.

In this pointing practice, it is best to draw the pistol from the pocket or a holster, extending it directly toward the target and cocking the revolver at the same time it is drawn.

After practice has taught you to line the gun up accurately on objects in this manner, the next thing is to practice snapping as you line up the gun, so as to preserve the knack, which has already been learned, of just contracting the hand without any twitch that will throw the gun off.

The next step is to test your ability by actual firing without looking at the sights. If you have a place where you can shoot into the water there is nothing better, as it shows you where your shots are going. A tin can or bottle thrown in the water and blown rapidly away from the shore by the wind makes a first-class object to practice on; but in this kind of practice be sure you are shooting in a safe direction, because bullets may glance from the water and go a considerable distance.

A number of years ago, when living in Florida, I used to carry a .22-caliber revolver in a holster at all times, and as I was in a rather wild part of the country, I could always shoot whenever I wanted to without danger of hitting anyone. The use of the .22-caliber cartridge was adopted because it was the only way to keep the expense down to a reasonable amount and still be able to use the number of cartridges it seemed necessary and desirable to use. In going through the woods anything that offered any kind of target was usually shot at, especially white mushrooms and toadstools, tin cans or bottles.

Another practice that I indulged in with this .22 was shooting at these same white objects at night. Along the beach white shells on the sand make a fine target for this kind of work, and a splash of the sand will generally show where you have hit; but it is utterly impossible to see the sights even in the moonlight.

Such practice as this, especially if you will stick to one particular gun, will rapidly train the subconscious mind so that the hand will always hold and point the gun so as to send the bullet into the right place.

It is surprising how soon you get so that you can simply extend the gun toward the object in question, at the same time smoothly contracting all the muscles that do the trigger pulling, and strike just about the mark.

We have mentioned several times, both in this chapter and elsewhere, that the best way to aim is to extend the revolver straight out at the object you are going to shoot, and not swing it from the shoulder in the old western style. This gesture had a reason in those early western days and was necessary. The reason was that the muzzle-loading or cap-and-ball revolvers were used, and when a cap was exploded it split in fragments which were liable to get into the revolver mechanism and clog the works. Swinging the gun with the muzzle vertical when cocking allowed these pieces to fall off of the nipple and drop to the ground.

Hip-Shooting

Another form of instinctive pointing embraces what is known as "Hip-shooting." This is simply the firing of the gun from the level of the hips, without ever raising it to the level of the eyes. The old .45 Colt Single Action has the barrel set at such an angle to the grip that when held with the hand on the hip the barrel naturally points straight forward. For very close range work deadly shooting could be done in this way with that weapon. It was thus best adapted for the type of shooting sometimes practiced in the old western days—that of shooting through the bottom of the holster.

Hip-shooting is spectacular and interesting; but I do not consider it to be of much practical value. Much closer pointing can be done, and the shot fired just as quickly, by extending the gun toward the target, as above mentioned. Try pointing the finger at some object, holding it at the hip, and you will find it is not as easy as holding it off. You are likely to deviate from the direction intended. But a considerable amount of proficiency can be obtained in hip-shooting if you only practice it.

Recently an especially effective method of hip-shooting has been taught to the police of San Francisco and other western cities by Capt. W. H. Sweet, U. S. Army.

In Capt. Sweet's system, the gun is worn on the left side, in either a belt or a shoulder holster. It is drawn by the right hand and grasped by the right hand in the usual manner; but instead of being extended in the usual manner, it is held close against the body at the waist, pointing directly to the left. At the same time the left hand grasps the frame of the gun, with the thumb on top, over the cylinder, and the first two fingers of the left hand on the bottom, the first finger just forward of the trigger guard, and the second finger under the guard. The left hand thus holds the gun firmly, and steadies it against the body. The gun itself does not touch the body, but both hands holding it do.

As the gun is brought into action, the body is turned so that the left side is directly toward the target, thus bringing the muzzle of the gun into that direction, and also presenting a smaller target toward the adversary. The shooter does not look at the gun at all, but looks at the target, and when things seem to be lined up about right, he pulls the trigger.

Lots of practice is what really counts in acquiring ability in hip-shooting. When the Model 1917 revolver was first adopted samples of these weapons were tested to destruction by the Government under the writer's supervision. These guns stood up for five or six thousand rounds. In one of these guns I fired nearly all of the 5,000 rounds of the test personally, shooting from the hip into a bank of sand at targets, cartons, etc., and soon learned to make a high percentage of hits.

Another thing learned in this test, which is only mentioned here as a matter of interest and not because it has any utility, is the fastest way to discharge six cartridges in a revolver. It can be done in a fraction of a second, and so fast that it will mystify people greatly if you do it without letting them see how it is done, because it almost sounds like only one explosion. It is done by taking the revolver in the left hand and placing the right forefinger on the trigger, thus using both hands. Pushing the hands together works the double action and makes the cartridge go off and at the same time the spring of the trigger will move the gun to its former position, and also push the hands apart. This motion can be repeated with great rapidity; try it with an empty gun some time.

Never try hip-shooting with the .45 Automatic. It will eject the empty cartridges straight into your face and may inflict serious injury.

Long Range Shooting

The limit of effective revolver range is usually considered to be about 75 yards; but this is not because the gun will not carry farther. It is because of the difficulties of aiming a one-hand gun, with its short sight radius, so as to hit an object at the longer ranges. The bullet from a revolver travels comparatively slowly, and therefore the trajectory is high; that is, the bullet drops considerably except at very short ranges. Revolver bullets will carry up to 1,000 yards and over with the heavy calibers, and at these ranges are capable of killing. At 50 yards the average revolver is capable of grouping its shots in a six-inch circle or less, and at 100 yards you could hit an object the size of a beer keg, provided you could hold steadily enough. At 300 yards, you can still put all of your shots, with the ordinary large caliber revolver, onto an object about the size of a barn door.

Recently, the capacity of the revolver for long range work has been considerably increased by the introduction of high velocity loads in the .38 caliber. The regular .45 Colt drops 131 inches in going 200 yards, and the .38 Special drops 108 inches; but the new .38/44 drops only 69 inches at the same range, and the sighting of the gun compensates for about 25 inches of this drop, so that by holding about four feet over the target at 200 yards with this gun we should be able to get a hit. By steadying the gun when shooting, we should be able to get a group not much over three feet wide. For all long-range shots it is advisable to rest the revolver in some way in aiming. One way is to shoot with both hands by grasping the revolver in the right hand and taking hold of the wrist with the left hand, so as to steady the arm as much as possible. Another way is to lie down flat and rest both elbows on the ground, and hold the gun with both hands. Still another way is to use any solid object for a rest, and resting the wrist or hand on the object. In using a rest to steady a revolver, never rest the barrel or frame of the gun on the object, as this will give a different kind of recoil, and therefore the grouping will not be the same as when shooting offhand. In shooting at an object over about 75 yards away, you must allow for the drop of the bullet by aiming above the object, as revolvers are always sighted for short ranges, not over 50 yards. The amount of this allowance for drop varies with the velocity of the bullet and its wind resistance. A table of drop for the various calibers at different ranges is given in Chapter 9.

CHAPTER 15

HINTS ON USING HAND ARMS FOR DEFENSE

THERE is one vital necessity in the everyday life of the average citizen that is filled by a revolver, and can hardly be filled in any other way. This is the need for an arm of defense. This is the real reason for the existence of the revolver or pistol today.

Some of the circumstances under which it may be vital to have one of these arms on hand are in the case of families living in detached houses in the country, where the women folk are likely to be left alone when the men are away on business or in the fields. What man would want to go away and leave his family with no means of protection against the ordinary tramp or marauder who otherwise could work his will unmolested?

Efforts to Disarm the Citizen and Their Effect

There are a number of individuals who at the present time are devoting a world of energy to an attempt to regulate the pistol or revolver out of existence by means of drastic laws forbidding the sale or possession of such weapons. They argue that the regularly organized police departments are sufficient protection, and that anyway, the citizen, if held up, should not resist, as some one might get hurt. The efforts of these misguided and pusillanimous individuals have resulted in making holdup, robbery, attacks on couples in parked cars, etc., safe and easy. The criminal knows that he has little reason to expect resistance from his victims in cities and states where there are drastic firearms laws. Such states and cities have accordingly become the happy hunting grounds for criminals of all kinds.

The theory that the police will always be available for protection in such cases is so ridiculous as scarcely to deserve notice. Even in a city, there are hundreds of times and places where no policeman is on hand; and in rural districts, the holdup man's chance of encountering the forces of the law are nil. In such cases the possession of a revolver and the knowledge of how to use it are the only safeguards of the law-abiding citizen.

For example, I knew of a case in the outskirts of a small southern town where everybody was away from home except a young woman about 18 years of age. She happened to glance out of the window and saw two colored men stealing peaches off of the trees

The Smith & Wesson .32 Hand Ejector. This excellent little revolver, chambered for the .32 S. & W. Long cartridge is a duplicate in design of the large Military Models. The round butt is a most desirable feature, as it makes the revolver less bulky to carry, and moreover, is a more comfortable handle to use. The .32 H. E. is especially desirable as a self-defense gun for use by women.

in her garden. She went out and told them to go away, but they merely laughed at her and continued to pick peaches. It just happened that this young woman was a crack shot with a revolver. She disappeared into the house and a moment later she stepped out of the door armed with a .38 Smith & Wesson Military and dropped a shot through the bucket that one of the colored men was carrying. The pair dropped the buckets and stood not upon the order of their going. It was rumored that a couple of colored men in that vicinity were several shades lighter in complexion than they were before.

Another and more common incident will be quoted. On the outskirts of a city a woman of my acquaintance called up the police department late one night and complained that a man was trying to get into the house and asked for assistance at once.

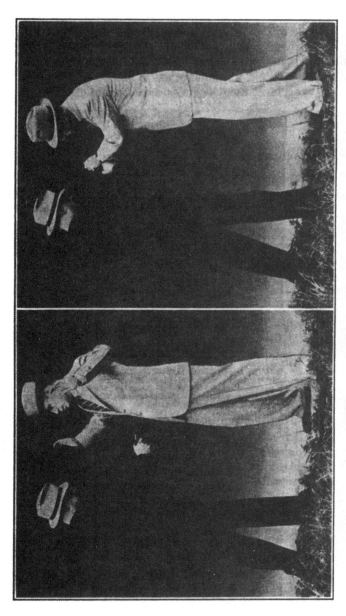

FOILING AN ATTEMPTED HOLDUP. SERIES A. BANDIT IN FRONT OF INTENDED VICTIM, WITH GUN POINTING SLIGHTLY TO THE RIGHT OF CENTER OF THE VICTIM'S BODY.

Left: Position 1. The bandit points the revolver at the intended victim, who notes that it is pointing (slightly to the right of the center of his body, and starts to raise his hands as commanded.

Right: The intended victim, noting that the muzzle of the gun is pointed slightly to the right of the centerline of the body, drops his left hand quickly onto the gun, pushing it to the right before it can be discharged. At the same time he turns the body slightly to the left, so that if the bandit succeeds in discharging the gun the bullet will pass to the right of his body. As he drops his hand on the gun and pushes it to one side, he grasps the barrel, and then places the other hand under the butt as shown.

These and the other pictures in this series were posed by Lieut. H. Laurence Gau, Ordnance Reserve, and the author. Lieut. Gau, seen holding the gun, is Pistol Instructor of the Maryland State Police.

SERIES A, NO. 3. FOILING AN ATTEMPTED HOLDUP, POSITIONS NO. 3 AND 4.

Left: With the right hand under the butt of the gun, as shown in position No. 2, hold the bandit's hand firmly onto the butt of the pistol, and swing the muzzle vigorously upward and to the left. This will put a painful strain on the bandit's wrist and throw him on the back of his head, and will leave the gun in the possession of the intended victim.

Right: As the bandit is being thrown, as described in No. 3, he may be further disabled by striking him with the knee as shown, if opportunity offers.

She was informed that they were sorry but her house was outside the city limits and they could not send a policeman there as it would be off his beat. Fortunately, she had a pistol and was able to frighten the intruder away.

What would either one of these women have done without a revolver in the house? Yet there are people who are today agitating the passing of laws to prevent anyone from having a pistol or revolver for any purpose.

Another place where it is desirable to have a means of defense is in an automobile. I knew a man whose car ran out of gasoline on a wild and lonely road several miles outside of a large city on a bitter cold night. He had to leave the car there and walk about a mile for gasoline, and his wife, who was in the car with him, had the alternative of either sitting in the car by herself or walking with him in the snow and bitter cold. This man happened to have a .45 Automatic with him, which he placed in his wife's hand and said, "If anyone bothers you, shoot first and ask questions afterwards." Yet the anti-firearms agitators would have left that woman perfectly defenseless on a wild and lonely road.

A revolver or pistol is a necessity for storekeepers, paymasters, bankers, jewelers, etc.

The agitators who have been working on this anti-firearm legislation have succeeded in having drastic laws passed in several States forbidding the possession of hand firearms of any kind, except by officers of the law or members of military organizations. Any one of these States is a Mecca for crooks and thugs of all kinds, because the law practically assures them that they will be able to ply their trade of holdups without the slightest danger of being shot. The crook, of course, cares nothing for laws against having firearms, and he knows that the law-abiding citizen will obey the law; therefore he is safe.

A man starting out on a career as a holdup artist always examines carefully the laws of all different States and goes to the one where his trade will be the safest, and that is the State which has the anti-firearms laws, which will assure the thug that he will find his victim unarmed, and therefore he will be in no danger of being either resisted or shot.

One of the most drastic anti-firearms laws is on the statute books of Illinois, and we have all heard of the Herrin murders, which recur with startling regularity, and of the activity of the famous Chicago bandit gangs. These revolver laws, of course, simply play into the hands of the thugs and the lawless element.

One of the most notorious of these laws is the Sullivan law of New York State. This law forbids the owning of a revolver or pistol without a permit. Of course, it can not bother the crook who has only to go on a short trip out of the State and get his gun whenever he wants it. Revolvers are cheap, and he will not be caught with it on him after a crime. The professional murderer, who is out to "bump off" a selected victim, ties his revolver onto the end of a string, steps up to his victim and shoots him, gives the revolver a couple of whirls on the end of the string and lets go. The revolver flies over the nearest row of houses and lands in some back lot, like a stone thrown from a sling. The crook sticks his hands in his pockets and goes merrily on his way. If arrested he is deeply surprised and hurt, and of course no evidence is found on him.

The following examples will show some of the practical effects of this law: An acquaintance from New York related that a small storekeeper in Brooklyn was robbed several times in succession; so finally he decided to sit up all night and wait for the robber. He got a pistol and sat in his store waiting. In the small hours of the night he made the rounds to his front door, and a police officer on the beat, who was a friend, saw him inside and knocked on the door. He let the officer in and passed a few words with him, mentioning the fact that he was trying to catch the man who had been robbing his store. The officer asked how he was going to catch him if he came, and the storekeeper replied that he had a gun. The officer at once placed him under arrest and rushed him off to the station house for violation of the Sullivan law.

It is said that a widow looking through her husband's effects after his death found an old revolver. She knew about the Sullivan law and did not want to be a lawbreaker, so she telephoned the police and told them about it and asked them if they would come and get it. She was arrested for having a gun in her possession.

The following Associated Press dispatch from New York, under date of September 28, 1926, speaks for itself:

"Aurelio Valdes, a painter, examined some second-hand furniture which he had bought for his home and discovered a revolver in a table drawer. Being a law-abiding man, he took the weapon to police headquarters, where he explained the circumstances and said he wanted to turn in the pistol. The police promptly placed him under arrest for violation of the Sullivan law, and on that charge Valdes was arraigned in night court. Again the circumstances were explained, and Detective Schmuckler corroborated Valdes' account of his visit to headquarters. Magistrate Glatzmayer said he had no recourse but to hold Valdes for trial in Special Sessions, but that he would fix bail at the lowest possible amount—$25. Mrs. Valdes said that even that sum could not be obtained. They had a child, she said, and she had to work, as well as her husband, to keep the family together. Bail was given finally by Magistrate Glatzmayer himself."

In spite of the drastic manner in which law-abiding citizens are disarmed in New York State, no one who has his feet on the ground and knows what the conditions around a large city are would expect the crook to be disarmed, but he would be rather surprised to know that prisoners in Tombs Prison, under the direct personal care of all the guards, would be able to have firearms, yet, about 3 p.m. on November 3, 1926, three desperate criminals in this prison, while being taken to the infirmary on their pleas of illness, drew automatic pistols and shot their way to the prison yard and killed the warden and one keeper before being finally cornered. They were finally subdued after a battle lasting nearly an hour, in which more than 200 policemen were engaged, who used machine guns, rifles, pistols and gas bombs from the wall of the prison and windows of skyscrapers. If an anti-firearms law will not disarm the prisoner in a cell, who has been searched before he was placed there, how can it be expected to disarm the thug who roams at large?

We have mentioned some of the abuses that the anti-firearms law has led to in New York State. In some other States it has been said to have led to even greater abuses. It has led to the corruption of officials and the institution of wholesale graft, according to capable writers who investigated conditions in these places.

For example, one such law forbade the possession of hand firearms except on the issuance of a license, revokable at will, and issued by a justice of the peace on the payment of a fee, which went to the justice himself. There are justices and justices. Most of them are, of course, absolutely straight, but money talks, and it was found that under this system many dangerous crooks who were arrested had perfectly valid licenses for having guns in their possession. It is said that conditions became so bad that the law was revised, doing away with the licenses, and forbidding all hand firearms except in the hands of members of military organizations, police officials and certain deputies.

Of course, it is an extremely easy matter for any enterprising crook to get a revolver or pistol when there are antirevolver laws in one State and the next one allows free traffic in these articles. The advocates of laws restricting the sa e of revolvers and pistols suppose that by making a uniform law for all States, prohibiting the manufacture or sale of hand firearms, it will stop anyone from obtaining them. This is not a well-founded supposition at all, because it is a very easy matter in a few minutes to cut off a rifle to a pistol-barrel length and whittle off the stock in such a manner as to make a pistol out of it. The smuggling of firearms and the bootlegging of pistols would grow to be a very profitable business, and there would be plenty of them to be had if only the price were forthcoming.

Even if anti-firearms laws were enacted which succeeded in suppressing all firearms, there would sti 1 be plenty of easy ways to commit suicide or murder. When a criminal is bent on committing a homicide he merely chooses the easiest way to do it. If that method is not at hand, he chooses another method.

At the present time most suicides are by means of illuminating gas, and if no pistols were to be had, it would still be possible for everyone to get hold of knives, hatchets, or other deadly weapons, and these have the advantage over the pistol or revolver for the perpetration of a crime, in that they do not make any noise and thus raise an alarm. If all pistols and revolvers were suppressed, murders and suicides would not decrease, but there would be a large increase in the number of knife murders and "cuttings."

Already it is noticeable that the common ten-cent store ice-pick is becoming popular as a stiletto. Its cost is practically nothing, it can be purchased or carried by anyone with no danger of legal difficulties and without interference from anti-firearms laws; it deals death silently and swiftly, and moreover it cannot be identified by rifling marks, etc., and its cwnership proved, as can so often be done with firearms. And even if ice-picks were abolished, anyone could make a similar deadly weapon in five minutes by sharpening a piece of wire.

In spite of all that has been said, it must not be concluded that all legislation regulating the sale, use and possession of firearms is undesirable. On the contrary, I do not see how anyone can dispute the necessity for safe and sane laws that will disarm the

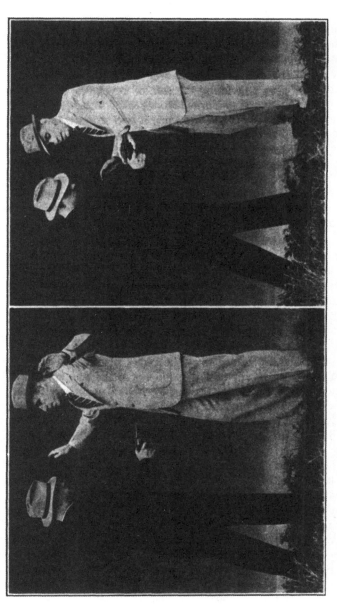

FOILING AN ATTEMPTED HOLDUP. SERIES B, WITH BANDIT IN FRONT, AND GUN POINTED SLIGHTLY TO LEFT OF CENTER OF VICTIM'S BODY.

Left: Series B. Position No. 1. Posed by Lieutenant H. Laurence Gau, Ordnance Reserve, (holding the gun) and the author. Bandit commands Hands up! and points revolver at victim, muzzle directed slightly to left of center of body. Victim starts to raise his hands.

Right: Intended victim suddenly drops left hand onto gun, pushing it to the left, and at the same time turning the body slightly to the right, so that if gun is discharged, bullet will pass by the left side. As hand is dropped onto the gun, the cylinder is grasped firmly, so that the trigger cannot be pulled unless gun is already cocked. Thumb and finger of bandit's hand grasping revolver are also grasped at the same time.

FOILING AN ATTEMPTED HOLDUP, SERIES B, POSITIONS NO. 3 AND 4.

Left: The right hand, instantly following up the action of the left as shown in Position No. 2, is placed under the butt of the gun, clasping the bandit's hand firmly in position on the handle of the gun. Then with the right hand under the butt as a pivot, and using the barrel in the left hand as a lever, the muzzle is swung sharply to the left, so that the muzzle points away at all times, and a bullet would pass harmlessly if the gun should be discharged. At the same time the bandit should be struck a disabling blow with an upward motion of the knee, as shown.

Right: As the muzzle of the gun is swung upward and to the left as described in the last position, the bandit's finger in the trigger guard will be broken, and he will be thrown to the ground by the pressure exerted on his finger by using the barrel of the pistol as a lever. The weapon will remain in the possession of the intended victim.

criminal and at the same time allow law-abiding citizens to have arms for defense.

Crimes of violence can be greatly discouraged by taking all possible steps to disarm the criminal element; but if at the same time the law-abiding element is deprived of means of defense the good effects of the law will be more than nullified, and crime will become comparatively safe, as it now is in New York and Chicago under the present laws of New York and Illinois.

The subject of legislation which will accomplish the desired result has been carefully considered by the United States Revolver Association. Some very brilliant legal talent has been obtained on the committee to consider that subject. The conclusions are that any law, to be effective, must be uniform in all States, so that it can not be evaded merely by stepping across the border.

Desirable legislation would allow anyone who does not have a criminal record to possess pistols or revolvers without restriction, but would make it a crime for anyone who has once been a criminal to possess one. Moreover, it would provide severe mandatory penalties for crimes of violence committed with firearms, and would make the mere possession of a firearm during the commission of any crime greatly increase the penalty that would otherwise be inflicted.

It would allow anyone with a clear record to purchase firearms, but would require an application to purchase to be filed at least 24 hours before the gun could be delivered by the dealer. This would prevent many of the impulsive suicides or other acts of violence that may otherwise be committed under the compulsion of emotional stress. The sale of all firearms, with the name and address of the purchaser should be recorded.

In view of all the various firearms laws now on the books of the various States, it is necessary for the householder, autoist, storekeeper, or paymaster who contemplates using a pistol for self-defense to become acquainted with the laws of his own community and obtain a permit before taking his gun in localities where a permit is required. Further, before carrying a weapon concealed for any purpose, an additional permit for carrying concealed weapons is usually necessary and this should always be obtained. In most cases valid reasons are—

First. Protection.

Second. The fact that you habitually carry large sums of money.

Third. That you habitually carry valuables; for example, jewelry salesmen.

Fourth. That you are in fear of your life by reason of threats, etc.

Such of these reasons as apply to your case, or any other valid reasons, should be quoted in applying for a permit.

Banks and Jewelry Stores

A field where hand firearms are very important for protection is in the case of stores, banks, jewelry establishments, etc. Small stores, such as drug stores, which are open until late hours at night, are particularly subject to holdups. As emphasized above, if a gun is kept it should be loaded and where it can be instantly reached. Holdups of this nature are easier to combat than those of banks or jewelry stores.

In the case of a drug store the amount to be obtained is small, and generally it is the private work of an individual or a pair who are not well organized and generally do not know how to use firearms very well.

In the case of banks and jewelry stores the possible haul for the robbers is so much greater that the robbery is usually the result of the efforts of an organized gang. It is generally hopeless for one man to try to cope with a raid of this nature. One of the best precautions is an alarm system which can be put into action at the same time that the teller is complying with the bandit's demands. In some Middle Western localities, vigilance committees have been organized for this purpose.

In a recent holdup a gang of bank robbers descended on a small town and ordered the teller to turn over all the cash he had. He stepped on the alarm button and proceeded to turn over the cash as directed, which the robbers hastily put in a satchel and then made a rush from the bank to their car, which was waiting outside, but on arriving at the door they were met by a volley of gun fire by the citizens who had responded to the alarm, and were all killed. In localities where these vigilance committees have gone into effect insurance rates have been greatly reduced.

A very great protection in banks and jewelry stores is a bulletproof glass which has recently been developed which will withstand the direct charge at short range of the heaviest revolver or automatic pistol made. The writer has conducted many tests on this glass for the manufacturers of it, and the latest samples withstood successfully two shots from an Army automatic in the same

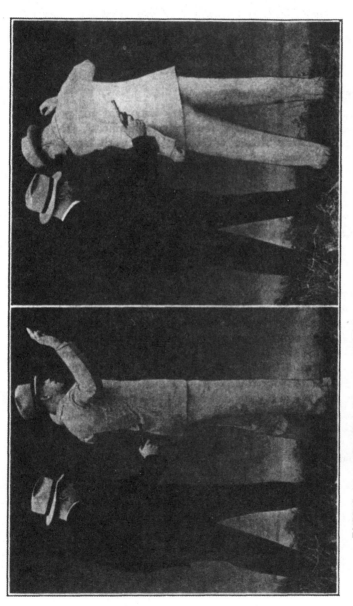

FOILING AN ATTEMPTED HOLDUP. SERIES C, WITH BANDIT BEHIND INTENDED VICTIM.

Left: Position No. 1. Victim receives command "Hands up!", and feels muzzle of revolver pressed against his back, slightly to the right of center. He starts to raise his hands as directed.

Right: The victim whirls suddenly to the left, at the same time throwing the left arm downward so as to push the gun away from the right side of the body, which is moving to the left at the same time, so that the bullet cannot strike the body when the gun is discharged. As the intended victim steps backward in whirling, to the left, he should endeavor to step on the bandit's foot.

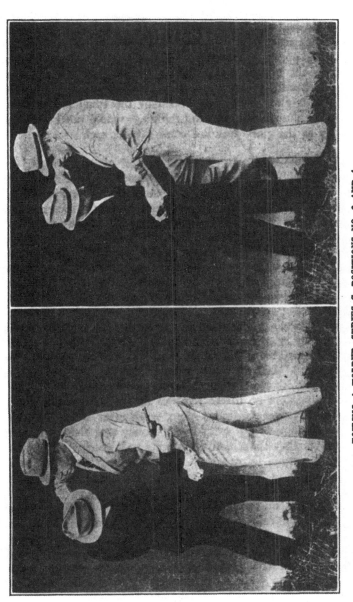

FOILING A HOLDUP, SERIES C, POSITIONS NO. 3 AND 4.

Left: As the intended victim whirls to the left he brings his right fist crashing against the jaw of the bandit.
Right: If the intended victim is balanced favorably as he whirls, he may strike the bandit a disabling blow by an upward motion of the knee, as shown.

spot. Also, the famous German Mauser is powerless to penetrate this glass. A bank teller behind such an enclosure is perfectly safe from revolver bullets. The thicker size of this glass will withstand even a service rifle bullet, and the bandit who shoots upon it is in for a very unpleasant surprise, for the surface glass which is shattered by the impact will fly back at the shooter and cut him severely. A bandit attempting to hold up a bank and firing against a sheet of this glass would be blinded by the small pieces flying in his face, while the teller behind the glass would not be injured in any way as the glass does not come off the back.

Pay-Roll Robberies

A matter which deserves very serious thought is the subject of pay-roll robberies. Most paymasters carry a revolver, it is true, but most of them do not know anything about how to use it and they would really be better off without it. I have many times had occasion to investigate the measures that paymasters or their clerks take to prevent robbery. Frequently, especially those who carry small sums of money, will have a revolver of small caliber in the satchel along with the money. If anyone should ask them to stand and deliver, he would get, not only the money, but the revolver as well.

The only place a revolver does any good for a person who is carrying money is in his hand and actually cocked ready to shoot. If he is walking, his hand could be in his coat pocket with the gun in the hand. If he is riding in an automobile, the gun can be in his hand and his hand on his lap all ready to shoot.

Many paymasters go to the bank in an automobile, frequently in a closed car, over the same route, week after week, and they think because they do not carry much money that they will never be held up, or they think that no bandits will know that they are making these trips. Most of them consider that they are in no danger, and this is the reason why many do not take any precautions.

This is a very mistaken notion. In the first place, organized gangs of pay-roll robbers have a very well worked out system of espionage and information. They collect from every available source all the information they can on pay rolls—what kind of protection is used, what route the paymaster takes, what hours he goes, etc.—and they frequently pay well for this information and keep it for future reference. You never know when someone in your own organization may either knowingly or unconsciously give away this information to the representative of one of these gangs. Another thing is that having once obtained this information they first hold up those pay rolls that appear to have the least protection.

The paymaster may think that he can not cope with a gang of bandits anyway; so he may as well take no precautions and merely stand and deliver. This is a very dangerous attitude and may lead, not only to the loss of your money, but of your life, because these gangs are getting more and more in the habit of making out a schedule of where they will meet the pay roll, and suddenly appearing on the scene with a volley of shots, giving the paymaster no chance to put up his hands and deliver the money. They merely shoot down everybody in the way, and then get away as fast as they can with the bag.

Now it may be possible that a gang may be well enough organized to take even a well-protected pay roll, but they will not take it as long as there is one less carefully protected that they know about. On the same principle that if there are two automobiles standing on the curb, one of them locked and one of them not locked, a thief will not take the trouble to pick the lock when the other one can be driven away with no trouble. In the same way, they argue, if there are two pay rolls, one protected poorly, the other not protected at all, grab the unprotected one and take no chance of being hurt. Therefore, if you take every step possible to protect your pay roll, and let it be known that you are doing so, the chances are you will not be held up. They will take someone who is not giving any attention to protection.

Among the protective measures that are very effective are always changing the time and route at which you go to the bank, and not letting anybody know when you are going and what route you are going to take.

If you use a car do not use a closed car unless it is an armored one protected with bulletproof glass, because a closed car can be shot into by a Thompson sub-machine gun but it can not be shot out of. Use an open car and have your messengers with their guns right in their hands. It is always best, where possible, to use two cars and have the money sometimes in one and sometimes in the other, so that it is not known which car it is going to be in.

An excellent way to avoid pay-roll holdups is to pay by check wherever this mode of payment can be used, and remember the knowledge that your pay-roll guard is receiving instruction in pistol practice never attracts any bandits.

Protection of the Home or Car

Guns intended for the protection of the home should be kept in a place where they will be readily accessible. There is no use keeping a gun on the top shelf of the closet in the spare room, or any similar place, because it will not be at hand when needed. From the situation of your own home, figure out where you will be likely to need a gun, then put your gun where it will be convenient to that place.

Moreover, the gun should be loaded, and the fact that it is loaded should be thoroughly understood and should be made known. You will never need the gun unless you need it loaded, and when you need it you will not have time to hunt up the cartridges and put them in.

Moreover, all impressions to the contrary notwithstanding, loaded guns that are known to be loaded are safest. No one takes any liberties with them. It is only with guns that are supposed to be unloaded that anyone will point at people or pretend to shoot, frequently with fatal consequences because of some cartridges that in some way remained in a supposedly harmless arm.

In a home all occupants should know where the revolver is kept; but it should be kept out of sight to prevent strangers from picking it up and handling it.

In a home where there are children they should be made to understand that revolvers are loaded and the harm they will do and generally they will never touch them. However, there are certain guns, such as the Smith & Wesson Hammerless, that a small child can not possibly discharge, and if small mischievous children are in the home this is the type of gun that should be chosen.

In the automobile the gun must be carried in some place where it can be easily reached and should be carried where it is out of sight or it will be stolen. In an open car an excellent place is in a spring holster, fastened inside the top just under the padding that is found in the curved part of most automobile tops. If you are held up you can stick up your hands as directed, then take hold of your gun. A spring holster lashed onto the steering post on top and in front of the dashboard in many makes of cars is out of sight, and is a convenient place to reach for. Remember that if your gun is not where you can get it instantly you are better off without it. Then look over your own car and find out where you can best put it.

Protection of the Person

Protection of the person involves the consideration of how best to carry a gun, and in most cases at least, it involves the carrying of the gun concealed.

For protection against holdups the very best place to have it, and, in fact, about the only place where it will do you any good is in the outside pocket of a coat or overcoat. If you have it in your hip pocket or under a lot of clothes, there is no chance to get it when you are held up.

Holdups generally occur in lonely places and dark sections. When passing one of these have your gun in your outside overcoat pocket, your hand on it, if you have any reason to anticipate a holdup. If you are asked to stick up your hands, make out you are going to do so, start at once to raise your hands, carrying your pistol in your right hand and start to shoot. Then drop to the ground and continue shooting from that position. If in defending your life or valuables you ever find it necessary to shoot at a man quickly at close range, the point of aim should be the center of the body. If you shoot at the head you may miss, especially if it is dark and you can not see the sights. A shot directed at the center of the body is not likely to miss and, moreover, it will have a paralyzing effect if it strikes in the region of the solar plexus.

The chances are one hundred to one in your favor if you are expecting a holdup and are armed, because the success of all holdup men depends on finding their victims unarmed and not expecting anything of the kind. The majority of them are rotten shots, armed with the cheapest kind of weapons, and generally the safest thing in the surrounding landscape is the thing they are trying to shoot at, as they are pretty certain to yank their trigger and pull their gun pretty far from their intended line of aim. Moreover, the holdup man is on the wrong side of the law, and the minute an alarm is raised—for instance, if you fire a shot—he is going to get out of there as fast as he can, and that means that he will cut and run. While running he can not fire at you. On the contrary, while he is running you can stand still and absolutely bring him down if you wish to by taking deliberate aim.

Remember never to run after a man you are trying to shoot for any reason. A bullet will go as far in a second as a man will go in a minute; so instead of running, just stand still and take careful aim and you are bound to get him.

As stated above, if you are carrying a gun for a special occasion,

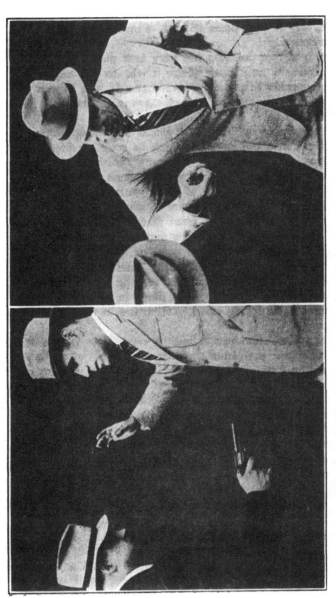

FOILING A HOLDUP. SERIES D, VICTIM HAS ONE HAND IN POCKET WHEN HELD UP.

Left: Position No. 1. Victim, walking with his hand in his pocket, is confronted by a bandit, who commands "Hands up!" This is a dangerous situation, for the gunman may shoot if the victim may have his hand on a gun in the pocket. Victim starts to raise his left hand.

Right: Foiling a holdup, Series D, Position No. 2. Bandit's entire attention is concentrated on victim's left hand, wondering if it may contain a weapon. Victim suddenly drops his right hand onto the gun, pushing it to the left, and at the same time grasping firmly around the cylinder and also around thumb and trigger finger of bandit holding the gun. As hand drops, body turns to the left, away from the possible path of the bullet if gun should be discharged. At the same instant, the muzzle of the gun is swung upward and to the left away from the body, throwing the gunman onto his back through the strain exerted on his wrist through the leverage afforded by the grip on the gun.

as for an anticipated trip through a questionable neighborhood, carry it in your outside pocket with your hand on it. However, if you are going to carry a gun habitually concealed, there are just two places where it can be carried conveniently and effectively. One of them is in a spring shoulder holster under the left arm. This is particularly suitable for large weapons. Another place is in a small belt holster inside the waistband of the trousers, diagonally across the abdomen. When carried in this way the weapon is not noticeable, is not inconvenient to carry and can be drawn with very great speed. Moreover, this is not where anyone looks for a gun when "frisking" you.

Revolvers can be fired from the outside coat pocket without removing them from the pocket if the emergency warrants this action. In this case the aim is likely to be poor. It is good for only an extremely short range emergency. This method of shooting with an automatic pistol invariably results in a jam because the empty cartridge can not be properly ejected.

Foiling an Attempted Holdup

Everyone should know that a determined man with a knowldge of firearms can often disarm a bandit or holdup man. This requires nerve, determination, and dexterity, but there are today a dozen men in our various police forces who are teaching such methods as a matter of routine, and it is really wonderful how quickly they can get the better of an armed man.

There are whole books written on this subject,* and they are well worth while to the police instructor, or to the man who is willing to take the time to study and practice this art. No attempt will be made here to go into the matter exhaustively, but a few examples are given in the accompanying illustrations and their descriptions which will show what can be done. It is well to practice each of the movements shown, but the caution is given that it must be done slowly and carefully at first, for an assistant is required, to represent the bandit, and his finger may be broken or the tendons in his wrist may be pulled very easily if the movements are executed quickly and without precautions to prevent injury to him. However, the fact that such injuries may occur is proof of the efficacy of the movements described.

The student of these exercises may never have occasion to use them, but if he has his nerve they will insure him against figuring in such headlines as one noted several weeks ago to the effect that a university athlete was held up by a girl bandit who poked a

---

*Example, *Scientific Self Defense*, Fairbairn, D. Appleton & Co., $3.50.

gun into his ribs and then marched him into a house where an assistant locked him in while the couple stole his car and money. If the young woman in question had tried that on some people that I know who have practiced this instruction, she would have wound up in jail with a broken finger and probably with concussion of the brain from being thrown onto the back of her head. One such experience would probably do more to turn a bandit's mind from the subject of hold-ups than any number of terms in jail.

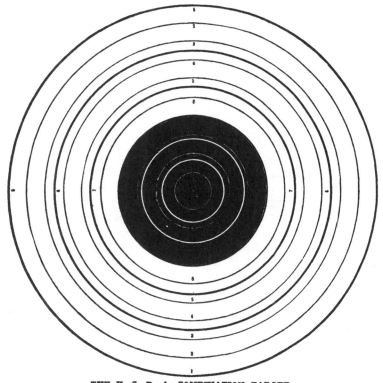

THE U. S. R. A. COMBINATION TARGET.

Used in all the championship matches at 50 yards. Standard American Target rings in heavy lines. International Union Target rings in light lines.

CHAPTER 16

THE PEACE OFFICER AND HIS GUN

PROFICIENCY in the use of hand firearms is of vital importance to all guardians of the law, whether they be uniformed policemen, plain clothes detectives, or federal agents. The police officers of our large cities are, of all people, the ones who are most likely to have to use a hand firearm at any or all times.

A few years ago, the greatest menace to the safety of the police officer was the rowdy inebriated celebrant, who was likely to resent interference of his method of celebration by fisticuffs, or at worst, by throwing relatively harmless missiles such as the half of a brick. Now, however, the officer must be constantly on the alert for the dapper young man, faultlessly attired, who nevertheless is a gunman of the worst and most dangerous kind, who will shoot without warning at the slightest sign of police interest in him or in his actions.

A few years ago, the average police officer did not know very much about shooting, and did not have much incentive to learn; but the case is very different now. The National Rifle Association has co-operated fully and efficiently with the heads of the larger police departments in giving marksmanship instruction to the various members of those organizations; and the men, as their interest has become aroused, have responded by becoming the finest body of pistol marksmen, as a whole, in the world. In most of our revolver matches today, the majority of the honors go to police officers. Of course there are still hundreds of small town policemen who have never had the opportunity or the desire to learn to shoot; but the average city police force is now highly efficient in the use of hand firearms.

Nevertheless, the attitude of the press and of the public is all too often one of criticism of the Police Officer and his method of handling his gun.

513

This is because with the hundreds of thousands of policemen in this country being constantly obliged to cope with bandits of all kinds in crowded cities there are bound to be rare cases where someone else gets hit with a policeman's bullet besides the thing he aimed at. The thousand times he hits what he aims at with his gun or accomplishes his purpose is not "news," and very little notice is taken of these incidents in the press; but if the thousand and first time he shoots, the bullet hits an innocent pedestrian who comes around the corner just as the holdup man reaches it, this, or any other similar untoward accident, is big news and the most is made of it, not only by the newspapers, but by many other self-appointed critics.

Recently, in the case of the shooting of the desperado John Dillinger in Chicago by two Federal Agents, much criticism of the Department of Justice, and of the authorities generally was seen in the press because two women were slightly wounded. The impression given by these accounts was that there was a volley of random shots fired by the officers, striking the outlaw as well as everyone else in that general vicinity. Actually, as the outlaw drew his automatic pistol from his pocket, the Federal Agents fired three shots, one of them striking Dillinger in the left eye, one in the heart, and one just below the heart. These latter two bullets struck a brick wall, and one of them inflicted a flesh wound in the leg of a bystander, while the other caused a chip of brick to strike the ankle of another innocent passerby. The injury to these two victims was unfortunate, but unavoidable. The emergency made it imperative for the Federal men to shoot immediately when Dillinger drew his gun, not only to save their own lives, but to avoid a gun battle in the crowded theatre district, with no one knows how many possible fatalities. They acted with superb efficiency and marksmanship, and only bad luck caused the two bullets to do further damage after passing through the body of the outlaw.

Let us take a look at this whole subject of policemen and guns from the Police Officer's viewpoint, and see if there isn't another side to it. Let's dismiss for the moment the fact that ninety-nine out of a hundred of the critics themselves know nothing whatever about shooting. Let's look at it for a time as against the police officer and the man who actually does know something about shooting. The self-satisfied marksman takes a black paper bull's-eye, beautifully outlined against a perfectly white target at a fixed distance of 50 yards, and what is more, his target is usually standing absolutely still. If he can hit this there is real cause for congratulations, because the large majority of our citizens that have not tried to do it would hit the ground halfway to the target. We thus see that it is a fairly hard job to hit an ideal target of the type mentioned; but let us compare the target that the policeman has to shoot at. Nine-tenths of the time it is a moving target, and a rapidly moving one at that, for a policeman does not shoot at a man who is standing still. He only shoots when the criminal is trying to get away, or is drawing a gun, or committing some other overt act, and when a criminal is committing some such act he is far from being still. He is a moving target, and a rapidly moving one at that, and nine times out of ten he is a very indistinct target, for he is either in the dark, where neither he nor the sights of the gun can be seen by the policeman, or he is in a rapidly moving automobile trying to get away, or else he is around a corner or making his escape through a crowded street.

Even the average expert marksman when confronted with a job of target practice under those conditions, would be absolutely flabbergasted, and add to it that your target is shooting back at you, and you have a combination that is not at all conducive to the finest results as to marksmanship. As to the question of shooting innocent bystanders, make a mental picture of a bandit making his get-away in any down-town street of some of our big cities, and you will see that the criminal is silhouetted entirely against targets that will be damaged if the bullet misses him or if it goes entirely through him.

A most unfortunate phase of this situation is the fact that the law gives the criminal the first shot at the policeman in every case. This seems like a queer statement, but a little reflection will show how true it is and why. The police officer can not start shooting before he has attempted to make an arrest quietly; but the mere fact that he is approaching a criminal puts the criminal on his guard, who at once makes up his mind whether or not he wants to shoot; and the officer can not start shooting unless the criminal starts the trouble, and by that time the officer is at a big disadvantage. As a matter of fact, the policeman's job in any of the large American cities is an extremely dangerous one. The casualty lists of policemen killed or wounded in the performance of their duty has grown so common in the daily newspapers that they pass almost unnoticed by the average citizen.

A policeman never knows when he may be up against a proposition like this: Just recently the newspapers in Philadelphia carried an account of a policeman who saw a car with four occupants speeding down one of the well-known streets of that city at an early hour in the morning. He commandeered a taxicab and overtook the car; halted it and started to ask the driver his name. Another occupant of the car stepped up behind him and shot him without warning and for no apparent reason. But I am glad to say he was caught and executed.

Another example is the case of Sergt. Frank S. Harper, of the Los Angeles Police Department. Several years ago he located a car said to have been stolen, and while watching it saw a well-dressed man about to enter it. He went up to the car and asked the man for his name and driver's card. Without a moment's warning the man whipped out a revolver and shot the officer through the shoulder. However, he picked the wrong man this time, for Sergeant Harper was a graduate of the recently established School of Marksmanship, conducted for the Los Angeles Police Department, and was an expert rapid-fire pistol shot. As he was falling he drew his gun and fired five times. Four of the shots pierced the bandit's heart and lungs and the fifth went through his hat. We are glad to be able to record that the sergeant recovered very promptly from his wound and was decorated for bravery.

These two incidents show extremely well at what a disadvantage the ordinary patrolman is placed. Neither one of these two men had any reason to anticipate shooting. They couldn't even draw a revolver and approach the other man thus prepared because the presumption was in both cases that the driver was a reputable citizen, and if the police started the habit of going up to reputable citizens whom they had to question, with a drawn revolver in one hand, their job on the force would not last very long. The moral of these incidents is that the public places the policeman in a position of deadly peril, and his only hope when danger comes is to be able to use his revolver accurately and use it quickly. For him to have an even chance he must be trained in the use of hand arms, and his training must not be merely perfunctory, but must be so thorough that his use of the pistol will be instinctive and automatic.

It is the duty of the public, who places these men on this dangerous duty, to provide them with facilities for getting training. The policeman can not do this for himself. In the first place, he has neither the time nor the money to spend on pistol practice, because he is a hard-working individual, his hours are long and his pay is small. He can not afford to use up in pistol practice the few hours that he has off duty and in addition put up from three to four cents a shot for cartridges out of a salary that probably is not sufficient anyway to keep up life insurance for his wife and children against the time when the other fellow gets in the first shot. Suppose, however, that he does decide to take off the necessary time and put up the necessary cash to perfect himself in shooting. Just where would he practice? Pistol-shooting is something that you can not do in your own back yard in a city. Suppose that he decides to take enough time to take a street car out to the country. Even that is questionable, because there are very few places in the vicinity of a large city where indiscriminate pistol-shooting can be practiced. In many parts of the East you can ride by street car or automobile from one large city to another and never be out of sight of a house.

The answer is that unless the public does its part the police officer will not be trained in one of the most important parts of his profession, which is the quick and accurate use of hand arms. This is becoming more and more realized in late years, and most of our municipalities have established revolver ranges for the police, where a regular course of instruction is given to all members of the force. The instructions come during the hours of duty, and the necessary ammunition is paid for by the city. In places where this has been done the results have been remarkable in the reduction of crime. Gangsters and gunmen will not stay in a city where the police force has a reputation for quick and accurate shooting when there is another city near by where there is a poorly trained police force. An example of what happens to a crook in such a place is well illustrated in the incident of Sergeant Harper, given above.

Another important result of this policy has been to greatly reduce the premiums for burglar insurance in many localities where this training has been given. This item of insurance reduction alone is great enough to pay for the total cost of the instruction many times over.

The problem of training a police force in shooting is rather a big one for several reasons. One of them is that nine times out of ten the policeman must shoot in the dark or in a very poor light and cannot see the sights of his gun. His targets are practically moving targets, and moving quickly at that. In a great many cases they are shooting back at him. It means that he must undergo the most difficult sort of training in order to be able to win out in a game like this.

Primary Requirements

As a matter of fact, before the training of the Police Officer even starts there are certain other requirements that must be met. In the first place, he must have a suitable weapon. Rapid progress has been made along this line in the last few years. A few years ago the police officer was allowed to carry any gun he wanted to. Of late years, however, the subject has received a considerable amount of study and in many police departments there are excellent requirements as to the type and caliber of arm to be used.

The first requirement is that the gun should be of sufficient caliber to have ample stopping power. This means that it should not be smaller than a .38. Only the highest grade of pistol or revolver is good enough for the use of the policeman who may owe his life to the functioning of his gun. All guns in a police force should preferably be of the same kind and caliber. There is no telling when an officer may have to use a comrade's gun, and if they are all of the same make there will be no failure owing to unfamiliarity. Among the uniformed members of the force the only place a gun should be carried is on the outside of everything else, where it can be got out easily without having to get under an overcoat and a lot of other clothes to get at it. It should be carried in an approved type of quick-draw holster. Every man on the police force should be taught at city expense, and on city time, to use his gun proficiently, and after he has obtained proficiency he should have actual firing practice at regular intervals to keep up his knowledge. This practice should also, of course, be on city time and at city expense.

There should be a certain allowance of ammunition for every member of the police force armed with a revolver or pistol, and there should be a requirement which will provide that old ammunition be used up in practice and that new ammunition will be kept available for actual service use. Unless this point is watched the officer may carry the same old cartridges in his gun, and then from the effects of dampness or oil soaking into the cartridges they may fail at the critical moment.

Carrying cartridges openly in a cartridge belt is a practice not to be recommended for the police force. In one of our large Eastern cities the regulations require each member of the force to carry twelve cartridges in this manner in the holster belt, which is worn outside of all other clothes. These cartridges must be kept shined up for inspection, and there is plain evidence around the primers in many cases of the metal polish that has been used to keep their cartridges bright and shiny. This metal polish generally contains gasoline, which will ruin the primer if any of it soaks in. The cartridges are carried in the belt, primer end up, and naturally the primers will be the first place for moisture to collect in any rain or dampness, and if the waterproofing is not perfect or if it has been removed by the polishing of the cartridges, it is conceivable that the ammunition may fail when needed, with possible disastrous consequences.

Marksmanship School for Police

The instruction that the police should receive in the handling and use of hand arms should include full information on the different kinds of firearms, how they are made, the names and func-

The National Rifle Association Police School at Camp Perry. Police Officers on the firing line executing "Rapid Fire."

tions of each part, and especially safety precautions, and how to handle them without danger of accident. This instruction should be followed by the teaching of proficiency in both slow and rapid fire as described in Chapter 13. This training in target marksmanship will form only the groundwork on which the policeman's real pistol training should be built. This target training gives him a confidence in his arm and an ability to let off shots without disturbing his aim. It gives him the co-ordination of the shooting hand and arm that will never be obtained in any other way.

After this regular marksmanship training has been learned the next thing is to teach him rapid fire, using the sights, and after that, rapid fire without using the sights. Then he must be taught all kinds of emergency firing, such as shooting at night, in dark hallways, etc. His training must be so thorough that at any time he can point his gun at an object in the same way that you can point your finger and that this can be done automatically and without thinking of the sights at all. A course of pistol training should include the above-mentioned subjects in about the following sequence:

1. Description of pistols, and instruction as to handling and safety precautions.

2. Explanation of sights and sighting, followed by aiming exercises.

3. Instruction in the method of holding the gun, followed by snapping exercises.

4. Slow-fire practice with the .22 caliber until proficiency is attained.

5. Slow-fire practice with full charges.

6. Rapid-fire—aimed shots.

7. Rapid-fire without using sights.

8. Instruction in drawing the gun from the holster—practice in drawing and shooting at "Man" targets.

9. Drawing and shooting at moving targets.

10. Raid practice.

A description will be given of each of these headings.

1. The student should be given a simple description of the principle of firearms and of the different kinds of arms, such as automatic pistols, single-shot pistols, revolvers, etc. The principles of construction of the various arms should be explained and the reason for the different parts, such as the hammer, trigger, cylinder, rifling, etc. The difference between right- and left-hand rifling should be explained, and the student should be shown bullets that have been fired from guns, with rifling marks on them. The cleaning and care of the gun should also be fully explained. For information on these points the instructor is referred to Chapter 5.

2. Aiming exercises. The instruction and use of the various sights should be explained and the student should be put through a course of aiming triangles as described in Chapter 13.

3. Method of holding, and snapping exercises. This subject is also fully described in Chapter 13, and instruction will, of course,

depend somewhat on the type of arm with which the force is equipped.

4. The practice of slow and rapid fire should also be taught as described in Chapter 13.

7. This brings us to No. 7—rapid-fire without using the sights. This is a course of practice which is particularly necessary for the police. The student should be taught to face his target squarely at all times and to swing the arm directly up in line with the bull's-eye, letting the shot off as soon as the arm reaches the horizontal position. For success it is essential that one particular grip on the gun be learned and be adhered to. For this practice it is advisable to use a 50-yard standard American target placed about 5 yards away. Facing this target, the arm holding the revolver should be swung up straight toward the target from the position of the holster on the belt, cocking the gun as it is swung up, and when it is in line with the bull's-eye the trigger should be pulled. It is well to practice this extensively before doing any actual shooting in this manner. In actually shooting at this target shots must be expected to hit the floor at first and sometimes to go to either side of the target or above it, so it is well to hold this practice in a place that is arranged so that no damage will result if some of the shots do not strike the target. After practice is had in simulating fire of this kind actual shooting should be done, one shot at a time until such proficiency is reached that the shot can always be placed in the bull's-eye. It will be found that with a little practice quite a knack can be acquired, so that swinging the arm upward and letting the shot off at the bull's-eye is almost like tossing a ball at it. When this point is reached the secret will have been mastered.

8. Instruction in drawing and shooting at the "Man" targets. The best targets of this kind are the Langrish Limbless target and the Colt Police Silhouette target. Both of these targets represent the outline of the upper part of a man's body, and they have various scoring zones with different values accorded the hits. The man target should be placed about 5 yards away for the first practice. Before beginning the practice the student should be carefully instructed in regard to holsters, the manner of drawing, and cocking the gun while drawing, and then should be allowed to practice with an unloaded gun at this target until smoothness in getting the weapon into action is attained. Afterwards this practice should be conducted with one cartridge in the gun, shooting one shot at a time at the target. After proficiency has been obtained in rapidly

putting one shot on the target, the distance should be increased to 10 yards, and the practice repeated. Finally, the target should be moved to 15 yards, and the marksman should be required to fire six shots, slow fire, keeping the shots in a small group in the center of the figure.

Next, rapid fire should be practiced, cocking the gun for each shot; then rapid fire, using the double action; that is, cocking the gun as well as firing it, but pulling the trigger.

When the officer under instruction can draw his gun and fire six

Police Training School conducted by the National Rifle Association at Camp Perry. Police officers examining the targets and recording the scores after a string of "Rapid Fire." Note the automobile target in the foreground. It is arranged on a track so as to move rapidly away from the firing line. The body of the car is buff, but the important aiming points, such as the tires and gas tank are black.

shots into the center of the man target at 15 yards in ten seconds he will be a formidable antagonist for anyone in a gun-fight.

9. Practice with moving targets. For this purpose the target carrier is arranged to travel on a trolley in a line parallel to the firing-point. On this traveling target clamp a Colt Man target is hung. The trolley for the target carrier to travel on is arranged to travel across an opening about 10 feet wide, the target being about 10 yards away. In the first practice with this traveling target the student loads his gun with one shot and stands ready, gun in hand and cocked, and the target suddenly appears and travels across the opening. During the time it is traveling across he is supposed to place the shot somewhere in the target. After proficiency is ob-

tained with one shot the student is allowed to load his gun fully and see how many shots he can get in while the target is traveling across. The last practice with this traveling target consists of allowing the student to have his gun in the holster loaded with one cartridge. As soon as the target appears the shooter draws his gun, cocks and fires one shot.

10. The last practice in this course is the "raid" practice, representing conditions encountered in raiding a dwelling or vice den

"Hogan's Alley" at Camp Perry. By pulling the levers the operator can make figures appear at unexpected places in the doors and windows, and from behind the chimney of Bud Peagler's Place.

of any kind. This course is taken from the description given by Commander Baum in the December 1, 1924, *American Rifleman*, where he states:

"This string is fired inside of a bombproof to prevent wild shots from injuring anyone. The shooter takes his position outside of a door which leads into a dark passageway. Upon opening the door he is permitted to draw and cock his pistol. The passageway is dark and littered with chairs, boxes or short stairs, in fact, many things to cause extreme care in walking. At the end of the passageway is another door leading into a dimly lighted room. Immediately he steps into the room he must be prepared to shoot at whatever target he sees representing a human being. As soon as the shooter clears the threshold, firecrackers, confetti, sticks or other objects are thrown at him; then someone yells into his ear, pistols are fired behind him and everything possible is done to shake his nerve and disconcert him. A target representing the head and shoulders of a man swings out from behind a wall, remaining in sight only momentarily, a moving target slides across the end of the room, and a head is dropped into the room from above to represent a man springing down. Only three targets are shown and the shooter is permitted only one shot at each target."

There are not many places where the exact course suggested by Commander Baum can be arranged, but the general idea may readily be grasped from what he has said, and something of the kind is

Police Officer practising in "Hogan's Alley," at Camp Perry. A figure has just appeared in the window, and another will appear in the door in an instant.

exceedingly valuable in rounding out any course of marksmanship and in making a really practical police shot.

Something on this general order is found in the so-called "Hogan's Alley" range which is part of the great Police School conducted by The National Rifle Association at Camp Perry each year. This is an outgrowth of the "French Village" at the National Matches at Caldwell, New Jersey, in 1919, just after the close of the World War. This French Village was constructed by Captain Deming, who was an artist by profession, and during his war service contributed much valuable material in the way of landscape targets. He made a section of canvas representing part of a ruined village in France, with houses, streets, etc. Back of this there was a pit for the scorers. Each of these scorers had a cardboard figure, resembling the head and shoulders of a man, nailed on the end of a long stick. The shooter took his place at the firing-point, gun in hand. Suddenly, at the windows or the corner of a wall, or some other unexpected place, one of these figures would be poked up and exposed for three seconds, then withdrawn. The firer never knew just where a figure was going to appear. It was his business to watch for these figures and the instant one appeared to shoot it. This is a very hard thing to do, and it shows up different shooters in different ways, which is quite a revelation. It is especially confusing when two figures are shown at different parts of the target. This is actual practice for quick shooting with the pistol already in the hand. "Hogan's Alley" consists of several sham buildings erected on the target line, to represent a street in a slum section of a town. There are, of course, numerous doors and windows, and there are chimneys, etc., behind which gangsters might be supposed to be lurking. The officer under instruction walks down the street, with his gun loaded. There is a target operator with a number of levers at his command, by means of which he may cause silhouette figures to appear in the various doorways and windows, and to lean from behind the chimneys on top of the various buildings. As each figure appears in some unexpected place, the officer fires at it. His endeavor is to place a shot on every figure that may appear.

A man who has been intelligently put through a course of instruction similar to that described under the above headings will be a very dangerous adversary indeed and will get the better of any gunman in a shooting fight. The description given above is only an outline and is intended to be modified to suit various conditions. It should be supplemented with as much general instruction on the subject of firearms and their use as can be made available.

Useful Knowledge

There are many things that it would be very useful for the policeman to know about the use of guns. For example, in moving-picture shows the commonly accepted method of intimidating one with a pistol appears to be to push it against his ribs in readiness to shoot. The user of an automatic pistol should know that when the muzzle of the gun is pressed hard against any object the slide is pushed back slightly and consequently the gun cannot be discharged at all.

Again, if a revolver is pointed at you closely enough so that you can grasp it tightly around the cylinder it is impossible to cock it because in cocking the revolver the cylinder must rotate.

This danger is avoided if when approaching a man to effect an arrest with drawn gun you advance toward him left side first, with the right hand holding the gun near your own body, pointing at the prisoner, but well back away from his reach. If he should make a move for your gun, you can hold him out of reach of it with your left hand, as you fire with your right. This may sound cold-blooded, but as you value your life, never approach a man with a gun in your hand unless you have made up your mind to shoot if necessary, and then at the first sign of trouble let him have it.

Moreover, if you are known to be armed, don't draw your gun until the case demands drastic action and you are willing to shoot. Unnecessary display of a revolver weakens your position. But if you do have to draw a gun in making an arrest, take the offensive, and walk boldly up to your man. Somehow the fact that you have made up your mind to shoot at the first violence not only settles your own mind and makes you act with more force and decision, but it also communicates itself to your opponent and, so to speak, "gives him a chill." If you have fully made up your mind to shoot if you have to, the chances are that you will not have to.

The revolver is also a useful weapon in a hand-to-hand fight, even if not loaded. It can be used very effectively to strike an assailant with, and for this purpose it is not necessary to turn it around in the hand and strike with the butt, instead strike with the barrel, especially if it is a heavy gun, such as the .45.

In towns where gun-fights are common one of the most noticeable things to a stranger is that at the first shot everybody gets down as flat to the ground as possible. Once, in a Western town a good many years ago, I saw a "bad man" shoot up a restaurant by firing all the cartridges in his revolver into the door at random because the proprietor would not cash a check for him. I was passing when the first shot occurred, and what I noticed most was that at the first shot everyone in the street was down as flat as possible and most of them were in the gutter. The man was standing in the door of the restaurant firing his gun into it, and just as he got the last shot fired he was collared from behind by a soldier belonging to the Army detachment stationed there at that time and was dragged off to the lockup. His exhibition of fireworks did no harm aside from putting a few holes in the walls and ceiling of the restaurant, because at the first shot everybody in the restaurant was down flat on the floor. A number of other times when I have seen shooting affrays in places where they were common I have been impressed with the fact that everybody gets down as quickly as possible and that often no one is hurt.

There is a lesson in this. If you are mixed up in a gun-fight of any kind and have to stay in one place the best thing to do is to get down as low as possible, as you can fire a gun just as well from this position and your chances of being hit are practically nil. Another good thing to remember is that if, for any reason, you do not get down, do not stand still when somebody is shooting at you. Either move toward him or away from him, or side-wise, but move in some direction and move as rapidly as possible as this will disturb his aim. Stop when you are going to fire, because you can fire much more effectively when you are still. Never shoot while you are running after a man. If you shoot while you are running your fire will be ineffective. If you are trying to stop a running fugitive, stand still and take deadly aim and you will get him every time as a bullet can overtake a running man very easily.

If you ever have to fire your gun to scare anyone or as a warning, never fire it onto the pavement, as the bullet will bounce and may kill someone. The safest way to fire it is almost straight up, because then the bullet will spend most of its energy overcoming air resistance and will fall harmlessly to the ground.

The author shooting Mr. R. F. Sedgeley's Colt New Service .22 Hornet.

INDEX